Serve the Power(s), Serve the State

Serve the Power(s), Serve the State:

America and Eurasia

Edited by

Juan Carlos Garavaglia,
Michael J. Braddick
and Christian Lamouroux

Cambridge
Scholars
Publishing

Serve the Power(s), Serve the State: America and Eurasia

Edited by Juan Carlos Garavaglia, Michael J. Braddick and Christian Lamouroux

This book first published 2016

Cambridge Scholars Publishing

Lady Stephenson Library, Newcastle upon Tyne, NE6 2PA, UK

British Library Cataloguing in Publication Data
A catalogue record for this book is available from the British Library

ISBN (10): 1-4438-8877-X
ISBN (13): 978-1-4438-8877-6

TABLE OF CONTENTS

PROLOGUE

HISTORIES AND BUREAUCRACIES: ADMINISTRATE AND SERVE THE STATE

JUAN CARLOS GARAVAGLIA,
MICHAEL J. BRADDICK
AND CHRISTIAN LAMOUROUX

This book arises from the international conference held at the Pompeu Fabra University in Barcelona in March 2011, which was itself part of a twofold initiative. The project directly at the origin of the conference in Barcelona was primarily pedagogical in intention: a team of young historians, who had been initially educated in Latin America, was formed to study systematically the history of the state, within the framework of fellowships funded by an advanced grant from the European Research Council.[1] The method that underpinned their course of study was based on a principle that most doctoral programs have implemented: "Teaching research by doing research". Their program aimed at deepening current knowledge of the history of the state in the Luso-Hispanic worlds, the main field of research for historians studying Latin America.[2] But, secondly, it was essential to offer to them access to new approaches, using different historical sources and drawing on different scholarly traditions. The conference held in 2011 was an important part of that second initiative, and this book represents its conclusion.

In this prologue we set out several themes on which general discussions during the conference focused. Many of the participants were cautious in the face of the challenge inherent to the second undertaking:

[1] *A Comparative History of the State Building Process in Latin America (1820-1870)*, Advanced Grant 230246, European Research Council, FP7.

[2] The results are presented in Garavaglia and Pro 2013.

that of comparative analysis. Such caution was a necessity for the pedagogical program but a key purpose of the conference was to broaden the students' horizons. Contributors set out to compare the conditions in which the Latin American states emerged from the Iberian empires and were consolidated with those that prevailed in other imperial realms: the English colonial rule from which North America was liberated, but also Russia, whose references to the European state continue to be ambiguous, and far from the European experience, the Asian world, in work on India, Japan, and China. The chronological spectrum was thus also obviously very broad: the Chinese bureaucracy emerged and its hegemony was already in place, according to Sinologists, almost eight centuries before the Latin American states were built up. The book is therefore based around a core of chapters offering a longitudinal view of Iberian government, and its expression in Latin America, from the 15th to the 19th centuries, around which are set comparative studies ranging Song China and Tokugawa Japan, via early modern England to nineteenth century USA and India.

These comparative discussions confront two particular methodological difficulties: to juxtapose the cases presented by the successive papers; and to generate some unity among each participant`s particular conclusions and remarks by employing useful but not excessively general categories derived from sociology or political science. One unifying theme was the attempt to understand the state 'from within'. The very title of the conference "Serve the Power(s), Serve the State" prompted us to approach the history of the state through its functioning and from the perspectives of the actors in charge of running its operations. Hence the figures of bureaucrats and the bureaucracy that have haunted historians and sociologists of the state since Max Weber, were naturally able to unify our considerations. Our discussions certainly revealed that we were often tempted to resort to these categories elaborated by the eminent sociologist because generally speaking such categories allow historians to grasp effectively the role that the public services and bureaucratization played in the integration and formation of the state. As many authors point out, however, it is important to employ such categories with caution in order to avoid any distortion of the facts within the diverse historical experiences.

As historians, we are indeed convinced that the realities we study form part of our present, and that the comparison between the political cultures of different societies is enlightening.

Max Weber was therefore an important point of reference on several occasions during our discussions, and it is perhaps appropriate to recall here that he was above all interested in elaborating a theory of domination.

As a consequence, we could not be satisfied by an approach consisting of describing events, analyzing the coherence of operations, and the actors' social framework for action, as if they had been determined by some sort of preconception about the bureaucracy's political or institutional efficiency, or even in search of rationalization or modernization. Such an approach would just replicate the general perspective employed by the sociology of domination as envisioned from the experience in the West. By contrast the essays collected here follow a recent tendency for histories of the state to pay more attention to the human interactions that constitute what states actually do than to overarching institutional and constitutional structures. We might gloss this as a desire to consider state activity as a kind of 'social practice', mediating between material conditions, linguistic resources and the skills and capacities of the individual actor.[3] The roots of this turn may be found in the linguistic turn, the rise of cultural history or the sociology of Foucault or Bourdieu (or in a more restricted field, of Goffman), but they have converged around the deconstruction of abstract notions of the state in favour of the study of these more problematized and complex patterns of social action. This literature is more clearly concerned with state practices or, we might say, with the state as practice (or process), rather than structure.[4] A by-product of this shift of attention is to turn attention away from moments of revolution, and tectonic change in political 'structures', towards the more routine negotiation of the relationship between political power and social interests, and a more organic account of historical change.

If we made a point of employing bureaucracies in the plural, it is firstly because the papers are often written with comparative approaches explicitly in mind. In this context the methodological contributions made by the first German school of social studies, which was already concerned with fostering dialogue between sociologists and historians, are of particular importance, above all perhaps, two central ideas defended by Otto Hintze (1861-1940), which subsequently became widely accepted.[5] Firstly, if the bureaucracy is a central phenomenon of the political life, just like all other political phenomena, it should be contextualized by taking into account its social dimensions. Secondly, if historians studying the

---

[3] Reckwitz 2002; Schatzki 1996.

[4] Gorski 2003.

[5] We were largely inspired here by the stimulating issue of the on-line journal, "Max Weber et la bureaucratie", *Trivium*, 7, 2010, see http://trivium.revues.org/3757, consulted on 15/12/2014

bureaucracy draw natural benefit from political sociology, it becomes not only legitimate but quite simply essential for them to study diverse historical regimes of authority.

Of course no one today would venture to look at these regimes as the stages of a unique process which evolves from monarchy to aristocracy and finally to democracy. A kind of developmental perspective in which the key categories of patrimonialism, clientage and bureaucracy are drawn into a teleological account of modernity now seems inadequate to capture and explain historical experience. For example, Andújar Castillo shows in this volume, how the apparent distinction between a judicial Hapsburg monarchy of the seventeenth century and an administrative monarchy in the eighteenth, dissolves on close inspection. Such large-scale schematic distinctions are difficult to sustain when exploring the world of concrete action, in which personal incentives of various kinds operated by the rules of a patrimonial order. It is hard to maintain a strong distinction between putting people in a position where they could derive benefits and offering them direct financial reward—and the sale of offices was a way of mediating the difference. Many of these studies show how it was the problem of reward that underpinned the failure to materialize the ideals of a bureaucratic order, of uniform and transparent conduct of office in return for defined benefits. The essay by Carré can be read in this way, tracing attempts to achieve more within constraints of patrimonial administration, leading to modulation, rather than rapid structural change in the relationship between social groups and political power. The powerful imprint of nineteenth century scholarship nevertheless remains, often leading historians to conceptualize evolutions as “regimes”, in which comparable social factors are combined: professional groups, operators and classes granted with statuses. One way of avoiding essentialising bureaucracy, as Hintze himself studied it in the Prussian form, is to see it as a force field: the forces which can merge within this field relate to a functional implementation but remain fundamentally shaped by the pattern of each local political tradition.

Several chapters in this book attest that the state’s agents were not necessarily civil officers. It is consequently essential to grasp how some groups were more apt to construct and fulfill functions that served as the foundation of the bureaucratic regime of government. In Lamouroux’s account of the early Song case we can see in the intertwining influence of military and civil functions how bureaucracy can be seen as institutionalized force—the exercise of legitimate violence by other means. But this affinity between government and legitimate force is not the only reason for the close association of fiscal-military development and bureaucracy. As Caselli and Ruiz Ibañez also note, in the absence of large and dependable tax flows, closely defined salaries (in respect of closely defined limits on the exercise of office) are difficult to achieve. This is perhaps one more reason why there is an affinity between bureaucratization and fiscal-military power, leading to the assertion that it is warfare that drove the development of the state; a relationship illustrated by Garavaglia's contribution. The monetization of war allows perhaps for the monetization of the administration of war, and that permits the development of a monetized bureaucracy at large.[6] In other contexts, securing collaboration, or co-opting elites as other literatures have it, entailed ceding monarchical control over the detail of administration.[7]

If we were to put this back into Weberian terms, it would probably not be through the construction of developmental typologies, but through the question of legitimation: historians have been more interested in the process of legitimating political action, and how that process interacts with social interests and linguistic resources, than in the progressive achievement of the monopoly of violence or the establishment of bureaucracy. Certainly, this is a question at the core of this book. However, at the heart of studies of the state are institutions, and varying institutional outcomes over time and across space, and the implications of these forms for social and economic life. This emerging literature would tend to see institutions as the outcome of dialogues of various kinds: regularized and routinized forms of legitimate action that successfully negotiate the conditions in which political power is sought and exercised.

Bureaucracy remains therefore at the heart of these questions. For a long time it was treated as something beyond social relations, but that is to accept its central legitimating myth—that the bureaucrat is transformed by his or her position into a neutral instrument of the public good, and that public good has been agreed and instantiated independently of the action in hand. In British history we might think of the contrast between a seventeenth century magistrate, acting as father of his country, or a village constable implementing a local 'concept of order', using their 'discretion' to see justice done in the light of local conditions and norms; and the modern bureaucrat operating uniform and transparent rules, with governed criteria of inclusion and exclusion, explicitly without discretion, in order to ensure equality. The bureaucratic legitimation of routine political action

[6] Tilly 1990; Brewer 1989.
[7] Beik 1985.

depends on the assertion that bureaucracies are free of social interest, discretion and are efficiently directed toward the public good. Braddick's essay problematizes this distinction by examining the quotidian realities that lie behind these legitimations—the complex relationships between public good and private benefit, and the battles for status and position in the administration. Caselli examines this issue in detail, exploring the social practice of a particular group—judges and judicial officers in 15th and early 16th century Castile—revealing how, but considering them as 'agents', serving the monarchy, but also exercising their private office, reveals the tensions around their personal benefits. They negotiated the complex rules and legitimations that shaped their service of the Crown, and also the rewards they were allowed in return for that service. The forced tolerance of potentially ad hoc and informal payments created an area of contest, in which judges secured their own livelihood, and also incurred costs in defending it.

Many of the essays approach routine bureaucratic action as a social practice, particularly in contexts in which it can be seen as emergent, a newly agreed settlement on how to exercise political power in a routine way. In doing so they draw attention to the gap between legitimating languages and social practice—a gap in which the negotiation of political power took place. Ruiz Ibañez explores an equally fundamental political task in similar terms—the practice of personal participation in defence as a negotiation of complex and overlapping networks of influence and authority. Defence was only in the most abstract way service of the monarchy—much else was introduced into this practice by the dialogue with other social and personal interests. There is a mismatch between overarching studies of the Empire as an abstract institution, and local realities: "a far too institutional vision continues to predominate in most of the studies about concrete political realities; they therefore do not pay attention to the ways in which the local realities were inserted into the monarchy" (43). In one sense these complexities served to restrain the power of government: for Caselli, for example, provision of justice in fifteenth century Spain was an *act* of government, not simply the "procedural implementation of a predefined regulation or regulations" (3), and that entailed complexities which were on occasion formally resolved by the artful order to "obey but not to comply".

As Garavaglia concludes on the basis of his wide-ranging analysis of the emergent Latin American regimes: "The notion, sustained repeatedly in many studies … of the bureaucracy as an *apparatus* is totally inappropriate, as there was no apparatus external to society; there was only a *network of social relations*" (113). Ingerflom goes further, demonstrating on broadly the same grounds how limited is the utility of the term state—that it embeds a model of "state-society" relations in our analysis, which bears little relation to the realities of social and political life in any period before the twentieth century (and, some would suggest, occludes our understanding of modern states too). The translation and substitution of *gosudarstvo* to or by state reflects the attempt to translate into the modern metaphor of an apparatus something that was not there, and that act of translation prevents us from seeing what is there. The same goes for the transformation of the East India Company, the subject of Raj's essay. The dramatic transformation of one regime into another disappears on close inspection of the practice of the "company state"—what is often presented as a transition from commerce to empire reflects a more organic development from a corporation which conducted both to a directly state-controlled imperial presence.

Thus, we could see the negotiation of power as a contest between those exercising political office and social interests defined in terms of class, gender, age, ethnicity, and religious identity. How a social problem is defined, and how a deployment of political power is agreed as a solution to that problem, reflects in part the differential capacity of social groups to deploy political power. Administrative action bears the imprint of differentials in social, cultural and economic power. A particularly telling example of this might be the history of measures taken in relation to disease or poverty. For example how the plague bacillus, acting in broadly similar ways on all human bodies, came to be treated as a moral or religious problem, with clear class dimensions.[8]

On this view, of state action as a kind of social practice, there is an inherent connection between the formation of the state—the development of routines of legitimate political action, and the continuous negotiation of their interpretation and of innovation—and the development of political languages and material possibilities. Many institutional economists take this for granted, but tend to reify institutions: here we would see the development of state and economy as dynamically interconnected. Economic change affects the material conditions in which political action takes place—creating risks and opportunities, class interests and class conflicts—but the realm of the economically possible is also a product of the institutionalized practice of political power, which is the outcome of past negotiations of material conditions. A political or economic science

[8] Slack 1985, 1988.

which seeks to isolate institutional forms from the social environment in which they are practiced will ignore the potential for particular rules and practices to be interpreted and used in very different ways in varying social contexts.

In recent studies of early modern England, these approaches have tended to come together around the analysis of the negotiation of power.[9] As Ruiz Ibañez put it "the king's authority was absolute in his sphere of powers, but defining this sphere, and the hierarchy that was constructed among the powers that depended on his legitimacy, was contingent on the traditions and political culture of each one of the agents that participated in the administration of royal domination" (47). Such an approach does not dissolve the general entirely into a myriad of particulars; however, it can also reveal an underlying process to which the many local negotiations and outcomes were particular responses. From a governmental perspective, this might look like the mobilization of local energies in order to make a reality of claims to legitimacy, of which Will's study of Qing administration offers a particularly enlightening example.

The essays presented here approach the exercise of public power from the perspective of the political actor. Refusing any sort of determinism, most of the participants chose to reflect upon the paths followed by groups which were aggregating to defend shared interests, develop alliances, resist or submit to forms of authority, create methods of intervention and fields of expertise, all these groups being differentiated by the specific vocabulary and body of knowledge they jointly developed. Thanks to archival documents, but also to the accounts that they wrote themselves, to the correspondence they carried on, and to statutory obligations or chronicles, we are able to catch a glimpse of these men's practices and to tackle the question of their role. It is therefore possible to understand their motivations and ambitions, their ideals and sense of group consciousness that they advanced (or did not advance) within corporate organizations that were already established in the society. We can likewise reconstruct the alliances that they invented or consolidated as social and political resources, thanks to family ties, of course, but also through the relations which provided the basis of their sphere of activities and expertise. These groups created their identity partly through activities that allowed them to exercise long-lasting and diverse forms of domination: men of the law in Castile at the end of the fifteenth century or office-holders on both shores of the Iberian Atlantic; merchants and brokers of the East India Company

[9] Braddick and Walter, 2001; Griffiths Fox and Hindle 1996.

in the shady world of Calcutta; clerks serving at the mint of Kanazawa in Edo Japan; private agents at the service of the tax authorities in seventeenth-century England; officers "attached to the palace" who set up a military bureaucracy in eleventh-century China. Moreover we can reverse the perspective: it is worth recalling that starting in the nineteenth century, the liberal state in the United States was built up durably under the pressure of communities that were organized in order to contest the legitimacy of the fiscal administration, and hence resorted to the most extreme forms of violence.

Beyond the content of all these historical cases, several approaches, which were often dictated by the sources, reveal how most of these groups sought to distinguish from each other and set themselves apart from the mass of those whose interests they "served"; they were capable of conceiving themselves as members of a professional milieu, which had its specializations, hierarchies, and standards for recruitment. We also saw how they could consolidate their own positions and make their interests coincide with those of the collectivity, how they chose (or did not choose) to put themselves at the disposal of the established powers, whom they recognized as eminent insofar as these powers were able to guarantee the long-term stabilization of their collective endeavor and nascent identity. In short, each contribution obviously strove to give substance to the "bureaucracies" thanks to the "networks" their agents constructed.

How then, on the basis of the history of the state "from within" might we explain the trajectories followed by particular states? We must avoid civilizational determinism, but perhaps take account of the way in which history, while not repeating itself, can often "rhyme" (Ollé, 415). Rather than invoke such essentialist arguments, and in place of developmental teleologies, we might instead trace how this local and negotiated history creates a kind of path dependency in political development. For example, Lamouroux traces how early Song bureaucracy had a situational logic in the demands of establishing dynastic authority in the localities using power that was in origin military, but without losing the administrative legitimacy of the central administration. One outcome sets the parameters for a future negotiation, with the result that different institutional environments have different situational logics—in the modern period, different national traditions. It is institutions that do this, by routinizing political power and setting the limits for the negotiation of any particular issue: plague, financial crash, technological changes affecting individual privacy and so forth. Huret shows how the negotiation of a tax administration which could generate sufficient money at an acceptable political cost during the nineteenth century created a pattern of state finance in the US with which twentieth century politicians then had to work. Raj traces the evolution of Indian bureaucracy in a similar way, seeing changes to the educational formation of bureaucrats as a formalization and standardization of skills that company administrators had developed previously, and a pattern of skills which informed the political practice of the post-colonial state too. Garavaglia shows how regimes in Latin America were transformed by their rupture with the European past, and their trajectories shaped by the conditions of their own existence—for example a high dependency on foreign trade—but also how their encounter with the future was shaped by the legacy of past negotiations of power. Patterns of accepted and routine political action persisted as the basis on which to navigate the future, in this case, particularly, the persisting importance of family to the appraisal of suitability for bureaucratic office. In a complex polity like the Hapsburg Monarchy, as Ruiz Ibañez shows, this means though more than national diversity, a point that emerges more clearly for English historians by considering the diversity of settlements under Stuart authority beyond the English core—in Scotland, Ireland and the colonies of settlement.

On many of these paths the route taken reflects a negotiation between the interests of centre and locality. Pro looks at the development of public administration in the national state which only gradually emerged from the traumas of the Napoleonic period and its immediate aftermath. Here the emergent state entered into negotiation with peripheral regions which by virtue of their physical distance or relative weight, retained considerable powers to administer local affairs. The apparent uniformity of the emerging national state was thus diluted by inherited outcomes of negotiated power. Prior to 1890 local administration was the key to the actual functioning of the national state. Huret unpicks a similarly complex relationship in the USA during the same period, although one in which the hierarchy of powers was more formally defined and institutionalized. Here, the term state-building is perhaps more helpful than state formation, since there was a more purposeful creation of new patterns of political authority through the creation of the groups that were responsible for its exercise, rather than the more organic and undirected process which some other studies seem to have revealed. In Spain, from the late nineteenth century onwards, the full unfolding of a national administration was allowed by the development of a new cadre of individual officers, and we can observe a similar development in China in the wake of the turmoil of the 10th century. This process was actively resisted in the USA in the nineteenth century, as it had been, for example, in England in the seventeenth. Tax gatherers were a focus for the contestation of power, and were gradually replaced by a tariff approach: collection at the point of production or transport defusing resistance and therefore lowering a transaction cost.

Underlying many of our discussions then was the analysis of the functioning of the state as a process and it is a theme that runs throughout the essays in this book. This process could be described as the "institution" of the domination of different groups, which is renewed through alliances, conflicts, innovation, and the sedimentation of various forms of their authority; in this way, the hierarchies historically imposed by these forms are progressively transformed as natural and legitimate regimes of authority. We thus reconsidered questions that have been the subject of long-standing debates: the relations between private interests and public service; the structuration of authorities at the service of leaders whose the leadership itself was open to competition in the context of a society of orders organized by hierarchical statuses; the identification of new forms of domination, whether they were institutionalized, for example, in the form of offices or they took shape when communities organized themselves to fight against this domination; the creation of routines and standardized procedures. But rather than trying to establish a unique model or set of typologies—charismatic and patrimonial domination or bureaucratic rationalization—of which the force of gravitation would explain the accretion of private dominations into a legal domination, we sought to demonstrate this accretion from the historical (thereby somewhat unpredictable) interaction between these groups, which were all in positions to exercise different forms of power. This approach also, perhaps, holds a potentially optimistic message. By considering these institutionalisations as the outcome of agency, and negotiation, we highlight the history of change and the mutability of the state. Structures of state are an extension of social relations and express ideas and values—institutions are an outcome of social practice, and changed social practice can create new, and better, institutions, and also the possibility of managing relations with large and complex polities in accordance with local realities, and aspirations. Behind this process lies a dynamic apparently capable of transforming "particular" collective interests, and not simple private ones, into public interests. The accretion of particular interests is made possible by the force of organized groups, well aware of their authorities and function, avid to conquer new positions while stabilizing those that brought them to the attention of the established powers, whether they were imperial, regional or simply local. Readers are therefore encouraged to keep in mind some of these questions while considering each particular case explored here: how could the interests of a group embody, rightly or wrongly, the collective interest? How did this group succeed in particular in founding the defense of its own interests as the way of ordering the collectivity? How did this institution, in a self-aware and historically uncertain process, engender a powerful administration of things and at the same time, become a central element in governing men? In these conditions, how did a specific power take the form of a specialized service? How were the agents able to transform the prestige of the service owed to the public authority into a reproducible routine, inseparable from the power of the state? And, finally, how did that enable, but also limit the future negotiation of power in that particular polity?

Paris/Barcelona/Sheffield,

December 2014-October 2015

References

Beik, W., (1985), *Absolutism and Society in Seventeenth-Century France: State Power and Provincial Aristocracy in Languedoc*, Cambridge, Cambridge University Press.

Braddick, M.J., and Walter, J.D., (2001), *Negotiating Power in Early Modern Society: Order, Hierarchy, and Subordination in Britain and Ireland*, Cambridge, Cambridge University Press.

Brewer, J., (1989), *The Sinews of Power: War, Money and the English State, 1688-1783*, London, Unwin Hyman.

Garavaglia, J.C., and Pro, J., (2013), *Latin American Bureaucracy and the State Building process (1780-1860)*, Cambridge, Cambridge Scholars Publishing.

Gorski, P., (2003), *The Disciplinary Revolution: Calvinism and the Rise of the State in Early Modern Europe*, Chicago: Chicago University Press.

Griffith, Paul, Fox, Adam, and Hindle, Steve, (1996), *The Experience of Authority in Early Modern England*, Basingstoke, Macmillan.

Reckwitz, A., (2002), "Toward a Theory of Social Practices", *European Journal of Social Theory* 5: 243-63.

Schatzki, T., (1996), *Social Practices,* Cambridge, Cambridge University Press.

Slack, P., (1985), *The Impact of Plague in Tudor and Stuart England*, London, Routledge, Kegan, Paul.

—. (1988), *Poverty and Policy in Tudor and Stuart England*, London, Longman.

Tilly, C., (1990), *Coercion, Capital, and European States, A.D.990-1990*, Oxford, Blackwell.

CHAPTER ONE

RENDERING JUSTICE AND ADMINISTERING THE OFFICE: JUDGES AND JUDICIAL OFFICERS IN CASTILE DURING THE REIGN OF THE CATHOLIC MONARCHS

ELISA CASELLI

Justice in late medieval Castile has been studied countless times and from innumerable angles. The same observation could be made about the reign of the Catholic Monarchs [1475-1516] and the changes that occurred throughout the Hispanic world during this period. The spheres of governance were reorganized and, among them, the administration of justice received particular attention (Calderón 1999).

On this occasion, my objective will be to revise the fundamental characteristics of this essential area of governance and analyze, through the use of examples, the everyday activities of the judges and judicial officers. I will do this by studying normative sources (preferably law codes and rulings from the *Cortes**) and in particular by examining lawsuits and *cartas ejecutorias** that recount judicial trials. Particular attention will be paid to demonstrating the manner in which these agents served the monarchy and at the same time *privately* administered their own office. Firstly, a very short description of the organization of the judiciary in Castile during that period will be presented, as well as the salient traits of the Royal Council and Chanceries as the highest tribunals of the kingdom. Finally, I will emphasize two exceptional aspects of the judicial offices: the conviction of judges for having proceeded inappropriately, and the use of the courts to procure the effective payment of judges' salary and defend the benefits of their office. Most of the time, both aspects, which were used to safeguard and sustain the position, constituted two sides of the same coin; for example, when a judge tried to seize property that had been confiscated as a consequence of a judgment that he himself had pronounced. On these occasions, the magistrate could move from being judge to being the denounced party (and the litigant) in the course of the same lawsuit. It should be clear that such incidents were not contingent on the judgment issued during a *juicio de residencia**, when it was applicable.

The absence of a centralized tax collecting system meant that the monarchy's servants received their pay through *situados** or orders of payment from the treasury, which were to be drawn from royal duties that a tax farmer or local tax collector had to pay (Ladero 2002). In addition, the practice was tolerated whereby the agents guaranteed their own livelihoods through the daily exercise of their office. This *forced tolerance* was a consequence of the impossibility of carrying out effective audits, and of the almost chronic deficit of the Royal Treasury. Specific cases will be cited here to illustrate how these public servants administered, privately or individually, their pay and emoluments; they had to bear the costs and expense of defending them, even the judicial procedure that it could entail.

Justice and its Administration

"Justice is one of the virtues by which the world is best and most veraciously governed…" The definition of "Justice" is introduced by these words in Hugo de Celso's compilation, which was published around 1538 (De Celso 1538). For Díaz de Montalvo, justice was the most perfect of all virtues; a virtue that consisted essentially in giving to each individual what he deserved.[1] I should begin this section by emphasizing that *juridical inequality* was one of the principal characteristics of the period that concerns us here. This fact should be borne in mind when addressing any

---

[1] "*Porque la justicia es muy alta virtud e por ella se sostienen todas las cosas en el estado que deben e es perfecta más que todas las virtudes porque comunica e participa con todas e distribuye a todos e a cada uno su derecho*." "Because justice is a very lofty virtue and thanks to it, all things are maintained in the state that they should be in and it is more perfect than all the other virtues because it communicates and participates with all the other ones and distributes to everyone and to each one its right ". Díaz de Montalvo, Alonso [This untitled original work is generally known as *Ordenanzas Reales de 1484*; it is a compilation of laws and pragmatic sanctions that Díaz de Montalvo assembled, so as to comply with an order from the Catholic Kings and which he finished writing, according to what the manuscript states, in Huete in 1484].

subject related to justice, as it implies that everyone possessed a *quality* acquired by birth, and reflecting the estate they were born into; their social horizon was shaped according to it. This *quality* was difficult to modify but was in no way immutable, and it is important to emphasize this aspect. To affirm the contrary would be to deny the existence of any type of social mobility and nothing could be less true. Changes did take place, and these variations often meant a modification of the person's juridical status, which in turn involved alteration to what the individual was thought to deserve, namely, what he *should* receive in accordance with his new social condition. That was what was *just*.

The quotation which opened this section, however, contains another idea that deserves to be underlined: justice was conceived of as an *act of government*. The absence of a division of powers meant that, as Professor Tomás y Valiente (2000: 89) rightly noted, the act by which a court pronounced a sentence was seen as something more than a judicial act in the strict sense of the word, to wit, a unique, procedural implementation of a predefined regulation or regulations, as the prevailing tendency has defined it since the Enlightenment. Such a sentence also represented "an act of government, in function of which the judicial act was permeated by a series of considerations, which transcended the simple, singular justice of the case that was being considered and resolved procedurally". In addition to dispensing justice, each agent that served as a judge was entrusted with various tasks related to governance. He could be in charge of supervising the maintenance of streets, preserving public order or appointing men to certain offices, to cite a few examples. This duality of the judge's attributes was present on both the local level for the *alcaldes ordinarios** or *corregidores**,[2] as well as on the highest echelons for the members of the Royal Council or the Chanceries.[3]

At this point, it is essential to keep in mind a concept that is fundamental when we refer to justice in this context; it is *inherence*[4] in the most literal sense of the word, between religion and political power, for it defined the Spanish kingdoms for centuries. Its most evident expression can be found in the conception of the monarchical institution as sacred and

---

[2] An interesting analysis of a case can be found in Cortés 1999.

[3] As for this institution, see Gómez 2003, *passim*.

[4] According to the *Diccionario de la Real Academia Española*, "*inherencia*" (from the Latin, *in haerentia*) can be defined as a union of things that are inseparable because of their nature, or that only can be separated mentally and through the process of abstraction.

the king being designated by God. It was believed that he was God's vicar on earth so as to render justice in the divinity's name. According to the theory of the jurists of that era—including those that have been cited above—*divine grace* endowed the king with the *monopoly of grace*, from which the royal prerogatives were derived (among them, for example, the competence to suspend the implementation of a law in certain cases); his was the highest rank of justice in the kingdom. Dispensing justice in itself was consequently an act of government and the image of the "Just King" was one of the most enduring representations of the monarch (Hespanha 1989: 220). As we know, the king was, above all, a judge. He possessed supreme jurisdiction over the kingdom. Thanks to this *summa potestas*, the king could delegate *jurisdiction*, both in *señoríos** and in cities. Each jurisdictional sphere reproduced the act of *governing* that space when dispensing justice; it could even be considered the principal act.

Within these parameters, justice acquired a dual dimension. On the one hand, as *distributive justice*, it depended exclusively on the monarch; by virtue of it, he could make use of his magnificence and liberality by awarding graces and *mercedes** to individuals according to their merits. On the other, *commutative justice* dealt with the cases that involved negotiations over conflicts that men had amongst themselves; in such cases the king had the last word. Thus, prescription presupposed that the administration of justice functioned (or *should* function) according to a pyramidal order, in which the monarch would be placed on the vertex (Calderón 1999: 31).

Along with the king, the members of the *Consejo Mayor del Rey** or *Royal Council* had supreme jurisdiction; they could, in turn, appoint judges to carry out inquiries (*jueces pesquisidores**) or serve as their delegates with the specific mandate to pronounce sentences (*jueces delegados**). In addition, the *Alcaldes de Casa y Corte** formed part of the personal sphere of royal justice (they did not generally hear appeals nor did they send investigators more than five leagues beyond the site where the Court was established).They also had the authority to hear the same types of lawsuits as the aforementioned judges and together they made up what can be considered as the highest legal authority. The *Royal Chanceries* (or *Court and Chancery*) and the *Audiencias** would be found next (with the difference that their members had to reside permanently in the institutional seats).

Below this were the *Adelantados** or the *Alcaldes de Adelantamientos**—the *adelantamientos* or *merindades** corresponded to territorial divisions that originated in the thirteenth century and were appointed by the king to "rule and govern" in his name. They had the power to judge and try the appeals that were lodged before the *alcaldes* of their province.

On the local level, *alcaldes ordinarios**, *alcaldes mayores**, *corregidores** or their deputies could administer justice in the first instance; *adelantados**, governors or their assistants heard appeals (and also in the first instance, provided that they resided in the jurisdiction). The institutions that were appointed to hear specific cases, such as the *Alcaldes de las sacas y cosas vedadas**, *Alcaldes de la Mesta y cañadas** or the *Alcaldes de la Hermandad** should also be included here.

All of the offices that have been introduced so far presupposed two fundamental attributes. Firstly, they were functions that derived, directly or indirectly, from royal instances, that is, they were administrators of royal justice. Secondly, these offices were defined as being *ordinary*, which meant that these judges heard all cases that occurred within the area of their jurisdiction. In contrast, there were also *delegated judges* or *commissioned judges*, who, again by royal mandate, were assigned to take responsibility for a particular case. The royal notaries and accountants of the Royal Treasury should not be overlooked here, for they also had the authority to act as judges, especially when the lawsuits had to do with royal revenues (De Celso 1538; De las Heras 1996; Calderón 1999).

The orbit of the administration of justice did not end there. Broadly speaking, an identical administrative organization was replicated in the jurisdictional spaces that the monarchy ceded to the lords who, in turn, delegated powers to govern, including the authority to levy taxes and render justice (Bernardo 1996: 52). Although variations existed based on the size of the *señorío*, we would generally find there: *alcaldes ordinarios* (generally chosen by the lord, at the proposal of the council), *corregidores* (selected by the lord), *audiencias* (with their judges and sometimes with the office of president and judges) and the lord, as the highest instance in his jurisdiction (García 1996: 215-216). The law stated that under certain conditions, a vassal could subsequently appeal to the royal justice. The highest royal tribunals were obliged to respect seigniorial justice, and limit themselves to hearing appeals, as long as all the instances had been exhausted within the lord's jurisdiction or if the lawsuit involved the lord himself. Nevertheless, if a vassal managed to prove that his rights were not necessarily going to be respected, he could appear directly before the *Audiencia*.

The administration of justice did not entirely derive from the monarch. As is well known, there existed, at the same time, the very active system of ecclesiastical justice, which had no qualms about interfering in the spheres of royal jurisdiction—a principal object of concern during the reign of the Catholic Monarchs. It is not at all fortuitous that in the description of each one of the aforementioned judicial offices, those that wrote the laws of this period took care to remind the men that held offices that it was their responsibility to prevent the "ecclesiastical judges" from interfering, and to defend the royal justice that they represented. In the ecclesiastical *señoríos*, both the juridical foundation (canon law) and judicial organization (the Court of Justice of the Diocese) acquired specific characteristics, and needless to say, their legitimacy did not derive from royal justice. In practice, the ecclesiastical administration functioned in a similar manner, with offices such as judges, deputies, royal prosecutors, notaries, and lawyers; they even spoke of the "bishop's *alcaldes*" or the "bishop's *oidores**" in the procedural jargon. As for appeals within the system of ecclesiastical justice, the verdict of the bishop or archbishop was appealed before the primate of the ecclesiastical province and afterwards, an appeal could only be made to Rome (sometimes the procedure went directly to Rome after the bishop's ruling). Nevertheless, in the workings of everyday justice, the sentences pronounced by bishops could equally be appealed before the *Audiencia*. When the right to appeal was not granted, the appellant could make a direct presentation to the *Audiencia*; if the judges accepted his appeal, a jurisdictional dispute could certainly arise between the instances of ecclesiastical and royal justice.[5]

Concurrent Jurisdictions: Indeterminacy and Conflicts

Jurisdictional overlaps, which were so common in the period under consideration, led to incessant conflict. It needs to be emphasized that these clashes were not limited to disputes between the royal, ecclesiastical, and seigniorial legal spheres, for they also occurred within the realm of royal justice. Jurisdiction (*iuris dictio*) in itself implies the power to construct, in the words of Pérez-Prendes: "a value judgment masked by coercion" (1996: 144). In order to make use of a jurisdiction, however, it is

[5] This assertion, just like others that are expressed in this article, refers to aspects of procedural practice revealed in the trials or by the positions of diverse social agents expressed in them, except if a specific source is cited; I have made these assertions based on the careful reading of more than six hundred lawsuits, *cartas ejecutorias,* and reports about cases to the judge (*relaciones de causas*), that are preserved in the *Archivo General de Simancas* and especially the *Archivo de la Real Chancillería* of Valladolid.

necessary to have "cognizance", which is first defined by considering for whom and for what reasons a specific judge can intercede, and, then, at what moment or instance in the course of the lawsuit he has this right (Pérez-Prendes 1966). The functions and levels of jurisdiction that were assigned to each one of the judicial offices were frequently replicated in different posts, or they were not defined with the requisite clarity. This ambiguity meant that in the same town, for example, different officers considered themselves legally qualified to try the same case. In other words, a crime could become *judgeable* by diverse judges (or "justices", as they are called in the documents). This lack of precision allowed the litigants to take legal action before different judges, which could lead to parallel lawsuits or a jurisdictional dispute for the continuation of the lawsuit. In this respect, the *fuero** (derived from factors such as belonging to the Church or military, or having a specific place of residence) constituted a fundamental aspect. According to how it is appreciated, a *fuero* can easily be considered a *competence*, seen from a tribunal that was mindful of its jurisdiction, or a *right*, seen from the point of view of the defendant, who could contend that he was being deprived of his rights and privileges.

Lawsuits that reveal concurrent jurisdiction are certainly not scarce.[6] They not only document the clash of the ecclesiastical, seigniorial and royal justices when they invade each other's jurisdictional sphere, but also confrontations among the agents who exercised royal justice. Let us take as an example the *Alcaldes de la Hermandad*, who could only hear cases that involved the theft of personal property or damage to it, as well as the kidnapping and rape of women (if they were not prostitutes); they also judged assaults, murders, and wounds that occurred on routes, provided that they occurred in virtually uninhabited areas (meaning fewer than thirty *vecinos**). Nevertheless, this restriction was no longer applicable if the case involved any member of the *Hermandad* or his family members; in these situations, they could hear both civil and criminal cases (De Celso 1538; López 1921; Martínez-Gómez 1996). They could also intervene in all the crimes that were committed in the town where the *Hermandad* was in session. In practice, this lack of definition led to interminable conflicts with *alcaldes ordinarios* and *corregidore*s.

The provable overlaps did not end with the aforementioned examples. As Hespanha rightly points out, documents also reveal vestiges of the

[6] This phenomenon did not just occur in the Hispanic Monarchy. For the case of France see Toureille 2013.

vigorous coexistence of oral justice (1993: 21). It has also been called a lay justice (or even "unlettered"), or an "infrajustice" (Mantecón 2002), which did not leave any trace other than tangential references in the written lawsuits. It was a form of justice that complied with an alternative juridical order. The men that judged were not generally career officers but *honorable* people that were local notables, chosen on grounds of prestige and not for their technical qualifications. Their profound knowledge of what was *just* or *unjust*, defined in terms of local custom, was not easily replaceable. The parties involved selected these "arbiter judges" or "compromise judges" by mutual consent; the arbitrators could proceed "as if they were ordinary judges" and pronounce their "rightful verdict according to the merits of the lawsuit", that is, they followed the course of a trial even if it were conducted orally. There were also, however, the so-called "amicable arbitrators", who "because of their goodwill" sought to "extricate the dispute" without having to have recourse to a real lawsuit.[7]

This lay justice aimed to create a consensus among the disputants and sought to avoid the definitive, irremediable defeat of one of the sides; by trying to get both parties to give up something, it tried to procure the maintenance of a stable equilibrium (Hespanha 1993). In any case, even if both sides initially agreed that the arbiter judge should intervene, it was not uncommon that one would accept him at first, but later would appear before the *corregidor* or *alcalde* even while the case was still being argued; two overlapping sentences could thus be pronounced. Another possibility was that one side could appeal to the formal system of justice after the oral sentence. Thanks to the petitions, appeals or depositions of witnesses that refer to these situations, we possess written testimonies about the oral intervention that "compromise judges" made.

It is also important to point out that while religious minorities existed in Castile, both the Jewish and Muslim communities had their own judges, who possessed the power to resolve internal disputes. They could try civil as well as criminal cases, although from the last quarter of the fifteenth century, their authority tended to be restricted to cases of civil law. The official course of appeals would lead first to the *major judge* of each community and then to the Royal *Audiencia* or Council. Nevertheless, the litigants appealed to the tribunal that would best accommodate their interests, just as the Christians did. They did not therefore restrict themselves to the judges of their own communities, which at once gave

---

[7] The expressions that have been put in quotation marks in this paragraph were taken from Hugo de Celso 1538.

rise to jurisdictional overlaps and parallel lawsuits were frequently pursued (Caselli 2008).

The Highest Tribunals of the Kingdom

It was only in the provisions that were issued by the *Cortes* of Toro in 1369 and 1371 that the objectives for the *Audiencia* were established and fixed, even if documents dating back to the first half of the fourteenth century have been located that speak of "the judges of the king's *Audiencia*" (Díaz Martín 1997: 20). In the ordinances from those years the mission of the *Alcaldes de corte* was defined, and it was resolved that an *Audiencia* would be formed. Seven judges were assigned to it. They were to meet "to hold *Audiencia*" where the king was and, in his absence, in the church where the Chancery or royal seal was. Although it was decreed in 1447 that the Chancery would have its permanent seat in Valladolid, the real organization of the high tribunal was only undertaken during the reign of the Catholic Monarchs.

From the moment of its establishment, the *Audiencia* represented the person of the king; consequently, the decisions that the judges took collegially became unappealable. The documents state: "in our Court and Chancery, before the judges of our Royal *Audiencia*". The institution possessed a unitary status, although each name had a distinct meaning: *Audiencia*, the supreme royal tribunal; *Chancery*, the keeper of the seal, and *Court*, to manifest the pre-eminence that the royal presence, symbolized in the seal, conferred on the *Audiencia*. The authority that the Chancery had in the kingdom was founded on the fact that it was the keeper of the *king's great seal*. The origin of this elevated position can be found in the division that was instituted at the end of the thirteenth century, during the reign of Sancho IV, when it was decided the highest tribunal of justice would keep the seal, while the "secret" seal would remain with the king in his residence. The king's great seal, which was used to validate with lead the most solemn ordinance and privileges written out on parchment, was complemented by metal seals for validating letters and provisions issued on paper. The seal represented not only royal *potestas*, but the king himself; the ceremonial that accompanied the use of the seal existed precisely to remind the onlookers of this fictitious presence (Garriga 1994: 221-229).

In its origin, the jurisdictional confines of the Chancery of Valladolid (the first to have been created) were coincident with the jurisdiction of the king and Royal Council. In 1494 it was divided on the establishment of the

Chancery of Ciudad Real, which was later moved to Granada. The new *Audiencias* that were created starting in the sixteenth century had more strictly demarcated jurisdictional spaces, at least in Europe. It was certainly not the case in America, where the magnitude of the territory made it necessary for each institution to oversee much vaster areas with diverse levels of jurisdiction. In any case, their inclusion allowed for a greater proximity to the highest tribunals of royal justice.

The *Audiencias* and Chanceries fundamentally tried, in the first instance, what were called "court cases". Also, they were authorized to hear lawsuits that originated within five leagues of the place where they resided [the so called *rastro* jurisdiction], in competition with the local ordinary justice. In spite of the restrictions that the Catholic Monarchs attempted to impose on judges and *alcaldes* in the matter of ordinary cases, so as to advantage the local agents of justice, confrontations continued between the *regidores* and *alcaldes* of Valladolid (the same also occurred in Ciudad Real and then in Granada), which proves that the magistrates did not easily resign themselves to losing their competence. On the level of appeals, they heard all those that were lodged against sentences pronounced by any ordinary or delegated judge. As instances of royal jurisdiction, they were also authorized to hear appeals issued from areas that formed part of *señoríos*.

During the period under analysis, the Chancery of Valladolid was composed of a prelate[8] as presiding magistrate, four *oidores*, though they were soon increased to eight (they passed sentence in two courtrooms with four judges in each one), three *alcaldes de Corte y Chancillería*, commonly called *alcaldes del crimen** (although the distinction between jurisdiction in civil and criminal cases was not always clearly respected), the major judge of Vizcaya, who paid special attention to the appeals lodged from the *señorío* of Vizcaya, two *alcaldes de hijosdalgo* and three provincial notaries, who instituted proceedings in lawsuits about royal taxes (Garriga 2007: 39). The composition of these tribunals was rounded off by the presence of clerks (for hearings and receiving evidence, a task that could involve making copies for its commission), investigating officials, a collector, public prosecutor, a lawyer, attorney for the poor, two doormen or porters at the front door of each courtroom, two officers of the seal and registry, a bailiff and a jailor (de Celso 1538).

---

[8] The requirement that this highest authority of the *Audiencia* was a bishop was maintained at least until the middle of the sixteenth century, which did not mean necessarily that he was no longer an ecclesiastic after that date.

The functioning of this institution lacked regularity. Neither the president nor the judges appeared assiduously at the tribunal. Their repeated absences frequently provoked complaints, especially from the *Cortes*, where on more than one occasion the participants insisted on the need for the judicial officers to be present on the days and at the times when hearings were supposed to be held. A bishop always presided at the *Audiencia*, but would be frequently absent because he was tending to his own diocese (where he in turn assigned judicial matters to his vicar general). What is more, the prescribed procedure for choosing new judges was not followed: the nominations were not made through an annual election as the provisions stated. When the process was finally carried out, the same men were often selected, which frequently meant that they held the post in perpetuity. The bachelor Pedro de Frías represents a clear example of this tendency, as I detected him serving as a judge from 1483 to 1489 or the doctor Martín de Ávila, who exercised the same office from 1485 to 1492.

The presence of honorary judges, that is, without salary, should also be noted: they were permitted to perform judicial acts as lawyers while they were training for their future posts. They obviously often did so in the lawsuits that they would subsequently try and sentence as judges (Varona García 1981: 47). All of these irregularities followed the timing set by the alliance maneuvers of the groups competing for supremacy in the local and supra-local political power relationships; the terms of reference of that informal exceeded by far its institutional setting.

Let us cite an example: *doctor* García Gómez de Castro, a professor at the University of Valladolid, was named judge in May 1492. Nevertheless, I found a lawsuit dated 1489 (in which he confronts another *vecino* about a property) where he already appears identified as a "judge of the Royal *Audiencia*", asserting his *quality* as such.[9] It is probable that at that point he only served as a "judge without pay"; it is evident, notwithstanding, that he had possession of the prerogatives of the position. I even discovered a sentence with his signature dated February 1492, that is, three months before his official nomination so he was not yet authorized to sign it.[10] In March of the same year, the president and judges were summarily dismissed (an act that did not affect Gómez de Castro, as he had not yet been designated). No official document revealing the causes of these dismissals exists, and the dismissal is only documented by chronicles and

---

9 ARCHV.RE.1489-25-28

10 ARCHV.RE.1492-43-27.

the verification of the signatures that the final judgments contain. According to Garriga, this incident formed part of the process the kings successively undertook to try to control the Chancery as they endeavored, unsuccessfully, to make their agents obey the applicable regulations (Garriga 1994: 144-145). This explanation probably describes the monarchs' intention.

Nevertheless, according to the documents that I have located, it is more likely that the cause of this general dismissal was linked to the confrontations between corporations and even individuals that were happening on the local level. One of the judges that was included on the new roster would be the same García Gómez de Castro, who was by then officially invested. There were permanent clashes between the members of the tribunal and professors from the University of Valladolid because the former assumed the right to intervene in the appointments of posts at the university. Various lawsuits about the naming of professors and the director of the university, one of which directly involved Gómez de Castro, reveal an undercurrent that would call into question any interpretation that I could try to develop here about the real reasons for the mass dismissal. But these documents do undoubtedly illustrate vividly the circumstantial confrontations that disrupted the institution.

As for the Royal Council (which also had to include a minimum number of prelates), I should say that its powers were not radically different from those assigned to the *Audiencia* and Chancery, which led to concurrent jurisdictions within the sphere of royal justice itself. At its onset, the Council was not given specific authority to administer justice, but it obviously had them, for I have already explained how the administration of justice was considered to be intrinsic to governance. A proclamation that Juan II issued in 1427 recognized the Council as an organ of justice, and in the Ordinances of 1459 it was mentioned as the supreme tribunal of the kingdom (Calderón 1999: 34). During the reign of the Catholic Monarchs, Ferdinand and Isabella, important changes occurred in different areas, especially in the terrain of justice. The provisions proclaimed by the Cortes in Toledo in 1480 clearly reflect the Monarchy's intentions of endowing the judicial institutions with greater effectiveness. These dispositions grant the Council vast judicial faculties, which allow it to try almost any lawsuit, a measure that meant that the institution was placed on the same level of jurisdiction as the Chancery. It was conceded extensive discretionary latitude to sign documents and provisions in the name of the kings, even though they made clear which cases they would judge themselves,[11] and expressly indicated that they would be present on Fridays to attend to those matters.

In most of the cases, litigants had recourse to the Council in order to obtain a summons addressed to the opposing party in which that party was ordered to modify its stance on the disputed point, or was to be required to make reparation for an act that had been committed. The summons could also be used to request a writ of protection or precautionary measure in the face of a possible act by the adversary (to mention only the most common cases). In practice, this possibility resulted in the institution trying innumerable lawsuits, although they were not always carried out procedurally. Summary proceedings became the typical channel for processing lawsuits before the Council (Calderón 1999). It sometimes sent commissioned judges to hear a particular case, but it did not necessarily proceed in this fashion, as, according to what was prescribed in 1480, the Council was authorized to act in both civil and criminal cases without the need to "commission them to others" and "without the mode of a trial"; "once the truth was known" the judges could simply decide and pronounce their sentences, for which the only possible appeal was a *suplicación** (*Cortes* of Toledo, item 26). This same provision revived a law, issued by Juan II, which required a bond of one thousand and four hundred *doblas** (later increased to one thousand five hundred) in order to be eligible to go to retrial to appeal the verdicts pronounced. Clearly, the aim was to restrict this legal instance to very important cases.

---

[11] The Catholic Monarchs prescribed: "we want to make known which matters we want to sign with our own names, which are these that follow: the charges of our own House, daily alms, *mercedes* for inherited or lifelong annuities, lands, tenures, and remissions of debt, legitimations, first authorized registers of sale, the sustenance of ambassadors that have to leave our Kingdoms to go to other lands, offices for the cities, towns, and villages of our kingdoms, new notaries, appeals from prelates and other benefices, rights of patronage, chaplaincies, offices of sextons, *corregidores*, investigators of cities, towns and villages of our Kingdoms with suspended offices" / "*queremos declarar cuales son las cosas que nos queremos firmar de nuestros nombres e son estas que siguen: oficios de nuestra casa, mercedes, limosnas de cada día, mercedes de juro de heredad e de por vida, tierras e tenencias e perdones, legitimaciones, sacas, mantenimiento de embajadores que hayan de ir fuera de nuestros reinos a otras partes, oficios de ciudades, villas e lugares de nuestros reinos, notarias nuevas, suplicaciones de perlados e otros beneficios e patronazgos, capellanías, sacristanías, corregidores, pesquisidores de ciudades e villas e lugares de nuestros reinos con suspensión de oficios*" Cortes de Toledo de 1480, ítem 24.

These measures were intended to put in order and regulate a tribunal that was obviously overwhelmed by the profusion of lawsuits that were processed before it. The delays and stays that the litigants faced were the object of reiterated complaints and a subject of discussion in the *Cortes*. One of the provisions of 1480 ordered the court reporter to post on the Council's door a scrip that indicated the matters that would be dealt with that day, so that only the interested parties need remain there, awaiting their dispatch, and the others would not needlessly waste time and could attend to their other business. I have indicated that the most typical way in which the Council processed lawsuits was by dispatch, but nevertheless, cases were also judged in full-fledged trials. The progress that the Council made in this terrain led the Catholic Kings to order the remission, on diverse occasions—the last one during their reign in 1498—of the pending lawsuits to the Chanceries; according to Carlos Garriga, such attempts were intended to curtail the Council's judicial expansion (1994: 236).

The *Audiencia* Chancery and the Royal Council could obviously try similar cases because the definitions of their respective areas of jurisdiction lacked precision and this led to a constant overlapping as the judicial activities unfolded. One of the most serious problems that this overlapping caused was the emission of two royal documents which contradicted each other about the same lawsuit. It should be kept in mind that both the Council and the Chancery signed with the royal seal. Countless examples of such predicaments were found in the course of this investigation. For example, during the course of a lawsuit processed before the *Audiencia*, one of the parties could present a plea before the Council and thus obtain a summons notifying the opposing side, or ordering the local agents of justice, to execute a legal procedure. Once the trial was over, the judges pronounced their verdict and issued a *carta ejecutoria* about the same case, which was not always or necessarily coincident with the one that the Council expedited. From the official point of view, only the *cartas ejecutorias* were the result of a trial (*res iudicata*); however, both (*cartas ejecutorias* and summons) were pronounced in the name of the Kings, began with the same heading ("Ferdinand and Isabella, by the Grace of God...") and bore the royal seal. It could also happen the other way around, namely that the litigants first went to the Council and then the Audiencia, even if both cases could give rise to the creation of parallel lawsuits and the ensuing pronouncement of overlapping sentences.

As I have explained, these contradictory orders were formulated in the name of the kings. The summons and second injunctions (in fact sometimes the third ones) abound, stressing that a decision was clearly not being complied with. The reason for this lack of obedience can be found in the compliance to another writ, which was also issued *by royal order*. It is clear that in the face of two conflicting mandates, only one could be *complied* with, although it was officially declared that both should be *obeyed*, as it was a matter of royal orders. Ferdinand and Isabella were not indifferent to this situation. The *Cortes* had already discussed this subject over a long time and periodically legislated so as to prevent documents issued from the heart of the monarchy from hindering the functioning of its highest tribunals. It is timely to clarify that I am referring here to documents that address lawsuits between private individuals and not those that impacted upon *fueros* or local customs, for claims made to the *Cortes* about these latter cases date back to an earlier period; this particular question has been thoroughly studied.

The first clear declaration in relation to this can be found in the acts of the Cortes held in Burgos in 1453. The seventeenth item denounces the postures of those that, inventing a pretext, obtained a summons with the royal signature so as to be dismissed from a lawsuit, or to be able to withdraw one from the Chancery or the ordinary instances of justice which were pending, with the evident intention of bringing the case before judges that would favor them. It adds that such documents should "be obeyed and not complied with notwithstanding any affirmations they might contain". As we can see the well-known expression "*obedézcase pero no se cumpla*" [obey but do not comply with]" encompassed "transactions between individuals" just as the regulations signalized. The law then warned the notaries or secretaries that they should not allow such documents and provisions to be executed, under penalty of deprivation of their offices. Almost identical texts reiterated this law according to the acts of the *Cortes* held in Toledo in 1462, Salamanca in 1475, Burgos in 1515, Valladolid in 1523 and Madrid in 1528 and 1534. And it would even be renewed with greater precision in the *Novísima Recopilación de las Leyes de España* of 1805.[12]

This subject was also an object of concern for Isabella and Ferdinand. They tried to curb the emission of documents that were "against the rights", as they were also known, and prevent them from being understood as being against the rights of one of the parties. A measure issued in 1480 aimed to restrict the presence of lawyers or extraneous individuals in the tribunals so as to prevent them from influencing others in this respect. It explained that if some men needed to enter the court to deal with their own

[12] Libro III, Título IV, Leyes IV a VII.

matters, they should leave promptly and "neither hear other affairs nor expedite our documents", except if they were "archbishops or bishops or dukes or counts or marquis or grand masters of military orders, because they form part of our Council because of their titles, and we want them to be able to be in our Council when they so desire" (Toledo *Cortes* of 1480, item 32). The eloquence of this quotation almost exempts me from making any additional commentary about it. During this period the institution of the monarchy undoubtedly became stronger, though, as this one aspect of its functioning demonstrates, this strengthening in no way meant that the clergy and nobility vanished from the political scene; on the contrary, they clearly intervened (and would continue to interfere) in the areas where decisions were made. I should add that the repetitions of similar provisions are evidence that this measure was not complied with, as is the verification of documents issued to contending parties when a trial was underway.

The question that must arise is: who was effectively behind the signing of these royal documents? The kings' confidants were obviously not the only ones involved, nor was it just question of those that "because of their titles" could exert their influence. Networks based on clientelism or lineage, friendships or enmities, alliances or rivalries, which were always contingent, shaped a network of bonds constituted by services provided and asymmetrical compensations, which one way or another impacted the administration of justice. These intrinsically aleatory ties were further modified by the shifting of the agents – the majority of whom were pursuing their own careers within the administration. This web was not just confined to the highest royal tribunals but encompassed all those that administered royal justice. In reality, the web should be simply described as the administrators of justice, in order to include in the expression those that formed part of the seigneurial and ecclesiastical systems of justice. It should be born in mind that the aforementioned nobles and bishops could not only exert their influence, but they and their vassals could also dispense justice in their respective jurisdictions. At the same time, they frequently subscribed as members of the Royal Council or the Chanceries; these gentlemen and prelates consequently could be found hearing cases simultaneously as judges in the seigneurial and royal jurisdictions.

In the midst of these jurisdictional conflicts, each agent maneuvered through the uses and customs and general laws, and fulfilled his office, safeguarding the common good whilst all while taking care of his own. Without neglecting those to whom he owed favors, he was constantly trying to increase his own symbolic and material capacity in order to gain a better position in the network of relationships or, in other words, to be placed more advantageously within the relationships of power. The monarchy's government rested, and was administered, on the basis of this complex network, which was traversed by *permanent negotiations*. Each judicial officer juggled a *public* side, which consisted of dispensing justice in the name of the king and therefore participating in the operation of the monarchy itself, and a *private* side, which involved optimizing his own profit. Both were inseparable and indispensable for their mutual survival.

Men of the Law and the Administration of Their Office

"Judges take the place of the king and the judge's arms are the voice of the king…". Hugo de Celso expressed this relation thus in the previously cited work. In order to be feared, the magistrates did not need any other weapon than the voice of the king, which was expressed through the justice they rendered. It was expected that the judges "were loyal and had a good reputation and without evil greed and that they had wisdom so as to judge the lawsuits rightly… and have good sense and above all that they feared God…".[13] These expectations were clearly not always met. Those men were charged with dispensing justice, which was in Montalvo's words "the highest of virtues". As in all offices (and I could almost say in all walks of life), there were, however, those that fulfilled their mission perfectly, those that attempted to do so, and those that only looked out for their own interests.

Within the realm of Castile, each judge knew that the authority of his verdicts derived from the reference to the royal power they contained and was therefore perfectly aware that any one of his acts *formed part of* the administration of the monarchy. At the same time, each judge was also the proponent of *his* own office. This point attests to one of the characteristics that most specifically defined the system of justice during this period. As I have maintained, every decision that an agent (judges, clerks, prosecutors, etc.) took in his judicial practice, represented an act that had a public aspect (as part of the governance of the monarchy) and a private one (the regulation of his own position), within a quite broad spectrum of possible ploys. The margins for these maneuvers were as flexible as the capacity and ductility that the agent possessed to further his undertakings. In this dual mission, the least competent (or perhaps the least discrete and unscrupulous) often transgressed the regulations, dispatched their tasks with "exorbitances" (in the terms of the epoch) and caused disgruntlement

[13] *Partida III*, Título IV, Ley III.

and complaints that frequently reached the *Cortes*. The reclamations arising out of breach of trust and bribery inundated the petitions, and therefore the ordinances issued, during these years.

Nevertheless, all of these aspects, that is to say the lawsuits the agents of justice brought forward and the claims from the attorneys, formed part of the mechanism of negotiations. All of them composed power networks, which on the local level were played out in factious struggles. The complaints proceeded from those that saw their interests the most directly altered and managed to make themselves heard. It should not be overlooked that due to their very essence these relations were changing configurations (Dedieu 2000: 24-25). It could then transpire that the following year the local situation had been reversed and those that the day before were complaining then had in their hands the authority to dispense justice. They could then assail their rivals with the same abuses they had previously denounced. In other words, these were the agreements and dubious compromises that tend to characterize that particular form of political power.

Let us return to the question of the administration of the office itself, which was mentioned above. The regulations established the mechanisms for appointing judges and officials, as well as their respective salaries and who should pay them. When making these appointments, they had to take into account, in addition to age, other specific physical requirements (blindness, deafness or insanity were some of the handicaps that barred men from these positions), as well as ethical ones (being just, upright men, and possessing the aforementioned virtues was necessary), sociological requirements (the exigency of holy orders for certain offices, the *limpieza de sangre**, and, of course, being a good Christian, so that the excommunicated were ruled out, as well as those that had performed manual labor). During this period, the attainment of an academic degree and experience were considered desirable criteria (Roldán 1989: 41-87), and being a ¨native¨ of the area of jurisdiction was ruled out, as the *Partidas* stipulated that it would be "a sacrilege" that someone could "acquire the position of judge or any other one in his birthplace", as it would call his impartiality into question.[14]

Given that royal justice is primarily being examined here, I should point out that the appointments were the king's responsibility, whether they were made by his direct decision or by those that were authorized to do so in his name. In very succinct terms, it could be said that the offices

[14] *Partida I*, Título XVIII, Ley XI.

of the supreme tribunals, such as the *Alcaldes de la Casa y Corte*, judges of the Royal Council or *Audiencia* or *alcaldes* of the Court and Chanceries, were all conferred directly by the monarch. In the same manner, the office of *corregidor* was designated directly by the king (and then the officer was responsible for appointing his own deputy), although the law indicated that he could only be appointed if the city, town or village thus requested it.

On the contrary, the *alcaldes mayores* were elected (through different procedures according to the epoch) by the cities and towns/*villas*, and the choice was then presented to the king so that he could confirm them. A similar process was followed for the designation of the *Alcaldes de la Hermandad* or *merinos** and *adelantados*. Once the royal appointment was obtained, however, through diverse contrivances, these positions could be alienated,[15] transferred (the most common way was through a resignation accompanied by a proposal for a successor) or could be rented out, as if it were question of any other type of property. These transfers took on extremely diverse variables (Dedieu 2011: 23); for example, the appointment of a deputy could in fact be used to as a way of resigning the charge (López Díaz 2011: 132). In the *Cortes* of Burgos of 1453 (item 16) the complaint was generalized: "*corregidores*, *alcaldes*, bailiffs, *merinos*… rent the aforementioned offices", which represented a "disservice" to the monarchy and implied "great damage" to the cities, for the lessees were not inclined to actually hold the offices and, in addition, often committed severe abuses. In the aforementioned work of Hugo de Celso, in his entry "leased or rented", when he refers to the contracts truncated by the death of one of the parties, he included judges, *alcaldes* or lawyers, and specified the conditions under which the heirs could continue to rent the office.

This *private* character of the judicial offices was not only expressed, however, in the possibility of renting them. In addition to the benefits received from tax exemptions, the right to be lodged, and honorific recompenses, judges and judicial officers generally could count on incomes from their salaries or wages, court fees for each procedural act,

---

[15] This vast question, which obviously is not included in this article's subject matter, has already been widely and excellently studied. It suffices to cite the classic works by Francisco Tomás y Valiente or Benjamín González Alonso; we should also include the more recent analyses of Inés Gómez González, which are included in the bibliography and Francisco Andújar Castillo, in this same book just to mention a few examples. Cfr.: Jiménez Estrella 2012.

ten percent of the seizures and a proportionate share of the fines which was added to the share destined for the accuser when he acted *ex officio*, that is, when the case did not originate in an accusation. In return, when a judge proceeded unacceptably in the first instance, he could be condemned by the court of appeals to pay the costs of the trial, for example. The judges and judicial officers had in their own hands the means to optimize their revenues, but they also could be condemned to pay from their own pocketbooks the costs engendered by their errors or abuses. These two aspects, which could be seen as two sides of the same coin, constituted the private administration of the office. The prolonged existence of this specific practice, which succumbed only in the light of nineteenth-century constitutionalism, and its impact on the everyday functioning of the legal system and beyond it, means that it should be considered as one of the most prominent characteristics of justice in the Ancien Régime.

Condemned Judges

I have just said that if a judge acted unacceptably in the first instance, he could be sentenced to pay the costs of the next suit. Let us examine an individual case in order to confirm that it was in effect true and not only applicable to the magistrates that represented royal justice.

In 1489, Miguel Sánchez de Ainzo, a *vecino* from Navares de las Cuevas near Segovia was sued by his creditors because he had failed to pay a debt. Sánchez's own guarantor in the initial transaction also joined the suit. The lawsuit was initiated before the *alcalde mayor* of the bishopric of Segovia, who, ordered that the debtor's property should be sold, even though he was not present. Sánchez appealed before the judges of the Royal Council, which at that time was in Málaga. It issued an ordinance in his favor, which revoked the attachment because, as the writ stated, he had left to serve the kings by performing military service, in fact in Málaga. As the royal summons was ignored, Miguel Sánchez then turned to the judges of the *Audiencia*. In his presentation he denounced the existence of a fraud, in which the guarantor himself had taken part. The creditors and guarantor in connivance had claimed what Sanchez no longer owed. This was not all: as his solicitor added, the trial was riddled with errors. According to the denunciation, the *alcalde*, Tome Ferrand, in concurrence with the creditors, had ordered that the sentence was enforced so that Sanchez's belongings would be sold at very low prices and he could "get them for himself". In other words, the magistrate had clearly prevaricated and committed abuse. In addition, the auction had been carried out for an amount that included "the *pena de doblo**", even if the sentence had not stipulated it.

In the Royal *Audiencia*, the judges ruled in favor of Miguel Sánchez, and condemned his creditors to pay the costs. This first sentence was appealed. It is important to underline that the creditors, the guarantor, and the ecclesiastic *alcalde* lodged the appeal together, and were represented by the same solicitor. At that point, it became evident that the "*alcalde del corregidor* of Segovia" had also acted, as he had ordered the sale in response to the judges' direction. That is, as often happened, the same lawsuit had been tried simultaneously by secular and ecclesiastical judges. The ecclesiastical *alcalde* attempted to excuse his act by blaming the *alcalde del corregidor* for the decision to sell Sanchez's belongings. In addition, it is interesting to observe that in cases such as this one, the judges of first instance went on to constitute part of the lawsuit in the appeals, by sending solicitors to justify their acts and decisions. The previous sentence was confirmed by other judges in the retrial; in the verdict, they ordered Tome Ferrand, the ecclesiastic *alcalde* and Juan Gonzalo Pérez, the *alcalde del corregidor*, to pay the costs of the appeal because of their erroneous acts.[16]

Alcaldes were not the only judicial officials that could be ordered to pay the costs of their mistakes. In 1492, Alfonso Martínez de Granadilla denounced Álvaro de Cuellar and his men for seizing twenty-one of his cows from a pasture within the jurisdiction of Badajoz on the contention that he owed them "certain *maravedíes** of sales tax". Denying that such a debt existed, Martínez had recourse to Gonzalo Fernández del Castillo, *corregidor* of Badajoz, who accepted the action and jailed Cuellar and his men. However the official erred in accepting guarantors that were not sufficiently solvent to justify releasing the men, which he nevertheless did. Alfonso Martínez then appealed to the *Audiencia* presenting a brief in which he denounced the magistrate's negligence for not demanding "creditable" guarantors. The insolvent guarantor was ordered to appear before the judges of the *Audiencia* or send a solicitor in his name. The notice however also included a summons for the *corregidor* himself, in which it was asserted that he had acted incorrectly because he had not protected Martínez's rights. Therefore, it was ordered, as a precautionary measure, that "all the amounts that were due to the *corregidor*" should be seized. After having examined the lawsuit, the judges pronounced a sentence that ordered that all of Cuellar and his partners' belongings be

[16] ARCHV. RE. 1489-24-4

auctioned off and, if it were necessary, they should continue by selling off the guarantor's property. They also ordered the *corregidor* to pay the costs of the appeal even if it were very unlikely that the plaintiff was able to make him pay them. Upon further research into the magistrate, I discovered conflicts that set him against the *alcaldes de la Hermandad* and some members of the Council of Badajoz; in both cases, the differences arose over designations to positions. I also learned of his unhappy fate: in July 1493, when he was on his way to mass, Gonzalo Fernández del Castillo was ambushed and murdered, dying of six stab wounds. The case analyzed here had extended over some time; the final judgment of the *Audiencia* is dated 1494. It has not been possible to establish if Alonso Martínez de Granadilla demanded what he was due from the murdered judge's heirs.[17]

It should be emphasized that such convictions were not exceptions. It is very common to find them, especially in the verdicts pronounced by the judges and *alcaldes* of the Royal *Audiencia* and Chancery. The judges' abusive conduct or negligence in the first instance was not always silenced. When the wronged parties had the opportunity to make their case known, they did so and could even demand to be compensated for the offense. They could include the claim in the same appeal, as they did in the examples cited above or expressly file a new lawsuit.

For example, Pedro Gómez de Manrique, *corregidor* of Zamora, was sued in 1486 before the *Audiencia* by Jacob Haya and his wife, *doña* Elvira, both Jewish, for the abuses he had committed against them. The magistrate had extracted a confession from Jacob under torture, and then without having confirmed it once the torture session had ended, as the law required, he insisted on having guarantees and guarantors, whom he also tortured, until *doña* Elvira managed to amass the sum he had required. The *corregidor* sent his solicitor to defend him before the high tribunal where the advocate maintained that the judge "had acted correctly, in conformity with his office". Nevertheless, the judges rejected his plea and ordered the *corregidor* to repay the two thousand silver *reales* he had received, in addition to ordering him to pay the costs of the trial.[18] This case had not been the only occasion when Gómez de Manrique had taken advantage of his position. The previous year, he had used a similar strategy against Martín Sánchez and Juan Sánchez de Mateo; according to what their

[17] ARCHV. RE 1494-78-3 / AGS. RGS. 1493-08-206 / AGS. RGS. 1493-08-44 / AGS. RGS. 1494-04-468

[18] ARCHV. RE. 1486-5-45

children and son-in-law respectively complained about, he had them shackled and cruelly tortured in prison until they handed over twenty-five gold *doblas*.[19]

Another case that can be cited is that of García de Peñaranda and Alonso de Eizmar, *alcaldes ordinarios* of Valencia de Alcántara; they were accused in 1492 before the *alcaldes del crimen* of the Chancery. The relatives of a murdered man denounced them for not having acted quickly enough against the assailants of the victim and so allowing them to escape. The accusation was for "fault and negligence … for not having wanted to make them comply with the law". Given that this case took place on land belonging to the *señorío* of the Order of Alcántara, the first argument that the solicitor of the *alcaldes* made was that the case came under the jurisdiction of the Grand Master of the Order. Nevertheless, the *alcaldes* of the Chancery declared themselves the judges of the case and condemned the *alcaldes ordinarios* to be banished. In their verdict they explained: "so that for them it would be a punishment and chastisement and for other *alcaldes* and judges an example of how to administer and enforce the law…" The sentence was appealed and the retrial ratified it, thereby adding to the condemnation a fine of four thousand *maravedíes*, two thousand for the "stand of the prison"—that is, indirectly, for the *alcaldes* of criminal cases—and two thousand for the expenses of the party making the accusation.[20]

It should be made clear that most of the sanctioned magistrates continued exercising their functions. Established by the law in very general terms, these punishments sought to curb the abusive conduct of the many judges that, in pronouncing sentence, thought more about their pocketbook than about imposing exemplary sentences. The question that arises here is evident: what happened with the sentences pronounced against judges that did not proceed in a proper fashion? The pronouncement of a sentence in every case was not synonymous with enforcing it, as it was necessary to possess the *strength* to make it come into force.[21] And the cases of the judges being judged were certainly no different. Although the law stated it should be otherwise, the *alcaldes* or *corregidores* formed personal ties in the cities where they exercised office, and thereby became an important force in local power relations. As a

[19] AGS.RGS.1485

[20] ARCH.RE.1492-43-2

[21] A very suggestive analysis of this subject can be found in: Garnot-Lemesle 2012: 12-16.

result, it is not easy to confirm if the verdicts pronounced against them were eventually carried out; the outcome also depended on the identity of the accuser or the plaintiff that obtained the favorable legal opinion. In addition, there were also cases in which the condemned judge held his office in the ecclesiastical or seigneurial sphere, in which case, the outcome wound up depending on the strength of the protective mantle that his lord could offer or not. In any case, I am inclined to believe that no one acted just out of sheer zeal. If these petitions were drawn up it was because it was anticipated that some sort of compensation or indemnification could be received, or that there could be redress for the harmful experiences meted out by judges that made *bad use* of their office. The fact that this type of denunciation remained a widespread practice in the Peninsula until at least the seventeenth and eighteenth centuries strengthens this perception, and Tomás Mantecón's studies convincingly demonstrate its validity (2002b).

Optimizing the Returns of the Office

This abuse and negligence committed by judges was directly related to the different procedures that they could use to optimize their income or, in other words, to make their office yield more. It should be pointed out that although it might seem paradoxical, this objective was not always or necessarily at odds with the satisfactory administration of justice; the outcome depended clearly on the abuses committed by each judge or judicial officer and their moral values.

In the highest tribunals of the kingdom, the judges received their salary or income by means of promissory notes drawn on the royal treasury. They also had what were called "*ayudas de costas*" (complementary allowances for their expenses), which generally weighed less in their total income, although in some cases they could almost equal the salary itself. Both the salaries and allowances were fixed per year, even if they were generally paid at three different intervals. The considerable sums of money that these salaries represented (for example, 200,000 *maravedíes* for the presiding magistrate of the *Audiencia*, 120,000 for the judges, 100,000 for the Council judges, 50,000 for the *alcaldes de Casa y Corte*) meant that actually paying them turned out to be fraught with difficulties, resulting in frequent complaints. With the intention of limiting such claims, in 1480 the Kings established an annuity of 500,000 *maravedíes* that was drawn on from the sales taxes that the city of Valladolid collected (Varona: 208). However, this turned out to be insufficient and therefore, promissory notes were placed on the treasuries of other cities or villas. On the other hand, it should be remembered that even though an Accounting Office and Royal Treasury did exist, there was no centralized collector's office for the royal taxes. Therefore, the salaries of the judges and the officers of the highest tribunals, as well as those of other agents of the Crown, were paid with the promissory notes issued on the royal revenues collected by tax farmers and private collectors scattered throughout the kingdom. Such an arrangement could mean that an agent would be paid by a draft issued on a locality that was not the one where he was posted; the actual payment of his salary therefore largely depended on his good luck, as we shall shortly see. To palliate this almost chronic deficit, the allowances for expenses were taken directly from the revenues from fines that each institution received, the administration of which was in the hands of the receiver. However, there was not always enough of a balance to cover the allowances. The case that José Luis de la Heras cites is quite illustrative of this problem: several officers were to receive the sum of 500 *ducados,* but as the money in the cash box had run out, the secretary advised them to take on ¨a transaction¨, that is to say, a judicial case, so that its pecuniary sanction could be used to pay them (de las Heras 1991: 50).

The rest of the officers (clerks, court reporters, registers, accountants, chancellors, doormen, etc.) were paid based on the specific proceedings they undertook according to the list of established rates. In the *Cortes* of Madrigal of 1476, the prices that each one could collect per act were defined, so as to put an end to the "greed of the officials", who did nothing other than "inflate these sums". For example, both the chancellors of the *Casa y Corte* and Chancery were ordered to keep a register of the ordinances and fees for seals that they would charge thereafter. In this respect, the most frequent complaints were about the abuses committed by the notaries and court reporters; at different moments between the end of the fifteenth century and the beginning of the sixteenth, a set rate was established for each sheet of paper. They were ordered not to transcribe deeds or other unnecessary documents in the final judgments, which they often did with the obvious purpose of lengthening them.[22]

Nevertheless, such measures did not settle the matter. The reproductions that follow correspond to the two judgments that were issued almost simultaneously by two clerks of the Royal Chancery of Valladolid. As can be seen, there were notaries that certainly knew at any

[22] OCHV. Libro II, Título IV.

rate how to boost their income, just by spacing out and lengthening their handwriting.[23]

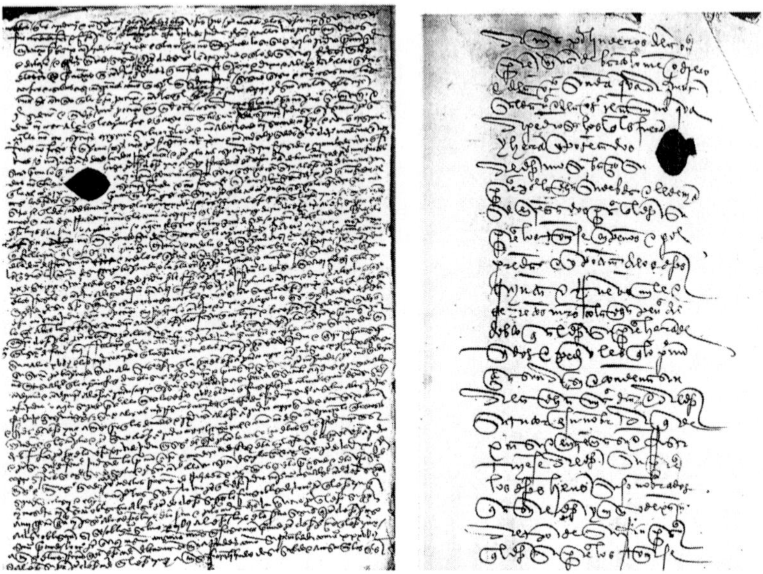

Fig. 1-1 Fragments of documents issued around the same time – the dimensions of the original pages are identical.

On the local level, the cities were supposed to pay the salary that the judges (*alcaldes mayores*, *alcaldes ordinarios* and magistrates) received; these expenditures were covered by encumbering the *propios** or establishing *special levies* on the *pecheros**. These judges also charged a series of fees for specific acts and proceedings, as just explained. Given the difficulties that the cities had paying these salaries, the resources that derived from the proceedings themselves constituted more of the judges' overall income than the salary itself, which was almost never completely paid; the situation of these local magistrates was therefore quite different from that of the high court judges. How then did these agents manage to make sure their office was profitable? The fees for the judicial acts were not at all substantial: to give only a few examples, a voucher for receiving

---

[23] For the diverse aspects of the office of notary and its importance during this period please consult: Villalba-Torné 2010.

witnesses would earn them two *maravedíes*, four for a peremptory order in a civil case, two for a summons, and twelve *maravedíes* for a final sentence (de Celso 1538). Fines undoubtedly provided the most significant part of their income. The terms established for imposing them lacked homogeneity; the share assigned to the presiding judge varied depending on the crime. The distribution of the monies could be a third for the Chamber, a third for the judge and a third for the accuser or a third to be divided up between the judge and the accuser and two thirds for the Chamber. If the perpetuation of the crime included a religious offense or had affected communal properties, a third went to the *fabrica ecclesiae*, to a charitable foundation or to the city (according to the case at hand), another third to the Chamber and the remaining third to the judge. Other cases provided for a division by halves: one half for the Chamber and the other to be equally divided between the judge and the accuser. When there was no accusing party and the judge acted *ex officio*, the share that would have gone to the accuser was added to his income, as was prescribed in all the cases and maintained without alteration until the *Novísima Recopilación* in 1805.

In connection with these fines, the laws repeated endlessly that their division and allocation could only be carried out once the verdict had been pronounced, that is, for property that had been *confiscated* through a judgment and not for *preventatively seized* property. When a judge had dictated his sentence, only then and not before, was it permissible to sell the belongings, which was generally done by a public auction. This point reminds of another important resource for the justice officers: the tithe of execution. In effect, the bailiff, *alcalde* or whoever was in charge of seizing the property, kept for himself ten percent of the total that the auction yielded. Another provision that was also reiterated on numerous occasions dictated that no judge could impose fines that would be assigned to the Chamber, with the secret intention of making off with them. Needless to say, the provisions condemned any imaginable form of bribery, as well as other "lucrative activities" that were against the law, such as issuing falsified documents. Nevertheless, these illegal payments did exist and as Richard Kagan rightly points out (1991: 60-61), their importance should not be underestimated.

Now that the general background has been traced, let us examine through a few concrete examples how the everyday practice of justice could transpire. In July 1485, Juan Fernández de Paternina, *alcalde ordinario* of the city of Vitoria, ordered the arrest of a *vecino* of the city for blasphemy. Basing his case on a rumor, he proceeded *ex officio*. To confirm his suspicion, the *alcalde* summoned the son-in-law of the accused to testify; as he refused to give evidence, he was taken to prison. When being questioned, he answered that his father-in-law "was innocent and without guilt". Not at all convinced by such a response, the *alcalde* decided to send him to the rack. Not satisfied with the results of the first session that only yielded from the forced witness a deposition that was identical to the first one, the *alcalde* ordered the son-in-law to be tortured a second time until the testimony was obtained that would allow him to accuse the suspect formally. The use of torture to force witnesses to testify in criminal cases (including blasphemy) was provided for by the law, but first-degree relatives, and sons-in-law and fathers-in-law, could not be forced to testify and much less could they be tortured (it should be borne in mind that this case was not being tried in an Inquisitorial court).

After this the accused himself was faced with "interrogation by torture", where he was subjected to water torture. He confessed that during an argument with his wife and his children about some *fanegas*[24] of wheat, he had become extremely angry and abnegated God. Nevertheless, once he was out of the torture chamber, when asked if he would reaffirm what he had testified, he roundly denied it. The irate *alcalde* told him that he was denying the truth and that "he would not let him get away with it"; he immediately sent the man back to be tortured until he confirmed his confession. The *alcalde,* then, on "that same day and month and year" pronounced the penalty. He contended that in accordance with the laws of the kingdom, he should condemn the man (as he did) to having his tongue cut off in public and to receiving fifty lashes while astride a mule so that he could be exhibited in the sites set up for that purpose. He was also required to forfeit half of his belongings.

In these cases, the *Partidas* enacted punishments in conformity with the status of the guilty party.[25] The nobility and gentlemen were to forfeit part of their property, but always in proportion to their rank (I should make it clear that this was not a principle of equity but quite the contrary for the highest-ranking members were the least encumbered). Inhabitants of cities and villages were to be condemned to forfeiting at the first case of blasphemy a quarter of their property; at the second one, a third part; and for a third case half of their belongings. If they re-offended, they were to be "banished from their homeland". The worst punishments were reserved for those that possessed nothing: namely, for the first offense, fifty lashes;

---

[24] *Fanega*: ancient measure= 44 kg for wheat

[25] *Partida* VII, Título XXVIII, Leyes I a VI

the second, their lips branded with a hot iron; the third, "having their tongue cut off". The punishments for "lesser men" underwent certain alterations in the *Ordenanzas* issued in 1484: for the first occasion, a month in prison; for the second, banishment for six months; for the third, "that his tongue be nailed".

According to the laws then, as it was first time that this *vecino* was accused of blasphemy, his punishment should have been the forfeiture of a quarter of his belongings, but as we have just seen, the *alcalde* interpreted the laws rather peculiarly. He did attribute the confiscated property as the law indicated: half for the Royal Chamber and the other half for the accuser. He added however that the part allocated to the Royal Chamber could be granted to the judges and agents of the royal justice—which was not true. As already pointed out, such an arrangement was explicitly forbidden by royal law. And he added that as there was no accuser, his share should be apportioned to the agent that had acted *ex officio*, which in this case was himself. The *alcalde* ordered the immediate execution of the sentence, both with respect to the property, which was taken to be sold, and the guilty man himself. After receiving fifty lashes, the convicted man was led to the main square of the city, where "his tongue was nailed"; he was kept there until heeding the entreaties of the people that were gathered there, the *alcalde* ordered that "the tongue was unnailed".

The incident was denounced before the *alcaldes* of criminal cases of the Chancery, where everything that had occurred was expounded. Fernández de Paternina was summoned on various occasions but never reported to the court. When the appointed period of time had elapsed, the judges dictated their sentence, restoring to the convicted man "his honor and good reputation" and ordering the return of his property. At this stage, several months had already elapsed since its sale, which makes it quite difficult to imagine that they managed to carry out the sentence. Fernández de Paternina had no reason to be at all concerned because he had not appeared before the *Audiencia*, having powerful enough connections that backed him. Some years before, when acting as a notary, at the request of the Royal Solicitor he had drawn up the property survey of 1481 for Vitoria, and in 1495 his son and namesake was granted the office of "clerk and public notary of the Court" for the duration of his lifetime.[26]

Another case: on January 7, 1514, after having received certain information, the prosecutor of the town of Arévalo requested the bachelor

---

[26] ARCHV. RE. 1486-4-15/ AGS. RGS. 1485-72/ AGS. RGS. 1485-154 / AGS. RGS. 1495-08-16

Fernán Dianez de Lobón, *corregidor,* to initiate an investigation about a *vecino* of the town who apparently had committed "a sin against nature with some men". Based on the declarations of various witnesses, the judge issued an order of detention and prepared the immediate seizure of all his belongings "for having committed the crime of sodomy". Juan Gutiérrez de Hontiveros was put in charge of the task, for he acted alternately as bailiff or *alcalde*, according to what was necessary; it is not surprising to find the same person holding both offices even though various laws prohibited it. He could not arrest the accused, who had managed to flee. Gutiérrez de Hontiveros then proceeded as speedily as possible to seize his property, which, after an inventory, was placed under the guardianship of two *vecinos* who accepted responsibility for its safekeeping; it should be pointed out that the depositing of sequestered goods in the hands of third persons, generally *vecinos,* was the customary procedure.

Miguel de Arévalo, the *promotor fiscal** who acted in the name of the Queen, suspected that some belongings were missing, so he requested that the accused's wife and daughter be subjected to arduous questioning about this matter. Both described the fear that they and their maid had when the *alcalde* turned up close to midnight to effect the seizure—which in itself was not out of the ordinary, as once the mandate to seize the belongings, was released, he had to act quickly so there was no time for property to be hidden. When the order was given to seize "all the belongings", it effectively meant all, without exceptions (obviously including real estate). Inventories of such acts contain descriptions of beds, mattresses, pillows, sheets, blankets, large and small tables, drinking vessels, cauldrons, a brazier, etc., including personal items such as toilet articles. Scenes such as this one must have been frequent at those times, when not only secular justice commonly ordered this kind of measure, but also the Inquisition.

The day after these events, January 9, the fugitive defendant's wife presented before the *corregidor* a petition which made it known that all the property that was seized because of the her husband's supposed crime was really hers, as it formed part of her dowry and therefore should be returned to her. At that point, a new lawsuit was initiated, which was a civil one, in which this woman confronted the *promotor fiscal* in defense of her dotal property. Two extremely long lawsuits ensued, in which innumerable witnesses made an appearance. To summarize, in the criminal lawsuit, both in the first instance tried before the *corregidor* and then the appeal before the *alcaldes* of the Chancery, the accused was found guilty. He was condemned in his absence and by default "to die in open flames" and all his property was to be seized (that is, if he actually had belongings of his own). At the same time, the *corrigedor* recognized the wife's rights in the civil suit, and ordered the suspension of any proceeding involving the seized property. The prosecutor then requested the right to appeal and appeared before the judges of the *Audiencia,* who after having examined the case, ruled that all the property should be returned to the plaintiff. This sentence was appealed by the presiding prosecutor in the Chancery, but it was upheld when retried.

Nevertheless, while this case was being tried in Valladolid, the guardians of the property in the villa of Arévalo were in quite a fix. According to their subsequent testimonies, when they were interrogated in the *Audiencia*, the prosecutor insistently and violently harassed them until they handed over to him the possessions "in kind" that equaled his annual salary, in addition to that of a "counsellor of the treasury" that accompanied him. This incident took place while the belongings were "in abeyance", awaiting the judge's decision. As the agent was a prosecutor attached to the Court, his salary should have been theoretically paid through an order of payment drawn on royal taxes, but as already explained, such payments were irregular and the agents complained because they did not always receive their salaries. Therefore, it is quite probable that those items extracted from the seized property went towards paying their salaries, even if it cannot be known for sure. In any case, salary or not, it is evident that for fear of a ruling that would return the property, the prosecutor decided to guarantee himself a considerable deposit of money for himself. Of course I do not know how much of her dotal property the unfortunate woman was able to recover.[27]

Another example is provided by Alonso Ramírez de Villaescusa, who was a *corregidor* in Valladolid and its jurisdiction for eight years, starting when he was appointed in June 1491.[28] As is well known, the law stated that *corregidores* could not hold office for more than one year in the same locality, so that they would not forge bonds with the local inhabitants. Rarely was the law respected. The office of Ramirez de Villaescusa was successively renewed[29] even after his first *juicio de residencia.*[30] All this time, he was living with his wife, Inés Méndez, in Valladolid. The different lawsuits that the couple initiated during those years confirm it, as

27 ARCHV. PL. CV. QUEVEDO 1514-1412-4

28 AGS. RGS. 1491-06-41

29 AGS. RGS. 1492-06-65/ AGS. RGS. 1493-11-37 / AGS. RGS. 1494-10-50 / AGS. RGS. 1496-7-224

30 AGS. RGS. 1493-08-28/ AGS. RGS. 1493-11-93

both are mentioned as *vecinos* of Valladolid.[31] The *corregidor* was obviously very well connected. Near the end of 1490, as prosecutor of the Council, he and Martín de Yanguas (archdeacon of Zamora and royal chaplain) were asked to carry out a *visita** of the Royal *Audiencia* and Chancery, so that they could report on how justice was administered there and establish whether the *Ordenanzas* of 1489 were being observed. It is believed that the report of the *visita* brought about the dismissal en masse of the president and judges (Garriga 2007: 44), referred to earlier. Even after having been appointed *corregidor*, he continued to be considered a member of the Council. In 1498, he proceeded *ex officio* against a credit venture, which, according to his information, had collected interest at usurious rates (it should be remembered that usury was punished by the law). Upon intervening, he confiscated the far from negligible sum of 400,000 *maravedíes.*[32] As he was acting *ex officio*, he, as "accuser and denouncer", set aside for himself a third of the sum, and assigned the other two-thirds to the Royal Chamber.

Now, although the loan had been made to *vecinos* of Valladolid, the transaction itself was carried out in the town of Dueñas, where the creditor lived. The *corregidor* had proceeded to seize the money from the debtors when they arrived in Valladolid. The problem was that to transform the seizure into a real confiscation, a judicial sentence was needed and the *corregidor* was acting outside of his jurisdiction. Dueñas not only fell under the jurisdiction of the Conde de Buendía but was also the seat of the *señorío*. Ramírez subsequently appeared before the judges of the *Audiencia.* He requested that they make the seizure effective and above all, safeguard the third part of the sum that he was entitled to because he had acted *ex officio*. To justify his intervention, he presented witnesses that corroborated the fact that the transaction had been carried out in Valladolid. Nevertheless, the judges ruled that he did not succeed in justifying his "intention" and they lifted the seizure on the money.[33]

That same year, Ramírez's second *juicio de residencia* was assigned to the bachelor Luis de Polanco, who at that moment was an *alcalde de Casa y Corte,* though earlier he had served for two years as *alcalde del crimen*

---

[31] ARCHV. RE. 1498-130-22 / ARCHV. PL. CV. PÉREZ ALONSO (F). 1504/1506-0083-436-1

[32] In order to provide the reader with a rough idea of what the sum really represented, I would say that the average price for a house was about fifty thousand *maravedíes*.

[33] ARCHV. RE. 1498-125-22

in the Chancery of Valladolid. What it came up with did not at all favor the *corregidor*. The principal objections it contained did not focus on his work as a judge, but rather on his undertakings as an administrator. As I emphasized at the beginning of this chapter, the administration of justice was simply another task entailed for the agents that were charged with governing. It can be deduced from the report that the *corregidor* was in charge of tasks such as supervision when certain streets of the village/town were "paved with stone" and making sure that the men hired to "pursue malefactors" did their job. According to the report that the judge of the *residencia* issued, Ramírez de Villaescusa should be required to explain the discrepancies that appeared in his administration's accounts. Among other irregularities, it was not at all clear how the *sisas* [excise levied on merchandises entering the city] had been spent nor what exactly were the "works" in which the considerable sum of 436,528 *maravedíes* had been invested between May of 1494 and July of 1497, according to his register.[34]

The judges and judicial officers did not always optimize their resources by trickery, nor by such abuse and arbitrary acts as in the cases just recounted. Sometimes they only tried at their own expense to effectively ensure that their salary was paid.[35] It is essential to underline this point. Although the salaries were paid by promissory notes backed by the royal treasury, if the benefitting judge did not manage to actually receive his pay, he had to bear the cost of the procedure so that his salary would materialize, even if he had to initiate a lawsuit, in the same way as if it were an ordinary debt *between individuals* and not the salary of a public official.

Let us consider an example: the bachelor Gonzalo Sánchez de Castro was an *alcalde* at the Court. In 1491, the Royal Accountant's Office issued an order of payment for 50,000 *maravedíes* for his salary, drawn on the revenues derived from *merindades* of Burgos and Medina del Pomar. The tax farmer and collector of these taxes made it known that the sum could not be paid all at once, but rather in three installments, as was customary. When the "last third", that is 16,000 *maravedíes*, was due, Sánchez de Castro sent his son to receive the outstanding balance. The tax collector

---

[34] AGS.RGS.1499-02-06

[35] Several studies about the administration of justice in France also reveal the existence of lawsuits that were carried out between judges as they argued about the returns that resulted from cases or the fees that were charged for them: Follain 2002: 45-47; Toureille 2013: 188-189.

only paid him 6,200 *maravedíes*, though "with tricks and malice" he made the youth give him the payment order, which served as a receipt for the total sum.

Once Sánchez de Castro learned about what had happened, he sent his solicitor to lodge a claim before Diego Martínez Quitano, *alcalde ordinario* of Medina del Pomar, where the process was started though it would subsequently be appealed before the Chancery. This case raises two questions that should be highlighted. On the one hand, the promissory note was drawn on both Burgos, a royal city, and Medina del Pomar, which at that time belonged to the *señorío* of Velasco.[36] On the other, even if an *alcalde de Casa y Corte* was at the center of the process, a circumstance that supposedly granted him a privileged legal status, Sánchez de Castro had to present his demand to the *alcalde* of the *señorío*.

When the tax collector was summoned before Diego Martínez, he presented a petition in which he denied absolutely everything, including even being the tax collector of that town. Ultimately the *alcalde ordinario* considered that the tax collector had not provided sufficient evidence and ordered him to pay the outstanding balance. Various months had passed, however, and Sánchez de Castro claimed that he should be paid, in addition, the costs of the lawsuit. With the trial closed and sealed, as was fitting he lodged an appeal before the judges of the *Audiencia*, thereby requesting that they change the previous sentence to include the expenses that had been incurred in the suit against the tax collector. Nevertheless, the judges limited themselves to confirming Sánchez de Castro's right to collect the outstanding balance, and they did not order the payment of his expenses. In other words, expenditure incurred on a suit to enable his salary to be collected remained at the judge's cost and expense.[37]

Final Considerations

Before ending this analysis of justice and the agents of justice in Castile during the early Modern Age, I would like to return to some of the points that it underlined. The transcendence, and permanence over time, of the figure of the monarch as a judge was emphasized. We also examined the conception of justice as an *act of government* and the division, as expressed by the jurists of the period, between distributive justice, which

---

[36] It is extremely complex to map out how royal taxes were collected during this period. Cfr.: Ladero 2002: 426; Diago 2007: 173-215.
[37] ARCHV. RE. 1492-48-2

gave to each individual his due according to his social condition and commutative justice, which dealt with the matters that led to men confronting each other. This was followed by a succinct description of the judicial system in late medieval Castile, pointing out the jurisdictional overlaps and frequent indeterminacy of jurisdictions. In order to exemplify it, I focused on the highest tribunals of the kingdom, and showed how the Catholic Monarchs' policies sought to renovate these particular instances of law making and to instill more discipline into them. Particular attention was paid in this section to the form in which royal documents were issued by the Royal Council and Chanceries, which often gave rise to contradictory directives about the same case; they could likewise interfere in the judicial trials.

The second half of this study was devoted to the activity of judges and judicial officers; I stressed two questions that are fundamental when reflecting on the differences that characterized the system under consideration and the bureaucratic administrations that surged after the Enlightenment. On the one hand, it was possible for judges to be ordered to pay the costs of the trials if it was decided that they had proceeded inappropriately or had "passed judgment incorrectly". On the other hand, judges were also able to plead in front of tribunals on their own behalf in defence of their salaries and other benefits of their office. On occasion, both sets of circumstances could coincide; for example, a judge that had delayed a proceeding could be accused of negligence and condemned to pay the costs in instances of appeal. In these cases, the magistrate could find himself forced to send a solicitor in his defense, as part of the same lawsuit that he had sentenced as a judge. In other cases, the wronged parties might present an independent suit, and request reparation for the magistrate's unacceptable acts or decisions, even as he continued to exercise the functions of his office. It could also happen, however, that the judges would appear before the law to safeguard their office or protect the emoluments they received for their work, or those they thought they were entitled to. In the juridical terms of the epoch, they went from dispensing justice in the monarch's name in order to reconcile parties, to participating, as litigants, in the realm of commutative justice, by litigating for the wages of their office, as if their case were a private matter.

All of these proceedings were closely related to the absence of a centralized fiscal system or municipal treasuries that were able to sustain effectively the local judicial officers, and to the impossibility of implementing effective controls. The monarchy's agents received their salaries through promissory notes from the royal treasury to be drawn on taxes that were to be collected in specific localities. Even if judges and judicial officers were generally assigned a salary, as we saw, it was not necessarily easy to get it paid. They therefore rounded off their income with fees, and the proportional shares of monies they were assigned from their daily activities (the question is whether these ¨extras¨ in fact really made up most of their income). Optimizing their benefits constituted the private aspect of the office, even at the risk of committing excesses that could lead to a sentence against them. In other words, it meant that they were privately responsible for the administration of the public position they held; both dimensions, of course, co-existed simultaneously. As Professor Tomás y Valiente aptly emphasized several decades ago, "the office was, then, a double-fronted reality" (1972: 36).

The concurrent jurisdictions and lack of clear definitions of cognizance provoked an infinite number of conflicts. They often occurred because the parties, trying to make sure that their side was favored, appeared simultaneously before different "justices"; the judges or officers, however, were receptive to such appeals. Thus, trying a lawsuit meant, for example, charging fees, receiving the ¨tithe¨ of executions, a proportional share of seizures, and even more if the judge had acted *ex officio*. This feature of the judicial system is essential to the case. When the Royal Council issued a document in response to a petition from a party so that a judge could not intervene in a case, it was obviously to his detriment, but all the while it created the possibility of benefit for another magistrate, as it simply *reoriented* the destination of the fees and the fines that the presiding judge had the right to collect.

If the magistrate that was prevented from trying a case formed part of the sphere of royal justice, the first argument used to retain the case was that royal justice was being subjugated. And it was certainly true. The argument was valid both to defend the royal jurisdiction as well as to safeguard his interests. Here I underline one of the aspects that this study sought to emphasize. These officers formed part of patronage networks with their friendships and enmities, their alliances or rivalries. I say that without slighting those to whom the officer had pending debts for favors received: each agent sought to increase his own symbolic and material capacity to gain a better position in the web of relations. These bonds were circumstantial, as they were constituted by the services and asymmetric compensations that made up the complex network of power relationships on which the monarchy's government was sustained and developed. Thus, each judicial office juggled a *public* side, which consisted of administering justice in the name of the king and therefore participating in the operation of the monarchy itself, and a *private* side, which involved optimizing his own profit. These aspects could not be separated, for they were understood as being *naturally* associated. Such customs and style represented a weakness if they were viewed from the vantage point of the monarchy interested in centralizing its power; the problem was to maintain sufficient control so that personal ambitions did not exceed certain limits. To make that happen, the kings had necessarily to be open to the negotiations with each and every one of the corps and estates that made up society. I believe that the investigations, *visitas*, and other control mechanisms should be considered within these parameters. They did not aim to eliminate the private interests of the public officials, but rather to maintain a certain social *consensus*, or re-establish one, whenever a magistrate's acts threatened it (Schaub 1998: 49). It implied that margins of regulation had to be flexible, and adapt to the individual becoming the subject of the regulations. In other words, the key for those who had committed excesses was to be able to count on someone having the power to "turn a blind eye", allowing the offenses to be overlooked. As I pointed out, however, these relations were mobile and support was never lasting; fidelities and protection mutated and were redirected. In moments of weakness, the excessive benefits that a judge procured for himself could collide with a judicial sentence that on such an occasion would most probably be executed. For a judge or judicial officer, the possibility of optimizing his benefits depended on his dexterity and prudence, as did the possibility of remaining in the service of the monarchy.

Abbreviations

ARCHV. RE.: Archivo Real Chancillería de Valladolid. Registro de Ejecutorias.
ARCHV. PC.: Archivo Real Chancillería de Valladolid. Pleitos Civiles.
AGS. RGS.: Archivo General de Simancas. Registro General del Sello.
OCHV: Recopilación de las Ordenanzas de la Real Audiencia y Chancillería de Valladolid.

References

Lopez Carrasco, F. - Flores Varella, C. – Martin Galan, M.M. – Serrano Morales, R., (prol.), (1999), *La administración de justicia en la Historia de España. Actas de las III jornadas de Castilla-La Mancha sobre investigación en archivos*, Guadalajara: Junta de Comunidades Castilla-La Mancha.

Andújar Castillo, F. - Felices de la Fuente, M. del M., (2011), *El poder del dinero. Ventas de cargos y honores en la España del Antiguo Régimen*, Madrid: Biblioteca Nueva.

Bernardo Ares, J. M., (1996), "Jurisdicción y villas de realengo en la Corona de Castilla", in Martínez Ruiz – Pazzis, *Instituciones de la España Moderna. 1 Las jurisdicciones*: 51-69.

Brizay, F. and *al.*, (2002), *Les justices de Village. Administration et justices locales de la fin du Moyen Âge à la Révolution*, Rennes: Presses Universitaires de Rennes.

Calderón Ortega, J. M., (1999), "La justicia en Castilla y León durante la Edad Media", in Lopez Carrasco et *al.*, *La administración de justicia en la Historia de España. Actas de las III jornadas de Castilla-La Mancha sobre investigación en archivos*: 21-38.

Caselli, E., (2008), "La administración de justicia y la vida cotidiana. Judíos y cristianos en el ámbito jurisdiccional de la Corona de Castilla (siglo XV)", in *Historia Social*, 62: 3-28.

Castellano, J. and *al.*, (2000), *La pluma, la mitra y la espada. Estudios de Historia Institucional en la Edad Moderna*, Madrid: Marcial Pons.

Cortés Ruiz, M., (1999), "El corregimiento de Molina durante la Edad Media", in Lopez Carrasco et *al.*, *La administración de justicia en la Historia de España. Actas de las III jornadas de Castilla-La Mancha sobre investigación en archivos*: 51-70.

De Celso, H., (1538), *Las Leyes de todos los Reinos de Castilla: abreviadas y reducidas en forma de Repertorio decisivo*, Valladolid.

Dedieu, J.P., (2000), "Procesos y redes. La historia de las instituciones administrativas de la época moderna, hoy", Castellano, *La pluma, la mitra y la espada. Estudios de Historia Institucional en la Edad Moderna*: 13-30.

—. "Acercarse a la 'venalidad'", in Andújar–Felices, *El poder del dinero. Ventas de cargos y honores en la España del Antiguo Régimen*: 19-28.

De Las Heras Santos, J., (1991), *La justicia penal de los Austrias en la Corona de Castilla*, Salamanca: Universidad de Salamanca.

—. (1996), "La organización de la justicia real ordinaria en la Corona de Castilla durante la Edad Moderna", *Estudis: Revista de historia moderna*, 22: 105-39.

—. (2007), "La incidencia de la fiscalidad de la monarquía en el territorio riojano durante el reinado de los Reyes Católicos", *En la España Medieval*, 30: 173-215.

Díaz Martín, L. V., (1997), *Los orígenes de la Audiencia Real castellana*, Sevilla: Universidad de Sevilla.

Follain, A., (2002), « Justice seigneuriale, justice royale et régulation sociale du XVe au XVIIIe siècle: rapport de synthèse », in Brizay, *Les justices de Village. Administration et justices locales de la fin du Moyen Âge à la Révolution*: 9-58.

Fortea, J. - Gelabert, J. - Mantecón, T. (eds.), (2002), *Furor et rabies. Violencia, conflicto y marginación en la Edad Moderna*, Santander: Universidad de Cantabria.

García Hernán, D., (1996), "La jurisdicción señorial y la administración de justicia", in Martínez Ruiz – Pazzis, *Instituciones de la España Moderna. 1 Las jurisdicciones*: 213-227.

Garnot, B. - Lemesle, B. (dir.), (2012), *Autour de la sentence judiciaire, du Moyen Âge à l'époque contemporaine*, Dijon: Editions Universitaires de Dijon.

Garriga, C., (1994), *La Audiencia y las Chancillerías castellanas (1371-1525)*, Madrid: Centro de Estudios Constitucionales.

—. (2007), *Recopilación de las Ordenanzas de la Real Audiencia y Chancillería de Valladolid*, Madrid: Consejo General del Poder Judicial.

Gómez González, I., (2000), *La justicia en almoneda: la venta de oficios en la Chancillería de Granada (1505-1834)*, Granada: Comares.

—. (2003), *La justicia, el gobierno y sus hacedores. La Real Chancillería de Granada en el Antiguo Régimen*, Granada: Comares.

González Alonso, B., (1981), *Sobre el Estado y la Administración de la Corona de Castilla en el Antiguo Régimen*, Madrid: Siglo XXI de España.

Guerra, F.X. and *al.*, (1998), *Los espacios públicos en Iberoamérica. Ambigüedades y problemas. Siglos XVIII-XIX*, México: Centro de estudios mexicanos y centroamericano.

Hespanha, A., (1989), *Vísperas del Leviatán. Instituciones y poder político (Portugal, siglo XVII)*, Madrid: Taurus.

—. (1993), *La gracia del derecho. Economía de la cultura en la Edad Moderna*, Madrid: Centro de Estudios Constitucionales.

Jiménez Estrella, A., (2012), "Poder, dinero y ventas de oficios y honores en la España del Antiguo Régimen: un estado de la cuestión", in *Cuadernos de Historia Moderna*, 37: 259-72.

Kagan, R., (1991), *Pleitos y pleiteantes en Castilla. 1500-1700*, Salamanca: Junta de Castilla y León [1st English edition: 1981].

Ladero Quesada, M., (2002), "La receptoría y pagaduría general de la Hacienda regia castellana entre 1491 y 1494", in *En la España Medieval*, 25: 425-506.

López Díaz, M., (2011), "Tráfico de cargos y oligarquías urbanas: de lo 'público' a lo 'privado' y lo contrario (siglos XVII y XVIII)", in Andújar – Felices, *El poder del dinero. Ventas de cargos y honores en la España del Antiguo Régimen*: 119-44.

López Martínez, C., (1921), *La Santa Hermandad de los Reyes Católicos*, Sevilla: Imprenta Vilches.

Mantecón Movellán, T., (2002a), "El peso de la infrajudicialidad en el control del crimen durante la Edad Moderna", in *Estudis: Revista de Historia Moderna*, 28: 43-75.

—. (2002b), "El mal uso de la justicia en la Castilla del siglo XVII", in Fortea and *al.*, *Furor et rabies. Violencia, conflicto y marginación en la Edad Moderna*: 69-98.

Martínez Ruiz, E. - Gómez Vozmediano, M., (1996), "La jurisdicción de la Hermandad", in Martínez – Pazzis, *Instituciones de la España Moderna. 1 Las jurisdicciones*: 143-70.

Martínez Ruiz, E. – Pazzis Pi, M. (coords.), (1996), *Instituciones de la España Moderna. 1 Las jurisdicciones*, Madrid: Actas Editorial.

Pérez-Prendes, José M., (1996), "El Tribunal eclesiástico (sobre el aforamiento y la estructura de la Curia diocesana de justicia)", in Martínez - Pazzis, *Instituciones de la España Moderna. 1 Las jurisdicciones*: 143-170.

Roldan Verdejo, R., (1989), *Los jueces de la Monarquía Absoluta*, Santa Cruz de Tenerife: Universidad de La Laguna.

Schaub, J.F., (1998), "El pasado republicano del espacio público", in Guerra and *al.*, *Los espacios públicos en Iberoamérica. Ambigüedades y problemas. Siglos XVIII-XIX*: 27-53.

Tomás y Valiente, F., (1972), *La venta de oficios en Indias (1492-1606)*, Madrid: Instituto Nacional de Administración Pública.

—. (2000), *La tortura judicial en España*, Barcelona, Crítica [1st edition 1973, *La tortura en España*: Ariel].

Toureille, V., (2013), *Crime et châtiment au Moyen Âge, Ve-XVe siècle*, Paris: Seuil.

Varona Garcia, M. A., (1981), *La Chancillería de Valladolid en el reinado de los Reyes Católicos*, Valladolid: Universidad de Valladolid.

Villalba, E. - Torné, E. (eds.), (2010), *El nervio de la República. El oficio de escribano en el Siglo de Oro*, Madrid: Calambur.

CHAPTER TWO

IMPERIAL ADMINISTRATION AND LOCAL DEFENSE IN THE HISPANIC MONARCHY*

JOSÉ JAVIER RUIZ IBAÑEZ

Although service to the Hispanic Monarchy is usually defined as direct participation in the royal administration, the subjects of the Catholic Kings found several ways of negotiating with the monarchy while serving their ruler. Their idea of service went beyond a simple feudal pact and included negotiation with the monarchy as part of government (Mazín Gómez 2004: chapter 1). The medieval tradition on which the monarchy was constructed between 1470 and 1530 guaranteed that an essential part of the functioning of the imperial administration was devolved to the traditional institutions that maintained a corporative subordination. The link that was consequently established between the monarch and the corporations represented more a new kind of loyalty than a simple feudal pact to their lord (Mousnier 1972). They were entrusted with keeping order, collecting taxes, and contributing to the implementation of royal justice (Ruiz Ibáñez & Sabatini 2009). This relationship included helping to defend the monarchy, even if the nobility progressively felt less enthusiastic about this function (Thompson 2007). The local powers, both *regnícola*[1] and urban, were also required to participate. At the end of the Middle Ages, the insertion of urban corporations in the monarchies whose territorial administrations continued to be very limited was based on the guarantee of defending the

*This study was developed as part of the "Hispanofilia" Research Projects, Ministerio de Economía y Competitividad/Ministry of Economy and Competitiveness, code HAR2008-01107/HIST, HAR2011-29859-C02-01 and and HAR2014-52414-C2-1-P.

[1] "Regnícola", literally "of the kingdom", makes reference here to several of the "kingdoms", such as the Kingdom of Valencia or Principality of Catalonia, which formed part of the composite monarchy

territory. It could certainly serve as a way to gain exemption from other fiscal impositions and guarantee that the presence of the king's direct power was limited. Service to the community itself, and the defense of its collective honor as a corporation, were therefore tied to a complex political network based on multiple services. Although it did have the king as the ultimate head, its hierarchy (and the identity that derived from it) was not stable. Studying these practices and its evolution by focusing on personal participation in defense allows us to examine the diverse realities of monarchy that were constructed in the sixteenth and seventeenth centuries. (I have already dealt with this subject in 1995 and 1996, and refer to these studies for a more exhaustive description).

The Historiographical Limits to the Study of the Expansion of a Nonprofessional Defense in the Hispanic Monarchy

One of the commonplaces that historical studies have accepted about the territories that the Hispanic Monarchy occupied is the absence of organized systems of defense on the majority of its borders until the eighteenth century—except for the system of protection created for the empire itself, namely the armies in Flanders and Chile, fortresses garrisoned by soldiers, galley fleets, systems of defensive towers and the royal navy of the Atlantic, noted as *Armada del Mar Océano* (the first global vision of it was provided by Thompson, 1976). Until recently, historians have insisted on the lack of protection that local populations had in the face of threats that structurally weighed heavily on the majority of the monarchy's borderlands. Even if it might appear paradoxical given such reasoning, these threats could be contained to varying degrees thanks to the defense initiatives undertaken by local institutions. It is surprising that a historiography that on occasions openly claims to be Weberian or Post-Weberian has not stressed such an assertion, or at least drawn theoretical conclusions from it. It could thereby situate the political power in these local powers' effective exercising of violence as it was legitimized by the king (see a global overview in the studies collected in Ruiz Ibáñez 2009 and in Brunet and Ruiz Ibáñez 2016).

The reasons that can be advanced in order to explain such an oversight, and the inherent limitation it imposes when trying to understand how the monarchy functioned, are numerous. In the first place, even if studies are increasingly addressing political practice (Pardo Molero 2001; Truchuelo

García 2004), a significant divide continues to separate studies about local realities and those that offer a global vision of how the empire functioned. This is due to the fact that a far too institutional vision continues to predominate in most of the studies about concrete political realities; they therefore do not pay attention to the ways in which the local realities were inserted into the monarchy. At the same time, the accounts that explain the monarchy as a whole continue to ignore the conclusions that the local studies offer. Secondly, even if findings reached by the now distant debate about the history of the state are generally accepted, the development of the monarchy somehow continues to be associated with the direct administration of resources. Studies only deem it worthwhile to describe processes that involved explicit formation of defensive systems, such as those that proposed specific types of reforms or the establishment of new models. The mechanisms of local defense are consequently delegated to a purely residual position as a sort of medieval heritage. They are by definition anti-modern, though this obviously appears to be contradicted by their extension to America and their effectiveness (albeit always complex and imperfect) throughout the sixteenth and seventeenth centuries. Thirdly, the weight of national history in its local dimension, which focuses on the singularity of the cases, should not be (Cardim, Herzog, Ruiz and Sabatini 2012), as it seeks the specificity of its own genealogy in them. Such an approach has prevented us from distinguishing for these cases the development of a tradition of defense that was often tied to the urban world itself. Its active functions corresponded to institutions that did not depend directly on the royal administration. In the fourth place, it should be highlighted that there are still many gaps in studies about how the monarchy's different borders were really defended on a daily basis. Finally, the lack of knowledge concerning the organization of the urban military in the majority of the cities, and the social consequences of this, continues to be considerable. It perhaps originates in the excessively rigid divisions that compartmentalize military, social, and political history.

As can be concluded, most of these analytical problems are not rooted in the quite complex difficulties research about such questions entails. They can rather be attributed to the limits created by the evolution of historiography (due to its basically national character, analytical hierarchies, as well as to professional and academic specializations), that prevent historians from grasping a history that turned out to be much more global. In any event, recent research convincingly confirms the importance of local organizations in guaranteeing the protection of imperial spaces

(Prak, 2015); they especially originate in complementary perspectives about the political organization of the monarchy as an unstable collection of appendages. The most obvious approach is to cite the cases when cities and towns were defended from threats that could not be driven back by the somewhat professional defense system that depended directly on the king, because of the absence of troops or the small size of the localities. It was thought that the protection of the contiguous territory (and in some cases the mediate lands) was the responsibility of the inhabitants as organized by the institutions run by local government. Most of them were autonomous of the central government. In many cases, the royal presence was limited to exercising justice and to the legitimization of the aforementioned defensive actions through the leadership of the king's direct agents stationed in the territory.

It is interesting to verify that systems of intervention were established on the monarchy's different borders through the professional defense forces organized in the *situados**. At the same time, systems of defense were consolidated that were based on the obligatory nature of mutually binding assistance between localities in the interior of the territory and positions on the borders. This duty was bound to the enjoyment of privileges that founded the territorial articulation of the Monarchy and was entirely linked to the definition of collective honor. Thus, for example, cities in the *adelantamiento** of Murcia had to help those on the kingdom's coast and also contribute to the defense of Oran in northern Africa. Such practices were employed in all the monarchy's territories, even in those where there were professional army garrisons, and this strengthened relations with the local institutions; a significant part of the territorial protection was devolved to the inhabitants even in an area as highly militarized as western Flanders.

Defenders of Borders… and the Social Order

The presence of professional forces was essentially symbolic on the monarchy's borders because of fiscal restrictions and/or respect for privileges of the localities. The king's subordinates found themselves with the imperious necessity of counting on the armed forces, albeit generally poorly armed, that the localities could levy. Just as it happened, for example, in the narrations of Drake's voyages (Wernham 1994: chapter 3; Kersey 2002: chapters 12 and 13), in accounts about the different sorts of incursions launched by irregular troops, corsairs and pirates (from the Mediterranean to the Caribbean, from Italy to Flanders), the intruders were always confronted by local forces (whether they were to crush the natives or be stopped by them). These local forces were at least able to try to defend their territory even if they did not appear to be particularly well-prepared. The presence of local forces therefore became a decisive factor for maintaining order on and beyond the monarchy's borders. In addition, they not only had to guarantee the defense of a city or small locality from the almost continual raids by their external enemies, but also defend the king's authority when it was threatened from within, either directly or because of the calling into question of public order and the political framework that maintained it. It is significant that most of the cities in the Low Countries rose up at the beginning of the revolt against Phillip II when the dissidents managed to win over the urban militias (Knevel 1994: chapters 2 and 3).

The Hispanic Monarchy was the setting of a long tradition of urban revolts. As scholarly attention has been focused on the Iberian areas, it appears that those that occurred elsewhere have been forgotten, thus limiting the possibility of reflecting upon them along with other European realities as a global phenomenon. When these revolts broke out (in Flanders, Valencia, Catalonia, Andalusia, Naples, Portugal, or America), the meagre forces that were at the disposal of the king's direct agents (viceroys, *corregidores**, governors) were unable to repress the insurgents in the majority of the cases if the representatives were not actively supported by the local military organization, or if the bond with the governing authorities had been weakened or shattered (a general revision in Gil Pujol 2006). Either because of some inhibition they felt, or their decision to join the insurrection, the members of these urban forces were to decide whether a locality should remain under the king's direct orders. If the revolts took on an especially dangerous social tone for the *citizens*, as happened in Mexico City in 1692 (Silvia Prada 2007: 99-102, 313, 321 and 333), the local forces swiftly organized and put an immediate stop to the disorder. The very stability of the monarchy was therefore converted into the objective of a corporation that defined itself as civic in the use of arms. The choice of the term *citizens* is completely deliberate here, as at least in areas where the use of arms was not just for mere ostentation, and the presence of royal troops continued to be limited, these citizens were in charge of defense (Gil Pujol 2002). In other words, a real citizen (defined as an inhabitant with the political rights that were attributed to a *vecino**) was the man that had both the obligation and right to bear arms.

A perspective that encompasses the Middle Ages can perhaps make it easier to understand that this distinction was anything but subtle, as in societies as tense as those of the Modern Age, providing the ultimate guarantee of public order (*ergo* of imperial order) was the very essence of the leading role conferred on the political agents. Defining who controlled defense meant confirming who was responsible for regulating everyday life (Prak 2015: 123-124). If this same phenomenon of transferring the responsibility for defense against external forces to the local political sphere happened in the Flemish cities at the end of the Middle Ages (Boone 2005), it similarly appeared at the beginning of the Revolt of the Brotherhoods (Pardo Molero 2001, pp. 89-92). It was also present when *suspicious* populations were disarmed for religious or social reasons, or when the Mediterranean was being defended (Ruiz Ibáñez 1995: 223-225; Lomas Cortés 2010), as well as during the colonization of America or the Wars of Religion in Europe. The rhetoric about the city being "in order", which was proclaimed on occasion of urban rituals, had an underlying political function as it linked the definition of the individual and the corporative socio-administrative entity with the very construction of the Monarchy and service to it (Thøfner 2007).

The manner in which the mechanisms of urban and territorial defense evolved during the sixteenth and seventeenth centuries progressively favored the royal systems of protection that were based on professional units or royal militia troops. Their aspiration to establish a territorial base eroded the very definition of the urban republic in two different ways. As these militias were dependent on the royal administration, the local authorities lost their capacity to mobilize and organize the civic community. If it happened to have a corporative base (for example, the militias of blacks and mulatos in America), the legal capacity to define who ultimately had the right to bear arms was transferred from the city to the king. The progressive appropriation by the royal administration of the means of exercising legitimate violence should obviously not be seen as the construction of a mechanism that was coherent in its intentions and disciplined in its conduct. Internal conflicts continued to define the process of how local violence was handled, only now the protagonists were changing and the old territorial entities were giving way to new realities (Zúñiga 2006).

Administering Defense in Times of Turmoil

It is necessary to situate the king's different agents, namely the administrators of his authority, in this unstable framework, all the while bearing in mind that the representation of what can be understood as *this* authority would depend on the point of view (political, territorial, cultural, and social) of the individual defining it. In the end, the king's authority was absolute in his sphere of powers, but defining this sphere, and the hierarchy that was constructed among the powers that depended on his legitimacy, was contingent on the traditions and political culture of each one of the agents that participated in the administration of royal domination. A royal delegate, a powerful local citizen or a simple *vecino* were all considered to be the king's servants, but each one would define that service according to his own representation and political culture (for the constitutive pluralistic network of identities see Gil Pujol 2004). We therefore need to return to the study of practices so as to understand how each component that formed part of the monarchy interacted with the others, evolving in a way that, in many cases, did not turn out as anticipated. We start with the premise that the three political positions outlined above reflected their own social aspirations that affected the stability and the mutability implied by the monarchical regime.

Although narratives inspired by *grande histoire* tend to leave out local political life, both currents seem to intersect when international politics appear in one form or another. At that point, the individuals providing the backbone of the accounts of such moments act in a setting that is made up of urban powers and the daily exercise of their authority. The forces that drove back Drake's incursions into the Caribbean in the mid-1590s, or those that succumbed to the Duke of Cumberland's attack on Puerto Rico in 1598, can be described in this way. The American territories that were incorporated into the crown of Castile were not the only territories where coordinated collaboration of country man and armed citizen proved to be decisive for repelling the great threats that characterized the wars between princes.

Two of these instances of cooperation, which took place in the Iberian Peninsula between 1596 and 1597, were particularly significant. The first one confirmed the weakness of the defensive systems located on the coast of the Peninsula when confronted by a major raid. It reawakened the feeling of fear that had been left hanging in suspense after the Counter-Armada was easily resisted in 1589. Then, the capture of Cadiz by Essex's British-Dutch fleet made it obvious that the territorial heart of the Monarchy was terribly vulnerable. Terror spread throughout the different Atlantic and Mediterranean ports, as their inhabitants felt sure that they were going to be attacked very shortly, not only by the Low Countries and Elizabeth of England's navy, but also by the Great Turk's fleet, which appeared to be waking up in the center of the Mediterranean after periods of inactivity and complacency. Given this prospect, the inhabitants unleashed an intense flurry of activity, which was expressed by hectic agitation as the local authorities rushed to buy gunpowder, guarantee succor from the inland areas, organize the men fit for fighting and prepare plans to evacuate those who could not contribute towards the defense. Everyone was well aware that if the forces of another prince, or of the Dutch rebels, managed to cross the lines of defense that were marked by the army in Flanders, the galley fleets, and the *Armada del Mar Océano*, the only way to stop an invasion, aside from fortresses, was to call to duty the traditional local and noble military corps (except for the case of the kingdom of Granada), though no one was particularly optimistic about their effectiveness. In order to reorganize and rearm them, it was essential to have the cooperation, or, better yet, the encouragement and participation, not only of the authorities delegated by the king, but even more importantly, of those entities that coordinated the local populations (Ruiz Ibáñez 1997).

Catalonia in 1597 came to represent a particularly significant case though it was far from being unique. The Duke of Feria, the viceroy, was quickly taught the need to cooperate with local powers when he was faced with the dissolution of the League in southern France and the beginning of a direct threat to the north of the Principality in 1597 (Pérez Latre 2003: 239-245; Valencia Rodríguez 2010: 243-266). Although the war had been officially declared in 1595, and the king had taken the preventive measure of writing to the nobility, towns, and important ecclesiastics, it was not until the surrender of Narbonne to the first Bourbon that the Rossellon became the front of the war between the Bourbon army and the Catholic king's meagre garrisons. As the threat of a French offensive grew (Larquier 1996: 189; Larquier 1996b: 531-538), the viceroy had to negotiate with all of the entities of the Principality in order to mobilize sufficient troops to resist even if there were only scarce military resources in proper order in the south of France (Souriac 2008: 239, 395). The arming of the territory was carried out by invoking the mobilization act of 1595 and feudal rights; at the same time, the local and regional entities were recognized as interlocutors. In the end, the viceroy, the former ambassador to the General Estates that held Paris in 1593 (the Duke of Feria) did not have many options, and with the collaboration of local powers, he managed to send a considerable military force to the border, and at the end of August deterred the threat on Perpignan. The French conquests of the following year were limited to capturing Opol, and the fortification of the Salvaterra castle took place the year after that. The best that the monarchy could do was to promise to send some funds, order the galleys from Genoa to move to the coast to provide assistance, transfer guards from Castile, and send veteran soldiers to help the duke.

According to the duke, the country had mobilized between 13,000 and 14,000 infantrymen and 1,000 horses. The words that the son of Charles V addressed to Feria reveal that such an effort only represented what was due to him, as he wrote to his viceroy that: "I highly value what is rightly your solicitude and the good will with which the natives are ready to serve me on this occasion, which is in accordance with what should be expected from you and them, and for this reason I give you great thanks and would wish for you to thank them on my behalf and I trust in God and in the good wits that you will be granted so that our enemies will receive the just punishment for their insolence...".[2] Maintaining the state of irregular war until the month of June meant that, as all the promised reinforcements did not arrive from Castile,[3] the defense against real—or simply feared—attacks from the French troops fell to the forces sent from the capital of the Principality, lords and the *Diputació del general**; the duke obviously had to carry on complex negotiations with all of them.

The Duke of Feria's situation, between impotence and dependency, was similar to those that the king's different agents faced to varying degrees in the territories, where there was an increase in belligerence during the 1590s on almost all of the monarchy's borders. Viceroys, *corregidores, bailíos**, and governors found themselves having to make concessions and acknowledge that it was the local powers that were in a position to mobilize the population, and this led to massive, disorganized and slightly frenetic negotiations on all of these borders. It should be added that the local defense mechanism generally worked well, for in a period when incursions on the monarchy's different fronts substantially increased, except in the aforementioned cases of Cadiz and Puerto Rico, the Catholic king had to lament few losses, due to luck, the effective weakness of the attackers, and the existence of a means of protection.

---

[2] ACDM, AH leg 166, Caja VII, 8/17 "Yo estimo en lo que es raçon vuestro cuydado y la buena voluntad con que los naturales se disponían a servirme en esa ocassion, que es muy conforme a lo que de vos y dellos se devía esperar y por ello os doy muchas gracias y vos se las dareys a ellos de mi parte y confío en dios y en la buena maña que os dareys que los enemigos llevaran la pena de su atrevimiento…".

[3] ACDM, AH leg 166, Caja VII, 8/10 and 8/25; Pérez Latre 2003, pp. 242-243

Armed Civilians: Between Cities and Kings

The royal administration drew the obvious conclusions about its weakness in the middle of the 1590s. On the one hand was the state of defenselessness that characterized the territory itself, unless national policy stationed military resources on the borders of the monarchy. On the other, its agents lacked the capacity to mobilize armed men without an expensive and slow mechanism of negotiation. This reinforced the image of political autonomy on the part of the local authorities, and the emotional tie that united the king with the local powers. In addition, the alternative of replacing the non-professional defense systems by an effective militarization of the borders was simply inconceivable, given that it would be decades before the fiscal revolution would start in Europe. The result was to modernize the mechanism of semi-professional defense (the territorial militia) that had been devised during the mid-sixteenth century; it was not only implemented in the multiple territories of the Spanish monarchy and other European kingdoms (Boynton 1971). These units consisted of the formation of corps of privileged civilians that would be organized under direct royal authority; they would be, in theory, better trained, mobile, and more available for territorial defense. It should be clarified that the semi-professional corps gave the king a greater degree of autonomy in the territory, and perhaps some of its members would even accept the discourse about direct service to the king. The studies that are available, nevertheless, clearly demonstrate that the posts of officers were almost all quickly incorporated into the patrimony of certain families; this finding should dismiss any idea that their creation meant a mechanical or bureaucratic dependence on the sovereign power. It is, however, also questionable whether this process of familiar "hoarding" automatically indicated that the administration totally lost control of these posts. Lacking more specific studies about this question, I now feel that, thanks to these designations to the captaincies, the monarch was able to expand his direct clientele, making more families dependent on the royal administration and extending the social base on which the presence of his power was sustained (Jiménez Estrella 2004: chapters 7-8).

The generalization of this type of corps (in Castile, southern Italy and Valencia) incited the active resistance of the local authorities, who quite rightly saw their possibilities of negotiation with the court and means of personal promotion threatened; even their indisputable control of the territory was jeopardized. This opposition was reinforced by the continuous conflicts over jurisdiction that the militiamen and their officers had with the local powers, whether they were city-based or issued from the traditional royal administration. In addition, the different peace settlements reached in Europe between 1598 and 1609 seemed to make the modernization of the system of defense much less urgent. By the next decade, the new territorial militias had been restricted to those areas where they were very useful due to the persisting threats of irregular warfare, or they languished in an almost purely phantasmal existence that did little or nothing to disrupt the local balance of power. Nevertheless, a precedent had been set and it would soon be invoked when international unrest put the monarchy's secondary borders into a predicament. Once again, Cadiz was dealt the first blow.

Although the English navy failed resoundingly when it attacked Cadiz in 1625, mainly due to its notable incompetence, it should not be overlooked that, unlike what had happened almost thirty years earlier, this time the localities of Lower Andalusia managed to mobilize a considerable number of men. In spite of these encouraging results obtained by the military that year, nothing seemed to indicate that the pressure of the other maritime powers on the monarchy's coasts was going to diminish. It meant putting into operation plans for collective defense by reactivating the traditional forms of defense and revamping the territorial militias that would even be extended to new territories. This general mobilization was possibly extended to New Spain (Celaya Nández 2010: 115-116), where the central government decided not to comply with the viceroy's proposal of forming a battalion with "companies of two hundred *vecinos* from that city".[4] The central government preferred to maintain the professional troops, that were already in place, in spite of the "hatred that the populace has for them".[5]

What was actually under discussion was who should organize the participation of the civilians in defense and what that meant exactly. The creation of a semi-professional corps always came up against the self-interested resistance of local powers, as they tended to view the corps very negatively if the troops were not immediately useful. Their understandable argument was that these corps meant a loss of power on the local level to the detriment of the royal administration. In addition, the corps were already used as an instrument for increasing royal fiscality, a role that they would take on even more distinctly starting in the 1630s. The semi-

[4] "compañías de a dusçientos veçinos de la dicha çiudad".

[5] AGN RCO 1, no. 41 and 42, 20-II and 28-VI-1630, Madrid, Philip IV to the viceroy the Marquis of Cerralvo, "odio que la tiene el pueblo".

professional units, unlike those that depended on the cities, were more mobile and could remain in service during longer periods of time without having to receive authorization from the *cabildos**. Even worse, the integration into these corps was not based on a relationship that defined its members as part of the urban corporation, but rather as the king's subjects. The enormous changes fostered by the fiscal revolution of the 1630s and 1640s altered the basis of this relationship: it was no longer based on gratuitous affection but was founded on the principle of obligation (Mackay 1999).

The transformation of the system of defense did not respond to a precise plan, but was rather the generalization of isolated responses carried out in concrete contexts in a common political-administrative framework. It produced the opportunistic modelization of other administrative solutions that had yielded more or less efficient results in other territories. When examining a monarchy as complex as the Hispanic, it is necessary to question the simple nominative implementation of political reforms as the instrument used to unify its administrative bases. It should not be forgotten that these programmatic reforms were very frequent from the 1550s onwards, and their effective application was invariably linked to the skills of territorial agents capable of putting them into practice and overcoming local resistance. Only in a state of war, and for other reasons that I have discussed in previous works, could these reforms be used for transmitting the effective increase of fiscality in the king's name. The result was not so much a tendency towards the planned equalization, but rather a local adaptation to new fiscal obligations, a process of adaptation that resulted from the unstable political equilibriums that characterized each territory and their representation. Of course, this evolution was not at all disassociated from the construction that the royal entourage was putting on such transformations by the end of the seventeenth century; they were not considered as the unlucky result of the fiscal chaos that accompanied the century, but rather as the expression of the *regalias** that, logically, were due to the king because of his royal dignity. Such a conceptualization proved to be a very effective line of political argumentation when the Bourbons were transforming the administration of their territories, claiming that it was not so much a violation of the division of the monarchical power, but rather its culmination (Muñoz Rodríguez 2010).

Serve the King and the City

It is often argued in the discourses seeking to gain exemption from fiscal duties, or at least their reduction, that were presented by the *señorios** and the Mediterranean, Flemish, and American cities, that the costs, suffering, and effort that the defense of their own lands implied should be discounted, or at least taken into account when their contributions were calculated. The reasoning was simple and easily understood; their defense of the borders directly saved the prince resources, and their providing this defense was not only their obligation as inhabitants, and a necessity as potential victims, it was also a service provided in defense of the royal dignity and power. As the kingdom of Valencia argued during the reign of Charles the V, there was no need to involve the kingdom's resources in the crusade against the Turks in the distant Danube valley, given that the war against the infidel was already being fought on east coast of the Peninsula (Pardo Molero 2001: 278-279). The concept of fulfilling the obligations to the city, or the *señorío* (Saavedra Vázquez 2007), was thus part of the complex imagery about service to a monarchy that was defined in terms of the local political culture, though from such a perspective a caesura between both forms of participation could not be recognized. In spite of being seen as corporations, the institutions that fulfilled this function, and the patricians that directed them, based their relationship with the king on affective ties that implied the recognition of their nobility (Centenero de Arce 2011: chapter 2).

Returning to the example of Catalonia clearly illustrates these ideas. Upon the mobilization of the Principality in 1597, Philip II insisted to his viceroy that "I was pleased to learn from your letter that you were heading towards the border and of the service that the *diputación* decided to perform for me on this occasion, and the determination and good spirits with which all, as a group and as individuals, have responded, which I value as being just and in keeping with its ancient fidelity and custom. You will thank them particularly for it on my behalf".[6] He also wrote to the cities of Girona and Barcelona expressing gratitude: "for the love and

[6] "holgue mucho de entender por ella que fuesedes ya caminando hazia la frontera y el servicio que la diputaçion se havia resuelto de hazerme en esa ocasión y la voluntad y buen animo con que todos, en general y particular, acudian que lo e estimado en lo que es razon y es muy acorde a su antigua fidelidad y costumbre. Vos les dareys mis particulares gracias por ello de mi parte…".

promptness with which you have attended to all matters of my service and that you have made known on this occasion the suspicion that the French have entered in Rossellon by offering me 1,000 infantrymen, whom for this purpose you sent to Perpignan and its border, as I value it even more being on this occasion, and it shows that it proceeds from how much you fulfill the duties of my service and the defense and security of this province, continuing to demonstrate your ancient loyalty as you have always and hence it is so natural for you, and the need will continue. I know that it is not necessary to charge you with continuing what has already been started until the cavalry and infantry reach the border, as they are hurrying to go to defend it, it will occur shortly, I can but trust that you will demonstrate in this matter what you have until now, for which I will receive a very welcomed service and the memory of the one and the other will remain with me, which is to be expected".[7]

Undertaking the defense was the responsibility of the *republicos** and by assuming it they affirmed that they represented the nobility of the city, as this role obliged them to respond to the king's call when the integrity of the kingdom was threatened. Of course, on the local level, the monarchy could also administer directly; this presence was reduced, in the majority of cases, to small garrisons, except partly on the principal war fronts, at least until the mid-eighteenth century.

The cause of this situation was twofold. On the one hand, the privileges of the cities normally protected them from the introduction of professional garrisons. On the other, the king simply lacked a direct administration that was capable of being present in all the threatened areas. In the best of the cases, and in the face of an imminent threat, specialized agents could be sent to augment the defensive forces and allow local leaders to organize the mobilized troops better. This strategy was

[7] ACDM, AH, Box VII, 8/22. "el amor y prontitud con que acudis a todas las cosas mi servicio y que os aveis señalado en esta ocasión de sospecha de entrada de franceses en Rossellon con servirme con mil infantes q para este efecto aveis enviado a Perpiñan y su frontera q siendo en tal ocasión lo extimo en tanto mas y echo de ver q procede de lo mucho que zelais mi servicio y la defensa y seguridad de esa provincia, siguiendo vuestra antigua fidelidad y lo que siempre aveis acostumbrado y pues esto os es tan natural y la necessidad se va continuando se que no será menester encomendaros la continuacion de lo començado asta que llegue a la frontera la cavalleria e infantería q se esta aprestando para yr a su defensa q sera con mucha brevedad, sino confiar que os mostrareis en ello los q hasta aquí en que recivire muy acepto servicio y de lo uno y lo otro me queda la memoria que es razón".

implemented in Catalonia in 1597-1598, when soldiers such as Captain Juan Ortiz were sent to fight. He was described as "one of the veteran soldiers that I told you would be sent. I have ordered that he go to serve me on this occasion as I am very satisfied with this person because of how well he served me in Flanders".[8] Other soldiers that were sent included Antonio de Corral y Rojas, Juan de Urreta, the second lieutenants Alonso López de Agüero and Jusepe Gutiérrez Velarde, the captain Rafael Luis Terrades, of whom it was said "certainly his presence there will be of great benefit", and the lieutenant of the captain general of artillery, Captain Pedro de León.[9] Such a plan meant, in the best of cases, the arrival of a few dozen veterans, who would almost immediately be at odds with the local authorities. The king could also send arms [10] although this contribution complemented those that had been manufactured (Pérez Latre 2003: 241) or purchased either by institutions or individuals,[11] and this obviously reinforced the Mediterranean arsenal after 1596.

Using the King and the City

If defending the city was defending the monarchy, the discussion as to who was responsible for leading and managing this function acquired a clearly political overtone, although it was expressed through a disorganized multiplicity of conflicts about protocol and confrontations over jurisdictions. It was no longer just about guaranteeing the local social hegemony of an established elite, for it also involved identifying the different "parcels" of power that existed on the local level and the corporative, personal, and institutional means of insertion in the monarchy. While these questions were settled in other administrative or geographical areas with an even level of emotional intensity, they took on a new dimension in these spheres of conflict, as they had an evident repercussion on the monarchy's very security. Areas in danger were also territories in which the services to the king should be rewarded, but it was crucial to

---

[8] "es uno de los soldados platicos que se os avissó se os enviaran… al que e mandado vaya a servirme en la en la ocassion que ay se ofrecce es persona de quien tengo satisfacion por lo bien que me ha servido en Flandes".

[9] ACDM, AH, Box VII, 8/14 "por cierto que su asistencia ay sera de mucho provecho".

[10] ACDM, AH, Box VII, 8/25.

[11] ASMi CS 344, sn, 1-4-1598, request of Clemente Galcerán.

decide who had sufficient standing to perform those services, that is, to be able to be awarded a position of some status upon completing them.

When the members of the urban and territorial patriarchates that inhabited the monarchy's borderlands presented petitions for *mercedes*, they did not hesitate to make it known that both they and their ancestors had led the local defense, losing in many cases members of their lineages due to such deeds. It was not uncommon for these narrations also to allude to other relatives that had served the king in the regular army on American and European battle fields. These powerful locals expressed a self-interested confusion as they insisted that all these deeds stemmed from just one unique source of merit; serving in both the local and imperial spheres, they appropriated the same logic they used as rulers of the cities, though now they cast it in terms of lineage and personal service. A unified vision of their relationship with the king and service to him, which is based on domestic bonds, subsists in this "confusion", which obviously surpassed the division between imperial and local administrations.

From the very moment when the Modern Age began, it appeared to have been established that the action of the non-professional forces outside of the city walls was subordinated locally to the king's direct agents (viceroys, governors, *corregidores*, mayors, *bailíos*, etc.) once it was handed over by the city. Furthermore, once the armed corporation was constituted, there were sometimes discussions (which inspired a notable casuistry) about who had the ultimate authority over it within the city walls. It was the king's agents' responsibility to lead it during the solidary defense of the territory, and once the immediate need for the defense had passed, it was the king's duty to sustain it. It did not imply however that the corporation's members were actually professionalized. It was an even more complicated matter to identify the men that were to be in charge of the organization, training, and local leadership of the units that this armed corporation directed. Robert Descimon has shown the importance of the military leaderships of the Parisian militias as a unifying force in both cultural and political terms. The vertical and horizontal ties that were created played a crucial role when it was time to pick sides during the Wars of Religion (Descimon 1987, 1993). This line of research (that incorporates social, political and cultural realities through the study of administrative questions) has not been particularly taken up by the historiography of the territories the Hispanic Monarchy ruled. Nevertheless, it appears that the local patriarchates and territorial elites were much more aware than historians have been of how physical and symbolic power could be reproduced and consolidated through the prestige and patronage that the direct control of the urban forces permitted and conferred.

It was, perhaps, too much power, and this could explain why the kings attempted to keep these functions in the hands of subsidiary corporations, such as the *jurados** of Murcia,[12] so that they would not depend directly on the hegemonic groups that dominated the *ayuntamientos**. It was evidently necessary to maintain a certain equilibrium that would not upset the urban order that the monarchy relied on, as the memory of rebellions such as the Revolt of the Brotherhoods [*Germanías*] had not faded. It appeared that the position of the royal authorities was generally to rely on the oligarchical groups although the power of the local rulers to mobilize the population was reduced. The royal tribunals' willingness to defend the rights that the low-level municipal administration possessed perhaps just reflected their dogmatic respect for the Monarchy's foundations and past; in any case, it managed to restrain effectively any aspirations to monopolize the local power and royal *merced** that the *repúblicos* had. In the cities where the royal representatives did not manage to take over this function despite their insistence, they at least tried to divert it through the articulation of the instrument of military mobilization, and this allowed them to surpass the institutional limits and remain within a purely municipal model, at least until the 1640s. It meant establishing *ad hoc* companies, which even if they did articulate the services of the cities or *señoríos*, did not do it as an expression of their insertion in the Monarchy, but rather as an extraordinary service. This posture allowed them to avoid formal institutional limitations and to arbitrarily designate officers, depending in many cases on personal and financial involvement. It thus guaranteed that the elite could manage the acquisition of services from the king.

Continuing to Serve the King in the City

The sovereign's direct ordinary delegates in the cities believed that their natural leadership would be demonstrated in the area of defense (or at least in the articulation of the local forces) as a form of promotion that formed part of the services they had been providing professionally to the king. It was logical that a considerable proportion of these positions originated in the army, or were *capa y espada**, given that the representation of royal authority in areas of conflict saw defense to be one

[12] AGChG, Caja 2033-001.

of their primary functions. These former soldiers found themselves placed in the midst of a society that was already beset by numerous tensions involving groups that fought for the control of defense in its interior as well as royal delegates with extraordinary powers trying to mobilize the civilians more efficiently and with greater coordination—though this new articulation would not necessarily be more bureaucratic. Against these royal delegates the cities and *señoríos* tended to make common cause with representatives of the king that defended a *status quo*, the undermining of which would reduce their capacity to obtain the central administration's attention. The ambivalent position of *corregidores* and mayors and their ensuing resistance to transformation was decisive in curbing the reformist measures that the imperial governments tried to implement from 1590 to 1620. Such attempts had to be abandoned, which meant that new political spaces had to be sought for negotiating fiscal measures with the population.

All in all, the position of these delegates was extremely tenuous, as they were defending an administrative structure that they could only change if they were particularly effective, could direct the local divisions in their favor, or count on the king's resolute support. Imbued with the administrative culture that characterized the army, in which the royal *merced* and a certain meritocracy really existed, the veterans that came from the fronts could easily consider these positions in the area of justice and defense as an opportunity to bolster their careers, and do it by making use of their military experience. It was not unusual to find these veterans, whose careers we have only recently started to study,[13] developing ambitious plans to improve the city stronghold, putting to use their technical knowledge, and providing a service to the king on the local level just as they had previously done in a professional environment. This example shows that the logic of identifying local defense as an imperial realm was not exclusively for the patriarchs. There were certainly multiple ways of carrying out these improvements, such as reinforcing the defenses, increasing the urban forces' training and drilling, improving the officers and their coordination by promoting those inhabitants that had military experience in European wars, bettering the armament, and strengthening

[13] Pardo Molero and Lomás Cortés (2001) serves to clarify even more the relations between these direct agents of the king and the territories where they exercised their mandate. See also Domingo Centenero de Arce, *¿Una Monarquía de lazos débiles? Veteranos, militares y administradores 1580-1621*, unpublished doctoral thesis, IEF, Florence, Italy, 2009.

the ties among the communities in anticipation of solidary defense. Strengthening of the defense was the way to guarantee stability in the Empire for the imaginary of this kind of *capa y espada* delegate. This objective could not, however, be achieved without problems.

Of course, in the key years (1596, 1625 or 1691) when troops were mobilized on the secondary borders in reaction to the dramatic increase of external threats, the local authorities were ready to overlook momentarily the implications of relinquishing the operations to the royal officials belonging to the new or old administration, so as to obtain an effective protection in the face of an extremely real menace. Nevertheless, upon gaining excessive effective power, the king's direct agents questioned the socio-administrative hierarchies (appointing veterans to executive positions), and exacted taxes for assuring the defense that, in the opinion of the *repúblicos,* was unnecessary once the urgency had passed. The local leaders then did all that was possible to recover their former positions, or to oust the royal officials who were extremely dependent on the natives' cooperation. The delegates were consequently forced to check their yearnings for reform or face a particularly hostile *juicio de residencia**, once the local men in power mobilized all their possible contacts at the court.

The downfall of Captain Diego de Villalobos y Benavides during his term as *corregidor* in Malaga represents an exemplary case of the perverse effects that excessive zeal could have on the career of an official, though it was far from being unique. It was a fortified town that seemed singularly vulnerable at the beginning of the 1620s, when the presence of the British and Dutch navies in the straits could not be effectively opposed by the Spanish fleets. Born in Mexico City and a veteran of Flanders, Don Diego did all in his power to make headway in his *cursus honorum* by mobilizing the city and its surroundings so that they would be able to drive back an attack by the navies from the north, not an unreal threat given what had happened in Cadiz. Don Diego was not the first *corregidor* to have difficulties with the military organization of a city that was considered particularly prone to conflict; in addition, there were chronic problems with the administration of justice in the countryside around Malaga. Although the *corregidor* also held the title of war captain, in no time his defensive measures created conflict with the local civil and religious authorities, as well as with the envoy that the court sent to administer Olivares's political reforms more strictly. Having to confront all the other authorities and lacking protectors in Malaga or at Court, the *corregidor* soon found his political position to be untenable. The condemnation he and his collaborators received attests to the eldermen's capacity for political resistance and to the royal power's lack of autonomy when having to contend with them (Vallejo Cervantes and Ruiz Ibañéz 2012)

Villalobos y Benavides's downfall co-incided with the implementation of the new administration that Olivares was trying to put in place in order to have effective control of defense and the means of mobilizing the nonprofessional soldiers, as the global reactivation of the territorial militia had not resulted in the formation of a defense system that could dissuade the monarchy's enemies from attacking its borders. This failure did not mean that the local entities could completely recover their capacity to defend their city, even if, in the difficult years of the 1630s, any measure appeared good if it tried to respond to the ever-increasing threats that the monarchy faced.

As isolated responses to isolated aggressions, the modernization of the urban defense systems ran counter to two elements that were particularly discernable in the cities' situation. The progressive monopolization of power by a reduced group of individuals had broken down the political ties that united cities as groups of *vecinos* and this meant that a full renovation of military services was going to be seen as a new form of fiscality. This would only receive popular support with difficulty as it lacked a wide social base. Also, it is necessary to take into consideration the growing urban discontent that can be detected in different territories, obviously related to the institutional drive (Gil Pujol 2006).

Rearming a population in a context of increasing mobilization against rising fiscal pressure could not be imagined as a particularly wise action. Therefore, neither the central government nor the *ayuntamientos* looked favorably on this possibility. It was clear that the only option was to construct new forms of fiscality. This would allow the elites to maintain their capacity for mobilization and local control by capitalizing on the legitimacy that the monarchy gave to an increase in taxes that in the end would benefit the king (Thompson 1998).

Though it could seem paradoxical, the cities that continued to be armed were those that had been previously armed, and where the exercise of collective defense had maintained an urban articulation that compensated in part for the elites' accumulation of power. These borderlands appeared more unshakeable in the face of political disorder than those in the interior, since it was necessary in the borderlands to reckon with a part of the population that was organized for defense, *ergo* armed, and therefore not completely excluded from power. Therefore, the process of making decisions, even though it was controlled by the ruling elites, had to take into account the political position of a population with full rights. Significant political and social discipline could thus be maintained in a century that was in fact chaotic. This feature can be made clear by pointing out that whenever uprisings took place, it was in these "armed" areas that they were relatively easily controlled. Also, when the urban elite took sides by making a political decision, they possessed the means to make the entire population both participant and protagonist in that decision. Nevertheless, this urban entente was limited to what had been traditionally the realm of defense. It could not be expected to cover the monarchy's *new* defense requirements, and this meant that they had to be financed by new fiscal measures just as had been the case in the interior.

Conclusion

The sphere of local defense made it possible to identify the different agents that, one way or another, participated in guaranteeing local security as defenders of the whole Empire and the king's direct servants. Unlike those posted in the territories of the interior, the monarchy's agents could not defend a line of argument that sought to justify fiscal contributions by invoking the protection against the external aggressions that the imperial structure guaranteed. On the contrary, service to the monarchy on the borders was both an individual and collective form of participating in the royal realm and making it the base of their self-identity, and this allowed these armed subjects-*vecinos* to play upon their different political identities. The same individual or family could claim that the services performed at the local level had a strictly urban meaning while sustaining before the central power the argument that these very actions also corresponded to the exercise of their duties as the king's direct servants. This fluidity between the two stances nevertheless had its consequences.

One issue was that the powerful men demanded that the king recognize their services at the local level and that the corporations asked for the exemptions that derived from their involvement in defense; a quite separate matter was whether the sovereign would be willing to do so, and, if so, how he would go about doing it. It could appear somewhat paradoxical that the elites requested that they could claim as individuals and subjects the same services performed as the recognized leaders of their privileged republic. The separation that logically divided the two spheres of services became unified because of the course taken by political practice. The monarchy's central administration was aware of the need to reward individuals' involvement in its service, especially in those places where its military presence was particularly weak and those in which the king's base of clientalism consequently had to be expanded. By granting pensions, *señoríos*, *mercedes*, licenses for arms, robes of the military orders, perpetual captaincies, or the ennoblement of specific persons as the men in charge of their communities' territorial defense, the king not only partially fulfilled the hopes of those involved, but also (equally important) changed the established local social order by creating small fissures in the forms of urban self-recognition. No one claimed that local powers were static, or that the search for their stability really existed, or that there was an illusory return to the "old good times", even if chorographical rhetoric in this sense flourished in the cities.

If the protection of the adjoining territory was recognized by the king as the serviceable, though not obligatory, defense of the monarchy, it could be rewarded as a personal service to the sovereign. In turn, the beneficiary's status changed; a position originating in the community was transformed into one that reflected the dignity that the king recognized. It also occurred when royal venality was exercised or taxes were conceded to the king. However, military services were performed in a framework in which the population participated, a factor that was not present in the former local instances of personal service. In addition, as services of this nature conjured up the principle of nobility being acquired by armed service, their accumulation could be particularly appealing in symbolic terms. When each royal favor or award was granted, the very nature of the services performed by the *señoríos* and principalities was transformed. Their elites could claim with greater credibility that their preeminence was due more to their nature, recognized by the king himself, than to their integration in the community.

The interested agents accepted that service was the way to obtain recognition, but this service could be defined in various spectra and on different scales. The interpretative malleability that arose concerning the defensive actions shows how each one of the king's servants (those on the local level as well as those from his own administration) appropriated their participation in the area of defense from an opportunistic stance, implying their position in a specific conception of the monarchy. It is very significant that when these direct dependents describe their services, they always take on the leading role that ensured the good coordination of the defense; no space is left for the deeds that the virtually faceless local authorities accomplish, for they were reduced to fulfilling their simple obligation. The letters sent by the cities or *señoríos* narrating the same operations insist that their gratuitous and serviceable acts originated in the collective honor of the community and aggrandized it. Above all, they confirm the honor of the corporation that led them. The inclusion of individuals worthy of special recognition is always complex and perforce negotiated. As has been indicated, the petitions presented by individuals insisted that the service derived from an individual or family, leaving aside the local collective honor (Sabatini 2000).

Serving the king and the Monarchy was therefore not a neutral act; it could not be reduced to the simple framework of direct service. It did not depend only on theoretical formulations, nor was it developed in rigid compartments that the different jurisdictions defined. The multiple ways in which service could be understood defined the local construction of the Monarchy. The everyday acts that ensured defense in the different territories demonstrated a similar dynamic in America and Europe, and in many cases were even inter-related. Such similarities clearly show that the global projection of the foreign policy generated common processes, although they could have different rhythms. It was often through the silent evolution of the use of this power, whether it was active or latent, that the modern urban world evolved and a reality was constructed in which service would eventually be defined only in a top-down hierarchy.

Archives Cited

AGN: Archivo General de la Nación, Mexico D.F., Mexico.
ACDM: Archivo de la Casa Ducal de Medinaceli, AH [Archivo Histórico] (Sevilla-Toledo)
ASMi: Archivio di Stato di Milano, Milano, Italia, RCS [Registre delle Cancellerie dello Stato (e di Magistrature diverse)]
ARChG: Archivo de la Real Chancilleria de Granada, Granada, Spain.

References and Sources

Álvarez-Ossorio, A. - García García, B., (eds.), (2004), *La Monarquía de las Naciones. Patria, nación y naturaleza en la Monarquía de España*, Madrid: Fundación Carlos de Amberes.

Bernal, M. - De Rosa, L. - D'Esposito, F., (eds.), (2000), *El gobierno de la economía en el imperio español*, Sicilia: Fundacion del Monte.

Bernand, C. – Stella, A., (ed.), (2006), *D'esclaves à soldats. Miliciens et soldats d'origine servile, XIIIè-XXIè siècles*, Paris: L'Harmattan.

Boone, M., (2005), "Armes, coursses, assemblees et commocions. Les gens de métiers et l'usage de la violence dans la société urbaine flamande à la fin du Moyen Âge", *Revue du Nord*, 87/359: 7-33.

Boone, M. – Prak, M., (eds.), (1996), *Statuts individuels, statuts corporatifs et statuts judiciaires dans les villes européennes (moyen âge et temps modernes)/Individual, corporate and judicial status in European cities (late middle ages and early modern period),* Leuven: Garant.

Boynton L., (1971), *The Elizabethan Militia, 1558-1638*, London: Newton Abbot.

Brunet, S. - Ruiz Ibáñez, J. J., (ed.), (2012), *Les milices dans la première modernité,* Rennes: Presses Universitaires de Rennes.

Cardim. P. - Herzog, T. - Ruiz Ibáñez, J. J. - Sabatini, G., (2012), *Polycentrics Monarchies. How did Early Modern Spain and Portugal Achieve and Maintain a global Hegemony?*, Eastbourne & Porland & Vaughan: Sussex Academic Press: "Introduction": 3-10.

Celaya Nández, Y., (2010), *Alcabalas y Situados: Puebla en El Sistema Fiscal Imperial 1638-1742*, México, D.F.: El Colegio de México.

Centenero de Arce, D., (2011), *De repúblicas urbanas a ciudades nobles. Un análisis de la evolución y desarrollo del republicanismo castellano (1550-1621)*, Madrid: Biblioteca Nueva.

Descimon, R., (1987), "Solidarité communautaire et sociabilité armée: les compagnies de la milice bourgeoise à Paris (XVIe-XVIIe siècle)" in *Sociabilité, pouvoirs et société (Actes du colloque de Rouen, novembre 1983)*, Rouen: 599-610.

—. (1993), "Milice bourgeoise et identité citadine à Paris au temps de la Ligue", *Annales ESC* : 885-906.

Dubet. A. - Ruiz Ibáñez, J.J., (eds.), (2010), *Las Monarquías española y francesa. ¿Dos modelos políticos?*, Madrid: Casa de Velásquez.

Gil Pujol, X., (2002), "Republican Politics in Early Modern Spain: The Castilian and Catalano-Aragonese Traditions" in Van Gelderen, M. – Skinner, Q., (eds.), *Republicanism and Constitutionalism in early Modern Europe*, vol. I, Cambridge: Cambridge University Press: 263-288.

—. (2004), "Un rey, una fe, muchas naciones. Patria y nación en la España de los siglos XVI-XVII", in Álvarez-Ossorio - García García, (eds.), *La Monarquía de las Naciones. Patria, nación y naturaleza en la Monarquía de España*: 39-76.

—. (2006), "Más sobre las revueltas y revoluciones del siglo XVII y sobre su ausencia" in Parker (coord.), *La crisis de la Monarquía de Felipe IV*: 351-392.

Jiménez Estrella, A., (2004), *Poder, ejército y gobernación en el siglo XVI. De la Capitanía General del Reino de Granada y sus agentes*, Granada: Universidad de Granada.

Jiménez Estrella, A. - Andújar Castillo, F. (ed.), (2007), *Los nervios de la guerra. Estudios sobre el ejército de la Monarquía Hispánica (siglos XVI-XVIII): nuevas perspectivas*, Granada: Comares.

Kelsey, H., (2002), *Sir Francis Drake. El pirata de la reina*, Barcelona: Ariel.

— . (1994), *Burgers in het geweer. De schuterijn in Holland, 1550-1700*, Hilversum: Verloren.

Larquier, G., (1996), "Devenir une ville frontière: Narbonne, XVe-XVIIe siècles" in Menjot, (coord.), *Les villes frontière. Moyen-Âge, Époque Moderne*: 177-195.

—. (1996b), *Le drap et le grain en Languedoc: Narbonne et Narbonnais 1300-1789*, Perpignan: Presses universitaires de Perpignan.

Lomas Cortés, M., (2010), "El Marqués de los Vélez y el desarme de los moriscos de Murcia (1601-1605)", *Manuscrits*, 28: 45-70.

Mackay, R., (1999), *The Limits of Royal Authority*, Cambridge: Cambridge University Press.

Martínez Ruiz, E. – Pazzis Pi, M. de (dirs.), (1998), *España y Suecia en la época del Barroco (1600-1660)*, Madrid: Consejería de Educación y Cultura.

Mazín Gómez, O., (2007), *Gestores de la Real justicia. Procuradores y agentes de las catedrales hispanas nuevas en la corte de Madrid*, Mexico: El Colegio de México.

Menjot, D., (coord.), (1997), *Les villes frontière. Moyen-Âge, Époque Moderne*, Paris-Montreal: L'Harmattan.

Mousnier, R., (1972), "Les concepts d''ordres', d''états', de 'fidélité' et de 'monarchie absolue" en France de la fin du XVe siècle à la fin du XVIIIe", *Revue Historique*, 502: 289-312.

Muñoz Rodríguez, J., (2010), "El superintendente austriaco y el intendente borbónico. La evolución de un modelo de gestión de los recursos fiscales en la Monarquía Hispánica", in Dubet - Ruiz Ibáñez, (eds.), *Las Monarquías española y francesa. ¿Dos modelos políticos?*: 131-144.

Pardo Molero, J.F., (2001), *La defensa del imperio. Carlos V, Valencia y el Mediterráneo*, Madrid: Sociedad Estatal para la Conmemoración de los Centenarios de Felipe II y Carlos V, Colección Historia.
Pardo Molero, J.F. - Lomás Cortés, M., (2001), *Oficiales reales. Los minstros de la monarquía católica (siglos XVI-XVII)*, Valencia: Universidad de Valencia.
Parker, G., (coord.), (2006), *La crisis de la Monarquía de Felipe IV*, Barcelona: Crítica-Instituto Universitario de Simancas.
Pérez Latre, M., (2003), *Entre el rei i la terra. El poder polític a Catalunya al segle XVI*, Vic: Universitat de Vic/Eumo editorial.
Piceu, T., (2008), *Over vrybuters en quaetdoenders: terreur op het Vlaamse platteland (eind 16de eeuw)*, Leuven: Davidsfonds.
Prak, M. (2015), "Citizens, soldiers and civic militias in Late Medieval and Earlu Modern Europe", *Past & Present*, 228: 93-125.
Ruiz Ibáñez, J.J., (1995), *Las dos caras de Jano. Monarquía, ciudad e individuo. Murcia, 1588-1648*, Murcia : Universidad de Murcia.
—. (1996), "Sujets et citoyens: les relations entre l'Etat, la ville, la bourgeoisie et les institutions militaires municipales à Murcie (XVIe-XVIIe siècle)", in Boone – Prak (eds.), *Statuts individuels, statuts corporatifs et statuts judiciaires dans les villes européennes (moyen âge et temps modernes)/Individual, corporate and judicial status in European cities (late middle ages and early modern period)*:126-156.
—. (1997), "Monarquía, guerra e individuo en la década de 1590: El socorro de Lier de 1595", *Hispania. Revista Española de Historia*, Madrid, LVII/I, 195, 1997: 37-62.
Ruiz Ibáñez, J.J. - Sabatini, G., (2009), "Monarchy as Conquest: Violence, Social Opportunity and Political Stability in the Establishment of the Hispanic Monarchy", *Journal of Modern History*, 81/3: 501-536.
Ruiz Ibáñez, J.J., (ed.), (2009), *Las Milicias del rey de España. Política, sociedad e identidad en las Monarquías Ibéricas*, Madrid: Fondo de Cultura Económica.
Saavedra Vázquez, C., (2007), "Los protagonistas de la actividad militar en Galicia: nobleza, ciudades y Juntas del reino (s. XVI-XVII)" in Jiménez Estrella - Andújar Castillo (ed.), *Los nervios de la guerra. Estudios sobre el ejército de la Monarquía Hispánica (siglos XVI-XVIII): nuevas perspectivas*: 121-148.
Sabatini, G., (2000), "La trasmissione delle informazioni dal regno di Napoli agli organismi centrali della corona. Le relazioni delle autorità vicereali, le memorie delle magistrature, le suppliche delle comunità"

in Bernal - De Rosa - D'Esposito (eds.), *El gobierno de la economía en el imperio español*: 211-232.

Silva Prada, N., (2007), *La política de una rebelión. Los indígenas frente al tumulto de 1692 en la ciudad de México*, Mexico: El Colegio de México.

Souriac, P.-J., (2008), *Une guerre civile. Affrontements religieux et militaires dans le Midi Toulousain (1562-1596)*, Seyssel : Champ Vallon.

Thompson, I.A.A., (1976), *War and Government in Hapsburg Spain, 1560-1620*, London: Athlone Press.

—. (1998), "La movilización de recursos nacionales y la tesis de Downing. La guerra y el Estado en España a mediados del siglo XVII" in Martínez Ruiz – Pazzis Pi (dirs.), *España y Suecia en la época del Barroco (1600-1660)*: 279-306.

—. (2007), "Consideraciones sobre el papel de la nobleza como recurso militar en la España Moderna" in Jiménez Estrella - Andújar Castillo (ed.), *Los nervios de la guerra. Estudios sobre el ejército de la Monarquía Hispánica (siglos XVI-XVIII): nuevas perspectivas*: 15-36.

Thøfner, M., (2007), *A Common Art: Urban Ceremonial in Antwerp and Brussels during and after the Dutch Revolt*, Zwolle: Waanders Publishers.

Truchuelo García, S., (2004), *Gipuzkoa y el poder real en la Alta Edad Moderna*, San Sebastian: Diputación Foral de Gipuzkoa.

Valencia Rodríguez, J.M., (2010), *El poder señorial en la Edad Moderna. La Casa de Feria (siglo XVI y XVII)*, 2 vol., Jaraiz de la Vega: Diputación de Badajoz.

Vallejo Cervantes, G. - Ruiz Ibáñez, J.J., (2012), "Viviendo 'sin dexar parte donde las Cruzes españolas no hayan sido conocidas'. Don Diego de Villalobos y Benavides en la administración imperial de la Monarquía hispánica", *Historia Mexicana*, Vol. 243, 61/3: 1109-1170.

Wernham, R.B., (1994), *The Return of the Armadas. The Last Years of the Elizabethan War against Spain 1595-1603*, Oxford: Clarendon Press.

Zúñiga, J.P., (2006), "Africains aux Antipodes. Armée et mobilité sociale dans le Chili colonial", in Bernand – Stella (ed.), *D'esclaves à soldats. Miliciens et soldats d'origine servile, XIIIè-XXIè siècles*: 115-132.

CHAPTER THREE

THE VENALITY OF OFFICES AND HONORS IN SPAIN AND AMERICA IN THE EIGHTEENTH CENTURY[1]

FRANCISCO ANDÚJAR CASTILLO

Until fairly recently, historical studies presented the dynastic change of 1701 as the beginning of a process of reforms that introduced profound changes in the model of the state prevailing under the Hapsburgs. For many years these studies interpreted the modifications imposed by the Bourbons as the passage from a model of "judicial monarchy" to one of "administrative monarchy". This interpretation then formed the basis of innumerable studies that analyzed the Bourbons' policy of reforms, principally in matters of treasury, army and government, concluding that the new dynasty that accompanied the change of century substantially modified the inherited structures. The creation of the ministerial system of the *Secretarias de Despacho**, which were to assume the power that the *Consejos** had previously held, was considered the most conspicuous symbol of this change.

Several recent studies have revised this thesis in order to emphasize more the elements of continuity linking the two dynasties (Dubet 2007). For, even if important reforms were effectively introduced, many of the bureaucratic practices and the political-administrative mechanisms were unchanged. In essence, there was no modification of the nature of a state that, at the dawn of the eighteenth century, tried to reconcile "patrimonial" logic and a timid "rationalization" of the government's structure, just as it had in previous centuries. This is what happened with the sale of offices at

[1] This study was carried out as part of the Research and Development Project *Between the corruption and the venality during Old Regime* (HAR2014-55305-P), financed by the Spanish Ministerio de Ciencia e Innovación.

all levels, from the humblest posts in towns to the highest positions of government. The monarchy constantly struggled with the necessary rationalization of the system of naming its agents and the forces that opposed this intention, some of which were inherent to the internal constitution of the monarchy itself. The "rational" option, if this term can be used, would have been that the king, when naming those who served him, recompensed merit, virtue, experience, years of service and good performance in the positions that made up the bureaucratic, judicial, political or military careers. In practice, however, other elements that were more characteristic of a patrimonial state continually annulled or interrupted this course of action. In the first place, there were the eternal financial needs of a monarchy always keen for resources to sustain innumerable wars and the equally expensive royal estates. As expenses always exceeded revenues, the appeal to "extraordinary measures" compelled the king to alienate, either temporarily or permanently, a significant number of the monarchy's offices. It was a quick way of collecting funds, which could represent considerable amounts of money for the royal coffers, without having to tax the population additionally.

On the other hand, the very nature of the economy based on *mercedes** (Olival 2011), in which the king exchanged services and merits for *mercedes*—be they honorific, monetary or in the form of offices—made it necessary on occasion to disrupt any intent to "normalize" the bureaucratic career. One example was dowry gifts. They were places, principally on the Councils and in tribunals of justice and treasury, conceded by the king to female retainers so that when they left the palace they could make an advantageous marriage. Their future husbands would become councilmen, judges, or auditors of the Major Accounting Office because of the mere fact of having married the women that had received these *mercedes* (Andújar Castillo 2010). The *mercedes de paso de oficios*, the right to transmit offices from fathers to sons or sons-in-law, functioned in a similar way although they were restricted to the confines of the palace itself; they represented another distinctive way that service to the monarchs bestowed greater privileges on their most intimate circle. In the spheres of the courtiers, remuneration for services operated as a separate world, governed by particular conventions and specific control mechanisms. They clearly differed from the rest of the exchanges that took place between the king and his civil servants in the framework of the economy of *Gracia**. Hence, both the dowry gifts and *mercedes de paso de oficios** would become one of the principal expressions of royal patronage that always considered the administration of the kingdoms as a component of the king's own patrimony.

In any case, the nature of monarchy itself, basing, as it did, a good part of its exchanges on the clientele system that culminated with the king as the great patron, formed one of the fundamental curbs to any attempt to rationalize the processes of creating an administrative system regulated by "modern" principles of capacity and merit. The presence of clientele networks at the summit of all power is a subject that recent historiography has emphasized (Imízcoz Beunza, 2007). I myself have shown the enormous weight that clientele relations had in the distribution of judicial magistratures and equally important positions on the principal *Consejos* during Charles IV's reign, especially during the period that encompasses Floridablanca's last years and the first phase of Godoy's reign as the royal favorite (Andújar Castillo 2007).

This clientele system was implemented by frequently dispensing with the "obligation to seek advice" represented by the consultative bodies. The king and his close associates, in other words the *Secretarías del Despacho*, used instruments that allowed absolutism to flower in all its forms, notably by resorting to the well-known "executive decrees" or "decisive decrees". They were nothing less than direct orders from the king to the *Cámaras** of Castile or the Indies. These orders named government agents without the individuals having to display any other merit than their belonging to the clientele group of a powerful minister or courtier. In this fashion, the procedure of the executive decree acted as the best way to create clientele and consolidate political loyalties, as it permitted the formation of solid power networks that revolved around access to public offices and subsequent promotions by a channel not accessible to all the king's servants.

Nevertheless, as I have demonstrated in other studies, there was something else behind these executive decrees, which almost always altered the *cursus honorum* to fill positions in justice or magistracies of the Councils, than the mere establishment of clientele relations between the king and/or his ministers and their subjects (Andújar Castillo 2008a). The use of this executive channel frequently hid a more evident reality: the traditional system of remuneration for services and merits was essentially being modified by a financial transaction. In other words, when it was time to remunerate merit and services, the "pecuniary service" became the basis and the essence of the relationship between the king and his subjects, that is, it was often fulfilled by granting subjects the monarchy's principal offices in exchange for money. In respect of this, it should be recalled that this practice had a long tradition in the administration of the Hispanic monarchy. It was found every time that clientele relations started to alter the ordinary systems or *reglados** and whenever money, which obviously had to be accompanied by an equally important capital constituted by relationships, was behind the naming of an agent of the government or, in the realm of honors, behind the concession of a title of nobility.

In this context, the sale of offices—the same as the dowry gifts, *mercedes de paso de oficios*, the quasi "legacies" present in the transmission of some positions—worked, during the periods that they proliferated, to frustrate the rationalization of the bureaucratic system of the monarchy's government. And they did it in a manner that was very similar to the logic imposed by the system of clientele networks. This is my thesis, which obviously in essence implies engaging in a debate about the forms in which power is exercised. In fact, Jean Pierre Dedieu has put forward a thesis that takes the opposing view: he considers venality as simply another part of a system of exchange of services and merits for *mercedes*, with the supreme arbitrator being the king. He argues the system was founded on personal relationships, which were based on a domestic type of convention that led to other conventions, for example commercial ones in the form of the sale of public offices. In this way, the sale of offices would be an additional rationalization of the granting of *Gracia* by the king (Dedieu 2010, 2011).

Sale and Benefice: Two Facets of the Same Reality

Until fairly recently, classic historiography maintained that the sale of offices had practically ceased following the change of dynasties. Only Domínguez Ortiz took into consideration a certain prolongation of venality during the War of Succession, as well as the alienation of *regidurias** in the municipalities, even if most of these cases corresponded to private transactions (Domínguez Ortiz 1985). The origin of such a thesis can be traced back to two problems of varying importance. On the one hand, it can be attributed to the lack of monographic investigations of the reign of the Habsburgs. This has only started to be redressed very recently thanks to research carried out by different historians (Marcos Martín 1999, 2003, 2007, 2011; Gelabert 1997; Hernández Benítez 1995, 1997, 2007; López Díaz 2011) on the sale of municipal offices and, at the other extreme of the bureaucratic hierarchy, on the sale of the positions in the upper-level administration (Andújar Castillo 2011a; Marcos Martín 2007).

The second problem is even more substantial, as it has a direct impact on what the historiography has hitherto been able to ascertain concerning the sale of public offices. I am alluding to what was understood at that time, and what historians understand in the present, as a "sale". The existence in the documentation of an assimilated term such as "benefit" has not only concealed the concession of numerous offices—and honors—for money but it has also led some historians to consider that the "benefit of the offices" and, by extension, that of the honors, was not the same as a sale of the same offices and honors.

The differentiation between "benefited" and "sold" offices was formulated years ago by American historiography; it pointed out that by means of a "benefit" the Crown received a certain amount of money for an office even if this office did not become the property of the beneficiary, who could only use it during a set period of time (Yali Román 1972; Muro Romero 1978). On the contrary, the sale of an office was only considered to have occurred when the king alienated it as a part of his royal patrimony, that is, selling it in perpetuity and thus giving the buyer the power to bequeath it or sell it. In other words: the offices that were "benefited" did not grant patrimonial rights to their title-holders, while those that were "sold" moved from being part of the king's patrimony to being the purchaser's "private" possessions. As for the case of America, a distinction was made between the "saleable and alienable" perpetual offices and the "benefited" ones. While the former were primarily negotiated in America, the latter were awarded during the seventeenth century in exchange for money as either temporary positions in the political government or as life-long positions in the areas of justice or treasury.

Other historians have recently specified even more precisely the differences between "benefited" and "sold" offices by noting that the former were only held temporarily and could include the administration of justice. They were justified as representing "an economic service performed for the king" by donating or lending money (Sanz Tapia 2009). Accepting the juridical difference between "benefit" and "sale", I contend that the "donation"—the donated money—was only the euphemism used to conceal the obtainment of offices in exchange for money, or if one prefers, for "a pecuniary service". Handing over a "donation" to the king made it appear that money was not the principal lever used to obtain an office. On the other hand, with regard to the "benefited" offices as well as those that included judicial powers, suffice to note that this term was generalized throughout the seventeenth century. It was eventually employed to designate all types of offices exchanged for money, including titles of nobility that were sold and that obviously did not involve administering justice.

In my opinion, regardless of the judicial differences between "benefited" offices, which were conceded for a set time as the king maintained the ownership, and "sold" offices, which were alienated in perpetuity, both concepts corresponded to the same reality: the payment of a quantity of money in exchange for the designation to a position. Whether the king "benefited" or "sold", what he was actually doing was designating as his "subjects" men who had presented a certain quantity of money as their principal merit; they had offered a "service", although it was clearly pecuniary. Both the "benefit" and the "sale" of offices boiled down to obtaining public positions in exchange for money. I consequently refer to venality of offices whenever the monarchy names a man as its agent in reward for "pecuniary merit" and that is a decisive component in the royal will to proceed to a designation.

These considerations lead me to affirm that all the offices conceded for money were "benefited", understanding by that term that the person that was "benefited" was the seller, namely the king in public transactions, and individuals in private deals. In this way, when referring to the public transaction, in the game of exchanging *mercedes* for services, the principal merit for obtaining offices was the availability of hard cash. As a result, the distinction between "benefit" and "sale," based on the amount of time the offices could be used, or their ownership, does not invalidate the concept of both as two expressions that share a common origin: venality. In any case, the essential difference consisted in the fact that "benefited" positions always originated in the public sphere, since the king conceded them, whereas the sale of offices for perpetuity was only public in its first alienation. From the moment the offices were privatized as the property of an individual, they formed part of the families' patrimonies and therefore became transmissible possessions; they sometimes even ended up being auctioned off publicly to the highest bidder.

In short, by selling offices for money, the king far too frequently disturbed the ideal of distributive justice by damaging the rights of the individuals that served in the same institutions as those who had purchased their posts but who could only claim "non-monetary" merits. Therefore sales and benefits formed part of a common phenomenon that was the naming of offices for money, venality. And for this reason, both in the case of sales as well as the "benefits", the buyers tried to hide the pecuniary service. There were also "secret benefits", "secret donations" or "reserved favors" in the function of the offices to be purchased (Andújar Castillo 2008a).

The Sales of Offices in the Eighteenth Century: Conjunctures and Spheres

To understand the problem of venality during the century of the Bourbons, one has to start with an essential question: which positions that belonged to the royal patrimony still remained in the king's hands? In other words: which patrimonial elements did the monarchy have that could be alienated so as to take on the considerable expenses that originated in the dynastic war that started the century? Which official positions had been preserved from the "auctioning off" of posts that took place during the reigns of the previous two Hapsburg kings?

The answer to both questions is complex for a fundamental reason. Even if the historiography about such topics has made progress in the past few years, the lack of monographic research makes it impossible to understand the scale of the process of alienating official positions in perpetuity that had been carried out in the previous centuries, especially during the seventeenth century. If I restrict this analysis to positions that had been sold in perpetuity and therefore had been privatized without the king once again taking possession of them, I can confirm that the sales had been concentrated in two principal institutional areas. Firstly, an enormous number of transactions in municipal offices and positions took place during the sixteenth and seventeenth centuries; these included practically all the positions in the territorial administration at the local level, encompassing even the prized *regidurías*. At the other extreme of the hierarchy, there were sales of positions in institutions such as the *Consejos* (Andújar Castillo 2011a), tribunals of justice (Gómez González 2000), Inquisition (Lera García 1988) and *Casa de Contratación** (Schäfer 1935). It is impossible to evaluate these sales quantitatively, but there is no doubt that these were the principal areas where alienations took place, along with the complex network made up by administrative positions in the treasury.

Many of the monarchy's posts remained in the king's power. Some of them were only the object of a "benefit", under which the king could recover his property once the individuals had ceased their temporary occupation of the positions, or once the titleholders of the positions held for life died. Thus, for example, whenever new military corps—new *Tercios**—were formed, they frequently resorted to selling the posts of officers by the system of "benefit", and this was generally done by the individuals that enlisted the new troops (Rodríguez Hernández 2007). The only positions that were perpetually alienated in the military sphere were the *Alcaldías de Fortaleza** (Jiménez Estrella 2004). The positions of the upper administration in the areas of treasury, accounting and the *Consejos'* treasuries were similarly "benefited" as offices to be held for life, except for those with the greatest value, which were sold in perpetuity. In relation to justice, it is known that the secondary positions were alienated, as many were sold in perpetuity. As for the more senior positions such as magistrates, *oidores**, *alcaldes de crimen** and *alcaldes de hijosdalgo**, we only have data about their sale during the reign of Charles II, in the Italian tribunals (Álvarez-Ossorio 2000, 2007), in Spain during the period 1706-1711 (Andújar Castillo 2008a), and in America during the period 1687-1750 (Burkholder-Chandler 1984). In relation to positions on the *Consejos*, I have previously been able to prove that some were sold during the reign of Charles II, but it does not appear that their sale was a generalized policy of the crown. Certain *Consejos,* however, such as those of Italy (Álvarez-Ossorio 2003), the Indies, and the Treasury did seem to be more susceptible to these practices (Andújar Castillo 2011a). Finally, at a lower echelon of the monarchy's political government, the *corregimientos** were not granted in exchange for money until the period marked by venality that started between 1704 and 1711, although it is essential to bear in mind that we lack definitive studies of this.

At the same time, the "American market" experienced an extraordinary period of sales during the last third of the seventeenth century as hundreds of offices of the political government, from the general captaincy to the *alcaldias mayores** of New Spain and the *corregimientos* of the Viceroyalty of Peru (Sanz Tapia 2009) were granted by "benefit". The viceroys had previously sold the positions directly for their own profit. Money then became the principal lever that was used to obtain temporary political offices, which were sometimes alienated several times in the same year via the system of "futures". In fact, these positions were purchased even though their buyers would not be able to occupy them until the preceding "future" holders had vacated them, which could take ten or fifteen years from the moment of the investment. In addition to these positions in the political government, a considerable number of posts related to the treasury were also alienated, such as positions in the royal counting-houses distributed throughout the principal cities of America, and the two high tribunals of accounts in Lima and Mexico (Bertrand 1999), as well as numerous judicial magistratures in the American

*Audiencias**. In these high courts, it was possible to buy exemptions or licenses that, for example, allowed the purchasers to work as judges in areas where they could not legally do so, such as the territories where they had been born, or to marry women that were natives of the same jurisdiction over which they presided, or to possess property in the same area (Burkholder-Chandler 1984).

It was also possible to acquire "supernumerary" positions in the areas related to both the treasury and the judgeships that were alienated for one lifespan with the possibility of being promoted in the same hierarchy. This option meant that the buyer started to occupy the post once there was a vacancy in one of the "numbered" positions. The "benefit" of some of the military positions and of a good number of the positions that made up the Route of the Indies (of which the extensive personnel went from admirals to the *maestres de plata**) completed this particular "market". Its principal point of sale was in the court in Madrid, though at the same time the equally active sale of the so-called "saleable and alienable" positions continued, as it had from the sixteenth century onwards, in America. The posts of the *Casa de Contratación* itself in Seville serve as a gauge to demonstrate the dimensions of this "American market", for all of them, with the exception of the Presidency and those posts that administered justice, were alienated in perpetuity throughout the seventeenth century.

Three dates that marked the reign of Charles II can be used as points of reference for these exceptional sales. The first would have been around 1674 when, alleging the rampant corruption inherent to the designations made by the viceroys, the crown wrested this power away from them. However it did not proceed to grant the posts to the most meritorious men but rather to sell the great majority of them to the highest bidder. The second date could be 1683, when not only "minor" positions were put up for sale but also the general captaincies with the additional posts of the presidencies of their respective *Audiencias*. In particular, Gil Cabrera Dávalos acquired the general captaincy of New Granada with the presidency of the *Audiencia* of Santa Fe for 30,000 pesos – 12,000 as a donation and the rest as a loan; Gabriel Curucealegui received the presidency of the *Audiencia* and the Philippine government for 40,000 gold pesos—10,000 as a "gracious donation" and the rest as a loan; and Tomás Marín de Poveda did the same with the general captaincy of Chile and the presidency of its *Audiencia* for 44,000 pesos—with 22,000 as a "gracious donation" and the rest as a loan (Andújar Castillo 2011b). The third date could be 1687, according to Burkholder and Chandler, when judicial magistratures in the American tribunals began to be sold, thus initiating a process that would continue with only a few lulls until 1750 when the last ones were alienated. This initial date of 1674, however, should be changed to 1683 when the positions of *fiscales* protectores de indios* sold in the Audiencias of both Lima and Quito; the latter one was acquired by Ignacio Aybar Eslava in a "package deal" that also included a "future" position as an *oidor* of that *Audiencia* (Herzog 1995). This system would reach its zenith when the viceroyalties themselves began to be the object of negotiation so as to be conceded for "pecuniary merits" (Domínguez Ortiz 1965).

In the face of such a situation, Phillip V followed the instructions of his grandfather Louis XIV and decided to put to an end these sales that were exceptional in both qualitative and quantitative terms. A decree dated 6 March 1701 ordered that the sales of public offices be suspended. In addition, all positions that involved the administration of justice, including the political positions in the Indies that had been obtained for money, were cancelled if the buyers had not yet taken office, and their money should be returned. The suspension was retroactive for all the positions that had been granted during the ten years preceding the decree. It further specified that as it was impossible to know with certainty which positions had been acquired with money as the purchaser's principal merit, all the titles conceded by "decisive decrees" or "executive decrees" were to be annulled, namely all those that had not been an object of consultation in the *Cámara* of Indies. The publication of this decree led to an error in Spanish historiography about the Modern Age, as the interpretation was that this date signified the end of the sale of offices. It was thought that the new dynasty, symbolized in the person of Phillip V, put an end to the system in force during the reign of the Hapsburgs, which consisted in alienating the posts that belonged to the royal patrimony and conceding for pecuniary services positions that ranged from offices in the highest echelons of the monarchy to subaltern posts in local administration. The error persisted for a long time and generally little was known about specific cases, except for the sales of *regidurías* that were documented at the end of the 1830s (Torras i Ribé 1983) and some studies centered on municipal positions (García Monerris 1991; Hernández Benítez 2007). This decree of 1701, and the discourse that it engendered, served to reinforce the idea that the policies of reform and rationalization were the decisive hallmarks that the new dynasty imposed on the monarchy's bureaucratic and political system.

No interpretation, however, could be further from the truth. Recent research has been able to prove that the decree of 1701 was very soon a dead letter. Scarcely two years later, Phillip V, with the coffers empty and in the midst of a war that was going to require substantial resources to pay the huge army that had to be levied, found that he had to forgo his grandfather's advice. The sale of all types of positions was therefore begun again in order to deliver extraordinary resources to the royal treasury; the definition of what was saleable was even expanded. The first blow occurred in November 1703 when the presidency of the *Casa de Contratación* in Seville was sold to the Count of Miraflores for a "service" of 300,000 *reales*.[2] After a suspension in sales that barely lasted a year, in September 1704, Phillip V returned to the same dynamic that had characterized his predecessor on the throne, even though he did not annul the decree of 1701. And he was going to revert to previous practice, not only by maintaining the extensive venal market that had functioned during the last decades of the previous century, but by widening it considerably to obtain the greatest possible economic resources in order to finance the costly war that set him against the archduke of Austria.

A colossal sale of offices and honors unfolded from September 1704 until the end of 1711. Given the scarce number of positions that the king still possessed, necessity forced him to put on the market positions that had not yet been sold, and above all to intensify the sales by attributing more "future" and "supernumerary" positions, especially in America. When compared to previous phases, this period of sales would be characterized by the great novelty of judgeships to be exercised in Spain and the concession of *corregimientos* in Castile being included in the exchange for "pecuniary services". With this expansion, Phillip V quite simply implemented in Spain the model of alienations that had been used until then only in America.

A vast operation of venal transactions was thereby launched, which made it possible to purchase any office that formed part of the monarchy's large bureaucratic complex. The personnel were obviously quite extensive. It included magistrates on the territorial level in chancelleries, the *Audiencias*, the *Sala de Alcaldes de Corte y Casa**, and the tribunals in the Italian kingdoms; even positions as lawyers on the *Consejo*s were put on sale. Thus, the members of the Councils, fundamentally the councilors of Indies and Treasury, saw how "new" men reached their cherished seats. Such appointments corresponded to considerable outlays of money, transacting positions that went from the presidency to the porter's post in what had been the monarchy's most important institutions. This picture of

[2] AGS, C.G., Leg. 79, fol, 105 v.; one *peso* = 8 *reales*.

venal undertaking was completed by the sale of positions in the area of treasury, such as those that formed part of the Major Accounting Office, *corregimientos*, a few political-military government posts, and some positions at the court. In addition to these offices, honors as important as titles of nobility and more than a hundred concessions of *hidalguía** were also exchanged for money, thus expanding the trail that had been laid out by the previous reign. Honorific titles were also sold for positions that did not need to be exercised but gave prestige to those that held them. A venal market, similar to the one that had been developed for designating government agents in the Indies during the last third of the seventeenth century, was continued from 1704 to 1711, when a small *alcadía mayor* in New Spain or a minor *corrigimiento* in the viceroyalty of Peru or even the general captaincies, including the presidency of the *Audiencia*, were all sold for "pecuniary services".

In fact, the aspect that most pertinently characterized this vast operation resided in the very system that alienated these offices and honors. A complex network of private financiers and middle men was commissioned to carry out these sales, so that the greatest amount of money could be amassed in the shortest possible period. At the same time, the "clink of coins" was to be kept distant from the court, where such matters were supposedly not negotiated. Considerable resources—more than 75 million *reales*—were obtained by these procedures under the direction of the Secretary of *Despacho* José Grimaldo and the supervision of the French ambassador Amelot; the all-powerful Princess of the Ursines intervened when the most substantial cases were being negotiated. These funds were used to cover the expenses of the war that legitimatized these sales, although an important amount of this money ended up being destined to the House of Queen Maria Louisa of Savoy.

After 1712, it was generally considered that these venal transactions had ended. There are many ways of explaining this change, but what stands out is the turn of events that took place in 1711 in favor of Philip's troops, and the recoupment of the ordinary sources of revenues, which obviously allowed more resources to make it to the royal treasury and, in particular, to the Queen. On the other hand, the market for venal transactions was practically saturated, as very few offices remained to be sold. For example, even the third "future" of some *corregimientos* and *alcadias mayores* in America had already been sold. In spite of this outlook, the sales of political offices and posts in the treasury for the American territories continued throughout 1712 on a very reduced scale;

in addition, some honors and offices in Sicily could still be purchased, although the alienation of offices in Spain was completely halted.

The year 1712 therefore marks a caesura in the sale of offices in Spain, though it continued in America. A double standard, a dual form of governing, which dated from the last decades of the seventeenth century, was about to be established in the heart of the monarchy. The *corregimientos*, *alcadias mayores* and governments of the two American viceroyalties (New Spain and Peru) continued to be sold, whereas the *corregimientos* and political-military posts of Spain were once again granted on merit; the *Cámara de Castilla* was even consulted for the nominations for *corregimientos*. Preliminary research points to such findings, as the "vacuum" in the historiography about such questions after the War of Succession makes it impossible to draw definitive conclusions.

The case of America was even clearer. The sale of the offices involved in political government, treasury and justice continued until 1750 when the Marquis of Ensenada put an end to this practice at a juncture that, as a consequence of the new period of peace, was characterized by a diminished need for cash for the royal treasury. Different stages, nevertheless, can be distinguished in the long period spanning 1712 to 1750. A first stage would cover 1712 to 1719, during which the sale of offices related to treasury and political government continued; it therefore followed the pattern inherited from the reign of Charles II. An important new development emerged during this period as the sale of judgeships ended, just as had happened with those exercised in Spain. The system once again established limits, which for the judicial offices meant returning to the *status quo ante* that had been shattered in 1687 when the alienations of positions as *oidores* and *alcaldes del crimen* in the American *Audiencias* had begun to happen regularly.

In turn, within the period 1712-1719, the years 1712-1713 continued the situation that had preceded, and whilst an interruption was recorded in 1714, it was resumed during the following two periods of 1715-1716 and 1718-1719, according to the first data available (Sanz Tapia 2006 and Martos Crespo 2011). But 1719 did see the end of the intense venality that had been created by the posts of government and treasury in America. As has been shown, the "market" was exhausted; there were numerous "future" and "supernumerary" designees waiting to exercise the positions that had been purchased years earlier. From then on, only a slow trickle of sales was registered and did not exceed three offices per year.

The appointment of José Patiño in 1726 to the *Secretaría de Despacho* of State, Navy and the Indies marked a new direction in the sales policy for American positions, although change did not really materialize until 1728. The reasons for resorting once again to venality as a form of extraordinary financing have still not been studied, although evidence seems to suggest that it was part of Philip V's ministers' project to overcome the monarchy's financial difficulties and to lower the permanent budget deficit. Once the door was opened again to the "benefit" of offices in 1728, the following year a new reason for an extraordinary demand for funds appeared when the king moved to Seville, where he resided until 1733. The transfer of the court meant additional expenses, so a special treasury was created, whose coffers were filled in great measure by the sale of offices and titles of nobility (Andújar Castillo 2008b).

The dynamic created by this policy of venality in the offices to be exercised in America was continually maintained until the end of 1750. A new factor nevertheless appeared in 1739 that aimed not only at maintaining the standards set during the preceding years but at increasing the sales. The general suspension of payments that occurred that year forced the royal authorities to look for even more resources in order to deal with the dramatic situation of the royal finances. Just as had happened in the past, the "benefaction" of offices would be once again one of the handiest means to use in a time of great need. In 1740 a new venal venture was started, when a *Junta de Medios** agreed to put offices in Spain and America on sale. One of the most fevered debates that this *Junta* focused on was whether the offices that administered justice should be sold, as had been the case during the War of Succession. In the face of the need for money, the debaters were silenced as the sale of offices of *oidor* and *alcalde de crimen* in America was begun again; some judgeships in the existing tribunals in Spain were also secretly sold. Thus, for example, it is known that Francisco Javier del Arco paid the sum of 160,000 *reales* in 1740 for a "supernumerary" position as an *oidor* of the *Casa de Contratación*.[3] In the ordinary tribunals, the Chancelleries of Granada and Valladolid and the other *Audiencias*, various individuals would be registered for positions of *oidor* and *alcaldes de crimen* as "supernumerary" designees, therefore awaiting vacancies. They were named by executive decrees, which implied that the *Cámara* of Castile was not consulted about their nomination. The "benefitted" men could then accede at very young ages to judicial posts that for others required long years of service. In the case of the tribunals in America, from 1740 to 1750 the sale of magistracies was intensified; this new trend culminated in

[3] AGI, Contratación, Leg. 5786, Lib. 2.

some feeble attempts to alienate such offices—two positions as *oidor* and one as *alcalde de crimen*—that took place in 1728, 1733 and 1736.[4]

Meanwhile, in the light of the available research, there do not seem to be records, at least not systematic ones, of any massive transactions in the remaining positions of the monarchy that were to be served in Spain during the first half of the eighteenth century. The exception was military positions and they had their own particular venal dynamic. This trend appears to continue during the second half of the century, although the documentary voids force us to proceed with caution when addressing this topic, especially given the lack of records from the state economy. Also, it is possible that money was diverted from venality to corruption, namely that the ultimate destination of the buyer's money was not the public treasury's coffers but rather the "pocket" of the person that "engineered" the sale. These types of maneuvers could have happened during an exceptional period such as that between Floridablanca's last years and the first phase of Godoy's reign as the royal favorite, when the *Cámara de Castilla* was excluded from participating in many designations for offices and was replaced by "executive decrees" or "decisive" decrees that emanated directly from the king. All available information indicates that nepotism and clientele relations imposed on councils and judgeships the sale of a considerable number of posts that before then had been put forward to the king by the *Cámara de Castilla*. Nevertheless, the idea should not be ruled out that money was by then circulating outside of the institutionalized channels where the funds buying offices had previously moved. Consequently it was no longer just a question of positions for money, but something much closer to corruption.

In relation to designation by executive decrees, it should be pointed out that this "marginalization" of the *Cámara de Castilla,* so as to impose the absolute will of the king without further ado, is almost always documented as coinciding with periods of upturns in venality. Thus, for example, in comparison with an average of about twenty executive decrees to concede offices and honors by the king to the *Cámara* before 1728, in that very year when the sale of offices begins again in America, there are 32 decisive decrees. And such a spike happens again in the years around the crisis of 1739. In 1737, compared to the 22 decisive decrees issued during the preceding years, the total reaches 42. An average of 40 decrees per year is maintained until 1742.[5] It is almost impossible to trace the presence

[4] AGS, TMC, Leg.1945; Burkholder-Chandler 1977.

[5] AHN, Consejos, Legs. 678-682.

of money because the transactions take place in a private market and when the sums were actually deposited in the treasury, they were calculated as a lump sum, without any breakdown of the total.

It is particularly interesting to study the numerous "supernumerary" and "future" designations to the *Consejos* of Treasury and the Indies that were made during the first half of the eighteenth century. I have confirmed the sale of various positions of *capa y espada** *consejeros** on the *Consejo* of the Treasury from 1704 to 1711. Between approximately 1711 and 1750, a total of 36 councilmen were designated as "supernumeraries" and "futures" to the Treasury; a considerable percentage of them had "pecuniary services" as their principal merit. Thus, financiers, tax-farmers, contractors, and businessmen in general managed to accede to the *Consejo* of Treasury. Even if the positions they "acquired" were *capa y espada* and not the robed ones that had a place in the hall of justice, they invested a part of their fortunes to sit in the very institution that, as the highest justice tribunal in matters of treasury, supposedly controlled their individual activities and above all resolved disputes and lawsuits. There were fewer exceptional designations to the *Consejo* of the Indies—a total of 14—than to the Treasury—but they were likewise primarily carried out during periods that coincided with upturns in venality, in particular after the years that followed 1728 and after the general suspension of payments in 1739.

The fact that some positions as councilmen or judges were sold had to be kept quiet so that the payment did not "stain" their merit and, above all, so that their peers did not know the real reasons why some new members of a *Consejo*, a Chancellery or an *Audiencia* were appointed. This "particularity" helps to explain why the documentary trails of such transactions completely disappeared. In addition, the *Gaceta de Madrid* took particular care to keep these pecuniary merits quiet when the newspaper announced the appointment of the principal agents of the monarchy's government. It either did not publish certain appointments or else announced that the appointments corresponded to the grantee's merits and services, void of any pecuniary ones. The latter was exemplified when Manuel Salcedo Sierralta obtained a position as a *capa y espada consejero* on the *Consejo* of the Indies for his "merits as captain of the Guards and governor of Yucatan", according to the *Gaceta de Madrid*. In reality, this appointment was in return for the pecuniary service of 135,000 *reales* that had been paid secretly; it therefore completely disappeared from his title as *consejero.*[6]

[6] AGS, DGT, Inv. 16, g. 19, Leg. 8.

On the other hand, a particular space where venality prevailed, which had been functioning from the seventeenth century, is also documented during the first half of the eighteenth century. It comprised the positions that administered the treasury, fundamentally the "accountants of designations" and the "accountants of results" of the Major Accounting Office, as well as additional posts in other accounting offices in institutions such as the *Consejo* of the Indies. In this sphere there were many designations of "supernumeraries"—some corresponding to dowry gifts made during those periods that the positions comprising the Major Accounting Office were held (Andújar Castillo, 2010). Once again, I am proposing hypotheses, but it appears more than likely that some of these appointments corresponded to pecuniary merits, just as had happened during the reign of Charles II and the War of Succession. This idea, that venality reached the high administration, can be demonstrated by the case of Juan Cristóstomo Bonavia, whose father, the financier Juan Bautista Bonavia, bought a position for him as accountant in the General Accounting Office of the *Consejo* of the Indies for 120,000 *reales.*[7] Another example is provided by José Osma Haro, who paid 60,000 *reales* in 1744 for a position as accountant in the Major Accounting Office. The venality of such positions seems to end during the reign of Ferdinand VI while the same dynamic will persist, between 1760 and 1788 when Charles III reigned, except, as we shall see, in the army. It will be difficult to dispel doubts about the reign of Charles IV raised by preliminary research, and in particular about the period of Godoy, because, as has already been mentioned, the documents produced by the royal treasury were lost.

The Persistence of Venality: Military Posts

The monographic research that I have dedicated to the Bourbon army and the sale of military posts reveals that throughout the eighteenth century, the military world prolonged the practices that had been in force in the previous century. A significant novelty, however, was about to be introduced into what had been, until then, an omnipresent reality in the organic structures of the armies of the Hispanic monarchy. Insofar as during the seventeenth century venality was almost always linked to recruiting, namely the concessions of blank military titles to those that levied new armed corps to "encourage" recruitment (Rodríguez Hernández

---

[7] AGS, TMC, Leg.859 and DGT, Inv. 16, Guión 19, Leg. 8 respectively.

2011; Jiménez Estrella 2011), this same dynamic was maintained during the Bourbon period. At the same time, on at least three occasions, military posts were "beneficiated" directly by the Secretary of the War Office. This change meant that the royal offices in the Court became the site where the commissions for the ranks of sublieutenant, lieutenant, captain, lieutenant colonel, and even colonel of the royal armies were sold (Andújar Castillo, 2004). Of course, the system was not in any way exclusive to the Spanish army, as studies about the military institution in France (Gorau 2002; Rowlands 2003; Drevillon 2005) or England (Bruce 1980) demonstrate.

Both procedures—sales to form new regiments and those conducted directly in the royal offices—guaranteed the purchasers of military posts that, at the very least, they would hold the military rank they had acquired throughout their lives. They could also advance in the military hierarchy, not only without obstacles but even from a privileged position, as seniority in rank, rather than seniority in the army, regulated promotions. This rule produced a glaring paradox that was at the same time a disheartening contradiction for the men in arms that served the king. For example, an individual that had reached the rank of captain after twenty years of service and whose title was dated 1 April 1763 was less "senior"—and therefore relegated in the hierarchy—than another man that had entered the army for the first time by purchasing his title of captain on 31 March of the same year. Consequently, in addition to the inequalities that venality generated in the core of the regiments themselves, the system allowed men without any military experience to don the chevrons attributed to the captain or colonels of the royal armies from one day to the next.

Formation of Regiments and Venality

Following the model of the France of Louis XIV, the reform measures that were implanted in the army of Phillip V had as one of their guiding principles the intention of strengthening the prestige of the military career by creating the cadets as an exclusive way to gain access to the rank of officer. Individuals had to prove that they were *hidalgos*, thereby clearly differentiated from men without noble blood, who had to join as simple soldiers and face a very limited professional mobility, with promotion practically closed to any rank above captain. Social origin acted therefore as an essential element of a military institution that the new dynasty tried to dignify by creating a space reserved for a "nobility of service" that made the military its principal profession. Family and lineage should form the basis of the social structure of a military institution that would faithfully reflect society. Such a system was regulated in the military ordinances and we historians have concurred in such an interpretation for a long time.

Nevertheless, recent research has demonstrated that a more rapid and direct way to obtain the rank of officer existed and made it possible to join the army in positions that ranged from second lieutenant to colonel, without having to prove irrefutably the possession of blue blood. In any case, the candidates did not have to demonstrate it to the individuals that were enlisting the new regiments, who always put their own economic interests before any excluding social factor that would impede the applicant from purchasing a post. I am alluding to the venal path to the rank of officer in the Bourbon army that was established throughout the century as one of the most commonly used levers not only to gain access to the military, but also to become socially mobile. Many families longed to see their sons dressed up in a uniform representing a career that yielded prestige, power and a privileged legal status that set them apart from the rest of society, in addition to a salary. In fact, one of the keys to the sale of military positions was the limited control that the royal agents, whether they were private enlisters of regiments or army officials, exercised on the purchasers of official posts. At times this regulation of the purchasers' social origins was even practically non-existent. Therefore, the individual that bought the rank of captain acquired at the same time a privileged status assimilated to social position of a *hidalgo*.

From a chronological perspective, two phases can be differentiated according to the venal processes that were in place within the institution of the military throughout the century of the Enlightenment. Corresponding to the early years of the century, the first phase occurred when the cities and kingdoms, principally, levied new regiments as a consequence of the War of Succession, although there were also some private initiatives. Venality was evident during this period as official posts were freely allocated to the clientele and family members of the elites that dominated the municipal *regidurias*, as well as to those that were present in the *Juntas** and *Cortes** of the different kingdoms that provided troops. These elites could opt to access these posts as officers "graciously" or buy them in order to defray, at least partially, the costs of forming the new military corps. From 1710 onwards, however, a second stage came into operation and meant that a profound change occurred simultaneously in the model of recruiting and selling the posts of army officers. From this moment on, the Crown would take over most of the companies that created new regiments. In the great majority of cases, the royal officials resorted to privatization via a system of contracts *(asientos)** similar to the ones used in the seventeenth century. This system was also employed to supply other goods to the State (Andújar Castillo 2006a). In essence the system consisted of assigning the formation of new army units either to officers that aspired to thrive in their military careers by "enlisting regiments" in order to contribute towards the king's needs, or to men without any military experience that pursued the same professional goal. As they promised in their contract to form a new regiment, they managed to accede directly to the rank of colonel in the royal armies even though they had never seen a weapon and lacked even the slightest knowledge of the profession.

The essence of these private companies was very simple. An individual promised to recruit a certain number of soldiers, normally in uniform and armed, and have them ready in the previously agreed upon time and place. In exchange, the king granted him the rank of colonel, in addition to giving him the written appointments for most of the other official posts so that by selling them, the "army contractor" or "troop enlister" could cover the expenses he had already incurred. Some positions were reserved for men with military experience. The army contractor absolutely had to sell the blank designations that the king had signed so that his own operation could be financed. Money was therefore the crucial issue, and other matters such as how well versed the purchasers were in the art of war, or their hypothetical noble origin, were certainly secondary.

This explanation illustrates the general model, even though I have been able to document diverse types of venal transactions. They range from small ones, for which a civilian or official offered to recruit a company at his own cost, to contracts to levy a complete regiment, including large-scale *asientos* to recruit soldiers from abroad. Even if the contracts for the latter tended to define a set sum of money in exchange for each man recruited, they also often included blank designations for officers so that their sale would "stimulate" the general recruiting process.

The figures that I have gathered demonstrate that this venal system weighed significantly in the selection of officials. According to my estimates, approximately 90 regiments were created in Spain between 1702 and 1711. In addition, new infantry, cavalry and dragoon units were formed in Flanders in 1701, Italy in 1702-1703 and the Kingdom of Aragon before its adhesion to the cause of the Archduke Charles of Austria (Andújar Castillo 2008c). It is known that they were formed in Flanders with the same venal procedures that very shortly afterwards extended throughout Spain (Glesener 2011). Thereafter, a second wave of regiment units and sales of military posts occurred between 1718 and 1719 when 31 new regiments were formed because of the beginning of war against Sardinia and Sicily. It started when a significant number of the troops that had been levied during the War of Succession were being demobilized. The third recruiting period started in 1734 and 1735 on the occasion of the War of Italy; it meant once again the alienation of hundreds of posts of army officers. It created 20 regiments, 18 of which were formed by contracts. And even the reign of Phillip V was to see a final venal operation, for in 1742 twelve infantry regiments were enlarged with a third battalion, an operation that meant the sale of 460 officer posts.

After the "break" that was ushered in by the period of peace that accompanied the reign of Ferdinand VI, a new phase in the formation of cavalry and dragoon regiments took place between 1762 and 1771, due initially to the onset of the war against Portugal. This recruitment was carried out by "mixed contracts", also known as *capitanes proponentes**. Then, the infantry was enlarged with new units by creating eight regiments plus a few additional companies, which were used, among other functions, to replace the units that had to go to America as reinforcements. Finally, the last example of the creation of new army units along with the sale of officer posts is documented between 1793 and 1795, when 16 regiments were formed to face the war against the French Convention; seven were created selling the posts and three by a mixed system in which some officer positions were sold and others awarded for meritorious service.

The Sale of Offices in the Court

In the absence of more studies on the seventeenth century, I would now contend that the primary novelty that the Bourbon century introduced was that offices and posts were sometimes sold directly from the Ministry of War, from the *Secretaría de Despacho*, in addition to the venality inherent to the process of forming regiments. The contradiction could not have been more flagrant. Military legislation prescribed that in order to be promoted to an officer post it was necessary to have previously held the lower rank, and it regulated only cadets becoming officers. Nevertheless, the very system that defined such rules ultimately violated them by selling posts as army officers directly from the Court.

The beginning of these direct sales coincided with the Treasury crisis of 1739, even though other similar operations can be documented, such as those that took place during the War of Succession. The latter operations consisted, in particular, of providing a certain number of horses in exchange for an army officer post. Legitimized by the need for cash to pay for the war in Italy, the king directly alienated his "*Gracia*" in exchange for money, namely his sovereign right to designate those that would serve him in the army; the army officer ranks could consequently be obtained in the Secretary of War's "hovel". During these years, the so-called "benefit of ranks" or "benefit of posts" was carried out as part of a vast series of sales of the monarchy's offices that was controlled by a *Junta de Medios* led by Cardinal Molina, president of the *Consejo* of Castile, and the Duke of Montemar, the Minister of War. Payment for these ranks could be made directly for the designated price of each one, or by its equivalent in recruits, a formula that concealed the purchase of the post, as most of the candidates ended up paying in cash. Nevertheless when posts in the army were alienated, they were almost always disguised by the "laudable" justification that the king was selling them because he did not have enough cash to cover the costs of the war.

The enormous venal operation developed between 1744 and 1748 was going to be even more substantial as more than one hundred posts were sold in order to finance a general levy to complete the infantry corps. The operation was directed by an expert in the sale of offices, José Manuel Vázquez Prego, and solidly backed by the minister, the Marquis of the Ensenada. It was structured following the same model as those of the preceding years, which meant essentially with payment in cash or recruited soldiers so as to conceal even more surely the "clink of coin". In addition to the social composition of the purchasers, who were the sons of personnel from the central administration, the titled nobility, newly-rich *hidalgos,* and members of the commercial bourgeoisie of the most active mercantile centers, this operation was particularly remarkable because its proceeds were not deposited in the General State Treasury. They were rather placed in a special cash box or the "private treasury office" of a business house in Madrid, which then designated this money to cover the expenses of the general levy.

A new venal episode would take place during the reign of Charles III during which offices were sold directly at the Court, just when the military ordinances of 1768 were being finished. These ordinances were to enjoy such success and longevity in the Spanish army that they remained in force until 1975. Between 1766 and 1772, a special account office was set up in the Secretary of the War Office for receiving the proceeds of the sale of military posts, an operation that was controlled directly by the minister Juan Gregorio Muniain in close collaboration with the infantry inspector Antonio Manso. As had become customary, it was once again managed by the office of another businessman from Madrid, Manuel Iruegas. The money generated by the sales was therefore not transparently for the royal treasury, as it was managed by the minister's orders that were always in perfect harmony with the aforementioned inspector. That operation, however, was not the only venal transaction underway. During these same years the system of payments for officer posts was enlarged to "payments in kind" in exchange for ranks up to colonel, in order to finance a series of military works such as the defensive constructions on the coast of the Kingdom of Granada or civil ones (Andújar Castillo, 2002). Practically anything was exchangeable for the rank of officer, as exemplified by services as diverse as the construction of the customs house in Cadiz, or the colonization of the *Sierra Morena* by peasants organized by Juan Gaspar Thurrieguel. It sufficed to offer a "service" to the king or, when appropriate, to the Minister of War. During these years an active market functioned with many points of sale, as at the same time the enlisters of regiments sold a range of officer posts and several recruiters also sold them to finance the private levies they carried out abroad.

The problem created by so many different points of sale was extremely serious, as it almost brought about the complete parallelization of the military promotion ladder due to the excessive number of "benefited" posts. Drawing a parallel with the title of Burkholder and Chandler's study, I have called the period between 1762 and 1772 a veritable "age of auction" of military posts (Andújar Castillo 2004). These sales would be taken advantage of by social groups on the rise that emerged from families with clearly identifiable origins. The candidates were often the sons of the mercantile bourgeoisie (especially from Cadiz), bureaucrats in sectors such as public finance administration, *intendentes**, war commissioners, and families that had become rich in America; a few also came from military families or the titled nobility. And of course there was also a long list of *hidalgos* and "powerful" candidates that wanted to take the plunge of entering the royal service via a career of honor and arms. Many of these families already had solid experience in buying positions.

The last phase of venality took place on the occasion of the war against the French Convention between 1793-1795. Its most decisive trait was that the number of posts for sale exceeded the number of potential candidates that could guarantee their condition as *hidalgos*, a social rank that the ordinances, at least theoretically, required. Consequently, the Crown had no other alternative than to openly diminish this mandatory social status. Thereafter, an army post could be sold to any individual that could prove his *"limpieza de sangre"**, a condition that was clearly diluted by the end of the century. This change obviously marked the triumph of money over the importance of blood, or the victory of the bourgeoisie sectors on the rise, as opposed to the traditional values that had provided the backbone of Spanish society during the Old Regime.

It is difficult to quantify this long process of venal operations that occurred in the Bourbon army comprehensively, especially because the percentages fluctuated depending on the military units and the exact historical moment under consideration. Nevertheless, my estimates, based on the study of several hundred service records of army captains serving in different situations, allow me to confirm that during the first half of the century, for example, around 50% of those that reached the rank of captain in the infantry had purchased one post such as second lieutenant, lieutenant, or that of captain during their career. This figure drops to 25% for the period 1772-1776, only to decrease again to just over 20% during 1784-1789. As far as the cavalry is concerned, the findings are similar for the first half of the century and close to 25% for the second half. These percentages are the result of a large number of regiments that were created during the reign of Phillip V through the system of "*asientos*". They decreased from the middle of the century because of the suppression of officer posts arising from new levies. They would only be compensated for by the direct sales that took place starting in the 1740s, especially during the reign of Charles III. Multiple forms of venality, such as those that derived from the creation of new military units or the sales undertaken by the Ministry of War, would converge during this period.

The Sale of Honors: From "*Hidalguías*" to Titles of Nobility

Apart from the system created to sell offices, the Bourbon monarchs followed the precedent set by the House of Austria by alienating—and sometimes intensely—honors of all types, from *hidalguías* to titles of nobility, including on at least one occasion the *Grandeza de España**, the highest honor the monarchy conferred. They constituted an aggregate of *mercedes* that were described by a contemporary as being "political favors", and included, additionally, the robes of military orders and the keys of the *gentilhombres de cámara**.

As for the *hidalguías*, a considerable number of privileges that they proffered were put on sale during the first decade of the eighteenth century following a tradition that was fully established in the sixteenth century (Thompson 1979). It turned out to be a total failure, partly because there already existed at that time numerous other ways to gain access to the social space that had been growing extraordinarily during the preceding centuries. On the other hand, it does not appear that the robes of the military orders were the object of transactions during the Bourbon period even though they had been during the "reign" of the Count Duke of Olivares (Jiménez Moreno 2009). As they represented a privilege with a religious component, their alienation would have meant the Crown committing the crime of simony (Giménez Carrillo 2011). Nevertheless, at least during the first years of the Bourbon century, it is almost certain that the *mercedes de hábito** continued to be sold through a private market, that was almost always controlled by the secrecy required for such formally "prohibited" transactions.

Outside of this system of social hierarchy that went from *hidalguías* to titles of nobility and included the members of the military orders, other honors were also alienated during the eighteenth century. Two little known examples of such *mercedes* were those attributed to the *gentilhombres de cámara* and *gentilhombres de boca**. When these titles did not include the *derecho de entrada y ejercicio**, they were only honorific titles that could be purchased and were indeed alienated during periods of intense venality (Andújar Castillo 2008a). This same phenomenon happened with some honorific appointments to offices, such as those of the king's *consejeros* or secretaries; their possession did not imply really taking on the responsibilities related to these positions though they were also sold in periods of venality along with other offices and honors.

In this field of honors, the most active market without a doubt involved the sale of titles of nobility. Although there are no monographic studies on the seventeenth century, preliminary research indicates that, after some titles were sold during the reign of Phillip IV, an authentic boom in sales occurred during the last third of the century thanks to multiple modes of sales. For example, based on research in progress, I would estimate that just during 1679 and 1680 alone, years in which a "profit fund" was created to finance the royal wedding, approximately 35 titles of marquis and count were sold. A significant number of them were acquired by the commercial bourgeoisie of Seville. The high total of new titles of nobility that were registered also around 1693 corresponds to the number of titles sold, as a decree issued that same year declared that all titles that did not surpass the sum of 30,000 *ducados** for the sale of such a *merced* would only be valid for one lifetime (Rodríguez Hernández, 2010). The mechanism of obtaining a title of nobility by "pecuniary service" had been fully established by this period, whether it consisted of paying in cash or financing other "services" for the monarchy. One of the most notable services consisted of investing in the creation of new military units, which could yield, if such were the terms of the agreement, a title of Castile in exchange for recruiting soldiers and providing them with uniforms and arms (Rodríguez Hernández 2011).

As happened in many other areas of the monarchy's government, Phillip V did not change the dynamic of venality that he inherited from his predecessor on the throne. In theory, marquisates and earldoms should be attributed to men of illustrious lineage, and of course reward the services carried out for the monarchy by those that aspired to such honors. In practice, they ended up being destined to parvenus, social groups on the rise, such as residents of the Indies that had become rich in mining and commerce. In short, they were brought by a universe of individuals whose principal merit lay in having so much cash on hand that it could be invested in titles that were then worth between 20,000 and 30,000 *ducados*, although some titles were acquired for sums higher or lower than these averages.

The need for cash caused by the War of Succession made Phillip V pay individuals and territories with titles of nobility in order to foster loyalty, just as it can be exemplified by those that were granted after the *Cortes* of Catalonia in 1702 (Molas Ribalta 2004) or to cities in Andalusia in 1711 (Andújar Castillo 2006b). In addition, he tried to fulfill the aspirations of some of his principal subjects by granting titles in exchange for money. In my study of the period 1704-1711, I registered numerous alienations of titles to residents of Spain, as well as individuals from the active American market (Andújar Castillo 2008a). Research currently underway by María del Mar Felices de la Fuente reveals that a third of the noble titles conceded by Phillip V were the result of pecuniary services, or, in other words, they were purchased. These figures are low estimates, because, as she has demonstrated, tracing money and services incompatible with the condition of titled noble is difficult since they were systematically hidden in order not to "stain" the honor that had been attained (Felices de la Fuente 2010b).

The monarch could successfully award such eminent distinctions in exchange for money because bureaucratic measures were implemented that facilitated this process right from the time the practice became widespread. Executive decrees were used to grant the immense majority of the titles of nobility conceded for money, just as almost always happened when an element of his patrimony was alienated. The king therefore dispensed with consulting the *Cámara de Castilla*, the institution that theoretically should monitor the social origins and previous activities of those that sought titles (Felices de la Fuente 2010a, 2011). As there was no consultation, the king awarded the title without verifying beforehand the "qualities" of the beneficiaries. In this way, the sale of titles of nobility was facilitated by the system, as the only requirements were the deposit of the sum of money agreed upon and the executive decree that turned the individual donating the sum into a count or a marquis.

At times the relation of deposit to title was not so direct, as it could vary depending on where the alienation was implemented. Many of the titles were sold after the king had signed them without including the name of the individuals; therefore, anonymous subjects were named marquises or counts. These blank titles were then transferred for their sale to the viceroys in America, where there was a greater demand for such honors and more wealth available for investment in them, or they were devolved to convents and monasteries that had requested them to defray the cost of repairing or even constructing their edifices with the proceeds (Andújar Castillo-Felices de la Fuente 2007). These cases entailed a considerable transfer of the king's authority to other institutional spaces, even if finally the official document that contained the appointment was issued by the royal offices. In practice, the transaction was formalized between the royal "commissioner", whether it was the viceroy or an ecclesiastical institution, and the individual eager to reach the pinnacle of the pyramid of honors and able to do so thanks to his potent fortune.

Thus, the active formula of alienating titles of nobility through religious institutions continued without interruption until 1761, since its beginning, insofar as is known, in 1623. There was an exceptional sale in 1790 to José Antonio Roche, who bought the title of Marquis of Roche for 22,000 *ducados* from the monastery of San Jerónimo of Zaragoza, which had kept the blank title signed by the king in 1755.[8] Nevertheless, the Bourbon century was principally characterized by the extraordinary intensification of the sale of titles to residents of the Indies, which had already started at the end of Charles II's reign (Maruri Villanueva 2009). It is undeniable that the extensive American market, in particular the viceroyalty of Peru, had emerged as one of the most active sources of demand for the purchase of titles of nobility. One of the nuclei of this new titled nobility was formed by American estate owners, merchants, miners, and even some bureaucrats that managed to accumulate a fortune by carrying out other functions in addition to their official positions as the

[8] AHN, Consejos, Leg. 8978.

king's administrators. Numerous channels obviously existed to facilitate such purchases, including the viceroys, monasteries, convents, and individuals that could transact them privately; other options included the exchange of titles for direct monetary investments made at the Court, or as compensation for loans granted to the royal treasury.

The sale of a noble title had no costs for the Crown but it did represent an important revenue at the time of the operation, plus the rights of the *media-annata** and the annual payment of the "lance" tax. Given the high price of titles, their sale became one of the most commonly used resources whenever one-off financing was needed for any reason whatsoever. This importance is proven by the proposal made by the Marquis of la Mina and Secretary of the War Office in 1765 when they were trying to finance the enlargement of the dragoon corps, as they were not sure whether they should sell military posts or titles of nobility (Andújar Castillo 2004). And a similar dilemma was present when four noble titles were sold a few years earlier by the viceroy of Peru, Manuel Amat, to finance the fortification of the Araucanian territories and their settlement.[9] The fact is that the sale of offices and honors bore the weight of a burden that would have otherwise fallen on the royal treasury.

Final Considerations about the Political Implications of Venality

Although there are still not enough studies that evaluate the weight of venality in the history of the Ancien Regime in Spain, its role was evidently far more important than the one that it was assigned by the historiography when analyzing the different mechanisms that underpinned the economy of *Gracia* and the exchange of *mercedes* for services and merits. I am at least in the position to confirm that, in some periods, venality surpassed other factors that have been emphasized until now, such as clientele relations or the absolute power of the monarch—demonstrated in its maximum expression as judge and supreme arbitrator of the entire complex network of relations forged with the government's agents.

This question clearly leads us to reconsider the reflections that were initiated a number of years ago concerning absolutism, a practice that had been considered both as unchangeable and as distinctive of the political systems of the principal European monarchies ruling during the

[9] AGI, IG, Leg. 545, Lib. 4.

seventeenth and eighteenth centuries. The theoretical construction of "imperfect absolutism" has been introduced quite productively so as to make it clear that the concept of absolutism does not always correspond to the imposition of the king's will, nor to the model of the centralization of political power (Potter 2003). The prescribed manner of establishing consensus with the kingdoms,[10] for example, when negotiating their fiscal contributions, or the negotiations carried out via the *Cortes*, can be seen as signs of this "imperfection", or, put more simply, of the necessity of collaborating with the elites. It was pointed out previously that there were different ways of negotiating with the elites, intermediate powers, and nobility when asking for collaboration in recruiting soldiers. They almost always entailed delegating the king's power to these intermediaries, whether they were kingdoms, *Cortes*, or private businessmen, members of the nobility, or individuals hoping to receive titles of nobility.

These considerations obviously propound the idea that absolutism did not always correspond to the model based on the imposition of the monarch's will. Royal decisions were almost always influenced by a series of factors interposed between the monarch and his subjects. It has been pointed out that numerous decisions were often made by those of his inner circle, even if the king adopted them formally. They were almost always strongly conditioned by the authentic spider's web that power networks formed in the Court and that connected individuals by clientele, family, or local origin ties. Such negotiations were activated in the institutionalized, regulated sphere of the official mechanisms through which the monarchy controlled social actors with clearly defined functions. The importance of other external factors with less clear functions also has to be taken into consideration such as, for example, the so-called "business agents", about whom very few studies exist (Álvarez-Ossorio 2000); as they were removed from the institutional level, we have fewer documents about them.

In my opinion, even if venality represented the ultimate expression of royal absolutism, at the same time it clearly reflects the weakness of that very system. When the king named to official posts in exchange for money, in certain measure he was almost always forced to do it because of the imperious "urgencies" of a treasury that was too frequently incapable of defraying the monarchy's substantial outlays. In this sense, purchasing public offices and honors could be seen as a form of necessary

[10] The "kingdoms" are the components of the "Composite Monarchy" (editor's note).

"collaboration" with the king (albeit self-interested) by individuals who had sufficient wealth to invest in these special "goods". In the same way, it would also express the weakness of the monarch's absolute power, as he yielded to the numerous clauses that were included in the contracts whenever the offices were sold; the posts in perpetuity, particularly, illustrate this debility (Andújar Castillo 2011c). In fact, their alienation meant their privatization for the subsequent appointments did not depend on the king's will but on the price agreed upon by two private individuals, the seller and buyer.

On the other hand, "benefited" offices were equally conceded for money but either for a predetermined period of time or the buyer's lifetime. In practice they signified a loss of royal attributions as the king often "named in blank". The titles were consequently issued to anonymous subjects that were not going to accredit any merit other than the money invested in the acquisition of the offices. In fact, in the case of these blank appointments that the king signed before the name of the appointee was even known, which were so common for the army during the eighteenth century, the commissioner really effectuated the final appointment. These business agents, intermediaries, or contractors that specialized in the formation of new regiments only knew about the prices of the posts. In relation to this reality, the opinion that the seventeenth-century jurist, Juan Bautista Larrea, put forward in his *Allegationes Fiscales* is unequivocal since he wrote that the sale of offices wronged the sovereign "*puesto que lo privaba de una de sus prerrogativas principales, la de conceder plazas y oficios ejerciendo su liberalidad, y provocaba por ello una disminución de su autoridad*" ("given that it left him without one of his most important prerogatives, that of conceding posts and offices in exercising his liberality, thereby causing a diminution in his authority") (Valpini 2010).

The sale of offices was established as a system of funding after having been transformed from a mechanism to be used only for special political and economic needs to an almost normal source of revenue because it was resorted to so regularly. The monarch was forced to alienate his patrimony, or just his power in the case of the "benefited" offices, in terms that demonstrated his debility as opposed to the purchasers' strength. If an office or honor becomes a means of producing credit for the monarchy, the pecuniary merit comes before any other consideration, such as the potential purchaser's competences or experience. Therefore, the true nature of the transaction was perfectly concealed by the use of the euphemism "pecuniary service"; the service was in this manner assimilated to the "merit" of having contributed funds to the king when he most needed them. It is clear that even if the proceeds were always demarcated as extraordinary resources, it would have been difficult to sustain the royal treasury at such critical stages as periods of war without the substantial revenues that venality generated. Consequently, without this self-interested "collaboration" that the up-and-coming elites offered, as they had enough wealth to invest in offices and honors, the "edifice" of absolutism would have had difficulties surviving. The problem was that such collaboration simultaneously entailed a certain weakening of the monarch's *auctoritas.* Such a statement however invalidates a postulate that is obvious, namely that the king possessed the absolute right to name his agents in exchange for money, or to distinguish certain subjects with the highest honors of the reign as an illustrious expression of his extensive power. It is certainly a different question that this power carried with it unmistakable signs that the system of absolutism itself had debilities as well as all-embracing power.

Abbreviations Used

AGI: Archivo General de Indias, Sevilla
AGS: Archivo General de Simancas
AHN: Archivo Histórico Nacional, Madrid
CG: Contadurías General
DGT: Dirección General del Tesoro
IG: Indiferente General
TMC: Tribunal Mayor de Cuentas

References

Actas del IV Simposium de Historia de la Administración, (1983), Madrid: Instituto Nacional de Administración Pública.

Alvarado, J., (coord.), (1997), *Poder, economía, clientelismo*, Madrid: Marcial Pons.

Álvarez-Ossorio Alvariño, A., (1997), "Pervenire alle orecchie della Maestá: el agente lombardo en la corte madrileña" in *Annali di Storia moderna e contemporanea*, 3:173-223.

—. (2000), "La venalidad de las magistraturas en el Estado de Milán durante el reinado de Carlos II" in *Archivio Stórico Lombardo*, CXXVI: 111-261.

—. (2003), "De la plenitud territorial a una prolongada agonía: el Consejo de Italia durante el reinado de Felipe V", in *Cheiron, Materiali e strumenti di aggiornamento storiografico*, 39-40:311-392.
—. (2007), "La venta de magistraturas en el reino de Nápoles durante los reinados de Carlos II y Felipe V", *Chronica Nova*, 33: 57-94.
Andújar Castillo, F., (2002), "Galones por torres. La financiación del sistema defensivo de la costa del Reino de Granada: una operación venal del reinado de Carlos III", in *Chronica Nova*, 29:7-25.
—. (2003), "La privatización del reclutamiento militar en el siglo XVIII: el sistema de asientos", in *Studia Historica. Historia Moderna*, 25:123-147.
—. (2004), *El sonido del dinero. Monarquía, ejército y venalidad en la España del siglo XVIII*, Madrid: Marcial Pons.
—. (2006), "Empresarios de la guerra y asentistas de soldados en el siglo XVII", in García Hernán – Maffi (coord.), *Guerra y sociedad en la monarquía hispánica: política, estrategia y cultura en la Europa moderna (1500-1700)*, v. II: 375-394.
—. (2006b), "Servicios para la guerra, mercedes para las oligarquías: las recompensas de la Guerra de Sucesión en Andalucía", in Bernardo Ares (ed.), *La Sucesión de la monarquía hispánica, 1665-1725*: 43-74.
—. (2007), "Nepotismo, clientelismo y fidelidad. De Floridablanca a Godoy (1789-1798)", in *Cuadernos de Historia Moderna*, Anejos, VII: 165-197.
—. (2008a), *Necesidad y venalidad. España e Indias, 1704-1711*, Madrid: Centro de Estudios Constitucionales.
—. (2008b), "Vender cargos y honores. Un recurso extraordinario para la financiación de la Corte de Felipe V", in Castellano Castellano - López-Guadalupe Muñoz (eds.), *Homenaje a don Antonio Domínguez Ortiz*, v. III: 89-110.
—. (2008c), "La financiación de la Guerra de Sucesión. El coste de la formación de un nuevo ejército", in Edelmayer - León Sanz - Ruiz Rodríguez (eds.), *Hispania-Austria III. Der Spanische Erbfolgekrieg*: 108-129.
—. (2010), "Mercedes dotales para mujeres, o los privilegios de servir en palacio (siglos XVII-XVIII), in *Obradoiro de Historia Moderna*, 19: 215-247.
—. (2011a), "La venalidad en los Consejos durante el reinado de Carlos II. De las plazas de consejero al oficio de archivero", in Marcos Martín (ed.), *Hacer historia desde Simancas. Homenaje a José Luis Rodríguez de Diego*: 73-96.

—. (2011b), "Tiempo de venalidad. Tomás Marín de Poveda y la venta de cargos en Indias", in Andújar Castillo - Giménez Carrillo (eds.), *Riqueza, poder y nobleza: los Marín de Poveda, una historia familiar del siglo XVII vista desde España y Chile*: 79-92.
—. (2011c), "Los contratos de venta de empleos en la España del Antiguo Régimen", in Andújar Castillo - Felices de la Fuente (eds.), *El poder del dinero. Ventas de cargos y honores en la España del Antiguo Régimen*: 59-78.
—. - Felices de la Fuente, M. del M., (2007), "Nobleza y venalidad: el mercado eclesiástico de venta de títulos nobiliarios en el siglo XVIII", in *Chronica Nova*, 33: 131-153.
—. - Felices de la Fuente, M. del M., (eds.), (2011), *El poder del dinero. Ventas de cargos y honores en la España del Antiguo Régimen*, Madrid: Biblioteca Nueva.
—. - Giménez Carrillo, D.M. (eds.), (2011), *Riqueza, poder y nobleza: los Marín de Poveda, una historia familiar del siglo XVII vista desde España y Chile*, Almería: Universidad de Almeria.
Bernardo Ares, J.M., (ed.), (2006), *La Sucesión de la monarquía hispánica, 1665-1725*, Córdoba : Universidad de Cordoba.
Bertrand, M., (1999), *Grandeur et misère de l'office. Les officiers de finances de Nouvelle Espagne, XVII-XVIIIe siècles*, Paris : Publications de la Sorbonne.
Beik, W., (2005), "The absolutism of Louis XIV as social collaboration", in *Past and Present*, 188: 195-224.
Belenguer Cebriá, E. (coord.), (1999), *Felipe II y el Mediterráneo*, v. II: *Los grupos sociales*, Madrid: Sociedad Estatal para la Conmemoración de los Centenarios de Felipe II y Carlos V.
Bruce, A., (1980), *The Purchase System in the British Army, 1660-1871*, London: Royal Historical Society.
Burkholder, M.A. – Chandler, D.S. (1977), *From impotence to authority: the Spanish Crown and the American audiencias, 1687–1808*. Columbia: University of Missouri Press.
Carzolio, M.I. - Fernández, R.I. - Lagunas, C. (coords.), (2010), *El Antiguo Régimen. Una mirada de dos mundos: España y América*, Buenos Aires: Prometeo Libros.
Castellano Castellano, J.L. - López-Guadalupe Muñoz, M.L., (coord.), (2008), *Homenaje a don Antonio Domínguez Ortiz*, Granada: Universidad de Granada.
Dedieu, J.P., (2010), "El aparato de gobierno de la monarquía española en el siglo XVIII, elemento constitutivo de un territorio y de una

sociedad", in Carzolio - Fernández - Lagunas (coords.), *El Antiguo Régimen. Una mirada de dos mundos: España y América*: 39-62.

—. (2011), "Acercarse a la 'venalidad'", in Andújar Castillo - Felices de la Fuente (eds.), *El poder del dinero. Ventas de cargos y honores en la España del Antiguo Régimen*: 15-24.

Díaz López, J.P. -Andújar Castillo, F. - Galán Sánchez, Á., (eds.), (2010), *Casas, Familias y Rentas. La nobleza del Reino de Granada entre los siglos XV-XVIII*, Granada: Universidad de Granada.

Domínguez Ortiz, A., (1965), "Un virreinato en venta", in *Mercurio Peruano*, 453: 43-51.

—. (1985), *Instituciones y Sociedad en la España de los Austrias*, Barcelona: Ariel.

—. (1985), "La venta de cargos y oficios públicos en Castilla y sus consecuencias económicas y sociales", in Domínguez Ortiz, *Instituciones y Sociedad en la España de los Austrias*:146-183.

Drevillon, H., (2005), *L'impôt du sang. Le métier des armes sous Louis XIV*, Paris : Tallandier.

Dubet, A., (2007), "¿La importación de un modelo francés? Acerca de algunas reformas de la administración española a principios del siglo XVIII", in *Revista de historia moderna*, 25: 207-233.

Edelmayer, F. - León Sanz, V. - Ruiz Rodríguez, J.I., (eds.), (2008), *Hispania-Austria III. Der Spanische Erbfolgekrieg*, Vienna: Oldenbourg Wissenschaftsverlag.

Felices de la Fuente, M. del M., (2010a), "La Cámara de Castilla, el rey y la creación de títulos nobiliarios en la primera mitad del siglo XVIII", in *Hispania: Revista Española de Historia*, 70, 236: 661-686.

—. (2010b), "Silencio y ocultaciones en los despachos de los títulos nobiliarios. Análisis crítico de su contenido", in *Chronica Nova*, 36: 229-252.

—. (2011), "Procesos de ennoblecimiento. El control sobre el origen social de la nobleza titulada en la primera mitad del siglo XVIII", in Andújar Castillo - Felices de la Fuente (eds.), *El poder del dinero. Ventas de cargos y honores en la España del Antiguo Régimen*: 243-269.

García Hernán, E. - Maffi, D., (coord.), (2006), *Guerra y sociedad en la monarquía hispánica: política, estrategia y cultura en la Europa moderna (1500-1700)*, v. II, Madrid: Consejo Superior de Investigaciones Científicas.

García Monerris, E., (1991), *La monarquía absoluta y el municipio borbónico. La reorganización de la oligarquía urbana en el ayuntamiento de Valencia (1707-1800)*, Madrid: Consejo Superior de Investigaciones Científicas.

Gelabert, J.E., (1997), "Tráfico de oficios y gobierno de los pueblos de Castilla (1543-1643)", in Ribot Garcia – De Rosa, (eds.), *Ciudad y mundo urbano en la Época Moderna*: 157-186.

Giménez Carrillo, D.M., (2011), "La venta de hábitos de las Órdenes Militares en el siglo XVII. Entre la ocultación y el delito de simonía", in Andújar Castillo - Felices de la Fuente (eds.), *El poder del dinero. Ventas de cargos y honores en la España del Antiguo Régimen*: 297-309.

Glesener, T., (2011), "Venalidad y fidelidad en los Países Bajos durante el reinado de Felipe V", in Andújar Castillo - Felices de la Fuente (eds.), *El poder del dinero. Ventas de cargos y honores en la España del Antiguo Régimen*: 187-205.

Gómez González, I., (2000), *La justicia en almoneda. La venta de oficios en la Chancillería de Granada (1505-1834)*, Granada: Comares.

González Lopo, D. - López López, R.J. (coords.), (2003), *Balance de la historiografía modernista, 1973-2001. Actas del VI Coloquio de Metodología Histórica Aplicada (Homenaje al Profesor Dr. D. Antonio Eiras Roel)*, Santiago de Compostela: Xunta de Galicia, Dirección Xeral de Patrimonio Cultural.

Gorau, F., (2002), *La vénalité des charges militaires en France au XVIIe et XVIIIe siècles*, Villeneuve d'Asq: Presses universitaires du septentrion.

Hernández Benítez, M., (1995), "Y después de las ventas de oficios ¿qué? (Transmisiones privadas de regimientos en el Madrid moderno, 1606-1808)", in *Anuario de Historia del Derecho Español*, v. LXV: 705-748.

—. (1997), "Cuando el poder se vende: venta de oficios y poder local en Castilla. Siglos XVII y XVIII", in Alvarado, *Poder, economía, clientelismo*: 71-95.

—. (2007), "Venalidad de oficios municipales en la Castilla del siglo XVIII: un ensayo de cuantificación", in *Chronica Nova*, 33: 95-129.

Herzog, T., (1995), *Los ministros de la audiencia de Quito, 1650-1750*, Quito: Ediciones Libri Mundi.

Imízcoz Beunza, J.M., (2007), "Elites administrativas, redes cortesanas y captación de recursos en la construcción social del Estado Moderno", in *Trocadero*, 19: 11-30.

Jiménez Estrella, A., (2004), "El precio de las almenas: ventas de alcaidías de fortalezas en época de los Austrias", in *Revista de Historia Moderna. Anales de la Universidad de Alicante*: 143-172.

—. (2011), "El reclutamiento en la primera mitad del siglo XVII y sus posibilidades venales", in Andújar Castillo, F. - Felices de la Fuente, M. del M. (eds.), *El poder del dinero. Ventas de cargos y honores en la España del Antiguo Régimen*: 165-186.

Jiménez Moreno, A., (2009), "Honores a cambio de soldados, la concesión de hábitos de las Órdenes Militares en una coyuntura crítica: la Junta de Hábitos (1635-1642)", in Soria Mesa - Bravo Caro - Delgado Barrado (coords.), *Las élites en la época moderna: la monarquía española*, v. 3: 155-172.

Lera García, R., (1988), "Venta de oficios en la Inquisición de Granada (1629-1644)", in *Hispania*, XLVIII/170: 909-962.

López Díaz, Ma., (2011), "Tráfico de cargos y oligarquías urbanas: de lo 'público' a lo 'privado' y lo contrario (siglos XVII-XVIII)", in Andújar Castillo - Felices de la Fuente (eds.), *El poder del dinero. Ventas de cargos y honores en la España del Antiguo Régimen*: 115-140.

Marcos Martín, A., (1999), "Oligarquías urbanas y gobiernos ciudadanos en la España del siglo XVI", in Belenguer Cebriá (coord.), *Felipe II y el Mediterráneo*, v. II: *Los grupos sociales*: 265-293.

—. (2003), "Enajenaciones por precio del patrimonio regio en los siglos XVI y XVII. Balance historiográfico y perspectivas de análisis", in González Lopo - López López (coords.), *Balance de la historiografía modernista, 1973-2001. Actas del VI Coloquio de Metodología Histórica Aplicada (Homenaje al Profesor Dr. D. Antonio Eiras Roel)*: 419-443.

—. (2007), "Las ventas de oficios en Castilla en tiempos de suspensión de ventas (1600-1621)", in *Chronica Nova*, 33: 13-35.

—. (2011), "Las caras de la venalidad. Acrecentamiento, 'criaciones' y consumos de oficios en la Castilla del siglo XVI", in Andújar Castillo - Felices de la Fuente (eds.), *El poder del dinero. Ventas de cargos y honores en la España del Antiguo Régimen*: 81-114.

—. (ed.), (2011), *Hacer historia desde Simancas. Homenaje a José Luis Rodríguez de Diego*, Valladolid: Junta de Castilla Y Leon.

Martos Crespo, J., (2011), *Venalidad y elites de poder. Los gobernadores de Yucatán en tiempos de Felipe V (1705-1742)*, Almería ("Memoria de D.E.A.", unpublished).

Maruri Villanueva, R., (2009), "Poder con poder se paga: títulos nobiliarios beneficiados en Indias (1681-1821)", in *Revista de Indias*, 246, v. LXIX: 207-240.

Muro Romero, F., (1978), "El 'beneficio' de oficios públicos con jurisdicción en Indias. Notas sobre sus orígenes", in *Anuario de Estudios Americanos*, 35: 1-67.

Olival, F., (2011), "Economia da mercê e venalidade em Portugal (séc. XVII e XVIII)", in Andújar Castillo - Felices de la Fuente (eds.), *El poder del dinero. Ventas de cargos y honores en la España del Antiguo Régimen*: 341-353.

Potter, M., (2003), *Corps and clienteles: public finance and political change in France, 1688-1715*, Aldershot: Ashgate Pub Ltd.

Ribot Garcia, L. A. – De Rosa, L., (eds.), (1997), *Ciudad y mundo urbano en la Época Moderna*, Madrid: Editorial Actas.

Rodríguez Hernández, A.J., (2007), "Patentes por soldados. Reclutamiento y venalidad en el ejército durante la segunda mitad del siglo XVII", in *Chronica Nova*, 33: 37-56.

—. (2010), "La creación de Títulos de Castilla durante los reinados de Felipe IV y Carlos II: concesiones y ritmos", in Díaz López -Andújar Castillo - Galán Sánchez (eds.), *Casas, Familias y Rentas. La nobleza del Reino de Granada entre los siglos XV-XVIII*: 168-169.

—. (2011), "La venta de títulos nobiliarios a través de la financiación de nuevas unidades militares durante el siglo XVII", in Andújar Castillo - Felices de la Fuente (eds.), *El poder del dinero. Ventas de cargos y honores en la España del Antiguo Régimen*: 270-296.

Rowlands, G. (2003), *The Dynastic State and the Army under Louis XIV. Royal Service and Private Interest, 1661 to 1701*, Cambridge: Cambridge University press.

Sanz Tapia, A., (2006), "El acceso a los cargos de gobierno de la audiencia de Quito (1701-1750)", in *Anuario de Estudios Americanos*, 63/2: 49-73.

—. (2009), *¿Corrupción o necesidad? La venta de cargos de gobierno americanos bajo Carlos II (1674-1700)*, Madrid: Consejo Superior de Investigaciones Científicas.

Schäfer, E., (1935), *El Consejo Real y Supremo de las Indias. Historia y organización del Consejo y de la Casa de Contratación de las Indias*, Madrid.

Soria Mesa, E. - Bravo Caro, J.J. -Delgado Barrado, J.M. (coords.), (2009), *Las élites en la época moderna: la monarquía española*, v. 3 (Economía y poder), Córdoba: Universidad de Cordoba.

Thompson, I.A.A., (1979), "The purchase of nobility in Castile, 1552-1700", in *Journal of European Economic History*, 8: 313-360.

Torras i Ribé, J.M., (1983), "La venta de oficios municipales en Cataluña (1739-1741). Una operación especulativa del gobierno de Felipe V", in *Actas del IV Simposium de Historia de la Administración*: 723-747.

Volpini, P., (2010), *El espacio político del letrado. Juan Bautista Larrea, magistrado y jurista en la monarquía de Felipe IV*, Madrid: Universidad Autónoma de Madrid.

Yali Román, A., (1972), "Sobre alcaldías mayores y corregimientos. Un ensayo de interpretación", in *Jahrbuch für Geschichte Lateinamerikas*, 9: 1-39.

CHAPTER FOUR

SERVING THE STATE IN LATIN AMERICA DURING THE EIGHTEENTH AND NINETEENTH CENTURIES

JUAN CARLOS GARAVAGLIA

The birth of the countries of Latin America at the beginning of the nineteenth century can be considered as the last, distant (and attenuated) echo of the great wave of revolutions that started to shake the Western world on both sides of the Atlantic in 1776. Even if after three centuries of domination by Spain and Portugal the culture of their white elites was deeply rooted in Iberian traditions, they were also strongly anchored locally in the indigenous population that in several cases (Mexico, Guatemala, Ecuador, Peru, Bolivia) descended from eminent civilizations more ancient than those of Western Europe. With regard to the role of their administration and the personnel that served the state, who always belonged to the white-tinged minorities, the Iberian imprint was the fundamental cultural matrix in which the overwhelming majority of the men that would lead the revolt against the colonial powers had been formed.

In this study, we will rapidly sketch a panorama of the situation of the functionaries that served the power before and after the revolutions for independence between 1810 and 1825. We then follow them until the 1850s – 1860s, when the process of state-building entered the phase of completion and consolidation. We will focus almost exclusively on the case of the former Spanish colonies,[1] even if some brief references to Brazil will be made.

---

[1] And in particular, on the examples of Guatemala, Costa Rica, Colombia, Ecuador, Chile, Argentina, and Uruguay, which are the countries that have been the center of the *State-Building in Latin America Project* sponsored by the ERC.

The Hispanic Administration Crosses the Atlantic

Just as had occurred in the "kingdoms" that made up the composite Hispanic monarchy (Kingdom of Valencia, the Principality of Catalonia, etc.), the first institutional forms that structured the exercise of power and jurisdiction in America were successively governors (Hispaniola and *Tierra Firme* were the first seats of government established shortly after Columbus's voyages), and *Audiencias**—*the* first one was founded in Santo Domingo in 1511. This high tribunal was the fourth *Audiencia* founded in all the territory dominated by the Crown of Castile on both sides of the ocean (it was preceded by the chanceries founded in Valladolid in 1475,[2] in 1480/1484 and Ciudad Real in 1594, that was then transferred to Granada in 1505). In short, the judicial framework of Castile was extended to America very early. In 1527 the *Audiencia* de la New Spain (México) was established.

The viceroys were introduced immediately afterward when Don Antonio de Mendoza was appointed viceroy of New Spain in 1535. The experience in establishing this role that had already been acquired in Aragon, Naples, Valencia and, to a certain extent, in Catalonia provided a solid tradition for these primogenital institutional forms that were established in the Indies. It is essential to underline that, at least during the first century of domination, contemporary sources do not refer to a "viceroyalty"; there was, of course, a viceroy, but he governed the "Kingdom of New Spain", just as he would govern the *kingdom* of Aragon or Valencia—and more than one of these men would actually follow such a trajectory. New Spain was just one of the many *kingdoms* that formed this extensive composite monarchy. Serving as the viceroy of Aragon or Catalonia—with their ancient consolidated juridical traditions, *utsages* (mores) and customs—was obviously not the same experience as exercising the charge in the Indies, a context in which the viceroy only had to face a group of fierce conquistadors, plus their relatives, allies, and followers, and the vanquished indigenous societies that were subject to the right of conquest. The real power of the American viceroys consequently turned out to be much less counterbalanced than that of their peers stationed in the rest of the Hispanic monarchy. After its foundation in 1524, the Council of the Indies would assume a role in the peninsula largely similar to the one that the Council of State exercised in Castile, or

---

[2] During a preceding phase, this *Audiencia* was itinerant, that is, it followed the monarch as he traveled.

the Council of Aragon in that kingdom. During the entire period of Hispanic domination, the power that governed Hispanic America would center on three pivots—the Council of Indies, the *Audiencias*, and the viceroys. There were also other functionaries that governed, such as general captains and governors, though they were generally held accountable to the viceroys.

By the late eighteenth century, there were thirteen *Audiencias* scattered across the Americas, and it is here that we find quite a few elements of a true bureaucratic career, as defined by Max Weber (Weber 1978). Of course there were different phases in the evolution of these careers in the *Audiencias*, as shown in a pioneering study from some years ago (Burkholder and Chandler 1977), but here our aim is to reveal the "model" character of this judicial institution with regard to the subject that concerns us. In the 1780s these true bureaucrats (true precisely because of their proximity to the Weberian model; i.e., they were qualified professionally, had followed a career with successive promotions, were highly respected for their services to the empire—wherever they were actually posted—and had weaker links to local elites) were the first to leave or to be expelled when the revolutions for independence broke out. There was little tying these true bureaucrats to their overseas posts, where they often felt their presence was transient, and a great deal tying them to a crown to which they had sworn allegiance. What happened to them in Quito, Santafé de Bogotá, Santiago de Chile and Buenos Aires, differences aside, is a clear example of what we are talking about: for one reason or another, with few exceptions, the prosecutors and judges of the *Audiencias* soon disappeared from the scene. In other cases, such as in Guatemala, the judges were divided between those who favored and those who opposed independence (those with strong local ties resumed their judicial careers in the new state configurations). We should recall that the *Audiencias* were empowered to assume governmental functions, standing in for the viceroy or captain general in his absence. It was clear that the project to build an independent state in opposition to the crown could not leave an instrument as powerful as the pinnacle of the judicial system in the hands of senior officials loyal to that crown. This was a key factor in all governmental tasks geared towards creating what has been called the "legal statute" of the state (O'Donnell 2007).

But we recall that the true pinnacle of political power was the viceroy, a figure which appears in the Americas after the establishment of the first two *Audiencias* (Santo Domingo in 1511 and New Spain in 1528), while Peru and New Spain had viceroys from the 1530s and 1540s; Toledo,

Velasco and quite a few of the other early viceroys served successively in both viceroyalties and, in some cases, viceroys had already held similar posts in Galicia, Aragon or Italy. In the first 150 years of colonial rule, it was common for the viceroys to belong to the nobility or, in cases such as the Mendoza, Alburquerque, Mancera, and Manríquez families, to the high nobility. Let's take one example, almost at random. In 1680 Don Tomás Antonio de la Cerda y Aragón, the third Marquis of La Laguna, was appointed twenty-sixth viceroy of New Spain. Not only was he the younger brother of the powerful Duke of Medinaceli (a member of the high nobility, one of the *Grandes**), a favorite at the time of Charles II, and the leading member of a family that presumed to date back to Alfonso the Wise and Louis IX of France, but he had also married the Countess of Paredes, Doña María Luisa Manrique de Lara y Gonzaga. She was the daughter of Vespasiano Gonzaga de Mantua and María Inés Manrique de Lara, of the House of Manrique, also a descendant of one of the Castilian nobility's oldest and most powerful families. But this did not prevent our Marquis from pursuing a military and bureaucratic career as captain general in Andalusia and as a member of the Council of the Indies before becoming, due to his powerful brother's influence, viceroy of New Spain. We should not be surprised by this fact: according to one expert in seventeenth century Spain, in all of Europe in this period it was the Spanish aristocracy that played the biggest role in running the state and in society in general (Kamen 2005).

During the colonial period, bishops often simultaneously held the position of viceroy because of the death or disablement of their predecessors, as happened on at least five occasions in Mexico during the seventeenth century and once in Peru during the same period. It happened three more times in Peru before the mid-eighteenth century, and, between 1710 and 1716, one archbishop succeeded another one in governing the vice-royalty. In some cases, these temporary appointments could last for quite a number of years, such as when Friar Payo Enríquez de Rivera replaced the deceased viceroy of Mexico, the sixth duke de Veragua, from 1673 to 1680. And this same phenomenon occurred even in "late" vice-royalties such as New Granada (1734).

In this respect, Pedro Moya de Contreras's career is noteworthy. He was born in a small town in Andalusia around the 1520s. When he was very young, he entered as a page in the service of the licentiate Juan de Ovando who was at that point a very powerful personage at the court and president of the Council of the Indies. Enjoying the favor of Ovando, Moya de Contreras completed his studies at the University of Salamanca, where he graduated as a doctor in both laws. He then went successively from a minor post at the cathedral of the Canary Islands to that of inquisitor in Murcia, until he was sent in 1571 to oversee the establishment of the Tribunal of the Inquisition in Mexico City. He was ordained as a priest in that city and named archbishop of the archdiocese in 1573. From 1583 to 1585, he also held the position of viceroy, because of the vacancy that occurred after the Count de la Coruña died. He was then appointed general *visitador* of all of New Spain and upon returning to the peninsula he was named to the Council of the Indies, where he concluded his long career as its president. Moya de Contreras's trajectory is obviously exceptional, but it does show us once again the intricate web that linked the church to the civil power; it also demonstrates how difficult it really is to try to distinguish unequivocally between both aspects of the imperial state's power in the Indies during the sixteenth and seventeenth centuries.

The trajectory of Don Fernando de Arias Ugarte, who was named archbishop of Lima in 1630, is seemingly just as impressive. He was born in Santa Fe de Bogotá into a family that belonged to the elite. He studied in Salamanca and Lerida in Spain. Upon returning to America, he became an *oidor* in the *Audiencias* located in Panamá, Charcas and Lima, following the typical career path for a judge up until that point. However, he would subsequently be ordained as a priest and be successively conferred the miters of Quito, Santa Fe, Charcas, and Lima. We once again discern a complex dual itinerary, both civil and ecclesiastical. Of course this is also found during those same centuries in the peninsula, starting with the very foundation of the first *Audiencia* in Castile. While it was still in its itinerant stage the *oidores* were ecclesiastics as well as university graduates and, in its earliest phase, its presiding magistrates were generally bishops.[3] Let us take as an example Pedro Manso, who died in Madrid in 1610 as the patriarch of the Western Indies. He studied at the University of Salamanca before becoming vicar-general for his uncle, the bishop of Calahorra as well as archdeacon in Bilbao; he was subsequently named *oidor* of the *Audiencia* of Pamplona, the Chancery in Granada, *alcalde de corte*, president of the Royal *Audiencia* of Valladolid, and ended his career as the president of the Council of Castile. It should not be forgotten that the *Audiencias* and viceroyalties of all the Hispanic Empire were encased in what has quite rightly been called "a monarchy within the church".

[3] See Elisa Caselli's study in this volume.

As early as the eighteenth century, in the new viceroyalties such as New Granada (1734) and Río de la Plata (1776), we begin to see the rise of the figure of the "bureaucrat" viceroy. Generally speaking, he was a *hidalgo* of *capa y espada** who had pursued a long bureaucratic and military career with successive promotions in Spain and the Americas, whether as a governor, *Audiencia* president or captain general, and who was then named viceroy of a place different to where he had previously served (or, alternatively, the same place, as in the cases of Ceballos, Vértiz, Arredondo and Sobremonte in Río de la Plata). We offer two examples of such nomadic careers. Nicolás de Arredondo, born in 1726, fought in wars in Italy, Gibraltar and Menorca; in 1780 he travelled to the Americas, occupying the post of governor in Florida and Cuba. In 1787 he was *gobernador intendente** in Río de la Plata and in 1789 he replaced the Marquis of Loreto as viceroy, holding this post until 1795; subsequently he returned to Spain, where he served as captain general of Navarra, then of Valencia and Murcia, where he was also president of the *Audiencia*. Similarly, Joaquín del Pino, after serving as governor of Montevideo from 1776 to 1790, became president of the *Audiencias* of Chile and, in 1795, Charcas, and then returned to Chile as governor; in 1800 he was appointed viceroy of Río de la Plata. It also happened that sitting viceroys were shifted from one viceroyalty to another, as in the case of Manuel Antonio Flores who was transferred from New Granada to Mexico in the 1780s. The studies offer ample evidence of how intertwined military and bureaucratic functions were in these types of careers, a fact Max Weber understood and highlighted in his work (Weber 1978: 221). What is clear is that the functions of order, discipline, hierarchy and obedience, the archetypes of military conduct, are not in any way removed from the issue that concerns us here.

But we also find lower officials, below the levels of judges and viceroys, whose careers in service to the crown were equally long and nomadic. Let's take a relatively minor figure, again chosen somewhat at random, by the name of Bernardo de Veyra. In 1782, while living in Sonsonate, he presented a request for confirmation of his record, according to which he had been an official paymaster for workers at the sieges of Tortona and Plasencia in the Duchy of Milan at the time of the Italian campaigns between 1740 and 1748, during the War of the Austrian Succession. He later served in the Hospital de la Pasión in Madrid as an officer of the Royal Treasury before travelling to the Americas to assume the post of *alcalde mayor** of the Province of Sonsonate. Subsequently, he was appointed militia colonel in the Nicaragua battalion. Here we have a truly mid-level official with a career in service to the Spanish Empire lasting more than forty years.

In August 1804, when Gaspar Lozano, a high-ranking accountant whose full title was Accounting Minister in the main Treasury of the *Intendencia** of Córdoba del Tucumán, requested “that the aforementioned job fall to his son Narciso Lozano y Goyechea,”[4] he already had a truly exceptional career behind him in terms of its longevity: fifty-two years in service to the crown in seven cities of the vast Hispanic empire from Cádiz to Córdoba, by way of Buenos Aires, Lima, Jujuy, Chuquisaca (Charcas), and Mendoza. For much of his career he served in San Salvador de Jujuy, where he married María Teresa de Goyechea, who was a member of what had been one of the largest and most powerful families in the city since Martín de Goyechea’s arrival there from Navarra in the 1670s (and we should point out that Lozano, originally from Pamplona, was also Navarran). Here we see an example of a very common practice in the careers of bureaucrats born in the Iberian Peninsula during the colonial era, i.e., of officials marrying into prominent families in the towns where they served. The law expressly prohibited this practice among members of the *Audiencia* and other senior officials (Mariluz Urquijo 1988, 344-350), but, even in such cases, this legal constraint was nonetheless often overlooked, as previous research has shown (Burkholder and Chandler 1977). The reasons for this are quite self-evident: both sides derived obvious benefits from such relationships, and this highlights some of the specific limits to any true process of “rational” bureaucratization in the Spanish Empire. This is, of course, hardly surprising given the importance in this society of kinship networks in the process of the constitution of the mechanisms of power.

This example shows us a complex course; it involved, on the one hand, a career in the bureaucracy with progressive promotions, in Spain as well as in America, and on the other, the insertion of the same bureaucrat in a family network that supported him, and that he would undoubtedly protect when the occasion arose. When Gaspar Lozano was ready to retire, he proposed his eldest son as his successor and recommended his other son for a minor position in the administration, successfully obtaining both placements. In this society, it would not appear to anyone that such intercession devalued at all the applicants’ own specific merits. What is more, it would even seem to be undeniable proof that they were indeed suitable men to hold those offices. It was not uncommon for an applicant

[4] All citations for Lozano are from AGI-Buenos Aires 28.

during this epoch to mention the positions that his father or other ancestors had held as one of the important antecedents of his own professional curriculum.[5] The archives house dozens of applications for posts in which the applicant's family background is one of the key elements that would supposedly be taken into account.[6] Here, we will mention only one of many possible examples: in 1800, the customs administrator in Montevideo, when formulating his request to hold the same post in Buenos Aires, did not hesitate to mention his uncle's heroic military feats, as well as those of his father-in-law and brother-in-law. Given the relevance of what can be called the "military families", this tendency was even more widespread among those engaged in military careers. In 1783, Miguel and Antonio Marín, two brothers who were respectively second lieutenant and cadet in the squadron of the dragoons, submitted a request in New Guatemala to be transferred to Barcelona so that they could study mathematics. The only antecedent they included in it was that Antonio Marín, their father, was a military engineer and Miguel Marín, their grandfather, made it to field marshal.[7]

It is also important to point out that certain principles concerning the evolution of careers and professionalism generally appear to have been respected earliest in the Department of Accounting and Royal Treasury, and it is not at all surprising given that this kind of work required specific qualifications. We should not forget, however, that the phenomenon of a genuine career in the bureaucracy for functionaries that did not work for the judiciary would be relatively late, and the "sales" and "benefits"[8] of positions would continue to be very common throughout the entire eighteenth century.[9] The history of the Aíoz family may be an example of this, since it shows us another side of the bureaucrat's career. In 1740, Pablo de Aioz assumed the post of Major Bailiff of the Royal Treasury of

[5]An example among many others can be found in AGI-Buenos Aires 27; there, Juan Manuel Alcalá García Ríos y Rojo, applicant for a post in the Indies, recalled "that his parents, grandparents and uncles were always devoted to royal service". Mariluz Urquijo, 1998: 49-56, points out that this was common currency in the Hispanic world from the seventeenth century on.

[6] Several examples for the River Plate at the end of the eighteenth century can be consulted in AGI-Buenos Aires 27.

[7] AGS, SGU, legajo 6933, 34.

[8] The difference between "sale" and "benefit" is clear, as in the former case, the office became part of the buyer's patrimony, while in the latter case, he only acquired the right to hold it temporarily.

[9] See Francisco Andújar's study in this same volume.

Potosí and La Plata, handing over "un servicio pecuniario" ("a pecuniary service" or, in others words, a payment, as the sources discreetly put it) of 14,000 pesos—the post had been awarded by auction since its creation in 1659 (Araujo [1803] 1908, 396)—at the moment in which the second wave of post selling began in the imperial context of a Crown plagued by the costs of the War of the Austrian Succession (Burkholder and Chandler 1977). Pablo de Aoíz, of Navarran origin and born in 1709, had sailed to Buenos Aires at an early age with the merchant ships of Martínez de Murguía in 1717, and was very close to the powerful group of Bruno Mauricio de Zabala. He married Tomasa de Larrazabal in 1737, thus linking himself to an extensive and prestigious family of peninsular and Buenos Aires military officers. Pablo de Aoíz, who appears with the title "merchant" on one of his voyages from Cádiz, stayed on as *alguacil mayor* (major bailiff) until his son Tomás, the true recipient of the post, came of age (Tomás would have been 3 or 4 years old when the post was bought). In 1763, Pablo returned to Cádiz once again with the title of Corregidor* of Larrecaja. It is no coincidence that in this same year his son Tomás, who was probably going to work with his father in the business of distributing goods in Larrecaja, transferred the post of bailiff of the Royal Treasury of Potosí to his younger brother Fermín, by a process that, from a study of the information given by the source, is not clear (apparently the decision was his father's, probably as an advance on his inheritance). A few years later, in 1770, Tomás also returned to Cádiz with the post of *corregidor* of Chayanta, which is quite indicative of this family group's financial means and relationships.

In 1773 Fermín, who received a salary of 3,240 pesos a year as *alguacil*, agreed to pay his brother Tomás, who was still *corregidor* of Chayanta, 600 pesos per annum through an extrajudicial arrangement. When the Crown decided in 1780 to eliminate the post of bailiff, Fermín, who had spent all those years in Potosí and knew almost everyone in the public administration, was named official accountant at the Treasury of Potosí in January. He then decided, since the original post no longer existed, to stop paying his brother Tomás the salary of 600 pesos. In 1781, Tomás brought a complaint demanding this payment, and we learn that Fermín was no longer even living in the frozen climes of the Altiplano, but had moved to Buenos Aires and left in his place a substitute (whose name does not appear in the dispute) receiving a portion of Fermín's salary. We will leave this story here (in 1786 Fermín and his sister-in-law, Tomás's widow, finally agreed on the sum of 300 pesos, to be paid to her yearly). One of Tomás's sons, Mariano de Aoíz, also pursued a career in the state offices, and in 1792 began working at the Tobacco Accounting Office without remuneration; by July 1793 he had been named deputy inspector of the Tobacco Office, and in 1798 he was appointed third official of the Secretariat of the Audiencia, where he continued in service at least until 1803; in 1818 his name appears on the list of retired employees.

As we see, these examples show that this form of "inheriting" a post in the administration, or claiming it based on the merits of family members, was not at all uncommon. What is important to note, besides the phenomenon of the family networks that we have examined in these three cases, is this kind of private arrangement (remember that Lozano, too, offered to split his salary with his son Narciso prior to his retirement so that following his death he would succeed him) by means of which the post—more so in the example of the Aoíz family, since the original post had actually been bought—could be passed down as if it were a simple asset, by means of these rather peculiar arrangements. All of this gives a very accurate sketch of the type of bureaucratic career that these functionaries actually had, and we should point out that we are already at the threshold of the revolution leading directly to independence, when the functioning of the Spanish imperial bureaucracy is considered to be closer to the "rational" model. Indeed, we note several factors pointing in this direction, such as the obligation to present service records and qualifications obtained over the course of a period of employment, and the consideration of seniority in granting appointments. As we can see, on the eve of the revolution, the imperial administration was at a truly transitional juncture in its long history, between "patrimonial" logic—the sale or benefit of the positions—and a timid "rationalization", as Francisco Andújar rightly states in his chapter in this volume. We could say that we are midway between those Weberian models of two opposing ideal types: the "patrimonial" bureaucrat and his opposite, the "rational" bureaucrat. As we have said, many aspects of this peculiar bureaucratic phenomenon would persist largely unchanged in the period that followed. The notion, sustained repeatedly in many studies on the issue in Latin America, of the bureaucracy as an *apparatus* is totally inappropriate, as there was no apparatus external to society; there was only a *network of social relations*.

Latin American Bureaucracy after Independence

Changes in the organization of the bureaucracy

According to Alexis de Tocqueville (Tocqueville 1848, Dreyfus 2000), the continuity between the state and the past (which seemed to be refuted in his day by the political revolutions occurring from 1789) rested on the stability of the administrative structures that endured despite the profound political changes that took place after the French Revolution of 1789. The state bureaucracy, then, would be the link between the "past" of the former regime and the revolutionary "present," and thus the main thread of continuity between the two periods. Clearly, Tocqueville's observation gives rise to the first questions that one must ask regarding the independentist revolutions in Ibero-America: Did they overturn the bureaucratic structures? And if so, how were these structures rebuilt and bureaucratic functions resumed over the course of the revolution? Finally, what happened to the bureaucrats' careers when revolution came, whether or not there was continuity from one period to the other? It is clear that the answer to these questions can only come from the sort of detailed analysis found in each of these case studies; there can be no a priori answer, given the different circumstances, not only with respect to moments of rupture (1810, 1817, 1819, 1821, 1824), but also with respect to the form—violent or relatively peaceful—of this rupture. In this regard, Chile and Buenos Aires appear as polar opposites to Guatemala and Costa Rica. Brazil also represents a very singular example, as in that case, there was not even a rupture in the sovereign legitimacy, for Don Pedro, the king's son, was proclaimed emperor. He would govern with personnel that seemed to be characterized by a certain degree of continuity even though debate about this question is very lively in Brazil today (Murilo de Carvalho, 2006; Jancsó, 2005).

An important initial consideration is the matter of loyalty to the incipient new order. Both in Río de la Plata and in the beginnings of the *junta* established in Chile, strict allegiance to the "American" cause was demanded of bureaucrats who had served in the colonial period. Buenos Aires started by barring access to all "public jobs for anyone not born in these Provinces" except, logically, "current European employees," as long as they demonstrated "good conduct, love of country and adhesion to the Government." This provision speaks for the first time of "city rights" [sic], adding that "all the nations justify this rule… for in none is the government divided with disaffected men."[10] Before long, naturalization papers called "*cartas de naturaleza*" were implemented, and in 1812 the first triumvirate created an *ad hoc* form.[11] According to Barros Arana, in Santiago de Chile a provision from September 1811 stated:

> After this government has published the sacrosanct rules that define its system, indifference would be the highest crime for any member of the state; but this would be more serious for those with the honour of meriting immediate trust due to the posts by which the motherland has distinguished them. It is therefore not the belief of this power (the *junta**) that such low ideas are held by any class or individual of this privilege; however, it has resolved, in performing the duties of this high office, that hereafter the second entry in all service records shall be completed indicating the quality of patriotism, regarding which only well-grounded opinions will be considered valid; that indifference will be a crime meriting termination of service (Barros Arana 1887: VIII, 401).

As we know, in both cases, Chile and Río de la Plata, when open war broke out, the confiscation of property and in some cases the imprisonment of "European Spaniards" not sympathetic to the regime, was an indisputable fact, but we lack the sources to understand the extent to which Spanish inhabitants of the peninsula who quit their posts or retired did so willingly. The Buenos Aires *Registro Oficial*, throughout its pages, repeatedly records provisions excluding "suspicious" bureaucrats from public jobs, and some were not even allowed to retire (others were, but without remuneration). In Chile, the above-cited provision of 1811 states that "those who, regrettably, might act otherwise will be looked upon and treated as guilty of an offense against the state." In contrast, in Central America the transition to the new order, beginning in 1821, was relatively smooth, ensuring a certain degree of stability within the bureaucracy, and apparently did not include massive dismissals of officials (Sarazúa 2013; Rodríguez Solano 2013).

Yet there is another key issue here. As the link with the motherland breaks, it is vital that this bureaucracy under reorganization be aware that it is at the helm of a new political experiment (the construction of a sovereign state), and therefore that it must renounce being a small, passive branch of the big tree of imperial bureaucracy and learn to think ahead. We could call this change in the mindset of the state bureaucracy

---

[10] *RORA*, I: 91-92, (1810).

[11] *RORA*, I: 172, (1812); AGNA-X- 23-4-8 and X-3-8-10.

structural. This is no trifling thing, as it presupposes a transformation from a deeply-ingrained mentality, especially since, in the early years, virtually the sole concern was…paying the troops. All of this also presupposes a rather profound change in the organization of state offices. It is clear that this reorganization could not happen from one day to the next, but in two early cases, Buenos Aires and Chile, and from the very beginnings of the revolution, departments (also called ministries or secretariats) were created, and this meant a radical change in the structure of the state bureaucracy.

Three days after the coup d'état of 25th May 1810, Buenos Aires began to reorganize its government—for the moment, leaving untouched the legacy of the colonial period—creating two departments: Government and War, and the Treasury. An undated document from the Buenos Aires archives—probably from this same period—lays out a set regulation, accompanied by a short list of officials for each department. In Chile, as López Taverne (2013) relates, "four sections within the government, equivalent to the future secretariats or ministries of Government, the Treasury, War and Police," were created on 19th May 1811. In the Oriental Province of Uruguay, as Mario Etchechury (2013) points out, during the Artigas period the ministry of the Treasury existed by 1815, but this did not prevent the colonial tax-collection system from remaining largely in force. Again, given the different dates of independence, similar public entities were established in New Granada in 1819 (called the General Treasury *Superintendencia**) and in Central America from 1825 onwards, as Pablo Rodríguez Solano's research shows. What is important to highlight here with regard to the impact of independence on the bureaucracy is this actual reshaping of state offices. Furthermore, the reshaping was focused on two fundamental objectives that, as we know from data we have studied on the evolution of state finance, constituted the pillars of state-building throughout this period: the exercise of violence—whether internally or externally—and the search for adequate means to pay for it.

Employees, Administrators and the Forces of War: How Many and Where?

Let us begin by briefly reviewing the principal resources that the young nations born of the rupture with Spain possessed. More than 85 percent of the fiscal revenues of the two states that were established in the

Río de la Plata (the Argentine Confederation and Estado Oriental del Uruguay) depended almost exclusively on foreign trade and in particular, the level of imports, as they (and not exports) were the principal object of taxation, that is, these taxes would really be paid by consumers when they purchased imported merchandise. The same occurred during the brief experience when the Argentine Confederation confronted the State of Buenos Aires[12] (1852-1861). This phenomenon would extend to all the Latin American cases as they were being introduced in the tide of world trade. And we would point out that those imported goods, such as textiles, wine and spirits, tobacco and other similar products, were destined for mass consumption, which meant essentially that the great mass of the population supported the process of financing the state. This first group of experiences in state-building, which depended on the income derived from foreign trade for more than 70 percent of their revenues during this initial period, or better said, during the first decades of their existence as independent nations, also includes the Empire of Brazil and Venezuela.

A second group, consisting of Chile and Peru, would come next; in these two cases, at least half of the state's budget was financed by income generated by foreign trade, and that was followed in value by a number of taxes such as those that we will list shortly when discussing the remaining countries. The situation in Mexico was distinct, given its federalist, or rather, confederate structure. The federal state had customs duties as its principal resource (the *contingencia* or contingency, the percentage of the taxes collected by the states, was supposed to go to the federal government although it had very little effect on its total revenue), but in just a few years those resources derived from customs constituted more than 50 per cent of the total revenue during the period from 1820 until 1860.

Finally, the last group includes the rest of the Latin American states, which would have multiple and varied sources of financing: taxes levied on foreign trade–which was still in its infancy during this period for economies whose entry in the world market was more of a promise than a reality—the traditional colonial monopolies on specific products (salt, tobacco, liqueur, gunpowder), tributes paid by the indigenous population, tithes and ecclesiastical *censos**, partially expropriated by the state, old taxes on the circulation of merchandise, such as the *alcabala*, etc. It is essential to keep in mind that even in the 1850s, that is, decades after independence, taxes paid by indigenous peoples covered a substantial part

[12] The province of Buenos Aires constituted an independent state separated from the Argentine Confederation between 1852 and 1861.

of the state's budget in Bolivia, Peru, and Ecuador, as well as in various states in Mexico (Chiapas, Yucatan, and Oaxaca) and in the province of Jujuy in Argentina. This point shows us the extent to which the legacy of colonial fiscality continued to be ever-present in the middle of the nineteenth century in many Latin American nations, as we should not forget that, in addition, in Costa Rica, Guatemala, and El Salvador,[13] as well as in Equator and Colombia, the state monopolies continued to be one of the pillars of the fiscal system until the end of the nineteenth century.[14]

The Department of the Treasury

Taking into account what the preceding pages reveal about the new countries' finances, we should not be at all surprised to find that the Department of the Treasury constituted the "heart" of the state's bureaucracy in almost all the cases we have studied. Having inherited several institutions from the colonial period (the Tribunal of Accounts, Accounting Department, *Junta* of the Royal Treasury, customs house, etc.) and made up essentially in their first decades by employees that had worked for the previous administration—who possessed a *savoir faire* that could not easily be replaced—this department would become for all the post-revolutionary governments "the apple of their eyes". It is also of the greatest interest to verify how, in several examples (Costa Rica and New Granada [Colombia]), the offices inherited from the colonial epoch—in these two cases, they would respectively be the Tobacco Monopoly and the post office—fulfilled, to a certain extent, the function of backbone for the rest of the state bureaucracy and constituted the "model" for their future development. The examples the following table contains show the relative weight of the Department of the Treasury in the bureaucracy as a whole during the first decades of the era of post-independence.

It is necessary to recall, however—and the example of Uruguay almost illustrates the extreme in this regard, as its government went as far as to lease the right to collect customs duties (which constituted its primary source of revenues, as we already explained)—that a "parallel" bureaucracy also existed complementing the formal one. It was nevertheless assigned to collecting a series of farmed taxes (monopolies, sales taxes, bridge taxes, etc.); the merchants and financiers that collected these taxes had

[13] For the case of El Salvador, see Acosta Rodríguez, 2007.

[14] For an in-depth analysis, see Garavaglia 2010; also the studies included in Jáuregui 1998 and 2006, as well as in Aboites Aguilar and Jáuregui 2006.

their own workers, who were obviously not registered as state employees. And this authentic "bureaucracy in the shadows" was related to taxes that, as just explained, were in several cases (Colombia, Ecuador, Guatemala, Costa Rica, El Salvador, Chile) a substantial percentage of the fiscal revenues collected during the first five decades after the revolutions.

Table 4-1: Civil Employees of the State

	Ecuador 1843	**New Granada 1843**	**Chile 1845**
Government and Foreign Affairs	68	216	129
Justice and Education	31	146	176
Treasury	338	469	440
Total	**437**	**831**	**745**

Civil Bureaucracy and "Armed Bureaucracy"

As we have already seen, Max Weber thought that a close bond linked the history of the bureaucracy in the West (and in the East, as this very volume reveals[15]) and that of the military organization. Indeed, as it has been explained, the functions of order, discipline, hierarchy, and obedience, the archetypes of military behavior, were not at all foreign to many of the fundamental questions that shaped the history of the bureaucracy. In addition, we know that the independent states of Latin America primarily concentrated their spending on sustaining the forces of war and those of control or repression (police, night watchmen, customs guards, etc.) as well as on repaying the debts incurred by war.[16] It is therefore not surprising that most of the individuals that were paid a salary by the state formed part of one of these forces of war or repression.

The second table shows us several examples from the cases of the State of Guatemala (that is, as an autonomous state within the Confederation of Central America), province of Buenos Aires (a state that had complete constitutional, financial, monetary, and administrative autonomy in the framework of the Argentine Confederation) and New Granada (Colombia). As it can be observed, these data clearly indicate how dependent the

---

[15] See Christian Lamouroux's article about Song China in this volume.

[16] See Garavaglia 2010.

process of state-building in Latin America was on the activation of the forces of war and repression in its early stages.

Table 4-2: Civil Bureaucracy and "Armed Bureaucracy"

	Control, Repression, and Standing Army		***Civil Bureaucracy***		***Overall Totals***
Guatemala 1837	1.577	90%	180	10%	1.757
Buenos Aires 1841	9.222	97%	296	3%	9.518
New Granada 1843	7.006	89%	831	11%	7.837

And even though these examples might seem to represent only the most extreme examples, the phenomenon appears similarly in the rest of the cases that were studied. In Chile in 1850, there were 2,634 salaried members of the armed forces. If we compare this with 802 civil employees in the same year, we see that 76.6% of the salaried employees were in the military. However, we note that the police operated in cities and towns. In 1842, the Santiago police force had 255 employees (guards and watchmen), and in 1845 the newly structured police force of Valparaíso had 206. In other words, if we assume there were around 500 policemen and watchmen for all the cities and towns (a number that is clearly very low, but that doesn't matter for this particular argument), we see that around 80% of those who received a salary (whether state or municipal) were part of the military or forces of repression. We find the same in the State of Uruguay in 1838–1839, where 93% of the 2,831 people who received a state salary were in the military or the police (Etchechury 2013). We see similar proportions in Costa Rica in the Braulio Carrillo period at the end of the 1830s, with 969 members of the army and navy compared with around 90 civil employees (of these, about 50 belonged to the Treasury). We must also stress here that bureaucratic growth in Costa Rica was actually quite spectacular, despite the low figures, since it had only a handful of civil servants when it became an independent state (Rodríguez Solano 2013). In other words, in all the cases for which we have data, we see that in the mid-nineteenth century, state personnel were divided between a very small civil bureaucracy and a huge cohort of soldiers, police officers, night watchmen, rural watchmen, etc.

Kinship Networks and Bureaucracy after the Colonial Rupture

A case study of kinship networks and bureaucracy in Río de la Plata, (Garavaglia 2013) presents various examples of families of public servants that survived independence relatively intact. That said, the question should be: is it possible to extend this family paradigm to public servants from lower echelons of society? This question is hard to answer, because it would require meticulous research of source materials in order to unearth the family and social connections of those bureaucrats who were not from families of sufficient status to leave traces in the usual documents and genealogical studies. In other words, we would have to work with parish records and other types of documentation, and this is only possible when dealing with a tiny number of cases. If such an undertaking for a town of, say, 2,000 inhabitants would require endless hours of painstaking research, for a city like Buenos Aires, Santiago de Chile, Santafé de Bogotá or Montevideo in the mid-nineteenth century, with populations in the tens of thousands, it would likely exceed the powers (and perhaps the lifetime) of a single researcher. Moreover, the types of material sources relevant to this issue in Latin America in the nineteenth century are not comparable with what we have for Europe in the same period. For example, Maurizio Gribaudi has worked in France with a collection of letters of introduction and files on the individual careers of all the health personnel who worked in three ministries from 1803 to 1910 (Gribaudi 2009). So far, we have found no comparable source materials in the archives of the different countries we deal with here, and furthermore the colonial practice of keeping service forms in general fell into disuse, thus depriving us of a valuable tool for analysis. All of this leaves us, for the time being, without avenues for broadening the study of the relations between family ties and bureaucratic careers in the nineteenth century for less wealthy and powerful families.

In any event, one thing seems clear to us: in the latter stages of the colonial period, despite the obstacles inherent in bureaucratic careers which typically started in one city in the Iberian peninsula and continued at several other posts, in either the peninsula or the Americas, family networks had a major impact, something that was no longer true once these "itinerant" imperial bureaucrats disappeared. Indeed, after independence and the break with the metropolis this sort of transience largely disappeared too, with the evident result that bureaucrats had the opportunity to establish family ties within the society where they worked, and, as far as we know, there were no obstacles to doing so. In other words, it seems safe to assume that, with independence the weight of kinship relations in bureaucratic careers became even greater than it had been in the colonial era. The case of Ecuador demonstrates a peculiarity that reinforced the need to be immersed in a social network that had a certain relevance, as those that applied to become functionaries of the treasury were required to present a guarantee backed by a real estate in order to assume a post. Though it might appear obvious, we should point out that this obligation did nothing but reinforce the relations between the applicant to a job and the social networks that sustained him.

Bureaucracy from One Epoch to Another: Continuity or Rupture?

There are dozens of specific examples of families, such as the Portales in Chile that provided four generations of servants to the colonial power and later to the republican one, from the seventeenth and the mid-nineteenth centuries. Other examples would include the los Lessaga family in the province of Santa Fe in Argentina, who also served during the long century that spanned from the mid-eighteenth century until the 1860s, or the Acuñas de Figueroa in Uruguay, who worked in branches of the treasury during the colony, and then, without any difficulties, joined diverse administrations, such as those based in Buenos Aires and Uruguay, or the governments headed by Artigas and the *Cisplatina Republic**. We have been able to respond partially to this question for the case of Buenos Aires (Garavaglia 2013). There, we discovered a certain continuity for at least a third of employees working in the middle and lower echelons of the state's administration, but of course, with some changes in the organization of the offices and departments. It is, however, very difficult to be sure about this given the nature of the documents that have been preserved about it. But we can point out that Linda Arnold's study of Mexico between 1742 and 1835 reveals a similar panorama (Arnold 1988: 31-45). In any case, all the examples we studied clearly revealed that the functionaries working in the areas related to the treasury demonstrated the greatest stability between the two epochs examined. This specificity must be directly related to the evident necessity of possessing a certain level of training or education in order to be part of an office in this area that proved to be so essential for the construction of the state; as we have already stated at various points, fiscality constituted the heart of the process of forming the new states, in the European experience as well as in the American one.

Bureaucrats, jobs and *empleomanía**

Yet beyond family ties (and often as a continuation of them), we find ties to the social networks common to all people. This is where friendships, acquaintances and recommendations come into play. In his introduction to *La carta de recomendación*, Eduardo Wilde (1872: 132-133) wrote rather fittingly:

> For Castilians, a buen acomodo means a job where you work little but earn a lot. This explains the vast number of applicants for each vacant post. Getting a job requires determination, good relations. One would think that to obtain a position one needs aptitude, but this, which seems right at first glance, is sophistry in Buenos Aires. Aptitudes are the qualities given the least consideration. Favors, recommendations and patronage are growing at an alarming rate and have made this society ill. Truly, in Buenos Aires, the value of merit has disappeared or been adulterated. Having friends (who doesn't have friends in a country in which we are all equals!) is the greatest of advantages. Positions in which one earns money pass round among circles of friends.

This sounds like an echo of certain points from the 1843 report from the Treasury of New Granada (Memoria de Hacienda, Nueva Granada, 1843):

> As descendants of a people for whom empleomanía has been and continues to be an illness, we seek in jobs, not a productive occupation, but rather a comfortable means of subsistence. Hence the laziness and indolence in public service. Jobs are a sort of sinecure to which we all believe we have rights, and in whose performance collecting one's pay is the primary mission.

A little further on, the report adds:

> The Government finds itself molested and harassed by a swarm of foolish applicants who claim shamelessly to possess merits and abilities which they lack, and when it fills positions, it earns enemies in equal numbers to those excluded from the offices, and the appointee is either ungrateful or acts selfishly to avoid losing the job.

Finally, given the nature of bureaucratic organization in the colonial era, and despite the crown's attempts at reform in the late eighteenth century, it is no coincidence that the new citizens viewed state jobs through this particular lens.

Let's examine this matter of *empleomanía,* or "public sector job fever," more closely. The following table (3.7) shows the data we have gathered on the numbers of state officials per thousand inhabitants. Of course, this brings up countless problems—from the limited reliability of population data to the question of the limits on the types of jobs selected. We decided to count only bureaucrats who worked for the main state bureaucracy, that is, excluding provincial (or departmental, depending on the nomenclature of the country) and municipal employees. And these people all held "office" jobs, and thus we also exclude customs guards, night watchmen and all other personnel attached to any armed corps.

Table 4-3: Number of state employees per thousand inhabitants

Country	Year	
State of Guatemala	1837	0.3
Colombia	1843	0.6
Chile	1854	0.7
Ecuador	1839	0.7
Costa Rica	1848	0.9
Empire of Brazil	1877	2.6
State of Buenos Aires	1861	2.7

As we can see, comparing our data with those for Brazil in the study by Murilo de Carvalho (who disputes the well-known statement from Joaquim Nabuco [1883] regarding the imperial bureaucracy, "a burocracia era a vocação de todos" (Murilo de Carvalho 2006)), it does not seem that the charge of *empleomanía* is founded on real data. But, we note that these quantitative comparisons—so cherished by economists and sociologists—are often misleading, since the popular perception of this phenomenon generally comes from urban areas, precisely where bureaucrats were found in their greatest numbers. By basing our data on the entire population of independent states, at a time when the majority of the population was rural, we avoid an essential part of the question, which is, as we have said, the popular perception of bureaucrats: How much contact would a Guatemalan or Ecuadorian Indian have had with office-bound state officials at that time? In the case of the State of Buenos Aires (which is notable for having the highest rate of such public personnel), in 1861 the ratio of bureaucrats per thousand inhabitants would treble if we limited our base to the urban population. Moreover, a person living in the Buenos Aires countryside knew very well who the parish priest and justice of the peace were, but neither of these people received a real salary, and thus are not included in the table. As we said before, this indicator has its defects.

However, there is another way to view the ties within family groups, social networks, friendships, and state employees. Nobody would claim that being "from a good family" was actually a disadvantage with respect to the quality of the work that a candidate would have to perform; the very fact of being "from a good family" meant that he had the vote of confidence of his relatives, and the employer could approach these relatives if the employee neglected his duties. This is hardly surprising in an Iberian society in which family relationships played a central role in shaping social relationships. Of course this is far from Weber's ideal. In any event, certainly there were areas of work in office where specialized professional training and aptitudes were essential; no one works in land surveying at the topography department without knowing how to draw maps or without being an engineer (Gautreau y Garavaglia 2011). Nor was it easy to be a high-ranking employee at the Department of Public Works without possessing the indispensable technical knowledge, or as a professor at a university or clerk in the accounting office of the Treasury without having the required preparation.

By Way of Conclusion: Doubts, Questions, and Unfinished Business

Throughout this text, it has been a question of "functionaries" and "employees", as well as of "jobs", "salaries", "wages", etc. Sources in Spanish use these diverse terms although it is not always clear how they can be concretely differentiated for each one of the cases studied here. We think that *almost every individual that was paid wages or a salary by the state* falls within our area of interest, whether he was a civil employee—designated as a *functionary* or not—or a member of the armed forces or the diverse, varied security corps (urban and rural police, night watchmen, customs guards, etc.). The tables that have been presented here encompass posts from the superior head of the ministries—the employee that was ranked just below the minister, who was not always a permanent functionary—to the lowest-ranking doormen who, it should not be forgotten, often had the "magic key" that provided access to the arcana of their department. They do not include deputies, representatives, senators, etc., namely, those persons that belonged to political sectors, nor interest groups that temporarily represented those that exercised the rights of citizenship.

What, therefore, are the principal conclusions that we have drawn about this subject? Firstly, given the existence of a certain continuity in the lower and middle echelons of the administration—that was particularly visible for the functionaries of the treasury—the changes in the bureaucracy during this initial period relate above all to the structural aspect: they reorient the administration and above all, the fiscality, toward the objective of constructing a state/nation, thereby giving up its place as a little branch of the mighty Hispanic Empire. Secondly, the totals that we have arrived at reveal the existence of a bureaucracy that is slender compared to the overwhelming numbers made up by the forces of war and repression: 75 to 90 per cent of the individuals that received a salary from the state were included in those two rubrics. These findings appear normal in view of the need for a growing monopoly on the use of force at that stage when some of the traditional components of symbolic domination that had prevailed in the preceding period were starting to "falter". If we look at the figures included in Juan Pro's study, we see that the quantitative relation between civil functionaries and the military and repressive forces was not very different in the case of Spain.[17] The construction of the new components of symbolic domination would take time, and it was impossible "to do everything all at once", given the limited fiscal resources that were available. The dilemma was iron-hard: if canons had to be paid for, it would not be possible to build schools.

The subject of municipalities and other forms of local government should be addressed in the future. Indeed, aside from a few exceptions, the material that we have been analyzing at this stage of our research project has not allowed us to observe a substantial part of the process of state-building and that remains concealed from view when we use the memoranda and documents that were produced at the level of the state. That is, the town councils and mayors' office—which in many cases had quite an important role in the urban police, public hygiene, some public works and even in education—have not yet been taken into consideration

---

[17] See the study "The Origins of the State's Bureaucracy in Nineteenth-Century Spain" included in this book.

in our study. We once again refer to Juan Pro's work, when he writes of "A model of an Unwritten State" in the case of Spain. This question of the "lower echelons" of the bureaucracy continues to represent an unresolved matter for Latin American historiography on this subject, especially for places such as Mexico, Central America and the young Andean republics (Ecuador, Peru and Bolivia), where, for historical reasons, the towns and villages have maintained a long tradition of self-government. And we should not overlook the fact that for all of those experiences that were strongly influenced by the decisions taken at Cádiz (the cases of Mexico and the Central American countries are representative in this sense, see Acosta Rodríguez 2008), the role of the "constitutional" town councils, which were the inheritors of the constitutional charter written in Cadiz in 1812, was extremely important.

In our work, we likewise touched on a number of individuals that *exercised functions related to the construction of the state*, even if they had neither an official salary nor the real status of *functionaries*: notaries, surveyors, change agents, assayers of precious metals, etc., but at this stage we generally did not spend much time analyzing them. It would therefore be necessary to examine the role of these individuals in the future.

There also exists another very special category, made up by the ecclesiastics that undoubtedly exercised functions closely linked to the construction of the state, in the context of these societies where the church played a central role as the real *total institution*. A substantial part of family law was to remain in the hands of the ecclesiastical jurisdiction until civil codes were enacted (most of them were issued after the 1850s). This was also the case with education, where the church occupied a privileged position, as it did throughout the Catholic world of that epoch, even beyond the Iberian nations.

Archives

AGI Archivo General de Indias, Sevilla
AGS Archivo General de Simancas, Simancas
AGNA Archivo General de la Nación, Buenos Aires
AHN Archivo Histórico Nacional, Madrid

Published Sources

Araujo, J.J. de, [1803], (1908), *Guía de Forasteros del Virreinato de Buenos Aires…*, Buenos Aires: Junta de Historia y Numismática Americana.

Barros Arana, D., [1884], (2006), *Historia jeneral de Chile*, Santiago de Chile: Editorial Universitaria.

Henry, Á.A., [1815], (2000), *El oficinista instruido ó práctica de las oficinas reales...*, Madrid: Centro de Estudios Políticos y Constitucionales.

Memoria del Secretario de Hacienda de Nueva Granada al Congreso Constitucional de 1843, [1843], Bogotá: Imprenta de J. A. Cualla.

RORA, *Registro Oficial de la República Argentina...*, [1883], t. primero, Buenos Aires.

Wilde, E., [1872], (1935), "La carta de recomendación", in *Obras completas*, Buenos Aires: La Facultad: 123-39.

References

Aboites Aguilar, L., and Jáuregui, L., (eds.), (2006), *Penuria sin fin. Historia de los impuestos en México*, México: Instituto Mora.

Acosta Rodríguez, A., (2007), "Hacienda y finanzas de un estado oligárquico. El Salvador, 1874-1890", in García Jordán (ed.), *Estado, región y poder local en América Latina, siglos XIX-XX*: 17-79.

Annino, A., (coord.), (1995), *Historia de las elecciones en Iberoamérica, siglo XIX,* México, Fondo de Cultura Económica.

—. (1995), "Cádiz y la revolución territorial de los pueblos mexicanos 1812-1821", in Annino (coord.), *Historia de las elecciones en Iberoamérica, siglo XIX,*: 177-226.

Burkholder, M.A. - Chandler, D.S., (1977), *From impotence to authority: the Spanish Crown and the American audiencias, 1687–1808*. Columbia: University of Missouri Press.

Dreyfus, F., (2000), *L'invention de la bureaucratie. Servir l'état en France, en Grande-Bretagne et aux Etats-Unis (XVIIIe-XIXe siècle),* Paris, La Découverte.

Etchechury, M., (2013), "Taxation without Bureaucracy? Republican Governments and the Old Fiscal Regime in the Estado Oriental del Uruguay: An Approach through Tax Farming, 1828–1852", in Garavaglia - Pro Ruiz, *Latin America bureaucracy and the State Building Process (1780-1860)*: 373-403.

Garavaglia, J.C., (2010), "Algunos aspectos preliminares acerca de la 'transición fiscal' en América Latina: 1800-1850", *Illes i Imperis*, 13: 160-92.

Garavaglia, J.C. - Gautreau, P., (eds.), (2011), *Mensurar la tierra, controlar el territorio. América Latina, siglos XVIII- XIX*, Rosario, Editorial Prohistoria/State Building in Latin América.

Garavaglia, J.C. - Gautreau, P., (2011), "Inventando un nuevo saber estatal sobre el territorio: la definición de prácticas, comportamientos y agentes en las instituciones topográficas de Buenos Aires, 1824-1864", in Garavaglia – Gautreau (eds.), *Mensurar la tierra, controlar el territorio. América Latina, siglos XVIII- XIX*: 63-96.

Garavaglia, J.C. - Pro Ruiz, J., (2013), *Latin American Bureaucracy and the State Building Process (1780-1860),* Newcastle upon Tyne: Cambridge Scholars Publishing.

Garavaglia, J.C., (2013), "The Bureaucracy in Río de la Plata: Buenos Aires, 1760–1861", in Garavaglia - Pro Ruiz, *Latin America bureaucracy and the State Building Process (1780-1860)*: 240-272.

García Jordán, P., (ed.), (2007), *Estado, región y poder local en América Latina, siglos XIX-XX,* Barcelona: Publicacions i Edicions de la Universitat de Barcelona.

Jancsó, I., (2005), (ed.), *Independência: história e historiografia*, São Paulo, Hucitec/Fapesp.

Jáuregui, L., - Serrano Ortega, J.A., (eds.), (1998), *Las finanzas públicas en los siglos XVIII-XIX*, Instituto Moro/El Colegio de Michoacán/El Colegio de México.

—. (2006), *De riqueza e inequidad: el problema de las contribuciones directas en América Latina, siglo XIX*, México: Instituto Mora.

Kamen, H., (2005), *Spain, 1469-1714: A Society of Conflict*, London: Pearson Education Limited.

López Bejarano, P., (2013), "Organization and Uncertainty: the Administrative Dynamics of the *Secretaría de Hacienda* of Nueva Granada (1806-1851)", in Garavaglia - Pro Ruiz, *Latin America bureaucracy and the State Building Process (1780-1860)*: 134-165.

López Taverne, E., (2013), "The Structuring of a Bureaucratic Corps in the State-Building Process: Chile 1810 -1860", in Garavaglia and Pro

Ruiz, *Latin America bureaucracy and the State Building Process (1780-1860)*: 212-238.

Mariluz Urquijo, J.M., (1998), *El agente de la administración pública en Indias*, Buenos Aires: Instituto de Investigaciones de Historia del Derecho.

Murilo de Carvalho, J., (2006), *A construção da ordem*, Rio de Janeiro: Civilização Brasileira.

O'Donnell, G., (2007), *Disonancias. Críticas democráticas a la democracia*, Buenos Aires : Prometeo.

—. (2007), "La poliarquías y la (in)efectividad de la ley en América Latina", in O'Donnell, *Disonancias. Críticas democráticas a la democracia*: 151-78.

Rodríguez Solano, P., (2013), "State Metamorphosis: the Evolution of Institutional-Bureaucratic Structures in Costa Rica, 1786-1842", in Garavaglia - Pro Ruiz (2013): 100-133

Sarazúa, J. C., (2013), "Formation and Expansion of the Bureaucracy in Central America: the Federation and State of Guatemala (1823-1840)", in Garavaglia and Pro Ruiz, *Latin America bureaucracy and the State Building Process (1780-1860)*: 73-101.

Socolow, S.M., (1987), *The Burocrats of Buenos Aires, 1769-1810: Amor al Real Servicio*, Durham: Duke University Press.

Weber, M., (1978), *Economy and Society: An Outline of Interpretative Sociology.* Vol. 1. Berkeley: University of California Press.

CHAPTER FIVE

THE ORIGINS OF THE STATE'S BUREAUCRACY IN NINETEENTH-CENTURY SPAIN[1]

JUAN PRO

After the loss of its fleet in 1805, the French invasion of 1808, and six subsequent years of war and occupation, the fatally damaged Spanish monarchy witnessed the collapse of most of the bureaucratic apparatuses that had sustained it during almost 300 years. The succession of intermittent absolutist and liberal political regimes between 1810 and 1833 did not allow for either the reconstruction of the structures that had gone, or their replacement by more modern ones inspired by the experiences of England and France, as the Spanish revolutionaries had hoped. It was a dark time, in which the territorial administration was exceedingly tenuous and poor, as was expressed not only by contemporary attestations, but also by the documentary traces that have remained in archives. These administrative records were fragmented, or notably less extensive than those created during the reign of Charles IV (1788-1808).

The national state whose construction began during the 1830s and 1840s thus took this void—relative of course—as its foundation. If the political definition of the new State's institutions was fixed during the decade 1834-1844, its administrative definition was established during the following decade, from 1844 to 1854. This process was not finished by 1854, for only the key functions of the Spanish state were defined and these would remain essentially in place until the first third of the twentieth

[1] The writing of this article was assisted by the research project HAR2012-32713 of the Spanish National Plan of R & D, and it is a result of the collaboration of its Principal Investigator with the European Research Council Advanced Grant 230246 (2008 StateBgLatAmerica SH 6) as an associated researcher.

century (and in some important aspects until the last quarter of that century).

It is important to emphasize that unlike other historical examples of state-building, Spain's experience was based much more on the administration than on other aspects, such as the territory, national identity, political representation, and judicial protection of rights. The creation and progressive expansion of the public administration provided the backbone for the state and nation that identified with it. As a consequence, the rhythms of the country's political, social, and cultural life were inevitably marked by the process of the material construction of the State, in other words, by the creation, consolidation, and perfection of the public administration that supported it. As has just been stated, this process experienced its most intense period from 1834 to 1854, though it continued at least until 1870. It reached its declared objective of controlling the centralized territory in the last decades of the nineteenth century. The process can be considered as having been finished by the first decades of the twentieth century.

What constituted that administration, charged as it was with concretizing the Spanish Liberals' plan for a nation? What human resources could be used to reconstruct *Spain* in a territory that had been drastically reduced because of the loss of most of her American empire?

A Bureaucracy in Evolution: Between the Kingdom and the Nation

The bureaucracy underpinning the Kingdom of Spain that Ferdinand VII (1808-1833) inherited was barely the shadow of one that had sustained his predecessors, Charles IV (1788-1808) and Charles III (1759-1788). The king, however, was reluctant to accept the lack of continuity with the epoch that had preceded the Napoleonic wars. That continuity had been destroyed as a result of the cycle of revolutions and wars that the French Revolution had initiated in Europe and America. Therefore, he vainly aspired to maintain the political and administrative models that emanated from the reforms that the House of Bourbon had introduced in the machinery of the aging Spanish monarchy.

This determination essentially meant relying on a bureaucracy that had five fundamental components:

- Justice: with its network of *consejos** and *audiencias** that structured the territory, reinforced the king's sovereignty, and maintained equilibrium among the interests that existed in the society;
- Treasury: even if the eclectic assortment of taxes it administered was always insufficient, it managed to perform, year after year, the miracle of making sure that the kingdom survived;
- Army and Navy: although they were progressively weakened due to this lack of resources, which made it impossible to think of establishing an independent foreign policy, they at least performed relatively efficiently the repressive function that allowed the king to preserve the unity of the territories that were still his, namely, peninsular Spain, the two adjacent archipelagoes, and overseas empire; it was still believed in 1814-1815 that it would be possible to restore the Spanish crown's power in the American territories;
- The Church: it carried out extremely important administrative functions as a specific institutional complex, which was both part of the royal bureaucracy and external to it. It assured the registry of births, marriages, and deaths, shared the function of collecting taxes with the Royal Treasury, controlled the use of the printing press, exercised police functions, and indoctrinated the population on a daily basis about loyalty to the monarchy and the acceptance of a common identity that was much more Catholic than Spanish;
- The municipalities: a network of thousands of organs of power and administration that, even if they represented the interests of the local oligarchies, which were solidly implanted in the councils and *cabildos*,* they also served as the principal framework for supervision and control of the population, a source of collective identity, and intermediaries for most of the transactions between the monarchy and its subjects: towns, families, individuals.

An exception would have to be made regarding the colonial Administration in Cuba, Puerto Rico and the Philippines, which acquired special characteristics after the refoundation of the Spanish empire in 1836, and was even framed under its own Ministry – the Overseas Ministry - in the period from 1863 to 1899. But this exception, which will not be considered in detail in this chapter, was overwhelmingly the result of a militarized colonial Government, and so it can be considered in the general picture as a dimension of the action of the Army and the Navy (Fradera, 2005).

These five superimposed administrative networks had traditionally assured the functioning of the Spanish monarchy, even in its "modern" incarnation as the *Kingdom of Spain* after the eighteenth-century reforms. The first three—Justice, Treasury and the Army—were able to assert directly the crown's power. The fourth, the Church, remained a tremendously efficient power structure, as it was the only one whose hierarchization assured that it exercised centralized control over the entire territory via its own agents. In return, it was a network with a certain degree of autonomy, as the crown shared control over it with the Papacy. The last-mentioned administrative network, the municipalities, in fact constituted the key to the kingdom's administration, for without their support, the crown was incapable of enforcing laws, obtaining information about the kingdom's inhabitants and resources, collecting taxes or even recruiting soldiers.

In spite of all the efforts to centralize and standardize the kingdom that the eighteenth-century kings and their reformist ministers made, Spain continued to be a conglomeration of municipalities in 1800. So, when in 1808 the French invasion made all the monarchy's centralized apparatuses disappear at the stroke of a pen, resistance against the occupants spontaneously took the shape of local revolutionary *Juntas**, which expressed the fundamental identities and legitimacy of the municipal powers in the political-military sphere.

The defeat of Napoleon and José Bonaparte in 1813-1814 brought about the restoration of the Bourbon monarchy, with Ferdinand VII as the absolute monarch. Nevertheless, the royal bureaucracy and the legitimacy of its institutions had reached such a degree of deterioration that it was not possible to restore them completely. The Treasury, for example, was bankrupt, and all the efforts to rectify it by administrative reforms and better management failed when faced with an ideological prejudice that obstructed any structural change. This resulted in indebtedness and ultimately the suspension of payments in 1836. The Army and Navy could not be reconstructed after the rout of 1808-1810 due to the lack of financial resources. In any case, they had been shaken to their foundations by the logic of six years of war against the French and the continuation of the conflict against the American rebels. This new logic imposed recruitment and promotion based on merit, and that put an end to the privileges and hierarchies of the Ancien Régime. The system of justice, which had previously constituted the backbone of territorial control, was discredited because of its slowness and inefficiency, especially when its organs such as *consejos* and *audiencias* were compared to the more executive mechanisms of government, such as secretaries, *intendentes**, governors, and general captains. The justice system's disrepute was so extreme because of the ambiguity that the institutions of justice had displayed when confronted by the French invasion, when many of its members had surrendered to the invaders. The king himself had given the *coup de grace* to the traditional idea of justice when he made an exception to the logic of a full restoration of the Ancien Régime, by assimilating into the crown the jurisdictions that had corresponded to the *señoríos** until 1811. The destruction of the *señorios*, as the last link in the traditional chain that constituted the system of justice, was initiated by the *Cortes** of Cadiz in 1811, confirmed by Ferdinand VII in 1814, and consummated by the progressive liberals in 1837. It laid the foundations for the creation of a new system of justice, entirely run by the state, which would be constructed very slowly between the Constitution of 1812 and the Organic Law of Judicial Power in 1870.

As for the Church, after having been divided, it withdrew to an ambiguous stance during the French invasion, and lost its connection with the monarchy's secular institutions during the war (1808-1814). Both the administration of José I and *patriots* loyal to Ferdinand VII, who took refuge in Cadiz, started to recover for the state the functions that were its own, as well as its control over the national church. The successive initiatives to disentail the Church's property, which were launched by José I, the liberals of the Constitutional Triennium (1820), and, finally, the Progressives (1835-36, 1841, 1855), put an end to the ecclesiastical patrimony, weakened the clergy's material and human bases, discredited the Church's intervention in civil matters, and ended up reducing the clergy to the condition of state employees, as they received their income from the government. Ferdinand VII himself contributed to the progressive annulment of the Church as a civil power when, after his second absolutist coup in 1823, he made a second exception to his intention of fully restoring the Ancien Régime by maintaining *de facto* the abolition of the Inquisition.

In almost all of the kingdom's administrative areas—Treasury, Justice, Army and the Church—rupture rather than continuity predominated in the first third of the nineteenth century. In the fifth of these aforementioned areas—the municipal sphere—continuity prevailed over rupture, assuring the reproduction of mechanisms and groups of power from the Ancien Régime in the new national state.

Thus, the Spanish national state that was constructed in the nineteenth century was neither the result of the reconstruction of the administrative apparatuses inherited from the monarchy of the Ancien Régime, nor the product of their reform. It doubtlessly had elements of continuity, because the territory, population, and cultural habits required it. But these elements persisted, as has been pointed out, particularly at the local level. This level continued to have a fundamental importance throughout the nineteenth century, having constituted the base of the kingdom's government under the Ancien Régime. The monarchy's large centralized institutions collapsed and were replaced by new ones: a new army, a new treasury, and a new system of justice would form part of the State. There was also a new national church that resulted from the process of reforming the clergy that the revolutionaries began in 1835-1836. It was completed by reaching an agreement with Rome through the Concordat of 1851.

The Reform of the Church and Construction of a National Army

The destruction of the Church's secular power was the key that allowed the Spanish liberals to promote the construction of entirely new state institutions during the second third of the nineteenth century. In the first place, it opened up public spaces that the Church had previously occupied; the State could then take them over by implementing its own bureaucracy. The abolition of the Inquisition—de *facto* in 1820 and *de jure* in 1834—made it possible for the state police to be installed in a sphere that the Church had previously occupied and for the government to control the printing press. In addition, charity, public education, population censuses, civil registries, and many other aspects of the State's administration all grew on the ruins of the former ecclesiastical structures.

Reforming the Treasury was a prerequisite, not only for constructing a viable state, but for making sure that the essential functions of controlling the territory and covering the court's expenses were completed. The process of state-building was equally conditioned by the possibility of removing the Church from the realm of power and by wresting resources away from it, though it was not possible, for ideological reasons, to initiate such changes when an absolute monarch still ruled. When Ferdinand VII died in 1833, the only option his widow had that would allow her to retain the throne for their daughter was to permit the Liberals to take power. They were only ones that could carry out the profound reform of the Treasury that was needed to balance, to the greatest possible extent, revenues and expenditures.

Having lost its American empire and the financial means that the transatlantic commerce and remittances of precious metals provided, the monarchy could only be sustained—which meant basically, in this period, financing its army and navy—by direct contributions imposed on internal productive activities, basically farming and raising livestock. This project of generating a far-reaching direct contribution that would ensure the kingdom's financial solvency had been launched years earlier by the Marquis of the Ensenada (with the Unique Contribution of 1749) and tried out several times by the Liberals when they ruled (1810, 1813, 1821, 1837, 1841 and 1842). However, it collided with an insurmountable obstacle: the existence of another direct contribution that had been efficiently collected during centuries, though it was attributed to the ecclesiastical treasury rather than the royal one. The tithe already taxed internal productive activities, especially those involving agricultural products and livestock, so that it was not possible to impose another direct tax on them. Such a reform of the Treasury, which was gradually turning out to be the only remedy for the fiscal bankruptcy of the monarchy, depended on the prior abolition of the tithe, and that implied confronting the Church and searching for alternative resources that could be used to finance the clergy.

The Liberals launched a first attack against the ecclesiastical tithe in 1821, by reducing it by half, which served to start the process of its discredit and led to difficulties when collecting it. These acts made it easier subsequently to abolish the tithe, initially in 1837, and then definitively in 1841. At that moment, the obstacles that had impeded a tax reform until then were overcome, and reform was carried out in 1845, creating a system of direct taxes inspired by the one that had been started in revolutionary France. This fiscal change had very important consequences, because it determined the type of bureaucracy that the new state would have—developed from the model of a treasury designed to administer these direct taxes—and, at the same time, the type of control that would be exercised over the territory and the relationship that would exist between the State and citizens.

At the same time, the abolition of the tithe in 1837-1841 made it necessary to seek an alternative model for the economic sustenance of the clergy and Catholic religion. The reform was propelled by a state that continued to be denominational, and by political leaders that were, in their great majority, practicing Catholics, even if they were progressive liberals and could be anti-clerical. They knew that they lived in a Catholic country with very few religious minorities. It should be born in mind that at the same time as the Church was despoiled of the tithe, the collection of which had supported the clergy and financed religion during the previous centuries, those same Liberals nationalized almost all the Church's possessions, depriving it of an immense patrimony that had been accumulated during centuries.

The Church was offered the option of having the state take charge of sustaining its activities, through the Contribution for Religion and the Clergy that turned the clergy into salaried state employees. After several successive reforms in 1840, 1844 and 1849 that progressively implemented this new *entente*, the Concordat signed with the Holy See in 1851 appeased Church-State relations. It made the Church accept the sale of its lands, the abolition of the tithe, and the clergy's economic dependency on the state budget as *fait accompli,* as well as the correlate that the government acquired the power to oversee, discipline, and reform the clergy.

The creation of a national army completely independent from the old royal armies could seem to be unrelated to the question of church—state relations, but it was, in fact, closely related to it. The so-called *Mendizábal Sale of the Church's Lands* in 1835-1836 marked the first phase of ecclesiastical disentailment in Spain. It allowed the State to acquire enough extraordinary resources to embark on the formation of a permanent army. This army was thus an imperious necessity in order to affirm the triumph of the liberal alternative in the construction of the State, given that the absolutists' resistance had started to take form in 1833 around the pretender to the throne, Don Carlos. It sparked a civil war that was to last seven years, commonly known as the *First Carlist War* (1833-1840). Receiving considerable support from the Church and autocratic powers of Central and Eastern Europe, Carlism acquired strength throughout Spain and was hegemonic in large areas of the north. The course of the war seemed to favor the Carlist cause during its first years. Both a military and financial revolution were needed to defeat it; this revolution consisted, precisely, in the creation of a state.

Nationalizing the Church's possessions not only meant debilitating the adversary but also, simultaneously, acquiring a prodigious amount of resources to finance the creation of a large regular permanent army. These resources were mobilized in the long term by selling the Church's possessions in public auctions. In addition to gathering extraordinary funds, these sales made it possible to win over to the liberal cause the purchasers of Church's disentailed property who belonged to the upper and middle classes. In the short term, the credit would be used to obtain immediate financial resources by offering the patrimony of nationalized buildings as a guarantee.

Such resources would be used to carry out a levy *en masse*, which the government's propaganda would dub as the "levy of a hundred thousand men"; it allowed the State to send a massive contingent of armed uniformed men to the war front. 125,000 men were conscripted in 1835, as compared to the annual drafts of the previous years that only drafted 25,000. Military service was introduced at the same time to assure the permanent renewal of this army made up of armed citizens. A general staff was also created to organize and direct the army. And the very buildings that had been despoiled from the Church—churches, schools, convents and monasteries—served as expedient barracks where the army could be housed and trained while real quarters could not be constructed *ad hoc*.

This entire process was completed within three to four years, giving the operation the appearance of a veritable revolution. At its end, in 1839-1840, Carlism was defeated; the consolidation of a constitutional state in Spain was thereby ensured by warfare. This state had a standing army, patrimony sufficient to cover the fiscal deficit that had been inherited, and a number of buildings that had been attained by selling the Church's possessions. These buildings were used to house not only military quarters but also offices for the civil bureaucracy that began to be deployed throughout the territory, thereby making the new state present there. The Church had lost the material basis of its power and was forced to restrict itself to its spiritual labor. When peace was finally established (first when the Vergara Agreement was signed in the north in 1839, and then when the Carlists' defeat was consummated in their last stronghold in the east in 1840), the construction of a civil bureaucracy was begun, the second phase in the construction of the state, following the first that consisted of establishing a permanent army.

The Deployment of the Public Administration

If during the 1830s the strengthening of the State had taken a giant step in Spain when a national army was created and the Church's civil power repealed, a more "peaceful" phase of state-building started in the 1840s; it consisted in designing and extending the civil bureaucracy that sustained the public administration throughout the entire territory. The adversary that had to be defeated during this new phase was no longer the Church, restricted to its new dimensions and functions, but the local powers. They turned out to be a much more difficult rival, for they were not definitively defeated until the end of the nineteenth century.

The design for the new administration corresponded to a rational homogenous conceptualization. Based on the model of France, it was adapted to the Spanish reality with very few changes, these being due to fewer resources, and a less resolute will to make the territory uniform.

Expressed in a multitude of regulations, statements of purpose, parliamentary speeches and juridical manuals, the doctrine achieved its purest expression in the writings of Alejandro Oliván, a specialist in administrative matters from Aragón. He was integrated into the ranks of the Moderate Party and became spokesman for the project of a hegemonic state during the so-called *moderate decade* (1844-1854). He also wrote a treatise on the subject (Oliván 1843), in addition to implementing the principles that it contained while holding posts at all echelons of the administration. Another important Administration expert of the time, in this case Galician, was Manuel Colmeiro (1818-1894), who systematized for the first time the juridical doctrine developed as a correlate of the development of the State as Administration: *administrative law* (Colmeiro, 1850).

During the initial years, the bureaucracy was virtually non-specialized and structured simply by ministries. It was based on the classic schema in six ministries that assured the limited functions assigned to the state in the 1830s (State, War, Navy, Treasury, Justice, and Interior). These ministries had begun functioning in the rooms of the royal palace itself, as organs that executed the absolute monarch's will. Each *Secretary of State* had small offices set up in the palace until they started to move out in 1826 due to the lack of space. They were first transferred to nearby buildings (the Grimaldi Palace, in front of the Royal Palace in Madrid) and subsequently, in the 1840s, to others dispersed on the capital's most emblematic streets (Pro 2001).

The aggregate of these ministries located in Madrid formed the nucleus of the *Central Administration of the State*: about 72,000 employees at the beginning of the construction of the liberal State in around 1837. This total grew by 26% and reached 91,000 employees by 1870 in the following third of the century. It had about 110,000 employees, 21% more, in the following third of the century, until the end of the nineteenth century (Table 5-1):

Table 5-1: Personnel in the Service of the Central Administration: Spain 1837-1900

	Presidency of the Council of Ministers	State	Grace and Justice	War	Navy	Interior	Treasury	Development	Total
1837		133	2893	47822		3767	17369		71984
1850		309	2562	26339	13247	4404	22168	2249	71278
1870[1]	258	346	2497	31255	15135	13577	21728	6343	91224
1880[2]	157	350	2806	21689[4]	17235	25121[4]	22721[5]	5790	95869
1890[3]	166	361	3758	39188	15699	9424	22307[5]	8705	99608
1900	139	306	3082	55961	10240	9255	21086[5]	10613[6]	110682

Source: Table based on the data provided by Jordana and Ramió (2005), p. 1004, about the figures contained in the State's general budgets.

Notes:

[1] Budget for the fiscal year 1869-1870.

[2] Idem year 1880-1881.

[3] Idem year 1890-1991.

[4] In 1880 the Civil Guard personnel (between 16,025 and 16,101 men) were counted as employees of the Ministry of the Interior instead of the Ministry of War, as was usually done.

[5] In 1880, 1890 and 1900, the corps of the Customs Guards (14,519, 14,664 and 14,744 men) and that of the state-owned mines, which had previously been counted as part of the Treasury, were added to the Ministry of the Treasury's own personnel (6,951, 6,435 and 5,760), which was then considered as constituting "other organisms" (15,770, 15,872 and 15,326).

[6] In 1900, the employees of the ministries that had been divided up into Development (Agriculture, Industry, Commerce, and Public Works: 6,311) and Public Education and Fine Arts (4,302) were added up together.

In showing the distribution of the employees by ministry, the table reveals the structure and functions of the incipient Spanish state in the nineteenth century. It demonstrates that two-thirds of the personnel employed in the state's service were attached to the ministries of War and Navy, which included the Army and the Navy. Of 71,984 men in 1837, 47,822 (without counting the recruits) were in the army or navy; it was undoubtedly a period of civil war but also—for that very reason—the moment when the State, with its own bureaucracy and a standing army assigned to achieving compliance, started to assert its control over the territory.

The rest of the ministries that made up the civil bureaucracy slowly became larger, starting with the 24,162 employees in 1837 (33% of the State's employees) rising to 31,692 (44%) in 1850, once the Carlist war ended and the country was at peace. They numbered 44,834 (49%) in 1870; this total would be similar to the number of employees in 1890 and 1900. Throughout the nineteenth century, therefore, the civil bureaucracy did not exceed 50% of all the State's employees, as compared to the weight of the Army and Navy, which had to assure its essential repressive functions (including the colonial presence in Cuba, Puerto Rico, and the Philippines until 1898).

In addition to the Army and Navy, other armed forces existed that ensured the "monopoly of legitimate physical violence" on behalf of the State: the Civil Guard and corps of the Customs Guards, the military sectors of the Ministries of the Interior and Treasury respectively. As we shall subsequently see, the inclusion of personnel from these corps in the total number of employees of the ministries in which they served distorts the significance of these figures as representing the "civil bureaucracy", as it elevates the numbers of armed forces that were subordinated to both the Ministry of War and their own. These armed, organized groups, which were corps subject to military discipline, guaranteed the State's coercive power and, therefore, were crucial so that the civil bureaucracy—big or small—could support itself, act efficiently and assert its authority. Given the situation that existed before 1836, when there was not even a regular permanent army, the State's coercive power was rapidly asserted in the subsequent decades, to the point that in 1860 there were almost 200,000 men in arms (163,415 in the army, 8,176 in the navy, 11,586 in the Civil Guard and 12,962 in the corps of the Customs Guards, a figure from 1861).

The civil bureaucracy of the Spanish state maintained a small foreign service (133 employees in 1837, 306 in 1900), which was established in the Ministry of the State. Its administration was structured in three branches: civil, economic, and judicial (*Almanaque del Empleado*, 1868-1936).

Of the five branches, the *Judicial Administration* maintained the greatest continuity with the monarchy of the Ancien Régime. It was not organized strictly as an independent *judicial power*, but rather as a branch of the Central Administration, which commonly referred to it as the *Administration of Justice*. Its functioning was ensured by the Ministry of Grace and Justice that always suffered from a serious dearth of human and financial resources. The system was based on the division of the territory into 446 *judicial districts.*[1] Their tribunals administered justice in the first instance; 49 provincial *courts*, 15 territorial *courts* and a Supreme Court constituted the three successive instances to which one could appeal. In addition, there was a system of registries (Land Registry Office and Notary Publics), which was completed in 1870, when the responsibility for the civil registry was seized from the Church that had managed to hold onto it until that date.[2] The Ministry had only 3,000 employees to make this entire network function, a total that remained almost the same throughout the century. It is clear that deployment of the Spanish state throughout the territory did not rely significantly on the deeds of judges and tribunals, and this clearly differentiated it from the Anglo-Saxon model. In fact, the Administration of Justice clung to concepts inherited from the Ancien Régime until a very late date, or at least until the Organic Law of Judicial Power was passed in 1870.[3]

It was the bureaucracy of the Treasury rather than the judicial administration that secured the State's presence throughout the territory and directed the expansion of a public administration. This second branch of the government, known as the *Economic Administration*, was placed under the authority of the Ministry of the Treasury. This department had received an initial impetus from "the government action", strictly speaking from the Bourbon monarchy, and, for this reason, it ensured the State's active presence throughout the territory from the initial moments when the contemporary state was being constructed. Its 17,369 employees in 1837 constituted the bulk of the civil bureaucracy (71%), a total incomparably higher than that of any other ministry of that period, except for the Ministry of War.

---

[1] *Real Decreto* (Royal Decree) of 21-IV-1834; hereafter R.D.
[2] *Ley* (Law) of 17-VII-1870; hereafter L.
[3] Provisional Law of 15 September.

Both the number of employees it had and the essential nature of the functions it carried out—collecting funds and channeling them to cover the State's expenses—gave the bureaucracy of the Public Treasury a strategic place in the Administration. The fiscal bureaucracy enjoyed a high degree of autonomy with respect to the political power, and this allowed it to remain untouched by the upheavals caused by the war, revolution and the changes of regime during the first half of the nineteenth century (López Garrido 1984). The 17,369 civil servants that the Treasury registered in 1837 were the successors of the 14,300 that Lerena referred to during the reign of Charles IV: 10,729 employees in the tax section and 3,571 in Customs House Offices (Lerena 1789). Not only did the Treasury retain its importance, but it became more significant because of the major reforms of the 1840s, especially the tax reforms of 1845 and the standardization of its accounting system in 1850. As a result, in 1850 the Economic Administration could count on a stable hierarchical bureaucracy made up of 22,168 men (70% of a civil bureaucracy that was already quite stable).

Nevertheless, these figures about the Ministry of the Treasury are misleading if the weight of corps of the Customs Guards [*Cuerpo de Carabineros*] is not borne in mind as they made up more than 60% of its personnel. The guards came from from the night patrols and custom house officers of the Ancien Régime, as they constituted armed forces (about 3,500 men at the beginning of the reign of Charles IV in 1788, already almost 6,000 in 1820) assigned to defending the authority of the Royal Treasury and, especially, to combating smugglers. During the last years of the absolutist monarchy, these forces were replaced by the corps of the Customs Guards of the Coasts and Borders[4] that the Liberals reorganized in 1842 and renamed as the Corps of the Kingdom's Customs Guards. This corps, which employed 13,288 men in 1855 (14,744 in 1900), was military in nature and was subordinated to the Ministry of War, although it was functionally in the service of the Ministry of the Treasury. Even if this force contributed to the Economic Administration by providing it with a special power to obtain obedience, it is obviously problematic to consider this corps as part of the civil bureaucracy. Even without the Customs Guards, the Ministry of the Treasury employed between 7,000 and 8,000 employees, a total that continued to define it as the largest non-military ministry of that period. However, this total number of employees was much more comparable to those of the other ministries.

---

[4] *Real Cédula* (Royal Document) of 9-III-1829; hereafter R.C.

The Ministry of the Treasury had its central offices in Madrid. They were organized in several head offices that changed over the years: the office of Property Taxes, Incomes, Accounting, Treasury, Public Debt, and State Properties. The Ministry's force and capacity to intervene were, nevertheless, based on the fact that it had a peripheral network of employees organized and spread out all over the territory. In fact, only a small number of the Treasury's employees (fewer than 10%) worked in the central offices in Madrid, while the majority were placed in provincial branches. In 1839, out of a total of 19,353 employees, there were 17,997 in the provinces and 1,356 in Madrid (Nieto 1966).

The Treasury's personnel was distributed in this way because the Ministry had its own office in each province. This structure was inherited from the system of *intendencias* that dated back to the Ancien Régime and had been adapted to the new territorial division into 49 provinces carried out in 1833.[5] The fiscal reform of 1845 organized these offices, which were hereafter called the Provincial Administrations of the Treasury. In each one of these offices, an *intendente* supervised an administrator, treasurer, accounting department, official inspectors, and tax collectors. The structure of the judicial districts—which I referred to when discussing the judicial administration—was used to subdivide the provinces also for fiscal purposes, therefore distributing the sub-delegates, district administrators, and receivers throughout the territory. Subordinates, messengers and tobacconists made up the lowest level of this structure.[6] The system was perfected over time until the 1880s, when the *intendentes* of the Treasury were replaced by the *provincial delegates of the Treasury,*[7] and the administrations by *provincial delegations of the Treasury.*[8] *Subordinate administrations of the Treasury* were created in the important cities that were not provincial capitals.[9]

The fiscal bureaucracy also included the customs administrations (28 principal offices and 140 secondary ones, 11 offices of weights and measures, seven auditing offices for registries and three offices for free ports), Tribunal of Accounts for the Kingdom, Tribunal of Pensioners, Mint, National Stamp Factory, several state-owned mines (Almadén, Río

---

[5] R.D. of 26-IX-1836.
[6] R.D. of 23-V-1845.
[7] L. of 9-XII-1881.
[8] L. of 24-VI-1885.
[9] L. of 11-V-1888.

Tinto, Linares, Falset and the salt-mines of Torrevieja), eight tobacco factories (as fiscal monopolies) and lottery offices (Moral 2007: 38-53).

The Economic Administration that has just been described became so important not just because it guaranteed that the State's acts would be financed, but also as it offered an organizational model for the growth of the entire bureaucracy in contemporary Spain. The transfer of this model to the rest of the Central Administration took place in the middle of the nineteenth century, when Juan Bravo Murillo presided successively over the Treasury Ministry (1849-1852) and the Council of Ministers (1851-1852) (Pro 2006). During his tenure at the Treasury from 1849 to 1850, Bravo Murillo had carried out a number of essential reforms including the creation of a General Board for Contentious Matters specializing in defending the interests of the Public Treasury before the courts of law.[10] He also oversaw the standardization of the Ministry's departments, as they were re-redistributed into eight general offices: Public Treasury, Accounting, Contentious Matters, Direct Contributions, Indirect Contributions, Customs and Tariffs, Revenues from State-Owned Monopolies, and Fiscal Properties.[11] The Ministry's documents were gathered in one archive,[12] and an *Official Bulletin of the Ministry of the Treasury* was established so that its provisions would receive more publicity (as of 1-I-1850). There were also a number of minor regulations that defined the criteria for the daily operation of its offices and the subjugation of its personnel to a strict hierarchical order. The operational plan that was thus established and that the Moderate party considered to be a model, was "exported" to the remaining ministries. When Bravo Murillo was president of the Council of Ministers in 1852, he introduced a general set of regulations about civil servants inspired by the Treasury's administrative practice; it would regulate the civil service in Spain until 1918.[13]

The panorama of the Central Administration of the State was completed by a third element, the *Civil Administration*. This designation was employed for that part of the administration that came under the Ministry of the Interior. The bureaucracy of this ministry was not particularly large at the onset of the contemporary state: only 3,767 employees in 1837 (15% of the civil bureaucracy of the Central State at that moment). Such a first impression about its lack of importance,

[10] R.D. of 28-XII-1849.
[11] R.D. of 21-VI-1850.
[12] R.D. of 25-VI-1850.
[13] R.D. of 18-VI-1852.

however, is completely erroneous and should be redressed by four fundamental considerations.

The first consideration concerns the figures themselves, for the number of workers that Ministry of the Interior employed grew more quickly throughout the nineteenth century than that of any other ministry, as the total reached 9,255 in 1900. It represents a 145% growth from 1837 (as compared to 21% for the Treasury, 17% for War, or 6% for Pardon and Justice).

The second point is also related to the total number of employees, as these figures would be quite different if the Civil Guards were included as employees of the Ministry of the Interior. Just as was the case with the customs guards, the Civil Guard was a military corps that was organically answerable to the Ministry of War, but it was in practice at the service of the Ministry of the Interior. The regulation of public order had been previously entrusted to a small inefficient police corps (created during the last years of the absolutist monarchy), and to the National Militia during the revolutionary period. This extremely politicized corps of armed citizens was abolished by the Moderates when they took power and it was replaced in 1844 by something completely different to guarantee public order: a strictly hierarchized professional corps of civil servants, which was subject to the Central Government and military discipline.[14] This corps, the Civil Guard, would have a repressive function and would work very efficiently to help centralize the government's power throughout its more than 160 years of existence (López Garrido 2004).

The Civil Guard was initially defined as a corps of "rural guards", but it was also soon used for repressive functions in the cities. In any case, the control of public order in the rural areas turned out to be crucial for the State's operations in a country where the majority of the population lived in small towns and villages. Originally composed of 6,000 men, this corps grew rapidly and was deployed throughout the territory, ensuring the government's control over the country. In 1850 it already comprised 7,000 men, and it reached 10,000 in 1853, 15,000 in 1877 and 19,000 in 1900. Its deployment in the territory was carried out by a system of local military posts, provincial command headquarters, and regiments (clustering the provinces into 13 strategic zones); they followed the route of the rail networks that during the same period were being extended in a radial form from Madrid to the coasts, borders and provincial capitals. By adding the Civil Guard to the strictly civil personnel of the Ministry of the Interior,

---

[14] R.D. of 28-III-1844.

since they were efficient civil servants for introducing the State's presence wherever they were stationed, the Ministry went on to have, for example, 25,121 employees in 1880; it then become the largest ministry, as it had more employees than the ministries of Treasury (22,721 employees, including the corps of the Customs Guards) and War (21,689: see Table 5-1).

The third consideration refers to the establishment of a new ministry in 1847, the Secretary of State and Office of Commerce, Education and Public Works, which would be the seventh member of the Spanish Council of Ministries.[15] It would later be called the Ministry of Development.[16] This new ministry broke off from the Ministry of the Interior that had assumed excessively diverse functions. From then on, the Ministry of the Interior would be responsible for the more political aspects of territorial control (public order, supervision of local powers, organization of elections) and the Ministry of Development would focus on favoring the country's development and promoting economic growth (agriculture, livestock, commerce, industry, transports, and communication) and culture (public education and fine arts).

Since it had been divided between these two ministries, the Civil Administration was thus no longer restricted just to the Ministry of the Interior. As we have already seen, the Ministry of the Interior did not become smaller because of this division but, on the contrary, it experienced strong growth throughout the nineteenth century. Nevertheless, the growth of the entire Civil Administration was even stronger, as it was additionally reinforced by the expansion of the Ministry of Development. The latter grew from the 2,249 employees it had in 1850 to 6,343 in 1870 and 8,705 in 1890. At the end of the century, the Civil Administration totaled 38,851 employees: 9,255 civil servants of the Interior, 18,983 civil guards, 6,311 civil servants of the Ministry of Agriculture, Industry, Commerce and Public Works, and 4,302 of the Ministry of Public Education and Fine Arts. In fact, the original Ministry of Development was effectively divided into the latter two ministries in 1900.[17] As can be seen, the successive divisions of the Ministry of the Interior (the first one in 1847, the second in 1900, and many more later in the twentieth century) defined the restructuring and expansion of the Spanish government, so that it could be adjusted to the new tasks and responsibilities that were attributed to the

[15] R.D. of 28-1-1847.
[16] R.D. of 20-IX-1851.
[17] R.D. of 18-IV-1900.

State, especially those related to its role of favoring the economic growth of a country that was becoming increasingly aware of its backwardness. Even if it was not apparently the largest institution, the so called *Civil Administration* provided the governmental bureaucracy with a dynamic element, which fomented its modernization in the long term.

The fourth and fundamental reason that the Ministry of the Interior cannot be considered in any way as a secondary component of the Central Administration of the nineteenth-century state lies in the importance of the functions that it exercised. It is not necessary to underline how important the repressive functions of the apparatus controlling public order were for a state that had a marked lack of representation until 1931; the Ministry of the Interior directed them from the very center of power at the *Puerta del Sol* in Madrid (seat of the ministry from 1847 on). This Ministry was the government's "strong man" and the confidant of the President of the Council, for in addition to running the Civil Guard, the President of the Council was in charge of manipulating the elections and procuring—generally by a fraud—legitimacy for the position of the governing party with the illusion of an electoral victory and the ensuing majority in the parliament.

It should not be overlooked, however, that in addition to these political and repressive functions, the Ministry of the Interior was entrusted with supervising and controlling the local powers: *ayuntamientos** and *diputaciones provinciales**. This task was indeed crucial for the functioning of a state such as the nineteenth century Spanish one.

The Government and the Towns: A Model of an Unwritten State

In short, the Central Administration did not constitute the totality of the State's administrative instruments, and perhaps it did not even represent its most fundamental part. This factor should be taken into account when characterizing the Spanish bureaucracy in the nineteenth century and how that state functioned. When the national state began to be constructed, from the collapse of the monarchy in 1808 until when the new civil bureaucracy of the liberal state began to take hold in all the territory in 1840, the government had a limited capacity to act directly and control the population and its resources. It encountered difficulties completing tasks as necessary as carrying out the census, drawing maps, compiling statistics, collecting taxes, recruiting soldiers or simply making sure that the new legal provisions were obeyed.

This situation was especially marked in the outlying zones that were more difficult to access due to the complexity of the terrain, distances, and shortcomings of the transportation system. It also occurred in certain areas of less difficult access but because of their size and economic and demographic weight. They were capable of putting up resistance—even if it was passive—to the administration's few agents, who were poorly trained, paid, and provisioned. In extreme situations, people went so far as to say that His Majesty's government could not control things beyond the enclosure of Madrid (the wall that circled the capital for fiscal purposes).

This state of affairs actually existed during certain periods of the nineteenth century, as the administration was ruined by a series of consecutive wars, the collapse of the fiscal system of the Ancien Régime, and the excessive amount of time it took to replace it by an efficient tax system. The lowest point can perhaps be said to have been 1836-1837, when the government could not even effectively control a considerable part of the territory. This was due to the course of the civil war, which allowed the pretender Don Carlos to take up position with his troops at the gates of Madrid and threaten to occupy it. Given that the Treasury had suspended payments and the Church was ready to fight against the state because of the nationalization of its possessions and the abolition of the tithe, it is difficult to believe that civil servants could carry on normally in the provinces. There exists an extensive historiography about Spain based on this image of a weak state that was incapable of controlling the country, promoting economic development, or instilling nationhood in its population (Such a widely-spread thesis was synthesized in Riquer 1996 and in a more moderate version in Álvarez Junco 2001).

It would not make very much sense to continue the debate about this question as the positions that are principally argued depend on the different interpretations that are made of the same data. It is more important to understand that the deployment of the State consists of a process, and its dynamic aspects, tendencies, and rhythms of change have to be assessed; the state of affairs at the beginning was very different from that at the end. In order to simplify the complexity of the problem to a succinct schema of "phases", it could be said that the state's bureaucracy was extremely weak until the end of the First Carlist War (1840). It started to change very rapidly in the "moderate decade" (1844-1854) although it was only in the last decade of the nineteenth century and the first decades of the twentieth that the government managed to control the territory directly with its own Central Administration. What happened, then, during this long intermediate period that spanned almost all of the nineteenth century, when the government could not guarantee its presence throughout the country using its own administrative means?

The first observation that has to be made is that the state did function, even though it had a very limited number of employees and a restricted means of action. It functioned (taxes were collected, soldiers were conscripted, public works were constructed, most of the breaches of public order were suppressed…), but it was not in accordance with the theoretical model of a "dense state" that experts in administration, such as the aforementioned Oliván, had designed at the beginning of the process, before the onset of the "moderate decade". That "dense state", whose civil servants intervened following direct orders from the central government to establish order in all facets of the social, economic and cultural life, was beyond the power of an administration that did not have 100,000 employees until the 1890s. Growth was needed to make an administration similar to the one that Oliván had dreamed of in 1843 a reality, and was also needed to realize the development and perfection of the ministerial organizational charts, the professionalization of the corps of civil servants, the completion of the railroad network, and to complete the expansion of the Civil Guard.

Until this transformation took place—which was not before 1890-1900, as I have explained—the local administration was the key to the functioning of the Spanish state. Most of its administrative functions operated during the nineteenth century by using the municipalities and provinces as intermediaries, especially the municipalities, as they maintained direct contact with the citizens. This system reduced the administrative problems to manageable proportions, as it was no longer a question of directly reaching the country's 15,000,000 citizens, but rather of establishing contact with just over 9,000 municipalities that were asked to carry out tasks such as collecting taxes, compiling statistical information, or conscripting young men into military service. In fact, the problem was simplified even further, as the central government scarcely had direct relations with the municipalities, dealing with them through the far fewer 49 provinces.

The established chain of command went from the ministries' central offices in Madrid (especially the Ministry of the Interior as its seat in the *Puerta del Sol* was crowned by the central tower of the Spanish telegraphic network, in order to guarantee that its orders and information were efficiently transmitted) to the 49 provincial capitals where the governors resided. It then extended from the provincial capitals to the 9,000 municipalities into which the country was divided. If we think, for example, that in 1855—ten years after the fiscal reform—Spain remained divided into 9,085 districts for collecting taxes we can see the scale of the problem. The municipalities were virtually divided in half between the 4,555 in which the distribution and collecting of the taxes fell to the *ayuntamientos* and the 4,530 in which such tasks were carried out by private contractors. The collection *by administration*—that is, by the Ministry's own civil servants—that was the dream of all the experts in administrative matters, was not yet viable anywhere.

The provincial governors (initially called *Jefes Políticos** in the Constitution of 1812; then *subdelegates of development* in 1833; in 1834 *civil governors* and *provincial governors* in 1849) were the government's real agents throughout the territory.[18] They have been frequently considered as authoritarian agents that simply transmitted orders and imposed obedience to the government in their respective areas. Such a description perhaps fits the initial conception of this political-administrative figure. What we know about their real conduct, however, demonstrates that they spent more time keeping watch, informing, and negotiating than really imposing, because they scarcely had the means to impose in the initial phases of the process. They would go about taking control gradually, to the extent that they were backed by sufficient strength to sidestep the resistance of the local powers that controlled society. For example, the only personal memoirs that remain from one of these provincial governors (Guerola 1985, 1986, 1993a, 1993b, 1995 and 1996) demonstrate it. The governor probed, measured how far his forces could reach, struck deals, sought allies among the local elites, and was occasionally in the position to impose his decisions or punish someone. The Spanish state thus functioned in the nineteenth century with a system of bilateral negotiations centered on the figure of the governor, who had to negotiate, on the one hand, with the provincial *diputaciones* and, on the other, with the *ayuntamientos* of his province.

The design for the modern *ayuntamientos* had been initiated by the French administration based on the municipalities of the Ancien Régime.[19] Starting with the *Cortes* of Cadiz, they were reorganized by granting them an elective representation from the towns.[20] The *ayuntamientos,* which

[18] R.D. of 28-XII-1849.

[19] RR. DD. by José I of 21-VIII and 4-IX-1809.

[20] *Decreto* (Decree) of 23.VI.1813; hereafter D.

were the only "administration" that the majority of the citizens had contact with, functioned through the establishment of municipal *commissions* presided over by an *alcalde**. They were responsible for different areas, such as internal government, treasury, municipal taxes, budgets, urban police, public works, charity, education, statistics, and entertainment. These commissions were aided by specialized *juntas** that had a consultative role (according to Ponte, 2000, cited by Moral 2007: 76-77). The figure of the mayor, who was at the head of this municipal administrative network, was devised as the head of the local administration and, therefore, the State's delegate and representative. It was hence decided that, from 1835 on, the direct appointment of the *alcaldes* of Madrid and the largest cities was reserved for the government; the provincial governors would intervene in the other appointments (Castro 1979; Hijano 1992: 144-148).

The key to the organization of the municipal bureaucracy was the figure of the *secretary*, a municipal employee appointed by the corporation; he ensured the legality and administrative effectiveness of the decisions that the *alcald*e and councilors made. The secretary was not allowed to be from the locality itself so as to avoid connivances with interests other than those of the *ayuntamiento*. He was the head of a municipal administration whose functions went far beyond those assigned to the *urban police*, as he was responsible for the others that the state delegated to this local level, such as maintaining the roads, exploitation of the woodlands, financing public education, drafting soldiers, and collecting taxes. For all these matters and any additional ones that might appear when administering everyday life in the towns, the *ayuntamientos* had to notify the two provincial authorities, that is, without submitting their enquiries or demands to the central power: the *diputaciones* and governor.

The provincial *diputaciones* were a completely new creation of the liberal state, as opposed to the municipalities that were based on the precedent of the *consejos* that exercised local power under the Ancien Régime, even if they had received a new definition during the War of Independence (1808-1814). The provincial *diputaciones* were created by the Constitution of 1812, developed by the decree of 23-VI-1813 and later redefined by successive regulations that did not alter the original concept.[21] They coordinated the *ayuntamientos*, defined the municipal

[21] D. of 3-II-1823, L. of 20-VIII-1870, L. of 16-XIII-1876, L. of 2-X-1877, L. of 29-VIII-1882.

boundaries, and assigned to the local governments their respective share of taxes that the government or the *Cortes* had previously divided up between the provinces. They established the list of eligible voters and had powers that complemented those that the *ayuntamientos* exercised in matters such as the construction and upkeep of the roads, charity, public health, statistics, and public education.

To make sure that these tasks were carried out, the provincial *diputaciones* hired their own employees. Each provincial *diputación* had three administrative sections (Secretary's Office, Accounting, and Depository), where a secretary, depositary, head clerk, a junior clerk, archivist, copyists, office workers, and officials worked. There were also engineers, architects, and master builders in the largest ones. Doctors, and the staff assigned to the charitable establishments, were also answerable to the councils, as well as secondary school teachers and personnel and the staff of the provincial and local prisons.

Of these two levels of government—the municipal and provincial—the former doubtlessly formed the basis of the functioning of the Spanish state during the nineteenth century. The *ayuntamientos* had to take on so many crucial functions and tasks that the political definition of these institutions became a major question in the confrontation that divided the two parties of the so-called "liberal family". The progressives envisioned the *ayuntamiento* as a community of citizens that elected their own local representatives to manage their common interests and raise their voices to the higher-ranking instances on the national scene; to defend that ideal they embarked on the armed revolt of 1840.[22] The moderates, by contrast, saw the *ayuntamiento* as the State's administrative organ in the towns. They therefore tended to attribute it a less representative composition and insist more on its dependence on the chain of command that went from the minister to the provincial governor and from him to the mayor of each town. This conceptualization was reflected in the laws that regulated this matter during most of the century.[23]

The intensity of the argument about the definition of the *ayuntamientos* was not fortuitous as it was a question of the political and administrative key to a state under construction. And it is true that the nineteenth-century Spanish state was, in fact, a confederation of more than 9,000 local entities, although the constitutional texts vainly defined it in ideal terms as

[22] L. of 5-VIII-1856; L. of 20-VIII-1870.

[23] R.D. of 23-VII-1835, L. of 14-VII-1840, R.D. of 31-XII-1843, L. of 8-I-1845, L. of 2-X-1877.

a unitary and centralized state (that was, throughout the nineteenth century, only the expression of a desire, the formulation of an objective that created a tendency).

Seen in this light, the nineteenth-century Spanish state possessed a certain complexity: it was organized on three levels—local, provincial and national—with a central figure, the provincial governor, who, dependent on the national government, was entrusted with meditating among the three powers. If we take into account that, as has been indicated, a very high percentage of the Central Administration's employees were spread out throughout the territory, it is clear that only a limited number of the civil servants that made the state function on its three levels resided and worked in Madrid. For example, in 1866-1867 in Spain, the municipal administration employed 95,865 employees and the provincial administration 9,591 (*Anuario Estadístico,* 1866-1867). These totals add up to 105,456 employees in addition to the, at least, 90,000 that the Central Administration retained, of which very few were civil servants. Therefore, if the civil servants from the provincial level and, especially, the municipal ones are added to the total number, the Spanish state's capacity for action, albeit indirect action, was easily doubled.

We know that this predominance of the local administration over the central one was slowly being reversed, at the same time that the expansion of the state bureaucracy was completed; it underwent a watershed at the turn of the century. The figures now available effectively indicate that once the first decade of the twentieth century had elapsed, the Central Administration's civil servants outnumbered those that the local administration employed: 76,248 compared to 75,936 in 1913 (Moral 2007: 131-134). This new balance of power would coincide with the moment when the Central Administration started to be able to dispense with the *ayuntamientos* as intermediates in their relations with citizens; it thus shifted to a model of direct administration, which would have not only tremendous administrative consequences, but also political and social ones.

The Civil Service in Action

Most of the Central Administration's civil servants—those that strictly speaking can be considered as members of the State's bureaucracy—graduated from secondary schools; they did not consequently have university degrees. During the political debates about the definition of public education, this direct association between secondary education and the production of the employees that the state needed was taken for granted.

These individuals joined the ministries that structured the government, which were at first six ministries, then seven, and by 1900 already eight, without including the Overseas Ministry that only existed between 1863 and 1899 as it specialized in colonial affairs.[24] In each one of these ministries, under the minister (officially called the Secretary of State and Dispatch until 1851) there were a number of general directors who were in charge of the different administrative areas defined in accordance with a bureaucratic and political logic that progressively changed over time. The general directorates were divided in turn into *sections*, and these were broken down into *departments*, the smallest unit of administrative operation. Departments, sections, and general directorates had their respective directors and were organized in accordance with a strict chain of command.

The employees that worked in all these offices were classified by *corps*, according to the professional skills and education, employment regime, and wage rate of each one. In short, this idea of organizing the civil servants into corps derived from military tradition. It was generalized to the civil bureaucracy by the decree of civil servants that Bravo Murillo issued in 1852.[25] This regulation was important because, on the one hand, it established order in the public civil bureaucracy by using ideas and principles that derived from the Ministry of the Treasury's specific experience, as has already been explained. On the other, even though it was just a simple decree that the executive power dictated provisionally, its perdurance in the long term meant that it regulated the Spanish public bureaucracy during all the period when the contemporary state was being constructed, until it was replaced by the Law of 1918.[26]

The exposition of motives that Bravo Murillo addressed to the queen justified the decree and the urgency with which it was pronounced—without waiting for it to be passed as a law by the *Cortes*—by the government's need for:

- On the one hand, "trustworthy employees, given that without them it would be unfair to make the government bear, in most cases, the moral

[24] RR. DD. of 26-III-1863 and 25-IV-1899.

[25] R.D. of 18-VI-1852.

[26] L. of Rank and File of 20-VII-1918 and L. for Regulations for its Enforcement of 7-IX-1918.

responsibility that public opinion demands, or the material responsibility that article 42 of the Constitution imposes".
- On the other, promoting "order and discipline in the employees, classifying them in a clear and categorical manner. Thus, each one knows the place he occupies on the administrative scale, the rights he is allowed to enjoy, and the duties that he is entrusted with completing" (*Gaceta de Madrid*, 20 June 1852: 1).

It was therefore a question of reinforcing the executive power, by providing it with an administration that was obedient, disciplined, well organized, and trustworthy; a bureaucracy that would function as an effective machine, which was ready to fulfill its leaders' orders.

In order to achieve such a goal, it was ordered that all the civil servants should be organized by ministries. Also, each ministry was to be structured following the same scale composed of five levels: Superior Heads, Administrative Heads, Department Heads, Officials and Aspirants to Official. There was also a sixth level for the subordinates, who did not have the status of *government civil servants*; they therefore did not enjoy the rights that were legally established for these employees.

Every year the different ministries announced in the *Gaceta de Madrid* and their respective official bulletins a convocation for an entrance exam that would open the door to a career in the administration; it gave access to the category of *Aspirant to Official*. These exams took place in Madrid and the provincial capitals before the boards of examiners appointed by the ministries. These boards would publish the results as lists, arranged in order of the results, from the names of aspirants that "Passed unanimously with outstanding merit" to those that "Failed". The positions were progressively filled according to the order of the ranking, and if there were still candidates that had passed when all the positions were taken, they would remain on a waiting list. It would be used to fill the vacancies that subsequently appeared. To take these exams, the prospective aspirants had to be at least sixteen, demonstrate good moral character and possess an academic diploma. This presupposed that they had formal schooling (even if the decree did not specify the academic level, it was promptly identified as a secondary education).

In this way one began one's career as a civil servant. Afterwards, the aspirants could be promoted to officials by taking a public exam, or by the recognition of exceptional achievements when completing their work as aspirants. After six years of service as an official, a civil servant could then envision being promoted to the rank of department head. Promotions to the three higher-ranking categories of the civil service—those of department, administrative and superior heads—were not granted through public exams, but rather through a mixed system, which was based on seniority (two thirds of the positions) and direct appointment "for outstanding achievement, extraordinary services and circumstances or eminent services" (a third of the available positions).

As a consequence, it was expected that the principles of merit and personal capacity would be given precedence when recruiting civil servants on the lower end of the scale. Promotion based on seniority and merit would likewise protect them from their bosses' favoritism and the political vicissitudes experienced during the two previous decades. Nevertheless, upon climbing up the ladder and approaching the positions with more political weight, the civil servants faced the quota that was fixed so that ministers could appoint collaborators they trusted completely.

In addition, the decree established a precise pay scale, which was adjusted to the five levels of the civil service. It created a disciplinary regimen that was aimed at subordinating the civil servants to the requirements of the ministries, through the *Committee of Directors* and *General and Provincial offices,* which supervised the employees' behavior, evaluated the merits of each one, updated the work records, and established the promotion ladder in each ministry.

The *work record*, which had been used somewhat irregularly from the Ancien Régime on, was the document in which the civil servants' successive placements were registered, along with the starting and ending dates of each job. It was crucial for recording information such as processes of promotion and transfer, as well as requests and disciplinary reports.

The *roster* was certainly as important as the work record. It was a detailed list of the employees that formed part of a category, corps, class, department or ministry, which included the positions that had been held, order of precedence and corresponding salaries. This roster proved to be a useful instrument, therefore, for establishing the budgets of each one of the Administration's departments, but also for organizing the administrative careers, analyzing the availability of personnel, and estimating needs. As a result of the decree of 1852, all the ministries, sections, and departments had to define their rosters in addition to establishing internal regulations for their employees, by developing in detail the general provisions of the decree. The implementation of this decree meant that a great effort was made to organize the Spanish administration at its very core, and this took place at the same time as the establishment of the State's general system of accounting. Launched in 1850, it involved each transaction of funds, including expenditure for personnel that had to be rigorously recorded and submitted to the regulatory supervision of an inspector who made sure that the expense was legal and complied with what the general budgets had planned.

The decree of 1852 had many consequential aspects, although some of them just reinstated pre-existing practices and organized them in order to create a system. For example, it became obligatory that each civil servant had to serve in the successive placements of his category in any location in the national territory where the government sent him (in the peninsula and adjacent islands; the overseas territories followed a different set of rules). This regulation implied the creation of a corps of truly national civil servants, who would move in order to respond to the government's needs and priorities. From a cultural and social point of view, it became a useful component in national integration, as throughout the second half of the nineteenth century many families, following the placements of a civil servant father, moved from where they had been born and put down roots in different provinces.

Another important aspect of the decree was that, without a doubt, it clarified the right that public employees would have, after having completed a certain number of years of service and fulfilled certain requirements, to retire with a retirement pension. This right was applicable only to those that retired after having reached at least the category of official; neither aspirants nor subordinates were eligible for it. The Administration's heads and officials had the right, when they retired "due to the absolute impossibility of continuing to serve" (because of age or illness) to receive a pension from the State. Also the civil servants' families—once again for the category of official and above—could benefit from a *monte pío**, which paid pensions to widows and orphans. This right would create a significant financial burden for the budget, which would be called the burden of the *inactive classes*, the State's pensioners, a practice that has continued without interruption until the present. In any case, in a period when workers and professionals as a whole did not have access to any type of social security system, these measures represented very important social advantages that added to the relative security and stability that was created by the system of public exams and promotion based on seniority. They were measures that were aimed at dignifying the civil service, by reinforcing the State's authority and symbolic power, but they were also intangible social benefits that compensated for the somewhat limited pay that was obligatory because of the fiscal constraints.

In the same vein arose the idea of establishing uniforms for all the categories of the civil servants that would make it possible to identify, at first sight, the corps and grade to which each employee belonged. It would establish in them a visual, even intuitive, sense of authority. For the greater honor of the civil servants, the uniform was accompanied by a system of forms of address; they had the right to be addressed in a specific manner, which depended on their category. For example, Superior Heads would be addressed in the same manner as the members of the Royal Council (an extraordinary acknowledgement in a monarchy). The Administrative Heads, who were already the second highest rung of civil servants, would still have the right to be addressed as *Excellency*.

All of these aspects doubtlessly originated in the military tradition: the terminology—and the very idea—of a *corps*, with *heads and officials*, the *roster*, *work record*, promotion based on seniority, the uniformity, even the forms of address. All were a transfer to the sphere of the civil bureaucracy of those elements of hierarchy, discipline, order, and authority that had been proven to be effective in the Army and that they then wanted to exploit to the full in the sphere of the civil administration. The State's previous history had been that of an army and the tax and administrative system used to sustain it; it reworked that experience in its phase of consolidation and maturity in order to win new bloodless battles with the same arms.

All of these efforts to dignify the civil servants were perhaps not disassociated from the virtual campaign to discredit them that was underway from the beginning of the liberal period. In the epoch of the *Cortes* of Cadiz, a liberal as well-known as Martínez de la Rosa had already published a comic play that mocked those that joined the revolutionary cause only with the goal of ensuring their future by obtaining a position in the new administration (Martínez de la Rosa 1813). In a country in which uncertainty prevailed, the liberals fuelled even more—if it were possible—the mistrust of those who lived off the State's budget, the figure of the civil servant and *cesante** (who continued to collect from the treasury but no longer worked) became immensely unpopular. It was clearly shown by the press of all of the political colors during the Constitutional Triennium (1820-1823) and in speeches such as the one that Agustín Argüelles delivered in 1820, when he stated that "the Spanish Nation is a nation of employees" (Fuentes 2002). With the return of the liberal régime in 1834, this negative image once again started to circulate, making the concept of *empleomanía**, the equivalent of the French *fonctionnarisme,* commonplace. Without a doubt the tendency existed. But it is difficult to know to what extent its characteristics were exaggerated. There was certainly a tendency to seek employment in an ever-expanding public administration as a way to thrive socially and to ensure a future safe from fluctuations and economic cycles, or as a radical newspaper of the period stated graphically, “the obsession of preferring a post to any other honorable way of guaranteeing their sustenance” (*El Guindilla*, in 1842, cited by Fuentes, 2002: 272). For some people, the modern civil servant inherited the unpopularity of the inefficient, onerous *covachuelistas** of the absolute monarchy. For others, they grew rich and obtained personal privileges because of their self-interested adhesion to a party’s ideology. For many people, the jobs and benefits that they obtained formed part of the exchange of favors that fed the networks of patronage and clientelism that corrupted public life—the origin of what would later be called *caciquismo**. Finally, for some people, they created an artificial social class that lived off other people’s work and was the source of the century’s disorders and revolutions (Jaime Balmes in 1843, cited by Fuentes, 2002: 273).

At the beginning of the “moderate decade” (starting in 1844), the attacks against the employees and *cesantes* worsened when the State’s bureaucracy began to expand rapidly. We see it, for example, in writings such as those of Antonio Flores in 1850, in which he harshly criticized the abuses and vices of his society, including the unbridled search for public posts that were seen as sinecures or parasitic privileges, or the political favoritism that was used to hire and fire the State’s employees. He also included the ensuing figure of the *cesante*, a civil servant who, after being dismissed—generally as a consequence of a change in the government—was left unemployed and with the preferential right to be re-hired by a future Administration, so that his only hope lay in “his men” being returned to power (Flores 1968).

The decree of 1852, which took elements from previous legislation,[27] was in turn complemented by later ones, which perfected the system as it was being put into practice. Thus, in 1855 the requisite of the “sole occupation” was established for public employees, which prohibited them from receiving several salaries or executing several posts at the same time.[28] And in 1866 an organic regulation of the civil careers in the State’s

---

[27] Such as the *Real Orden* (Royal Order) of 19-VIII-1852; hereafter R.O. and the R.D. of 7-II-1827, that organized the Treasury’s employees.
[28] L. of 9-VII-1855.

service was established[29] and crystallized and developed the principles of 1852 in the light of the experiences of the preceding fourteen years.

The system of the five categories of civil servants ensured the everyday functioning of the ministerial offices, in addition to the subordinates, who were hired on fixed-term temporary contracts. Nevertheless, the necessity of establishing a special regime for some tasks that required more skills or education became evident, and the decree of 1852 recognized this by leaving certain areas outside of its scope (article no. 44). The areas and figures that were regulated by other legislation included the provincial governors (who were practically the government's political agents), diplomats, judges and magistrates, professors, military and naval personnel, and engineers.

Each one of these areas of the civil service has its own history, which is impossible to even outline here. It is nevertheless important to pause for a moment and analyze the mechanism that regulated them. It was a question of the creation of *special corps*, which were separated from the general corps of civil servants, whose set of rules I have just presented. Some of these special corps went a long way back, such as the civil and mining engineers that were deliberately mentioned as an exception in the decree of 1852. Such corps emerged directly from the schools specifically established for the education of these engineers. Overseeing the process of selection, the schools thus provided direct access to the professional corps. The Corps of Mining Engineers was the oldest one, as it had already been created under the Ancien Régime [30] because the Treasury possessed mines—in particular those located in Almadén, where the first school for mining engineers was established—and needed specialized personnel to administer them. The mining engineers functioned as an autonomous corps within the Administration, with their own roster, pay scales, and internal regulations; this autonomy was recognized by the liberal state.[31] The corps of ¨Roads, Canals and Ports¨ engineers, which functioned in a similar fashion after its creation in 1802, complied with this system of corporative functioning under the rule of constitutional state.[32]

The creation of these two corps of engineers paved the way for the others, and they adopted the same system of keeping themselves on the periphery of the general system governing the civil service as they were

[29] R.D. of 4-III-1866.

[30] R.O. of 14-VII-1777.

[31] R.D. of 2-II-1859.

[32] RR. DD. of 31-VII-1835, 28-IX-1853 and 10-VIII-1855.

defined as *special corps*. The first example was the Forestry Engineers.[33] It did not take long, however, for it to be followed by the special corps of University professors,[34] master builders,[35] telegraph operators,[36] forestry assistants,[37] agricultural engineers,[38] state lawyers,[39] diplomats,[40] doctors and pharmacists assigned to public charitable organizations,[41] agricultural experts,[42] and state industrial engineers.[43] These are only the most important examples as there were others.

The most important point to retain from this disparate history of how the administration's special corps, which continued into the twentieth century, were created, is that it constituted a way to increase the professionalization, skills, and education of the State's employees, by providing the Administration with flexible mechanisms and *ad hoc* solutions. Once the general regimen of ordinary civil servants was solidly established by the decree of 1852, and the measures that it enacted put it into effect, the Administration was launched. In addition to a quantitative dimension, it had another qualitative dimension that consisted of progressively adding the special corps to it. The internal mechanisms and characteristics of each corps were different, for they corresponded to the characteristics of their profession and the circumstances of their creation. All, nevertheless, had some features in common, which appeared to be "privileges", until the Law of 1918 extended such features to the entire administration and transformed them into general standards for its functioning. The special corps, therefore, were the models for the modern administration that, from the twentieth century on, replaced the one that had guaranteed the initial "unfolding" of the Spanish state during the nineteenth century.

---

[33] R.D. of 30-IV-1835 and 18-III-1843, RR. OO. of 12-VIII-1848 and 12-X-1853, and the R.D. of 17-III-1854.
[34] R.D. of 17-IX-1845 and roster of 22-VI-1847.
[35] R.D. of 24-I-1855.
[36] R.D. of 5-VII-1856.
[37] D. of 28-VIII-1869.
[38] RR. DD. of 14-II-1879, 20-I-1882, 9-XII-1887 and 20-IX-1900.
[39] R.D. of 10-III-1881.
[40] L. of 14-III-1883, after the precedent set by R.D. of 4-III-1844.
[41] R.D. of 23-XII-1884.
[42] R.D. of 10-VI-1894.
[43] R.D. of 23-III-1911.

References

Almanaque del empleado, (1868-1936), Madrid, Imprenta de Eduardo Zafra.

Álvarez Junco, J., (2001), "El nacionalismo español y las insuficiencias de la acción estatal", *Historia Social,* 40: 29-52.

Anuario estadístico de España, (1866-1867), Madrid, Imprenta Nacional.

Artola, M. – Bilbao, L.M., (eds.), (1984), *Estudios de Hacienda: de Ensenada a Mon,* Madrid: Instituto de Estudios Fiscales.

Carreras, A. – Tafunell, X., (coord.), (2005), *Estadísticas históricas de España. Siglos XIX y XX,* Bilbao: Fundación BBVA.

Castro, C. de, (1979), *La revolución liberal y los municipios españoles,* Madrid: Alianza Editorial.

Colmeiro, M., (1850), *Derecho administrativo español,* 2 vols., Madrid: Librerías de don Ángel Calleja.

Fernández Sebastián, J., - Fuentes, J.F., (dirs.), (2002), *Diccionario político y social del siglo XIX español,* Madrid: Alianza Editorial.

Flores, A., (1968), *La sociedad de 1850,* Madrid: Alianza Editorial.

Fradera, J.M., (2005), *Colonias para después de un imperio,* Barcelona: Bellaterra.

Fuentes, J.F., (2002), "Empleado", in Fernández Sebastián - Fuentes (dirs.), *Diccionario político y social del siglo XIX español*: 271-275.

Guerola, A., (1985), *Memoria de mi administración en la provincia de Zamora como gobernador de ella desde 12 de agosto de 1853 hasta 17 de julio de 1854,* Zamora: Instituto Estudios Zamoranos Florián de Ocampo.

—. (1986), *Memoria de mi administración en la provincia de Cádiz, como gobernador de ella desde el 31 de marzo hasta el 31 de mayo de 1863*, Cádiz: Caja de Ahorros.

—. (1993a), *Memoria de mi administración en la provincia de Sevilla como gobernador de ella desde 11 de junio hasta 24 de octubre de 1863,* Sevilla: Fundación Sevillana de Electricidad.

—. (1993b), *Memoria de mi administración en la provincia de Sevilla como gobernador de ella por segunda vez, desde 1 de marzo de 1876 hasta 5 de agosto de 1878,* Sevilla: Guadalquivir.

—. (1995), *Memoria de mi administración en la provincia de Málaga como gobernador de ella desde 6 de diciembre de 1857 hasta el 15 de febrero de 1863,* Sevilla: Fundación Sevillana de Electricidad.

—. (1996), *Memoria de mi administración en la provincia de Granada como gobernador de ella desde 27 de noviembre de 1863 hasta 25 de enero de 1864,* Sevilla: Fundación Sevillana de Electricidad.

Guía de forasteros (1811-1935), Madrid: Imprenta Real/Imprenta Nacional [the publication changed titles over time: *Kalendario manual y guía de forasteros en Madrid* (1760-1810 and 1814-1816), *Guía patriótica de España* (1811), *Guía política de las Españas* (1812-1813), *Calendario manual y guía de forasteros en Madrid* (1817-1820 y 1824-1837), *Guía de forasteros en Madrid* (1821-1823 y 1838-1864), *Guía de forasteros* (1865-1872), *Guía oficial de España* (1874-1935)].

Hijano Pérez, Á., (1992), *El pequeño poder. El municipio en la corona de Castilla, siglos XV al XIX,* Madrid: Fundamentos.

Jordana, J. - Ramió, C., (2005), "Gobierno y Administración", in Carreras - Tafunell (coord.), *Estadísticas históricas de España. Siglos XIX y XX,* vol. III: 973-1026.

Lerena, C. de, (1789), "Memoria sobre la naturaleza de las rentas públicas de España" in (1990), *Memoria sobre las rentas públicas y balanza comercial de España (1789-1790),* Madrid: Instituto de Estudios Fiscales.

López Garrido, D., (1984), "La autonomía del aparato hacendístico en la transición al régimen liberal (notas para un estudio)", in Artola – Bilbao (eds.), *Estudios de Hacienda: de Ensenada a Mon*: 355-372.

—. (2004), *La Guardia civil y los orígenes del Estado centralista,* Madrid: Alianza Editorial.

Lorente, M. (coord.), (2007), *De justicia de jueces a justicia de leyes: hacia la España de 1870,* Madrid: Consejo General del Poder Judicial.

Lorente, M., (2007), "Justicia desconstitucionalizada. España, 1834-1868", in Lorente (coord.), *De justicia de jueces a justicia de leyes: hacia la España de 1870*: 245-287.

Martínez de la Rosa, F., (1813), *Lo que puede un empleo: Comedia en dos actos en prosa, adicionada por Don Valentín de Foronda,* Coruña: Oficina de Don Antonio Rodríguez.

Moral Ruiz, J. del – Pro, J. – Suárez, F., (2007), *Estado y territorio en España, 1820-1930,* Madrid: Los Libros de la Catarata.

Moral Ruiz, J. del, (2007), "Las funciones del Estado y la articulación del territorio nacional: símbolos, Administración pública y servicios", in Moral Ruiz – Pro Ruiz – Suárez, *Estado y territorio en España, 1820-1930*: 17-358.

Morales, A. - Esteban, M., (ed.), (1996), *La historia contemporánea en España: Primer Congreso de Historia Contemporánea de España, Salamanca, 1992,* Salamanca: Universidad de Salamanca.

Nieto, A., (1996), *Los primeros pasos del Estado constitucional. Historia administrativa de la Regencia de María Cristina de Borbón,* Barcelona: Ariel.

Oliván, A., (1843), *De la Administración Pública con relación a España,* Madrid: Boix.

Pinto Crespo, V., (dir.), (2001), *Madrid. Atlas histórico de la ciudad, 1850-1939,* Madrid: Lunwerg - Fundación Caja Madrid.

Ponte Chamorro, F.J., (2000), *Administración y gobierno municipal en el siglo XIX: Madrid, 1845-1876. Un modelo de estudio de la Administración local,* Unpublished Doctoral Thesis, Universidad Autónoma de Madrid.

Pro Ruiz, J., (2001), "El Estado y la administración pública en la ciudad (1833-1936)", in Pinto Crespo (dir.), *Madrid. Atlas histórico de la ciudad, 1850-1939*: 270-299.

—. (2006), *Bravo Murillo: política de orden en la España liberal,* Madrid: Síntesis.

Riquer, B. de, (1996), "Nacionalidades y regiones en la España contemporánea. Problemas y líneas de investigación en torno a la débil nacionalización española del siglo XIX", in Morales - Esteban, (ed.), *La historia contemporánea en España: Primer Congreso de Historia Contemporánea de España, Salamanca, 1992*: 73-89.

Solla, Julia, (2007), "Justicia bajo Administración (1834-1868)", in Lorente (coord.), *De justicia de jueces a justicia de leyes: hacia la España de 1870*: 289-324.

CHAPTER SIX

THE CONTESTED STATE: REVENUE AGENTS, RESISTANCE AND POPULAR CONSENT IN THE UNITED STATES FROM THE EARLY REPUBLIC TO THE SIXTEENTH AMENDMENT (1913)

ROMAIN HURET

In Ohio, during the Civil War, a person who styled himself Thomas H. Hanner imposed himself upon a Revenue Officer of the 19th district as a special agent of the Bureau of Internal Revenue, and made "decisions as to the effect of the law, giving directions as to the management of cases involving large amounts and borrowing money upon the strength of his alleged position".[1] Another usurpation of identity occurred in Philadelphia where a person named Gillespie collected income taxes in the city.[2] In many States, an impostor under the name of Thomas Glanner also sought to collect taxes.[3] There were frequent appearances of false agents under the new war tax regime, and it sparked strong resentment against revenue officers during the Civil War. Such usurpation of identity reveals the

---

[1] Letter from Commissioner Joseph Lewis to Capt. Harrison, revenue inspector, OH, Jan. 25th, 1865, Inspectors Book, June 1st 1864 to May 17th 1865, Records for the Civil War Period, Letters sent to revenue agents and inspectors, 1864-1865, Record Group 58, National Archives [RG 58 hereafter].

[2] Letter from Commissioner Joseph Lewis to Whitman, Esqu. Jan. 27, 1865, Inspectors Book, June 1st 1864 to May 17th 1865, Records for the Civil War Period, Letters sent to revenue agents and inspectors, 1864-1865, RG 58.

[3] See letters from Commissioner Lewis on Jan. 28, Jan. 30, 1865, Inspectors Book, June 1st 1864 to May 17th 1865, Records for the Civil War Period, Letters sent to revenue agents and inspectors, 1864-1865, RG 58.

fragility of the bureaucratic system designed to collect taxes in the country. From the Early Republic to the Sixteenth Amendment, policymakers in the Federal Government sought to create a coherent and efficient cohort of officers.[4] To properly police his district, each revenue agent required "the utmost energy, industry, and vigilance of which he is capable" as 1878 instructions put it.[5] However, these federal employees were seen not only as federal intruders, but also as corrupt agents since they were paid a percentage of their collection or of the penalties collected. The fluid boundaries between private and public spheres sparked opposition at local and national levels. As a consequence, many taxpayers expressed their distrust by mobilizing politically. While most Americans accepted postmasters in their towns and counties, they frequently opposed the establishment of revenue officers to collect taxes.[6] In the field of taxation, opposition was the rule, and led to the dismantlement of each new tax regime during the nineteenth century, with the sole exception of the tariff regime.

By focusing on the very place of contacts between citizens and revenue officers at the local level, this paper demonstrates that the expansion of the Fiscal State was limited because of the inability of the Federal Government to select revenue officers based on their standing in the local community. As many scholars have argued, fiscal action requires, on the whole, administrative consent.[7] The recent scholarship on the nexus between state and society stresses reciprocal interactions between institutions and various social groups (Huret 2009, 2014). Citizens are more likely to comply and even give active consent when they perceive institutions as procedurally fair in both decision-making and implementation processes, and when they believe other citizens are also doing their share. Resistance, ranging from petitions to violence, occurred when opportunities to maneuver were no longer available for taxpayers. The local ineffectiveness of tax officials helps to explain the pressures behind the creation of entirely new social roles such as, for example, that of the exciseman or the custom officer. Such offices lacked a generalized legitimacy—their holders were active only as revenue agents and they

---

[4] On the nineteenth century tax regimes, see Brownlee 2004:13-57.

[5] Internal Revenue Agent Manual, July 1, 1878, Washington D.C., Government Printing Office, 1878, Historian's Books, Box 38, RG 58.

[6] For this "uncontested State" as Brian Balogh puts it, see Balogh 2008; John 1995.

[7] See for a general discussion of bureaucratic consent, Daunton 2001; see also, Martin 2008.

were presumed to have a direct personal interest in increasing yields. They were, thus, suspected of corruption and they were referred to in terms of invaders. The functional ineffectiveness of county officeholders in raising taxation had been a product partly of how they had understood themselves and of how others had understood their roles. In this paper, I focus on five categories of tax officers (gaugers, storekeepers, assessors, customs' officers, and deputy collectors) at different periods during the nineteenth century. By refusing to abandon the patronage system, and by implementing a hybrid system including private and public officers, the Federal Government paradoxically increased the number of tax opponents and created a strong distrust about institutions and bureaucracy.

Resistance against revenue agents and excisemen in the Early Republic (1780s-1830s)

In the spring of 1798, Fisher Ames wrote to the first Treasury Secretary Oliver Wolcott Jr to express his fears about the future of the young American Republic: "The chance of our future state is imprecise. All our good men should join their best efforts to keep this system from sinking".[8] A few months later, the metaphor took a vivid turn when more and more taxpayers opposed the 1798 Revenue Law. In eastern Pennsylvania, tax assessors were driven off by angry inhabitants when they tried to count and measure windows. Some women used a novel technique to drive them off: douse them with hot water. The wife of David Shaeffer—a tax resister from Macungie Township, Northampton County, who eventually died of yellow fever while in jail awaiting his trial—became one of the leaders of the "Hot Water War" (Newman 2004: 13-15). Meanwhile, thousands of petitioners criticized the new revenue laws and expressed their fears about the centralized government envisioned by the Federalists. A few years after the American Revolution, opposition to the Fiscal State had become entangled with a violent rhetoric and a larger debate about the meaning of the American Revolution. Both excise taxes and direct taxes were seen as unfair in their methods of collection, and in their apportionment. The crisis mentality, as historian Joanne Freeman has labeled it, raised doubts about the very nature of the revenue system in the country (Freeman 2003: 20-49).

[8] Letter from Fisher Ames to Oliver Wolcott Kr, April 22 1978, Oliver Wolcott Papers, Connecticut State Historical Society [hereafter OWP].

During the 1790s, a number of administrative changes carried out by Federalists were made, reducing the possibilities of concealing wealth from tax collectors (Edling 2003: 206-218). Tax excises sought to tax a very wide range of domestic items of consumption, on the argument that levels of consumption reflect levels of wealth. But such consumption is difficult to trace without entering every house in the country and recording its contents, or entering every retail outlet. This was inflammatory, and difficult to achieve, and the excise on whiskey led to rebellion in 1793 and 1794. Eventually, with the Direct Tax law of 1798, taxes fell on land and houses, which were also difficult to hide. But this created unfairness, in that land and houses were by no means the only form of wealth or income in the Early Republic, and to rely only on taxes on land was to unfairly burden particular sections of the population. As a result, resistance to the Window Tax, as it was generally called, spread throughout the country. The Federalists hoped to construct federal authority to work through local channels of influence and power so as to combine a new source of political power with preexisting, traditional sources of law and governance (Rao 2008). In the matter of personnel, for instance, Alexander Hamilton's Treasury Department turned to local elites to do the potentially divisive job of collecting federal duties. These elites had secured their status through inherited or acquired wealth, or through distinguished military or political records during the Revolution, and parlayed their social, political, and economic distinction into governance. In an era in which the legitimacy of a new federal government was tenuous at best, elite officeholders carefully balanced the national political economic imperative of collecting revenue against local economic vicissitudes and political circumstances (Dalzell 1991 and 1992: 355-388). The Whiskey Rebellion of 1793-1794 and the revolt against the Window Tax of 1798-1799 were the result of the inability of local elites to collect revenue taxes.

The Whiskey Rebellion sheds light on the difficulty the Federal Government had in imposing its own rules and regulations through local officers.[9] If the rebellion has often been portrayed as a heroic tale of American rebels or a crucial episode of civil disobedience, it was supported by many local elites who felt dispossessed by the Federalists' administration and feared losing their local power.[10] In the first two years of resistance to the excise, as small bands of farmers were terrorizing

---

[9] On the Whiskey Rebellion, see Slaughter 1986; Kohn 1972.

[10] On this heroic view, see Slaughter 1986; on civil disobedience, Bonsteel Tachau 1982 and 1978.

collectors along with distillers who complied with the tax (tarring and feathering the former, destroying the stills of the latter), inhabitants, residents of the western counties, repeatedly met to draw up remonstrances against the law. Nearly every one of the region's office-holding elite—representatives to the state assembly, local judges and justices of the peace, county commissioners, and even members of Congress—attended such meetings, signed petitions against the law, and joined "committees of correspondence" to coordinate the campaign across the four counties and any others that might choose to join the effort. Participants in these meetings ensured, moreover, that their proceedings were published in local newspapers, including the *Pittsburgh Gazette*. However, many of these early opponents of the tax were either indifferent or hostile to the mass mobilization that occurred later. Even John Neville, who accepted the post of excise inspector late in 1791, had initially joined the clamor against the law; and in 1794 men like Albert Gallatin and William Findley (both members of Congress) struggled for a peaceful solution rather than side with those who had mustered the militia. Some local notables decided to take up arms against the federal government; others didn't. The difference lay in the level of political integration of the elites. The resisters occupied structurally disadvantaged positions in the network of patronage relations that linked many of the region's prominent officeholders to one another. Disadvantage took two forms: either an elite officeholder had no connection to the local patron-client system, or his position in the system was threatened by the fact that his clients were also tied, directly or indirectly to federal officers. Of the 44 elites identified by Gould, seven played an active role as leaders of the Whiskey Rebellion: James Allison, David Bradford, John Cannon, Edward Cook, John McDowell, James Marshall, and Craigh Richie (Gould 1996: 413). A similar challenge of the patronage system occurred when Federalists decided to implement new taxes at the end of the 1790s.

The Direct Tax Act passed on July 9th 1798 by Congress, and commonly referred to as the "Window Tax", imposed a direct tax on property, which included all dwelling houses, lands, and large slave-holdings (See Edling 2003 and Brown 1993). To finance a quasi-war with France, Federalists had no other choice but to increase taxation through two taxes—Stamp Tax and Direct Tax. Republican Albert Gallatin, a western Pennsylvanian critic of the whiskey excise, thought that a direct tax would provide a fairer distribution of taxes. On April 4, 1796, the House resolved to direct Secretary of the Treasury Oliver Wolcott to draft a plan to lay and collect a direct tax and to present a report to the next session of Congress. Hamilton preferred a tax on dwellings, believing that houses were a more accurate index for assessing individual wealth, especially in cities and towns, and thus would provide a fairer distribution of the tax burden across class lines and reduce the risk of resistance or rebellion. When Congress passed an "Act to provide for the valuation of lands and dwelling-houses, and the enumeration of slaves, within the United States" on July 9, and five days later passed the "Direct Tax Act" authorizing collection, Hamilton thought he had corrected the error of his previous federal tax by giving careful attention to fairness in his graduated House Tax. Indeed, the House Tax was a graduated tax that applied a sliding scale to the tax rates from poor to wealthy by counting the number of rooms in a house and taxing extravagances such as chimneys and papered walls.

This direct tax called for the formation of a bureaucracy. Secretary Oliver Wolcott, Jr was in charge of appointing tax collectors. The law divided each state into several districts, each with its own commissioner. Each commissioner had several assessors, and of course each assessor had to have several assistants. The assessors were responsible for completing a schedule that included house measurements and value, land measurements and value, and the number of slaves. In addition, the 1798 law required the assessor to record the number and measurements of a dwelling's windows. There was to be no tax on windows for the meantime, but Hamilton and Wolcott saw the scheduling as an opportunity to collect information that might be useful should future direct taxes on luxuries be considered. In an effort to stave off ethnic tensions, President Adams and Wolcott appointed a fairly equal mixture of Anglo and German-American assessors. Federalist assessor for Pennsylvania, Jacob Eyerle, the defeated German Moravian candidate for Congress, received the post of commissioner for Pennsylvania's fifth district, while Seth Chapman, a Quaker and a relation of the Federalists, and another defeated congressional candidate, John Chapman, were commissioners for the third district. They subsequently appointed fellow Federalist Quakers and Moravians as assessors and assistants to levy the House Tax. Seth Chapman appointed his brother James to assess the northern district of Bucks and Montgomery Counties and James appointed several Quakers – John Roderock, Everhard Foulke, and Cephas Childs – as assistants, along with Samuel Clark. The procedure of enforcement and collection sparked a revolt during the winter of 1798. An auctioneer named John Fries incited a small rebellion in eastern Pennsylvania against the federal tax on houses. After U.S. Marshals arrested several men who had interfered with tax assessors, Fries organized an armed band to rescue the prisoners. President John Adams, like his predecessor, could not allow the challenge to federal authority to go unanswered and the militia marched again on Pennsylvania.[11]

Most tax resisters in Pennsylvania were local elites. Of the 211 identified resisters, ninety-nine owned taxable homes and ninety-eight owned taxable land. This figure sounds low, but the 211 identified resisters represent 172 households. Eight of ten resisters owed less than a dollar in tax on their homes. Most of them criticized not only the apportionment of taxes, but also the revenuers chosen by the Federalists. In Pennsylvania, assessor Everhard Foulke was rejected by the local population. The Foulkes family was an influential Quaker family in northern Bucks County and they held a variety of local offices. Many resisters also refused to trust officials who had been defeated in Congressional elections such as Jacob Eyerle and Seth Chapman. In the winter of 1799, Congressman Robert Brown brought before the House of Representatives a petition signed by 1,100 Northampton County men that declared the Federalist legislation "contrary not only to the spirit but to the letter of the Constitution".

In 1800, the Ways and Means Committee decided to repeal the infamous tax, referring to petitions sent in by citizens throughout the country: "A petition of sundry inhabitants of Madison county, in the State of Virginia, was presented to the House and read, complaining of the assessment of the property of the petitioners by the assessors appointed under the act, entitled 'An act to lay and collect a direct tax within the United States', and praying relief in the premises. Ordered, That the said petition be referred to the Committee of the Whole House to whom is committed the report of the Committee of Ways and Means relative to the expediency of repealing the act providing for the valuation of lands and dwelling houses, and the enumeration of slaves within the United States".[12] On April 6, 1802 Congress repealed the first internal revenue laws, effective from June 30, 1802. This action also resulted in the abolishment of the position of Commissioner of the Revenue and all offices concerning the collection of internal taxes. This marked the end of internal taxation in the United States until 1813. The Commissioner and Supervisors of the Revenue were to continue in office until all outstanding taxes had been collected. Indeed, the Federalist experiments did not work well and established precedents for future tax initiatives. As a result, tariffs

[11] On the Fries rebellion, see Newman 2004; Bouton 2000; Churchill 2000.
[12] *House Journal*, 27/01/1801, 775-776.

became the cornerstone of the revenue system, and the customs' officer its central actor.

Indeed, the federal government relied on tariff for two main reasons: it was easier to collect than other taxes and it subsidized the domestic producers of the goods that it taxed. Moreover, as Robin Einhorn has shown, it was the result of a political accommodation between Southern and Northern States (Einhorn 2006: 117-156). Between 1789 and 1815, the tariff revenues accounted for about 90 percent of total federal tax revenues. By July 4, 1789, Congress had created the Treasury, and President George Washington signed into law a tariff act designed to raise revenue for the new government. The act established a complex set of duties on imports, rebates for reported goods, and special favors for imports carried in American vessels. The act yielded more than $1 million a year. Alexander Hamilton, the first secretary of the Treasury, needed to expand federal tax revenues to accomplish the highest priority of his ambitious financial program: paying off, in full, the loans that foreign governments had made to the Continental Congress during the Revolution.[13] Facing tax resistance in the country, Alexander Hamilton perfectly understood the virtue of the tariff, both an invisible and a nonintrusive tax. Customs' officers who collected it at the nation's ports formed only a small cadre of officials. In the Early Republic, Hamilton's strategy proved valuable while customs' officers accommodated themselves to the procedures of enforcement. "If the bonds are not paid, as they fall due, they be immediately put into suit," explained Hamilton in 1789 to the new cohort of Customs officers. In other words, officials had to initiate suits against most violators so that the decision not to sue others was an exception to the norm.[14] Collectors of Customs, however, quietly ignored Hamilton's circular urging "the most exact punctuality" and instead continued, if not expanded "the relaxations" that had reigned under state revenue laws during the Articles of Confederation.[15] In the days of the Early Republic, accommodation became the rule in the customs house and that limited tensions between taxpayers and tax collectors. Therefore, until the Civil War, many Americans hoped that Thomas Jefferson's dream of a Republic without taxpayers would come true (Huret 2014).

[13] On Hamilton's tax policy, see Brownlee 2004: 21; Rao 2016.

[14] Alexander Hamilton, Circular to Collectors of Customs, December 18, 1789, Circulars 1789-1796, Container 1, Folder 1, Records of the U.S. Department of the Treasury, Manuscript Division, Library of Congress [hereafter, Treasury Records].

[15] For more details, see Rao 2016.

The "broad farce" of taxes: Resistance against revenuers during the Civil War

A few months after the end of the Civil War, Commissioner of Internal Revenue, Joseph Lewis, sent a letter to D.C. Whitman, a revenue agent living in Newark, New Jersey about the collecting of the Income Tax in the State. "Sir, It has been represented to this office that the assessment of the Income Tax in the village of Mahvah, N.J. and vicinity has been a "broad farce". As an illustration of his case, Lewis referred to a photographer, some wealthy farmers and other residents who "support family in excellent style", but "paid no income tax".[16] Many citizens criticized the collection of taxes, deploring both fraud and inefficiency. As petitioners from Ohio argued: "Income tax to be abolished, because unequal in its operation; but, if not abolished, we *urge* rigid means from its collection from all. Assessors being enjoined to call for full information, and make strict investigation before accepting sworn returns; but when accepted and paid, such returns to be *final*, unless fraud can be proven in a Federal Court. No publicity of returns allowed".[17] In his report sent on January 13th 1863, the Commissioner of the Bureau of Internal Revenue, George S. Boutwell, agreed on the weakness of the bureaucratic structure.[18] Clearly, the income tax posed the biggest collection problems. For its part, the Treasury Department was less than enthusiastic about the new tax. Secretary Chase did nothing to prepare for it, insisting that enforcement would be too expensive. And he was not alone in his concern about collection costs. Citizens also complained about the cost of the income tax. Their anxiety was expressed by newspapers. While generally supporting the income tax, the *New York Times* voiced unhappiness with its concomitant bureaucracy. Editors were appalled by reports of patronage-seeking applicants thronging the Treasury. As the war ended,

---

[16] Letter from Joseph Lewis to D.C. Whitman, Dec. 9th 1865, Inspectors Book, June 1st 1864 to May 17th 1865, Records for the Civil War Period, Letters sent to revenue agents and inspectors, 1864-1865, RG 58.

[17] Petition, Citizens of Waverly County, OH, 5 Mars 1862, Tray HR 37A-G20.8 (Dec. 4, 1861 to Jan. 22, 1863), Record Group 233, National Archives (hereafter RG 233).

[18] Report of Commissioner of Internal Revenue, George S. Boutwell, January 13, 1863, Folder Historical Misc. Materials, Historian's Records, Box 21, Record Group 56, National Archives (hereafter RG 56).

M. S. Beach, proprietor of the *New York Sun* newspaper, launched a petition for the remission of the income tax by three per cent.

The new Bureau of Internal Revenue reached into almost every hamlet and town through a network of 185 collection districts and became the most coercive civilian agency of the national government (Bensel 1991: 169). As soon as he was appointed at the head of the Bureau of Internal Revenue, George S. Boutwell was looking for "person of business capacity, of well-established character for integrity, and of gentlemanly bearing that the law may not in the manner of its administration be rendered odious to the people".[19] The men who collected revenues derived from excise taxes faced a particularly difficult set of problems, as the agents were often perceived as federal intruders. In 1863, Cincinnati brewers refused to let assessors see their books open since by so doing they would be required "to keep our doors unlocked and our houses exposed to the public, while other manufacturers can do as they please".[20] The ability to have access to the books entailed many tensions between tax collectors and taxpayers, and raised constitutional problems. In 1865, a dealer in leaf-tobacco, Blatchford J., was arrested since he refused to let tax assessors have access to his books. He accused civil servants of not respecting his constitutional rights: "The relator sets up that a criminal proceeding had been commenced against him for making such alleged false and fraudulent returns and that he cannot produce the books or give the testimony without criminating himself".[21] On the contrary, M. V. B. Wilcoxson for the relator and T. Symons, Assistant District Attorney, for the United States argued that taxpayers' information predominated over taxpayers' rights: "In this view there could be no excuse for stretching the power of the assessor as to invoke a violation of one of the fundamentals principles of justice that no person shall be compelled to give testimony which may tend to criminate himself. This may be done by exhibiting or disclosing an entry in a book as well as by testifying orally. The witness

[19] Letter written by George Boutwell, Commissioner of Internal Revenue, August, 2, 1862, to Dessle. Little, Esq., Assessor of Taxes, Great Salt Lake City, Utah, Vol. 1 A of 2, From Aug., 1st 1862, to Sept. 19, 1862. RG 58.

[20] Petition from citizens and Brewers of Cincinnatti, December 8th, 1862, Tray HR 37A-G20.8 (Dec. 4, 1861 to Jan. 22, 1863), RG 233.

[21] W. S. District Court, In the Matter of Leopold Lippman on Habeas Corpus, Undated, Copies of certain opinions of Attorney General, Solicitors of the Treasury, and Judges of the Courts. p. 161-164, Entry 50, vol. 1 of 1, Opinions of Attorney General, Re: IRS, RG 58.

must be the judge of the effect of the disclosure on testimony unless it is manifest that there is no ground for claiming the protection invoked". Some tax inspectors outreached their rights in many cases. In 1865, the Commissioner Joseph Lewis had to explain to one of his agents, Samuel Wilkinson, that he had "no power conferred upon you by law to make a seizure, as I presume upon you are aware, and the power of seizure vested in the collector is not one which can be delegate".[22]

During the Civil War, with accusations running from the very beginning of the war through the end, members of Congress, the press, and ordinary citizens identified dozens of government officers and contractors as perpetrators of illegal or immoral behavior. Henry Morford" *The Days of Shoddy: A Novel of the Great Rebellion in 1861* (1863) popularized the image of administration corruption in distributing contracts for military supplies (Neely 2002:137; Wilson 2006: 150). The Inspectors Book, which detailed inspection of tax assessors on the ground, reveals a high number of cases implying fraud and corruption for the year 1864 and 1865.[23] On June 2 1864, a citizen named Joseph Karned, living in Stephensville, OH, charged some of the officers of the 11th district of Ohio with various irregularities and stated that the income of certain individuals and establishments had not been returning in full.[24] Local newspapers also denounced cases of fraud and corruption and pushed the administration to launch an investigation on the alleged facts. On November 25, E. A. Rohing sent a copy of the *Philadelphia News* to James A. Briss, a revenue agent in New York, concerning the alleged attempt of Collector Harding to obtain an interest in the collecting process.[25] Two weeks later, another

---

[22] Lewis to Samuel Wilkinson, esqu. Revenue Inspector, Peoria, IL, Inspectors Book, June 1st 1864 to May 17th 1865, Records for the Civil War Period, Letters sent to revenue agents and inspectors, 1864-1865, RG 58.

[23] Inspectors Book, June 1st 1864 to May 17th 1865, Records for the Civil War Period, Letters sent to revenue agents and inspectors, 1864-1865, RG 58. Unfortunately, only one inspector's book is available at the National Archives. Denunciations are always biased since the Book contains only letters sent to or received by Inspectors from their bureaucratic hierarchy. Unfotunately, letters from citizens are not available.

[24] Letter from R.S. Corvin, esqu., Special Agent, Easton, PA, Inspectors Book, June 1st 1864 to May 17th 1865, Records for the Civil War Period, Letters sent to revenue agents and inspectors, 1864-1865, RG 58.

[25] Letter sent by E. A. Rohing to James A Briss, Revenue Agent, NY, , Inspectors Book, June 1st 1864 to May 17th 1865, Records for the Civil War Period, Letters sent to revenue agents and inspectors, 1864-1865, RG 58.

revenue agent was asked to investigate and to sort things out in the city of Philadelphia in connection with the "unfair assessment of Income taxes".[26] The rise in corruption cases led Lewis, the new Commissioner, to intensify the inspection of tax assessors. In a letter sent to many inspectors, he set out his intention of creating a team of honest tax assessors: "If within the limits of your district upon this of any collectors whom you have reason to believe is in the habit of retaining in his own hands any part of his collections for his own purposes, be good enough to furnish me with the name of such collector".[27] Lewis' wishful thinking was thwarted by the novelty of the tax collection system which led to more corruption and fraud. Moreover, citizens complained about the use of informers to enforce the new tax law, as well as about compensation for tax officials being based on the amount of revenue they collected. As early as 1862, when the new revenue laws were debated upon in Congress, Rep. William Holman, D-Ind., denounced provisions that awarded one half of any money recovered to the Bureau of Internal Revenue official who instituted proceedings against a tax cheat. Two years later, tax collectors, inspectors and informers were part of the daily life of citizens in the network of 185 districts created by the Bureau.

Difficulties in the collection of taxes made the Commissioner fear the development of fraud and tax evasion. Stamp taxes, probably the most ordinary tax of the Civil War since virtually every document was taxed, as were many proprietary articles such as matches, medicines, and perfumes, were counterfeited.[28] These have become collectibles and are a window onto the business and cultural world of the Civil War era in America. The Bureau of Internal Revenue was concerned about the possible loss of revenue from the washing (eliminating the cancel) and reuse of stamps, and various experiments using different colors on stamps were carried out in an effort to reduce this threat. In this context of fraud and corruption, the levy of penalties by tax assessors raised concerns among officials of

[26] Letter sent from D.L. Whitman, Esqu., Rev. Agent, Newark, N.J., Dec. 9th, 1865, Inspectors Book, June 1st 1864 to May 17th 1865, Records for the Civil War Period, Letters sent to revenue agents and inspectors, 1864-1865, RG 58.

[27] Joseph Lewis to A.N. Lewis, esqu., New York, Jan. 2, 1865, Inspectors Book, June 1st 1864 to May 17th 1865, Records for the Civil War Period, Letters sent to revenue agents and inspectors, 1864-1865, RG 58.

[28] On the stamp tax, see Gary Giroux, "Financing the Civil War: The Office of Internal Revenue and the Use of Revenue Stamp" (http://acct.tamu.edu/giroux/financingcivil.htm)

the Bureau. Commissioner Lewis often asked his agents to be more moderate. "As I find a large number of cases of fraudulent evasion of the internal revenue arising in your city, most of which after detection and exposure at the solicitation of the delinquent parties …While the system of internal revenue was new and many persons were ignorant of its provisions it was in my opinion unwise to enact with rigor the penalties provided for violations of law" he wrote to one of his agents in New York.[29]

In Southern States, collections of taxes also proved to be difficult. The Commissioner of Taxes reported in April 1864 that, of the 471 collection districts established, 133 were not administered because of military operations or enemy occupation. Judging from the fact that the War Department set up 1,440 collection depots for tax-in-kind, and that the assessments were made by Treasury Department appointees, it is possible to estimate that there were 1,440 appraisers. In addition, there were probably some laborers or other subordinate employees in some of the districts, but it has not been possible to determine the extent to which this may have been the case. However, the total employment figure of the department would have reached at least 2,780. Few states collected any tax at all, choosing instead to issue their own treasury notes or to borrow from their local banks. The Confederacy had neither the administrative capacity nor the political will, given the opposition to centralized power, to collect most of the taxes it imposed. Treasury Secretary Christopher Memminger reported,

> "the difficulties which are encountered in the collection can only be estimated by the ones who will inspect the mass of papers which are required for each return, and the inquiries necessary to be made of each individual taxpayer. The results of the tax will probably confirm the recommendation already made of a resort to a more simple system of taxation. The frauds and evasions, which cannot be discovered under the present system, are a perpetual drain upon the tax, which is necessarily increased by the number of officers who must be employed in its collection."

Assessors, collectors, and all their assistants were granted the power to search homes and businesses, authority that sat uneasily with many

[29] Letter from Secretary Lewis to Hon. Alex. N Lewis, special agent, NY, Inspectors Book, June 1st 1864 to May 17th 1865, Records for the Civil War Period, Letters sent to revenue agents and inspectors, 1864-1865, RG 58.

taxpayers. In addition, they had broad powers to proceed with assessment and collection when taxpayers were unwilling to file returns and pay appropriate taxes. Many of their actions were difficult if not impossible to appeal.

On January 13, 1865, more than two hundred thousand citizens of Springfield, Massachusetts, complained about the inequity of income taxes since “its burden shall fall more equal on the taxpayers. It is well known that in some cases the taxpayer represents none but himself; while in other case, he represents himself and a numerous family; and the exemption is alike in both cases. So while the bachelor, or the man with a small family pays his tax easily, and might pay more; it bears heavily on the man burdened with the support of a large family. It in fact offers a premium on bachelors and small families”.[30] The petition reveals the widespread feeling among Americans of unfairness as far as taxes were concerned. And so it is no coincidence that taxes should become very unpopular as soon as the war ended.

On December 1866, Congress charged a select committee with investigating "any frauds or evasions in the payment of internal duties" as well as the role of revenue officers in compromises, settlements, and underpayments. The committee issued a report the following year stating that "they doubted that the laws would ever be efficiently executed until there has been a reorganization of the revenue force." On March 31, 1868, heavy penalties were laid upon revenue officers and agents for gross neglect of duty or for defrauding the United States. The same penalties applied if the revenue officer or agent had knowledge of fraud committed by any person and failed to report it in writing. During March 1868 a new congressional committee investigated revenue frauds. The committee report accused President Andrew Johnson and his supporters of direct involvement in the fraud. On July 20, 1868 Congress passed a revenue act strengthening the administrative control of the Commissioner over his field officers. The Commissioner was authorized to appoint 25 “supervisors of internal revenue” who would have the power to transfer or suspend any officer or field employee of the Internal Revenue Bureau for neglect of duty, abuse of power, or fraud. The Commissioner was also given authority to hire 25 “detectives” to prevent fraud upon the government and assist in the collection of taxes.

[30] Petition of 2136 citizens of Springfield, MA for a modification of the Internal Revenue laws in respect to income, Jan. 13, 1865, Folder HR 38A – G24.12, 13, 14, Tray HR 38A-E24.11 to HR38A –E24.17, RG 233.

Many opponents of the tax regime stressed the necessity of implementing a civil service reform. In 1868, a businessman of Detroit, E.B. Ward, sponsored a new petition, signed by many representatives throughout the country and adopted by many other business organizations. The petition's prayer offered many expressions of tax resentment to which the organization was publicly committed. It didn't condemn a specific tax but addressed the system as a whole. Its goal was to attract as many opponents as possible. In most petitions, the analysis of governmental operations had still tended towards the negative, deploring both fraud and inefficiency. Petitioners asked for a modernization of the bureaucratic apparatus:

> Income tax to be abolished, because unequal in its operation; but, if not abolished, we *urge* rigid means from its collection from all. Assessors being enjoined to call for full information, and make strict investigation before accepting sworn returns; but when accepted and paid such returns to be *final*, unless fraud can be proven in a Federal Court. No publicity of returns allowed".

Led by E.B. Ward, businessmen from Michigan asked for what Mark Summers has labeled "a more activist judiciary [and] a professional bureaucracy" (Summers 1993). Another delegate, sent by the National Convention of Manufacturers at Cleveland, went to Washington to "urge Congress to discuss to adopting measures for the reduction of the taxes, now so oppressive of the whole country". What he discovered was the whole machinery of the Government:

> The first obstacle to any large reduction of taxation I met with was the influence and power of the great army of useless employees that the war had fastened upon the treasury. I found the War Department asked for \$95,000,000, exclusive of bounties and pensions; the Navy Department for \$47,000,000; the Civil Service for \$50,000,000, each department vying with the other to aggrandize itself at the expense of the producing class of the country. These enormous demands were in no instance accompanied with even a remote conference to the almost exasperated tax-payers of this country. The annual estimates for the wants of the Government are a disgrace to the Nation. I took special pains to ascertain what reductions ought to be made in the War and Navy departments, and so far as I could

in the Civil Service, and I am entirely satisfied that the number of ships in actual service should be reduced from 103 to not over 30 in all".[31]

The reduction of taxes went together with a reform of the Federal Government as one petition sent by businessmen put it:

1st. Pass the 'Civil Services' of Hon. T.A. Jeneckes.
2d. Complete and Pass the New Tax Bill, reducing taxation wherever possible
3rd. Reduce expenses in all departments, and decrease the proportion of costly officers in Army and Navy.
4th. Put all Indian Affairs in charge of the War Department to save cost and stop fraud.
5th. Let lands acquired by treaty from the Indians be sold at public land offices, and not in large tracts to speculators.
6th. Grant no subsidies in money or bonds to railroads.
7th. Stop large and useless appropriations for Custom House and Hospitals
8th. Adopt such measures as in your wisdom you deem best to turn the balance of trade in our favor, that our coin may be left at home as a means of resuming specie payments.[32]

However, if these civil service reformers rejected traditional patronage appointments in the North and the South, they did not replace it with anything like the European notions of expert and standing bureaucracies (Hoffer 2007: 118-143). They put the blame for the current state of affairs squarely on the Republicans, who had turned public offices into a political machine. The enlargement of government led naturally to a threat to republicanism and free institutions. Resistance to taxation rallied more and more supporters with the help of business organizations.

In 1872, lawmakers responded to the widespread complaints about assessors by eliminating the position entirely; duties were split between district collectors and revenue agents. The change left the collectors even more powerful. As presidential appointees, they remained largely independent of their nominal superiors in the Treasury Department and the BIR. Also in 1872, Congress experimented with the private collection of federal tax revenues. Lawmakers authorized the commissioner to hire

[31] 40th Congress, Febru. 24, 1868 to Feb. 26, 1868, RG 233.
[32] Trail HR 201 – H19.18, Feb. 27, 1968 to Feb. 1, 1869 & undated , 40th Congress, Committee on Ways and Means, HR40 A – H19.18, Tax reduction, July 8, 1868 to February, 1869 + undated, RG 233.

three private sector individuals to assist in collection efforts. These private collectors were to be paid from the taxes they actually collected. The commissioner approved several contracts for private collection, assigning 50 percent of collected taxes as payment for the services rendered. Two years later, however, Congress investigated the practice and discovered that these collectors were simply collecting taxes that would otherwise have been collected by federal officials. While lawmakers uncovered no corruption, neither did they see any reason to continue the arrangement, and legislators repealed the law in 1874. Despite these several changes at the Bureau of Internal Revenue, the agency remained relatively intact. The end of the income tax brought with it a rollback in agency operations, but most of its organizational infrastructure stayed in place. The post-war reform efforts, initiated by Congress in response to widely acknowledged problems at the Bureau, produced more tinkering than restructuring. An act of December 24, 1872 abolished the offices of assessors and assistant assessors. On May 20, 1873, these offices were closed and the records relating to the Civil War taxes were shipped to the commissioner of internal revenue in Washington, D.C. The Civil War experiment of taxation ended.

Assaults against excisemen during the Gilded and the Progressive Eras

In the fall of 1893, in Murray County, Georgia, Thomas A. McIntyre betrayed George Terry when he informed a deputy marshal about where to find Terry's still. Before the marshal took action, Terry learned that McIntyre had betrayed him, and he hastily removed his still. Several weeks later a band of white caps seized McIntyre from his bed and lashed his back over a hundred times (Holmes 1980: 589-611). In southern communities, lashing was the sentence for informers; arsons or shots were reserved for other revenue agents. As historian Edward Ayers put it, "the New South was a notoriously violent place".[33] Not only did African-Americans suffer from the widespread use of violence, but also white informers, deputy collectors and US marshals who sought to collect excise taxes.

---

[33] Ayers 1992: 155; on the violence in Appalachian region, see McKinney 1977: 131-44.

After the Civil War, excise taxes on whiskey became one of the cornerstones of the revenue system as taxes on alcohol and tobacco products were the only ones left in place after 1872.[34] Men who collected excise taxes were also contractors in so far as they were paid a percentage of their collections. For Republicans in power, the system provided hundreds of patronage jobs. If taxes on whiskey have always been unpopular, the "Whiskey Ring" scandal intensified local critics. Indeed, in 1875 Secretary of the Treasury Bristow investigated and broke up the conspiracy of distillers and internal revenue officials known as the "Whiskey Ring".[35] Orville Babcock, President Grant's private secretary was indicted and the President himself was implicated in this scandal. In the end, more than $3 million in taxes was recovered and 238 persons were indicted and 110 convicted. Such scandals pushed both Republicans and Democrats to reconsider the spoils system and envision a civil career system (Skowronek 1982: 47-84; 177-211). In many States, attempts to reform the civil administration in the 1870s and 1890s created more resistance and violence than consent, since many taxpayers considered excise taxes as unfair. However, the idea was not to create a European-style system of civil service since, as commissioner of Revenue Green B. Raum contended, "such a system would create a privileged class removed from the influences of popular sentiment, which in this country is a constantly opening force favorable to honest, efficient administration" (White 1958: 316-317).

While most internal taxes had disappeared, excisemen embodied the fiscal responsibilities of the Federal Government. In Northeastern States, their action and brutal methods of collection were denounced through petitions. Hundreds of petitioners signed a text advocating "the speedy consideration and passage of Hon. E.R. Meade's Internal Revenue Bill in the belief of the reduction of the tax of 50 cents per gallon, the reform of the official system, and the simplification of the present unwieldy method of collection, will decrease governmental expenses, increase revenue, prevent fraud, and encourage honest business".[36] Between March and May

---

[34] During the period 1911-1913, alcohol and tobacco taxes produced even more revenue than did tariffs. See Brownlee 2004: 37-38.

[35] On the whiskey ring and its impact on public opinion, see Summers 1993: 89-90; 184-185.

[36] Petition…, House Bill n° 2331: to define the powers and duties of officers of Internal Revenue and to further provide for the collection of the tax on distilled

1876, the petition was signed by 718 brewers in the country and sent to Congressmen. Elsewhere, notably in Southern States, resistance took a more violent turn in the years following the Reconstruction. From 1877 to 1915, more than one hundred of revenue agents, from informers and guides to deputy collectors, were wounded or killed in Southern States. The most violent years were between July 1877 and June 1878 and March 1895 and December 1899, as table n° 1 shows.

Table 6-1: Assaults against tax Revenue agents in Southern States (1877-1815)[37]

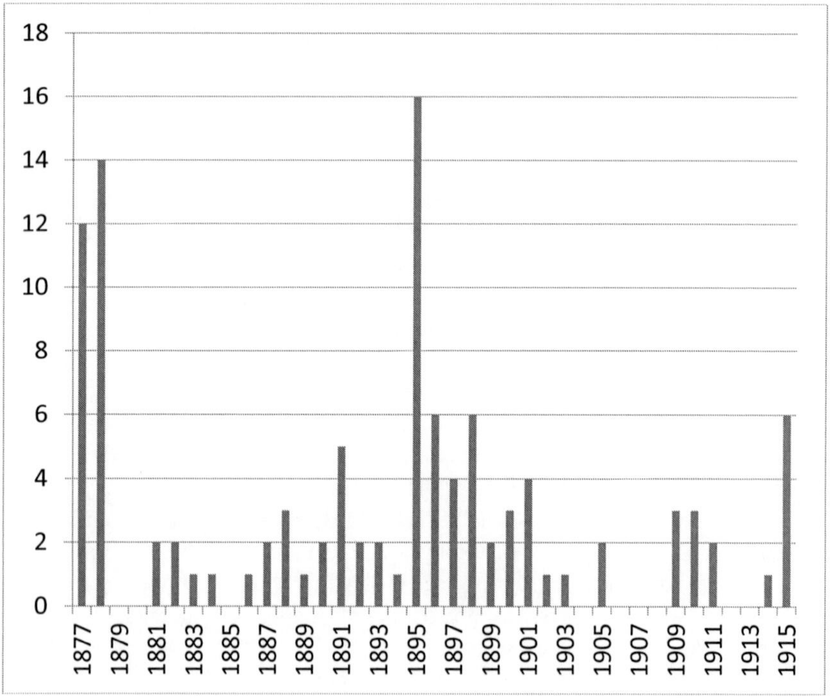

The main regions of tax resistance were located in Georgia and Tennessee, as table n° 2 shows. Attacks also occurred in the Cumberland

spirits, 44th Congress, Committee on Ways and Means, HR 44A-H20.8, Trail HR 44A – H20.6 to HR44A-H20.8, RG 233.

[37] The table is based upon annual reports of the Bureau of internal revenue.

Mountains of eastern Kentucky, West Virginia, and western Virginia. At the end of the nineteenth century, assaults against revenue agents were more concentrated in the rugged Blue Ridge-Smoky Mountain border areas of eastern Tennessee, western North Carolina, northwestern South Carolina, and northern Georgia.

Table 6-2: Assaults against revenue agents by States (1877-1915)[38]

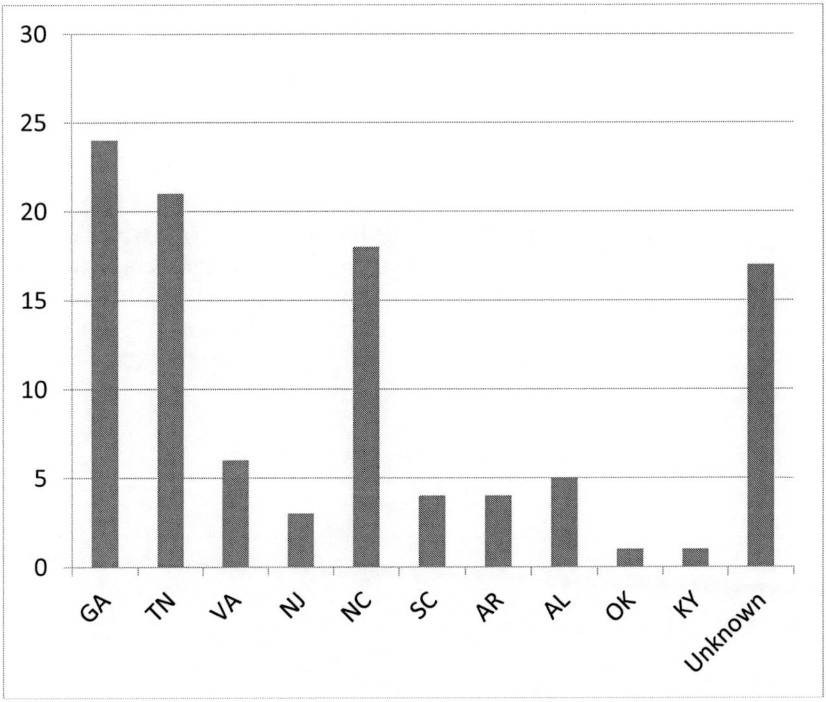

If the whole hierarchy of revenue agents had been victims of violence (see table n° 4 below), punishments depended upon the status of revenue agents. As they were members of the community, guides and informers were whipped, before being killed. Sometimes, revenue agents were only threatened and asked to leave the county. Mountaineers tried to frighten the revenue men by conspicuously following them, sometimes rescuing

[38] The table is based upon annual reports of the Bureau of internal revenue.

their prisoners.[39] Houses were dynamited, families were threatened. Shooting occurred during direct interactions between tax agents and distillers, and caused the death of many people on both sides.

Table 6-3: Types of punishment against tax agents[40]

Types of Punishment	Total Uses
Whipping	4
Arson and dynamiting of homes	8
Shot	54
Shot and killed	43

Campaigns against moonshiners were led by deputy collectors, appointed by the collector of the district. Usually based in the county seat town, they recruited for individual raids revenue agents who lived in town or nearby. These posse men rarely lived near the moonshiners, but knew them. Revenue posses were led by one or more deputy collectors and deputy marshals. The marshals served warrants on individual moonshiners and could also arrest, without a warrant, any blockaders they caught. Revenue officers usually relied on informers.

Table 6-4: Typology of tax agents assailed[41]

Functions	Total
Deputy Collector	36
Internal Revenue Officer	12
Revenue Agent	14
Informer	4
Guide	8
US Marshal	17
Posse man	17

[39] On small incidents, see Letter from J. A. George to Green B. Raum, April 28, 1877, box 897, Letters Received by the Commissioner, Records of the Internal Revenue Service, RG 58; report of G. W. Atkinson to Green B. Raum, May 18, 1877, box 895, RG 58.

[40] The table is based upon annual reports of the Bureau of internal revenue.

[41] The table is based upon annual reports of the Bureau of internal revenue.

The rise in tension was caused by many factors including general tension between the citizens and the Federal Government, the attempts by federal officers to impose new procedures of enforcement, and accusations of corruption made by citizens against revenue agents.

First, the aftermath of the Civil War complicated the process of tax collection. Federal officials who collected revenue in the South were frequently the same as had the duty of enforcing civil rights. Until the end of the Reconstruction, district attorneys, marshals, and soldiers were responsible for upholding Reconstruction and worked with revenuers in the battle with moonshiners. Therefore, tensions with tax agents were closely linked to Southerners' denunciation of the Federal Government as a whole. Many Southerners feared that Reconstruction would lead to a strong central government dedicated to protecting the civil rights of African-Americans (See Foner 1988; Summers 2009). In some counties shortly after the Civil War, Ku Klux Klansmen attacked people suspected of being revenue informers. After the government intensified its campaign against illegal distillers in 1876, tensions intensified in Southern States. A Raleigh, North Carolina, newspaper carried this theme further: "Excessive taxation in these United States without representation, is not carrying out in good faith the policy inaugurated by the Revolutionists" (Miller 1989: 200). From the 1890s onwards, the tax resistance movement was strongly linked to the whitecap movement, which defended the supremacy of the white race in Southern States.[42]

Second, attempts to improve the enforcement process sparked resistance. After the Civil War, a major reorganization of the collection system occurred leading to a paradoxical transformation: higher centralization of the Bureau and the use of new local agents (gaugers, storekeepers) to record the amount and proof of each barrel of liquor (Schmeckbier; Eble 1923: 7-27). On December 24, 1872, in response to the report from the Special Revenue Commission, Congress enacted legislation which abolished the offices of assessors and assistant assessors and transferred their duties to collectors. Most assessor's offices were closed by May 20, 1873. This act also required a reduction in the number of internal revenue districts to not more than 80. In 1885, the consolidation of collectors' offices that took place over the previous ten years resulted in the elimination of 98 separate offices. From a high of 225 collectors' offices in 1873, the Bureau of Internal Revenue ended this era with only 127. As a dramatic example of these reductions, the State of New York began this

[42] On the whitecap movement, see Holmes 1969: 165-185.

period with thirty two offices and ended with only seven. On May 21, 1887, by executive order President Grover Cleveland reduced the number of internal revenue districts from eighty four to sixty two. Various changes between 1887 and 1914 brought the total number of districts up to sixty seven. In 1868, gaugers were appointed to inspect distilleries and to make sure every gallon was taxed. Storekeepers, who measured and recorded other phases of the distillery's production, were also appointed. Gaugers and storekeepers were paid a flat fee per day, but the gaugers were also paid according to the amount of liquor they measured. To control local agents on the ground, Congress gave power in 1868 to new officials—supervisors—who had to prevent fraud and weed out incompetence. Supervisors could appoint "detectives" (renamed "agents" in 1872) to work in special investigations. Authority was also given to pay rewards of 10 percent of monies collected to informants. On May 18, 1875, the Commissioner established a Division of Revenue Agents, relieving Supervisors of the Revenue of all responsibility in relation to directing Revenue Agents.

On the ground, new procedures of enforcement and control were implemented. In 1876, President Grant appointed a new revenue commissioner Green B. Raum. A "war Democrat", he became a dedicated Republican after the war.[43] Until 1883, Raum launched a campaign against illicit stills and promised to improve the honesty of tax officials. On March 1877, he established a system of inspection of collector's offices which ranked each office against a uniform standard of a "First Class" Office. On August, the number of relatives who could be employed in each Internal Revenue district was limited for the first time. On June 19, 1878, an appropriation act included $75,000 for "detecting and bringing to trial and punishment, persons guilty of violating the internal revenue laws, or accessory to the same, included payments for information and detection..." In 1879, in order to improve knowledge among tax officials, the Commissioner published a compilation of all internal revenue laws and statutes to be used by judges, district attorneys, marshals, and officers of internal revenue. The centralization of control sparked resistance among moonshiners who were no longer able to find an accommodation with revenuers. As a result, they turned to violence until the departure of Raum put an end to the process. The second wave of violence between 1893 and 1895 was also caused by new procedures of enforcement. In the context of the 1893 Depression, more and more farmers turned to moonshining to

[43] On Green B. Raum, see Miller 1991: 97-100.

supplement their incomes. As the government also faced a loss of tax revenue, officials increased the number of revenue agents to collect excise taxes. In Georgia, in 1893, President Grover Cleveland appointed a new marshal and revenue collector, both of whom pursued more vigorous campaigns against illicit distillers than had their predecessors. Paul B. Trammell, the new federal revenue collector, intensified the campaign to seize illicit stills. Each week he published in a local newspaper a list of stills, kegs, and other distilling apparatus seized by his agents.

Eventually, resistance was caused by dissent among local people about the revenuers, considered as corrupt and inefficient. In many ways, the revenue agent was seen by local people as a threat to their social, racial and economic way of life. By denouncing the "Russian methods" of the revenue agents, moonshiners criticized the fluid boundaries between public and private. Paid on a fee basis, revenue agents could be suspected of arresting as many people as they could to make money.[44] They were also accused of using "professional witnesses" who were often relatives of the taxmen to give false testimony against local people. Investigations made by agents revealed the extent of corruption and negligence in the process of tax collection. In a manual for revenue agents published in 1878, the Bureau of Internal Revenue detailed the missions of the country's tax collectors. In States "infested with illicit distilleries", they had to collect information and to help arrest offenders. Revenue agents were reminded that they "had no power to make seizure or arrest". Only collectors and their deputies could undertake seizure and only US marshals could arrest tax delinquents.

Between 1876 and 1879, however, the Bureau of Internal Revenue reported a total of 165 of its officers prosecuted in State courts. Aware of the high level of corruption, policymakers tried to reform the procedure of measurement and assessment. An Act of August 15, 1876, empowers the Treasury Secretary to combine the duties of storekeeper and gauger in a single officer.[45] The appointment of gaugers proved to be difficult. "Whenever it becomes impracticable for collectors to secure the services of persons who will accept the office of gauger, owing to the inadequacy of the compensation, they will be permitted to nominate for appointment as gaugers one or more of their deputies, who will perform the work

[44] On the expression of Russian methods, see Holmes 1980: 589-611.

[45] *United States Internal-Revenue Gaugers' Manual embracing Regulations and Instructions and Tables*, March, 12, 1913, U.S. Government Printing Office, Washington D.C., 1913: 3.

without extra compensation or fees, but actual traveling expenses incurred for gauging will be allowed".[46] A deputy collector was not allowed to serve as gauger while acting as collector. On August, 15, 1876, an appropriation act provided for the transmittal of revenue stamps to collectors by registered mail, dispensed with the "gauging of packages of distilled spirits filled on the premises of wholesale liquor-dealers", and provided that such packages "shall thereafter be stamped under such regulations as the Commissioner of Internal Revenue may prescribe". Under the provisions of this act, the duties of the gauger and storekeeper could be combined into one position for the first time. The storekeeper recorded the times of emptying and filling the mash tubs and weighed the grain used in preparing the mash to make sure that the distiller's output matched what was recorded in the official survey of the distillery. The gauger was in charge of the cistern room, to which the spirits were piped after fermentation. His goal was to record the exact quantity produced and to test the proof of the contents of each barrel. He stamped each barrel with a serial and barrel number, the proof and gallon content, and his name and place. The barrels were then placed in a warehouse bond valid for up to a year. As the Charge Book for the period 1878-1883 reveals, it was easy to subvert the system by bribery.[47] Distillers bribed the storekeeper to allow the use of more grain than the law allowed and employment of "quick yeast" to speed fermentation to twenty-four hours instead of forty-eight. This doubled the output of whiskey although the storekeeper's records would show only the legal amount of grain and the usual fermentation period. The gauger was then paid to allow removal of unstamped barrels from the distillery or reuse of old stamps. Another method of corruption required the gauger to record only half the amount of unblended whiskey received on the stamp stubs.[48] As the charge book puts it, many gaugers were also accused of using "incorrect gauging rods".[49] On July 1, 1880, responsibility for the appointment of storekeepers, gaugers, and tobacco inspectors was shifted from the Commissioner of Internal Revenue to the Secretary of the Treasury. In January 1881, beginning that month, distilleries producing 100 bushels or less each day were placed under the control of a single storekeeper-gauger. Before this, the cut-off had been distilleries producing 60 bushels or less each day. On

---

[46] *Ibid:* 3-4.
[47] Charge Book from 1879 to March 1883, Vol. 1 of 1, Entry 326, RG 58.
[48] Charge Book from 1879 to March 1883: 16, 19, 24.
[49] Charge Book from 1879 to March 1883 29.

July 16, 1881, for the first time, the Bureau of Internal Revenue required applicants for positions of storekeeper, gauger, inspector, or other subordinate positions to submit applications in writing, including age, legal residence, place of birth, service in the Army or Navy, names of relatives employed in the government, experience, and previous work, accompanied by recommendations. However, such reforms didn't put an end to tensions between moonshiners and revenuers as the second wave of violence demonstrates.

Conclusion

In his second Inaugural Address of 1805, after many violent forms of resistance, from the Whiskey Rebels (1794) to the Hot Water War led by John Fries (1798-1799), President Jefferson was pleased to present his fellow-Americans with a tax paradise based upon tariff; he promised that it would be "the pleasure and pride of an American to ask, what farmer, what mechanic, what laborer ever sees a tax-gatherer of the United States?"[50] For many Americans from the Early Republic to the Civil War, tariff became the ideal tax: invisible in its collection, it subsidized the domestic producers of the goods that it taxed and prevented Americans from having to confront the issue of slavery and the taxation of property.[51] In 1888, Van Buren Denslow, then professor of Economics at the University of Chicago, still celebrated the virtue of tariff policy when he contended that the "most convenient time and manner in which to pay a tax is when we pay it without knowing it." (Denslow 1888: 461). Jefferson's view on invisible taxes also matched the vision of a proprietary democracy, rooted in local governments (Appleby 1992; Baylin 1967; Kerber 1985: 474-495). In a classical republican vision, property conferred the economic and political dependence that a republic required in its citizenry.[52] Therefore, the Federal Government should not intrude into the local and private affairs of republican citizens.

During the nineteenth century, most Americans believed in the Jeffersonian creed of the Republic without taxpayers and without tax collectors. Therefore, resistance to any forms of new taxes became

[50] "Second Inaugural Address", *A Compilation of the Messages and Papers of the Presidents, 1789-1908*, I, (Washington D.C., 1908), 379.

[51] On the idea of invisible tax and consent, see Balogh 2008: 380-381; on the links between taxation, tariff and slavery, see Einhorn 2006: 117-156.

[52] For a recent analysis of the ideal of proprietary democracy, see Ott 2011: 12-15.

prevalent in the American Republic. Resistance to new taxes was one of the reasons that Americans went to war against Great Britain. The threat of British functionaries violating the liberties of Americans was as unnerving to the colonists as the financial consequences of such taxes (Morgan 1953; Rabushka 2008; Richards 2004; Huret 2014). The bureaucratic legacy was also important. American policymakers still hesitated between using professional revenue agents or influential local people, between accommodation and centralization, between private and public spheres. As a result, they created a hybrid system mixing private and public officers. Gaugers, storekeepers, customs' officers, assessors and deputy collectors were always suspected of having personal interests in the collection process. Paradoxically, attempts to improve the system created more dissent than consent: the creation of a more centralized system sparked resistance among the population since it left no room for accommodation and negotiation. It was easier to reach an accommodation with local gaugers than with newly appointed deputy collectors. Importantly, bureaucratic reforms were seen as an attempt to dispossess local elites of their power. The distrust of bureaucracy will have a lasting impact on the construction of the revenue system in the twentieth century. The implementation of withholding at the source during World War Two will be the result of negotiations between businessmen and policymakers, who were perfectly aware of the failure of collection during the nineteenth century.

Archives

RG 56 Record Group 56, National Archives, Washington D. C.
RG 58 Record Group 58, National Archives, Washington D. C.
RG 233 Record Group 233, National Archives, Washington D. C.
OWP Oliver Wolcott Papers, Connecticut State Historical Society, Connecticut
Treasury Records Department of the Treasury, Manuscript Division, Library of Congress, Washington

References

Ayers, E.L., (1992), *The Promise of the New South. Life After Reconstruction*, New York: Oxford University Press.

Appleby, J., (1992), *Liberalism and Republicanism in the Historical Imagination*, Cambridge: Harvard University Press.

Balogh, B., (2008), *A Government Out of Sight. The Mystery of National Authority in Nineteenth-Century America*, Cambridge: Cambridge University Press.

Baylin, B., (1967), *Ideological Origins of the American Revolution*, Cambridge: Harvard University Press.

Bensel, R., (1991), *Yankee Leviathan. The Origins of Central State Authority in America, 1859-1877*, Cambridge: Cambridge University Press.

Bonsteel Tachau, M.K., (1982), "The Whiskey Rebellion in Kentucky: A Forgotten Episode of Civil Disobedience", *Journal of the Early Republic*, 2/3, Autumn: 239-259.

—. (1978) *Federal Courts in the Early Republic: Kentucky 1789-1816*, Princeton: Princeton University Press.

Bouton, T., (2000), "No wonder the times were troublesome": The Origins of Fries Rebellion", *Pennsylvania History*, 67, Winter: 21-42.

Brown, R.H., (1993), *Redeeming the Republic: Federalists, Taxation, and the Origins of the Constitution*, Baltimore: Johns Hopkins University Press.

Brownlee, E., (2004), *Federal Taxation in America: A Short History*, New York: Cambridge University Press.

Churchill, R., (2000), "Popular Nullification, Fries' Rebellion, and the Waning of Radical Republicanism 1798-1801", *Pennsylvania History*, 67, Winter: 105-140.

Dalzell, F., (1991), "Taxation Without Representation: Federal Revenue in the Early Republic", Ph.D. Dissertation, Harvard University.

—. (1992. "Prudence and the Golden Egg: Establishing the Federal Government in Providence, Rhode Island", *New England Quarterly*, 65/3 (September): 355-388

Daunton, M., (2001), *Trusting Leviathan. The Politics of Taxation in Britain 1799-1914*, Cambridge: Cambridge University Press.

Denslow, V.D., (1888), *Principles of the Economic Philosophy of Society, Government and Industry*, New York: Cassell.

Edling, M., (2003), *A Revolution in Favor of Government. Origins of the U.S. Constitution and the Making of the American State*, New York: Oxford University Press.

Einhorn, R., (2006), *American Taxation, American Slavery*, Chicago: University of Chicago Press.

Freeman, J. B., (2003), "Explaining the unexplainable. The cultural context of the Sedition Act", in Jacobs and *al.*, (eds.), *The Democratic Experiment. New Directions in American Political History*: 20-49.

Gould, R., (1996), "Patron-Client Ties, State Centralization, and the Whiskey Rebellion", *The American Journal of Sociology*, 102/2 (Sep.): 400-429.

Hoffer, W.H., (2007), *To Enlarge the Machinery of Government. Congressional Debates and the Growth of the American State, 1858-1891*, Baltimore: Johns Hopkins University Press.

Holmes, W.F., (1969), "Whitecapping: Agrarian Violence in Mississippi, 1902-1906", *The Journal of Southern History*, 35/2 (May): 165-185.

—. (1980), "Moonshining and Collective Violence: Georgia, 1889-1895", *Journal of American History*, 67/3 (Dec.): 589-611.

Huret, R., (2009), "All again in the family? Political history and the challenge of social history ", *Journal of Policy History*, 21/3: 239-263.

—. (2014), *American Tax Resisters*, Cambridge, Harvard University Press, 2014.

Jacobs, M., Novak, W., and Zelizer, J., (eds.), (2003), *The Democratic Experiment. New Directions in American Political History,* Princeton: Princeton University Press.

John, R., (1995). *Spreading the News: The American Postal System from Franklin to Morse*, Cambridge, MA: Harvard University Press.

Kerber, L.K., (1985), "The Republican Ideology of the Revolutionary Generation", *American Quarterly*, 37: 474-495

Kohn, R.H., (1972), "The Washington Administration's Decision to Crush the Whiskey Rebellion", *Journal of American History*, 59/3 (Dec.): 567-584.

Martin, I.W., (2008), *The Permanent Tax Revolt. How the Property tax Transformed American Politics*, Stanford: Stanford University Press.

McKinney, G.B., (1977), "Industrialization and Violence in Appalachia in the 1890s", in Williamson, *An Appalachian Symposium: Essays Written in Honor of Cratis D. Williams*: 131-44.

Miller, W., (1989), "The Revenue: Federal Law Enforcement in the Mountain South, 1870-1900", *The Journal of Southern History*, 55/2: 200.

—. (1991), *Revenuers and Moonshiners. Enforcing Federal Liquor Law in the Mountain South 1865-1900*, Chapel Hill: University of North Carolina Press.

Morgan, E; Morgan, H., (1953), *The Stamp Act Crisis: Prologue to Revolution*, Chapel Hill: University of North Carolina Press.

Neely, M. E. Jr., (2002), *The Union Divided. Party Conflict in the Civil War North*, Cambridge: Harvard University Press.

Newman, P. D., (2004), *Frie's Rebellion. The Enduring Struggle for the American Revolution*, Philadelphia: University of Pennsylvania Press.

Ott, J. C., (2011), *When Wall Street Met Main Street. The Quest for an Investors' Democracy,* Cambridge, MA: Harvard University Press.

Rabushka, A., (2008), *Taxation in Colonial America*. Princeton: Princeton University Press.

Rao, G., (2016), *National Duties: Custom Houses and the Making of the American State*, Chicago: University of Chicago Press.

Richards, L., (2004), *Shay's Rebellion. The American Revolution's Final Battle*. Philadelphia: University of Pennsylvania Press.

Schmeckbier, L.F., Eble, F.X., (1923), *The Bureau of Internal Revenue: Its History, Activities and Organization*, Baltimore: Johns Hopkins University Press.

Skowronek, S., (1982), *Building a New American State. The Expansion of National Administrative Capacities 1877-1920*, New York: Cambridge University Press.

Summers, M.W., (1993), *The Era of Good Stealings*, New York: Oxford University Press.

—. (2009), *A Dangerous Stir. Fear, Paranoia, and the Making of Reconstruction*. Chapel Hill: University of North Carolina.

Slaughter, T.P., (1986), *The Whiskey Rebellion: Frontier Epilogue to the American Revolution*, New York: Oxford University Press.

White, L.D., (1958), *The Republican Era: A Study in Administrative History*, New York: Macmillan.

Williamson, J.W., (ed), (1977), *An Appalachian Symposium: Essays Written in Honor of Cratis D. Williams*, Boone, N.C.: Appalachian State University Press

Wilson M., (2006), *The Business of the Civil War: Military Mobilization and the State*, Baltimore: Johns Hopkins University Press.

CHAPTER SEVEN

PUBLIC OFFICE AND PRIVATE BENEFIT IN EARLY MODERN ENGLAND

MICHAEL J. BRADDICK

At the heart of this volume lies the relationship between political authority and other aspects of social relations. The rise of the state is often narrated as the emergence of an institution charged with the service of the public good, isolated from social interests, but in pursuing this line of argument, the editors suggest, historians accept an ideological move—that public action really does reflect and serve the public good. In fact, as many of the essays here demonstrate, public action was a more complex phenomenon, involving multiple institutions and social interests. In this essay I respond to that discussion by considering the relationship between public action and the reproduction of social order from the point of view of state actors themselves, through the analysis of the relationship between private benefit and public good.

This point of departure grows out of an approach I have taken elsewhere to the problem of analyzing the relationship between political and social power, between the institutions of the state and other social interests. Many recent works have rendered the study of the state complicated by demonstrating a) how institutions were complex and overlapping, so that it is not easy to disentangle state institutions from other authorities and b) that the exercise of power by those institutions was frequently influenced by wider networks of social relations. In response to these and other problems, my own account of state formation in early modern England took as its point of departure a concentration on the kind of power peculiar to the state—political power—rather than any particular institutional form or functional purpose for the exercise of that kind of power. The key analytic question in such an approach became how to explain the forms and functions *assumed* by political power in a given society—how particular interests successfully harnessed political power, and the institutional forms and rhetorics which rendered those uses of political power legitimate (Braddick 2000).

The complexity of the relationship between political power and other social interests is not simply an analytic one—it is also a perennial problem for state actors seeking to legitimate their uses of political power. Crucial to the exercise of political power is the ideological move of presenting this action as a service of the public good. Legitimation of political action in terms of the public good is crucial to the naturalization of political power. By the same token, perceived abuse of power throws light on this process of legitimation: what kinds of abuse are possible, and how abuse is identified and expressed, reveal dimensions of the embroilment of political power in a wider web of social relations. In many European historiographies the material is available for an analysis of this kind in relation to the monarchy or great lords—what languages were used to define the personal abuse of power—but this is a less-developed theme at the lower levels of administration. In this chapter I pay more attention to the people exercising power in those day-to-day contexts that, according to Goffman, are where the world's work gets done.[1] The historical context for this discussion is a transformation in the fiscal structure of the English (and, from 1707, British) state, that created new forms of political action and new problems of legitimation, and much of the discussion will center on those raising or handling revenues in the name of the public good.

In one of the most influential books in eighteenth century English history published during the 1980s and 90s, John Brewer overturned the normal assumption about the relationship between strong state authority and absolutism. Instead, he argued, the lesson of English history was that effective fiscal power and elaborated bureaucracy could quite happily co-exist with representative government; indeed they were, in the English case, interdependent. At the core of the relationship was the national debt, and the distribution of benefits that it facilitated: taxation offered the security for spending on a hitherto unimaginable scale. Very soon after the key financial reforms of the 1690s the English state had access to credit on a scale which changed the nature and potential of its military interventions, raising spending power by 34% in the 1690s, and 40% during the eighteenth century. This national debt offered a permanent potential investment to tens of thousands of English people, who acquired an

[1] Goffman quoted in Burns 1992: 18.

interest in the persistence of the regime, and of its fiscal arrangements (Brewer 1989).

It is this question of benefits, and the relationship between benefits and political effectiveness that I want to discuss here. In many other national literatures there is a ready category through which to discuss this relationship, and its abuse: corruption. Joel Hurstfield wrote an influential essay on the subject many years ago, arguing that the key issue was the relationship between private benefit and public service. In a cash-poor monarchy it was inevitable that servants would use their position to generate benefits that could not be provided directly by the government. The key question was the relationship between this and their public service: "where gifts are accepted while holding judicial office; where state revenues are directed into private purses; where appointment and advancement in the public service are by favoritism, or for reasons other than the public interest".[2] Others interested in administrative history have subsequently taken up this problem, but this term is largely absent from the English historical lexicon. It seems to me, however, that the still larger question of how we think about the relationship between public service and private benefit, an issue by no means irrelevant to an understanding of the history of the English state, has attracted hardly any attention at all.

One feature of the system that Brewer describes that does not detain him very much is its hybridity. He pays a lot of attention to the bureaucracy of the eighteenth century, and in particular to the excise and customs services, but little to the patrimonial administration which underpinned the land taxes which were also crucial to the stability of the fiscal system. One thing I want to do in this chater is consider how private benefit and public service were discussed in that context. Another is to discuss an area of the English state in which the term corruption does have currency—the analysis of the conduct of those close to the royal court, and in particular those close to royal finances. Finally, I will look a little more closely at the career of John Cannon, who figures in Brewer's account of the excise bureaucracy. The real work of the image of bureaucracy in the early modern excise was, I argue, to insulate local officers from charges of personal financial benefit at the expense of the tax payer. Many other forms of private benefit persisted, in the excise and elsewhere, as did the notion of a "place" well into the nineteenth century.

---

[2] Hurstfield 1967: 34. There are some interesting reflections on the relationship between private profit and public good in Sacks 1990: 121-42.

Officeholders and private benefit in the administration of direct taxation, 1550—1640

The land tax was in one sense less important to the finances of the Hanoverian state than the excise: the latter was permanent and provided the security for long-term borrowing, whereas the land tax was granted for limited periods and purposes. In terms of aggregate value, however, the land tax remained very significant: between 1688 and 1714, for example it raised £46 million of the total of £122 million in tax revenues enjoyed by the Crown (38%) (Brewer 1989: 95). It was a partition tax administered by local gentlemen, acting to specific commissions: it relied on those men who were acting as magistrates in their localities, and whose service was generally taken to reinforce their local social standing. The land tax was "a locally domesticated tax whose workings were adapted as much to the needs of merchants, gentlemen, and the populace in the provinces as to the requirements of the Treasury Board in London" (Brewer 1988: 349).

The personal financial benefits of the positions were limited—a handling charge, or poundage, was customarily paid, and there is some evidence that the possibility of using the balances between the point at which they were collected and remitted was exploited by some individuals. It may, for example, have been one reason why Humphrey Chetham, a substantial cloth merchant, was chosen as collector of the Ship Money during the 1630s while, more generally, the origins of provincial banking have been related to the possibility of using cash balances from tax collection prior to remittance to London. Certainly, it seems that private credit was crucial to the transfer of funds: much of the money was accounted for in London was paid by tally, rather than in cash. Later on, this was systematized in paper credit, in order to limit the amount of cash that was being moved around the country. But this clearly created opportunities for those handling the money. As the Treasury Commissioners complained to the tax receivers in Norfolk in 1695, the large arrear on their collection (£17,000) arose principally from "the extraordinary advantages you insist upon and receive by return [i.e. payment to London] of the moneys".[3]

By modern standards, this seems a recipe for abuse, but it is characteristic of early modern states in general: lacking effective public credit, early modern monarchies relied on private credit, which they

---

[3] Shaw 1935: 1208. For the development of the exchange office see Braddick 1994: 162.

mobilized by offering favor to those with credit to deploy on their behalf. This is well-remarked upon in relation to royal borrowing, as are the private benefits that accrued to the individuals who were able to deploy personal credit on behalf of the Crown.[4] It has been less remarked upon in relation to the remittance of public money from the localities to the center. There is some evidence that the intermingling of personal credit and public finance led some individuals into trouble. John White, for example, collector of a large land tax in Oxfordshire in the mid-1660s, had received £5796, but was "altogether unable to make payment thereof in one entire sum", and there were similar problems elsewhere (Braddick 1994: 162-3).

However, the principal benefit of unpaid positions in the patrimonial administration of the land taxes was influence, and the principal abuse identified was favoritism. In the early seventeenth century governments had been concerned that this served to undermine taxation altogether: that local officeholders were courting a "vain popularity" by under-assessing their neighbors to the detriment of the public service. William Tooker launched a familiar critique, when he claimed that

> It is to bee feared some of those who are busied in this commission [of tax collection] that they know to much, others to little belonging to the service, some sitte for shew or ostentation, some for protection of their frendes, others utterly remisse and slacke, some other distast the service which their fellow commissioners undergo by reason of some peccant or malignant humour of popularitie or partialitie, last of all some post and hast away the service thrustinge all upon one day whereas the business requireth a longer session & more considerate valuation of the parties presented.[5]

There is evidence that conscientious officeholders could try to make moral judgments in apportioning taxes—to do the just thing—and this aligned with their self-image as fathers of their country (Braddick, 1994: 27-8, 29, 74 n., 111-12). Indeed, the evidence of the yields of taxation is that unless some limit was imposed on this discretion by the apportionment of fixed sums to each locality, then the downward pressure on tax assessments was relentless (Braddick, 1994: 78-117). To their critics the private benefits—of popularity, partiality and of an easy life—clearly outweighed the call of public service.

---

[4] Outhwaite, 1966: 289-505; Outhwaite 1971: 251-63; Ashton 1960.

[5] William Tooker, "A discourse touching the diminution of the subsidy", British Library, Harleian MSS 188, fo. 5v.

Caterpillars and locusts: private benefits in the local enforcement of royal rights, 1550-1640

For a generation the emphasis of local studies of state formation in England has been on these officeholders, and their counterparts at the village level, the constables. Their interests and rewards were not primarily financial, but those of standing, status and respect; the corollary was favoritism, idleness and partiality. In English historiography the term "corruption" seems to have been reserved primarily for those handling money, and specifically for inappropriate private benefit from that position, and is primarily associated with studies of the royal court, or those in the most senior legal and administrative positions. At the local level, however, similar patterns of abuse can be seen. The monarchy was cash poor, but had extensive legal rights that could be turned to advantage —these were important assets. Minor officials could be rewarded with opportunities rather than direct bounty. Elizabethan and Jacobean financial policy largely concentrated on restricting expenditure rather than maximizing revenue, with the result that receipts from many sources of royal income had declined in relative terms, and some of them absolutely. Cash-poor but in its legal rights asset-rich, the Crown had preferred to put people in a position from which they could make money rather than to pay proper fees and salaries. Direct government revenue was reduced but these arrangements met obligations to government servants with no direct monetary cost to the exchequer. In the early seventeenth century, however, the costs of government were rising, and this approach was increasingly an impediment. In order to raise cash the Crown sold more and more concessions—creating monopolies in the trade or manufacture of particular commodities, for example, which yielded a profit through the fines imposed for breaches of the monopolies—and more assets were sold. In the short-term the government raised cash, without the attendant costs of administration, but it came at the long-term cost of lost control of assets and legal rights (Peck 1990).

In the localities this created a space for a host of shady characters, such as common informers, or monopolists. Lacking a bureaucracy, or the means to create and fund one, particular legal rights or sanctions depended for their enforcement on the private benefit of particular individuals, as at Court. Particular people, or groups of people, were given licenses for these limited purposes, and their reward lay in securing fines or payments from those of their victims who wanted to avoid court appearances. Money was raised in this way from domestic industrial production (through patents of monopoly, with the possibility of collecting fines from those who breached them) and it was a means used to maximize revenue by, for example, farming out the rights to particular sources of revenue to individuals—the customs duties, for example (Peck 1990: chapter 6). Beyond this lay an even more loosely connected group, the common informers, who lived off the rewards available under the law to those who brought information of legal infringements before the courts. This was particularly important in the enforcement of economic regulations of various kinds. The rewards took the form of a share of the fines, or direct "composition" with offenders, which allowed them to avoid a court appearance in return for a payment (presumably less than their full legal liability in court). In general, the relationship between the private interest of the informer and the larger purposes of good government was, at best, indistinct: as a result "the marriage of justice with malice or avarice which helped to discredit common informers in the eyes even of those who were not lawbreakers".[6]

Those enjoying these licenses and powers were often accused of avarice and cheating, and were abused as greedy or dishonest: rogue, caterpillar or knave, for example, were favored terms of abuse.[7] Purveyors and saltpetermen, who secured supplies for the Crown, found themselves in the same position. Purveyors could take up supplies for the royal court at the King's price, rather than the market price, the latter being of course much lower. This meant that the burden of supplying the royal court fell unevenly—on those who the purveyors could successfully coerce. As a result there were moves to regulate the right to purveyance, by making a cash payment of the difference between the King's price and the market price (Woodworth 1945: esp. 18-26, 37-38; Smith 1974: 293-302).

The saltpetermen were charged with collecting the crucial ingredient of gunpowder, and had the right to dig where they thought it might be had. This was widely regarded as an invitation to abuse—showing scant regard for property rights, being surly with property owners and local officeholders, and being not particularly good at clearing up after themselves. As Robert Bowyer put it

> Abuse of such as have commission to make Salt Peeter is exceeding great to the Subject in digging up their Dove Houses at unseasonable tymes, and other Houses at their Pleasure; And in takeinge their carts, and their wood

---

[6] Beresford 1957: 221-38 (quotation at p. 221). See also Williams 1979: 148-51.
[7] Braddick 1996: 169-70, 207-9, 220-2; for another example see Peck 1990: 145.

up and other things in more violent and unlawfull sort now, then in tyme of warr.[8]

One final group is worthy of note in this context: the "hunters after concealed lands". Crown lands had been, over the centuries, haphazardly administered, so that there was not always a sound sense of their limits, or the Crown's rights over them. As a result it was possible to make money from Crown service in seeking out encroachments and false titles. Sir Thomas Sherley of Wiston, Sussex, was licensed by James I for this purpose in September 1617 in these terms: because of the "manye alienacons aswell of estats of Inherytaunce as for lyves of mannors lands and tenements holden in Chiefe" had been made since the end of the reign of Elizabeth. In return for an annual rent of £400 Sherley was given power to seek out these alienations for fifteen years from that Michaelmas; his reward was to be two thirds of the proceeds.[9] In touching so closely on property rights, and so clearly in return for direct personal benefit, these commissions were very unpopular. Elizabeth revoked them in 1579 because of their "great misusage" which had convinced the queen that by pretence of law "a great multitude of her loving subjects ... in many cases (though not offending) to have been greatly vexed and molested, and the laws not thereby anything the better executed ... nor any such profit recovered or obtained to her highness' use".[10]

The personal financial interests of monopolists, saltpetermen, purveyors, patentees, licensees, hunters after concealed lands and informers made them all objects of great hostility. The terms of abuse were consistent. The denunciation of the purveyors in the House of Commons in 1604 was characteristic: "they have rummaged and ransacked since your Majesty's first coming in far more than any of your royal progenitors: there hath been no prince since Henry III except Queen Elizabeth who hath not made some one law or other to repress or limit them" (Tanner, 1922: 227). It resonates strongly with the language used by John Culpeper to describe monopolists in 1641 ("nest of wasps, a swarm of vermin which have overcrept the land ... like the frogs of Egypt they have gotten possession of our dwellings ... these are the leeches that have sucked the common wealth so hard it has almost become hectical") and with that used to describe

---

[8] Quoted in Stewart, 1996: 82, n. 6. See now, Cressy 2011: 73-111.

[9] Henry E. Huntington Library, San Marino, CA, EL 1452. See, more generally, Kitching 1974: 63-78.

[10] Hughes and Larkin, 1969: 451-53, at 451-52, dated 15/12/1579.

excise men from the mid-seventeenth century onwards ("what malignant ill-affected persons, what enemies, pests, vipers, locusts and caterpillars to the kingdom and nation" as one writer put it in 1653).[11]

Corruption and royal service at the heart of government, 1550-1640

Much of this hostile comment is accepted more or less at face value by modern commentators, who cannot see this kind of government by license as anything other than an abuse. By contrast, corruption in the central administration is often seen more ambiguously, as a matter of judgment. Two general studies of central administration and court politics provide the point of departure here: Gerald Aylmer's study of *The King's Servants* (in fact the first volume of what became a trilogy) and Linda Levy Peck's *Court, Patronage and Corruption*. The grey area of fees and perquisites was what made these positions attractive, and allowed powerful patrons to build up followings (Aylmer 1961, 1973, 2002; Peck 1990).

As Aylmer makes clear, offices in central government were economic resources, although they carried little by way of salary. Sale of offices was common, although it was usually to those who already had some claim to serve in government, and once in place they could sell more minor offices in order to recoup their investment. For those in office a variety of sources of income presented themselves—fees for standard or particular services, and gifts, for example. In a heroic act of archival retrieval Aylmer was able to estimate that between £273,000 and £373,000 p.a. was received in fees and gratuities by officers in the central administration: a substantial sum, inefficiently distributed, that secured the functioning of the administration in the absence of effective taxation. For the sake of comparison, it is worth noting that the total ordinary royal revenue during the early 1630s, was around £618,000 p.a. Direct payment by the Crown to its officeholders was in the range £320,000 to £340,000: perhaps half of the cost of the central administration was borne by those paying fees for its services (Aylmer 1961: 239-52, esp. 246, 248). Clearly this is a long way from a salaried bureaucracy, and offered plenty of room for maneuver by individuals seeking to maximize the returns from their offices.

Peck discusses the boundaries of what was legitimate in this world in terms of a balance between patronage and favoritism. A widespread

---

[11] Quoted in Braddick 1996: 208-09, 221-22.

language of patronage and bounty, drawing on classical sources, expressed the ideal of the circulation of largesse in return for loyal service. This was workable partly because it was difficult to restrict, or even impose a pattern on, the disposition of court offices. But when too much bounty was directed in a single direction then it appeared to contemporaries as an abuse. This was increasingly the case as the Duke of Buckingham rose in the King's favor in the late 1610s, for example. Unable to reward its servants with salaries, the Crown allowed them perquisites; but how hard to press those perquisites, and how far access to them was regulated by an ultimate interest in the good of the commonwealth or by private favor, were matters of judgment. The fall from power of influential figures was frequently accompanied, or justified, by the claim that they had dipped too deeply into these streams of benefit and patronage, that their own private benefit had taken precedence over their service to the King.

A leading early Stuart example is that of Lionel Cranfield. His fortune had been made at the intersection of justice, patronage and public finance. The son of a mercer and Eastland merchant, Cranfield had by 1612 amassed a significant fortune: first as a mercer and trader and then more latterly on the basis of a more diverse range of activities, including extending credit to individuals. At this point, with his international interests looking less promising or secure, he entered the lucrative world of government credit and contracting.[12]

For Cranfield and others like him, with ready cash, early Stuart royal finances presented a world of opportunity. Starting with some minor speculation in the disposal of Crown lands, and prompted by the fate of his international commercial interests, Cranfield moved into the world of government contracting full-time from 1613. His entrée was facilitated by the earl of Northampton, with whom Cranfield had had some dealings in relation to a starch monopoly. When the Treasury was put into Commission in 1613, to try to get a grip on the Crown's dire financial position, Cranfield made a mark by showing that rents for the customs farm could be increased. This lost him friends in commercial circles, but gained him influence at Court, and he was rewarded with the position of chief surveyor of the customs, a new post worth £200 p.a. He built on this favor effectively, proposing retrenchments and improvements to the revenue, and securing a knighthood, a Mastership in the Court of Requests, and by 1615 he was enjoying the support of the Duke of Buckingham, James I's favorite. Over the next few years Cranfield played

[12] For the following paragraphs on Cranfield see Prestwich 1966.

an important role in commissions which substantially reduced Crown spending, although they failed to solve the financial problems. In 1618 he became Master of the Wardrobe and made considerable savings. As Master of the Court of Wards, a position to which he was appointed in 1619, he brought greater strictness, but with less spectacular savings and remained useful to the government in negotiating leases for the customs farms. In 1619 he became a treasury commissioner.

The success of all this retrenchment did not make Cranfield universally popular, of course, and as he rose in court circles, so this kind of resentment increased. Meanwhile, as he reduced the opportunities for others, he was himself benefitting considerably. These enmities came to matter because he became vulnerable at Court. The outbreak of war in Germany in 1618 produced a divided response: the fate of the Palatinate was essential to the Protestant cause at large, but active involvement in the war threatened financial ruin. In the parliaments of 1621 and in 1624 these issues were very contentious and court politicians became vulnerable to attack. In 1621 the medieval process of impeachment was revived and in 1624 Cranfield became one of its victims. In 1621 he successfully rode the storm, appearing as a champion of the fight against waste, elimination of which would allow parliament to grant funds for war secure in the knowledge that the money would actually be spent in support of the military effort and not simply to "pour water into a leaky cistern". In July 1621 he was elevated to the peerage as Baron Cranfield, in September he became Lord Treasurer and the following year he became Earl of Middlesex.

He was unable to make further progress in improving public finances in his years as Lord Treasurer, although his personal fortune continued to improve. He built up his estate on credit secured against his public position at the Court of Wards and as Treasurer, so that, although he did not take more from those offices than previous incumbents, he was vulnerable to accusations of abuse. He had preferred not to pay for his estates in cash, but to borrow, and it was not clear that this had been against his own profits rather than the King's assets. This was held against him in 1624, when parliament met again, against a background of the deteriorating position of Protestantism, and divisions at court over the correct diplomatic posture to assume. Buckingham, a key figure at court, switched sides from a pro-Spanish position (favoring engagement with the Spanish, and a marriage alliance, as the means by which to advance Crown interests) to the promotion of active intervention in the war. Cranfield remained on the side of retrenchment and diplomacy, and was thus, increasingly, in Buckingham's way. He was accused of corruption, and accepting bribes, and lost office, resulting in his exclusion from public office, exile from the court and a fine of £50,000.

Although careers such Cranfield's have been discussed in terms of corruption, there is a standard contrast with other European monarchies, in that English offices were not bought or sold. They were signs of favor, and officials worked hard to secure that favor, but the absence of venality has been said to offer a contrast between English government and, for example, the contemporary French state. The contrast is not complete—there was no regularized sale of office, or tax on its fruits—but offices were certainly sold in seventeenth-century England. Again, however, they were sold not by the Crown, but by its officials—another key asset that had been alienated in return for service. The French state provided more offices, which were systematically exploited as a source of revenue (Aylmer 1961: 440-1). And, of course, England was very similar to other contemporary European states in depending on forms of reward other than salary in order to fill its offices (Aylmer 1961: 439-53).

Interest and corruption in the fiscal-military state, 1640-1700

Prior to 1640 the monarchy, short of cash but relatively rich in other assets, had rewarded its agents in ways that created forms of benefit quite distinct from the rewards for service in the patrimonial administration, and this had created distinct problems of legitimation—charges of corruption as opposed to favoritism or the seeking of popularity, for example. They were not entirely distinct, however, since the possibilities for personal enrichment in these fiscal offices frequently depended on the continued enjoyment of political favor. During the mid-century crisis the fiscal regime was transformed—government revenues increased dramatically, and the taxation granted by parliament came to dominate total revenues. This increased the government's credit-worthiness too.

Overall, this transformation of public finance created new opportunities for experts. During the 1640s and 1650s the revenue and credit needs of governments increased dramatically—the percentage of national wealth being taxed probably doubled, and the flow of funds through central coffers was smoothed by new instruments of short-term credit. Crucial to this new world were City merchants and traders, able to offer short-term credit on their own account, secured against credible commitments from the exchequer to repay the credit reliably. Under Charles II the so-called "Goldsmith bankers" were crucial to the smoothing of public finance. A number of such figures were also able to secure farms of the revenue, so that their short-term credit was absolutely secure—they controlled (and took a profit from) the flow of revenue that was, in the end, the security for the credit they advanced to the regime. Customs farmers during the reign of Charles I had been creditors as much as tax collectors, and during the 1640s a number of merchants had secured positions of this kind, particularly in the early excise administration. Martin Noell, for example, who made a fortune as a shipper in the West Indian trade, but who in the 1640s and 1650s was able to secure goods and services for the government on the basis of his personal credit. From the later 1640s he bought up excise farms, a move which on his own account was the first step on the road to a massive personal fortune.[13]

Perhaps the outstanding example from the later seventeenth-century, however, was Sir Stephen Fox, who rose from comparative poverty to become the richest commoner in England as a result of his dominance of this crucial nexus of government revenue, disbursement and credit.[14] Born into a family on the lower margins of gentility, he had attended the choir school at Salisbury, with the support of a prosperous relative, until the age of 13. Rather than pursuing his education he went to court, joining his brother John who was a musician there. As a page-boy he was evidently popular, and began a long association with the household of the Prince of Wales, with whom he went into exile following Royalist defeat in the civil war and the execution of the King. When Mazarin persuaded the exiled court to leave France in 1654, paying a pension in order to be rid of the embarrassment, it was Fox who was entrusted with its management. In 1658 he was knighted for his service in husbanding the meager resources of the exiled court and he accompanied Charles back on his return to England in 1660, restored to his Crown.

Others of higher status, if less loyal service, had prior claims on the juicier positions at court, but he did secure positions that put him in a much more comfortable position than he had enjoyed during the 1650s. What made him rich, however, was the need to find regular payment for the King's Guards, formed in 1661. Since the position of Paymaster had not previously existed, it could go to Fox without disappointing a more established court figure. His immediate problem was that there was no

[13] Hughes 1934: 133-5; Aylmer 2004.

[14] For the following account of Sir Stephen Fox's career see Clay 1978.

money to pay the £123,000 bill for the guards. Fox was issued with Exchequer tallies for the money, which he sold on at a discount in order to raise the money to actually pay the soldiers. In this way, and using some of his own money advanced to the commanders with interest, he was able to pay the bills. This was soon regularized as an "Undertaking" whereby an individual would guarantee to advance the soldiers their full wages on time in return for 12d in the pound (5%) of their wages (the "poundage"). They would then recover the money from the exchequer when it was available. Fox soon took it on himself, claiming 5% on all the sums, but only paying interest on what he needed to borrow. As his personal wealth grew he paid less and less in interest, while still claiming 5% of the total pay bill for the Guards. The government benefitted, since it was effectively receiving interest free credit for the wages bill, while soldiers received regular pay in return for a 5% commission. When it became clear that the government was falling into arrears it was agreed to pay Fox interest on money that was more than two months in arrears in order to cover the cost of his own borrowing. This took much of the risk out of the operation and Fox was increasingly able to use his own money, thereby reducing his costs. As he ploughed the money back he accumulated a fortune at an accelerating rate, and was able to advance money to other Departments. In the late 1670s he secured control of the receipts of the excise. It was the basis for a prominent role in government office from the 1680s onwards, secured by a shrewd distance from involvement in politics.

Fox escaped with a relatively unsullied reputation, although he had clearly benefitted considerably from his office, on terms which were of his own devising. In fact, he denied his successor the same opportunities by revising the terms of the "Undertaking". What had protected him was insulation from the national and court political scene and that his personal benefit was largely restricted to the formal arrangement of the "Undertaking".

At the same time as the increasing importance of public credit created new opportunities, the increasing reliance on taxation rather than other forms of revenue raising swept away much of the twilight world of monopolists and other licensees in favor of salaried office holding. Tax farming was abandoned in 1683 and the number of salaried offices grew rapidly thereafter: in the excise from 1,211 in 1690 to 2,778 by 1716 and 3,466 by 1726; and in the customs administration from 1,313 to 1750 and then 1,911 (Brewer 1988: 353). In the excise these offices were organized with great precision. By 1770 the country was divided into 53 "collections", each with a clerk and collector and a more junior officer learning the ropes. There were 253 supervisors below them, overseeing the work of 2,704 officers on the ground, either footwalkers or outriders. These local officers worked hard—covering 12-16 mile footwalks and much longer rides, and putting in long and arduous hours. They were moved frequently in order to prevent them becoming too friendly with the people they were taxing, and their rewards were salaries, pensions and a defined promotion ladder (Brewer 1989: 101-14).

The rise of the salaried officeholder, however, created a new set of concerns about the relationship between private benefits and the public good. A key feature of the attack on the "Robinocracy" (the self-perpetuating Whig government dominated by Walpole) and on "Old Corruption" generally, was hostility to "placemen", those members of parliament whose tenure of office and attendant vested interests made them political supporters of the regime and a burden on the people.[15] They were at the forefront of the more general suspicion about the distribution of benefits from the fiscal system, and about the reasons for its persistence. This was primarily a concern about access to office and its structural effects, rather than its conduct, however: the corruption here was of the constitution, not the malpractice of particular officeholders in their daily operations.

It is clear that in the excise administration considerable emphasis was placed on drawing a clear line between the agreed private benefits of office and the handling of public money. John Cannon figures in Brewer's account of the striking professionalism of the Hanoverian excise (Brewer 1989: 104-5, 109), and it is certainly the case that Cannon's career in the excise was shaped against the background of this commitment to precision and accuracy.

The son of a prosperous farming family, with local social pretensions, Cannon was a promising pupil in village schools. His hopes of progressing through grammar school, perhaps to University, were cut short by the kind of misfortune against which there were few protections in eighteenth-century England, even for the better sort. Family illness led to a reliance on John, the eldest of sons and the more physically robust of the two, to carry on much of the work on the farm. Further family misfortune led him to enter domestic service to an uncle, effectively as an agricultural laborer. While this equipped him with a thorough knowledge of local agrarian practices, his frustration at this "clod-hopping" life was palpable; indeed

[15] Plumb, 1967: esp. 143-49; Speck 1977: esp. 15-16; Brewer 1989: 155-61.

he seems to have borne a regret about the disappointment of his academic ambitions for the rest of his life. [16]

It was perhaps these frustrations, as well as an inappropriate romantic embroilment, that lay behind a fatal breach in the relationship with his uncle. An argument over the correct way to plough a field led John to leave the farm and seek his fortune elsewhere. Here the excise bureaucracy came to his rescue. The demands it made on its officers—for numeracy, literacy, accuracy, precision and order in the written record—all spoke to the kinds of academic skill for which agrarian labor offered little outlet. Cannon's life was turned around by the opportunity that this offered for a clever man of relatively limited education, but with the ambition to enter the ranks of the local worthies.

An incident soon after he was commissioned, in 1707, reveals the importance of this image of precise professionalism to the dignity of the service and its officers. George Spong, his supervisor, met him on the road having spotted his professional instruments, which marked him out as an excise man, "one of their tribe". They travelled on together a little way in pleasant conversation when "On a sudden", Spong stopped, and called Cannon to him. "Young Man, is nothing on the ground (pointing thereto) belonging to you? (it being the ivory head of my dimension cane by accident luckily fallen off just then), and looking on my cane found that it was the same". He picked it up and the two men, at Spong's insistence, travelled on together to Clifton, where they drank "several pints of ale". Spong asked him about his background and career "giving me instructions & good admonitions seeing me very young & charged me strictly to be mindful & careful in the charge & business I was now entering upon". The memory of this lesson in professional diligence and attentiveness clearly lived with Cannon for many years thereafter, and has been taken as emblematic both of the corps loyalty of the excise service and of the values it cultivated (Money 2010: li-lii, 76).

Shortly afterwards Cannon got himself into quite a panic over a breach of these values. Having recorded some barrels as containing Strong Beer (which paid a higher tax rate), when in fact they only contained Small Beer, he tried to correct the record. Allowing the record to stand "were injustice … and put upon me a rash undertaking to remedy it".

[16] For what follows see John Money 2010 which includes Money's extensive analysis, 'Reading John Cannon's Chronicles': xxvii-cxlviii.

> In order to make my stock charge & the gauges compare and agree, I took out my penknife & razed out the character [wrongly entered]… & badly made the character [which should have been entered] in the room thereof which when done, it did not please me. Therefore with my knife I endeavored to amend it, but made it much worse, & yet not content went on to write it & made it still worse & worse till at last it became so shamefully bad for that by scraping so often with my knife I had made a perfect hole through the leaf which not only damaged the said stock but ruined & obliterated a gauge on the other side belonging to one John Gregory...

Clearly by now in something of a panic, fearing the next visit from his supervisor, "I strived yet to do something to make it look plausible".

> At last I took up a resolution to cover all by burning the same with a coal or candle in such a manner as it might be took for an accident & to make it palpable I wrote against it in favor of such a construction yet well knew that scratching or razing or altering any figure in stock or gauge was not only notorious but almost unpardonable, and as often as I beheld it, the more I contemned it & reflected on my folly & dreaded the coming of my supervisor which I hourly expected. And what was worse was by my so often visiting this page I had made the book so pliable that it would open itself at the very page where now my folly was done as if it had vowed to be a witness against me to discharge me ...

When Spong did visit to audit his accounts they met sociably and discussed how things were going generally.

> On a sudden, Mr. Spong ordered a fire & candle in his room & turning to me said Now, my lad, let's see how the twos & threes stand, & forthwith, we went upstairs, & sitting down, he took up my stock book first of all to examine. And as before, so now, the book opened at the very page as before exposing to his view a dismal object which he steadfastly beholding said My Lad, what's here, heyday, what now? What has thee been doing here? How came this to pass? I believe we need not trouble further for our night's work is here cut out.

While Cannon stuck to his story, Spong was plainly unconvinced, and Cannon was strongly advised never to do anything like it again (Money 2010: 84-6). The tension of this petty drama is palpable, and the vividness with which Cannon recalled it twenty years later bears testimony to the damage that could be done to an excise career by any suggestion of inaccurate or false accounting.

Perhaps, however, this was cultivated by Spong for his own purposes: John Money, the expert on Cannon's life, notes that no record of the lapse appears in the Commissioners' records—hinting that Spong was putting on a front of some kind (Money 2010: liii). Perhaps, for example, Spong kept it to himself, knowing that he had assured himself of Cannon's loyalty and obedience: he was later reduced (demoted) for favoritism, and perhaps this was an attempt to cultivate one such favorite.

This interpretation, that the internal politics of the service affected how such lapses were treated, certainly fits the rest of Cannon's time in the excise. As he noted of his time at Watlington, "I continued with all care & caution to following both my business, & as yet being amongst strangers, minded nothing else but how to oblige my superior officers" (Money 2010: 83). He had a successful, even a promising, career in the excise over the next 15 years, but was dismissed from office in 1721 for another apparently minor lapse, but in circumstances in which he did not have the protection of a loyal boss like Spong.

A maltster called Bartholomew Manchip conceived a plan to embarrass him, having previously been fined for malpractice. In the summer it was the practice for excise men to visit the maltsters every five or six days, rather than every day, but to record their work as if they were visiting constantly. However, it was possible to malt barley in less time than that. Manchip, according to Cannon, deliberately malted some barley between visits of the excisemen, hoping thereby to catch them out—their records would miss this batch and they would be exposed as falsifying their own records. Cannon visited with his Supervisor, who duly found some batches of malting that were not recorded, and asked Cannon how it came to be. Cannon explained the usual practice, and left all his books with his Supervisor. Manchip, however, had (according to Cannon) bribed a minor officer to take a record of this malting in his pocket, and to claim that he had forgotten to hand it over. Thus, Cannon was returning two maltings in arrear when in fact the duty had been, apparently, paid. Confronted with this neglected record Cannon immediately suspected a plot; an argument ensued and his Supervisor, Harmsworth, did not take Cannon's side, attributing all the blame to him. Unlike Spong in the earlier case, Harmsworth showed no mercy. Spong had recorded the misdemeanor in his Diary but had not informed the Commissioners. Harmsworth instead wrote privately to them, meaning that there was no opportunity to remedy the problem, and Cannon was dismissed from the service. An important consideration, according to the letter of dismissal, was that Cannon owed £6 to Manchip, and was much more widely indebted (Money 2010: 164-5). This malpractice in relation to public funds seemed to be related to his private finances.

Again, this bears testimony to the rigidity of the rules, but there is evidence that such sins did not merit punishment in all cases. John Money draws attention to the career of William Bateman, for example: reprimanded twenty five times, admonished twenty times and demoted once before his eventual dismissal in 1717. The final offence altering "a minute by scratching, a date changed both in book and specimens, several surveys appearing so foul that there is great reason to question his sobriety when they were made" (Money 2010: lii-liii). Cannon himself felt he had been "unjustly and villainously discharged" (Money 2010: lxxv).

The background to Cannon's discharge does indeed seem murky, as John Money's painstaking reconstruction demonstrates. At the time of his dismissal Cannon was working in Bridgewater, a town like much of the region, in which political tensions were high. Cannon had earlier helped John Oldmixon (the customs officer) to seize and dispose of goods belonging to the nephew of the mayor. Excise men had greater powers in this respect. Later, when Manchip had been brought to court the mayor had mitigated the penalties. These local tensions, presumably not that unusual, intersected with local religious and political divisions. The Mayor was associated with Tory views, sympathetic to the claims of the exiled Stuarts and hostile to the protestant sects. John Oldmixon was a Whig publicist as well as the customs collector. There had recently been riots in the town, on the Pretender's [the exiled Stuart claimant] birthday, and the dragoons sent to keep order and take down Jacobite decorations claimed that they had been attacked. The local authorities "had gone through only the motions of their duty" in the run-up to this tense anniversary. By crossing the Mayor's nephew in alliance with Oldmixon, and possibly in his dealings with Manchip, Cannon had become embroiled in local party politics, at least by implication (Money 2010: lxxi-lxiv). In this case, as in others, there were other considerations that affected perceptions of transgression, or at least the channels through which it was handled, and this was a fertile breeding ground for suspicions of hypocrisy, or corruption.

Ezekial Polsted's earlier satire on the excise service sought out this ground, strenuously asserting the ideals of the excise to the point that they seem patently ridiculous. The title was *Kaloz telonesantai* ("here lies an honest publican [tax collector]"), the epitaph for Sabrinus, a rare example of such a thing. It referred to the reputation of Roman tax collectors: usually sub-contracted and doubly-hated therefore as both oppressors and traitors. In Mark chapter 2, for example, publicans are bracketed with sinners as surprising company for Jesus. The epigram to Polsted's book came from Dryden's translation of Juvenal's satires, published 4 years before his own work. It is a remarkable text in the sense that this bitter satire is sustained over 120 pages: one can only imagine what they had done to him. But in Polsted's satire is preserved the image the excise service sought to promote: excise men are free of human faults and ambitions, unswayed by affection or hostility, immune to spite and vengeance, detached from politics.[17] These were not realizable standards, but in setting them out, and publicly aspiring to them, a model was set against which excise men could become vulnerable—even minor slips like that made by Cannon were potentially disastrous to those who did not have protection.

One reason these standards are ridiculous is because the men who were in the excise service were of course subject to characteristic human weaknesses. The ideals to which they were held in their official duties were patently at odds with what could reasonably be expected of a living person. Here, the career of John Cannon is particularly interesting, since his diary not only juxtaposes these professional commitments and his human weaknesses, but also embeds his excise service in the larger trajectory of his life and personal ambitions. The borrowing which got him into so much trouble in 1721 had arisen from his addiction to books: "It hath been said often that by my purchasing of books etc. I had reduced my circumstances, that to keep up in my reputation I often borrowed money" (Money, 2010: 164). His reputation—the crucial standing as a member of the middling sort which was his birthright—was precarious. His own father's injury and illness had cut short Cannon's prospects, and now dismissal from the service pitched his own family into danger of poverty. He took up business as a maltster but, saddled with his father's debts, was unable to make a success of it. He suffered chronic sickness and by 1729 his family was reduced to poverty. A temporary placement in the excise that year, however, seems to have restored him, even though he was then felt to be too old for permanent re-engagement. For the rest of his life he undertook a number of local roles appropriate to a middling-sort professional—as an accountant, scrivener and village schoolmaster

[17] Polsted 1697. I am grateful to Prof Hugh Pyper for his help in decoding the joke in the title.

(Money, 2010: lxxv-lxxvii). Nonetheless, this remained a precarious living and on 26 December 1741 he undertook an onerous 30 mile journey to Bristol in connection with the sale of most of his books. On the way home he was lost and in some peril on the Mendip Hills, and was accompanied on the final part of his journey by his two eldest children who, concerned about his well-being, had gone out to look for him (Money, 2010: xxvii). Two years before his death, his condition remained a precarious one: the personal benefits of a secure excise career must have been obvious.

Fiscal transformation, private benefits and corruption in early modern England

The fiscal transformation of the seventeenth century—the growth of tax revenues and borrowing, the rise of the "tax state"—was associated with a tendency to pay for public service more directly rather than by providing officeholders with "opportunities".[18] This shifted the question of the relationship between private benefit and public service into new terrain. John Cannon lived in terror of technical error, which could be fatal to a man's career prospects, for which he depended on continued favor. Arguably, however, this had just placed one remove between his personal benefits—and his wider biography demonstrates exactly what those were—and political or personal favor. Certainly, the question of the relationship between personal benefit and public service remained a complex one, articulated on the one hand in terms of accuracy and, on the other, in terms of "place": the corrupting influence of a dependence on state employment for political independence. Accuracy was the key legitimating term for excise men, and to be publicly exposed as failing in that regard was to risk loss of place. But it was not automatic. Similarly, the separation of personal financial interest and the public service was crucial, and it was this that really did for Cannon, but it was lethal as the result of a wider set of considerations.

The practices of a salaried bureaucracy, and more particularly the ideals satirized by Polsted, can be seen as an attempt, partly rhetorical, to contain the private benefits of public office, and particularly the private benefits of handling public money. It was on this point—that his private finances and those of the public service had led him to falsify the excise

---

[18] I argue for this transformation in Braddick 1996. The argument is summarized in Braddick 2002: 69-87.

records—that Cannon lost his office, although it seems likely that much else lay behind the decision. Securing and retaining a "place" however, and of gaining further preferments, remained a highly political issue, one which the Northcote Trevelyan report of 1853 sought to address, in the name of efficiency. That report sought to recruit and promote public servants on merit, and to establish a clearer hierarchy between operational and strategic public servants. In this context we might read that as a further elaboration of the ideals of the excise service—to reduce the dependence on favor for continued job security.

It is for the narrow circle of direct financial benefit from office that English historians have tended to reserve the term "corruption", and for the use of influence to secure direct financial benefits such as cash payments or preferential contracts. The much larger issue of the relationship between private benefit and public service has attracted less attention, and certainly little comparative attention, but it was one very familiar to early moderns through their reading of the classics. For current purposes it offers another route to the heart of the relationship between political power and social interests. The changing functions, forms and languages of political power create new kinds of private benefit for those who exercised it. Analysis of the nature of these benefits, and their legitimate limits, can throw into sharp relief the chief pressure points and key arguments about the proper relationship between private benefit and public good. This was a crucial concern for contemporary political actors and successful negotiation of this issue was essential to the effective exercise of their political power. It is also another means by which to address a key issue in this volume—that is the relationship between political power and the social interests with which it is inevitably embroiled.

References

Aylmer, G., (1961), *The King's Servants: the Civil Service of Charles I*, London: Routledge, Kegan & Paul.

—. (1973), *The State's Servants: the Civil Service of the English Republic*, London: Routledge, Kegan & Paul.

—. (2002), *The Crown's Servants: Government and Civil Service under Charles II 1660-85*, Oxford: Oxford University Press.

—. (2004), "Noell, Sir Martin (*bap.* 1614, *d.* 1665)", *Oxford Dictionary of National Biography*, Oxford: Oxford University Press.

Ashton, R., (1960), *The Crown and the Money Market 1603-1640*, Oxford: Clarendon Press.

Beresford, M.W., (1957), "The Common Informer, the Penal Statutes and Economic Regulation", *Economic History Review,* 2nd series, 10: 221-38.

Braddick, M.J., (1996), *The Nerves of State: Taxation and the Financing of the English State, 1558-1714*, Manchester: Manchester University Press.

—. (1994), *Parliamentary Taxation in Seventeenth-Century England: Local Administration and Response*, Woodbridge: Boydell and Brewer.

—. (2000), *State Formation in Early Modern England*, Cambridge: Cambridge University Press.

—. (2002), "The Rise of the Fiscal State", in Barry Coward (ed.), *A Companion to Stuart Britain*, Oxford: Blackwell, 69-87.

Brewer, J., (1988), "The English State and Fiscal Appropriation, 1688-1789", *Politics and Society*, 16/2-3: 335-385.

—. (1989), *The Sinews of Power: War, Money and the English State, 1688-1783*, London: Unwin Hyman.

Burns, T., (1992), *Erving Goffman*, London: Routledge.

Clay, C., (1978), *Public Finance and Private Wealth: the Career of Sir Stephen Fox, 1627-1716*, Oxford: Oxford University Press.

Cressy, D., (2011), "Saltpetre, State Security and Vexation in Early Modern England", *Past and Present*, 212/1: 73-111.

Hughes, E., (1934), *Studies in Administration and Finance 1558-1825 with Special Reference to the History of Salt Taxation in England*, Manchester: Manchester University Press.

Hughes P.L., Larkin J.F. (eds.) (1969), *The Royal Proclamations*, II, *The Later Tudors (1553-1587)*, London.

Hurstfield, J., (1967), "Political Corruption in Modern England: the Historian's Problem", *History*, 52/174: 16-34.

Kitching, C.J., (1974), "The Quest for Concealed Lands in the Reign of Elizabeth I", *Transactions of the Royal Historical Society*, 5th Series, 24: 63-78.

Money, J. (ed.), (2010), *The Chronicles of John Cannon, Excise Officer and Writing Master, Part 1: 1684-1733 (Somerset, Oxfordshire, Berkshire),* Oxford: Oxford University press/British Academy.

Outhwaite, R.B., (1966), "The Trials of Foreign Borrowing: the English Crown and the Antwerp Money Market in the Mid-Sixteenth Century", *Economic History Review*, 2nd series, 19: 289-505.

—. (1971), "Royal Borrowing in the Reign of Elizabeth I: the Aftermath of Antwerp", *English Historical Review*, 86: 251-63.

Peck L.L., (1990), *Court, Patronage and Corruption in Early Stuart England*, London: Routledge

Plumb, J.H., (1967), *The Growth of Political Stability in England: 1675-1725*, London: Macmillan.

Polsted, E., (1697), *Kaloz telonesantai or, The excise-man Shewing the excellency of his profession* ... London, Ann Arbor: UMI.

Prestwich, M., (1966), *Cranfield: Politics and Profits under the Early Stuarts: The Career of Lionel Cranfield Earl of Middlesex*, Oxford: Oxford University Press.

Sacks, D.H., (1990), "Private Profit and Public Good: the Problem of the State in Elizabethan Theory and Practice", in Schochet and *al.*, *Law, Literature and the Settlement of Regimes*: 121-142.

Schochet, G. J. - Tatspaugh, P. E. – Brobeck, C., (eds.), *Law, Literature and the Settlement of Regimes*, Washington, D.C: Folger Institute.

Shaw, W.A., (ed.) (1935), *Calendar of Treasury Books*, X, pt. 3, London: HMSO.

Smith, A.H., (1974), *County and Court: Government and Politics in Norfolk 1558-1603*, Oxford: Oxford University Press.

Speck, W.A., (1977), *Stability and strife: England, 1714-1760*, London: Arnold.

Stewart, R.W., (1996) *The English Ordnance Office: a Case-Study in Bureaucracy*, Woodbridge: Boydell and Brewer.

Tanner, J.R., (1922), *Tudor Constitutional Documents, 1485-1603*, Cambridge: Cambridge University Press.

Williams, P., (1979), *The Tudor Regime*, Oxford: Oxford University Press.

Woodworth, A., (1945), *Purveyance for the Royal Household in the Reign of Queen Elizabeth*, Transactions of the American Philosophical Society, 35, Philadelphia.

CHAPTER EIGHT

THEORETICAL PREMISES AND COGNITIVE DISTORTIONS FROM THE UNCRITICAL USE OF THE CONCEPT OF "STATE": THE "RUSSIAN" CASE

CLAUDIO SERGIO NUN INGERFLOM

Aims of the paper

The concept of "State", used to define a political reality or as a heuristic category to investigate the past (the well-known "state-building"), is at the center of historical studies. It is usually examined through the analytical "state-society" paradigm, which has dominated our discipline since the mid-nineteenth century. The importance granted at times to the "State", and sometimes to "society", as the "engines of Russian history" has varied over time. However, such nuances have challenged neither the relevance of these two concepts as categories for analysis, nor the validity of the paradigm.[1] In the following pages, we

---

[1] In parallel to this dominant tendency, some were more cautious when using the concept of "State". The construction of the State is thought to have been left unfinished in the nineteenth century and even in the 20th century, and the Soviet political organization is not considered to have fallen within a state order. See Lowit 1979: 431-466; Amstrong 1982: 129-130; Catalano 1986: XVIII – XX; LeDonne 1984, VII, 13-17, 349; LeDonne 1991: 19, 56-7, 60, 92, 112, 311; Rieber 1988: 31; Ingerflom 1994: 125 – 134; Ingerflom 2004 (I), 28: 53-60; Ingerflom 2013; Rosenberg 1994; Markwick 1999: vol 15, 4:111-130; Dixon 1999: 256; Hosking 2001: 190, 240; Kharkhordin 2001, vol. 40, 2: 206-240, now in Kharkhordin, 2005: 1-40; Getty, 2013, to my knowledge, the paradigm's relevance to the Russian history has not been the object of any specific debate. Nevertheless, we had a stimulating exchange of views on "Should historians call Russia a State?"

specifically discuss Russian history. Nevertheless, to the extent that the theoretical premises on the use of the paradigm are not limited to Russian history—actually, Russian historiography borrowed it from "Western" historiography—this contribution is inserted into a wider debate, currently underway, on the conceptual apparatus of our profession.[2] Any research on "serving the State" in Europe, if related to the times prior to the French Revolution, requires us to take into consideration the historical boundaries of the concept of State.

The recurring use of both concepts to examine all periods in history, even the earliest times, coupled with the scarcity—or even absence—of critical awareness of the contemporaneousness of these concepts, has spontaneously granted to them an almost meta-historical status of neutrality and extraterritoriality in the research and interpretation of the past.[3] However, this paradigm has, as French wine and cheese, a "Protected designation of origin (PDO)": it is a tributary of a precise political context, i.e. the first half of the nineteenth century in Western Europe.[4] Far from being neutral, using it produces an impact on the choice, treatment and interpretation of the sources. Yet, the durability of the paradigm in time, as well as the uncritical use of the concept of "State",[5] have ended up veiling its original context, hiding the fact that the paradigm and its concepts are dated both historically and theoretically.[6]

---

at the round table held at the American Association for the Advancement of Slavic Studies (AAASS) in New Orleans in 2007, presided over by Valerie Kivelson, with the participation of Nancy Kollmann, John LeDonne, Daniel Rowland and the author of this paper.

[2] For a comprehensive view of the renewal of the political history of modernity and the State, see the articles written by Schaub, 1995: 9-49; 1996: 127–181 and 2005.

[3] To state "all times in history" is not an exaggeration. For instance, the "State" was a key novelty at the end of the third millennium B.C.; Forest 1996: 241 – 244, quoted by Huot, 2005. See also: "During these four thousand years (from the end of the 17th century to the end of the third millennium), we have gone from a feeble fabric of villages to a State in the modern sense of the word. The period we are analyzing lies between pre-history and history" (Huot 2005: 973).

[4] I use the word "Western" out of convenience, bearing in mind the heterogeneous nature of political constructions in Europe and other places.

[5] Recently, a Hellenist wrote that "Historians hardly ever define their concepts, and in historical contexts the term state is used in a fairly broad sense referring to any highly organized political community" (Hansen 1998: 35).

[6] This article only discusses the State. The study of the historiographical use of the other essential concept of the paradigm—society—would require a specific

Characterized by explicit reluctance to reflect upon its conceptual baggage, this historiography raises anachronism as a model.[7]

The second part of this paper will unveil what architects call a "hidden vice" of construction: the paradigm subjects the reading of sources to theoretical premises accepted in the nineteenth century, though for long incompatible with the achievements of human and social sciences. I hope equally to demonstrate that critical work on the concept of "State" used by the Russian historiography reveals the tensions between the use of this concept and the empirical material contributed by that same historiography. In the latter goal, there is no nominalistic claim. In other words, I do not attempt to define the State in order to confront what we know about Russian history with that definition and find out if they agree or not. The logic of my thinking is different. The historiographical tradition very often identifies a "State" in the Muscovite political system (fifteenth century – the beginning of the eighteenth century), and in a Saint Petersburgian Russia (beginning of the eighteenth century – 1917), it identifies an "abstract and de-personalized State", also called the "Modern" State. An attempt will be made to establish whether there is isomorphism or, on the contrary, some heterogeneity between what historiography itself teaches us about these two periods on one hand, and the features it attributes to the concept of "State", on the other. The third and last section presents a cognitive distortion inherent in the uncritical use of the concept of "State". The purpose is not to expose a mistake, as we researchers can all make mistakes, but rather to show how the uncritical use of this concept leads to false conclusions. Let us be clear: I here designate under the formula of "cognitive distortion" a thinking that, guided by that uncritical use, increasingly detaches itself from the sources until it elaborates conclusions

research study. In relation to the absence of a civil society in Russia, at least prior to the second half of the nineteenth century, and in order to conduct this debate efficiently, see Kimmerling Wirtschafter 2004/ 2007: 373-381.

7 We have heard recently that the frequent use "d'un *langage anachronique* pour nommer les […] éléments du pouvoir de l'Etat : information, propagande, bureaucratie, politique économique…" was a "*procédé fécond* […] *qui affirme d'emblée la modernité de l'Etat*" in the fourteenth and fifteenth centuries, Carbonell, 1993 : 311, my emphasis. See also Monsalvo Anton 2000. The title of Chapter 3 is "Idea y representaciones políticas sobre el rey, la corona y el reino (el caso castellano)". However, the author, eminent expert in the Spanish Middle Ages, noted that he "decided not to discuss conceptual digressions and renounced to any "detailed and theoretical definitions" of the concepts he uses, such as "politics, culture, power, state, political society, etc." (p.13).

that not only lack any relationship with the sources but contradicts what can be read in them.

The "State" Paradigm

A western teleological construction

The view of a country's history as a state-building process and, at the same time, as the evolution of relations between the State and Society started during the first half of the nineteenth century in Western Europe. This vision, brilliantly theorized by Hegel, was framed in a political situation dominated by the building and/or consolidation of the Liberal State in the contradictory process started in 1789. Although not all historians of the time ran a government, as did Guizot, many of them were committed to politics and had responsibilities in Parliament and other areas of government. Under those conditions, the formula of the "Modern state" ("*moderne staat*") was shaped and, according to Stephan Skalweit, it appears in German thinking between 1830 and 1840 in reference to the "constitutional State" (Skalweit 1975: 17-18).

The present was the apogee of history. To prove it, historians described a past time in which they isolated a large number of factors from their original structures and aligned them teleologically to present them as precedent, leading to the State, as if the acts of the past had been intended to produce what happened later. The path between early modernity and contemporary times was conceived as evolutionary. From this perspective, the revolution became something that had not been necessary. A cumulative account of "historical precedents" justified the present as the result of the past. History was made in the West and ended up in the State (Iggers 1988). Intellectuals from the countries located on the margins of the West were able to read their favorite philosopher stating that in "the history of the World only those peoples came under notice which form a state".[8]

[8] Hegel 1956: 39. For a recent update on "Hegel et la Russie", see Siljak 2001: 335-358. For Hegel's influence on Russian historians in the nineteenth century, see also Medushevskii 1988: 103 – 115.

The paradigm in Russia: the concept of the State (*Gosudarstvo*)

This western paradigm was introduced in Russia by the "statist school", also called the "legal" school: Serguei Solov'ev (1820-1879), Constantin Kavelin (1818-1885) and Boris Chicherin (1828-1904) in the first instance. [9] Since then, most research has been framed in this paradigm.[10] Hegel's place in the view of the State held by the founders of the school is well known.[11] Following Hegel, Chicherin asserts that the State stands above the particular interests of social estates and the selfishness of the *homo economicus* (Hamburg 1992: 101). The State exists if it can be clearly differentiated from civil society; it is the ultimate realization of freedom and the rights of the individual.[12] For Chicherin, who witnessed the abolition of serfdom (1861), there is no State where one group of the people is subject to another group under particular contracts; in other words, where the forms of domination are not defined by contemporary Law. There is a State if all citizens are subject to general laws and these laws do not change with every particular situation that arises or varies with the region or the stakeholders. The state political system involves a society aware of its social unity, rather than a conglomerate composed of individuals defined by a dignity inherited at the time of birth. The State is a higher power that stands above the powerful

---

[9] Prior to these historians, the term *gosudarstvo* had already caused controversy, but used in the sense of centralized power and independent territory. According to Polevoi, the *gosudarstvo* only appeared after the Mongol yoke; his work is entitled *Istoriia Russkogo naroda*, vis-a-vis Karamzin's *Istoriia Russkogo gosudarstva*. See Miliukov 1913: 301-2. Kavelin criticizes Pogodin and Karamzin's superficial political history of *gosudarstvo*, ignoring its internal structure as well as the confussion generated by Pogodin between politics and history, which turned the latter into a guarantor of the current order; (Kavelin 1897: 231, 235). On the relationships between Karamzin and the statist school, (Black 1973: 509 – 530).

[10] On the school's current status, see among others, Kitaev 1972 and 1995: 161-164; Beyerly 1973; Kollmann 1987: 9-11; Kivelson 1996: XV; Bushkovitch 2001: 1-2.

[11] Medushevskii 1988: 103-13.

[12] The course on Hegel delivered by Chicherin at the University shows what elements of Hegel's *Philosophy of Right* were privileged by the historian, as well as the way in which he presented them (especially, § 182-262). See Chicherin 1877: 573-609.

and the weak alike. Every particular interest is subject to the general interest represented by the State.[13]

In search of the Russian State

To be put into practice, political history needs to identify an autonomous political domain. As the concept and historical reality of the "State" stemmed from the autonomization of politics in the West, projecting the concept of "politics" to Russia raises more questions than answers: when does the political become autonomous in Russia or, so to say, when does the political become autonomous from religion?

The paradigm premises

History had barely become a discipline in Russia when its experts began searching for the Russian State in the past, using a borrowed analytical concept/category—the "State" (*gosudarstvo* in Russian)—that synthesized a radically new historical Western structure, constructed *against* the Ancien Régime (let's think of the people's sovereignty against that of the monarch, among others). Going back to the sources, they found that the word *gosudarstvo* appeared everywhere. They knew its meanings in Muscovite Russia.[14] They were also aware of the radical difference between the meanings of the *word* (*gosudarstvo*), as used in the sources, and that of the *concept* (*gosudarstvo*) used as a category of analysis. The word was considered as embodying an idea with a *permanent core meaning* that, at the same time, evolved with the passage of time, thus reflecting evolution. The researcher had to reconstruct this evolution, and that itself confirmed the validity of the word for the whole period, from the final centralization of the Russian principalities around Moscow (fifteenth

---

[13] Chicherin 1858a: 234, 236, 369; 1858d: 213, quoted in Kitaev, 1972: 100. See also Skinner 2002: 386, n.236, 407, 409-10, 413.

[14] Let's remember that *gosudarstvo* –first spelt as *gospodarstvo*– was used with two meanings: the dignity of the *gosudar'* (*dominus*, owner, master), be it the Great Prince first, or the Tsar soon after, and their estates. It designates a territory following the model of Polish *panstwo,* which was based on the Latin words *dominum* and *dominatio*. See Zoltan András, 1987. It also means the *gosudar'*s power over his property, giving it the sense of government (*pravlenie*) and the *gosudar*'s possessions, especially land and its dwellers; Tolstikov 2002: 296. It could also mean the "throne" (Krom 2006: 60-61).

and sixteenth centuries). The difference between the old word and the nineteenth century concept was blurred, thus increasing the risk of investing the former with the meanings of the latter. Likewise, "statist school" historians knew that, during their time, Russia—with its serfdom, its lack of freedom, and being legally fragmented into different estates (until February 1917)—practically ignored all components of the historical structure contained in the concept of State. Why, then, did they try to reconstruct the history of Russia through the history of the State?[15] The answer is that research was based on those paradigm premises and they had the capacity to produce an impact on interpretation. Historians interpreted Russian history through the lens of the construction of the state, because they assumed that Russia was following, with some delay, the footsteps of the West. Their point of reference was "the English system based on the respect for the Law" and the "French thinking about State" (Chicherin 1858a: 385). In this regard, a possible otherness was immediately excluded: believing that Russia was following the Western path was enough to conclude that autocracy was not, for instance, "Oriental despotism", as believed by "Western Europeans" (Kavelin 1846: t. 1, 637-8). Since "the State that moves forward without deviating from the predetermined path" is the realization of History, these historians adapted the past to this *telos*: "the development of the State was the main task of ancient Russia" (Chicherin 1858a: 386, 377, 380-1). The three summarized premises of the *state-society* paradigm are then: eurocentrism, evolutionism and teleology.

The tension between the concept of "State" and the sources

According to Kavelin, "the appearance of the State (*gosudarstvo*)", as well as the existence of a "state sphere (*gosudarstvennaia*)", was already confirmed in the fifteenth century. The story alternates between an already existing State and a State-building process. The words of a historian of Law come to mind: "The state is literally preconceived. It is its epiphany, not its history, that results".[16] Society and State already existed. They were inherent in Muscovy, with the only exception that they would be *completed* with new forms (Kavelin, 1866: 651-2). Contradictions within

---

[15] Disagreements exist between these two historians. However, I will not make any reference to that since they share the paradigm premises.

[16] These words, written in relation to the traditional historiography of the "Modern State" in the West, characterize the paradigm at a global level (Clavero 1987: 963).

this logic are inevitable. State and Society are *a priori* data, whose "deep sense" in Russia would be the isomorphism between the private and the political (Kavelin, 1866: 637). However, the distinction between these two was underscored in other papers of the same school as one of the State's distinctive features! (Chicherin, 1858a: 234). The State already existed, but "the idea of State" was not only "almost invisible under the old established forms", i.e. under the clan order and the master-property (*votchina*) relationship, but also "imbued by them".[17] This status continued for over two hundred years—until Peter the Great's time in the eighteenth century—in which time the past was strongly shaken, though not destroyed (Kavelin 1846: 45). In fact, when analyzing the seventeenth century, Kavelin talks about the "State" (in his contemporary Western sense), but showing that what was understood as *gosudarstvo* in the seventeenth century was *master's domain (*Kavelin 1866: 636-7). Along these lines, guided by his professional instinct, Kavelin described for the seventeenth century a system where the State was an alien institution, rather than a higher echelon. However, given that Peter the Great's transformations were about to take place, Kavelin retrospectively organized the materials of the past: "Under the Great Prince's *votchina,* the State is revealed […]; in the Muscovite State, under the old forms, a new content was already developing" (Kavelin 1846: 46). This "new content" is embodied in Peter and his work, opening up a period of transformation which has just finished, concludes Kavelin in 1846.

A clear tension exists between the meanings embedded in the concept of State that preside over the analysis, and description of a system—the Muscovite monarchy—to which it is alien. Kavelin tries to solve this tension by breaking up the system: he diminishes certain Muscovite elements to the rank of traces about to disappear, and raises others to the dignified level of embryos of a developing State. The historian reconstructs what he thinks was an anticipation of the future. In fact, this tension reveals a difficulty in conceptualizing the past alterity, a sort of

[17] The *Votchina* was a domain, owned by the Lord (the Great Prince, the Tsar or members of the old nobility such as the boyars). The *pomest'e* was the lands that newer nobility (*dvoriane* : from the word *dvor*, meaning "court") received as usufruct in exchange for the services provided to the Monarch. The distinction between these two types of ownership was dropped in the eighteenth century. The word "master" was one of the main meanings of *gosudar'* (for example, in the formula "master of his slaves"). The *votchina–gosudar'* relationship makes reference to the patrimony dimension of power in Muscovy.

analytical deficiency hidden under the use of the words "State" and "Society" in a common sense. Nevertheless, the resistance of the excellent researcher Kavelin, regarding the a-priori nature of his interpretation is exposed in the text, behind the author's back, in those places where the predicate weakens the subject: "By the end of the seventeenth century, the Muscovite State (*Gosudarstvo*) found itself in an abnormal situation" (Kavelin 1866: 651). This tension is constant: the research reconstructs a system alien to that contained under the concept of "State", while the theoretical premises impose the retrospective use of the latter. However, this tension can only be perceived by readers who are aware of the distinction between the historical structures summarized in the *concept* of *Gosudarstvo,* the paradigm itself, and the realities contained in the meaning of the *word gosudarstvo* in the past.

In sum, the authors of the teleological view state that the presence of the State takes us back to the fifteenth century. They discard everything they consider does not follow history's path, reducing it to the status of disappearing vestige. They take from every period what they think anticipates the future, i.e. they isolate from their system—and thus denature—the factors that gradually appear in an accumulation produced by the evolutionist view. They assume that these factors acquired their maturity when they became a State under Nicholas I (1825 – 1855). In the tension between historians' concrete knowledge and the premises of their thinking, the latter prevail at the moment of conceptualizing. The idea of alterity does not exist.

The Paradigm Falls Apart

Chicherin was mainly a legal historian, who undertook to explain and teach what Western scholars understood as a State. He was also committed to liberalism and that required him not to ignore freedom as an essential element of the State. As a result, probably of a combination of all these elements together, coupled to his sensitivity towards sources, the tension between the sources and the paradigm premises took a different direction from that proposed by Kavelin, turning this founder of the State paradigm into one of its first gravediggers. I believe that, on this last point, Chicherin has not been duly appreciated.

Through his work, Chicherin focused on the difference between the unlimited power the tsar claimed and the real world, in which too many things actually got out of hand and the monarchy's measures, intended to fight against the lack of organization, corruption, and some injustices, were unsuccessful (Chicherin 1858b: 383-5). Chicherin showed that neither the central power nor the local administrations can cover the extent of the territory they claim. Administration and law are not uniform, and contradictory institutions coexist (Chicherin 1858c:577-8). In the seventeenth century, the old ways of managing the country coexisted with the new ways, the relations between institutions and their employees were not governed by a single rule, but on a case-by-case basis, resulting in inequalities in the administration of the regions. The statement is indisputable: "When a developed State establishes a social order, it places all social life phenomena on the same level, reducing them to general categories, defined by state necessities. However, such general categories (…) did not exist in the Muscovite *gosudarstvo*" (Chicherin 1858c: 579). His conclusion is logical: "…in the Muscovite *gosudarstvo*'s regional administration, we see (…) the absence of a state (*gosudarstvennii*) system" (Chicherin 1858c: 585). Here, the noun *gosudarstvo* seems to go back to its meaning in ancient Russia, while the adjective *gosudarstvennii* (which I translate as state) seems to refer to the attributes of the historian's contemporary concept.

Notwithstanding the above, Chicherin keeps a teleological approach, analyzing the situation from the point of view of the "insufficiency" (Chicherin, 1858b: 385) of a State that, some day, will be "developed". But he also points out, with no ambiguity, the radical difference between a patrimonial Muscovy where, in his view, political relations are built on private relations, and a contemporary, nineteenth-century, system in which the existence of a society, conceived as such, makes the State's existence possible (Chicherin 1858a: 236). This difference partly overcomes the paradigm premises without removing them, since Chicherin sees the State as history at its peak. Nevertheless, thanks to this difference, the tension between these premises and erudition is solved in favor of the latter. In fact, in a manuscript from 1878, not published until 1906, Chicherin stated that the failure to establish a "constitutional monarchy" marked the failure of the State—this "new construction, whose natural achievement is political freedom". [18] He remains optimistic, though, as he sees the

[18] Chicherin 1906: 9. According to Chicherin's liberal thinking, the historical novelty represented by the State is not possible without political freedom. At the same time, freedom and personality can only be developed "within the State", Chicherin, 1858a: 368. It is notable that he defends the opposite from what is claimed by Kavelin and his Memoires, he considers Nicholas I and his "despotic government". Quoted by Hamburg, 1992: 95.

possibility that the emperor "may summon his subjects to take part in the state administration", but the only means to ensure such participation is to establish, even in a limited manner, popular involvement.[19] According to Chicherin, in 1878, Russia was still not a State. What was missing for it to become a State was not the technical modernization of its governance, but two essential features of political modern life: people's representation and political freedom.[20] In other words, an institutional and legal body different from the tsar and his subjects is not necessarily a State, though its goal may have been proclaimed as the search for common good. The political conditions for the common good to be defined democratically by the people are still not present (the real degree of democracy is a different problem).[21] The de-personalization of power is necessary, but not

[19] Chicherin 1906: 9, 11, 33, 26. This "representation" wasn't among Alexander II's intentions. And this happened well before Narodnaia Volia's terrorism. In 1861, he explained to Otto von Bismarck, the then Prussian minister in Saint Petersburg, who reported his words to Berlin: "The idea of taking counsel of subjects other than officials was not in itself objectionable and that greater participation by respectable notables in official business could only be advantageous. The difficulty, if not impossibility, of putting this principle into effect lay only in the experience of history that it had never been possible to stop a country's liberal development at the point beyond which it should not go […] To abdicate the absolute power with which my crown is invested would be to undermine the aura of that authority which has dominion over the nation […] I would diminish without any compensation the authority of the government if I wanted to allow representatives of the nobility or the nation to participate in it" (Lieven 1996: 142).

[20] At the same time, Chicherin (1906: 27-29) asserted he did not see any political people qualified to serve as the State personnel.

[21] The presence of the "common good" formula in the Russian discourse since the seventeenth century has confused those historians who have interpreted this as a proof of secularization and modernity, leaving behind the religious and ethical—not political—roots of this concept, as well as the reality behind the discourse. The lack of a sociological and political basis to translate this formula into Russian reality is mentioned by Kleimola 1979: 229 and by LeDonne, 1984: 12, 17 and 1991: 350. With regard to the discourse of power Kharkhordin was crystal clear. Commenting on *the Truth of the Monarch's Will* by Feofan Prokopovich, one of the chief ideologists of Peter the Great's politics wrote that: "Autocratic will is the ultimate mover of the Russian state, and no matter how much is said about the public good to which czar and people commonly aspire, a common 'fatherland' is instituted only on the order of the czar who must be obeyed due to the total patrimonial power of the gosudar' in his domain." (Kharkhordin 2005: 14-5).

sufficient, to turn the institutional and legal body into a State. Popular sovereignty is still missing. Chicherin suggests that democracy is inherent to the State, as democracy resulted from the French Revolution.

Serving the State or the tsar? The Paradigm and its cognitive distortions today

This paragraph reconstructs the fate of a statement made by the historian Serguei Solovev on the effects of the emergence of the State on the new government practices introduced by Peter and, as a result, on the collective representations of power. I have chosen this example as it illustrates the historiographical continuity between the start of the Statist school and our present times, as well as the influence of the paradigm on such continuity, and the cognitive distortion *inherent* in the uncritical use of the concept of State imposed by this paradigm. By cognitive distortion, I understand the progressive detachment of the historian from the sources until he loses all contact with them.

- According to Solovev, "the Russians heard the true ['nastoiashchoe' but let's remember that the polisemia of the term enables us to understand it as the 'current/present' C.S.N.I.] meaning of *gosudarstvo* for the first time under the rule of Peter the Great, when they had to swear an oath of allegiance to him".[22] Solovev was not far from the truth. On February 22, 1711, Peter instated the Senate and named its nine members. At that time, he was preparing to leave in order to start the military campaign against the Turks, aware of the dangers he was facing. Therefore, Peter writes the oath that senators, called upon to run the Empire during this absence, must swear. It is the *only* oath, among all of those I found, where the formula of "loyalty to the *gosudarstvo*" appears: each senator swears "loyalty to my Master/Lord[23] and to all *Gosudarstvo*", as well as loyalty to what the

[22] Solov'ev 1963: kn. IX (t. 17-18): 546.

[23] We are so used to *Gosudar'* being translated as Ruler or Monarch that the term Master may come as a surprise. However, the etymology of *gosudar'* goes back to the old Iranian *wis (clan, house), *wis-pati (clan chief) and *wis-ypura (son of the clan or the royal family, prince), as well as to *despótes* in Greek, and *dominus* in Latin. Benveniste 1969: t. 1: 88-91; F. Cornillot 1994. Also, the translation as "Master" respects its place in the discourse context and its use in everyday relations of authority and submissiveness. In *Lexicon pour voyageurs* (1764) de l'Académie de sciences, *dominus* is translated **as** "*gosudar'*"; Madariaga 1982. John

"interests of the Master/Lord and the *Gosudarstvo* require".[24] Peter explains the reason for this oath: to scare the senators in order to stop them from stealing public money or becoming corrupt (Anisimov 1997: 30). He knew who he was working with: out of nine senators, during the first six years of the Senate's existence, six were taken to court for serious felonies, with only two acquitted (Preobrajenskij 1997: 63). Leaving aside the problem of the meaning of *gosudarstvo* for Peter, to me it seems difficult to draw Solovev's conclusions about how the Russians understood its meaning in the creation of this oath. Taking into account the nine oaths I have found that were sworn during the rule of Peter the Great, we may conclude that:

- There is no separate oath of allegiance to the *Gosudarstvo;*

Alexander translated the words *gosudar' and gosudar'ynia,* used in oaths, as Master and Mistress respectively, in his translation of Anisimov 1993: 31. See also Bogatyrev 2000 v.307: 90; *Gosudar'ynia* was translated as *Domina* in the Latin version of Catherine the Great's title, see *Polnoe Sobranie Zakonov Rossijskoi Imperii. Sobranie pervoe s 1649 po 12 dekabria 1825g.*, Saint Petersburg (hereinafter *P.S.Z.*), 1830, t.22. n°15982, p. 107, title of Moldavian *gospodars*. As of the fourteenth century, *gosudar'* also acquired a political value (sovereign), although the sources certify that this title could be understood literally as "Slave Master". Thus, between 1477-1478, Novgorod elites reminded the great Muscovite prince Ivan III (1440-1505), who claimed to have over his city the same rights he had over Moscow—his family domain—of the difference between the word *gospodin* ("Lord" of free servants), which they agreed to use, and the words *gosudar'* or *gospodar'* (Master of unfree servants), which they refused to use. The difference between " Master" and " Lord" caused controversy in Moscow in 1533 after Vasili III's death, when his brothers refused to call their son—the incumbent Ivan IV—gosudar', choosing the word *gospodin* instead. Szeftel 1979:63; Khoroshkevich 1982: 74-75.

[24] Man'kov 1986: 157. See also *P.S.Z.*, t.4: 643, n° 2329. Boris Mironov relied on this source to state that "In 1711, Peter I introduced a new form of oath of loyalty not only to the *gosudar'*, as in the past, but also to the *gosudarstvo*", (Mironov 1999: 128). Certainly, the oath text did not reflect it being strictly aimed at senators. However, it was dated March 2nd, the day on which senators had taken the oath. It all indicates that this oath was not aimed at the administration in general but only at the senators. In Mironov, the verb "vvel", which led the English translators to write "Henceforth, subjects swore fealty not only to the tsar but also to the state", allows us to believe that the oath introduced in 1711 became the rule, Mironov; Ben Eklof, 2000, vol 2: 14. However, to my knowledge, it was never again used. As for the "interest of *gosudarstvo*", based on the sources, it is believed to have been defined within the framework of defense of autocracy's "rights and advantages" (Plotnikov 2001: 1).

- In only one oath, in 1711, did the nine senators swear loyalty to the "*Gosudar'*" and to the "*Gosudarstvo*", though at the same time and on the same phrase;
- In all the oaths, allegiance is sworn to the "*Gosudar'*";
- The word *Gosudarstvo* is missing in four oaths.[25]
- In four other oaths, below the reference to loyalty to the *Gosudar'*, we find the duty to combat the enemies of the "territories and of the *gosudarstvo* of His Majesty, the Tsar", and to *serve* the interests of the *gosudarstvo;*[26]
- There is no systematization in the introduction of loyalty to the *Gosudarstvo*.[27]

However, historians lost their course. Solovev's phrase was taken again a bit later by another prominent Russian historian, Vasili Kliuchevskii, as follows: "thanks to the instatement of the oath of loyalty not only to the *gosudar'* but also to the *gosudarstvo*, for the first time the people were offered the notion of the true meaning of *gosudarstvo*". Solovev had written "when they (the Russians) had to swear an oath of loyalty". He had also explained that it was not a "final" situation since, in practical terms, both during the rule of Peter and after him, what actually prevailed was the practice of serving the people in power and not the *gosudarstvo*. But with the word "vvedeniem", which I translate as "instatement" Kliuchevski introduces a statutory connotation which was missing in Solovev's work.

Next, Kliuchevski leaves us his own interpretation: "Peter distinguished (*razdelil*) between these two notions (gosudarstvo—gosudar'), giving the oath the status of law, distinguishing the *gosudar'* from the *gosudarstvo*".[28] By claiming the statutory nature of the oath, he detaches himself even further from Solovev, but without indicating what

---

[25] *P.S.Z.*, t.4, n°2267 (April 1710, The oath of the Military Navy). The oath of the general Administration in Lebed'ev 1937: 109-110. The oath of the Muscovite chief of police in *P.S.Z.*, t. 6, n°4047. The succession Manifest in Lentin, 1996: 132-133

[26] The War Rulebook (1716), in Man'kov, *Zakonodatel'stvo,* 328. The oath of magistrates (1721) in *P.S.Z.*, t. 6, n° 3708. The War Navy in *P.S.Z.*, t.4, n°2267. The oath of Swedish prisoners (1721) who wanted to settle in Russia in *P.S.Z.*, t. 6, n° 3778.

[27] The preceding lines summarize a more detailed study of oaths and the meaning of *gosudarstvo* in the eighteenth century: Ingerflom, 2013.

[28] Kliuchevskii 1989: 187, 193.

source leads him to conclude that Peter the Great turned the oath to the *gosudarstvo* into a rule.

Western historians have often quoted Kliuchevski's book on Peter the Great, but in general through its translations. The Russian statement "Peter distinguished (*razdelil*) these two notions" was justified, as Peter made the Senators take the oath to the *gosudar'* and the *gosudarstvo.* However, it is necessary to be precise that this distinction took place within *the same and single* oath and, to my knowledge, this was the *one and only* oath to include such a distinction. The verb *razdeliat' means—in general—"to* distinguish / separate the parts (*delit' na chasti)* of the whole", but the distinction can be made inside the whole. I have translated the word *razdelno* as "distinguish". Now, the translations made of Kliuchevski's book in French and English make him say what he has not actually said, and they widen the distortion of Solovev's statement. In the French edition, we can read "Pierre divisa ces notions, par une loi exigeant des serments séparés pour l'Etat et pour le souverain" (Klioutchevski 1991: 248-49). The word "separate (*séparés*)" gives the reader the right to think that actually two different oaths were taken. The English version is more explicit in that regard: "Peter insisted on two oaths, one to the State, and one to the Monarch" (Klyuchevsky 1984: 259). Thus, the historiographic account changed from swearing an oath of loyalty to the *gosudar'* and to *gosudarstvo* to the statement asserting that there are *two types* of oaths.

Likewise, the translation of the term *gosudarstvo* for État/State hides from today's reader the difference between the meanings of the *word gosudarstvo* in Peter's times and of the *concept* of *gosudarstvo* as used by Solovev and Kliuchevski following the steps of western historiography.[29]

---

[29] In the eighteenth century, the first meaning of *gosudarstvo* was the Empire or Kingdom (*tsardom*), or "country" (*strana*). According to the document dated August 27, 1747, the oath that foreigners had to take to become subjects of the Russian emperor expressed their loyalty to the Royal Majesty and the Russian Gosudarstvo's interests. The official translation into German made in the Russian court read: "Rusichen Reiche führen"; *P.S.Z.* t.12, 749. See also the Manifest dated November 7, 1742, on the appointment of Peter III, where the term *goduarstvo* was not used and the term "Empire" appeared instead. Ibid., t.11, 8658. At the time, the Germans used the term Reich to refer to their Empire, which was composed of many different entities such as the Herrschaften, equivalent to Russian *gosudarstva* (plural of *gosudarstvo*), with their particular princes, or the Reichsstädte, which were independent city-states. I am grateful to Professor Michael Stolleis for having provided this information. *Gosudarstvo* also means "a part of the country, a particular region, a province of the Russian Empire". For instance, it was common

The passage from one to two oaths, as well as the loss of meaning of the word *gosudarstvo* as a result of the confusion between the word and the concept, aggravated by subsequent translations into foreign languages, was adopted by contemporary historiography. It has been possible for historians to state that Peter "broke with the identification of the person of the Tsar with the State, and insisted on the fact that the population should swear two oaths, one to the Monarch and one to the State."[30] This tradition has resulted in statements such as this one that no longer have any links with the sources: the separate oath to the *gosudarstvo* might have been a rule during the government of Peter, who was the first European monarch to install a modern and impersonal State to which service and loyalty was to be paid. These mistakes are to be found in books about the history of the State in Europe.[31]

Conclusions

We have seen a series of successive historiographical inaccuracies caused by the endorsement of the paradigm, and based on the conviction that the *gosudarstvo* invoked by Peter is actually the State. The absence of a critical reflection on the use of the signifier *gosudarstvo* gave way to this chain of re-interpretations, where the sources, as well as concern about the historicity of the concepts are absent. Thus, Solver's prudent phrase is

---

to say "in the Siberian *gosudarstvo*" Kafengauz 1952: t. IX, v.1: 291. Apart from a long list of territories over which the monarch ruled simultaneously as an autocrat, Tsar and Great Prince, the official title included "other numerous *gosudar''stva* and land" of which he was "the heir, master (*gosudar*) and protector". The *Gosudar''stva* were part of the Tsardom, the Tsar's possessions. In this sense, its translation as "états" is correct and was used by Peter himself in French, see Lentin 1996: footnote 28, 285. The use of "states" to refer to the parts of a kingdom is not specifically Russian. Hanover's ambassador in Saint Petersburg, Friedrich Christian Weber, wrote that Peter's new policy was related to "*ses états* et pour humaniser son people". Bushkovitch 2001: 427. The title of the Prussian Code (1794), was "Allgemeines Landrecht für die preußischen Staaten": "the states" in plural. See the formulas "the King of Prussia and his states", or "his provinces". For sources in Russian, see for example "all *gosudar''stva* of the Russian Empire…", *Acta* announcing the election of Mikhail Romanov, in Pozdeeva 1996: n°1: 48. Other examples in *PSZ*, t.1, doc. n° 69, 114; Zhivov 2004: note 5, 82 (Letter of Aleksei Milkhailovich, 1677).

[30] Whittaker 1992: vol. 51, n°1: 82, 84

[31] Shennan 1980: 31.

turned into a statement of something that he never wrote and that did not exist, and the contemporary concept of "State" replaces the word *gosudarstvo.*

Loyalty and service paid—above all—to the Master/Lord and, depending on the circumstances, to the interests of the Empire[32] that belongs to him, is in harmony with the internal logic of a system in which such loyalty and service also have his footprint. This system is coherent and, at the same time alien to the State order that characterizes contemporary times. By isolating the formula of "loyalty to the *gosudarstvo*" and turning it into the first sign of contemporary state mentality, historians do not only fall into anachronism, but also neglect the internal coherence of the autocracy of Peter's times, and avoid making an evidently difficult analysis of its complexity. This arbitrary aging of "political modernity" feeds the incomprehension—not always void of underlying political intentions—of the revolutionary transformations that Russia will debate two centuries later.

Sources

Polnoe Sobranie Zakonov Rossijskoi Imperii. Sobranie pervoe s 1649 po 12 dekabria 1825g., Saint Petersburg: 1830.

References

Amstrong, J.A., (1982), *Nations before Nationalism*, Durham, University of North Carolina Press.

András, Z., (1987), *Fejezetek az orosz szókincs történetéből* (*Iz istorii russkoi leksiki*), Budapest, Tankönyvkiadó.

Anisimov, E., (1993), *The Reforms of Peter the Great. Progress through coercion in Russia*, New York and London: M.E. Sharpe.

Anisimov, E. A. (1997), *Gosudarstvennye Preobrazovanija i samoderjavie Petre Velikogo v pervoi chetverti XVIII veka*, Saint Petersburg, Dmitrij Bulanin.

Bartlett, R. - Lehmann-Carli, G., (eds.), (2007), *Eighteenth-Century Russia: Society, Culture, Economy,* Berlin: Lit Verlag.

Benveniste, E., (1969), *Le Vocabulaire des institutions indo-européennes*, Paris: Editions de Minuit.

[32] The "interest of the Empire" boiled down to that of autocracy, Plotnikov 2001: 63.

Beyerly, E., (1973), *The Europecentric historiography of Russia.* The Hague – Paris: Mouton.
Black, J.L., (1973), "The 'State School' Interpretation of Russian History: a Re-Appraisal of Its Genetic Origins", *Jahrbücher für Geschichte Osteuropas*, Band 21, Heft 4.
Blockmans, W. - Genet, J.P., (ed.), (1993), *Visions sur le Développement des Etats modernes*, Collection de l'Ecole française de Rome, v. 171, Rome: Ecole française de Rome.
Bogatyrev, S., (2000), *The Sovereign and His Counsellors. Ritualised Consultations in Muscovite Political Culture, 1350s - 1570s*, Helsinki: Supolaisen Tiedeakatemina Toimituksia Annales Academiæ Scientaum Fennicæ, Sarja-ser. Humaniora, v. 307.
Bullock, P. - Byford, A. - Nun-Ingerflom, C.S. and *al.* (eds.), (2013), *Loyalties, Solidarities and Identities in Russian Society, History and Culture*, London: School of Slavonic and East European Studies, University College London.
Bushkovitch, P., (2001), *Peter the Great. The Struggle for Power, 1671 – 1725*. Cambridge: Cambridge University Press.
Catalano, P., (1986), comments, *Popoli e spazio roamno tra diritto e profezia* Atti del III Seminario Internazionale di Storici " Da Roma alla Terza Roma. Documenti e Studi. Studi III (1983)", Napoli: Edizioni scientifiche italiane.
Carbonell, O., (1993), "Les origines de l'Etat moderne: les traditions historiographiques françaises (1820-1990)", in Blockmans and Genet, *Visions sur le Développement des Etats modernes*.
Chicherin, B.N., (1858a), *Dukhovnye i dogovornye gramoty velikkhx i udel'nykh knjazei*, in *Opyty po istorii russkogo prava*, Moscow.
—. (1858b), "O razvitii drevne-russkoi administracii" (Rech', proiznesennaia pri publichnom zashchishchenii dissertacii "Ob oblastnykh uchrejdenjakh Rossii v XVII veke"), in *Opyty po istorii russkogo prava, cit.*
—. (1858c), *Oblastnye Uchrezhdeniia Rossii v XVII veke*, in *Opyty po istorii russkogo prava, cit.*
—. (1877), *Istoriia Politicheskix Uchenii*, t. 4, Moscow.
—. (1906), *Konstitutsionnyi Vopros v Rossii. Rukopis' 1878*, Saint-Peterburg.
Chicherin., B.N., (1858), "Promyshlennost' i gosudarstvo v Anglii", *Ateneja*, 12, 1858, 213, quoted in Kitaev, *Ot Frondy k oxranitel'stvu. Is istorii russkoii liberal'noi mysli 50-60x godov XIX veka*:100.
Chistjakov, O.I., (ed), *Rossiiskoe Zakonodatel'stvo X-XX vekov*, t. 4, Moscow: Iuridicheskaia literatura.

Clavero, B., (1987), "De un estado, el de Osuna, y un concepto, el de Estado", *Anuario de Historia del derecho español*, t. 57, Madrid.

Cornillot, F., (1994), "L'aube scythique du monde slave", *Slovo*, 14: 27-127.

Dixon, S., (1999), *The Modernisation of Russia, 1676 – 1825*. New York: Cambridge University Press.

Forest, J.D., (1996), *Mésopotamie, l'apparition de l'Etat, VIIe – IIIe millénaire*, Milan, Jaca Book, Quoted by Jean-Louis Huot, "Vers l'apparition de l'Etat en Mésopotamie. Bilan des recherches récentes", *Annales, Histoire, Sciences Sociales*, 2005, 5: 953-973.

Getty, A., (2013), *Practicing Stalinism. Bolshevism, Boyars, and the Persistace of Tradition*, New Haven and London: Yale University Press.

Hamburg, G.M., (1992), *Boris Chicherin and Early Russian Liberalism 1828 - 1866*, Stanford: Stanford University Press.

Hansen, M.H., (1998), *Polis and City-State. An Ancient Concept and its Modern Equivalent*, Acts of the Copenhagen Polis Centre, vol. 5, Historisk-filosofiske Meddelelser 76, Copenhagen: The Royal Danish Academy of Sciences and Letters.

Hegel, W.F., (1956), *The Philosophy of History*, trans. J.Sibree, New York: Dover Books.

Hosking, G., (2001), *Russia and the Russians. A History from Rus to the Russian Federation*, London: Allen Lane, The Penguin Press.

Iggers, G.G., (1988), *The German Conception of History*. New Hampshire: [Wesleyan University Press, 1968] University Press of New England, Revised edition.

Ingerflom, C., (1994), "Oublier l'Etat pour comprendre la Russie ? (XVIe-XIXe siècles)" , *Revue d'Etudes Slaves*, 66/1: 125 – 134.

—. (2004), "Sobre el concepto de Estado en la historia de Rusia", *Historia Contemporánea*, "Pueblo, ciudadanía y otros conceptos políticos", 28: 53-60.

—. (2013), "'Loyalty to the State' under Peter the Great? Return to the Sources and the Historicity of Concepts", in Bullock and *al.*, *Loyalties, Solidarities and Identities in Russian Society, History and Culture*: 3-19.

Iorga N., (1940), *Histoire des Roumains et de la Romanité orientale*, Bucarest: Academia Romana, vol. 5.

Kafengauz, B.B. (ed.), (1952), *Pis'ma i Bumagi imperatora Petra Velikogo*, t. IX, v.1, Moscow: Nauka.

Kavelin, K.D., (1846), *Vzgliad na iuridicheskii byt' drevnei Rossii.*, in *Sobranie Sochinienii*, Saint-Peterburg.

—. (1866), " Mysli i zametki o russkoi istorii", in *Sobranie Sochinieniij, cit.*

—. (1897), "Istoricheskie trudy M.P.Pogodina", in *Sobranie Sochinienii, cit.*

Kharkhordin, O., (2001), "What is the State? The Russian Concept of *Gosudarstvo* in European Context", *History and Theory*, 40/2, 206-240, (now in Kharkhordin, *Main Concepts of Russian Politics*: 1-40).

—. (2005), *Main Concepts of Russian Politics*, Lanham: University Press of America.

Kitaev, V.A., (1972), *Ot Frondy k oxranitel'stvu. Is istorii russkoii liberal'noi mysli 50-60x godov XIX veka,* Moscou: Nauka.

—. (1995), "Gosudarstvennaia shkola v russkoi istoriografii: vremja pereocenki ?", *Voprosy Istorii,* 3: 161-164.

Khoroshkevich, A.L. (1982), "Istoricheskie sud'by belorusskikh i ukrainskikh zemel' v XIV - nachale XVI v." in Pashuto, Floria and Khoroshkevich, *Drevnerusskoe nasledie i istoricheskie sud'by vostochnogo slavianstva.*

Kivelson, V., (1996), *Autocracy in the Provinces. The Muscovite Gentry and Political Culture in the Seventeenth Century.* Stanford: Stanford University Press.

Kleimola, A.M., (1979), "Up Through Servitude: The changing Condition of the Muscovite Elite in the Sixteenth and Seventeenth Centuries", *Russian history / Histoire Russe*, 6, Pt 2, Leiden, Brill.

Klioutchevski, V., (1991), *Pierre le Grand*, Paris: Payot.

Kliuchevskii, V.O., (1989) *Sochineniia v deviati tomah*, t. IV, *Kurs russkoi istorii*, Chast' IV, Moscow: Mysl'.

Klyuchevsky, V. (1984), *Peter the Great*, London: Beacon Press.

Kollmann N., (1987), *Kinship and Politics. The Making of the Muscovite Political System, 1345 - 1547*. Stanford: Stanford University Press.

Koposov, N., (ed.), (2006), *Istoricheskie poniatiia i politicheskie idei v Rossii XVI – XX veka*, St Petersburg: Aletheia.

Krom, M.M., (2006), "Rozhdenie 'gosudarstva: iz istorii moskovskogo politicheskogo diskursa XVI v", in Koposov, *Istoricheskie poniatiia i politicheskie idei v Rossii XVI – XX veka*, St Petersburg: Aletheia.

Lebed'ev, V. I., (éd.), (1937), *Reformy Petra I*, Moscow: Gos-sots ek. Izdatelstvo.

LeDonne, J.P., (1984), *Ruling Russia. Politics and Administration in the Age of Absolutism 1762 - 1796*, Princeton: Princeton University Press.

—. (1991), *Absolutism and the Ruling Class: the Formation of the Russian Political Order, 1700 - 1825*, Oxford: Oxford University Press.

Lentin, A., (1996), *Peter the Great. His law on the imperial succession in Russia, 1722. The official commentary*, Witney: Headstart History.
Lieven, D., (1996), *Nicholas II. Twilight of the Empire*, New York: St Martin's Press.
Lowit, T., (1979), "Y a-t-il des Etats en Europe de l'Est?", *Revue française de sociologie*, 20 : 431-466.
Madariaga, I. de, (1982), "Autocracy and Sovereignity", *Canadian-American Slavic Studies*, 6/3-4: 376-385.
Man'kov, A.G., (ed), (1986), Zakonodatel'stvo perioda stanovleniia absoliutizma, in Chistjakov, *Rossiiskoe Zakonodatel'stvo X-XX vekov*: Iuridicheskaia literatura.
Markwick, R.D., (1999), "What kind of state is the Russian State - if there is one?", *Journal of communist studies and transition politics*, 15/4 (Dec.): 111-130.
Medushevskii, A., (1988), "Gegel' i gosudarstvennaia shkola russkoi istoriografii", *Voprosy Filosofii*, 3: 103 – 115.
Miliukov, P., (1913), *Glavnye techeniia russkoi istoricheskoi mysli*, S-Pb.
Mironov, B., (1999), *Sotsial'naia istoriia Rossii*, t. 2, Saint Peterburg: Dimitrii Bulanin.
Mironov, B., with Eklof, B., (2000), *The Social History of Imperial Russia 1700 – 1917*, v. 2, Colorado: Westview Press.
Monsalvo Anton, J.M., (2000), *La Baja Edad Media en los siglos XIV – XV. Política y Cultura*, Madrid: Síntesis.
Pashuto, V.T. - Floria, B.N. - Khoroshkevich, A.L., (eds.), (1982), *Drevnerusskoe nasledie i istoricheskie sud'by vostochnogo slavianstva*, Moscow: Nauka.
Polnoe Sobranie Zakonov Rossijskoi Imperii. Sobranie pervoe s 1649 po 12 dekabria 1825g., (1830), Saint Petersburg.
Plotnikov, A.B., (2001), "Ogranichenie samoderzhaviia v Rossii v 1730 g. : idei i formy", *Voprosy Istorii*, 1: 63.
Pozdeeva, I.V. (1996), "Pervye Romanovy i caristskaia ideia (XVII vek)", *Voprosy istorii*, 1/48: 48.
Preobrajenskij, A.A. - Novickaja, T.E. (ed.), (1997), *Zakonodatel'stvo Petra I*, Moscow: Izdatel'stvo "Iuridicheskaia literatura".
Rieber, A.J., (1988), "Landed Property, State Authority, and Civil War", , *Slavic Review*, 47/1: 31.
Rosenberg, W., (1994), "Social Mediation and state construction(s) in revolutionary Russia", *Social History*, vol 19-2/1:169-188.
Schaub, J.F., (1995), "La Peninsola Iberica nei secoli XVI e XVII : la questione dello Stato", *Studi storici*, 36/1: 9-49.

—. (1996), "Le Temps et l'Etat: vers un nouveau régime historiographique de l'Ancien régime français" *Quaderni Fiorentini per la storia del pensiero giuridico moderno*, 25: 127 – 181.

—. (2005), "La notion d'Etat moderne est-elle utile?", *Cahiers du Monde Russe,* 46/1-2 : 51-64.

Shennan, J.H., (1974), *The Origins of the Modern European State 1450 – 1725*, London: Hutchinson University Library.

Skalweit, S., (1975), *Der "moderne Staat". Ein historischer Begriff und seine Problematik,* Rheinisch-Westfälische Akademie der Wissenschaften, Opladen: Opladen Westdeutscher Verlag.

Siljak, A., (2001), "Between East and West: Hegel and the origins of the Russian dilemma", *Journal of the History of Ideas*, 62(2): 335-358.

Skinner Q., (2002), "From the state of princess to the person of sate", in Idem, *Visions of Politics*, II: *Renaissance Virtues*, Cambridge: Cambridge University Press.

Solov'ev, S.M., (1963), *Istoriia Rossii s drevneishikh vremen*, Moscou, kn. IX (t. 17-18).

Szeftel, M., (1979), "The Title of the Muscovite Monarch up to the End of the Seventeenth Century", *Canadian-American Slavic Studies*, 13: 59-81.

Tolstikov, A.V., (2002), "Predstavleniia o Gosudar'e i Gosudarstve v Rossii vtoroi poloviny XXVI – pervoi poloviny XVII veka", *Odissei*, Moscow: Nauka.

Whittaker, C.H. (1992), "The Reforming Tsar: The Redefinition of Autocratic Duty in Eighteenth-Century Russia", *Slavic Review*, 51/1: 77-98.

Wirtschafter, K.E., (2007), "A State in Search of a People: The Problem of Civil Society in Imperial Russia", in Bartlett - Lehmann-Carli, *Eighteenth-Century Russia: Society, Culture, Economy*: 373-381.

Zhivov, V.M. (2004), *Iz cerkovnoi istorii vremen Petra Velikogo*, Moscow: Novoe Literaturnoe Obozrenie.

Chapter Nine

From Merchants to Imperial Bureaucrats? Territorial Administration and the East India Company, Seventeenth-Nineteenth Centuries

Kapil Raj

It is all too well known that the British colonization of India in the mid-eighteenth century was not part of any state-sponsored imperial project but was initiated by the English East India Company (referred to henceforth as the EIC or simply the Company), a private consortium of London merchants founded in 1600 that held the lucrative monopoly of British trade conducted east of the Cape of Good Hope. It was this company that progressively established itself in South Asia as a commercial establishment and then acquired and governed territories in the region for a century, from 1757, in the wake of the battle of Plassey at the start of the Seven Years' War, to 1858, when it was dissolved and India became a crown colony under the direct rule of Britain. During these hundred years, the territories controlled by the Company had expanded from Bengal, an area considerably larger than the British Isles, and a few coastal possessions, such as Madras and Bombay, to large swaths of the Indian subcontinent, in other words more than a ten-fold increase. The issue that this chapter will address is the historical process through which the employees of a trading company, as such ostensibly versed mainly in purchasing, storing, and selling European and Asian goods on behalf of the Company, as well as for themselves, were able to successfully become a vast body of imperial bureaucrats and successfully administer the acquired territories from the mid-eighteenth century onwards. The question has a particular importance, since there are few *prima facie* similarities between the vocations of merchant and bureaucrat, apart from the fact that they both owe their existence to producing written documents and are organized according to hierarchical structures. Indeed, Max Weber, the great theoretician of bureaucracy and the emblematic reference for this collection of essays, did not see any genealogical connections between the two, identifying military organization as the model for modern bureaucracy, the buttress of rational-legal authority (Weber 1970: 196-244).

To be sure, the question of the transformation of the EIC from a trading corporation to a governmental structure is not new. However, it has been overwhelmingly conceived of in terms of a sharp rupture between two distinct periods, an "age of trade" and an "age of empire", i.e., post 1757, the transformation and the acquisition of the requisite skills occurring more or less unproblematically.[1] This is more than a hundred and fifty years after the initial contact with Asia, the earlier period being almost wholly characterized in this literature by the Company's commercial activity. It is only very recently that this transformation has been seen as a process that spans the two periods in the history of the EIC's—and more generally of Britain's—presence and evolution in India, most compellingly developed by Philip Stern (Stern 2011).

Like Stern, I shall in this essay argue that although the EIC's occupations were indeed primarily commercial, they also inevitably included a series of major non-commercial activities in fields such as treaty negotiation, revenue and tax collection, justice, urban planning and port management, all necessary for sustained trade relations. Indeed, right from the very first decades of its existence, the Company had to negotiate commercial and diplomatic treaties with Asian polities and merchant communities, and manage settlement enclaves called factories (however small and circumscribed these might have been). As such, its comportment was in fundamental ways that of a state. Territorial acquisition and sustained governance of the territories only accelerated this set of routine, obviously bureaucratic, activities. One might even say that the success of British colonization in the mid-eighteenth century was predicated upon the experience and skills accumulated and developed during the previous century of contact and interaction with South Asian commercial, political, administrative and fiscal regimes. However, in contrast to Stern, I shall emphasize the crucial role that the interaction with these indigenous

[1] The bibliography on the subject is too vast to be cited here at any length, but see, for example, Blunt 1937; Misra 1977; Chaudhuri 1978; Bowen 1991, 2006.

regional structures played in the way the EIC's non-commercial activities developed and evolved. In order to do so, I shall focus mainly on the settlement of Calcutta, not because it was inherently different from its older siblings, Madras and Bombay, but because of the normative role it came to play since the turn of the nineteenth century in the training of the British colonial bureaucracy.

This processual approach thus not only blurs the lines and chronologies of the "pre-colonial" and "colonial", but also brings to light the long-term evolutions and transformations that underlay the emergence of a British imperial bureaucracy. Since, at the same time, continued European presence in Asia, and South Asia in particular, was based on armed trade and militaro-diplomatic negotiations with local polities—indeed, this period has been qualified as an age of "contained conflict"—the EIC, like its other European counterparts, also had a substantial military presence in Asia since the very beginning, not least because European ships were heavily armed and did not hesitate to use their fire power to extort concessions (Subrahmanyam 1990: especially 252–54). As such, although its primary focus is the transformation of merchants into colonial bureaucrats in the process of the emergent British colonial state in India, this paper sits astride the whole of the *State-building in Latin America* project inasmuch as it does not underplay violence while focussing on the fiscal and legal systems.

The Recruitment and Activities of East India Company Servants

Direct contact between England and India dates back to 1600 when Elizabeth I granted a charter to a group of English merchants called "The Governor and Company of Merchants of London Trading into the East Indies", known throughout its long history simply as the East India Company. Having entered the Indian Ocean initially to participate in the growing spice supply to Europe, the EIC was soon driven out of the Malay Archipelago, the principal source of the most coveted spices, by the Dutch. It thus began to concentrate its efforts on trading cloth, spices, and luxury commodities from the Indian subcontinent. For this purpose, it set up entrepôts, or factories, in or next to a handful of already extant port cities along the Malabar and Coromandel coasts, and a few outposts in Bengal and the Gangetic plain.

Because trade between Britain and India was formally a monopoly of the EIC, these enclaves were manned by the Company's employees who were recruited in England and sent to India, where they lived for periods ranging between five to fifteen years—if they managed to survive the harsh tropical climate of South Asia. These were the men responsible for managing the company's trade, buying and selling its goods, negotiating commercial contracts conducting diplomatic negotiations and administering the first settlements, and ultimately, from the mid-eighteenth century onwards, explicitly assuming the responsibilities of governing the conquered territories. The vast majority of recruits to the East India Company arrived in India between the ages of fifteen and eighteen with the prospect of making a quick fortune.[2] Few of them were married, and those who were rarely had their wives with them until the latter half of the eighteenth century (Spear 1932: 13). To become a covenanted servant of the EIC these men had to be nominated by one of the Company's Directors. They were most commonly co-opted as "Writers" (or apprentices) anywhere between the ages of fourteen and seventeen, the only requirement being proof that the boy had been through "a regular course of arithmetick and merchants' accounts."[3] They were usually younger sons from (mainly London-based) mercantile families that vied with each other for procuring highly lucrative careers oversees for their offspring. In fact, the Company's owners had very early in its existence passed a resolution to the effect that gentlemen be excluded from employment in any place of responsibility (Thompson and Garratt 1934: 6).

As the servants progressively rose in rank from Writers to Merchants, the covenanted service took on a strongly hierarchical character. A series of graded ranks was fixed in 1706 into a form that was to last well into the nineteenth century. After serving for five years as a Writer, the next three years were spent as a Factor before becoming a Junior Merchant for another three years. They then reached the highest rank in the service, that of Senior Merchant. With the exception of outstandingly meritorious servants, seniority depended strictly on the year of arrival and, in due time, ten or so of the most senior of the Senior Merchants got to become members of the Factory Council. Finally, the most tenacious survivor could expect to become the President of the Council (Marshall 1976: 10).

---

[2] British Library, India Office Records (henceforth IOR), Court Minutes 1784-85, B/100, p. 216.

[3] IOR, Correspondence with the East, Despatches [sic], Letter Book 28, 1750-1753, E/3/111, p. 79.

These rules were quite strictly followed. In the words of one newly appointed writer reporting home from Calcutta to his brother in 1771 the Governor of Bengal "pays in general great regard to seniority of service… and indeed in the service here supercessions [sic] are not common. In an office if one is put over the rest all those are provided for and nobody serves under his junior."[4]

The covenant bound employees to obey the Company's orders, to deal fairly with their servants, to pay their debts to indigenous merchants before they left India, and above all not to trade in ways that infringed the EIC's monopoly.[5] All employees of the Company received salaries, which, however, made up a comparatively small part of their earnings. The greater part came from private trading. Indeed, virtually everyone was also a private merchant. The right to trade within limits laid down by the Company "without any lett, hindrance or interruption" was included in a Writer's covenant. Regulations on private trade were based on the distinction commonly made between trade of prime commodities, particularly Indian cloth, from Europe to Asia and vice versa, which was the closely guarded preserve of the EIC, and the "country" trade within Asia that European joint-stock companies had no way of controlling. On the contrary, allowing their employees to engage in inter-Asian trade meant that they would be satisfied with their modest emoluments while the Company could make money from the duties and levies on goods transiting through the ports they controlled.

The daily activities of these men consisted, then, of keeping records of the goods stocked in the Company's godowns and warehouses, paying salaries to their indigenous accountants, keeping track of ships and their loading and unloading. The more senior servants, in addition, had to maintain law and order amongst the English members of their settlements, usually through the instrument of the factory's council. And, they all had to negotiate with various intermediaries, usually their indigenous bankers, who put up a substantial portion of the finances for the European companies, and with individual traders to procure supplies of goods ranging from cloth and spices to opium, saltpeter, food grains, sugar and salt.

The business of the Company was thus conducted through indigenous brokers and middlemen, most commonly the *banyan*. The *banyan* not only

---

[4] Mitchell Library, Glasgow, Bogle MSS (relating to India and Tibet) George Bogle to Robert Bogle, 22 February 1771.

[5] For covenants from 1740 onwards, see IOR, O/1/1.

collected goods for export from local cultivators and artisans, but also advanced the sums necessary to procure these goods for endemically cash-strapped European merchants and companies. It was also he who traded the goods the English brought in for the Indian market. Not only was the Company's trade conducted by banyans, so was that of each of its European employees. William Bolts, a Dutch-German merchant (who spent many years in India) and keen observer of the affairs of the EIC characterizes the *banyans* thus:

> […] [T]hose Banyans have in fact a principal share, as deputies and interpreters, in every department of the government, as well as of the commercial concerns of the English East India Company in Bengal. …He is interpreter, head-book-keeper, head-secretary, head-broker, the supplier of cash and cash-keeper, and in general also secret-keeper. He puts in the under-clerks, the porter or door-keeper, stewards, bearers of the silver staves, running-footmen, torch and branch-light carriers, palanqueen bearers, and all the long tribe of under servants for whose honesty he is deemed answerable; and he conducts all the trade of his master, to whom, unless pretty well acquainted with the country languages, it is difficult for any of the natives to obtain access. In short, he possesses singly many more powers over his master, than can in this country [i.e. Britain] be assumed by any young spendthrift's steward, money-lender, and mistress all together; and farther serves, very conveniently sometimes, on a public discussion, to father such acts or proceedings as his master dares not avow[…] There have been few instances of any European acquiring such a knowledge in speaking, reading and writing the Bengal language (which is absolutely necessary for a real merchant) as to be able to do without a Head-banyan (Bolts 1772: 83-84).

The English were of course not exceptional in seeking indigenous intermediaries. Already when the Portuguese entered it at the end of the fifteenth century, the Indian Ocean was a highly organized space, a complex economic network with well-established land routes, shipping, and trade conventions. For a start, the Portuguese had to rely on the services of local Muslim pilots to direct them up the Swahili coast and then to Calicut, their final destination. And when, after initially carrying out armed attacks on local powers, merchants and populations, they finally embarked on sustained commercial exchange in the region, based on fortified littoral colonial settlements, private trade, and political and commercial treaties with regional polities, their interaction with the various communities and political authorities concerned was rendered possible only through the mediation of professional go-betweens with specific literary, technical, juridical, administrative and financial skills (Orta [1563] 1891: 26; Boxer 1969; Pearson 1988; Thomaz 1997, Subrahmanyam 1997; and Madeira-Santos 2016). This pattern formed the basis of subsequent European interaction and maritime settlements in the Indian Ocean.

As was the case, then, for all Europeans following in the wake of the Portuguese, the activities of EIC employees, and of the Company itself, were thus not limited to simple trade, but largely spilled over into the domains of diplomacy, general intelligence gathering, law, maintenance of civil order, negotiation with exotic specialist communities, of pilots and navigators, but also of accountants, translators and procurers of goods, services and manual, maritime and military labour (Bayly 1996. For intermediaries, Raj 2009). In the following section, we shall describe the consolidation and densification of these functions during the course of the seventeenth and early eighteenth century.

The presidencies and their specificities as contact zones

As the English share of the inter-Asian and Euro-Asian trade grew during the seventeenth century, the EIC began looking for firmer and larger tracts of coastal land on which to set up fortified entrepôts and townships of their own. In 1626, they were able to find a first fragile foothold in Armagon on the southeastern (or Coromandel) coast of the Indian subcontinent, just north of the Dutch establishment of Pulicat. However, in 1639, in exchange for a tribute to the local rulers, they succeeded in acquiring a sandy island some forty miles south of Pulicat on which they were allowed to construct a "fort and Castle". Madras, as it came to be called, was in its turn in the immediate proximity of the older Portuguese city of St Thomé. Madras gradually attracted weavers and other craftsmen as well as Taiwanese, Luso-Indian, Portuguese and Armenian settlers who settled down on the mainland facing the island, the population of the township rising to about 40,000 in 1670 (Wheeler [1878] 1972:48 et seq.; Love 1916 vol. 3: 557; and Stern 2011: 39).

In 1661, the English crown acquired the islands of Bombay as part of the dowry in the marriage of Catherine of Braganza to Charles II. However, effective control of the territory was difficult if not impossible for England, not least because of a lack of cooperation from the Portuguese establishment, which continued to be present on the islands. Not having a vision for the governance of these distant lands, the possession was leased to the EIC in 1668 for a rent of ten pounds per annum. As in the case of Madras, the site drew bankers and other intermediaries along with urban business communities and artisans from the western Indian Ocean and the South Asian hinterland, who added to the already existing population of about 10,000 Portuguese, Luso-Indians, indigenous Muslims and Hindus, the population quickly rising to around 60,000 in 1675 (David 1973: 24-38).

Finally, having been evicted in 1686 by Mughal forces from the port town of Hugly in Bengal, where they had a factory since the mid-seventeenth century, the EIC eventually managed to resettle some miles downstream in the market town of Sutanuti in 1690. In 1698 they gained *zamindari*, or rent farming, rights from the Mughal authorities over some few hundred hectares of land just south of Sutanuti on the banks of the Ganges, belonging to the Imperial exchequer. This was where the city of Calcutta was founded. Although the site was particularly unhealthy, this did not stop it from soon becoming the chief English station in the region and the main source of textile shipments, which, by the 1720s, made up over half the Company's exports from India. Its population multiplied from an initial ten thousand to around a hundred thousand by the middle of the eighteenth century.

All these settlements were then made up of populations of very diverse origins and instruments of orderliness needed to be devised. Mary Louise Pratt designates these heterogeneous spaces as "contact zones": spaces "in which peoples geographically and historically separated come into contact with each other and establish ongoing relations, usually involving conditions of coercion, radical inequality, and intractable conflict […] in terms of copresence, interaction, interlocking understandings and practices, often within radically asymmetrical relations of power." (Pratt 1992: 6-7). The concept of "contact zones" lends itself perfectly to this context. In order to maintain order and negotiate contracts in these contact zones that combined elements of economies of local and regional exchange with commercial institutions imported by central- and west-Asian merchants and European long-distance trading corporations such as the EIC, legal questions involving a plethora of different systems were of primordial importance from the very outset.[6] Given the very different juridical situations of the EIC in each of the three settlements, it is not surprising that the respective legal instruments of were also very different.

---

[6] For the functioning of such composite economies, see in particular Bayly 1983: 52 et seq.

In Madras, for example, the EIC was a tenant of only a very narrow length of island. In order to attract artisans, traders and other segments of the surrounding population to come and settle in its vicinity, the settlement was conceived of as a civic space that incorporated different components of its heterogeneous population. A municipal corporation chartered in 1687 thus integrated not just English residents but also representatives of indigenous commercial and professional groups, including various laboring communities. It was this body that took charge of the everyday governance of the city, its wellbeing and welfare, and determined the nature and extent of taxation and protection (Wheeler [1878] 1972; and Balachandran 2008).

Bombay, on the other hand, being English crown territory, the Company was supposed to administer it according to the laws of England. However, when the English obtained it, the territory already had a legal system established by the Portuguese over the preceding century. Accordingly, the first decades of the new administration were spent in trying to carve out a distinct judicial space from the one they had inherited from the Portuguese. However, in Bombay, as in Madras, the population was of very diverse origins, giving rise progressively to a number of courts with often overlapping and conflicting jurisdictions (Fawcett 1934; Khan 1922).

We shall treat the case of Calcutta in more detail below, but it is to be noted that minutes relating to all legal cases, all deliberations and decisions of the various courts and other decision-making bodies in each of these settlements had to be sent back annually to the Court of Directors of the EIC in London. Now, although the original charter granted by Queen Elizabeth I on 31 December 1601 instituting the Company vested it with legal authority, this authority had, until the acquisition of territory, mainly been exercised over wayward employees and seamen. The long-term management of these new heterogeneously populated spaces required much more than the delegation of legal authority from the English monarch. Thus, right from the mid-seventeenth century, the Company's covenanted employees slowly found themselves drawn into assuming the responsibilities of an administrative bureaucracy (Ogborn 2007).

Of course, this evolution had a direct impact on the writing, reporting, and accounting practices and the imperatives of the circulation of information within the EIC. But this evolution cannot be rendered intelligible purely within the logic of early-modern long-distance trading corporations. The indigenous groups with which Europeans had to interact and negotiate were themselves also constituted communities and held together through writing, reporting and accounting practices of their own. The Company's practices had thus to mesh in with the latter—and, more generally, all of them with each other. This interaction was at the core of the material functioning of the Company's warehouses, as an overwhelming majority of the accountants and storekeepers were indigenous. In the case of Madras, these forms of writing were largely the preserve, since at least the sixteenth century, of a professionally trained hereditary community of accountant-scribes called *karanams* (Tirumalai 1994). A polyglot group, the *karanams* composed variously in Dravidian languages such as Telugu and Tamil, but also in Sanskrit, Marathi and Persian, at times in a mix of scripts (Rao, Shulman and Subrahmanyam 2003). Similarly, in west and north India, scribal classes fluent in Marathi and Persian, had, by the seventeenth century, spread their presence into every aspect of the fiscal, commercial, religious, judicial, and other state administrations of these regions (Guha 2004; Alam and Subrahmanyam 2004). Many of the courts and administrative bodies in the European settlements, notably in Madras, Bombay and Calcutta, employed members of these literate and scribal communities in their administrations and courts as interpreters, scribes and legal specialists. Furthermore, Portuguese having acquired the status of a littoral *lingua franca* in many parts of the Indian Ocean, an indigenous Lusophone scribal community had developed in the course of the sixteenth and seventeenth centuries. This community was to find a significant place among the scribal groups associated with the European trading companies that followed the Portuguese into the region. Indeed, their place was to become so central that even many of the local polities of peninsular South Asia were to draw up treaties and other engagements with Europeans and their corporations in Portuguese.[7]

It has been persuasively argued that the skills and faculties of these "graphically literate communities," which developed in the dual contexts of early-modern state formation and commercial practices, and "who used writing as a medium, not [merely] for preserving or recording but also for communication", evolved in their close interaction with the East India Company in the centuries that followed (Rao 2004; more generally, Raman 2012. See also Kruijtzer 2002). Contrariwise, it is also arguable that the EIC's own writing practices were significantly shaped through the sustained interaction of these indigenous literate communities and its

[7] For a compilation of some of the treaties and other agreements signed between the English and political powers and communities of the Malabar, see Logan 1891; see also Hamilton 1727, v.I: xix-xx.

European employees. As mentioned earlier, the vast majority of the EIC's English recruits were employed and sent to Asia in their mid-teens with little other knowledge than “the rule of three and merchants’ accounts.” (Farrington 1976: 4). Few had been to university, a costly affair normally reserved for elder sons or for those seeking academic or clerical careers. They thus acquired the writing skills while in service in India from their senior colleagues, but also in a significant way from their indigenous scribal employees or commercial partners.

Calcutta *Zamindari*: Rent Farming and Administration of Justice, both British and Mughal

If the interaction between indigenous and English writing practices was common to all the EIC's entrepôts and factories in the Indian subcontinent, and was crucial in shaping the way its administration evolved from a purely commercial corporation to one which also had to manage the land holdings on which its warehouses and settlements were built, the specificity of the legal situation of the Calcutta enclave, and the place it was to acquire as the center of the first large tracts of territory that the English Company later captured, was to fundamentally give a new and unexpected direction to this shift. For while, as mentioned above, each of the three major settlements had their own legal statuses, Calcutta's specificity needs to be elaborated upon in more detail. In effect, in order to give some permanence to a shaky start in Bengal with a foothold in the market town of Sutanati, the EIC acquired the title of *zamindar* (rent farmer) in 1698 over about 770 hectares of Mughal lands extending southwards of it that were directly part of the Imperial exchequer, principally through the intermediation of a prominent Armenian merchant, Khwaja Israel di Sarhat.[8] It was on these lands that the city of Calcutta was to develop in the course of the eighteenth century. As *zamindar*, the Company would not only be empowered to collect land revenue, but also to levy taxes to defray the cost of the upkeep on roads and bridges, and incidentally to make a considerable profit on the *ghats* (river landing heads) and *bazaars* within its jurisdiction.

[8] For the role of Khwaja Israel di Sarhat in the negotiations to obtain the Calcutta *zāmīndārī* rights for the English, see IOR, Chutanuttee Diary and Consultations 1 December 1697 to 30 November 1699, G/7/3, f. 59r. See also Seth 1928: esp 110-113; and Wilson, 1906 vol. 1: 25 n. 3. More generally, Ferrier 1970: 439; Aslanian, 2006; Bhattacharya 2005; Seth 1937.

Most importantly, the conferment of a *zamindari* also carried a certain number of crucial obligations concerning the administration of justice over the population of the estate. As such, the Company also had jurisdiction in civil matters, while in regard to criminal cases it had to assume the powers of a magistrate to police. However, in this capacity, the Company was drawn into the jurisdiction of the Mughal Empire, and would be responsible for the good conduct of its several offices, under pain of revocation of its privileges.[9] Crucial to understanding the functioning of the Company on the ground, the composite nature of its constitution, at once English (as conferred upon it through the Royal Charter of 1601) *and* Mughal (as an imperial *zamindar*, has so far been neglected by historians).

The nucleus of the Calcutta settlement thus came to be the *zamindari kachahri*, or office (Wilson 1906 vol. 1: 14 n. 1), and the Company's servants found themselves having to run penal, civil and revenue courts as an integral part of their duties. These offices were modelled on the Mughal system in vigor in the rest of the empire: the main *Kachahri*, the *Fouzdari* (or *Zamindari*) *Kachahri* (for criminal cases) and the *Collector's Kachahri* (for fiscal matters) (Wilson 1906: vol. 1: 14 n. 1, also Patra 1962). It was only in 1727, almost thirty years after having been conferred the *zamindari*, that a Mayor's Court was founded on orders from the Court of Directors in London, when the population of the city had reached an estimated 300,000 (Firminger 1917 vol. 1: lxxiii et seq.). This court was supposed to rule on litigations amongst subjects of the British crown and their dependents, and those who by voluntary submission subjected themselves to that jurisdiction (Firminger 1917 vol. 1: lxxiii et seq.). However, as an examination of its records show, the Mayor's court soon found itself assailed with litigation between Asians and Europeans and between various Asian communities themselves.[10] To further complicate matters, the jurisdiction of the newcomer was almost immediately challenged by the city's other courts (Wheeler 1878).[11] Given the novelty of the situation, new laws had sometimes to be negotiated. Thus, Persian-

---

[9] For the roles, rights and obligations of *zamindars*, see Hasan 1969.

[10] IOR, Bengal Public Consultations, Mayor's Court Records, Dec. 1727 to Dec. 1728, P/155/10. For the controversy over the jurisdiction of the Mayor's Court and various other courts and authorities, see Proceedings for 1 and 8 June 1730, Mayor's Court Records, Jan. 1729/30 to Dec 1730, P/155/12 (no pagination); and John Browne to Court of Directors, 5 August 1749, Home Miscellaneous Series, H/420, pp. 13-21.

[11] For a detailed account of the administration of justice, see Sterndale 1885:12.

and Arabic-speaking literati and Sanskritist pundits versed in the various legal traditions and procedures in operation within the Mughal Empire made their appearance as notaries, scribes, or as minor employees in the growing administrative departments of the Company and of the city. Like the other communities in this urban space, these intermediaries were also part of larger diasporic communities some of which had a long heritage in seeking cultural accommodation between the different components of South Asian society.[12] The city's courts—along with the President and Council who were also responsible for the commercial dimensions of Company affairs—thus came to constitute the core of its intellectual and urban dynamic.

Two major events in the mid-eighteenth century—qualified in both contemporary Indo-Persian and English sources as 'revolution' (*inqilab*)—were to dramatically overturn the course of the subcontinent's history leading to the spectacular rise of Calcutta and the generalization of these nascent administrative practices over much of the subcontinent. First, the invasion of north India and the sack of Delhi in 1739 by an erstwhile Afghan tribal chief who had recently conquered Persia, Nadir Shah (1688-1747), rang the death knell of the ailing Mughal Empire, accelerating its virtual collapse and giving rise to a myriad of successor polities vying with each other to fill the power vacuum thus created. Secondly, the victory at Plassey in 1757 (in the first months of the Seven Years' War) of the EIC's army over the forces of Siraju'd-Dawla, the Nawab of Bengal, radically transformed the geopolitical complexion of the region, making Britain a major political actor in South Asia for the next two centuries. This conquest would also reshuffle the equilibrium between the administrative and commercial dimensions of the EIC in favor of the former.[13]

But, before discussing the boost of the administrative domain, let us keep in mind that both the commercial and the administrative aspects were inherent characteristics of the East India Company in the 150 years of its existence before territorial conquest. However, since Bengal was the first region to be thus acquired, the role of Calcutta in the future emergence of a colonial bureaucracy would turn out to be preponderant. We must then focus on the evolution of the city and its institutions in the decades that followed.

---

[12] On syncretic traditions in various currents of political thought in early-modern South Asia, see Alam 2004

[13] For contemporary perceptions of the times as being revolutionary, see Ṭabāṭabā'ī 1789, vol. 3: 161, [W. Watts/J. Campbell] 1760; and Bolts 1772: 150.

Having thus gained a portion of the subcontinent considerably larger than the total area of the British Isles, the Company very cunningly negotiated to sideline the local and regional polities and in 1765 to extort from the Mughal emperor the *Dewani* of Bengal, or the management of the revenues of the entire province. However, the consciousness of this new role was slow in coming for, in the years that followed the conquest of Bengal, EIC officials devoted their energies to ruthlessly plundering and devastating the land.[14] One of the first major acts by the Company was to plunder the Nawab of Bengal's coffers to finance its own trade, especially with China. It also began to mint its own money in the province and substantially reversed the flow of silver bullion and specie, which now started moving out of South Asia. The Company thus became less dependent on political and commercial inputs from indigenous trader-bankers and exchange agents for navigating between a multitude of currencies, although these latter continued to play an indispensable role because the new administration relied on them, not merely to underpin its residual trading operations, but to finance its administration and to guarantee the working of the land-revenue system. At the same time, the rise of British private merchants investing in inland trade under the protective umbrella of the EIC, meant that the intermediation of indigenous brokers shifted to these individuals, becoming more dispersed and making room for other communities of indigenous financiers to step onto the scene.[15]

This led indirectly to the collapse of a number of traditional urban centers. Calcutta was one of the few cities that prospered—it gained a new vitality to become, in the space of a few years, the capital of the East India Company's territories in India and soon the second-largest city of the British Empire. Its population and area quadrupled in a couple of decades (Nair 1990 vol. I: 23). Indeed, such was its perceived importance that when the Mughal Emperor Shah Alam II (reigned 1761-1805) dispatched an embassy to George III in 1766, his representative Mirza Shaikh I'tiṣam

---

[14] A comprehensive list of these 'most atrocious abuses that ever stained the name of civil government' may be found in 'Reports from the Committee Appointed to Enquire into the Nature, State and Condition of the East India Company and of the British Affairs in East India,' *Reports from Committees of the House of Commons, 1772-1773*, Vol. III, (London, 1803).

[15] For the economic consequences of the Company's control over Bengal, see Sinha 1981-84 vol. 1: 221-40; Datta 2000; and Chatterjee 1993.

al-Din (1730-1800), left from Calcutta instead of Madras, or Bombay, better situated on the sea route to London (Fisher 2004: 87-92).

But, after ten million lives, or a third of the population of Bengal (almost all peasants and artisans), had been lost in the space of three years—victims of a famine compounded with the ruthless policies of the Company's servants—attention was turned to stabilising the internal order of the province (Kumar 1982: 299). Under growing pressure from the British Parliament, which culminated in the Regulating Act of 1773 and the institution in Calcutta of the Supreme Court of Judicature for the administration of justice in the newly acquired territories, the Company and its agents grudgingly shifted from commercial plunder to more orderly and permanent forms of exploitation and government.

The Birth and Development of a Colonial Bureaucracy

It was in this context that the Court of Directors of the Company in London were prevailed upon in 1772 to appoint Warren Hastings (1732-1818)—a senior employee of the Company who had already served for 15 years in Bengal—as Governor-General of the province with the brief to take over and directly control the *nizamat*, that is, its whole civil (police and criminal) administration. The *diwani* (or the office for revenue administration) was transferred from the erstwhile capital, Murshidabad, to Calcutta which in the process saw itself transformed from a contact zone between Asian and European heterogeneous networks organized mainly around trade and urban administration, to become a locus of control and coordination of vast networks of territorial administration.

To Hastings' mind, successful administration required drawing up an inventory of the Company's territories. "Every accumulation of knowledge," he wrote, "and especially such as is obtained by social communication with people over whom we exercise a dominion founded on the right of conquest, is useful to the state…"[16] In addition to taxation and law—since, in addition to the conclusion and maintenance of legally viable commercial contracts with local traders and bankers, the Company was now obliged to administer civil and criminal law in the newly acquired territories—this knowledge was to include topography, natural history and antiquities, local customs, diet and general living conditions, in short all that was, in the coming decades, to go under the name of statistics (Cullen

[16] W. Hastings to N. Smith, Chairman of the East India Company, 4 October 1784, in Wilkins 1785:13.

1975: 10-11). However, Hastings also soon realized that the British would in no way be able to maintain sustained control over the territory by relying solely on the mere 1200 civil and military agents of the Company, poorly trained at administrative tasks to boot.

The collaboration between Britons and South Asians progressively broadened to include tax collection, administration of justice and finally education. And, although the British set up a variety of new intermediary relationships with native South Asians, they had to maintain many of the existing local administrative structures, and most of the "under civil servants".[17] Thus, the various revenue and judicial officials inherited from the Mughal and other princely administrations, continued to act in their official capacity as intermediaries between the British and local populations (Nagar 1942, 1940, 1954; Muhammad 1934; Cohn 1987: 320-342, 422-462; Bayly 1996). Once a contact zone between Asian and European heterogeneous networks organized mainly around trade and urban administration, Calcutta now also became a locus of control and coordination of vast networks of territorial administration. New institutions such as the *Munshikhana* (secretariat of the provincial administration) emerged in the footsteps of the Surveyor's office already established in the 1760s.

Giving the highest priority to a knowledge of the region's languages, Hastings devised a policy of handsome monetary incentives to those of his officials who were willing to study the languages and other aspects of South Asian society. This policy constituted the first step in the transformation of the study of exotic peoples from an individual activity—mainly of European missionaries—into a massive and institutionalized activity reflecting the vital concern it represented for the emerging rulers of the subcontinent. This was also the first step in the transformation of the emerging British empire from one held by force of arms to one held—at least in theory—by information and knowledge.

This demand for indigenous collaborators for language teaching as well as for administrative needs, particularly in the domain of justice, naturally attracted literati from the fast collapsing Mughal Empire as also from the new successor states, like Avadh and Hyderabad, and even from as far away as Iran. A significant number thus found employment translating learned texts of all kinds. One area where these texts were particularly crucial was in the administration of civil law, in part because

[17] I borrow the expression "under civil servants" to designate minor functionaries from Cohn, 1987:320-342, esp. 328 et seq.

of the rising flood of litigation between South Asians and Europeans ever since the new territorial conquest, and in part because British courts, as we have already remarked, offered new legal possibilities to indigenous litigants.

Indeed, it was the city's courts—which were already, as we have noted, at the heart of Calcutta's intellectual dynamism—that began to play a central role in the organization and construction of knowledge. In 1781, the Hastings administration established a *Madrassa* in the city center, a mile to the north-east of Fort William. This was in response, on the one hand to a request from "a considerable number of Musselmen of credit and learning" to promote institutions of traditional learning which "had been the pride of every polished court and the wisdom of every well regulated government both in India and in Persia [but of which] in India only traces… now remain, the decline of learning having accompanied that of the Mughal Empire" and, on the other, "with a view… to the production of officers for the courts of justice." The subjects taught were Arabic, Persian and Islamic law, with later additions, such as natural philosophy, astronomy, geometry, arithmetic, logic, rhetoric and oratory – "all according to Islamic culture."[18]

Now, although these policies began having their effects on the administration of the colonized province, especially in standardizing the indigenous under civil servants in Bengal through educating them in the Calcutta *Madrassa*, the European servants were left to their own initiative to instruct themselves in the intricacies of the administration and to benefit from the incentives offered through Hastings' schemes. It must be said that the situation was not so very different in Madras and Bombay as and how the Company acquired territory in south and west India, contiguous to these two Presidency settlements. However, this was to change at the turn of the nineteenth century in the wake of the Napoleonic wars and their repercussions in India.

The emergence of the colonial administrator: the College of Fort William

The Napoleonic wars gave rise to unprecedented antagonisms within British society. Radicals and reformers continued to criticize the

[18] Warren Hastings, 'Minute' 17 April 1781, Sharp, 1920: 7-9, 30; reprinted in Zastoupil and Moir, 1999: 73-5. For the petition, see *Calendar of Persian Correspondence* 1919-1949 vol. 6: 89; vol. 7: 2; Sanial, 1914: 83-112, 225-51.

government for adopting a hostile attitude to France and for allying with a confederation of absolutist monarchs. Already confused and divided on various issues, the British Government found its loyalties even further dissipated. In the wake of runaway inflation, crippling taxes, and trade disruption, radical whisperings grew more audible, growing numbers protested against the war, giving rise to massive strikes—a third of the eighteenth century's strikes took place in the 1790s—and naval mutinies. In retaliation, the Government responded by progressively abrogating constitutional freedom: suspension of the Habeas Corpus in 1794 and again in 1798; promulgation of the Treason and Sedition Act (1795), the Unlawful Oaths Act (1797), the Corresponding Societies Act (1799) and, finally, a ban on public meetings. But, however much British society was divided on the war, everyone in Britain seemed to agree that, in the light of the fragility of power in France, this was an ideal moment to capture profitable French colonies. Thus, along with the West Indies, the British lost no time in capturing all the French settlements in India.[19]

However, in pursuing these aims, Britain wastefully dispersed itself, and France not only held out but also managed to swing the war to its own advantage, taking control of the Mediterranean in the winter of 1796. In 1797, Britain found itself isolated in Europe. Its only ally, Austria, had capitulated; constrained to retreat from the Mediterranean, Britain narrowly escaped being invaded by a French expeditionary force operating in concert with Irish insurgents. A mutiny broke out in the Channel Fleet of the Royal Navy and soon spread to the Dutch and Spanish coasts and the Cape of Good Hope.

It was in this political climate that Lord Mornington, better known by his real name, Richard Wellesley (1760-1842), was appointed Governor-General of the Indian territories of the EIC in 1797. A convinced free-trader, this Irish aristocrat, like his younger brother, Arthur Wellesley (the future Duke of Wellington), was a fierce opponent of the French Revolution.[20] Having already served on the EIC's Board of Control, he was well abreast of the overall situation in the Indian subcontinent and of the supposed territorial ambitions of the French there.

[19] As Henry Dundas, Chairman of the Board of control and Secretary for War, wrote to Wellesley explaining his basic principle "that the way to defeat France is to take all her colonies and to destroy her trade." Quoted in Philips 1961: 101.

[20] See, for instance, his speech in Parliament to defend continuing the war with France in 1794, quoted fully in McCullagh Torrens 1880: 101-108.

Disquieting news awaited the new Governor-General on his arrival at Calcutta in 1798: from the local press he learned of Napoleon's project of attacking India from Egypt (Seton-Karr 1864: iii, 201-202). He was also informed of the landing of French troops and military advisors on the Malabar coast to help their most important Indian ally, Tipu Sultan the ruler of Mysore, mount an offensive against British interests in the peninsula.[21] He learned likewise of the presence of Frenchmen at the head of the Nizam of Hyderabad's 14,000-man army.[22] In November 1798, the Secret Committee of the EIC sent Wellesley a despatch informing him of Napoleon's conquest of Egypt.[23] And in spite of the reassuring news of Nelson's victory at the battle of the Nile, another letter asked him to seriously consider a pre-emptive attack on Egypt to "amuse [Napoleon] from the Red Sea with one of your Indian Brigades."

Wellesley lost no time in acting.[24] He despatched an embassy to Persia to persuade the Shah to offer his aid in the eventuality of a French terrestrial invasion. He organized a pre-emptive attack on Hyderabad, taking the French commanders completely by surprise, holding them prisoner and liberating the Indian troops.[25] And, he entrusted his brother, Colonel Sir Arthur Wellesley, with the task of containing the French push in the peninsula. The British armies, massively assisted by the Nizam of Hyderabad's troops, attacked Mysore in March 1799. Tipu was killed at Seringapatam in May, and Wellesley definitively put an end to the putative French schemes in India. Half of Tipu's territories were put under the direct rule of the Company and the rest restored to a puppet—the child heir of the erstwhile rajas of Mysore.

---

[21] IOR, Home Miscellaneous Series H/572, ff 5-7.

[22] See James Kirkpatrick, "A View of the State of the Deccan, 4th June 1798", British Library, Wellesley Papers, Add. Mss 13582.

[23] Despatch [sic], dated 26 November 1798, from the Secret Committee to the Governor-General in Council, and to the Governments in India, extracts from which are printed in *Review of the Affairs of India, from the Year 1798, to the Year 1806; Comprehending a Summary Account of the Principal Transactions during that Eventful Period* 1807:15. See also Despatch, dated 18 June 1798, printed in Martin 1836, Vol. i: 61-64.

[24] IOR, Home Miscellaneous Series, IOR/H/572, pp. 67-235: Governor-General's Minute concerning the political situation in India and measures to be adopted in reference to Tipu.

[25] Letter from the Earl of Mornington to the Court of Directors, dated 21 November, 1798, in Martin, ed. Vol. ii, 351-360.

Taking personal charge of an offensive against the French on the ideological and political fronts, Wellesley set about promulgating new laws to contain radical thought in Calcutta by imposing a draconian censorship on the local press, and visas for all Europeans unofficially present in India.[26] And in order to check the spread of the egalitarian message of the French Revolution amongst the junior servants of the Company, he drew up an astonishing scheme, using the change in the company's circumstances from a trading presence to a preponderantly ruling administration as a springboard to launch it.

In a Note dated 10 July 1800, Wellesley laid out his plan to the EIC's Court of Directors in London (Wellesley 1836a: 325-355). He began with an analysis of the nature of the Company. Its conquests in eastern and southern India in the latter half of the eighteenth century, he stated, now constituted an enduring empire larger in size than most European states and had radically transformed the nature of its activities and responsibilities. In particular, they called for certain specific obligations on the part of Company's employees: "To dispense justice to millions of people of various languages, manners, usages and religions; to administer a vast and complicated system of revenue throughout districts equal in extent to some of the most considerable kingdoms in Europe; to maintain civil order in one of the most populous and litigious regions of the world; these," he argued, "are now the duties of the larger proportion of the civil servants of the Company. The senior or junior merchants, employed in the several magistracies and *Zillah* Courts, the writers or factors filling the stations of registers and assistants to the several courts and magistrates, exercise, in different degrees, functions of a nature, either purely judicial, or intimately connected with the administration of the police, and with the maintenance of the peace and good order of their respective districts."

Wellesley then embarked on a description of the nature of court proceedings in Company-administered territories, pointing out that the pleadings were conducted in the various languages of the Subcontinent. Furthermore, the laws which the Company's servants had to administer were not those of Britain, but those "to which the natives had long been

[26] IOR, Home Miscellaneous IOR/H/537, pp. 339-359: Imposition of censorship 1799; and pp. 365-395: Special prohibitory orders issued 1801-1808 to Editors and Printers of the *Calcutta Gazette*, *Asiatic Mirror*, *Hircarrah*, Star, *India Gazette, Morning Post, Oriental Star, Telegraph, Orphan*, and *Mirror*. See also Mornington to J. Lumsden, 23 December 1798, in Martin, ed. 1836 Vol i: 386; Seton-Karr, 1864: iii, 17-18; and Cotton 1924: especially 77-79; and Maclean 1806.

accustomed under their former sovereigns, tempered and mitigated by the voluminous regulations of the Governor-General in council, as well as by the general spirit of the British constitution. These observations are sufficient to prove, that no more arduous or complicated duties of magistracy exist in the world, no qualifications more various, or more comprehensive, can be imagined than those which are required from every British subject, who enters the seat of judgment within the limits of the Company's empire in India."

The same applied to the reckoning and collection of taxes as well as to commercial contracts. All this demanded an understanding and knowledge of administrative, trading and banking conventions very different from those that operated in Europe (Wellesley 1836a: 327-8). Thus, training in the languages, laws, usages, and customs of the Subcontinent were henceforth indispensable for all servants of the EIC.

Although the "denominations of writer, factor, and merchant" were now "utterly inapplicable to the nature and extent of the duties discharged, and of the occupations pursued by the civil servants of the Company"—the more so since they were now required by solemn oath to abstain from any commercial activity—the vast majority of recruits to the EIC, arriving in India between the ages of fourteen and eighteen with only a rudimentary knowledge of merchant accounts, continued to carry these ranks and were thoroughly unprepared for this new role.[27] Moreover, without any education in traditional cultural and moral values, a large number of them succumbed to a life of "indolence, dissipation, and licentious indulgence." (Farrington 1976: 326-7). In these circumstances, and in order to discharge their wide-ranging duties, a novel system of education had to be conceived of, "involving the combined principles of Asiatic and European policy and government."

All this led up to Wellesley's main mission: according to him, it was incontrovertible that, "during the convulsions with which the doctrines of the French Revolution have agitated the Continent of Europe, erroneous

[27] Wellesley 1836a: Vol. ii - 326. (Cf. Burke's observation that "the India Company however still preserved traces of its original mercantile character; and the whole exterior order of its service is still carried on upon a mercantile plan and mercantile principles. In fact, it is a State in disguise of a Merchant, a great public office in disguise of a Countinghouse." Opening of Impeachment, 15 February 1788, in Burke 1991: 283. The rule of three and some knowledge of merchant's accounts was all that was required of aspiring candidates to the Company's service. See Farrington 1976:4).

principles of the same dangerous tendency had reached the minds of some individuals in the civil and military service of the Company in India; and the state, as well of political, as of religious opinions, had been in some degree unsettled. The progress of this mischief would at all times be aided by the defective and irregular education of the writers and cadets; an Institution tending to fix and establish sound and correct principles of religion and government in their minds at an early period of life, is the best security which can be provided for the stability of the British power in India." (Wellesley 1836a: 346). The Indian part of these principles was, in his scheme, to be taught by indigenous savants since they represented a strict hierarchical structure and would be the best bulwark against dangerous Gallic egalitarian ideas.[28]

For all these reasons, and because no appropriate educational institution existed at the time in Europe or in India to meet these desiderata, Wellesley wrote of his decision to found a college in Calcutta—at Fort William. Comparable in size and diversity of means to Oxford and Cambridge, it was formally inaugurated on 24 November 1800. Besides Latin and Greek, English and Natural History, Natural and Experimental Philosophy, Chemistry, Astronomy, Economics, Political Economy and Geography, the new recruits were to spend three years there from the day they set foot in India to learn Arabic, Persian, Sanskrit, six Indian vernaculars—Hindustani, Bengali, Telugu, Marathi, Tamil and Kannada—Hindu, Islamic and English law, European history—and Indian history and antiquities (Wellesley 1836b: 356-361). Many of these subjects were to be taught at Fort William by erudite indigenes.

Although these domains had never figured on the curriculum of any university in Europe, a precedent for their study did exist in India. Indeed, as we saw in the last section, Warren Hastings had devised a policy of large monetary incentives to encourage the Company's covenanted employees to gain knowledge of indigenous legal and fiscal thought and practices, as also of the region's antiquities, natural history, topography, local languages and customs, dietary habits, and the general living conditions. However, this policy only had a limited success inasmuch as most of the Company's employees, besides not having the intellectual wherewithal to tackle them, were not interested in these questions. The

[28] It is interesting again to compare this idea of stable hierarchical social structures to Burke's description of Hindu society and the parallels he draws between the Brahmans and the English nobility. See Burke 1991: vi, 303 et seq. See also his speech on Fox's India Bill, 1 December, 1783 Burke 1991: v, 389-90.

few who did respond to Hastings's scheme learned about local lore and languages from their *munshis* who already served them as interpreters, bankers, and intermediaries in their everyday dealings with indigenous merchants.[29]

In setting up his "University of the Orient", Wellesley was seeking on the one hand to make up for this shortcoming in making instruction in "orientalism" obligatory and, on the other, to institutionalize the relationship between the British and their indigenous intermediaries, which until then, as we saw earlier, had been constructed on an individual, and thus informal, basis. As instructors for this new institution, he chose members of the Asiatic Society and their autochthonous collaborators: British "orientalists" and South Asian savants shared the teaching. The College organized and encouraged expeditions into Company administered territories in order to look for, and acquire, new manuscripts for its own library. By 1805, its faculty had succeeded in systematizing the grammars and constructing dictionaries of a number of the region's vernacular languages. This standardization made it possible to teach these languages to large numbers of students.

The Board of Control was actually quite enthusiastic about the Fort William College project. Only a few Evangelicals protested against the dangers of losing Christian values on an intensive exposure to those of the Subcontinent. Desirous of introducing a training in natural and experimental philosophy and anticipating the difficulty of finding a suitable teacher over there, the Company's directors sent a Scottish savant, James Dinwiddie (1746-1815), to Calcutta at their own expense. One of the Board of Trade's experts on the East, Dinwiddie was also abreast of the latest French innovations in explosives (Proudfoot 1866: 98-9; Dinwiddie, 1789).

Wellesley's inordinate spending in the early years of the College's existence understandably did not go down well with the Company's shareholders, already deprived of dividends because of a severe financial crisis. The Governor General, however, received the unconditional backing of fellow Irishman and conservative, Lord Castlereagh, appointed Chairman of the Board of Control in 1802, who was quick to appreciate its potential anti-Revolutionary value. Unable to put a complete stop to Wellesley's initiative, the shareholders settled for a compromise: the teaching of European culture was to be shifted to England and dispensed before the cadets left for India. In the words of one of the Company's

[29] On *munshis*, see Alam and Subrahmanyam 2004.

directors, David Scott, "the College was sacrificed to the private trade agitation."[30]

In spite of this, Wellesley's plan of associating European and Indian teachers was maintained. When, in 1806, the East India College opened at Haileybury in England, Indian instructors were brought over in order to participate in the training of the Company's future employees, alongside great English savants like the political economist Thomas Malthus. Wellesley's scheme reappeared in the curriculum of the new metropolitan establishment (Philips 1961: 104-6). Between 1801 and its final dissolution in 1831, the College of Fort William received about forty cadets annually. They would then serve in Bengal as well as in other territories controlled by the Company, including Madras and Bombay. Crucially, this led to a standardization of administrative practices all over the emerging empire in India.

After having spent anywhere between ten and twenty years in India, these men would return to Great Britain to live as "nabobs", or serve as senior functionaries of the EIC or else as politicians—the more successful amongst them even got elected to parliament. Some even joined the exclusive fold of men of science (Holzman 1926; Nechtman 2010). Lastly, it is important to note that the spearheads of the educational reforms of the early 1830s in Britain and India, in particular James Mill and Thomas Babington Macaulay, were all leading protagonists in the debates around the College of Fort William. Wellesley's scheme for the Fort William College finally led to the spawning of a new middle class whose loyalty was to a professional network—skill, function, and organization being determinants of consciousness and identity.

At the same time, however, both British and Indian societies were changing rapidly in the first half of the nineteenth century, demographically as well as in terms of the rise of new professions and dimensions of state intervention. Large-scale public projects, such as canals, railways, and roads, were begun in both places and public health and agriculture began to receive particular attention from the state. This required new methods of recruitment and training, broadening the population from whom the servants of the Company were traditionally inducted, to include Indians by the latter half of the nineteenth century.

[30] British Library, Eur. MSS. E.176, f. 698, 23 April 1802. Grant wrote, "Wellesley himself inadvertently furnished the means of his defeat. His letter to the Court on enlarging the privilege of private traders arrived opportunely for that party to support their declining cause." Cited in Philips 1961: 127.

However, the general approach of an ongoing interaction between Indian literate elites and British functionaries was to continue and become even more entrenched in the training of personnel.

With the dissolving of the EIC in 1858 and the transfer of power directly to the British Crown, the training of Indian Civil Service probationers was shifted to Oxford. The Sanskrit inscription on the foundation stone of the Indian Institute, established there in 1883 and that until very recently housed the University's Modern History Faculty, acknowledged the common origins of worthy administrators on which the whole imperial apparatus was founded:

> This Building, dedicated to eastern sciences, was founded for the use of Aryas (Indians and Englishmen) by excellent and benevolent men desirous of encouraging knowledge. … By the favour of God may the learning and literature of India be ever held in honour, and may the mutual friendship of India and England constantly increase.

Conclusion

In this paper, I have attempted to make a brief historical presentation of the workings of the East India Company. In so doing, I have striven to show that, contrary to the commonly-held view amongst historians, there was no sharp rupture between its functionings in its "trading" and "imperial" periods. In line with recent research, especially by Philip Stern, this essay stresses that even in its early decades as a trading corporation, the Company had the trappings of a state and, as such, its overseas employees had the rudiments of both a commercial and a state bureaucracy. And, although there were significant contextual differences in the three main English settlements, which were later to become the nuclei of the three centers, or Presidencies, of British colonial power in South Asia, the fact of instituting a single training college, first in Calcutta, then in Haileybury, had the effect of standardizing the skills of the colonial bureaucracy as well as having a profound effect on the course of higher education and bureaucratic training in Britain itself. Finally, I have also tried to stress the enduring interaction and assimilation of modes of governance drawn from South Asian polities, a feature which preserved the specificity of this bureaucracy in the course of the nineteenth and early twentieth centuries and that at the same time formed an integral part of modern state-building.

Archives

British Library, India Office Records [IOR], London
Mitchell Library, Bogle MSS, Glasgow

References

Alam, M. - Subrahmanyam, S. (eds.), (1998), *The Mughal State 1626-1750*, New Delhi: Oxford University Press.

—. - Subrahmanyam, S., (2004), "The Making of a *Munshi*", *Comparative Studies of South Asia, Africa and the Middle East*, 24/2: 61-72.

—. (2004), *The Languages of Political Islam: India 1200-1800*, Chicago: University of Chicago Press.

Aslanian, S., (2006), "Social Capital, 'Trust' and the Role of Networks in Julfan Trade: Informal and Semi-Formal Institutions at Work", *Journal of Global History*, 1/3: 383-402.

Balachandran, A., (2008), "Of Corporations and Caste Heads: Urban Rule in Company Madras, 1640-1720", *Journal of Colonialism and Colonial History*, 9/2: *Project MUSE*. Web. 16 Feb. 2016. <https://muse-jhu-edu-s.sargasses.biblio.msh-paris.fr/>.

Bayly, C.A., (1983), *Rulers, Townsmen and Bazaars: North Indian Society in the Age of British Expansion 1770-1870,* Cambridge: Cambridge University Press.

—. (1996), *Empire and Information: Intelligence Gathering and Social Communication in India, 1780-1870*, Cambridge: Cambridge University Press.

Bhattacharya, B., (2005), "Armenian European Relationship in India, 1500-1800: No Armenian Foundation for European Empire?", *Journal of the Economic and Social History of the Orient*, 48/2: 277-322.

Blunt, E., (1937), *The ICS, the Indian Civil Service*, London: Faber & Faber.

Bolts, W., (1772), *Considerations on India Affairs.* London.

Bowen, H. V., (1991), *Revenue and Reform: The Indian Problem in British Politics 1757-1773*, Cambridge: Cambridge University Press.

—. (2006), *The Business of Empire: The East India Company and Imperial Britain 1756-1833,* Cambridge: Cambridge University Press.

Boxer, C.R., (1969), *The Portuguese Seaborne Empire, 1415-1825*, London: Hutchinson.

Burke, E., (1991), *Writings and Speeches*, Vol VI. Oxford: Oxford University Press.

Calendar of Persian Correspondence, 11 vols, Calcutta: Superintendent of Government Printing, 1919-1949.

Chatterjee, K., (1993), "Conflict and Collaboration: Bankers and Early Colonial Rule in India", *Indian Economic and Social History Review*, 30/3; 283-310.

Chaudhuri, K.N., (1978), *The Trading World of the Asia and the English East India Company, 1660-1760*, Cambridge: Cambridge University Press.

Chaudhuri, S., (ed.), (1991), *Calcutta, The Living City*, 2 vols., New Delhi: Oxford University Press.

Cohn, B.S., (1987), *An Anthropologist Among the Historians and Other Essays*, Delhi: Oxford University Press.

—. (1987), "The Initial British Impact on India: A Case of the Benares Region", in Cohn, *An Anthropologist Among the Historians and Other Essays*: 320-342.

Cotton, H.E.A., (1924), "The Story of James Paull", *Bengal Past and Present*, XXVIII July-December: 69-109.

Cullen, M.J., (1975), *The Statistical Movement in Early Victorian Britain. The Foundations of Empirical Social Research,* New York: Harvester Press.

Datta, R., (2000), *Society, Economy and the Market: Commercialization in Rural Bengal c. 1760-1800,* New Delhi: Manohar.

David, M.D., (1973), *History of Bombay*. Bombay: University of Bombay.

Dinwiddie, J., (1789), *Syllabus of a Course of Lectures on Experimental Philosophy*, London.

Farrington, A.J., (1976), *The Records of the East India College Haileybury & Other Institutions*, London: Her Majesty's Stationery Office.

Fawcett, C., (1934), *The First Century of British Justice in India*, Oxford: Clarendon Press.

Ferrier, R., (1970), "The Agreement of the East India Company with the Armenian Nation, 22nd June 1688", *Revue des études arméniennes*, n.s. 7: 427-43.

Fisher, M.H., (2004), *Counterflows to Colonialism: Indian Travellers and Settlers in Britain 1600-1857,* Delhi: Permanent Black.

Firminger, W.K. (ed.), (1917), *Fifth Report from the Select Committee of the House of Commons 28th July, 1812,* 3 vols., Calcutta: R. Cambray and Co.

Guha, S., (2004), "Speaking Historically: The Changing Voices of Historical Narration in Western India, 1400-1900", *American Historical Review*, 109/4: 1084-1103.

Hamilton, A., (1727), *A New Account of the East Indies*, London.
Hasan, S. Nurul, [1969] (1998), "*Zamindars* under the Mughals", in Alam - Subrahmanyam, *The Mughal State 1626-1750*: 284-98.
Holzman, J.M., (1926), *"The Nabobs in England: A Study of the Returned Anglo-Indian, 1760-1785"*, Unpublished Ph.D. dissertation, Columbia University, New York.
Khair-ud-Din Muhammad, M., (1934), *Tazkirat-ul-Ulama or a Memoir of the Learned Men of Jaunpur*, tr. and ed. M. S. Ullah, Calcutta.
Khan, S.A., (1922), *Anglo-Portuguese Negotiations Relating to Bombay, 1660-1677*, Oxford: Humphrey Milford.
Kruijtzer, G., (2002), "Madanna, Akkana and the Brahmin Revolution: A Study of Mentality, Group Behaviour and Personality in Seventeeth Century India", *Journal of the Economic and Social History of the Orient*, 45/2: 231-68.
Kumar, D., (ed.), (1982), *The Cambridge Economic History of India*, Vol. 2, Cambridge: Cambridge University press.
Logan, W., (1891), *Malabar*, Vol 3: *A Collection of Treaties, Engagements and Other Papers of Importance,* Madras: Government Press.
Love, H.D., (1916), *Vestiges of Old Madras, 1640–1800; Traced from the East India Company's Records Preserved at Fort St. George and the India Office, and From Other Sources,* 3 vols., London: John Murray.
McCullagh Torrens, W.T., (1880), *The Marquess Wellesley, Architect of Empire. An Historic Portrait,* London: Chatto & Windus.
Maclean, C., (1806), (Second Edition). *The Affairs of Asia Considered in their Effects on the Liberties of Britain, In a Series of Letters, Addressed to the Marquis Wellesley, Late Governor-General of India; Including A Correspondence with the Government of Bengal, under that Nobleman, and a Narrative of Transactions, involving the Annihilation of the Personal Freedom of the Subject, and the Extinction of the Liberty of the Press in India: with the Marquis's Edict for the Regulation of the Press,* London
Madeira-Santos, C., (2016), "O Império português face às instituições indígenas", in Palomo - Barreto Xavier - Stumpf (eds.), *Monarquias Ibericas en Perspectiva Comparada*, (forthcoming).
Marshall, P.J., (1976), *East Indian Fortunes: The British in Bengal in the Eighteenth Century,* Oxford: Oxford University Press.
Martin, R.M. (ed.), (1836), *The Despatches, Minutes and Correspondence, of the Marquess Wellesley, K.G., During his Administration in India,* 5 Vols., London: W. H. Allen & Co.

Misra, B.B., (1977), *The Bureaucracy in India: An Historical Analysis of Development up to 1947,* Delhi: Oxford University Press.

Nagar, R.N., (1940), "Employment of Indians in the Revenue Administration of the N.W.P., 1801-1833", *Journal of the United Provinces Historical Society*, Vol. XIII: 66-73.

—. (1942), "The Subordinate Services in the Revenue Administration of the North Western Provinces, 1801-1833", *Journal of the United Provinces Historical Society*, Vol. XV, part II: 125-34.

—. (1954), "The Tahsildar in the Ceded and Conquered Provinces, 1801-1833", *Uttar Pradesh Historical Quarterly*, Vol.II (n.s.).

Nair, P.T., (1991), "The Growth and Development of Old Calcutta", in Chaudhuri, (ed.), *Calcutta, The Living City*: 10-23.

Nechtman, T.W., (2010), *Nabobs: Empire and Identity in Eighteenth-Century Britain.* Cambridge: Cambridge University Press.

Ogborn, M., (2007), *Indian Ink: Script and Print in the Making of the English East India Company,* Chicago: University of Chicago Press.

Orta, G. da, [1891], (1563), *Colloquios dos simples e drogas da India.* Lisbon.

Palomo, F - Barreto Xavier, Â - Stumpf, R., (eds.), (2016), *Monarquias Ibericas en Perspectiva Comparada*, Madrid: Casa de Velasquez, (forthcoming).

Patra, A.C., (1962), *The Administration of Justice Under the East-India Company in Bengal, Bihar and Orissa,* Bombay: Asia Publishing House.

Pearson, M. N., (1988), "Brokers in Western Indian Port Cities: Their Role in Servicing Foreign Merchants", *Modern Asian Studies* 22/3: 455-72.

Philips, C.H., (1961), *The East India Company, 1784-1834*, Bombay: Oxford University Press.

Pratt, M.L., (1992), *Imperial Eyes: Travel Writing and Transculturation.* London: Routledge.

Proudfoot, W.J., (1866), *Biographical Memoir of James Dinwiddie LLD Astronomer in the British Embassy to China, 1792-1793*, Liverpool: Edward Howell.

Raj, K., (2009), "Mapping Go-Betweens in Calcutta, 1770-1820", in Schaffer - Roberts – Raj - Delbourgo, (eds.), *The Brokered World: Go-Betweens and Global Intelligence, 1770-1820*: 105-50.

Raman, B., (2012), *Document Raj: Writing and Scribes in South India*, Chicago: University of Chicago Press.

Rao, V.N., (2004), "Print and Prose: Pundits, Karanams, and the East India Company in the Making of Modern Telugu", in Blackburn, S., and Dalmia, V., (eds.), *India's Literary History: Essays on the Nineteenth Century*. Delhi: Permanent Black: 93-139.

—. - Shulman, D. - Subrahmanyam, S., (2003), *Textures of Time: Writing History in South India*, Delhi: Permanent Black.

"Reports from the Committee Appointed to Enquire into the Nature, State and Condition of the East India Company and of the British Affairs in East India", *Reports from Committees of the House of Commons, 1772-1773*, Vol. III, London 1803.

Review of the Affairs of India, from the Year 1798, to the Year 1806; Comprehending a Summary Account of the Principal Transactions during that Eventful Period, London.

Sanial, S. C., (1914), "History of the Calcutta Madrassa", *Bengal Past and Present* 8: 83-112, 225-51.

Schaffer, S. - Roberts, L. - Raj, K. - Delbourgo, J., (eds.), (2009), *The Brokered World: Go-Betweens and Global Intelligence, 1770-1820*, Sagamore Beach, MA: Science History Publications.

Seth, M., (1928), "Khoja Petrus, The Armenian Merchant-Diplomat of Calcutta", *Bengal Past and Present*, 37, pt. II, N°72: 110-126.

—. (1937), *History of the Armenians in India from the Earliest Times to the Present.* Calcutta: the author.

Seton-Karr, W.S., (1864), *Selections from the Calcutta Gazette,* 5 vols., Calcutta: Military Orphan Press.

Sharp, H., (ed.), (1920), *Selections from Educational Records* Part I: 1781-1839, Calcutta: Superintendent Government Printing.

Sinha, N.K., (1981-84), *The Economic History of Bengal: From Plassey to the Permanent Settlement,* 3 vols., Calcutta: Firma K.L. Mukhopadhyay.

Spear, P., (1932), *The Nabobs*. Oxford: Oxford University Press.

Stern, P.J., (2011), *The Company State: Corporate Sovereignty and the Early Modern Foundations of the British Empire in India*, Oxford: Oxford University Press.

Sterndale, R.C., (1985), *An Historical Account of 'The Calcutta Collectorate,' 'Collector's Cutcherry, or Calcutta Pottah Office,' From the Days of the Zemindars to the Present Time, With a Brief Notice of the Zemindars and Collectors of Calcutta, the Ground Tenure or Land Revenue System, Town Duties, Excise, and Stamp Revenue*, Calcutta: Bengal Secretariat Press.

Subrahmanyam, S., (1990), *The Political Economy of Commerce: Southern India, 1500-1800*, Cambridge: Cambridge University Press.

—. (1997), *The Career and Legend of Vasco da Gama*, Cambridge: Cambridge University Press.

Tabaṭaba'i, G.Ḥ.K., (1789), *Seir mutaqherin: or, View of modern times, being an history of India, from the year 1118 to the year 1194 of the Hedjrah, containing, in general, the reigns of the seven last emperors of Hindostan, and in particular, an account of the English wars in Bengal...* tr. Haji Mustafa (alias Nota-Manus), 3 vols., Calcutta.

Thomaz, L.P.F.R., (1994), *De Ceuta a Timor*, Lisbon: Difel.

—. (1994), "Estrutura politico-administrativa do Estado da Índia", in Thomaz, *De Ceuta a Timor*: 207-245.

Thompson, E.J., and Garratt, G.T., (1934) *Rise and Fulfilment of British Rule in India*, London: Macmillan.

Tirumalai, R., (1994), *Collected Papers: Studies in South Asian Epigraphy and History of Land Organisation, Development and Accounts and Select Chola and Pandyan Townships*, Madras: Department of Archeology, Govt. of Tamil Nadu.

[Watts, W., and Campbell, J.], (1760), *Memoirs of the Revolution in Bengal, Anno Dom. 1757,* London.

Weber, M., (1970), "Bureaucracy", in H.H. Gerth and Wright Mills, C., (tr. & ed.), *From Max Weber: Essays in Sociology*. London: Routledge & Kegan Paul: 196-244.

Wellesley, R., (1836a), "Notes on the Foundation of a College at Fort William, 10 July 1800", in Martin (ed.), vol ii: 325-355.

—. (1836b), "Regulation for the foundation of the College of Fort William in Bengal". in Martin (ed.), vol ii: 356-361.

Wheeler, J.T., (1972, originally published 1878), *A History of the English Settlements in India, as told in the Government Records, the Works of Old Travellers, and Other Contemporary Documents, from the Earliest Period Down to the Rise of British Power in India*, Calcutta. [reprinted London: Curzon Press.]

—. (1878), *Early Records of British India: A History of the English Settlements in India*, Calcutta: W. Newman & Co.

Wilson, C.R. (ed.), (1906), *Old Fort William in Bengal: A Selection of Official Documents dealing with its History*, 2 vols., London: John Murray.

Wilkins, C., (tr.), (1785), *Bhagavad Gita*, London.

Zastoupil, L. and Moir, M., (1999), *The Great Indian Education Debate: Documents Relating to the Orientalist-Anglicist Controversy, 1781-1843*, London: Curzon.

CHAPTER TEN

THE BUREAUCRATIZATION OF THE MILITARY ORGANIZATION IN SONG CHINA, TENTH - EARLY ELEVENTH CENTURIES[1]

CHRISTIAN LAMOUROUX

The wars and political conflicts that fragmented the Chinese Empire during the last decades of the Tang dynasty (618-907) and continued for seventy years after the demise of the Tang deserve to be viewed as a crucial moment in the building of a bureaucratic state in China. This assertion, which we will attempt to support in this chapter, nevertheless contradicts the heavily ideological reading of events by traditional Chinese historiography. The old discourse is haunted by the collapse of central power and by the societal decline under the long-term domination of illiterate and cruel generals. The present revisionist view which makes possible the positive reassessment of this history is largely based on the research of Japanese sinologists after the 1950s.[2] We will come back to the consequences of their work very soon.

To begin with, we should revisit the chronology of events. After the Tang, the North of the former empire was ruled by the ephemeral Five Dynasties (907-960), each succeeded by the next. During this period, in institutional terms, the North had become completely separate from the South, which in turn had broken up into some ten kingdoms between 907 and 975. This period of the Five Dynasties and Ten Kingdoms truly came to an end when political unity finally returned in 979 under the Song

[1] I express my gratitude to the two translators of my chapter, especially Xiaobin Ji who also provided me with advice concerning some translations of sources. Of course, all errors and misinterpretations remain mine.

[2] See a critical reading and a summary of these works in Tsang Shui-lung and Chiu Yu Lok, in Bao Weimin 2004: 165-228.

dynasty (960-1279). The Song founder had led a successful military coup against the last ruler of the Five Dynasties of the North. After twenty years of unification wars and about twenty more years of armed conflicts with the powerful Liao Empire, the new masters of the Song Empire imposed an effective long-lasting peace while creating a new regime of sovereignty. Without denying the institutional legacy of the Tang dynasty, the Song nonetheless created its own unique institutional framework by learning from the military governments that had directly preceded it. In this manner, the Song dynasty, whose rise was originally grounded on the violence of war, successfully dealt with the ever-present threats of internal palace intrigues and subversive alliances between regional powers.[3]

Since the 1920s, the period between the crisis in the middle of the Tang and the consolidation of the Song imperial rule has been considered by the Kyoto School as the emergence of "modern times," while at the beginning of the 1950s, the Tokyo School saw the same period as the beginning of the "medieval" age. Whatever the perspective, Japanese sinology has successfully promoted the enduring perception of a "Tang-Song transition" during which emerged an autocratic power centered on the person of the Emperor.[4] The institution of this new imperial authority, which was powerful enough to eradicate the influence of regional powers by violence and diplomacy, put the Song in a position to re-assure the regional elites over their security and offer them opportunities of upward mobility within the centralized system of public services that they had accepted. In fact, on the one hand, the new bureaucratic regime of the Song increasingly emphasized its dependency on the civil values supported by scholar-officials who were selected by an expanding system of examinations; on the other hand, the dynasty took advantage of the resumption of certain norms of control which military personnel had enforced in the heat of political instability and warfare. Thus, they formed around the sovereign a complex system of centralized command. It is precisely this structure that will be at the center of our analysis here.

---

[3] The history of the period is presented in the first two chapters of Twitchett and Smith 2009: 38-205.

[4] This question is summarized in Miyakawa Hisayuki 1955: 533-542. The nature of the transition is criticized by Paul Smith in the introduction of Smith and von Glahn 2003: 1-34. Another critical analysis of the "Tang-Song transition" is proposed in the introduction of Lau Nap-yin 2008: 3-42. See also several articles devoted to the transition in Li Huarui 2010.

Several recent studies, which are partly based on the results of Japanese research, have shed light on the transformation of a group of lower-ranking officers whose importance had been growing since the years 980-990 and throughout the first century of the Song dynasty. Despite the unclear contours offered by historiography, the origin of this group has to be found within the circles linked to the "inner posts" of the Royal Palace (*neizhi* 內職), which depended directly on the sovereign. The presence of these men in the palace can be documented at least two centuries before the Song dynasty, as they formed the immediate entourage of the Emperor from the second half of the Tang period. While the eunuchs certainly worked in parallel with the scholars, they also did so with technical specialists: astronomers and astrologists, sundry forecasters, doctors, calligraphic scribes, chess players, or officially appointed actor-musicians (*lingguan* 伶官). The growing influence of these technical specialists on government is inseparable from the weakening, and then the ultimate collapse, of the central administration of the dynasty.

These men took effective charge of diverse commissions within the palace so that their responsibilities progressively interfered with those of the regular administration. This interference increasingly confused the organization of offices, of which, from the seventh century on, two major categories could be distinguished: the "titular offices" (*zhishiguan* 職事官) that corresponded to effective functions; and the "classification offices" (*jieguan* 階官) or even the "prestige titles" (*sanguan* 散官). The first type articulated the real management of public affairs (justice and registration of households for taxes and corvée), and the others permitted the ranking of elites who progressively constituted themselves as a service aristocracy, alongside the powerful aristocratic lineages. During the second half of the tenth century, under the Song, this distinction was reaffirmed as an instrument of imperial power: the hierarchical classification of "titular offices" held by civil servants opened certain career possibilities to them while blocking others, but without systematically determining their assignments to posts in which they would have to fulfill real functions. Such assignments for a determined period of time were "commissions" (*chaiqian* 差遣), defined according to the needs of the Court. In other words, the titles held by officials did not always correspond to their functions. Moreover, many among them were supernumeraries, their titular office being never more than nominal. Only in 1082 did a great administrative reform partially remove this confusion which the Song had progressively perceived as dysfunctional, an institutional anomaly inherited from the disorder that had preceded the founding of the dynasty.

Our analysis will focus first on some essential facts, and then on the emergence of new government rules. On these rules was grounded the organizational capability to subdue the very group that had introduced these new principles of rulership: the military. We shall see, in addition, how the very notion of a "military bureaucracy" is a historical construction before it actually appears as an organizing principle or a model for political centralization, as sociologists have assumed. We will finish by insisting on the two major consequences of the bureaucratization of the military: the division between the administrative and military apparatus, and the social and political downgrading of the military function itself, something that was intimately related to the positive image of civil bureaucracy under the Song. Civil servants appeared, therefore, as the only officials capable of enforcing a new kind of sovereignty on the whole Empire, henceforth understood as a centralized territory. Ironically, this was the vision that the military had themselves promoted to the various emperors.

Men of the Palace: Eunuchs and Soldiers

The historical evolution presented in broad strokes hereafter covers the two and a half centuries that follow the great revolt of the Sodgian general An Lushan in 755.[5] This rebellion forced the Emperor Xuanzong 玄宗 (reign: from 712 to 756) of Tang to flee his capital Chang'an 長安 in 756 and find refuge in a neighboring province before abdicating in favor of his son. We will stop in 1005, once the Song dynasty (960-1279) agreed to bring about a long-lasting peace with the Liao Empire (907-1125), which permitted the civil administration to set its hegemony over the military apparatus.

Briefly, facing an uprising of several of its generals, the Tang Dynasty saved its Empire thanks to an army which came from the North-West. The Army of the "Divine Strategy" (*shencejun* 神策軍) rallied to Emperor Suzong 肅宗 (r. 756-762), the son of Xuanzong, and progressively became the Imperial Army. This force showed itself capable of stabilizing the military situation after the decade beginning 760, especially by the

---

[5] The general history of the Tang is studied in Twitchett 1979. The An Lushan revolt is detailed in Pulleyblank 1955. In general, on-line information such as Wikipedia articles is useful. Even though there are errors in detail, those articles provide biographies of the Tang, Five Dynasties or Song emperors, as well as the presentation of many events introduced in the present article.

definitive re-establishment of the authority of Daizong 代宗 (r. 762-779) over the capital, after having chased away the Tibetan troops who had occupied the city since 763. The decade of the 780s was marked by the reforms of the new Emperor Dezong 德宗 (r. 779-805): his fiscal reform resulted in the financial strengthening of the dynasty and so of its military capacity. In 784, the reorganization of the Army of the Divine Strategy was grounded on troop increase, the guarantee of better provisions, and above all by locking its command at the heart of the Palace: all the commanders of the different corps were eunuchs. From then on, this army was stronger than any of the armies controlled by the different regional governors, whose pretensions towards greater autonomy never ceased. Sure of this support at his back, Xianzong 憲宗 (r. 805-820) was thereby able to instigate several military campaigns which cut short such pretensions in many regions. The half century that followed is considered by Chinese historiographical tradition as a dynastic "restoration." The end of this dynastic revitalization came with the outbreak of a vast popular revolt, led by a certain Huang Chao 黃巢 (dead in 884): the movement began in 875 from the east of the empire, then the rebels took over the south and, finally, attacked the north-west to seize Chang'an, which fell into their hands in 881. Expelled from his capital, Xizong 僖宗 (r. 873-888) had no choice but to place himself under the protection of local governors, the strongest of whom had no scruples about forming strong factions in alliance with the eunuchs and their armies. The last Tang emperors could only stay on the throne by manipulating the balance of power between the most ambitious governors with whom they had accepted compromises. The governors were guaranteed a real autonomy, particularly in the matter of recruiting their own personnel, in exchange for their military and financial support. This new deal with the governors was enforced by the eunuchs who were appointed as Military Inspectors (*jianjun* 監軍) deputed into the governors' administration – and so often associated with them. This perilous equilibrium fell apart when two or three of the most powerful governors disputed the "protection" of the Imperial House. Zhu Wen 朱溫 (852-912) finally forced the last Tang Emperor to place himself under his protection before having the Tang emperor executed and proclaiming himself as Emperor of the Later Liang dynasty (907-923), the first of the Five Dynasties.[6]

[6] On the end of the dynasty and especially the period of division that followed it, the best reference book still is Wang Gungwu 1963/1995.

Following the works of Wang Gungwu, that were largely based on Japanese sinology, historians have cogently pointed out what interests us here.[7] Well before 755, a movement took shape in the heart of the Imperial Palace: some duties of the enormous central government, the "Outer Court" directed by the Grand Councilors, were progressively put in the hands of close servants of the Emperor who staffed the "Inner Court." These "Servants of the [Inner] Court" (*tingchen* 廷臣) formed a heterogeneous group of officials appointed as functionaries and officers of the "inner posts" of the Palace. One can find "Commissioners of the Various Offices" (*zhusishi* 諸司使) who, at the head of the organs of the Palace placed under their authority, served the Emperor and the Court in various areas: food, medicine, the presentation of guests at Court, the preparation and protocol of banquets, as well as the management of imperial horse stables and weapons, two domains which interested the military administration directly. There were also the "military servitors" (*shichen* 使臣), about whom we will speak at further length.

After 755, the administrative power of the "Outer Court" was increasingly eroded by that of the "commissioners" and their teams when the Tang emperors chose to assign to the eunuchs tasks which were previously entrusted to the "Outer Court" officials. Without going into detail, it is known that embassies, the inspection of armies, and the supervision of public monopolies devolved onto them. Even more decisive in terms of power in everyday operations was the introduction of procedures which placed the Palace "commissioners", and therefore some of the eunuchs, in a position to control the transmission of imperial directives from the Palace, where audiences were held, to the organs of government which depended on the "Outer Court." To this end, the post of Military Affairs Commissioner (*shumiyuanshi* 樞密院使) was instituted by Emperor Xianzong at the beginning of the ninth century.[8] The founder of the Later Liang Dynasty, from the moment of his seizure of power at

---

[7] On the history of the Commissioners and the officers assigned to inner posts, the literature in Chinese and Japanese is extensive. I refer throughout my text to two recent works that study this institutional system from the point of view of military organization: Chiu Yu Lok 1993 (this book is the result of a thesis obtained the same year by Chiu at the University of Kyoto), and especially Zhao Dongmei 2010.

[8] Tang Zhangru 1989: 244-272. Hucker remarks that the *shumi shi*, which he translates as "Palace Secretary" for the Tang period, was "a eunuch post created in 765 to coordinate and supervise the Emperor's paperwork", see Hucker 1985: 436.

the beginning of the tenth century, installed military officers from his personal retinue in positions formerly held by eunuchs whom he had executed *en masse* in 903. These officers, therefore, in their turn retained the powers once held by central civil officials.

One should see this episode as a military takeover of administrative responsibilities. This action deteriorated further the already weakened "Outer" administration that had guaranteed the older aristocracy both control of the statutes and the positions within the Court. At the same time, however, it should also be considered, as the historian Wang Gungwu showed almost half a century ago, that this meant the emergence of a new and lasting structure of central power. From that time on, it was the followers closest to the sovereign, his retinue composed of "bosom servants" (*fuxin* 腹心), who would fill the key posts of the central power. Here is a pen portrait of one of the Zhu Wen's servants in the *Comprehensive Mirror for Aid in Government*, completed in the 1080s:

> [The 8/06/907] The Master of the Memoranda regarding Martial Proclamations and Chamberlain for the Palace Revenues Jing Xiang 敬翔 took charge of the affairs of the Court for the Veneration of Governance […] to serve as counsellor and to debate strategy, to receive imperial directives from the Inner Palace, and transmit them by proclamation to the Grand Councillor so they might be carried out. If the latter had, beyond audiences as such, to submit a report or an answer after having received an order, everything would be consigned in memoranda by which the Emperor would be informed through the channel of the Court for the Veneration of Governance, and the Court, once having obtained the order from the Emperor, would respond by proclamation to the Grand Councillor. [Jing] Xiang was discrete and profound, clear-sighted and thoughtful. He had been a private secretary [to the Emperor] for more than thirty years […]. Whether the matter was military strategy or civil administration, he inevitably was put in charge by the Emperor […]. In the process of the devolution of power [from the Tang], it was Xiang who had fixed most of the strategic agenda.[9]

The Court for the Veneration of Governance was the very provisional name given by the Later Liang to the Bureau of the Military Affairs. Zhu Wen thus planned to adapt the model of organization staffed by the eunuchs as counselors and confidents of the Emperor by now entrusting the main tasks of any governmental cabinet to a commission directed by

---

[9]. Sima Guang 1957: chapter 266: 8674.

one of his followers: editing of written imperial orders, provision of information to the sovereign, transmission and probably preservation of the documents. The Palace Commissioners certainly had become the sovereign's spokesmen. Thus, from the Later Liang on, the "proclamations" (*xuan* 宣) that commissioners were in charge of acquired the enforceable power that until then had been the exclusive prerogative of the edicts that the Grand Councillor prepared under the authority of the Emperor to activate the administrative machinery.[10]

Each of the ephemeral Turkish dynasties which followed the Later Liang tended to increase the responsibilities of the Bureau of the Military Affairs that became a centralized organ directly supervising army inspectors during the unending wars of the period.[11] In fact, under the two emperors of the Later Tang dynasty (923-936), the two most important Bureau Commissioners were also appointed Grand Councilors. Therefore, they were naturally in charge of any liaison between the Emperor and the various offices of the regular administration, and were accordingly in a position to select local functionaries as well as Commissioners for State Revenue, and thus to supervise all the fiscal affairs under central government control. Lastly, as military advisers who were responsible for the security of the Palace, they were granted the privilege of re-transcribing audiences to be placed in the archives of the Bureaus of Historiography. By so doing, they had a chance to impose their own institutional perspective in the long term. After the founder of the Later Jin (936-947) made a short-lived attempt to return to a "regular" administration by abolishing the Bureau of Military Affairs (939-944), the importance of the Commissioners became quite obvious: the Grand Councilor who was in charge of the government had no choice but to recognize that he was unable to assume all the Court responsibilities, especially military matters—without which the Later Jin power could not survive. From that time on, the Bureau of Military Affairs was recognized as an institutional necessity. The last phase of the process preceded by a few years the foundation of the Song dynasty. First, as the Military Commissioner who was in position during the coup which overthrew the Late Han (947-950), Guo Wei 郭威 (904-954) was particularly aware of

[10] Two collections of "notes" (*biji*) make clear the conditions of this transfer of responsibilities: Shen Gua 2009: 62-64; Song Minqiu 1997: 46-47.

[11] On the evolution of the Bureau under the Five Dynasties, see Billy So 1995: 1-38. Many facts regarding the Bureau of Military Affairs have been collected in Liang Tianxi 1981.

the possible military threat upon the Late Zhou dynasty he had founded as Zhou Taizu (r. 951-954). So, from 953 onwards, he appointed Military Commissioners without any military pedigree or function. This policy was followed by his son and successor Zhou Shizong 周世宗 (r. 954-959), who paid great attention to limiting the influence of his own Military Commissioners. Shizong was aware of the Commissioner threat since Wang Jun 王峻 (902-953), who was his father's Military Commissioner had unsuccessfully tried to block his own accession to the throne. Shizong was able to explicitly limit the range of the Bureau's power: all of Military Commissioners' duties were strictly limited to strategic advice and the management of the armies.

Following Japanese historians, Wang Gungwu has argued that the institution of the Bureau and the structures of central government under the Five Dynasties had reproduced patterns established by regional military governments under the Tang. More recently, Billy So pointed out that such explanations were too general and too distant from the institutional mechanisms put in place to strengthen the position of Military Commissioners. So emphasizes the emergence of a new layer of political specialists, upwardly mobile from low-class origins, trained in the civil and military bureaus of the regional administration, and accustomed to handling army affairs. In practice, lacking academic pedigree and the prestige of passing the examinations, the Commissioners and their teams could not follow the usual career paths to success. They were therefore forced to emphasize their know-how, acquired in the unending conflicts that followed the Huang Chao rebellion and put to use in their service to regional governors' quest for conquest and security. Thus, for those administrators who appeared as especially efficient, the Bureau or more generally "inner posts" of the Palace, where they had been trained, offered a too-limited space in terms of promotion: this logic stimulated skilled personnel to take over more and more space within the regular administration that was under the Central Secretariat, in turn under the authority of the Grand Councilor.

Such a dynamic is even more visible if, like the historians Chiu Yu Lok and Zhao Dongmei, we focus on the category of low level Palace officers ranked below the Commissioners: the "military servitors." These officers did not depend on any agency as was formally the case for the Commissioners: they consisted of military followers of lower ranks attached to the physical person of the Emperor. Like the Commissioners, these petty officers, who stood quite close to the sovereign, were parts of the chain of command in administrative and military affairs. As such, they were no more than executive agents of the Emperor, as either "aides-de-camp" or "couriers." During the Five Dynasties, these officers were trustworthy followers, and this was the reason that they were regularly charged with missions outside the Palace and the capital. As deputies of the Emperor, they transmitted his orders, or supervised his troops stationed outside the capital, or even led armies, however many, and whatever kind of tasks were involved. They supervised army units; they controlled and, in fact, commanded them, especially in the course of special operations. Their missions also concerned the troops of the capital that the emperors had progressively tended to constitute as units of the imperial army and the troops of the Imperial guard. Often they acted by dissolving the better rival units, once these rivals had been defeated or had sworn allegiance. Thanks to their vigorous involvement in the supervision of armed forces in wartime, and their contribution to the reconstruction of an imperial army, the military servitors became identified as military officials (*wuguan* 武官), even though they continued to be appointed on "inner posts" of the Palace and still depended directly on the Emperor. Numerous biographies clarify the profile and career paths of these lower ranking officers. Following Zhao Dongmei's study, we have translated the biography of Xie Dequan 謝德權 which reveals several aspects of these men's common career paths (see Appendix 1).

Xie's biography shows his successes in terms of the steps in an exemplary career which took him from rank 9b, the lowest in the general hierarchy of the protocol, up to rank 7a, close to the highest ranking of the Palace Commissioners.[12] Xie entered public service following his father, from whom he inherited numerous qualities, markedly the attraction to the profession of arms. In fact, as has been remarked previously when alluding to "specialists," the profession of the warrior became largely hereditary after the beginning of the eighth century, when the Tang abolished conscription and, accordingly, began to recruit their soldiers. In recompense for the service merits of his father, Xie received his first appointment under the reign of Li Yu 李煜 (961-975), the last emperor of

[12] The career of the Commissioners of the Various Offices was subdivided into five classes (*deng* 等) and twenty-one qualifications (*zi* 資) while the military servitors' career followed a total of ten classification degrees (*jie* 階). In 1038, these two careers were ranked in a continuum of seven ranks (*pin* 品) between 6b and 9b in the protocol list of civil and military officials, which included a total of thirty ranks. See Gong Yanming 1977: 28-29, 33-36. See also the protocol list of 1038 in Kracke Jr. 1953: 229-235.

the Southern Tang (937-975), and evidently just before the demise of Southern Tang he offered his service to the Song dynasty in December 975. Xie was then quite young, just 22 years old.

Like his father, he was courageous, and able to infiltrate enemy lines. Even though the biography is a literary piece obviously compiled to reinforce an edifying message, this trait of bravery stressed individual superiority, and this could be easily understood as the transmission of a kind of skill, a way of acting which enabled the son to follow a pre-established plan in a difficult, even hostile environment. Accordingly, excellent soldiers came from outstanding families—a social norm that the new dynasty recognized, since it sufficed Xie to offer his services to be immediately accepted in public service, *i.e.*, only on the basis of his pedigree (the text reads "to present himself for service"). His career as an officer shows that the succession of titles he was granted corresponds exactly to the table of grades for officers appointed within the Palace, including a change of class, so that Xie was granted one of the titles of the Commissioners of Palace Services in becoming Vice Commissioner for Fostering Propriety (*chongyi fushi* 崇儀副使). In any case, it is clear that all these titles do not correspond to specific duties. Xie's posts, on the contrary, were temporary positions which took him from one region to another, from Shaanxi to Sichuan but especially to the capital, whereas the appointment as prefect of Sizhou 泗州 towards the end of his life looked like a punishment by the standards of his time.

These positions put him in a particular bureaucratic field that is of interest here: between the civil and the military, as Zhao Dongmei's book title underscores. As military inspector in Shaanxi, Xie strengthened a bridge. Then, called to the capital after his military exploits in Sichuan, he was put in charge of strategic warehouses for the army and the capital. Afterwards, he was granted missions of military engineering in the North-East, where his sagacity made him aware of the imminent danger of war and the urgency of preparing defensive works in the future theater of operations. Such discernment, which he took advantage of as an expression of his personal rectitude, was another important characteristic of his military career. Indeed, Xie regularly refused to compromise with the powerful, because he considered himself to be in the special service of the Emperor. In the matter of capital city planning, he was even so clever as to show the sovereign, who was ready to back down under the pressure of prominent individuals, that he should go all the way in his commitment in the name of an interest superior to private interests. This higher commitment appears to have been the background of his quarrel with Liu

Chenggui 劉承珪 (949-1012), one of the most powerful eunuchs in the Court of the Emperor Song Zhenzong (r. 997-1002). This conflict led to his punishment. As a soldier, Xie was clear-minded up to the end, and thus ready to oppose the Emperor's favorites, in particular the eunuchs. His lower-ranking status was stressed in the self-portrait he drew in the presence of the Emperor when leaving the Court. He had served his sovereign with an extreme loyalty, both within and outside the Palace, but this excessive loyalty had brought Xie a sinister reputation in Court circles, as the biographer concluded, not without venom. Still under the influence of the military values of the Five Dynasties and loyal to his chief, Xie was a man of action who died precisely when the threat of permanent war was vanishing. By then, the dynasty had been led to support new values and new men, a path that sealed the regime change.

A New Military Regime

During the early period of the Song dynasty that our present analysis will focus on, the profession of arms was perceived as it had been during the late Tang and the Five Dynasties periods: soldiers were specialists. Accordingly, as modern historians underline, military officers who often acquired their professional expertise through inheritance were increasingly identified as a professional group.[13] These men, whose social position had been reinforced throughout the endemic wars of the Five Dynasties, were officers appointed for "military assignments" (*junzhi* 軍職), and had the generic name of "military officers" (*wujiang* 武將 or *wuchen* 武臣), which distinguished them clearly from "civil administrators" (*wenchen* 文臣).[14] After the Tang, these military officers naturally maintained close ties with the men of the various "tent offices," and of course with their own soldiers.[15] They shared common interests and often joined their destinies in combats that created, so to speak, blood ties between them and their

---

[13] In his unpublished thesis, which is still quoted as a reference work today, Labadie stresses that he has "adopted Huntington's three criteria of military professionalism--expertise, corporateness, and responsibility", and he assumes that he tries "to demonstrate that they can be found, in one form or another, within the military establishment of the Sung dynasty," see Labadie, 1981: 20; 211-213.

[14] Among the plethoric studies devoted to Song military, one can point out two studies: Ho Koon-wan 2008; Chen Feng 2004.

[15] On the notion of "tent office" and the ties which linked the members of the military and strategic chain of command, see Shi Yuntao 2003.

men, obviously of a different nature but as solid and binding as those within the family circle. The practice of military patrons adopting their "men of the tent office" (i.e. members of a private retinue) as "sons" is evident throughout the late Tang and Five Dynasties periods.[16] Under such conditions, all the officers appointed on "inner posts" within the Palace, Commissioners and military servitors, were elements external to these groups of officers, even if a good number of the former, such as Xie Dequan, shared some of their values and their mindset, since they themselves had often come from families of "military officers."

Two phenomena should be underlined above all. One concerns the nature of the group of officers who staffed the "inner posts", the other the size of this staff. At the very beginning of the Song Dynasty, higher officials of ranks 1 to 5, both civil and military, who were the pillars of the new dynasty, were granted the privilege of having young members of their families entering the public service. This was called the *yin* 蔭, or "protection," privilege. Soon after his accession to the throne, in 977 the second Song Emperor, Taizong 太宗 (r. 976-997), decided to honor outstanding personalities recommended to him by the administrations of different regions. Seemingly in a gesture of allegiance, these men sent to the Court offered the finest products of their respective homelands as tribute. The Emperor granted them all honorific titles (*shixian* 試銜) or military ranks in the Three Ranks (*sanban* 三班), an institution to be discussed further on. Then, following the request of two Case Reviewers of the Court of Judicial Review, who had just been honored with this title, Taizong decided to go even further and, for the first time, allowed a quota of those who had been granted honorary titles to obtain a duty assignment by attending the appointment process (*fuxuan* 赴選).[17] One sees here the political opportunity through which Xie Dequan was able to enter public service. Whereas the founder of the dynasty, Taizu 太祖 (r. 960-976), had limited the privilege of "protection" to an elite endowed as a service aristocracy, his brother Taizong expanded this group in order to form a new basis for the recruitment of his officials. Taizong expressed this intention by honoring the young members of outstanding families from the whole empire with these titles that could open the door to real official posts. These families had until then formed the social basis of the provincial governments and independent kingdoms and thus had offered their administrative and military talents to serve these small polities. Now

---

[16] See in particular Dai Xianqun 2008: 121-135.
[17] Li Tao 1978-1993: 18.400.

their most talented sons could hope to benefit from a new position in the imperial administration. Besides this integration of various local elites into the rungs of imperial bureaucracy, there were other concerns as well. The Emperor wanted to bring under control a turbulent and arrogant group of youths forming part of the entourage of military governors who often had family ties with these youths. Last but not least, after his accession to the throne, Taizong and, to a lesser degree, each of his successors, appointed to "inner posts" several followers who had been members of his education staff in the Residence of the Heir Apparent (*donggong* 東宮).[18]

In brief, together with zealous and loyal men who were regularly promoted like Xie, there were officeholders coming from great families, youthful friends of the young sovereign, or the men the Emperor planned to maintain in a low-ranking position in the capital, far from their families. Of course, the practical management of these titles until the end of the eleventh century resulted in the number of these officers growing. From three hundred men during the reign of Emperor Taizong who could meet each of them in person, even know them personally, a generation later, at the beginning of the decade of 1020, their number had grown to 4,200 and in the years 1080 they were close to 16,000.[19] This growing number of officials created a significant problem in terms of long-term management: the duration of any individual career was stretching out, and the consequence was a long wait for promotions and more substantial government spending on salaries.

Obviously, Xie Dequan's career shows that the best officials could expect to change status during their career, by obtaining the title of Commissioner—and acceding to the corresponding remunerations and rewards, as is indicated by the self-seeking but apparently standard request presented by Xie when he was forced to leave the direct service of the

[18] Taizong's various decisions are presented by many authors. See for instance Chiu Yu Lok 1993: 131-139.

[19] These figures are given in a report that no doubt dates from 1080, by Zeng Gong, then administrator of the Bureau of the Lesser Military Assignment; see Zeng Gong 1992: 169. These figures are discussed by Ye Mengde 1984: 118-119. Zhao Dongmei offers estimations of the growth of the low-ranking officers administered by the Bureau of the Lesser Military Assignment, and on the rhythm of this growth throughout the eleventh century, see Zhao Dongmei 2010: 343-346. One can find more figures in Appendix 2.

Emperor.[20] Nevertheless, beyond the variety of origins and individual profiles, other factors explain the tensions encountered in the career management of all officers assigned to the "inner posts." Suffice it to consider the degree of specialization of the missions entrusted to the highest-ranking officials. For instance, the various Commissioners in charge of the audience protocol or the reception of "guests" coming from the provinces or neighboring kingdoms needed to master a comprehensive knowledge of codes of communications and Court ceremonial, while those who commanded imperial workshops had to be familiar with complex technology, especially for the production of weapons.

Since the range of bureaucratic titles and positions remained limited, and because the Emperor was interested in offering long careers to the officers assigned to "inner posts," it was necessary to add new ranks to the system of bureaucratic hierarchy. Granting honorary titles appeared to be a very practical solution, since it flattered officers by augmenting their ceremonial treatment. With the same logic, one could preserve old assignments, the effective function of which had disappeared: this was the case of the Commissioner for the Palace Corals and Stables (*xianjiushi* 閑厩使), who had not had in any way to deal with horses since the end of the Tang![21] The creation of new degrees within each rank similarly guaranteed the fractioning of emoluments. This evolution satisfied demands for promotion, while offering the sovereign a new range of rewards. The institution of the "Three Ranks", the very name of which went back to the decision of Taizong in 977 to integrate young men sent from the provinces and convoked to the capital, formed yet another part of the throne's response, given the heterogeneity and inflation of manpower among the officers who staffed the "inner posts."

From 981 on, the Emperor took measures to distinguish and formalize the rules regarding careers and appointments of the "military servitors" who composed the "Three Ranks." In 987 this institution was given the name of Bureau of Lesser Military Assignment (*sanbanyuan* 三班院) by

---

[20] Deng Xiaonan quotes a message that was sent the same year to the central administration by an official who felt angry at not having received the promotion he was supposed to get in view of the preceding events. Like Xie, he was on the verge of leaving for his prefectural assignment after punishment, see Deng Xiaonan 1993: 22.

[21] Zhao Dongmei 2010: 108.

the Emperor himself.[22] This new Bureau included well-defined rules which distinguished it clearly from the Palace administration, while it remained formally attached to the Emperor's person, as were all the other military organs, notably the powerful Bureau of Military Affairs. The Emperor thus disposed of an autonomous organ controlling this group of lower-ranking officers, the ranking scale of which furthermore received two new grades. These military servitors were thereafter seen as a group which, albeit not coherent, was at least managed in a coherent way. The system of ten titles through which they could rise constituted no more than military ranks, which guaranteed them a bureaucratic career and a wage-scale without further reference to a defined post or duty. They had become bureaucrats. Only a few among them could hope to remain within the immediate entourage of the Emperor and thus preserve their identity as Emperor's followers, a label that attached to officers assigned to "inner posts" under the late Tang and the Five Dynasties period. From then on, they, together with the other subgroup composed by "military officers" (*wujiang*), formed what was becoming the general category of "military officials" (*wuguan*).

In any case, even though they had the career of military men, "military servitors" remained outside the status of military officers assigned to "military posts." This phenomenon was in many ways the product of history. Their special position offered a model and, according to Chiu Yu Lok and Zhao Dongmei, even served as an institutional resource which permitted central power to establish the general organization of "military officials" on a new basis: army generals who were "military officers" found themselves deprived of a part of their power.[23] This mechanism certainly contributed to the stabilization of the Song dynastic power while it is also reputed, at least according to the historiographical tradition, to have weakened the military strength of the Song empire. This mechanism will be examined later, thanks to the analyses and conclusions by Zhao Dongmei who introduces this mechanism as the main source of the process of bureaucratization of the Song military.[24]

---

[22] Chiu Yu Lok writes extensively about the role of Taizong: see note 18. See also the entry on "Bureau of Lesser Military Assignment" in Gong Yanming 1977: 95-96.

[23] See Zhao Dongmei 2010: 100-103.

[24] The following paragraphs synthesized the first three chapters of Zhao Dongmei 2010: 31-151.

Turning Military Men into Functionaries

There was a real difference between the late Tang eunuchs and the Song officers of the "Three Ranks." The ties that bound eunuchs to the powerful armies they commanded were of the same nature as those existing between any general and his soldiers. Moreover, if some of them were sent as military inspectors to control governors, these missions aimed at informing the Court about the loyalty of army commanders without, therefore, questioning connections between unit commanders and their soldiers. By contrast, when the officers of the "Three Ranks" were sent from the Court with the title of "Military Director-in-Chief" (*bing-ma dujian* 兵馬都監) to oversee troops deployed on campaigns, their duty was to control the command of military operations. In practice, they used the model handed down from the end of the Five Dynasties, when military servitors' missions were to guarantee that orders given by the generals corresponded properly with Court policy. Their missions thus had a political dimension: they had to restore the authority of central power over any military organization, and the purpose of this mission was in contradiction with the absolute power "military officers" claimed over their men. Such continuous pressure had already put the Emperor of Late Zhou, the last of the Five Dynasties, in a position to oversee the nomination of governors' regional staff. As has been said already, it was thanks to these officers that the imperial power began to recruit a part of its military forces within the best regional troop units, with the advantage of weakening the power of military governors at the same time. By building a new frame for action which aimed at imposing the military prestige and authority of the imperial center, the "military servitors" who were "Emperor's men" were persistently perceived as a crucial element of the military hierarchical structure.

Under such conditions, the early Song troops led by officers assigned to "inner posts" received their orders from the central power whilst these officers' missions were merely temporary, limited in time. The "military officers" under supervision still were responsible for the discipline of their units, and, therefore, for their efficiency on the field, but they were progressively deprived of the general sense of overall operations.[25] The

[25] On the military organization during the early period of the dynasty, see three unpublished theses: Edmund Henry Worthy, Jr. 1976: especially chapter 4, "The Chou and Song Palace Armies. Agents of Centralized Imperial Power", pp. 137-

"military officers" who were in charge of the imperial regiments were no longer able to make decisions relative to marching orders. Moreover their periods of command lasted only as long as the specific campaigns they were assigned to. As a result, their close connection with their units, as well as the allegiance of soldiers to their officers, became progressively weak. Thanks to the officers assigned to "inner posts", the Palace created an organization able to break up military power. At the same time, their military assignments offered these officers a new field of action as well as a clear identity distinct from that of the "military officers." Their title still indicated that they enjoyed the confidence of the Emperor in so far as they were directly attached to the Palace, even though their growing number and their missions regularly took them far away from the Court.

This general change favored the emergence of a new group of military officials that joined together and reorganized the hierarchy of different imperial retainers: the officers assigned to "inner posts," whose ranks originated from the Tang, and other low-ranking followers, who were not holders of a regular office and were thus exterior to the regular procedures of evaluation and selection. This new group was named the "military appointed officials" (*wuxuanguan* 武選官). According to Zhao Dongmei, the status of these officials who could enter the process of "appointment" can be characterized as follows.[26] While "military officers" were military men on active duty, registered on army lists, and whose promotion depended on a procedure exclusive to the military, these "military appointed officials" remained regular officials without any registration on army lists. Under such conditions, like any other official, their assignments depended upon a system of "commissions" (*chaiqian*), a matter to which we shall return later. "Military officers" were not submitted to such a system. Finally, whereas the promotion of "military appointed officials" was managed by the Bureau of Lesser Military Assignment, the list of candidates for promotion was first directly proposed to the Emperor by military commanders--and, after 984, the sovereign himself took charge of the supervision and selection of these officials, which often seemed to be a very long process.

The institution of these "military appointed officials" strengthened the bureaucratization which had redefined soldiers' functions and the military

---

211; Labadie: 1981; Tsang Shui-lung1997: especially chapter. 4, 123-156. See also Fang Cheng-hua: 2009.

[26] See Zhao Dongmei 2010: 12. A synthetic definition of these officials is given by Gong Yanming 1977: 577.

organization of the Palace after the dislocation of the Tang Empire and the collapse of the old military aristocracy of the Tang. This institution reflected the emergence of a new bureaucratic system of military authority. According to Zhao Dongmei, two factors played a direct role in favoring this institutional evolution. Firstly, the giving of missions to the officers assigned to inner posts outside the Court limits, especially those missions involving military matters, was largely acknowledged and accepted as normal. This system reinforced the institutional disassociation between the official and his post, and this disassociation, over time, resulted in the transformation of any title granted to the holder of an "inner post" into a purely hierarchical sign, a simple rank (*pinwei* 品位).[27] Secondly, as has been pointed out already, the proliferation of nominations for the ranks of officers assigned to "inner posts" made any reference to Palace service a fiction. "Military appointed officials" were separated from the Palace insofar as they could enter the career track through several formal procedures: "protection" by high-ranking officials who had been granted this privilege, passing military examinations, transfer from military or civil status, and lastly transfer from the status of administration clerks which were selected from "outside the current" (*liuwai* 流外) to "enter the regular current" (*ruliu* 入流) of ranked official—according to systems of evaluation and recommendation that remained the rule for the vast majority of the officials.[28]

Obviously, this bureaucratization process stretched the links between the new group of officers and the Emperor and the Court. From the beginning of the dynasty onwards, one of the results was the devaluation of official titles that Zhao Dongmei has underlined by pointing out some of its expressions.[29] Zhao has especially mentioned the clear reduction in the number of nominations to such posts of those men previously assigned to the Residence of the Heir Apparent. Zhenzong appointed few men among his Residence retainers, while, by contrast, his father, Taizong, had generously offered promotion to his personal followers, a decision that is construed as a partial answer to the doubts and tensions surrounding his rise to power.[30] Apparently, in the course of just one generation, such titles came to seem insufficiently prestigious to reward men whom the sovereign

---

[27] See Zhao Dongmei 2010: 118-123.

[28] Gong Yanming 1977: entry "Military degrees" (*wujie* 武階): 577.

[29] See Zhao Dongmei 2010: 111-115.

[30] A long half century later, the censor Sima Guang (1019-1086) explicitly criticized this policy. See Zhao Dongmei 2010: 114.

wished to honor as being his regular attendants. Furthermore, since the beginning of the dynasty, the decisions of emperors facing frequent conflicts between officials assigned to "inner posts" and regular officials, in particular high-level military officers or civil servants, did not systematically favor men of inner posts. Lastly, whereas the promotion depended initially on the good will of the Emperor, who knew officials personally and thereby could distinguish them and grant them marks of his favor, the new system of recruitment of officials assigned to inner posts, which had been established as a direct consequence of the growth of this personnel, required these officials to be selected and evaluated through procedures systematized in the 990s and based on the number of years spent in each qualification and rank (*mokan nianxian* 磨勘年限). Officials assigned to inner posts were now no more than a group, among the lowest in the general hierarchy of public service, by the side of civil bureaucrats and military officers with whom they formed the group of "military officials."

The Military Bureaucracy and Institutional Tensions

Our description of the main aspects of the historical process through which the "military bureaucracy" developed and was reorganized between the end of the Tang and the rise of the Song, makes it clear that this change, even if it may be understood as the continuity of Tang and Five Dynasties military institutions, was definitively neither a restoration to the old regime nor a planned program resulting from a political agenda of predefined reform. Obviously, according to historiography, the restoration of imperial authority depended upon the dynamic which sustained the centralization of power. Therefore, although this dynamic developed as a major step in the construction of a new dynastic sovereign system, this historical dynamic by itself cannot be considered to be the result of a bureaucratic project. The state-building here was very much unplanned. Of course, this dynamic strengthened the hand of the Emperor on the military apparatus, so that civilians could exercise political hegemony and power. And above all, the evolutions summarized here were the response to the main question of the tenth century dynasts: how to ensure their authority over the army and over a territory which these troops were able to control?

Despite the influence of Chinese historiography, both pre-modern and modern, contemporary historians do not have any reason to favor the old idea—the old ideology, as one is almost tempted to speak of it—that saw China as always having had a natural tendency to imperial reunification, since a centralized Empire should be the only possible and legitimate political regime in tenth century China.[31] One may also ask if the process of reunification and centralization carried out by the Song was in fact the origin of an autocratic power, as Japanese historiography has frequently characterized the "Tang-Song transition." After the Meiji restoration, Japanese historians were able to impose this explanatory model of "transition" on a complex chronological sequence, and this notion has been recently recovered by historians eager to understand the transformation of the Chinese empire after the downfall of the great families' aristocratic power.

One could also turn back to the perception that tenth century contemporaries had themselves. They viewed the dynamic described here above all as an institutional disorder which gave way to a growing confusion within the administrative organization. There is also good reason to think that such confusion had become a constitutive dimension of political strategies, a resource in diverse struggles for power. Without any doubt, disorder in bureaucratic ranks was amplified when the Song sovereigns became conscious that they had found in such chaos a means of playing off different branches of their bureaucracy against each other, and hence tried to extend and systematize the fragmentation of both civil and military power. Two aspects of this tendency towards fragmentation are important here: the system allowing control of armed forces by the Emperor and the Court, and the redefinition of posts in civil administration.

First, what does the systematic control of the armed forces by the Emperor and the Court mean? One should look briefly at the structure of the imperial army and its command as it was when the system was established at the beginning of the Song Dynasty. It is indeed important to understand the impact of this organization on the bureaucratic regime as a whole. The role of the Bureau of Military Affairs in the management of military personnel, and the Bureau's power in terms of strategic decision have already been mentioned. In fact, from the beginning of the dynasty, military power was divided between two central institutions, since besides the Court there was another institution charged with handling imperial troops—estimated to have been between one hundred thousand and two hundred thousand men under Taizu. This other institution, or rather a collection of three institutions, refers to the "Three Military Commands" (*sanya* 三衙), which were set up between 960 and 1005. They included the

[31] Peter Lorge (Lorge 2005: 1-16) has elaborated on this argument in a slightly polemic fashion. See also Standen 2007: introduction and chapter one: 1-40. See these two authors' new findings in Lorge 2011.

Command of the Palace Corps (*dianqiansi* 殿前司) and the two Commands of the Imperial Guard, all of which were products of the division of the Command of the Emperor's Guard of the Palace in 1005: the Bureau of the Infantry Units of the Command of the Imperial Guard (*shiwei qinjun bujun duzhihui shisi* 侍衛親軍步軍都指揮使司) and the Bureau of the Cavalry Units of the Command of the Imperial Guard (*shiwei qinjun majun duzhihui shisi* 侍衛親軍馬軍都指揮使司).[32]

"The Bureau of Military Affairs controlled the file records of soldiers and the 'imperial tally of command' (*hufu* 虎符 – this should be understood as the imperial authorization issued to generals for troop movements); the Three Military Commands managed all the armies; the generals held formal authority over the troops."[33] This was precisely the synthesis that an upper class official, Li Gang 李綱 (1083-1140), drew up from the "Dynasty ancestors' times" when he was in charge of the defense of the capital during the collapse of the Northern Song Dynasty. Li concluded that such an organization had become "an inviolable rule for ten thousand generations." The logic of the division was thus clear. This division separated one or several bureaucratic organs under the Bureau of Military Affairs that was in charge of planning campaigns, ordering recruitments, dealing with careers and nominations for field operations, and the military command itself. This military authority was based on a chain of command that assumed the responsibility for preparing troops and putting them in the field, and general officers who were the only ones entrusted with the command of these forces on the field. Therefore, the discourse of Li Gang appeared, above all, as a rationalization of a process that will not be explored in detail here. Suffice it to say that, at the beginning of the dynasty, the areas of competence between the bureaus of the Three Military Commands that organized troops were partly similar and the hierarchy between them was not firmly established yet. In other words, it is quite difficult to distinguish what resulted from the confusion between concurrent powers and what depended on an institutional project.[34]

First of all, the tasks of the bureaus of the Command of the Palace Corps and those of the Command of the Emperor's Guard of the Palace, before its subdivision into two Commands, were encroaching on each other. They kept the records of their respective troops while guaranteeing

---

[32] See Worthy 1976: 238-245; and also Zhang Qifan 1993: 78-118.

[33] See Wang Zengyu 1983: 4.

[34] See Worthy 1976: 163-165 and 244-245.

training and handling career promotions. Troops under the Command of the Palace Corps, nevertheless, seem to have been assigned missions in the capital, especially for the defense of the Palace, while the units of the Command of the Imperial Guard were rather more engaged outside the capital city. It should be remembered, however, that the hierarchy set the Command of the Palace Corps in a subordinate position to the Command of the Emperor's Guard for a long time, until that order was reversed at the beginning of the eleventh century. In any case, after 960 the division of responsibilities between the Bureau of Military Affairs and the Three Military Command appeared as the result of a conscious strategy, certainly handed down from the last of the Five Dynasties. Neither the Command of the Palace Corps, nor the Command of the Emperor's Guard had authority over troop movements, nor regarding the allocation of troops, a responsibility that belonged to the Bureau of Military Affairs. This Bureau—whose leadership was entrusted exclusively to civilian functionaries after few years—was finally detached from the Palace, with a power of decision fixed at the same level as that of the central administration directed by Grand Councilors, of whom, nonetheless, military affairs remained independent.

Besides the task of planning campaigns, the Bureau of Military Affairs managed the soldiers' files and the careers of officers, while supervising the decisions taken by the Bureau of Lesser Military Assignment that, as already noted, was in charge of the control of lower-ranking officers. The effective management of troops was even more complicated by the presence of supplemental regional troops (*xiangjun* 廂軍) and service troops (*yibing* 役兵), who were in theory under local administration. These units regularly received orders to send their best men to reinforce imperial troop units.[35] Such bureaucratic entropy included the existence of a Ministry of War (*bingbu* 兵部), one of the six traditional ministries of the central government under the authority of the Grand Councilors. Even though the officials appointed to this ministry had little effective competence, their offices having become prestige titles in the bureaucratic hierarchy, the ministry was still charged with the organization of military exams, which represented one of the channels of recruitment for the "military appointed officials" (*wuxuanguan*). The extreme segmentation of military authority could be also traced to the attention paid, in a clearly political perspective, to reducing the autonomy of the Military Affairs

[35] The supplementary regional troops have been recently studied by Huai Jianli: 2007.

Commissioner. Besides the appointment of Vice Commissioners, in 979 there also appeared the new office of Controller-Signatory of the Bureau of Military Affairs (*qianshu shumiyuan shi* 簽署樞密院事): this official's functions seem to have "concerned the composition of documents as much as the devising of strategies."[36]

Directed by civil officials, the Bureau of Military Affairs possessed a vast area of military competences that were officially separated from civil responsibilities after the mid-950s. Up to the decade of the 1080s, the Song civil administration of the "Outer Court", always led by Grand Councilors at the head of government, was no longer in a position to question the fundamental split which determined the decision-making system. These two centers of authority were then designated by a term which stressed their differences: the "Two Administrations" (*erfu* 二府). It is well known, for instance, that imperial audiences remained distinct for the members of each of these 'Two Administrations," at least until the Grand Councilors had recovered a part of their supremacy by gaining the right to attend the discussions about military affairs.

What seems to be indisputable is the fact that the separation of powers, which was a historical legacy, became one of the resources the first Song Emperors used to stimulate the centralization of their own political power. This separation itself was one of the crucial mechanisms which enabled the reconstruction of the Emperor's authority.

In fact, it should be emphasized that the separation of civil and military affairs into two distinct areas was echoed not only by the split of military authority, but also by the fragmentation, even the disorder, of civil organization. As already discussed, that confusion was frequently denounced by contemporaries as the basis of malfunctions within the administrative system. Beyond the erosion of the Grand Councilor's power autonomy by the coordinated action of the Emperor and his Military Affairs Commissioner, officials saw it as a general obstacle of administrative efficiency and possibly a sort of uncertainty in the management of their careers. This division was directly reflected in the complexity and confusion of official classification that was the feature of the Song civil administration, a matter which will be mentioned later in more detail.[37]

---

[36] See Worthy 1976: 244. Deng Xiaonan (Deng 2002) has studied the personnel of the Bureau.

[37] See Deng Xiaonan 1993, quoted in note 20. In the huge literature devoted to Song civil service, see Kracke Jr. 1953. Basically, Gong Yanming's book, (Gong

As was made clear in the introduction, the civil administration "office" (*guan* 官) signaled rank and degree within the hierarchy of public service, and, therefore, any individual's position in the Court and in the central bureaucracy. A functionary bore the title attached to his office, much in the same way as a military officer carried the title which corresponded, as has been seen, to a grade in the military hierarchy. The possession of an office opened a career and directly impacted the assignment of the official who would possibly be appointed for a fixed period to manage actual functions, being "detached on commission" (*chaiqian*). In other words, "offices" according to which officials were ranked determined their social status and prestige and were the signs of that preeminence, badged by uniforms and privileges, salaries and gifts, and sponsorship rights for the upper-level class who could recommend young officials. And of course, this office contributed to defining the level of specific duty to which a titular could be assigned in the administrative organization. Nevertheless, and this was the advantage of the system made explicit in contemporary comments, the "commission" was the way to assign officials who had proven their skill to crucial or difficult posts, without their having the proper seniority in the civil hierarchy. Similarly, a high level official might be in charge of an inferior duty, markedly when he was sent to a local post to solve an affair that the central power wished to deal with directly.

This system relied upon the pre-Song distinction between "titular offices" (*zhishiguan*), "classification offices" (*jieguan*), and "prestige titles" (*sanguan*).[38] It is noteworthy that this distinction kept two structures quite separate: the administrative organization dealing with actual duties on the one hand, and the making of hierarchies within the elites on the other. From the Tang onwards, the use of "commissions" (*chaiqian*) had made the "titular offices" system more difficult to manage, since the official "detached on commission" bore the title of his regular office while assigned to a different post. This situation had gradually transformed the very nature of the "titular offices."

As a result, a part of the administrative content of the "titular offices" disappeared, so that these offices became simple marks of rank in a scale. The office-holders' corps was thus fragmented: many of them had still to administer the job corresponding to their office, while many others were charged with an actual duty distinct from their regular office, and others

1977) is an encyclopedia on the subject, including the part of the book devoted to technical vocabulary.

[38] We refer hereafter to Deng Xiaonan's analysis (Deng 1993: 2-22).

still were simply to receive the stipends attached to their office. The rigidity of the rules defining offices was thus stretched. These rules fixed a quota of office-holders for each "office," even though the officials who were granted this rank were not necessarily assigned to an actual job; but there was no quota for officials "detached on commission", regardless of their bureaucratic credentials, and their provisional duty assignments did not correspond to any given rank, thus no limit to these appointments existed. Thanks to this distinction between "offices" and "commissions", the late Tang Emperors were able to save the dynasty; but at the same time, provincial governors were in a position to select their own men, in clear violation of regular administrative procedures. The generalization of such nominations at prefectural level under the Five Dynasties has already been emphasized by historians working on Northern China or Southern kingdoms as well.[39]

Obviously, this system shared common features with the system of "commissions" on which the rise of "military servitors" appointed to "inner posts" had been based. An organic link existed between the two kinds of commissions, since these "servitors" were precisely the officers whose very existence had helped to undermine the whole purpose of the "titular offices" throughout the tenth century or, in other words, to separate the duty assignment designated by the office from its holder. During the whole of the century, because of the weakening of the "Outer Court" by the expansion of "commissions" secured for the men appointed to "inner posts", the separation between "offices" and "commissions" may appear as the main feature of the military officers who imposed, initially for the sake of their masters, the preeminence of the men from the Palace over the administration, and military power over civilian control. Then, the bureaucratization of the procedures connected to the commissions offered an opportunity to the "military appointed officials" to leave behind their role in Palace protection and enter into a regular military career. But, at the same time, from a broader perspective, the new system applied to the "Outer Court" blurred the distinctions between unemployed officials, who simply bore office titles, and officials assigned to duty posts without the required administrative credentials. In other words, the bureaucratization process allowed civil officials to benefit from the new regulations and maintained a fragmentation of power between civilians and military men. Thus the historical factor which prevailed was not so much bureaucratic rationality as the competition between civil and military administrations,

---

[39] Deng Xiaonan 1993: 15.

and such antagonisms between civilian and military could be manipulated by the Emperor for the sake of his own power. This separation had clear advantage for the imperial power, and this was precisely what Japanese historians interpreted as the "modern" affirmation of autocracy. By increasing the rivalry, and even the hostility between military commanders and civil officials, the Emperor enlarged the distance between the two bureaucratic organizations. This situation has been often described and analyzed, and is today something of a cliché in the Song studies.[40] It is therefore only necessary to insist on the existence of this specific bureaucratic space, between "civil and military," which determined the framework of the activities of "military appointed officials".

As Zhao Dongmei has demonstrated,[41] the missions entrusted to these officials can be divided into short-term and long-term missions. Among the occasional missions, embassies, or the accompaniment of ambassadors to the Song Court seem to have been one of their most frequent duties. Thus, "military appointed officials" fulfilled a function handed down from the "military servitors." Regarding their long term posts, they could serve as members of the retinue of army commanders, i.e. as upper class officials' escort officers. But their actual military missions remained inspections of armies and garrisons, especially on the borders where they could be appointed as prefects. However, Zhao has especially emphasized that many among them held the charge of State Monopoly Agents (*jiandangguan* 監當官) during their careers: they had to extract revenue from state monopolies on salt, tea, or alcohols, or to manage the mints and public warehouses. Because of these fiscal activities they were appointed as often in the capital as in the regions.

Finally, these jobs were similar enough to those of officials appointed to "inner posts" during the Five Dynasties. It indicates, above all, that such military officers formed a well-identified group, charged with various kinds of missions, without any real links between these different assignments. By their functions, many were undoubtedly linked to civil officials and many others to military commanders, but the group could not be confused with either one or the other. These Palace servitors who had

---

[40] Labadie's thesis (Labadie 1981) was the first attempt to summarize the main results on this topic. Recently, Chen Feng has investigated the Song military ideology, especially the two notions of civil and military, in several articles. His most important works are: Chen Feng 2005: 12-14; 2006: 12-14; 2007: 7-13; 2009: 38-50.

[41] See Zhao Dongmei 2010: 165-171.

become military officials were put in a position of imposing the ideal that service to the Emperor included not only security and public order, but also the proper management of local resources. Nevertheless, many among their missions can be viewed as contradicting the structural division between civil and military officials, and accordingly, confirming the confusion created by the selection of officers of military status for non-military posts. From the civil elites' viewpoint, the action of the "military appointed officials" was construed as the guarantee of internal stability, which indeed was the soldiers' duty; moreover, even though they shared the same career pattern as other military men, they helped to keep at bay the ambitions that army commanders could have been tempted to nourish according to the model of the tenth century. This twofold function fits the ideology of scholars in relation to armed forces quite well,[42] and this was certainly the reason that sources contain praise for the most eminent of these lesser officials, as well as disdainful references aimed at downgrading them as simply low-ranking officers who occupied the lowest ranks of the bureaucratic hierarchy.[43]

Conclusion

This chapter tackles the question of the emergence of a new imperial order, by focusing on the bureaucratization of military men. This approach has shed light above all on the internal logic of the bureaucratization of the dynastic state, but does not pay enough attention to other factors. Indeed, it is important to point out that other state traditions have definitely impacted the political centralization of the Song. After all, the Song dynasty inherited institutions from three Turkish Shatuo dynasties that had ruled

[42] On this ideology, see Chen Feng 2005.

[43] On the social hierarchy between literati and military, Zhao Dongmei quotes a story she read in a Song collection of jottings. The rich and elegant children of a military appointed official met with the poor children of a literati family, and the high official's wife who was hosting the two families forecast a limited career for the former and great honors of the highest positions for the poor children. The literati's children of course were preparing for examinations in the hope of a civil career, but military men's children have no such hope and, in any case, were simply promised to low level positions. See Zhao Dongmei 2010: 359-361.

Northern China for almost half of the Five Dynasties period.[44] Historians have already mentioned, for example, the practice of adoptions of the "men of the tent office" by their military patron, which was a custom well attested in Central Asia, among the Shatuo and Sogdian people as well.[45] Many examples drawn by Deng Xiaonan from the history of these three dynasties provide evidence that their elites presented themselves first as "men of the Tang" (*tangren* 唐人) before claiming their Turkic origins. These men were well aware of their differences, but they intentionally put emphasis on their membership of the Empire. Obviously, during the tenth century, the Empire was perceived as a composite polity, and the integration of its various peoples depended on mutual acculturations. Suffice it to say, for instance, that the superiority of Turkic or Khitan cavalry was determined by logistics, so that the hierarchy based on this logistics know-how might have influenced the organization of central armies under the Five Dynasties, in the same way that the organization by the Song of a fleet necessary for the conquest of the Southern Kingdoms might have favored the emergence of new military structures, and hence transformed the organization of the empire.

However, according to several studies that the present analysis is based on, one of the main processes which can explain the bureaucratic change of the dynastic state was the transformation of two specific groups: the servitors assigned to "inner posts" who formed part of the Emperor's entourage, and the "military appointed officials" whose role allowed the first Song Emperors to still use them for his own purposes. The result was confusion between two areas of competence, military and civil, at a time when these two areas were increasingly kept separate. By fulfilling missions as military inspectors, by checking performance and monitoring procedures within military units or civil offices, both in the center of the Empire and on its borders, these "military appointed officials" underlined the importance of controlling both men and the economic resources central for any government. Thanks to this specific group of officials, the ideal of service to the Emperor was progressively mixed with new perceptions of political order: order should be based on the service not only of elite officials but also of men of specific abilities. Independent of status, these

[44] The three Turkish dynasties were: the Later Tang (923-936), the Later Jin (936-946) and the Later Han (947-950). The father of the Later Tang emperor Zhuangzong was Shatuo and his mother Sogdian.

[45] An analysis of this Sogdian practice, exemplified by the case of An Lushan army, is presented by La Vaissière, 2007: 77-88.

abilities were to be adapted by petty officials to any aspect of government, whether central or local, civil or military.

From a broader and longer-term perspective, as the product of a period of fragmentation, the new regime seemed to have offered the sovereign the possibility of trusting various groups of his officials with the handling of local and central activities. These men were called upon to integrate "the four categories of people"—scholar-officials, farmers, craftsmen and merchants, according to the old classification—spread out through the vast and multifarious territory of the empire. In other words, the control of people was vested in two distinct civil and military administrations, and no local power or prominent family was able to deny the legitimacy of this control. The separation between civil and military affairs was the key that gave the central power the ability to stabilize, and redefine clearly, the civil and military links tying the imperial territory directly to the emperor.

Historians have construed the division between these two areas of competence as a systematic reinforcement of state bureaucracy. The purpose here is not to invalidate this conclusion, but to show that the historical process of bureaucratization does not result from a project, which would have been planned by one social category, the "bureaucracy," in search of its own reinforcement. First of all, it is crucial to keep in mind several simultaneous, even contradictory, processes which have generated substantial confusion regarding the different levels of power, both central and local. Given that the goal of the emperor and his court was to limit military influence, they had no choice but to rely on officials under the direct control of the emperor, able to act "between civil and military." This expression belongs to Zhao Dongmei, whose work has made it possible today to refresh analytic approaches to Song bureaucratic power. Secondly, while the Song emperors emphasized the importance of merit and competence, two cardinal values praised by soldiers, they were careful not to deprive their government of elements of stability such as statutes, titles or grades, which ranked the various bureaucrats and integrated them into the same system. In this way, the emperors could make manifest the supremacy that they wished to grant to their civil officials, and thereby confine military elites to low-ranking positions. Lastly, this process of bureaucratization was based on the ability of military officers to manage local affairs. However, their mission cannot be simply viewed as the transformation of local wealth into central resources, even though the written sources are literally saturated with this information. It is also necessary to tackle the question of those officials' capacity, especially those lower-ranking officers like Xie Dequan, to integrate local interests into the heart of central affairs and hence to give imperial matters a local dimension, as had been done before by the Tang aristocratic families for their own interests.

The group of "military appointed officials" played a crucial role in both practical and ideological terms by stabilizing the situation that resulted from the disorder between military officers and civil functionaries during the Five Dynasties. More than a question of autocratic centralization of power, and the so-called "modernity" of such a trend, which are the main ideas put forth by the Japanese historiography, it is the bureaucratization of various groups which has attracted our attention here. Similar approaches might contribute to the clarification of other moments in the ongoing process of state-building in imperial China, and to the historical analysis of the different regimes of imperial sovereignty. This analysis is still waiting for more refinement, since we do know that the supposed historical trend of demilitarization of the Song society has to be confronted with the moment of its remilitarization, imposed by the reforms under Emperor Shenzong (r. 1067-1085) in the 1070s.[46]

[46] Smith 2006.

Appendix A: Biography of Xie Dequan
Songshi (*History of Song*)
Beijing: Zhonghua Shuju, 1977,
Chap. 309, pp. 10164-10167

Xie Dequan, courtesy name Shiheng 士衡, was from Fuzhou 福州.[47] His father, Wenjie 文節, had first served the Wang family as the magistrate of Houguan 候官. Later, after the annexation [of Min] by the Kingdom of the Southern Tang,[48] Wenjie became Inspector-in-Chief of Extreme Loyalty and Commissioner of the Raozhou 饒州 militias. He gained a reputation for his valor and bravery. During Zhou Shizong's campaign against the Southern Tang,[49] Wenjie crossed the Great River alone in full armor to spy on enemy encampments. The people of Wu called him the Iron Dragon. He later commanded the defense of Ezhou 鄂州,[50] resisted Song troops, and died in combat.

His father having died on active service, Dequan was appointed by Li Yu as Vice- Commissioner for Estates and Residences.[51] After surrendering to the Song, he went to the Public Petitioners Review Office to present himself for service. He received the title of Palace Courier. He was later promoted to Aide-de-camp, and named Military Inspector in Shaanxi.[52] Thanks to his merits he gained his promotion to Right Palace Attendant.

---

[47] Fuzhou was the capital that the Wang dynasty chose after having founded the independent Min kingdom in South (909-945), in the present Fujian province.

[48] The Lis who founded the Southern Tang dynasty (937-975) ruled another kingdom in Southern China, and were able to annex the Min in 945.

[49] Zhou Shizong (r. 954-959) was the second emperor of the last of the Five Dynasties, the Later Zhou. This dynasty ruled Northern China between 950 and 960, the year of the foundation of the Song. Shizong has been considered by historians, including the Song historians, as the first ruler who had in mind the reunification of the empire and hence organized his military campaigns for this purpose. Thanks to several victorious campaigns, he was able to annex a part of the Southern Tang territories in 958.

[50] Ezhou was located on the middle course of the Yangzi River, close to the present-day Wuhan.

[51] Li Yu was the last king of the Southern Tang. In 975, he had no choice but to swear allegiance to the Song.

[52] Shaanxi is still the name of the same province located in the Northwest of China today. Near the present provincial capital, Xi'an, several spots served as former imperial cities for many centuries until the end of the first millennium.

When the floating bridge at Xianyang 咸陽 was wrecked, fiscal intendant Song Taichu 宋太初 ordered Dequan to plan the work.[53] Quickly the latter packed soil to reinforce the riverbanks and gathered stones to build a mooring berth. He copied the system of "Iron Bulls" established at Hezhong 河中, and firmly moored [the floating bridge to the Iron Bulls] with bamboo cords. After that there was no longer any damage.[54]

In the second year of Xianping (999) the Xi tribes 溪蠻 of Yizhou 宜州 rebelled.[55] Orders were given to Chen Yaosou 陳堯叟 to go there to handle the situation. Dequan joined the expedition. He entered alone on horseback into the lands of the tribes, whom he informed of the instructions of the Court so that all the populations submitted to these orders. After Yaosou had made his report, Dequan was promoted to the rank of Audience Usher and General Military Inspector of the Six Prefectures of Guang-Shao-Ying-Xiong-Lian-He. After his return to Court upon being relieved of this assignment (the inspectorship), he became Superintendent of the Granaries and Fodder Yards of the capital city. Just before that time, a large part of the food stocks rotted because of underground humidity. Dequan had brick shards piled up to form platforms to cushion the stocks. As a result, there were no more losses from rotting.

The back-streets and alleys of the capital were narrow. Dequan was ordered to widen them. From the moment he received the edict, he commanded the demolition to begin with the residences and houses belonging to the aristocracy and powerful people. Consequently, criticisms burst forth from all sides. An edict ordered the end of the operation. Dequan then made this request in person: "Your servant has received a mission that cannot be interrupted while underway. Today, all those who oppose the operation are powerful and eminent persons. They are very

---

[53] Xianyang was the first capital of the empire unified by Qin Shihuangdi, located on the Wei River, a few kilometers upstream from Xi'an.

[54] Hezhong prefecture was located in the modern province of Shanxi, in the Northwest of China. It was a strategic place as one of the crossing points from Shaanxi to Shanxi, just to the north of the loop that redirected the Yellow river towards the east and the great Northern plain. The "Iron Bull" was a piece of cast metal, immerged in the current at a chosen spot and fastened to the bank, as a protection from river erosion.

[55] Yizhou was the name of the present Chengdu, the capital of the large southwestern province of Sichuan.

attached to their houses and the rental income, that's all!" The emperor followed his advice. He therefore presented an itemized report on the dimensions of streets and alleys, and on the system of drums that announced the curfew from dawn to dusk.

Sometime later, the criminal Liu Ye 劉曄 and Monk Chengya 澄雅 accused some top government officials and certain inhabitants of Xuzhou 許州 to be secretly plotting to collude with the Xixia to commit treason.[56] An edict commanded Wen Zhongshu 溫仲舒 and Xie Mi 謝泌 to investigate, while ordering Dequan to supervise this inquiry. Very soon, his investigation showed that there was no basis [to the complaint]. The next day, during an audience in a non-ceremonial hall in the Palace, he explained the falseness of this accusation. Only [Xie] Mi claimed: "Only if we have pursued and seized the eminent officials [involved], will the report on this criminal case be complete." Dequan replied: "Mi hopes to make eminent officials fall! If innocent officials are humiliated, how can Our Sovereign employ such servants, and how can such servants serve Our Sovereign?" [Wen] Zhongshu concluded: "What Dequan reported is excellent." The Emperor endorsed it.

In the sixth year of Xianping (1003), he received the order to fortify the county seat of Xinle 新樂, and he was promoted to the rank of Palace Attendant. Orders were then given to him to dredge the moats of the Beiping 北平 stockade and to repair the walls of Puyin 蒲陰. One day, he went quickly riding post horses all the way to the Court in Kaifeng where he requested an audience. He declared: "Many border people have brought their clans into the city to settle down behind the city walls. Previous year, when the Khitans crossed the passes,[57] Fu Qian 傅潛 closed himself up in

[56] The name Xixia refers to the Tanguts who founded the kingdom of Xixia in 1038, long after the death of Xie Dequan. Living on the northwestern border of the Song Empire, these populations regularly opposed the Song by claiming their rights on the Ordos Loop, in the middle valley of the Yellow river, just to the south of Mongolia. The capital of the Xixia kingdom was destroyed by the Mongols in 1227.

[57] Khitan was the name of a Siberian proto-Mongolian population. They founded an empire at the very beginning of the tenth century after the collapse of the Tang Empire. The Khitan territory extended up to the present regions of Manchuria, Mongolia and the north of China, the present city of Beijing being their "Southern capital". The name of Liao was given to the Empire in 947 and remained in use until the end of the Empire in 1125. The Liao Empire became the powerful neighbor of both the Song Empire and the Xixia kingdom. The Song signed a peace treaty with the Liao in January 1005. According to this treaty, the two

his fortress to protect himself, and Kang Baoyi 康保裔 was taken prisoner, with the consequence that Your royal armies could not win any victory. Your servant thinks that the Khitan will certainly encroach upon our territory this year. Ordering border troops to remain concentrated in one place is really not expeditious. It is my hope that they be quickly divided into three columns at Zhen 鎮, Ding 定, and Gaoyang 高陽. The fortifications of Tianxiong 天雄 are spread out and far apart. [Your servant] asks that an urgent edict be sent--ordering the defenses to be concentrated into a tighter position, and furthermore ordering the city walls of Chanzhou 澶州 to be renovated and, further north, the walls and moats of the military prefecture of Deqing 德清 to be repaired. This will permit us to be prepared.[58] Your servant is convinced that the bandits will surely attack Puyin before the works at this city are finished." The Emperor sent him away with comforting words. Shortly afterwards, the Khitan indeed laid siege to Puyin. As soon as he learnt of an imperial edict ordering the construction of a royal lodge in Hebei, Dequan submitted a memorial by post horses requesting that the imperial carriage not cross the Yellow River. When the Emperor came to Chanzhou, Dequan rode alone to the royal encampment by taking a shortcut through a secondary road.

Shortly after, he was promoted to the position of Member of the Palace Honor Guard and became Controller of Military Personnel attached to the Finance Commission. Dequan established detailed regulations and equitably shared out the duties. A general officer was attached to the main warehouse of the eunuch intendance. Eunuchs memorialized [the emperor to request] that he be kept behind so as to permit him regular exclusions from the harshest services. Dequan, with the memorial in hand, reported to the Emperor and vehemently criticized favoritism. The Emperor praised him for such integrity. He was thereafter named Controller-General of the Four Bureaus of River Transport of the capital to direct the maintenance of the banks of the Bian 汴 [canal] and supervise the transports.[59] Before his

---

Emperors recognized each other as kinsmen and in order to maintain the peace, the Song agreed to offer the Liao an important annual gift of precious metals and silk.

[58] Located on the Yellow River, about one hundred kilometers to the north of Kaifeng, the Song capital, Chanzhou was the fortified city where the Song, under the leadership of the Emperor Zhenzong himself, resisted decisively the Liao forces before signing the peace treaty of 1005.

[59] During the Northern Song, the Bian was a harnessed river that made up the last part of the canal which connected the capital with the southeast regions of the empire. The canal was used for the transportation of the annual tribute in grain.

nomination, the annual *corvées* for repairs of the banks mobilized 300,000 drafted workers. Yet the officials in charge were accustomed to this routine: the protection levees were not solid, and the work was just to deposit yokes of sand for the protection of the banks. In case of flooding, the riverbed between the banks would be silted up again. Dequan required [the workers to] eliminate all the sand to reach the soil level, throwing all the sand beyond the dikes. He dispatched officers of the Three Ranks among whom he divided the work zones so that each one directed his own part of the work. Furthermore, he used a great pick to test the solidity of the dike, and, wherever the pick could pierce through, he immediately punished the responsible public agents on whom he had authority: many were demoted or fired. He had planted hundreds of thousands of trees to consolidate the dike. He suggested eliminating the mints of the capital, as well as moving the Western Kilns westward to Heyin 河陰—resulting in large savings in both labor and resources. His official status then changed as he became Vice Commissioner for Fostering Propriety and conjointly General-Manager of the Repair Offices of the East and West. Until then, construction projects often suffered from a shortage of labor, to the point that the projects remained unfinished for years on end. When Dequan supervised these projects, all were finished by the dates he set.

In the first year of Dazhongxiangfu (1008), the *Feng* 封 sacrifice (on Mount Tai) was discussed. [Xie Dequan], along with Liu Chenggui and Qi Lun 戚綸, were ordered to plan out the transport of supplies, and he was promoted to Commissioner of the Imperial Larder. He attended the construction of the Temple of the Resplendent Echo of Jade Pure. On that occasion, officials were continually removing commoners' houses so as to extend the site of the Temple, and Liu Chenggui proposed digging the ground to the depth of one *zhang* (approx. 3 meters) to reinforce the foundations of new buildings. Dequan was worried about the excesses of forced labor, and he angrily disputed with Liu daily. As he was unable to move [Liu], he asked to be relieved of his functions and took charge once again of the management of Granaries and Fodder Yards of the capital. He harnessed the Jinshui 金水 River, and made it flow westward from the imperial city while circling the Imperial Ancestral Temple, for a distance of more than ten *li*. In the third year (1010) he was named prefect of Sizhou. After he had established the best day for giving thanks, he himself

---

Sizhou, where Xie is appointed as prefect, is the city where the Bian connects to the Huai River, south to Kaifeng; whereas Heyin was located on the north branch of the Bian, upstream from its connection with the Luo River.

made the following remark to the Emperor: "Your servant has been for a long time in charge of various affairs of the capital, and is worried that the perception of those inside and outside of the Court might be that he is being sent out as a punishment, so he hopes to see himself granted with a slight promotion." An edict appointed him with a promotion as Commissioner of the Dyeing Service of the West. He died one month after he arrived at that post. He was fifty eight *sui* of age (born in 953). His son Ping 平 became Assistant Magistrate of Dingyuan 定遠, and was granted financial assistance for the funeral and mourning.

Dequan was honest and hard-working, enjoyed promoting efficacy and material advantages, and planned and organized many enterprises. Whenever he discovered an official seeking personal gain, he would invariably denounce the culprit to his face. As a result, wherever he went he was able to put things in strict order. Nevertheless, he liked to look for small faults in order to report them to the Emperor. As a result, he was detested by the opinion makers at Court.

Appendix B: Figures of Northern Song Officials belonging to the Bureau of Lesser Military Assignment and to the Public Service[60]

During the eleventh century the total number of officials increased five times, while the number of officers belonging to the Bureau of Lesser Military Assignment increased eight times. Obviously, the comparison between these figures suggests proportions that are scarcely credible. For instance, it is most unlikely that in 1080 more than half of all officials were affiliated with the Bureau. Figures for the total number of officials, like those of the 1090s, may be incomplete. A century later, in 1196, Li Xinchuan gave a total number of more than forty-two thousand civil and military officials and 18,070 for the officers of the Bureau, that is to say the latter accounted for close to 43% of the total.[61] In light of this data, it is reasonable to assert, nevertheless, that more than a third of the Song officials were affiliated to the Bureau during the eleventh and twelfth centuries.

---

[60] For the figures of the Bureau of Lesser Military Assignment, see Zhao Dongmei 2010: 343-346, and Wang Zengyu 1996; for the figures of civil officials, see Zhao Dongmei 2010: 254-255,

[61] Li Xinchuan 2000: 249.

Periods	**Personnel of the Bureau of Lesser Military Engagement**	**Public Service Personnel**	**Ratio**
Before 996	300		
1004-1008	600		
1017-1021	4 200	9 785 - 13 000	42%
1034-1037	4 000		
1038-1040	15 400		
1046	6 000	18 700 - 20 000	30%
1049-1054	17 300 - 20 000		
1050	5 297		
1053	7 703		40%
1055	8 112		
1060	8 800		
1064-1067	24 000		
1070	8 000		
1080	12 560	24 549	51%
1088	29 000 - 34 000		
1094-1097	4 848*		
1112	43 000		
1119	48 000		

*This figure given by Su Che is the total number of only four grades of officers belonging to the Bureau of Lesser Military Assignment.

Sources

Li Tao, 1115-1184, (1978-1993), *Xu Zizhi tongjian changbian (Long Draft of the Continuation of the Comprehensive Mirror for Aid in Government)*, Beijing, Zhonghua shuju.

Li Xinchuan, 1166-1243, (2000), *Jianyan yilai chaoye zaji (Note-book on the Court after the Jianyan Period)*, Beijing, Zhonghua shuju.

Shen Gua, 1031-1095, (2009), *Mengxi bitan (Brush Talks from Dream Brook)*, ed. Hu Daojing, reprint Taipei, Shijie shuju.

Sima Guang, 1019-1086, (1957), *Zizhi tongjian (Comprehensive Mirror for Aid in Government)*, Beijing, Zhonghua shuju.

Song Minqiu, 1019-1079, (1997), *Chunming tuichao lu (Notes Taken after an Official's Retirement from the Court)*, Beijing, Zhonghua shuju.

Toghto, 1314-1355, (1977), *Songshi (History of Song)*, Beijing, Zhonghua shuju.

Ye Mengde, 1077-1148, (1984), *Shilin yanyu (Banquet Talk in the Forest of Stones)*, Beijing, Zhonghua shuju.
Zeng Gong, 1019-1083, (1992), *Quan Song wen* (*Prose Works of the Song)*, Chengdu, Ba-Shu shushe, volume 29.

Modern References

Bao, Weimin (ed.), (2004), *Songdai zhidushi yanjiu bainian (1900-2000) (A Century of Research of the Institutional History of the Sung (1900-2000))*, Beijing: Shangwu yinshuguan.
Chen, Feng, (2004), *Bei Song wujiang qunti yu xiangguan wenti yanjiu (Investigations on the Group of Military Officers of the Northern Song and Related Questions)*, Beijing: Zhonghua shuju.
—. (2005), "Songdai zhuliu junshi sixiang yu bingxue pipan (A Critique of the Dominant Military Ideology and the Military Theories under the Song)", *Shixue yuekan*, 1: 12-14.
—. (2006), "Songchao de zhiguo fanglue yu wenchen shidafu diwei de tisheng (The Song Strategy for Maintaining Order and the Rising Status of Scholar-Officials)", *Shixue yuekan*, 1: 12-14.
—. (2007), "Zhengzhi xuanze yu Songdai wenguan shidafu de zhengzhi juese (The Political Choices and the Political Role of the Civil Scholar-Officials under the Song)", *Henan daxue xuebao*, 47/1: 7-13.
—. (2009), "Songdai zhuliu yishi zhipei xia de zhanzheng guan (The Concepts of War in the Dominant Ideology under the Song)", *Lishi yanjiu*, 2: 38-50.
Chiu, Yu Lok (Zhao Yule), (1993), *Tang-Song sanban guanzhi zhi yanbian (The Evolution of the Official System of the Three Ranks in the Tang and Song Periods*), Taipei: Wen-shi-zhi chubanshe.
Dai, Xianqun, (2008), *Tang Wudai shehui zhengzhi shi yanjiu (Investigations on the Socio-Political History of the Tang and the Five Dynasties)*, Harbin: Heilongjiang renmin chubanshe.
—. (2008), "Tang Wudai jiazi zhidu de leixing jiqi xiangguan wenti (Typology of the System of Adopted Sons under the Tang and the Five Dynasties and Related Subjects)", in Dai, *Tang Wudai shehui zhengzhi shi yanjiu*: 121-35.
Deng, Xiaonan, (1993), *Songdai wenguan renxuan zhu cengmian (The Different Levels of the Appointment System for Civil Office under the Song)*, Shijiazhuang: Hebei jiaoyu chubanshe.
—. (2002), "Jinchen yu waiguan: shixi Bei Song chuqi de shumi yuan jiqi zhangguan renxuan (Imperial Servitors and Officials of the Outer Court: A Preliminary Analysis of the Bureau of Military Affairs and Its

Personnel Assignments during the Early Northern Song)", in Qi (ed.), *Song shi yanjiu lunwenji*: 1-26, available on the Peking University website, http://www.hist.pku.edu.cn/person/dengxiaonan/tongshi_2/TD08/cankao/jinchenyu waiguan.htm, read on October 6, 2015

Fang, Cheng-hua, (2009), *Power Structures and Cultural Identities in Imperial China: Civil and Military Power from Late Tang to Early Song Dynasties (A.D. 875-1063)*, Saarbrücken: VDM Verlag Dr. Muller.

Gong, Yanming, (1977), *Songdai guanzhi cidian (Dictionary of Song Government Institutions),* Beijing: Zhonghua shuju.

Ho, Koon-wan (He Guanhuan), (2003), *Bei-Song wujiang yanjiu (Investigations on Northern Song Military Officers)*, Hong Kong: Zhonghua shuju (2nd edition, 2008).

Huai, Jianli, (2007), *Songdai xiangjun yanjiu (Investigations on the Regional Armies under the Song Dynasty)*, Zhengzhou: Zhongzhou guji chubanshe.

Hucker, C.O., (1985), *A Dictionary of Official Titles in Imperial China*, Stanford: Stanford University.

Kracke Jr., E.A., (1953), *Civil Service in Early Sung China – 960-1067*, Cambridge (Massachusetts): Harvard University Press.

La Vaissière, É. de, (2007), *Samarcande et Samarra: Élites d'Asie central dans l'empire abbaside*, Paris : Association pour l'avancement des études iraniennes.

Labadie, J. R., (1981), "Rulers and Soldiers: Perception and Management of the Military in Northern Sung China (960-*ca* 1060)", PhD dissertation, University of Washington.

Lau, Nap-yin (Liu Liyan), (2008), *Songdai de jiating he falü (Family and Law under the Song)*, Shanghai: Shanghai guji chubanshe.

Li, Huarui (ed.), (2010), *"Tang-Song biange" lun de youlai he fazhan (The Origin and Development of the Theory of the "Tang-Song Transition")*, Tianjin: Tianjin guji chubanshe

Liang, Tianxi, (1981), *Song Shumi yuan zhidu (The Institution of the Bureau of Military Affairs under the Song*), Taipei: Liming wenhua shiye gongsi.

Lorge, P., (2005), *War, Politics and Society in Early Modern China 900-1795*, London/New York: Routledge.

—. (ed.), (2011), *Five Dynasties and Ten Kingdoms*, Hong Kong: The Chinese University Press: introduction.

Miyakawa, Hisayuki, (1955); "An Outline of the Naitō Hypothesis and its Effects on Japanese Studies of China," *Far Eastern Quarterly*, 14/4, 533-542.

Pulleyblank, E.G., (1955), *The Background of the Rebellion of An Lushan*, London: Oxford University Press.

Qi, Xia, (ed.), (2002), *Song shi yanjiu lunwenji (Collection of Studies on the Song History*, Baoding: Hebei daxue chubanshe.

Shi, Yuntao, (2003), *Tangdai mufu yanjiu (Investigations on the Tang System of the "Tent Government")*, Beijing: Zhongguo shehui kexue chubanshe.

Smith, P.J., (2006), "*Shuihu zhuan* and the Military Subculture of the Northern Song, 960-1127," *Harvard Journal of Asiatic Studies*, 66: 363-422.

—. - von Glahn, R., (2003), *The Song-Yuan-Ming Transition in Chinese History*, Cambridge/London: Harvard University Press.

So, Billy, (1995) *Tang-Song fazhi shi yanjiu (Research on the History of the Legal Institutions on the Tang and the Song)*, Hong Kong: Chinese University Press:

—. (1995), "Wudai de Shumi yuan (The Bureau of Military Affairs under the Five Dynasties)," in So, *Tang-Song fazhi shi yanjiu*: 1-38.

Standen, N., (2007), *Unbounded Loyalty – Frontier Crossings in Liao China*, Honolulu: University of Hawaii Press.

—. (2011), 'Who wants to be an emperor? Zhao Dejun, Youzhou and the Liao', in Lorge (ed.), *The Five Dynasties and Ten Kingdoms*: 15-46.

Tang, Zhangru, (1989), *Shanju cungao (Manuscripts Preserved in My Mountain Residence),* Beijing: Zhonghua shuju.

—. (1989), "Tangdai de neizhusi shi jiqi yanbian (The evolution of the commissioners of the various inner offices in the Tang period)", in Tang, *Shanju cungao*: 244-72.

Tsang, Shui-lung, (1997), "War and Peace in Northern Sung China: Violence and Strategy in Flux, 960-1104", PhD dissertation, University of Arizona.

—. – Chiu, Yu Lok, (2004), "Tang-Song junzheng biange shi yanjiu shuping (An introduction to the studies on the change of the military administration from the Tang to the Song)", in Bao, *Songdai zhidushi yanjiu bainian (1900-2000)*: 165-228.

Twitchett, D.C., (ed.), (1979). *The Cambridge History of China, volume 3 – part 1, Sui and Tang China 589-906*, Cambridge/New York: Cambridge University Press.

Twitchett, D.C. - Smith, P. J., (eds.), (2009), *The Cambridge History of China, volume 5 – part 1, The Sung Dynasty and its Precursors 907-1279*, Cambridge/New York: Cambridge University Press.

Wang, Gungwu, (1963), *The Structure of Power in North China during the Five Dynasties*, Kuala Lumpur, University of Malaya Press (reedited with the title *Divided China – Preparing for Reunification 883-947*, Singapore/Hackensack/London: World Scientific Publishing Co. 1995).

Wang, Zengyu, (1983), *Songdai bingzhi chutan (Preliminary Inquiry into the Military Institutions of the Song Dynasty)*, Beijing: Zhonghua shuju.

Worthy Jr., E.R., (1976), "The Founding of Sung China, 950-1000: Integrative Changes in Military and Political Institutions", PhD dissertation, Princeton University.

Zhang, Qifan, (1993), *Wudai jinjun chutan (A Preliminary Study of the Palace Army in the Five Dynasties)*, Guangzhou: Jinan daxue.

Zhao, Dongmei, (2010), *Wen wu zhijian: Bei-Song wuxuanguan yanjiu (Between Civil and Military: Investigation on Northern Song Military Appointed Officials)*, Beijing: Beijing daxue chubanshe.

CHAPTER ELEVEN

THE 1774 ANNUAL AUDITS OF MAGISTRATE ACTIVITY AND THEIR FATE*

PIERRE-ÉTIENNE WILL

Paradoxes, impossibilities, and contradictions seem at first sight to characterize what had become of the system of local administration during the high Qing. In most regions a rapidly growing population had to be kept peaceful and secure, educated in the proper ways, and fed when times were difficult. The settled territory to survey and keep under control was fast expanding beyond the old plains and valley bottoms where most of the population had stayed concentrated until recently. A vibrantly developing economy needed to be monitored and taxed, encouraged in the directions deemed desirable, and provided with the necessary infrastructure. And all of this had to be accomplished by a handful of officials, whose numbers had stayed more or less constant since the Ming. What is more, these officials—the magistrates essentially—had to make do with ridiculously low operating budgets and with staffs which were not necessarily small, but were routinely considered unreliable and dishonest. In sum, ambitions were immense—not just extracting a little revenue and seeing to it that an appearance of order be maintained and that the regime not appear threatened, but civilizing the masses and controlling their lives. On the face of it, the means that were mobilized to attain such goals were exceedingly modest, and would have to stay so, since maintaining the administrative workforce and state expenditures at a low level was celebrated as a proof of good government and a manifestation of dynastic legitimacy.

* Previously published in *Late Imperial China*18:2 (1998), 1-50.

Quantity and Quality

All of this is well known, of course, as is the additional paradox that in spite of this quantitatively-limited governmental output the empire was, by and large, efficiently run for comparatively long periods of time, most strikingly the eighteenth-century Qing. How was this achieved?

A variety of methods, many of which have already been well described by historians, were used to offset the structural insufficiency of the regular bureaucracy in material means and human resources. Mostly, they come under the general notion of delegating or subcontracting specific tasks to state-approved non-bureaucratic agents. For example, local elites would be co-opted to monitor and educate the masses; citizens "honest and of means" would be selected to run granaries or other organizations; merchants known and respected and with sufficient assets would be entrusted with "liturgical" services like controlling their respective trades, policing the market-place, and levying commercial tax; landowners and merchants would be required to contribute funds to build and maintain infrastructures and services from which their communities were to benefit; systems of mutual surveillance and responsibility would be imposed on the populace to enforce self-discipline; and so on. Such techniques made it possible for the state bureaucracy to limit itself to setting examples, laying down rules and guidelines, and giving warnings, and to concentrate its organizational and financial efforts where scale and complexity required it. Thus, for example, coercion and repression would be applied selectively but harshly enough to discourage misbehavior, while state funds and an unusual concentration of field officials would be mobilized to combat natural disasters and famines, or direct public works of a regional scale.

Another type of approach was to try by every means to raise the efficiency, reliability, and output of the existing bureaucratic apparatus in the performance of its ordinary tasks. The present essay will be devoted to one method experimented with by the Qing government for a few years in the mid-eighteenth century—the so-called "things to promote and to prohibit" (*xingchu shiyi* 興除事宜) audit procedure, whereby magistrates were to tour annually every village in their constituencies and report in full detail on what they had been able to do to improve conditions. What I would like to emphasize in this introduction is that, in doing this, the Qing could avail themselves of a rather unique combination of mobilization from the top and activism among the rank and file; or, differently put, of an encounter between a succession of competent and interventionist emperors and a bureaucracy with at least an active minority of highly committed professionals, of which Chinese imperial history gives few other examples.

The Manchu emperors' hardworking habits and willingness to immerse themselves in the daily routines of managing the empire—down to Daoguang (1821-1850) at least, and with a special mention for Yongzheng (1723-1735) and Qianlong (1736-1795)—are well known to historians, and need not be expatiated upon here. One may ponder possible cultural, political, or even biological explanations for the contrast with a majority of their Ming predecessors. However, I would like to stress what seems to me a new streak of anxiety that was caused, in the eighteenth century at least, not by any particular external menace or threatening internal unrest, but by the sort of structural tensions alluded to above: the growing population on a limited cultivated area,[1] the increasing numbers of people on the move whose crossing of regional borders and settling in frontier wildernesses could not be controlled, the unabated inflation, the mounting level of litigation, and what was perceived as a rising trend of small-scale rioting. To cope with these challenges required more than the essentially conservative and minimalist approach to local government that was appreciated as non-oppressive by the theorists of benevolent rule, and as more comfortable to themselves by ordinary bureaucrats (those that the literature sometimes calls "vulgar officials", *suli* 俗吏). It required intervention, initiative, discipline, and above all an enormous amount of commitment.[2] And indeed, this is what the Manchu emperors were constantly hammering out in edicts which were, presumably, published in the *Beijing Gazette* and read by officials in every corner of the empire.

---

[1] I have discussed the Kangxi, Yongzheng, and Qianlong emperors' expressed anxieties on this particular problem in Will 1994.

[2] Some of the best formulations of what I call the "conservative and minimalist approach" are found in Huang 1981. Huang opposes this approach, whose main supporter in the book is Shen Shixing 申時行, the chief Grand Secretary during the years 1583-91, to the aggressive and interventionist style of Shen's predecessor, Zhang Juzheng 張居正 (chief Grand Secretary 1573-82): see in particular chapters 2 and 3. One important difference between Zhang's policies and the sort of interventionism I will discuss later in this essay might be their predominantly fiscalist bent.

Ordinary Officials and the Professional Elite

Such insistence had its reasons. A further cause for anxiety on the part of the court and of the most devoted high officials in the provinces was that, in their eyes, a majority of the local officialdom was insufficiently committed and, more often than not, incompetent. Opening the Kangxi, Yongzheng, Qianlong, or Jiaqing *Veritable Records* at random, one can be sure to find, within a few pages, some scathing imperial comment on the inefficiency and unreliability of department and county magistrates. They were as a rule suspected of doing very little beyond their mandatory fiscal and judicial duties and of trying systematically to camouflage their indifference and inadequacies, if not necessarily their abuses, under what was called "empty words", and much of what went wrong was routinely ascribed to their insufficient efforts. To be sure, the provincial governors, whom the Qing emperors tended to consider as their personal appointees, owing special devotion and loyalty, were not always spared: the throne was quick to attribute the magistrates' unimpressive performance to their superiors' laxness, thirst for popularity, and inability to put them seriously to work and control them. At the same time, it can be seen in the circulars and public addresses of a number of governors-general and governors that they, too, could use very harsh words denouncing the magistrates as lazy careerists who did not care much about the complexities and demands of local government.[3]

It should be obvious, though, that this scornful, even snobbish attitude in the top echelons of the state apparatus toward the rank and file local bureaucrats was in many cases unjustified, and in fact it was not

---

[3] Two famous eighteenth-century governors whose pronouncements are particularly eloquent in this respect are Tian Wenjing 田文鏡 (1662-1732) and Chen Hongmou 陳宏謀 (1696-1771). The fascinating collection of official correspondence and proclamations compiled in 1727 by Tian's assistants, the *Fu Yu xuanhua lu* 撫豫宣化錄 (Records of My Administration as Henan Governor), is crammed with denunciations of the magistrates' insufficiencies or even stupidity and gullibility. As for Chen Hongmou, we will mention later in this essay examples of his frequent exasperation with his subordinates. Incidentally, both Tian and Chen were products of the activist and reformist Yongzheng reign: in his Henan fief the former was a noted champion of the Yongzheng emperor's drive to discipline the bureaucracy and rationalize local finances, while the latter spent his formative years and held his first appointments—in the Southwest, notably—during the same period, building ties with some of the most eminent Yongzheng statesmen.

systematic. Governors in particular readily acknowledged the existence of competent and even outstanding local officials with whom they collaborated closely, moving them around to fill the more sensitive and difficult positions in the province, and warmly recommending them to the throne for promotion. Indeed, it seems to me possible to speak of an elite professional cadre among the Qing field bureaucracy—an elite to which belonged men of all venues, including not only ranking officials high and low, but also private secretaries (*muyou* 幕友), and even lay scholars whose views on local government were considered important and who could be invited by high officials to serve as informal advisors.[4] Since many of the values and ideas spread and discussed among this cadre are also in evidence in the audit and mobilization campaign that will be discussed below, a few more words about it may be in order.

As I suggested, it was a heterogeneous cadre, encompassing people sometimes very far apart in social standing and professional position. What is striking is how their shared passion for local government and its improvement brought them together, so that, one assumes, a man holding the exalted position of provincial governor or treasurer would freely communicate and consult with a modest magistrate or even an untitled private secretary to discuss questions of administrative technique and bureaucratic ethics. Admittedly, we do not have much concrete evidence of such intercourse; but a quantity of prefaces written for the specialized works produced in abundance by devotees of local administration indirectly bears witness to a sense of community and mutual respect, and occasionally to a familiarity, that cut across status lines and rank distinctions. In the same way, it is notable that some of the most often quoted and republished titles in this literature were by authors who had rather modest and sometimes fairly short careers in the county and prefectural administration.[5] Such men were representative of an influential

[4] Needless to say, the Qing was not the only regime where such professional bureaucratic culture flourished. But Qing bureaucratic culture definitely had its peculiarities, if only because, as suggested above, Qing administrators had to face peculiar challenges, demographic, environmental, or otherwise. Another distinctive feature might be the stifling authoritarianism of Qing political culture, as opposed to the flamboyant political style of the Northern Song or the late Ming, for example.

[5] Examples that come to mind (there are many others) are Huang Liuhong 黃六鴻, Yuan Shouding 袁守定, Wang Huizu 汪輝祖, and Liu Heng 劉衡, authors, respectively, of the *Fuhui quanshu* 福惠全書 (A Complete Book

elite minority of rank-and-file field bureaucrats whose commitment and professional expertise were admired and commended far beyond their immediate entourage.[6]

Handbooks

The specialized works just alluded to consisted principally of what I would loosely call "official handbooks", including not only the well-known guides for magistrates (*guanzhen* 官箴), but also the whole gamut of texts that were published or hand-copied in especially large numbers during the Qing to help novice administrators and staff members learn their trade, and those who were already into their careers, to perform more efficiently.[7] Many genres can be mentioned: collections of their administrative papers (such as proclamations, circulars, administrative correspondence, local regulations and "covenants", judicial sentences, and so on) published by individual authors for the instruction and edification of fellow officials—the so-called *gongdu* 公牘 anthologies;[8] biographical

Concerning Happiness and Benevolence, 1694), *Tumin lu* 圖民錄 (Planning for the People, 1756), *Xuezhi yishuo* 學治臆說 (Personal Views on Studying Government, 1793), and *Yongli yongyan* 庸吏庸言 (Ordinary Sayings from an Ordinary Official, 1830).

[6] Like the authors cited in the previous note—and to give a concrete example—Ye Zhen 葉鎮 (a *jinshi* of 1748) was only an obscure local official; yet his handbook, the *Zuoli yaoyan* 作吏要言 (Essential Words on Being an Official), was published with an enthusiastic commentary following a meeting where Chen Hongmou, the prestigious governor already mentioned, and an intendant by the name of Zhu Chun 朱椿, had discussed it. Chen, who had seen a copy of the work at the home of a vice minister of personnel that he knew, claims in his preface that it is superior to his own *Guanzhen batiao* 官箴八條 (Eight Instructions to Exhort Officials) that was published in the midst of the audit campaign described below. The *Zuoli yaoyan* is much quoted in the important anthology of magistrate handbooks, the *Muling shu* 牧令書 of 1838. (The version with Zhu's comments and Chen's preface is found as an appendix to the *Buzhu Xiyuan lu jizheng* 補註洗冤錄集證 [Washing Away the Wrongs, with notes and commentaries] edited in 1843 by Tong Lian 童濂).

[7] The Qing boom in composing and publishing handbooks and guides emerges clearly from the bibliographic work I have been pursuing for several years on this type of literature. Of the ca. 1,000 titles identified thus far, about four-fifths are from the Qing, and this does not simply reflect a higher rate of preservation.

[8] While the earliest published magistrate handbooks date back to the Song period, the *gongdu* anthologies seem to have made their appearance at the end of the

collections devoted to model officials; professional autobiographies; famine relief handbooks; handbooks for private secretaries (which were in general less ideological in tone and more technical in content, and frequently with a degree of provincial specialization). There was also a vast body of practical guides, abstracts of the penal code and administrative law, collections of model forms for administrative papers, and cribs of various descriptions, many of which were presented in forms easy to consult or to remember, such as mnemonic tables and rhymed adaptations.[9]

These texts offered a varying combination of ethical and practical advice to officials on such topics as how to behave properly, how to relate with their professional and social environment, how to master the details of local administration, and, importantly, how to keep control of their subordinates. The point is that, beyond its immediate practical aims—helping officials to stay afloat in the "sea of officialdom" (*huanhai* 宦海), avoid making mistakes, and not be manipulated by their underlings—it was a literature which conveyed a very high idea of the stringent behavioral and technical standards of responsible local government, as well as, in a large number of Qing works at least, an exalted sense of the devotion and personal commitment that were required to properly ensure the people's nourishment and education.

This last aspect, which is much less in evidence in the Ming handbooks I have been able to examine, is important for what follows. As I mentioned at the start, local officials were essentially alone in charge of vast constituencies, a problem that could only grow worse in the context of Qing demographic and territorial expansion. Increasing significantly the numbers of the formal bureaucracy and making its presence in the field more dense was, in practice, out of the question. Therefore, despite a lot of delegation and subcontracting in many domains, the basic functions of government still had to be accomplished by the magistrates themselves, with no better help than that of a staff of underlings who were considered

sixteenth century. Lü Kun 呂坤 (1536-1618) may have been one of the inventors of the genre with his *Shizheng lu* 實政錄 (Records of Real Government, 1598), which was highly influential during the Qing. Many Qing magistrate handbooks, beginning with Huang Liuhong's famous *Fuhui quanshu,* generously quote from their authors' administrative papers, and thus can be considered a mix of the *guanzhen* and *gongdu* formats.

[9] A full assessment of these works remains to be done. They are heavily used in the two classics on county administration, Ch'ü 1962 and Watt 1972.

both despicable and dishonest, and whose influence was hardly balanced by that of a handful of supposedly trustworthy private secretaries and attendants. To the already mentioned anxiety in the face of a rapidly expanding society and economy, which was shared by many of the best bureaucrats of the time, was added the anxiety, or even anguish, of having to make do with such poor means and—for the most idealistic at least—of not being able to accomplish the ambitious program of education and nourishment they had been entrusted with by the dynasty.

One of the basic aims of the handbooks and other aids was to dispense concrete advice, even to teach tricks, to help officials accomplish at least the basic tasks without committing errors and incurring sanctions. But for the most demanding handbook authors, even the larger "civilizing" ambitions of the state were not beyond the abilities of sufficiently trained, ingenious, and enthusiastic civil servants. At this exalted level, too, they suggested "methods" and proposed concrete examples to convince their readers that it was indeed possible. One of the basic problems, or so it was claimed everywhere, was that no self-respecting official would seriously consider allowing *yamen* clerks and other underlings to assume a responsible position in any of the nobler enterprises of the state, such as educating the people and promoting their welfare. Indeed, one striking feature of virtually all the policies championed by the supporters of what they called "real government" (*shizheng* 實政)[10] was that they were delineated precisely to prevent the clerks from interfering and, as far as was possible, to do without them. In other words, much energy and ingenuity in devising policies was spent on building protections against the encroachments and abuses of the very personnel who should have been the executive arm of the ranking bureaucracy.[11]

---

[10] The term may have been coined by Lü Kun in the title of his famous handbook, the *Shizheng lu.* In the Qing it is pervasive in the discourse on local governance. To give one example, all the authors of the prefaces to Tian Wenjing's above-mentioned *Fu Yu xuanhua lu,* all of them his subordinates in the Henan administration, wax enthusiastic about their boss's "real government".

[11] As is known, for Kyoto scholars such as Miyazaki Ichisada and Saeki Tomi the clerks were the actual rulers of "modern China" and the magistrate handbooks were basically collections of recipes for protecting oneself against clerical malfeasance. See for example Miyazaki 1950, or Saeki 1975, introduction. This seems to be an exceedingly limited view of that literature.

Communication

One of the outcomes of the felt necessity of keeping the clerks and other sub-bureaucrats at arms' length—an outcome that will concern us directly in this essay—is the ubiquitous and insistent theme of the desirability of direct and unmediated communication between officials and people and, more generally, of making oneself seen as much as possible. Touring the countryside and talking face to face with the small folk and their natural and legitimate leaders—the gentry and the so-called elders (*qilao* 耆老)—is in fact a "must" in most writings on the duties of local officials. Importantly, it was not just advocated by authors whom we might consider empty theoreticians, but also by old hands at field administration who revealed their own experiences and techniques. While a vast number of quotations could be given here,[12] it should be enough to emphasize that, in a general way, the insistence on being "close to the people" (*qinmin* 親民) reflected several sorts of preoccupations. One was simply to get acquainted with local conditions—a necessity for officials who, because of the law of avoidance, were by definition foreigners, and whom local personnel tended to keep as much isolated as possible from the society around[13]—and to figure out policies to improve them. Another was the more specific need to sound out the mood of the population and detect discontent: many edicts hold the magistrates responsible for having been unable to prevent popular violence flaring up. Yet another could be a sincere urge to indoctrinate the people in the true values, and lecture the notables on their responsibilities, by more effective means than simply posting proclamations—and for this, certain authors also discuss the

---

[12] To limit myself to authors I have already cited: Yuan Shouding in his *Tumin lu* (1839 ed., 2/25b-26a) recommends making oneself seen as much as possible in one's territory and finding ways to have as much contact as possible with ordinary people, both to discourage the abuses of the lowly personnel and to show off one's commitment wherever there are problems; one of the prefaces to Liu Heng's *Yongli yongyan* describes graphically (and charmingly, through the boyhood remembrances of the author) the "ordinary official" chattering with a crowd of excited schoolboys and respectful elders in some village—Liu's style was indeed bordering on the populist. Finally, Ye Zhen in his *Zuoli yaoyan* (quoted in *Muling shu,* 16/4b) makes a calculation of how many thousand people were "exposed in person to [his] speeches" during his tours of the countryside in any one year of his magistracies.

[13] For some striking citations on the solitude of the magistrate amidst his *yamen* personnel, see Will 1989:81-85.

problem of language, since they sometimes had to go through an interpreter.

Whatever the effectiveness of such direct communication may have been—those who recommended it concretely through their own example claimed it was great—it is easy to imagine that only a minority found the energy to practice it assiduously, assuming they were interested in it at all, if only because of the crushing amount of business they had to attend to in their offices. The tendency of magistrates to leave communication with their constituents to the sub-bureaucracy and gentry is indeed one of the classic complaints of activist officials in their handbooks, and of impatient governors in their circulars.

To be sure, direct communication and personal closeness to the people was only one aspect of the effort to raise the efficiency of the bureaucratic apparatus that was called for, as we saw, to compensate for its thinness and to meet the challenges of the times. But it was considered of paramount importance to attain the more specific goals of raising agricultural productivity, improving popular ethics and customs, promoting frugality, and discouraging litigation. In all these enterprises, if the activist elite of local officials could be relied upon as a vanguard, so to speak, it was still only that. Other methods of mobilization and control had therefore to be devised to make sure that the mass of "ordinary" bureaucrats would follow. Overall, everyone agreed that quality was not up to quantity.

Thus it was for the purpose of monitoring and mobilizing a local civil service that was seen as too indolent, short-sighted, and egoistic, to bring about the changes necessitated by an anxiety-ridden age that Yongzheng, his successor Qianlong, and some of their court dignitaries promoted a procedure of annual audits of local government. In its more activist (or maximalist) version at least, this attempted to raise the level of state intervention in the everyday life of the empire to radically new heights. In this respect it was to be qualitatively different from the routine procedures of annual and triennial magistrate evaluation. However efficient they may have been on the whole,[14] these last were obviously not designed to infuse the field bureaucracy with dynamic enthusiasm and active reformism.

---

[14] For John Watt (1970:24-25), "the Ch'ing government developed what must surely have been the most comprehensive evaluation system of any pre-modern administration".

The Mid-Eighteenth Century Audit Procedure

Origins

Not surprisingly, the history of the audit procedure begins under the Yongzheng emperor, whose reformist propensities and worries about the proper disciplining of officials are a well-known theme of his reign.[15] It started with an edict promulgated at the end of Yongzheng's first year of rule, in which the emperor expressed his concern that the many imperial edicts and memorials sent by high officials and approved by the throne that had been circulated since his accession were not always "sincerely" taken heed of and translated into "real" policies in the field.[16] He therefore gave one year to the high officialdom to make an assessment of how the new policies had been carried out, and report. Here is a full translation of this founding edict:

> The way of practicing government relies on devoting one's attention to reality (*wushi* 務實) without attaching importance to empty names (*xuming* 虛名). Ever since I have taken over the Great Heritage, I have spent every hour and moment pondering on the governance of the army and people by officials (*lizhi bingmin* 吏治兵民). About every affair big or small I have thought comprehensively and worried in detail, wanting to see things enforced in practice. Whatever [measure] could be of effective help to the empire became the subject of an edict and of repeated warnings. Whatever proposal from the court and provinces ought to be considered was always accepted. What was desired was that the officials in the capital and provinces effectively obey [their orders], so as to get results (*chengxiao* 成效). During the past year the edicts handed down and the proposals from the court and provinces issued to the Six Boards, Nine Ministers, Eight

[15] My assessment of this history is largely based on the succession of texts quoted at the beginning of a document I will describe more fully later, viz. Shulu 舒輅, memorial of QL 16/3/7 (hereafter SM), Beijing, No. 1 Historical Archives (hereafter NOHA), *Like tiben,* no. 314, bundle 55. The account found in the *Veritable Records,* to which I had to limit myself until I had access to further archival documents, including above all the copy of Shulu's memorial provided by Philip Kuhn, is too patchy to understand correctly the rationale of the system and the changes it went through. (Page numbers in SM citations below refer to the photocopies brought back from the archives by Kuhn, each sheet corresponding to four 6-column folds of the accordion-shaped original).

[16] Edict of YZ 1/11/-, in SM:2-4. A somewhat shorter version appears in *Da Qing Shizong Xian huangdi shilu,* 13/16a-b (dated from the 2lst day).

> Banners, and every province have been numerous indeed. If the issues memorialized about [and decided upon] by the different *yamen* at the capital and in the provinces have only been an occasion for sending a circular or putting out a proclamation, and left to empty words (*kongwen* 空文), so that in the end one has not seen any real result, then [it means that] there is no evidence and no trust (*bu zheng bu xin* 不徵不信). How could that accord with my utmost desire for "mutual help between neighbors" (*yipi xiangzhu* 倚毗相助)? If among the edicts and approved proposals there happen to be one or two things which do not entirely fit and need adding or removing, then of course I need to be informed sincerely.
>
> Let it be ordered to the Six Boards, Nine Ministers, Eight Banners, and the governors general, governors, and military chiefs of every province, that before the twelfth month of next year, for all the topics discussed in the edicts and approved proposals previously promulgated, an itemized and sincere assessment be made, clearly and in detail, of whether they have been implemented and, if so, what results have already been achieved. As for the secret memorials and secret edicts [in response], the detailed information [on implementation] will likewise be reported by secret memorial.
>
> The reason why I extend the time limit is that I want everyone to be able to make careful investigations and consider [the possibilities of] implementation, which will be of real help to administering the army and people. Let everyone improve himself, so as to meet my concerns.

This edict contains, explicitly or implicitly, all the elements that would be developed during the history of the audit procedure in the Qianlong period: the obsession with *shi* 實 (variously translated above as "real", "effective", "sincere", or "practical") in the implementation of directives, the natural inclination of officials to "send a circular or put out a proclamation" (*xingwen chushi* 行文出示) and leave it at that, and the need to make "real" investigations to check on results. What the text just translated does not say explicitly, but is indicated by the later documents that allude to it, is that the audit it was ordering would have to be performed and reported by the twelfth month *every year*.

Qianlong Revival

Indeed, what these later documents deplore is that over the years the procedure had become an "old convention" (*gutao* 故套), in other words that it had in effect (if not necessarily in name) fallen into disuse. As far as I can ascertain, the problem was not raised until twenty years later, at the beginning of 1744, when in an edict responding to the court dignitaries, themselves responding to the memorial of a censor by the name of Shi Jiqi 史積琦, the Qianlong emperor complained that only a few governors took it to heart to implement effectively the edicts about "teaching the people and improving customs" that were promulgated again and again: they only valued as "capable" (*neng* 能) those of their subalterns who knew how to obey decisions and were clever in answering questions, and tended not to show any further interest in matters for which regulations (*guitiao* 規條) had been established following imperial edicts.[17] It was therefore ordered (as it had been in 1723, although no explicit reference to that decision appears in the text) that the governors-general and governors carefully memorialize on the implementation of the decisions promulgated year after year by the throne concerning the education and nourishment of the people. They must indicate what had been done, and with what results; their answers would then be examined by the Grand Secretaries and Nine Ministers.[18]

What should be emphasized in this otherwise banal-sounding text is the sense that efficient government can only be dynamic and creative. Just running things as they are, however competently, ignoring in practice the exhortations and regulations handed down by an impatient and anxious throne, will lead to decadence.[19] The same notion of a dynamic approach is conveyed by the caption of Shi Jiqi's original memorial: "Magistrates are the officials close to the people and ought to take initiatives to educate and civilize (*yixing jiaohua* 宜興教化)"—introducing that essential link in the system, the people's "fathers-and-mothers", who were to be at the forefront of the effort described below.

To be sure, none of this appears very specific—just the sort of call for mobilization that was politely acknowledged and then quietly ignored by the bureaucracy. But later in that same year one senior official who had been a member of the Yongzheng inner court made much more precise proposals, and had them eventually accepted with the support of the Grand

---

[17] On the transmission of these regulations to the provincial governments and their distribution among local administrations, see Chen (1976). The first specific discussion of it cited by Chen is also dated 1744 (p. 29).

[18] SM:4, dated QL 9/2/-. So far as I know, Censor Shi Jiqi's original memorial has not been preserved.

[19] The text uses the rather strong phrase "this trend will get worse by the day, the people will ignore the rites and justice!" (*ze tuibo rixia, min bu zhi liyi* 則頹波日下民不知禮儀).

Secretariat and Nine Ministers,[20] causing some agitation for a few years in at least some provinces, as we shall see later. In a memorial submitted in the ninth month, the president of the Board of Personnel and Grand Secretary, Nuoqin 納親, developed the concerns expressed in Yongzheng's 1723 edict, to which he referred explicitly: the governors and magistrates do propagate dutifully the imperial edicts and court-approved proposals made by high officials, but apart from "less than twenty or ten percent of the cases" where there is substantial implementation, this is mere paperwork—"sending circulars and posting proclamations". The procedure ordered by Yongzheng to remedy this had become a mere routine: "One does no more than ordering the clerks to fill in the forms in conformity with precedent".

Nuoqin proposed to put an end to the 1723 system of "sending routine memorials on results achieved" (*juti chengxiao benzhang* 具題成效本章), which was based on the orders and instructions received by the provincial governments from above, and to replace it with a much more thorough and demanding procedure.[21] Now the effort would concentrate on the magistrates themselves, whom Nuoqin—in line with an attitude that we have seen was fairly common in higher circles—clearly designated as the weak rung in the entire system. He began by drawing up, first, a list of domains where results could be achieved if "sincere energy" was applied (*shili fengxing* 實力奉行): promoting schools, correcting literati behavior, improving popular customs, and the various "good policies" concerned with agriculture and irrigation—all of this "needs to be acted upon" (*yingxing* 應行). And second, he produced a list of things that "need to be prohibited" (*yingjin* 應禁): yeast- and spirit-making, gambling, litigation,

[20] This is the conventional phrase used in the original documents and in standard historical records, but the top dignitaries of these bodies were, first and foremost, members of the Grand Council. In 1744 and 1745 the three top Grand Councilors were the Grand Secretaries Eertai 鄂爾泰 (1680-1745), Zhang Tingyu 張廷玉 (1672-1755)—whose intervention in the history of the audit procedure we will discuss in a moment—and Nuoqin, the senior official just mentioned. All three had been members of the former Yongzheng inner court (Nuoqin only in an *ad hoc* capacity: see Bartlett 1991:94). On their positions in the Yongzheng and Qianlong inner courts, see Bartlett 1991, passim. On the composition of the Grand Council in 1744-45, see the table in Fu 1967:541-43.

[21] Nuoqin's memorial is briefly abstracted in the discussion of the court dignitaries (see below); there is a full Grand Council copy in NOHA, *Lufu zouzhe* microfilm, Qianlong, *Neizheng,* roll 5, frames 1149-51 (rescript of QL 9/7/29).

and violence. But all of this demanded careful consideration of local conditions, and results could not be hoped for overnight. On the other hand, banditry, vendettas, and heterodox sects could be rapidly eradicated with energetic intervention.

But, added Nuoqin,

> The reason why all of this is not successfully implemented is that the magistrates in the various provinces are only interested in registers and taxes. They do not concern themselves with knowing whether the populace in their constituencies is well-off or miserable, whether the terrain is rich or poor, whether the products are plentiful or scarce, what is the mood of the people (*minqing zhi quxiang* 民情之趨向), whether local customs are good or bad, and everything about mountains and rivers, plains and marshes, bridges and roads. Beyond [publishing] sets of exhortations (*tiaojiao* 條教) the officials do not give any [concrete] directive (*chishi* 飭事) to the people; beyond paying taxes the people have no dealings with the officials. The feelings from above and below do not connect with each other. How then could one expect to [implement] orders and prohibitions?

Hence Nuoqin's request: that the governors be ordered to make the local officials visit in person all the villages and hamlets in their constituencies within a year or a half-year (depending on the size of the county and the complexity of local affairs), ascertain the condition of every place, start whatever project needs to be started, put in order whatever situation needs to be put in order, and report in detail in a register on what they were or were not able to achieve. Their superiors would then check on these reports, and the governors would compile a year-end synthesis of what had been undertaken, county by county, and what the results had been, reporting in the form of a palace memorial.

This, in other words, was attempting, in a striking fashion, to legislate for some of the most cherished ideals of the local administration enthusiasts alluded to earlier: *everybody* would have to conform to the same exacting standards of commitment and performance, leave his office, and make contact with the real populace. Typical of a Yongzheng-trained high official, however, rather than dreaming of seeing every county magistrate internalize such standards, Nuoqin explained that it was pressure from above, the knowledge they would be evaluated on the basis of actual achievements, not of words, that would oblige every official to exert himself and avoid "telling tales". Besides, the ordinary tasks of local government would be performed much more efficiently: since the populace would now be able to convey its feelings and the magistrates would be obliged to get a sound knowledge of their terrain, it would become possible to deal with routine business like civil suits and tax delinquency more easily and with less paperwork, and, in case of natural disasters, damage evaluation and decision making would proceed more smoothly.

The emperor's rescript to Nuoqin's memorial ordered its discussion by the Grand Secretaries and Nine Ministers, and his approval of these dignitaries' conclusions was given exactly two months after that order.[22] The conclusions essentially followed the Board President's proposals, adding however a few details. For example, it was now specified that the magistrates would have to communicate to the governor the exact dates of their field trips and the name of the places they had visited. The Ministers also insisted on feasibility and effective implementation: the magistrates would take action with regard to the improvement and prohibition policies enumerated by Nuoqin only when they had been able to "see and hear", *i.e.* examine for themselves, the actual circumstances; and they would not impose short deadlines for results, which was only a pretext for careless implementation. The governors were to order the magistrates to send progress reports on each item within prescribed deadlines, indicating each time the previous circumstances, the date action had been started, and whether or not it had been successful. Then they would check on the magistrates' reports and, importantly, integrate the information into the year-end "itemized report on results" (*chengxiao shijian an* 成效事件案) that they were now to send as a palace memorial. In other words, the former "memorials on results" were not discontinued, as had been suggested by Nuoqin, but transferred from the routine to the palace memorial system and enriched with the new information gathered during the magistrates' field trips.

The Ministers also stressed an aspect that was not made explicit in the original 1723 procedure, namely, personnel evaluation: magistrates who had not demonstrated "sincere energy" in performing the audits and taking action would be censored (and of course, if it was found that the governors had failed to censor them, they would be punished as well). And, finally, they had a "further demand" to present: that the magistrates' auditing work be controlled not only by the governors-general and governors, who were too busy to exert more than nominal surveillance in the field, but also by the intendants and prefects—the intermediate rung between the counties

---

[22] See *Da Qing Gaozong Chun huangdi shili* (hereafter *GZSL*), 224/26a-27a (QL 9/9/27). A fuller text appears in SM:4-5.

and the provincial capital—who would make seasonal tours of inspection to ascertain that the magistrates were "implementing the order with sincere energy".[23]

First Results

The Ministers' proposal was approved by the emperor. Then, we may well ask, what happened? From there on, we have access to two sorts of information. First, we find in the *Veritable Records* and in the Qing central archives a limited number of entries and documents that make it possible to figure out, however spottily, the response in the provinces during the first few years after the court decision was handed down in the fall of 1744, and how the court tried to adjust its policies. And second, one especially responsive governor, Chen Hongmou, who was posted in Shaanxi at the time, has left in his administrative papers materials that enable us to give a comparatively detailed description of how the audit procedure, in its maximum interpretation, was implemented in at least one province.

The fact is, the court's instruction in 1744 could be interpreted in more or less demanding terms—either maximally or minimally—inasmuch as it was conflating two different but related procedures. One was the reports on the implementation of the edicts and approved memorials on "educating and nourishing the people" received from the central government over the years (first making up the delays accumulated since the original 1723 order, as censor Shi Jiqi had asked, and then reporting annually). The other, more demanding, procedure—designated by such phrases as *yingxing yingjin*—was having the magistrates tour their constituencies and report on the prevailing conditions following a pre-arranged list of topics, as well as on the steps they had taken to improve

[23] Shortly thereafter this part of the Ministers' deliberation was strongly criticized by a censor named Ou Kanshan 歐堪善, according to whom sending the intendants and prefects to make seasonal tours (that is, in addition to their routine trips) would only be a source of abuse and extra costs. In their rejection of his memorial the Grand Councilors estimated that, on the contrary, the collaboration of these officials with the magistrates would be quite fruitful, and that there already existed rules to make sure that the intendants and prefects were not making demands on the people and on their colleagues. See NOHA, *Yifudang* (Grand Council discussions) microfilm, roll 5, Grand Councilors' memorial approved by the emperor on QL 9/10/10.

these conditions. As we saw, the Secretaries and Nine Ministers recommended that the information on the magistrates' fieldwork be integrated into the annual reports on results (*chengxiao anjian* 成效案件) still to be sent—now by palace memorial—by the governors. The Board's instruction to the provinces clearly connected the two aspects when it said: "[To establish] whether all the imperial edicts and approved proposals from the court and the provinces over the years have been successfully implemented or not, it is ordered that the department and county magistrates travel through the villages in their constituencies to make precise investigations and report in registers; the intendants and prefects will make tours of inspection every season".[24] We shall see that a degree of confusion remained nevertheless, which provoked a discussion at court at the end of the first year of implementation.

In any case, the first one in the provinces to react to the new order seems to have been Chen Hongmou. In a memorial written at the beginning of 1745, the year following the order, he indicated that he had already sent a detailed questionnaire to all the magistrates under him several months before, and was now sending them a different version of this earlier questionnaire, adapting to Shaanxi conditions the standard list of issues established by the Board in the wake of the court decision discussed above. [25] Characteristically, Chen emphasized that such procedures served to "evaluate subordinates" (*kaoke shuli* 考課屬吏)—these are the terms in the caption of his memorial—knowing that "to keep the people in peace the most important thing is to check on officials" (*an min shou zai cha li* 安民首在察吏). The problem, he explained, was that province-wide checking on how the magistrates managed issues regarding the livelihood of the people and the improvement of customs was much more difficult than was the case with their judicial and fiscal results. The memorial also gave detailed information on how Chen had instructed the magistrates, prefects, and intendants to organize themselves so as to maximize the efficiency of the "going to the countryside" (*xiaxiang* 下鄉) program. Interestingly, it concluded on a sober note, stating: "I anticipate

[24] As quoted at the beginning of Huang Tinggui's 黃廷桂 memorial of seventh month, 1745, discussed below.

[25] Grand Council copy, NOHA, *Lufu zouzhe* microfilm, Qianlong, *Neizheng,* roll 5, frames 1502-06 (memorial of QL 10/1/25, rescript of QL 10/2/6). Abstract in *GZSL,* 233/17a-18a. Chen indicated that the court order based on Nuoqin's proposal had been received in Shaanxi as early as the tenth month of the previous year.

that, within the current year, even though the local officials' abilities vary and there are smarter and duller ones among them, still, they will [all] be able to familiarize themselves with the overall conditions of their constituencies and will get an occasion to manage some of the things to be promoted or discontinued".

There are a few indications in the sources of other governors commenting on the new procedure during its first year of implementation. Thus, an entry in the Grand Council log book indicates that during the second month of 1745 it received a memorial from Jiang Pu 蔣溥, the governor of Hunan, apparently devoted to his efforts to ensure sincerity in the "documents on the magistrates' field trips" (*zhouxian takan anjian* 州縣踏勘案件).[26] In the fourth month a memorial sent by the Shandong governor, Kaerjishan 喀爾吉善, and abstracted in the *Veritable Records*, quoted from an imperial rescript of the second month forwarded by the Board of Personnel to the effect that "All the provincial governors should send a detailed account of how the orders concerning the education and nourishment of the people received every year (*jienian suo feng jiaoyang baixing zhi shi* 節年所奉教養百姓之事) are presently being implemented, and whether or not there are results". This imperial rescript is not mentioned elsewhere, and its wording corresponds to the decision taken in the second month of the previous year, based on Shi Jiqi's memorial; in the *Veritable Records* abstract at least, Kaerjishan does not say a word about the field investigations that the magistrates had been meanwhile ordered to make.[27]

Then in the fifth month, Huang Tinggui, the governor of Gansu, sent in his turn a memorial whose contents were, in fact, not unlike those of Chen Hongmou's, in the sense that he, too, claims to have anticipated the new procedure by reaching directly to the magistrates and challenging them to

---

[26] NOHA, *Suishou dengji*, QL 10 vol., p. 33 (QL 10/2/26). The original memorial does not seem to be in the archives. Since the *Suishou dengji* volumes for QL 8 and 9 are missing, memorials on the audit procedure received at the end of 1744 may have escaped us; the volume for QL 10 stops in the middle of the seventh month, and there is no volume for QL 11. For the periods where it is available the *Suishou dengji* is supposed to record all the memorials received in the Grand Council, each entry indicating the caption (topic) of the memorial as well as the rescript.

[27] *GZSL*, 239/37b-38a. This is a very brief abstract, to be sure, including no more than a few well-balanced generalities on grain storage and local customs and concluding that magistrates should emulate each other in displaying their reverence and sincerity (kecheng 恪誠).

involve themselves in every aspect of local governance.[28] Huang's approach was typical of late-imperial activist local government: rather than allowing local officials to get lost in the maze of accumulated precedents and give reports which can only be "in name but not in reality", one should provide them with clear directives (*zhangcheng* 章程) in the form of "itemized models" (*tiaoshi* 條式) for every domain of activity (the memorial mentions sacrifices, agriculture, granaries and treasuries, taxes, bans, famine relief, prisons, canals, community granaries, tree-planting, spinning and weaving, charitable cemeteries, bridges, and roads), and order them to manage everything effectively under the surveillance of prefects and intendants. This is what he had done after assuming his post, when he could see the state of dereliction of local government in Gansu; the emperor had been informed in a memorial of the third month, 1744. Now that the new audit procedure had been ordered, Huang established with his colleagues a list of twenty items, already approved by the Board, and the magistrates were ordered to investigate and report, clearly and in detail, on what had been done regarding each of these.[29] What had prompted Huang's memorial, however, was that, Gansu being a very large province, sending the prefects and intendants on seasonal tours would keep them forever away from their offices. He requested, therefore, a reduced schedule of field trips for these officials, and the emperor accepted this on the condition that these tours be real investigations and not "empty words".

If interim comments and reports seem to have been scarce, we are told that at the end of 1745, reports were coming in. And here the confusion alluded to above becomes visible. An unsigned note of the Grand Council, dated from the tenth month, states that "as for the 'answering memorials on results' (*fuzou chengxiao* 覆奏成效) of the different provinces, from the eighth month of 1744 up till now seventeen have been received", of which eight were palace memorials and the rest were routine memorials; still missing were those of eleven governors-general and governors.[30] Two

[28] NOHA, *Lufu zouzhe* microfilm, Qianlong, *Neizheng,* roll 5, frames 1900-03 (rescript of QL 10/8/2). Abstracted in *GZSL,* 245/30a-b (QL 10/7/-). Huang Tinggui had been appointed to Gansu at the end of 1741 and was to stay there until 1748.

[29] This list is fairly close to Chen Hongmou's twenty-four items which will be detailed below.

[30] NOHA, *Yifudang* microfilm, roll 6, QL 10 vol., pp. 265-6, dated QL 10/10/20. The total number exceeds that of the provinces because governors, governors-

days later Nuoqin and Zhang Tingyu, the two chief Grand Councilors, profusely apologized because they had wrongly put the Henan governor among those late in reporting (to whom a reminder was about to be sent): in fact the governor had sent a routine memorial in the tenth month of last year, but it had been erroneously mingled with the "old memorials on results" (*jiu chengxiao ben* 舊成效本).[31] And, indeed, it does seem that neither the high officials in the provinces, nor the capital offices, were too sure of what was what in this rapidly changing system. Clearly enough, the first batch of memorials just alluded to corresponded to the "minimalist" option—in line with the decree based on Shi Jiqi's memorial—where it was just a question of updating the old procedure by listing edicts that had been received and indicating what had been done: that is to say, essentially, as seen from the governors' *yamen.* As a matter of fact, the demanding village-by-village field investigations decided upon in the ninth month of 1744 could not possibly have been completed and checked by that date (the Henan governor had memorialized one month after the decree!). Still, a certain number of governors had switched to palace memorials as ordered in the new procedure.

All of this was to be discussed seriously in the Grand Council early in 1746, at a time when it could be considered that the first year of the audit campaign was over, and when at least some of the memorials reporting on field investigations in the counties must have arrived.[32] It started with a memorial by Zhang Tingyu and others, which exposed again the problems

---

general, and Grand Canal and Tribute governors-general were all requested to memorialize.

[31] *Ibid.*, pp. 267-68, with a rescript of QL 10/10/22.

[32] As the *Suishou dengji* volume for QL 11 is missing it is impossible to assert how many such memorials (the palace memorials, at least) arrived, and when. The *Veritable Records* mention only one case, to wit, the report (received in the first month of 1746) in which the governor of Jiangxi, Saileng'e 塞楞額, submitted five items of policy to encourage, supposedly adapted to Jiangxi conditions, in addition to the standard list which (he said) he had duly ordered local officials energetically to implement; but he was rebuked by the emperor for "concerning himself with words and dispensing with reality" (*wu wen er qu shi* 務文而去實)—possibly the reason that it was mentioned at all in the *Shilu.* See *GZSL,* 257/15b-16b; in fact, the reason for the emperor's rebuke does not emerge clearly from this entry.

just referred to.[33] After recalling the origins of the procedure, they remarked:

> This rule of memorializing on results each year is a means of checking on the achievements of government and encouraging effective results, so as to avoid routinization (*yinxun* 因循). When it was originally established the method was perfectly sound; but sending these end-of-year memorials gradually became an old routine. This is why the governors-general and governors were ordered to check carefully on the reality [of the results reported] and to devote all their attention to replying point by point (*xixin tiaodui* 悉心條對). Now that the memorials of all the governors-general and governors are being received one after the other, [it can be seen that] as the case may be earlier and later affairs (*qian an hou an* 前案後案)[34] are either combined or separated in the exposition of the itemized results. Some use palace memorials and some use routine memorials; this is not standardized either. Moreover, even though all the items in the memorial are clearly set in order, there still is no true standard to prove the reality of affairs related to education and nourishment. If we continue to order that [the materials] be reported all together as usual (*zhaochang huizou* 照常彙奏), then a jumble of items will be put together on the spur of the moment, making camouflage easy, which is very contrary to the intention of striving for reality. One must order the governors-general and governors to devote all their attention to investigating in detail and strive to value effective policies. It is not necessary to set deadlines for results, which [would be conducive to] further empty documents and shirking of responsibilities. It is not necessary either to treat [earlier and later] affairs separately (*fen'an banli* 分案辦理), which causes confusion. [It will be enough to] report anew after two or three years, writing into a single palace memorial the results that will have been truly achieved or not.

[33] Quoted in SM:1-2 (where Zhang Tingyu is called a "Grand Secretary"); also in *Yifudang,* roll 6, QL 11 vol., pp. 21-24 (rescript of QL 11/2/5); shorter version in *GZSL,* 258/6b-7a (same date), where it is ascribed to "the Grand Councilors". The inclusion in the *Yifudang* shows that this was indeed a Grand Council discussion.

[34] *An,* "issues" or "cases", clearly refers to the edicts or directives received from the central government, on the implementation of which the governors were to report. What the text is saying is that when several instructions have been received over the years concerning the same problem, the governors either report on what has been done each time, or produce a synthesized assessment of their efforts.

The authors also asked that, as had been suggested by Shi Jiqi, the Grand Secretaries and Nine Ministers (that is, largely, themselves) deliberate on the memorials after all of them had been received, and moreover that they be ordered to establish directives to standardize the whole procedure.

To sum up, the Grand Councilors were stating that the results of the first year of the procedure had not been satisfactory, in particular that the lack of clarity in the directives sent around to the provinces only encouraged the usual tendencies to perfunctoriness and "glossing over" (*fenshi* 粉飾). And they asked for more time if any serious investigation into "reality" was to be made. The emperor granted two years: the reports from all the provinces would have to be sent by the end of next year (that is, 1747). For the rest he accepted the suggestions of Zhang and his colleagues, which, as we just saw, included a deliberation of the Ministers to put together clearer rules.

The text of this deliberation—literally, of this "proposal from the Grand Secretariat and other *yamen* in response [to the rescript]"—makes up most of the front part of the big "report on results" sent in 1751 by Shulu, the governor of Jiangxi, which will be described at the end of this section.[35] It includes lengthy quotations of several of the memorials and discussions analyzed above, beginning with the 1723 founding edict of the Yongzheng emperor. After reviewing the history of the procedure, the Secretaries and Ministers noted that in its three versions (that of 1723 and those of the second and ninth months of 1744) it boiled down to essentially the same thing: mobilizing the officials so as to achieve effective results in all areas of local governance. The problem was that the edicts and directives handed down over the years, excellent and useful as they were, needed to be adapted to local conditions, and that was the governors' duty to ensure. Now, reading the reports on results recently arrived, one could see that they always said that the directives had been implemented with success (*ju you chengxiao* 俱有成效), or at worst that success could not be achieved at once; they never said that something had been implemented unsuccessfully. "Such claims that in all cases there has been success really make one fear that among all the cases few are those for which there has been *real* success".

---

[35] See SM: 1-9; the proposal was approved by the emperor on QL 11/3/20. There is a brief abstract (ascribed to the Board of Personnel) in *GZSL,* 261/9b-l0b (same date).

As a consequence, the Secretaries and Ministers made several recommendations. First, keeping in mind that effective achievement could hardly be expected overnight, the governors should be required to distinguish carefully between (1) instructions that were presently being implemented with success, to which energy should be applied so as to avoid their ultimately falling into abeyance; (2) instructions that were being implemented but with no possibility of quick success, for which encouragement to strive for eventual success should be given; and (3) instructions that were definitely impossible to implement successfully because of local conditions, concerning which a clear explanation should be provided immediately upon receiving the instruction. In the cases corresponding to (1) and (2), a report would be sent at the end of next year, as ordered by the emperor; but thereafter reports would be sent only every three years, and in the form of a routine memorial.

Besides, and importantly, the dignitaries set apart the list of areas for local action proposed initially by Nuoqin. They did not mention any more the village-by-village field trips, but said that the governors would have to prepare a separate register indicating, county by county, what was the former situation regarding each of the issues, what had been undertaken, and when exactly. In other words, the procedure they proposed would make a clear distinction between, on the one hand, reports concerning the implementation of empire-wide orders received from above in the form of edicts or approved memorials, to be treated as they came; and, on the other hand, reports concerning specific policies implemented at ground level, corresponding to a standing list of issues. The two sorts of reports differed in their form, but would be sent together at three-year intervals.[36]

The 1751 Jiangxi Report on Results

Having been approved by the emperor, these proposals became the rule. If the details of their implementation are unclear, there are traces in

[36] The proposal further adds that the information written into the documents must be simple and clear and avoid discursiveness; that in provinces controlled by a governor and a governor-general the two officials must send a joint memorial (instead of one memorial each); that the provincial military commanders and regional commanders (*tizhen* 提鎮) also must report on policy implementation in their brigades; and, finally, that from now on the annual reports on results due by the ministries in the capital must dispense with duplicating information on the directives forwarded to the provinces

the routine memorials collection of the Qing archives—that is, the archives of the so-called Six Sections of the censorate, which kept copies of all the communications with the ministries. According to Philip Kuhn, a number of triennial reports on results can be found in the archives of the Personnel Section (*like* 吏科), apparently all of them dating from the middle of the eighteenth century, suggesting that the procedure did not survive beyond the mid-Qianlong years.[37]

The one such report I have been able to examine—the memorial sent by Jiangxi Governor Shulu in 1751—is a rather remarkable monument to the hardworking profession of scribe.[38] The text is spread over 669 six-column folds; apart from the front matter described above and a short conclusion, it consists entirely of apparently full quotations of edicts and approved memorials—197 entries in all[39]—on every kind of subject, having originated (for the memorials) in all the provinces of the empire,[40] circulated by the central government and received in Jiangxi between 1747 and the beginning of 1750.[41] Giving even a rough résumé of the materials quoted would be superfluous here. Suffice it to say that all areas of personnel management and field administration, civilian and military, high

---

[37] Since Kuhn's investigations in the archives were on a different topic, he did not collect systematic information on this type of document which, incidentally, seems to have puzzled the NOHA historians. Since I am not sure of when (if ever) I will have time myself to explore the immense *tiben* collection in Beijing, I have chosen to give the present account as it stands.

[38] Recall Nuoqin's criticism of what had become of the procedure instituted by the Yongzheng emperor: "One does no more than order the clerks to fill in the forms in conformity with precedent".

[39] Plus one that has been copied twice in a row, possibly by some drowsy clerk; but the short concluding comment is slightly different.

[40] A large number of these edicts and approved memorials start from some problem having occurred in a particular place and conclude with a decision enforceable everywhere in the empire. This is of course the classic process of creating "precedents". Certain of these precedents were hardly of any interest for a province like Jiangxi: a good example is a Zhejiang-inspired decision on repressing the smuggling of grain by sea (SM:84)

[41] The text says (SM:10) that the memorial dealing with directives received until 1746 has already been compiled and sent: now is the time for the triennial report covering the years 1747-49. This seems in contradiction with the above-mentioned 1746 decision that asked for a report at the end of "next year" (*i.e.*, 1747), to be followed by triennial reports. Perhaps Jiangxi was one year ahead of schedule.

and low, and all aspects of the people's life and behavior of concern to the state are represented.

How about implementation, successful or otherwise? Most entries are followed by a few words to the effect that the instruction has been forwarded to the prefectures and counties to be applied and is "on the record" (the typical, and minimal, formula being *tongxing zunzhao zai an* 通行遵照在案). Some add a few considerations or flourishes suggesting a degree of insistence on the part of the provincial government, and that the directive or new regulation has indeed been posted everywhere and, hopefully, integrated into local practice. A small number actually allude to conditions in Jiangxi, or at least insist that Jiangxi officials and citizens are particularly respectful of the law and eager to advance the policies supported by the central government—indeed, that "success has been achieved" (*yi zhu chengxiao* 已著成效).[42] But this is always very cursory, and specific details almost never appear; as a matter of fact, the document has practically no value as a source on Jiangxi. The overall impression, not surprisingly, is that of a province well administered by a disciplined bureaucracy and with no serious problem worth mentioning. One would tend to suspect that many provinces sent memorials of the same sort, and obviously the above-mentioned complaint that absence of success was never reported had been to no avail.

---

[42] See for example the comments added to entries on tax-levying methods (SM:15), tree-planting (SM:18), promoting harmony among the officials of the province (SM:20, "success has been achieved"), enforcing discipline during prefectural examinations (SM:38, same remark), controlling student behavior (SM:49, also a success), combatting speculation and hoarding (SM:60-62, where, interestingly, the comment insists that because of population growth there is no way to make prices return to their old level, but that by enforcing the directive and stopping public purchases of grain the Jiangxi authorities managed at least to check the rise), controlling underlings (SM:63-64, with "real success"), sending vagrants home (SM:65-66, 75-76, 83, same remark), making commerce flow freely (SM:7374, another successful implementation), enforcing the new 1748 ever-normal granary quotas (SM:81, 82-83, 85-86, 103-104), managing postal transmission (SM:104-105 [one of the very few entries to indicate concretely what has been done], 110-11, 112-13, 124-25, 12829), managing "life-saving boats" (SM:129-30), evaluating educational officials (SM:13940), selling ever-normal granary grain without incurring losses (SM:144-45), evaluating and moving around magistrates within the province (SM:149-50).

What is fascinating, in short, is the emptiness of it all, at least as far as the stated ambitions of the "accomplishments (*chengxiao* 成效) reports" were concerned.[43] Most entries are no more than a respectful and at the same time perfunctory acknowledgement of instructions received and passed on further down the administrative hierarchy. This may well have reflected actual practice in many cases—what we saw earlier was called "writing circulars and posting proclamations." To give but one example, an edict of 1748 concerning speculation and hoarding in Shaanxi complained that, while the governors-general and governors are required to make surprise visits and order the magistrates to strictly forbid such practices, "in fact, when [they] have received the Board's instruction they do no more than forward to the counties under them an order to issue prohibitions—it just boils down to one more proclamation; and whether the magistrates put all their energy into applying it, and if so, whether it has any effect on prices, there is no way to know".[44] In a way, the Shulu memorial looks like a sort of log book, or an "IN" file with a few words scribbled on each document received, rather than the critical account of active and creative response to the policies promoted by the throne it should have been, had the intentions of the procedure's inventors been met.

But this does not tell the whole story. The field investigations at county level were still supposed to take place. The Shulu memorial duly states in its introduction that, as soon as the order based on the "Grand Secretariat and other *yamen*" deliberation had been received from the Board, it had been forwarded to the intendants, prefects, and department and county magistrates, and that by now the registers based on their field investigations have gone through the required checks by the intermediary levels of administration and have been collected by the governor's office.[45] The memorial's conclusion specifies that while the previous field

---

[43] One should nevertheless stress that, for the general Qing historian, this account of everything that was circulated by the central government around the provinces during a period of three years is full of interesting information, much of it not found elsewhere.

[44] Quoted in SM:60.

[45] See SM:10-11. The court order was received in Jiangxi at the end of the intercalary third month of 1748. As I understand it, contrary to the 1751 "memorial on results" we are discussing here, the one "already sent" that concerned edicts and orders received up until 1746 was not accompanied by a *yingxing yingjin* register on local conditions.

investigation had followed a list of 24 items to be encouraged or prohibited, there are now only 23 items, since the one on "setting in order the officialdom" (*zheng guanfang* 整官方) is abundantly treated in the answers to the imperial edicts—that is, the "memorial on results" described above—and has been therefore removed. The registers compiled by local officials, indicating what was the current situation on each subject, what could be done to improve it, and so on—here Shulu is doing no more than reproducing the wording in the court's order—have been compiled into a "yellow register" to be presented to the emperor, "detailed registers" (*qingce* 清冊) being also sent to the ministries and censorate.

These registers from Jiangxi have apparently not survived—as a matter of fact, no register of the sort seems to be extant today. This is certainly to be regretted, since an examination of these documents would have helped us figure out, to some extent at least, how much hard information on local conditions was transmitted to the provincial government and, beyond, to the throne, and how much was simply "empty words". Indeed, it is the reality and contents of the entire campaign of audits at the county level—the village-by-village field trips envisioned by Nuoqin—that escape us. Was this all wishful thinking and phony reports, or did certain provincial governors "sincerely" attempt to mobilize the local bureaucracy under them?[46] It is here that Chen Hongmou's testimony, as we can read it in his administrative papers, adds a crucial dimension to our account.

The Audit Procedure in Shaanxi Province, 1744-1750

Chen Hongmou

At this point a few more words about Chen Hongmou may be in order.[47] Chen, whose reputation and influence went through a remarkable

---

[46] One telling detail is that Shulu's memorial was sent more than one year after the date of its last entry, which to say the least does not suggest much sense of urgency.

[47] The main authority on Chen Hongmou is William T. Rowe, who has published a book-length monograph on Chen's career and ideas (Rowe 2001). Rowe, who noted the paucity of studies on Chen (as opposed to studies making use of his writings), had previously published several articles where he figures prominently: see Rowe 1992, 1993, 1994. My understanding of Chen Hongmou and of his political and especially intellectual context owes much to Rowe's published and unpublished research. For an example of contemporary Chinese hagiography, see Zhang 1993.

revival starting with the rediscovery of his works by the "statecraft" scholars of the 1820s after a period of comparative oblivion, is an interesting character in many respects. A stern neo-Confucian and uncompromising Cheng-Zhuist—in the words of William Rowe, "abstemious and unusually straitlaced"—he was also a brilliant and devoted technocrat capable of sometimes startlingly reformist insights. As an official he accumulated a tremendous amount of experience in more than half of the empire's territory. After a few postings as prefect, circuit intendant, and provincial judge or treasurer, his career, which spanned more than forty-five years in all (from 1724 to 1771), featured a long series of provincial governorships (plus one relatively short governor-generalship in Liang-Guang in the late 1750s) that led him to about ten different provinces between 1741 and 1763. Above all, at least as far as the historian is concerned, Chen stands out because his son and grandson published that extraordinarily rich collection of texts on local government, spanning thirty years of his career in the provinces—the circulars, communications, and public addresses which compose the forty-eight chapters of the *Peiyuantang oucun gao* 培遠堂偶存稿 (surviving drafts from the Peiyuan Studio).[48]

During his lifetime Chen was famous, and considered a model official: he and his colleague and exact contemporary, the Manchu Yinjishan 尹繼善, were actually celebrated as the two best governors of the Qianlong reign.[49] They seem in fact to have been rather different types: while Yinjishan was easygoing and very popular with his colleagues, Chen Hongmou was definitively on the stern and vindictive side; indeed, he seems to have annoyed more than one person with his self-righteousness and high opinion of his own value, beginning with the Qianlong emperor himself, even though the latter could never fault him seriously and did

---

48 The *Peiyuantang oucun gao* (hereafter *PYTOCG*) is a typical example of the *gongdu* format alluded to above.

49 See for example the editor's comment following their biographies at the end of *juan* 308 of the Qing dynastic history (*Qingshi*, p. 4167). Although Yinjishan's was a little faster, the two men, who won their *jinshi* degree at a comparatively young age, had very similar careers, beginning and ending in the capital but with a long stretch in high provincial posts in between; they occasionally succeeded each other in the same province, or collaborated within the same governor-generalship. However, as a Manchu, Yinjishan was obviously closer to the center of things.

enthusiastically praise his work on many occasions.[50] Besides—and importantly for what follows—it is clear from his writings that the local officials of a province could scarcely hope to be left alone when he was the governor. Impatience and exasperation at the easygoing attitude and irresponsibility of so many magistrates comes across very frequently in the pages of the *Peiyuantang oucun gao.* One of Chen's favorite methods appears to have been to quiz the magistrates who came to visit him, only to realize that more than a few had not only failed to carefully read every one of the very important and very urgent circulars he had just sent out, but had not even the slightest idea of what they were all about.[51] One can easily imagine the feelings of a magistrate being grilled in this manner during an audience with his governor and having to admit his own inadequacies.

This forceful and impatient style is very much in evidence in the way Chen responded to the court order establishing the audit procedure and strived to enforce it in Shaanxi, where he was then governor. As we shall

[50] Chen Hongmou never incurred the dismissals and rank deprivation, sometimes imprisonment, that were not unusual in the careers of even able and successful high officials, but he was not without occasional political problems. One was his demotion in 1737 following what was deemed to be indiscrete lobbying for tax exemptions in his native Guangxi. A *Veritable Records* entry of early 1747 tells us that, when he had been Shaanxi governor (indeed, exactly at the time of the audit activity described below), he had been accused of "protecting subordinates" by the Shaan-Gan governor-general and proposed for cashiering by the Board, but in the end was maintained in his post out of imperial benevolence. Now, again, the board asked for the same sanction, apparently in connection with a case of corruption in his new province (Chen was then in Hubei). The emperor again kept him in office—for lack of another suitable candidate—but inveighed against his "lack of sincerity" when in Shaanxi, with the not too clear accusation of having "squandered his rich integrity allowance"; he was condemned to pay for the expenses of rehabilitating a city wall in Zhili (see *GZSL,* 285/5a-b). In 1754 again, the emperor accused Chen Hongmou (then in his second stay as governor of Shaanxi) of being too lenient in his evaluation of criminal cases for the Autumn assises and of being addicted to "fishing for praise" (*GZSL,* 423/2a).

[51] See *PYTOCG,* 20/16a-17a (concerning Shaanxi), and especially 32/36a-39a (concerning Fujian), where Chen inveighs against the magistrates who do not bother to read the documents and content themselves with having their private secretaries hastily prepare some notes just before they are to pay a visit to the governor. When pressed with questions by the latter, and having to admit that they know nothing of the issues, "their face becomes red and they start sweating".

see, the pieces collected in the *Peiyuantang oucun gao* provide us with a unique case study of how the procedure, which Chen took with extraordinary seriousness, was implemented in at least this province; and they also enable us to track its gradual routinization and disappearance over the next few years.

Questionnaires

When the decision taken by the court in the ninth month of 1744 was promulgated, Chen had been in the province of Shaanxi for several months—it was, in fact, to be the first of his four stays as Shaanxi governor, that totalled more than eleven years in all.[52] Significantly, he had somehow anticipated the order to have the magistrates of the province make thorough investigations in their respective territories. This is what he explained to the emperor in the memorial written at the end of the first month, 1745, that, as we saw, happens to be one of the very few detailed reactions to the 1744 order found in the record. Indeed, what Chen Hongmou had done was something of which there exist quite a few other examples in the literature, that is, sending out a detailed questionnaire to one's subordinates when arriving in a new post. Even though it may have been a fairly common practice, one can be sure that Chen's questionnaires were particularly demanding and that few were more insistent than him on getting "real" answers within the prescribed deadline, not perfunctory filling in with "empty words".

Much could be said concerning such questionnaires, whose authors clearly tried to gather more hard information on their new districts than could be gleaned following the standard recommendations found in all the official handbooks, such as reading the local gazetteer, examining the *Complete Book of Tax and Corvée,* requesting memoranda (*xuzhi* 須知) from the clerks in charge of the different *yamen* offices, and talking to local notables. Taking the initiative of circulating a detailed questionnaire certainly testified to the seriousness of the official assuming a new post. Still, one is somewhat puzzled by some of the questions, in the sense that officials like Chen Hongmou and many of his colleagues who advocated

---

[52] Chen, who was then Jiangxi governor, was appointed to Shaanxi in the tenth month of 1743; he exchanged posts with his replacement in Nanchang, Saileng'e, whom he went to replace in Xi'an. It seems that Chen reached Xi'an in (or perhaps slightly before) the third month of 1744, which is where the section of *PYTOCG* on Shaanxi starts.

the same method were requesting information much of which, one assumes, should have been readily available in their offices had government been reasonably well organized. This is the case with questions about the natural and man-made environment (the topography and hydrology, the distribution of settlements, population, and the various infrastructures), or the everyday functioning of local administration (such as fiscal quotas and surcharges, the number and location of subaltern officials, the distribution of troops, and so on). The same might be said of much of the information that Chen Hongmou ordered all the magistrates of Shaanxi to send him shortly after his arrival in the province in the form of detailed maps.[53]

In other words, one gets the disturbing impression that every new incumbent was facing a total blank, as if the information had to be collected each time from scratch, at least as long as one wanted to do more than simply close pending cases, recover taxes in arrears, and continue the routine. Indeed, it might well be that there was resistance from the clerical personnel and that the new incumbent had to earn his information, as it were. Besides, in the case of Chen Hongmou's questionnaires at least, there was an obvious and in fact explicit attempt at testing the goodwill and knowledgeability of the county magistrates, at evaluating their competence and commitment through the answers they would give to his very long list of questions.[54]

As already suggested, quite a number of such questionnaires are mentioned in the published papers (the *gongdu* anthologies) of officials of various ranks in the eighteenth and nineteenth centuries. Chen's collection cites three of them: the one just mentioned (in Shaanxi), one in Fujian, and

---

[53] See *PYTOCG,* 17/12a-15b. Chen is one among several officials who appear to have been particularly fond of representing administrative problems spatially and trying to plot as many data as possible on maps (another outstanding example is the famous early nineteenth-century specialist of local government and water conservancy, Wang Fengsheng 王鳳生: see his biography in *Xu beizhuan ji*, 34/12b-13a). Chen's instructions on how to design maps, what symbols and what colors to use, and so on, are extremely precise. He gave similar directives in Jiangxi, Fujian, Gansu, Liang-Guang, and Jiangsu (see *PYTOCG,* 12/22a, 34/15a-19a, 36/12a-18a, 41/27a, 44/5a, respectively).

[54] Referring, in the above-mentioned memorial, to his questionnaire of the 3rd month of 1744 and to the accompanying maps he had requested, Chen said: "Even those who are ordinarily sloppy (*pingri shuhuzhe* 平日疏忽者) will have to seek information and do research (*jiangqiu kaojiao* 講求考較) in order to answer the questions and produce the maps".

one in Hunan.[55] Other examples that have survived could be mentioned, from intendants, prefects, and magistrates. Of course we would like to know something of the answers. It may be that some file containing a set of answers to one such questionnaire lies dormant in some local archive, but, to my knowledge, none has surfaced so far. The only published example I know of is the summing up in 24 items of the information gathered by a late nineteenth-century acting magistrate of Funing in northern Jiangsu, a certain Ruan Benyan 阮本炎, who was apparently responding to a general (*i.e.*, Chen Hongmou-like) questionnaire sent around by the recently appointed Liang-Jiang governor-general, Zeng Guoquan 曾國荃.[56]

Some of these questionnaires basically concerned the technical functioning of the local *yamen* and the quality of the personnel therein.[57] Those which interest us here, by contrast, dealt primarily or exclusively with the territory and its people, and most of the time they were introduced by captions with the words "what should be promoted or eradicated" (*xingchu shiyi* 興除事宜), "things to promote and things to prohibit"

---

[55] The Fujian questionnaire, in thirty items, is in *PYTOCG,* 34/20a-27b. Interestingly, Chen circulated it in 1754, after two years in the province: he explains that this is an ungovernable place (an opinion shared by more than one Chinese official), that his information remains fragmentary, and that he therefore needs to know more about it. The Hunan questionnaire (in *juan* 37) was circulated after his arrival in the province in 1755.

[56] See Ruan Benyan, *Qiumu chuyan* 求牧芻言 (1884), 3/8a-15b. Zeng had been appointed at the beginning of 1884, at about the same time as Ruan Benyan. Ruan explains that he has allowed a few months to elapse so that he can tour Funing and become more familiar with its problems. Generally speaking, his observations (as most of the contents of the *Qiumu chuyan*) strike one as fairly competent and professional; it is true that Ruan had been a private secretary before becoming an official (probably by purchase).

[57] When he assumed his post in Xi'an, Chen Hongmou sent a first circular asking the prefects to evaluate the magistrates under them (lit. whether they were good or not, *xianfou* 賢否), and a second one to the commissioners and intendants (*sidao* 司道) asking them to evaluate the prefects. His third circular was the general questionnaire I am presently discussing. This was all hierarchically-ordered evaluation: Chen did not—at least, not publicly—send a secret questionnaire to the magistrates asking them about possible abuses on the part of their superiors. The only published such example I know of is found in the second batch of Tian Wenjing's 田文鏡 published administrative papers, the *Zongdu Liang-He xuanhua lu* 總督兩河宣化錄 (n.d.), 3/88a-91a.

(*yingxing yingjin* 應行應禁), "advantages and abuses" (*libi* 利弊), or other similar phrases. In other words, the attitude was interventionist and reformist, not just descriptive, and we have already seen that the same approach and the same terminology are characteristic of the audit procedure decided upon in 1744.

In questionnaires like Chen Hongmou's, a considerable array of topics was submitted to the magistrates' scrutiny, and in many cases one can see an effort to take local specificities into account rather than repeating a standard set of questions. Indeed, these lists of questions (or grids of investigation) are extremely interesting for the information they convey on the texture of the relationship between society and bureaucracy—or at least on what the elite high officials of the period deemed this relationship should be: hence the questionnaires, to make sure that everything was effectively covered. Such comprehensiveness will be apparent from the list of topics from Chen Hongmou's first Shaanxi audit in 1745, reproduced below. This is close to the arrival questionnaire he sent down to the eighty or so magistrates of the province in the third month of 1744, with instructions to answer thoroughly within two months. The latter was composed of 33 rubrics, some of which concerned the technical aspects of administration while the rest dealt with socio-economic issues. Apparently each question was followed by a blank space that the magistrate was to fill with his answer, although he was allowed to insert extra sheets if he needed.[58]

The First Stages of the Audit Procedure in Shaanxi

As Chen indicated in his memorial from the end of the first month of 1745, the new field investigations that the court was now ordering by way of the "audit" procedure were, in a way, duplicating the earlier questionnaire, the answers to which had already been received. Even though it was supposed to follow a standard list prepared by the Board, the new list of questions was basically an adaptation of the 33-rubric questionnaire of nine months before. However, since there were no more questions dealing with the technical aspects of local government, the number of entries was now only twenty-four, all of them concerning the people's condition and activities. The difference, above all, lay in the method, since in the present case the magistrates would have to go in

[58] For the text of the questionnaire, see *PYTOCG,* 17/3a-lla; the entry is entitled "Zi xun difang libi yu" 咨詢地方利弊諭.

person everywhere in order to retrieve the information, and at the same time mobilize their constituents to improve conditions.

This 24-rubric document is extremely interesting to examine. It occupies twenty double-pages of the *Peiyuantang oucun gao*,[59] significantly more than the earlier questionnaire, the reason being that each rubric—or question, if one interprets the captions as "what should be done about...?" or "what have you done about...?"—was accompanied by a sometimes quite lengthy commentary in which Chen developed the sort of problems the magistrates should concentrate on during their tours of investigation, discussed some Shaanxi specificities, and suggested what kind of answers and action he expected from them. The simple enumeration of the topics provides a sense of the range of problems in which it was considered that the state should intervene. They are as follows:

1. Regulating the scholars' customs (*xunchi shixi* 訓飭士習)
2. Emphasizing the [five] human relationships (*dundu lunchang* 敦篤倫常)
3. Taking marriage seriously (*shenzhong hunpei* 慎重婚配) (a criticism of certain marriage customs in Shaanxi, like levirate and elopement, of which, interestingly, we find the same descriptions in twentieth-century sources)
4. Extolling frugality (*chongshang jiejian* 崇尚節儉) (Chen notes that luxury and conspicuous consumption have been on the rise in Shaanxi lately)

After these articles on customs, we come to economics:

5. Opening uncultivated land (*kaiken huangdi* 開墾荒地) (dealing with marginal and non-taxable land that must nevertheless be registered with the government in order to avoid property conflicts)
6. Expanding sericulture (*guangxing cansang* 廣行蠶桑)[60]
7. Improving agricultural techniques (*xingxiu tiangong* 興修田功) (as a southerner, Chen had a very low opinion of the way Shaanxi peasants worked; this rubric also includes irrigation)

---

[59] *PYTOCG,* 119/21a-40a, entitled "Xunli xiangcun xingchu shiyi xi" 巡歷鄉村行除事宜檄.

[60] During his successive stays as Shaanxi governor Chen devoted much energy to reintroducing sericulture in the Wei valley (where it had been known in high antiquity): see Will 1994:894-97.

8. Planting trees (*guangzhi linmu* 廣植林木)
9. Disseminating community grain (*fenji sheliang* 分積社糧) (suggesting the creation of branch granaries in far-away villages;[61] this entry also deals with frugality, i.e., avoiding festive consumption in order to be able to store more)
10. Delivering taxes on time (*shuna qianliang* 輸納錢糧) (this entry also deals with the reimbursement of loans of government grain granted in times of high prices)

Then come infrastructures:

11. Maintaining the bridges and ferries (*xiuli qiaodu* 修理橋渡) (this rubric essentially deals with roads)
12. Repairing and building village walls (*xiuqi chengbao* 秀葺城堡) (walled villages were a characteristic of the region)

Then again customs:

13. Forbidding heterodox techniques (*jinzhi xieshu* 禁止邪術) (sorcerers and other medicine-men being apparently very active in the region)
14. Giving instructions on (proper) funerals (*shenchi sangzang* 申飭喪葬)
15. Forbidding plays at funerals (*jinzhi sangxi* 禁止喪戲) (another shocking Shaanxi custom)
16. Forbidding nightly operatic shows (*jinzhi yexi* 禁止夜戲) (also a Shaanxi specialty, at least if we are to believe Chen)
17. Severely investigating gambling (*yancha dubo* 嚴查賭博)
18. Curbing fights (*chana dajiang* 查拿打降)[62] (according to Chen, Shaanxi people are particularly violent; this, to be sure, is a cliché that one can find concerning all the northern provinces)
19. Prohibiting resistance against justice (*yanjin diaokang* 嚴禁刁抗)
20. Discouraging litigation (*quanxi songduan* 勸息訟端)
21. Warning against suicide (*qiejie qingsheng* 切戒輕生) (this also is introduced as a bad habit in Shaanxi, but the theme is universal in official writings)

And finally, security:

---

[61] The dispersion of settlements in Shaanxi is mentioned at the beginning of the document as one reason for the gap between officials and people.

[62] The term *dajiang*, which was also found in Nuoqin's original memorial, seems to refer to a kind of vendetta.

22. Interrogating traitors (*panjie jiangui* 盤詰奸宄) (referring to a particular brand of roving beggar-bandits called *guazi* 卦子, who appear to have been particularly aggressive in the region)
23. Controlling military exiles (*yueshu junliu* 約束軍流)
24. Checking unemployed vagrants (*jicha youduo* 稽查游惰)

Every one of these points would deserve further comment, considering especially that they are the subject of so many circulars and proclamations, both by Chen Hongmou himself and by a quantity of other officials in other provinces and at other times, who likewise published their administrative writings. This would go beyond the scope of this essay, however, and in the following I will concentrate, rather, on the methodological aspects of the audit campaign, and more particularly on its "communication" aspects, that is, how all this investigating and lecturing was supposed to have an impact on the population.

This brings us back to some of the considerations offered above on the methods of "educating" the people that were advocated by the more committed among officials. In the 1744 system of audits decided on by the court, the magistrates were supposed to visit personally each and every settlement (filling in forms indicating the date and place), instruct their inhabitants in the above-mentioned subjects, and initiate reforms—the so-called "promoting and suppressing" (*xingchu* 興除). Chen Hongmou strongly insisted that it should be done this way: as he says in one of his texts quoted below, the magistrates must "go all over and know everything" (*bianyue zhouzhi* 遍閱周知). This, again, was the crucial difference between that procedure and the more usual questionnaires, to which the magistrates could give honest and competent answers based on the files at hand and on the information provided by their staff—in other words, without moving from their offices.[63] The difference is also highlighted by the difference in deadlines: while Chen Hongmou allowed his magistrates no more than two months to answer the 33-rubric questionnaire composed at his arrival in the province, now, in line with the court's order, they will have six, or even twelve, months to do the annual audit.

[63] The difference should not be overstressed, however. Chen's early 1744 questionnaire was already strongly "action-oriented", since it required the magistrates not only to describe the current situation and identify the problems, but also to make proposals on how to handle the issues (*ruhe banli* 如何辦理).

Chen also made an important move to enhance the usefulness and efficiency of the field visits, which by definition could only be very cursory. He had the set of 24 rubrics just described printed in the form of "information booklets" (*shiben* 示本), which he sent to all the counties, where they were supposed to be disseminated among the village chiefs (the *xiangyue* 鄉約 and *dibao* 地保), who would in turn expound their contents to the populace, among whom everybody was then supposed to instruct each other.[64] In this way, when the officials came down, they would be able to dispense their instructions to people who *already* knew what it was all about and had had time to discuss the issues among themselves.

We may note that this reliance on the spontaneous dissemination of official information and instruction from person to person—by word of mouth, as it were (*zhuanxiang chuanshu* 轉相傳述)—is fairly common in the literature, and we may well wonder how it worked in reality. In the present case, at least, it seems to have been rather carefully organized, and indeed, Chen insists in several instances on the crucial importance of such preparatory steps for the eventual success of the entire operation. The persons who would be at the source of the propaganda—the village chiefs—had to be provided with the necessary materials, and their efforts would be carefully monitored by the officials. (We will see that, at the beginning certainly, the officials were not all up to the task). It is also worth stressing that, in Chen's and his colleagues' vision, the entire process was to concern the officials, the village chiefs nominated by the citizenry, and the citizenry itself (the "literati and people", as the phrase runs), exclusively: nowhere does the considerable apparatus of clerks and other *yamen* employees intervene in any way. As we recalled above, they were the ones to be carefully kept out of the process if any "sincerity" was to be guaranteed.

Before examining how this system of preliminary distribution of written materials may have worked, let me first say a word about the way Chen Hongmou envisioned the travels of the officials through the countryside. His already-mentioned first-month, 1745 memorial, for example, reports to the emperor how, on the one hand, he is urging magistrates to take advantage of every occasion to speak directly to the

---

[64] This is mentioned in the above-mentioned first month, 1745 memorial. There are more details in a later directive by Chen Hongmou: see *PYTOCG*, 21/2a-5a, dated 7th month, 1745 (see below).

people, while on the other hand they will have to make extra visits in order to meet the court's expectation of a total coverage of the territory:

> [What should be encouraged and what should be forbidden] I have enumerated in a proclamation which I have had printed and distributed. At the same time, I have ordered local officials who have to go to the countryside for public business to assemble the gentry and people in the more populous places among the villages nearby, to immediately settle conflicts, and to go in person to see whatever can be done as far as agriculture and irrigation are concerned. As for the villages in which there is no particular public business to attend to, the officials will make special visits later, within six months in counties easy to administer (*jian* 簡), and within one year in busy counties (*fan* 繁). They must absolutely go all over and know everything.

The same theme is developed in another text, this time found in a set of instructions on what their behavior should be, that Chen Hongmou circulated among all the officials of the province at the beginning of the first year of audit; that particular entry was entitled *Guang hua hui* 廣化誨, or, "To enlarge education".[65] The beginning deplores that the populace and the ranking officials have so little occasion to see each other, except for lawsuits or fiscal hearings, and that, consequently, it is so difficult to educate the people. Then, after having alluded to the "information booklets" just mentioned, Chen discusses the field visits of the officials in the following way:

> Whenever the magistrates have to travel to the countryside to attend to public business, they will gather the small folk in every village and hamlet along the road; they will select the most important points among the articles composing the directive (i.e., the 24-rubric questionnaire), will ask people about the current situation [relative to those articles], and will personally exhort them in the most insistent fashion; moreover, they will encourage them to propagate these teachings from one person to the next. And they will act the same way in the villages and hamlets they go through on their way back. If they go through the same places again, they will propagate the same directives anew and ask how things have been since their previous visit.

[65] See *PYTOCG,* 20/lla-24b, "Shenchi guanzhen baze xi" (dated 3rd month, 1745); "Guang hua hui" is the third of these "eight (in fact, ten in the *PYTOCG* text) admonitions to officials"; it was later anthologized in the *Muling shu,* 16/lb-3a.

Chen Hongmou also says that one must not hesitate to go out of one's way to visit villages not located on the road one is supposed to take. One should not, in his words, "just come and go (*sui lai sui qu* 隨來隨去) and hasten back to one's offices". What he advocates is trying to move as much as possible of the magistrate's activity to the countryside, especially where conflicts and lawsuits are concerned. Resolving conflicts on the spot saves both expense and trouble and, above all, it allows the magistrate to apply and celebrate the laws of the state directly in the villages, admonishing the populace accordingly. Only the treatment of important crimes should be moved back to the *yamen.*

There is much more in this directive, but here I will simply mention its conclusion, which sums up the philosophy of the entire operation. Through this intensive campaign of on-site instruction, officials and people will first know each other (*xiangzhi* 相知), and then trust each other (*xiangxin* 相信); as a result (says Chen), "big affairs will become small, and small affairs will disappear" (*dashi hua xiao, xiaoshi hua wu* 大事化小，小事化無). To this Chen adds the important notion that the people are the final arbiter: local officials occasionally can deceive their superiors over their actual behavior, but "no one can deceive the ignorant folk" (*bu neng yi qi yumin* 不能以欺愚民).

What is indeed remarkable in Chen's proclamations and instructions related to the audit campaign is this characteristic mix of, on the one hand, grand declarations of principles and quasi-utopian demands on his subordinates and, on the other hand, realistic assessments of the situation and of the difficulties involved. In a circular dating from the same month, Chen openly admits that the requirements of the central government—namely, that the magistrates visit every village in their district within six months and write down the places and dates in a register alongside their observations—are exactly of the sort that encourage local officials to fill in the forms without even leaving their offices. In line with Chen's ambition (not to say obsession) of inventing ways to force his subordinates to do more than just *pretend*, this circular attempts to introduce some flexibility into the process and to imagine methods that will allow them to make the field investigations fit into their already extremely busy schedules.[66]

[66] *PYTOCG*, 20/8a-l0b, dated 3rd month, 1745.

First Results

All this is very well, but were Shaanxi magistrates in 1745 up to their governor's exhortations and expectations? Interestingly, while at the start the process appears to have been rather slow to take off, thanks to the insistence of an exasperated Chen—and also because he was ready to allow magistrates some flexibility in their methods—results seem nevertheless to have been obtained within the first year of audit, with which even this ever-demanding man was not totally dissatisfied. In fact, he seemed rather pleased with what he had achieved.

The initial difficulties, obviously due to the fact that the magistrates were tired of being showered with questionnaires by governors like Chen Hongmou, are well in evidence in a circular of the seventh month, 1745 in which Chen discusses the mixed success met by his campaign to disseminate the "demonstration booklets" just alluded to.[67] The print run he had sent out to the counties clearly was not sufficient, and the magistrates' commitment (or lack thereof) could be seen in the way they reacted to this. On the one hand were those who ordered more copies at the provincial capital, or had more printed at their own expense, or even produced sets of posters based on the booklet: these were the serious magistrates that Chen warmly congratulated. On the other hand were those who did not really care. Some were content with distributing the limited stock they had received; others just kept it in their offices; yet others had duly distributed it but did not bother to check that the village chiefs were not keeping them in their houses and forgetting about it. In Chen's eyes, all these people were simply botching the preliminary stage of the campaign.

For the negligent magistrates Chen had very harsh words, and he ended his circular in exasperation, wondering, if there were such carelessness and indifference in the counties, how he was going to compile the register and compose the memorial he was supposed to send to the throne at the end of the year (the local investigations, he insisted, must imperatively be completed by the end of tenth month).

This outburst may have had some effect, since the later assessments of the campaign appear somewhat more optimistic. To be sure, they all use the same rhetorical balance as in the circular just mentioned: on the one hand are the good officials, of whom one can always be sure that (as the

[67] *PYTOCG*, 21/2a-5a. The text is a good illustration of how carefully Chen was controlling what was going on in the counties.

phrase goes) "they definitely also exist" (*gu yi you zhi* 固亦有之); on the other hand are all the others. But while in his seventh-month circular Chen said that the latter—those for whom the whole thing was no more than "empty words on a sheet of paper"—were "very numerous", implying, in fact, that they were the majority, the final assessment of the 1745 audit is of a fairly different tone.

This assessment is found in a circular of the fourth month of the following year.[68] According to Chen, all the counties had eventually sent in their registers (that is, the answers to the questionnaire), and the results they announced had been carefully checked by the provincial authorities. Thus, Chen had been able to compile a "yellow register" and to send it to the throne with a memorial of presentation.[69] He notes in the same document that, while some magistrates have demonstrated enthusiasm, efficiency, and obvious "sincerity", others have been indisputably more superficial and less thorough in their answers. But he claims that in every case one gets the impression that officials and people are getting closer to each other, and that in time one will be able to get an in-depth and operational knowledge of the field and of its inhabitants. How far this was wishful thinking we cannot know, but in any case in the eyes of militant field officials like Chen Hongmou it was obviously the ultimate goal.

Chen also states that even where the magistrates did not start improvement programs, at least the local populace could become aware of the problems and of what should be improved. For this "becoming aware", interestingly, he uses the term *ganwu* 感悟. Without going so far as to speak of "illumination" here, it remains that the notion of making ordinary people suddenly aware of advantages that lay in front of them, but that they are unable to see, is central to the theory and methodology of the program of agricultural improvement that mobilized much of the

---

[68] *PYTOCG,* 23/43a-46b. During the eighth month of 1745, already, a circular of a more technical nature (*ibid.*, 21/21a-22b) claimed that the magistrates were now actively "compiling their registers". Chen urged them to avoid generalities and verbosity and to expose the specific problems of each district (*xiang* 鄉) carefully; indeed, the circular said that two recently arrived reports had been turned down for being "simplistic and verbose" (*goujian fufan* 苟簡浮汎), while two more were retained as satisfactory. One may note that, while the county reports were supposed to be controlled and abstracted at prefectural level, apparently Chen Hongmou had copies directly sent for his own inspection.

[69] This memorial got the usual rescript *Zhidao le; ce liu lan* 知道了，冊留覽 ("Seen; I keep the registers to read them"), which sounds a little anticlimactic after all this excitation.

government's energies at that time[70]—and indeed, that informed the *xingchu shiyi* procedure as well. Without the intervention and push of the state and its officials, in other words, the society's potential for improvement and development could only lie dormant.

Chen, never one to be deluded by phony reports, had also to acknowledge that several reports were still as verbose as they were insincere—that is to say, their authors plainly had not done the investigative work that was requested of them, and a few more were simply trying to cheat by presenting a misleading account of their constituencies and of their work (*jiang wu zuo you, yi you wei wu* 將無作有以有為無).

The Follow-up

Still, as I said, the general tone of this lengthy assessment, which Chen says is based on a careful re-reading of the entire file of the preceding year, and which he reiterates elsewhere, is rather on the optimistic side, and this of course leads us to wonder what the follow-up may have been. Indeed, the main object of the circular just cited is not the 1745 campaign of audits, now concluded, but the new one for 1746 which has already been started. It informs (or reminds) its readers that the court has lowered its expectations somewhat, by agreeing that the reports be sent not at the end of this year, but of the next one. But Chen Hongmou was not one to allow the operation to lose momentum. In fact, even though the court is only expecting a report at the end of 1747, he now urges his own officials to deliver interim reports at the end of the current year, 1746, only to do it again next year; the two audits will be combined to produce the report sent to the throne.

In other words, what Chen Hongmou is trying to obtain from the magistrates of his province—in ordering them to constantly update their 24-rubric registers and also to show their creativity by adapting them to the local specificities of their districts—is to integrate the systematic annual field investigations and interventions originally required by the audit procedure into their routine activities and, one might almost say, into their style of working. This is the main point. Reading through all the proclamations and circulars produced by Chen during this episode, one gets the impression that he attempted to subtly transform the new procedure, the basic purpose of which was to evaluate the magistrates, into

[70] See Will 1994.

a tool to enforce his own ideal of interventionist and idealistic field government. Or, to put it differently, to transform routine managers, intent on preventing problems from occurring, into reformist activists. Had he succeeded in this extraordinarily ambitious attempt, it would without any doubt have been a small revolution.

It is clear that he did not, however, and indeed that he could not. Even though Chen's papers include some more documents discussing technical points and urging the magistrates to accumulate information and to take action, we do not know what the results of the 1746 and 1747 campaigns of audit in Shaanxi may have been. Before the end of 1746 Chen was transferred to Hubei, where he spent the entire year 1747 and where, interestingly, his administrative papers do not say a word of any *xingchu shiyi* campaign. The audit procedure had not fallen into oblivion, however. As we have seen when studying the memorial sent from Jiangxi by Governor Shulu in 1751, registers were still being compiled at county level, based on questionnaires. Chen Hongmou resumed the post of Shaanxi governor in the spring of 1748, and later during this year—in the ninth month—he did promulgate a slightly revised version of the 24-rubric list of topics for investigation which we have described earlier.[71] But we do not have any details on the methods adopted, on how the investigations were conducted, and on what the results were.

What we do know, on the other hand, and what may explain this absence of information, is that, shortly after this circular had been promulgated, much of the officialdom of Shaanxi was engulfed in the tasks and inconvenience of providing logistical support for the imperial army that was then proceeding through the Shaanxi core on its way to the Jinchuan theater (in western Sichuan). From the numerous documents about this found in the *Peiyuantang oucun gao* it is clear, and in fact, explicitly said by Chen Hongmou, that the administration of the province

---

[71] *PYTOCG,* 27/24a-49a. Compared with the original 24-rubric list, the new list shows some variants of wording and order. There are a few changes of content, too: for example, Chen mentions the developments produced by his campaign for promoting sericulture. He also seems to imply that the problem of Buddhist pilgrimages (*chaoshan* 朝山), which were a pretext for much agitation and for behavior profoundly shocking to someone like Chen (mixing men and women, etc.), has tended to grow worse: while people used to show their religious enthusiasm by firing rifles, now they are firing cannon. There is also a new entry on alcohol making.

was totally disorganized for more than half a year.[72] Subduing the Jinchuan rebels was a serious matter and, obviously, the auditing and investigating activity had to go by the board.[73]

And yet it did not disappear. More than one year later, in the third month of 1750, another circular of Chen's indicates that the magistrates had been required to send a new report at the end of 1749. The text in fact vehemently criticizes one of these reports, considered to be devoid of any substance.[74] It also recalls that at that moment the court only required triennial audits, not even biennial.[75] More importantly for our purpose, it is by now obvious that even in a province governed by a Chen Hongmou the procedure had by then become completely routinized. Magistrates were only required to mention changes that had taken place since the previous report, and Chen had to admit that in the eyes of most of them the procedure was useless: it only duplicated what they had to discuss in any case in their regular correspondence. Enthusiasm had clearly fallen away. The effort at communicating directly with the people, the ambition not to neglect one single settlement, which were at the heart of the audit procedure started in 1744, as it had been envisioned by Nuoqin and ardently supported by Chen, are no longer mentioned. In other words, it very much looks as if the audits had been emptied of their more original and militant contents.

---

[72] See in particular *PYTOCG,* 29/2a-b. All the *PYTOCG* entries from the 10th month, 1748 to the 4th month, 1749 are devoted to logistics, notably the furnishing of mounts to the army and the endless complications and abuses it entailed.

[73] Incidentally, the emperor was not completely satisfied with Chen Hongmou's performance in supporting the army. In an edict from the end of 1748 (quoted in SM:100-101) that assessed the work of the chief officials in the various North China provinces involved in logistical support, Qianlong remarked that Chen, "as a Chinese, is not particularly good at managing these things", for which reason he had sent Yinjishan (a Manchu) to take charge temporarily. In spite of his errors Chen was not punished because the emperor "remembered that the Chinese must not necessarily be entrusted with urgent public matters" (*ben bu bi ze yi jigong* 本不必責以急公). Manchu pride runs high in this and other edicts on the Jinchuan expedition that were circulated among all the provinces (hence their inclusion in SM, whose author had not much more to say than: "On record").

[74] *PYTOCG,* 29/32a-33b.

[75] As we saw earlier, this decision had been taken as early as the third month of 1746.

Conclusion

And there it stops, at least as far as Shaanxi is concerned. Although Chen Hongmou spent several more years administering the province, down to 1757, we hear no more of the annual *xingchu shiyi* field visits and reports in his papers. One can safely assume that the procedure in its more activist version very soon fell into oblivion and that what remained was mere paperwork. As for the paperwork itself, as we saw it is not known how long the triennial documents that purported to inform the central government of the implementation of its directives and of the work accomplished in every county of the empire continued to be sent. In any case it seems highly probable that they were discontinued at some point during the Qianlong reign.[76]

This failure is by no means surprising. The 1744 annual audit program is not the only example of the Qing court and its most activist bureaucrats attempting to enhance (and in this case, dramatically so) the level and intensity of the local bureaucracy's intervention in society. But at the same time, and again as in other similar cases, they did not increase its resources in terms of personnel or capital in any way. As usual, it was to be entirely a question of mobilization, of enthusiasm, and of devotion on the part of magistrates who were required to do the impossible, or at least the nearly impossible, if only to demonstrate their "sincerity". In the present case, while they were known to be overburdened by the tasks in their *yamen* and by the demands of their superiors, they were at the same time invited to travel up and down their districts like campaigning politicians who would simultaneously be social workers, field investigators, and missionaries. This tension between the constraints of everyday administration and a reformist enthusiasm actively encouraged by the throne, which wanted to get more with the same resources, is a characteristic feature of the high Qing approach to local government.

In spite of these contradictions, we may well ask what a provincial governor of the class of Chen Hongmou, who was prone to take the maximalist instructions of the court at face value, was able to achieve among his subordinates. For one thing, I am tempted to consider that, coming from the sort of person who is never satisfied, such as Chen Hongmou, who was constantly accusing his subordinates of sabotage or, at

[76] In this respect it is significant that, so far as I can ascertain, no trace of it can be found in the institutional compendia of the Qing dynasty, the *Da Qing huidian* and the accompanying *Da Qing huidian shili*.

best, indifference, the comparatively self-congratulatory evaluation mentioned above should not be overlooked. I do think that he achieved something, and that he was not without hopes that Shaanxi might soon enter a new age in terms of the quality, texture, and indeed nature of the relationship between local officials and their constituencies.[77] But what was he able to do exactly?

This is certainly not easy to ascertain. While Chen's account of the audit campaign in the *Peiyuantang oucun gao* is uniquely rich compared to the other sources on this episode, if still rather thin on detail about what actually happened in the field, as opposed to Chen's perceptions from his gubernatorial *yamen*. It is nevertheless possible to suggest some hypotheses—and I insist that what I propose here is decidedly on the cautious side. Even though Chen may have exaggerated a little in his various assessments of his own efforts, it seems obvious that he was able to give rise to a considerable amount of activity in much of the province. Knowing his insistence on being kept constantly informed, his no-nonsense attitude, and his manner of sending back reports that did not satisfy him, there cannot have been many places where, in effect, nothing happened. There might even have been some enthusiasm on the part of a minority of particularly militant magistrates. And this high level of mobilization continued for at least two years (1745 and 1746). In the process, a sizable proportion of the magistrates and prefects of Shaanxi—what proportion we cannot know—must have visited their terrain much more intensively than usual. Likewise, the quantity of hard information on local conditions (as opposed to generalities and "empty words") that reached Xi'an must have been exceptional, thanks to the systematic effort that was made to retrieve it. And finally, local improvement projects in such areas as irrigation, promotion of handicrafts, road maintenance, and so on, may have been accelerated due to the pressure that was put on magistrates not only to investigate but also to report on what had been realized.[78] After all this was, indisputably, a "campaign".

While the impossible level of mobilization attempted by Chen Hongmou—and perhaps by some of his colleagues as well, although we lack the information—could hardly be maintained for long, it cannot be

[77] Rowe has noted that in Chen Hongmou's career as a governor Shaanxi was, for a variety of reasons, including its specific intellectual tradition, a favorite province—almost a "model province".

[78] Only a careful examination of local gazetteers might possibly indicate whether the late 1740s saw a spur in local projects in Shaanxi.

altogether excluded that, through the institution of new guidelines, sets of local regulations, and other "covenants", for example, it did improve standards in a certain number of areas for a period that exceeded the audit campaign itself. This, again, can only be hypothetical. In particular, we cannot know whether officials got closer to the people, at least in the quasi-emotional sense meant by Chen and many local government enthusiasts, and whether popular consciousness and education (or "customs") were significantly changed by the episode. I tend to doubt that such could be the case in the long run, if only because of the usually fast turnover of officials (governors included) in the provinces. Still, it is quite possible that during the first stages of the campaign the inhabitants of Shaanxi (whose voices are nowhere to be heard in the sources, of course) realized that something special was going on, as it is possible, and even probable, that an unaccustomed proportion of them were reached by official directives and intervention, and perhaps also—since this was the gist of the entire effort after all—*saw* officials.

It would be far-fetched, however, to compare the *xingchu shiyi* campaign as it was envisioned and, as it seems, realized at least in part by Chen Hongmou, to one of those *yundong* that were imposed again and again upon the Chinese during the twentieth century. For one thing, the officials were the target of mobilization, not the populace, at least not directly. The populace was to be taught about what was in its best interest, and to be listened to in order that officials could learn of conflicts and areas of problem and ascertain the popularity of government policies. The populace was in no case intended to be—even in words—the leading edge of the movement and its inspiration.

Here the important distinctions proposed by Philip Kuhn in his classic essay on local self-government must be kept in mind.[79] Mobilization as it was understood by the late Qing constitutionalists—anticipating the "movements" of Republican and especially communist China—was meant to reach the mass of private citizens and enlist them in an overall effort at nation building and economic development under the leadership of the state. Patriotism and "Darwinian" energy mobilized locally would be the engine of what was considered to be a struggle, not against a difficult environment but against the forces that threatened China.

This is in total contrast with what was pursued in campaigns such as the one led by Chen Hongmou in Shaanxi in 1745-46, where it seems clear to me that the goal was (to use Kuhn's words when opposing the

[79] See Kuhn 1975:268-75.

traditional and the modernizing way) "the maintenance of a stable social and economic system". This system was felt to be in imperfect condition, and therefore ill-prepared to face the challenges of demographic and economic growth—hence the heroic efforts of activist emperors and idealist bureaucrats to restore official discipline, instruct the populace in the correct values, and improve the use of existing resources. If maintenance was the goal, improvement and adjustment were the immediate problem.

As we saw, the efforts spurred by Nuoqin's proposal of 1744, which in the case of Chen Hongmou were certainly heroic, appear to have been short lived and devoid of much long-term consequence. For this reason, the Qing institutional historian might be tempted to consider that this was just one more impracticable plan handed down by the court for "sincere implementation", but without any concrete measure to make it workable. It was therefore sure to be considered by a vast majority of officials in the field as "empty words on a piece of paper" and doomed to fast oblivion, in spite of a few earnest attempts at enforcement. And in a way it was just that. Does this make the episode less interesting or important to analyze? A superficial reaction after hearing of the audit procedure and its eventual and seemingly rapid failure and disappearance might be to ask: "Then what?" But, on the contrary, it seems to me that the process described above is of considerable interest.

It is, above all, interesting as an illustration of the anxiety that was felt by the Qing rulers and a significant part of the official elite in the face of the vast number of unresolved problems both in the empire and in the way it was governed, and of the reported inadequacy of the bureaucracy to meet them, at a time when the regime was supposed to be at its height. What makes the annual audit procedure more than a paper-producing, empty attempt at control from the top is that, in calling as it did for a surge in the activity and efficiency of magistrates, the court was meeting the preoccupations and ideals of the more activist, concerned, and influential segment of the field bureaucracy. There is no want of official handbooks, and especially of *gongdu*-type collections of documents (representing the efforts and achievements of individual officials, however embellished), showing people who did exactly that: desperately trying to know everything, reach out to the terrain, and improve conditions by a mix of moral-political persuasion and technical expertise and ingenuity. This is the case, not only during the mid-eighteenth century, but during the entire duration of the Qing dynasty, and also before.[80]

The 1744 attempt at reforming the working style of the most vital link in the field administration, making it more responsive to the challenges of the time and enhancing its output, was therefore not completely futile. Chen Hongmou's response at least demonstrates eloquently that activists could take advantage of such court orders to advance their own projects and methods, and these were fundamentally in harmony with the dynastic view of what local government should be.[81] The problem, of course, was the institutional conservatism that pervaded the system: no serious structural reform was ever contemplated that would have made the procedure workable—or, to put it in other terms, that would have made it both routinized and efficient, as no doubt Chen Hongmou dreamt it might become. As a result, after this brief episode of general mobilization, improvement in local administration could only remain as it always had been: a matter of individual initiative, possibly encouraged by activist provincial chiefs, and left to a minority of elite magistrates, whose visibility was certainly greater than their statistical significance among the vast majority of "ordinary" officials who ran the empire as usual.[82]

---

[80] To give just one example: The *Juguan bilan* 居官必覽 *by* Jin Yongzhai 金庸齋 (1757), which is an adaptation of Yuan Liaofan's 袁了凡 *Gongguo ge* 功過格 (Scales of Merits and Demerits) to administrative problems, has a large section on "promoting and discontinuing" (*xingge,* 1/15b-88b) that includes detailed discussions of all the improvement policies mentioned in this article, and more; for each undertaking the number of "merits" earned by the official is indicated. There are also lengthy sections on touring the county and visiting the people in person in order to "educate" them.

[81] As we saw, apart from Chen's testimony there exist only a few frustrating bits of evidence. Recall, however, the comments sent by Huang Tinggui, Chen's colleague in Gansu, in the fifth month of 1745. Like Chen, Huang had anticipated the procedure by attempting on his own initiative to mobilize the magistrates in his province, which may suggest that he, too, took advantage of the audit procedure to further his policies.

[82] There is obviously no way of asserting "statistically" the proportion of activists and reformists among the local officialdom. We can only follow the opinion of one of the most knowledgeable students of Qing local government, John Watt (1970:30-31), who speaks of a vast "center" of mediocre magistrates, with small minorities of "good" and "bad" officials on each side.

Acknowledgement

Earlier versions of this research were presented at Princeton University, at the University of California at Berkeley, and at Leiden University. Special thanks are due to Beatrice Bartlett, who gave precious advice on where to look in the archives; to Philip Kuhn, who provided one crucial document that will be introduced above; and to William Rowe, who communicated to me draft chapters from his monograph in progress on Chen Hongmou (since then published as Rowe 2001], some of which is of immediate relevance for my discussion here.

References

Bartlett, B.S., (1991), *Monarchs and Ministers: The Grand Council in Mid-Ch'ing China, 1723-1820,* Berkeley: University of California Press.

Chen, Fu-mei Chang, (1976), "Provincial Documents of Laws and Regulations in the Ch'ing Period", *Ch'ing-shih wen-ti* 3/6: 28-48.

Ch'ü, T'ung-tsu, (1962) *Local Government in China under the Ch'ing,* Cambridge, Mass.: Harvard University Press.

Elman, B., - Woodside, A., (eds.), (1994), *Education and Society in Late Imperial China, 1600-1800,* Berkeley: University of California Press.

Fu Zongmao, (1967), *Qingdai junjichu zuzhi ji zhizhang zhi yanjiu* (The Organization and Functions of the Grand Council in the Qing), Taipei: Jiaxin shuini gongsi wenhua jijinhui.

Huang, R., (1981), *1587, A Year of No Significance: The Ming Dynasty in Decline,* New Haven: Yale University Press.

Kuhn, P.A., (1975), "Local Self-government under the Republic: Problems of Control, Autonomy, and Mobilization", in Wakeman - Grant (eds.), *Conflict and Control in Late Imperial China*: 257-98.

Miyazaki, Ichisada, (1950), Introduction to Kyodai Toyoshi kenkyushitsu (comp.), *Kanshin mokuji sogo sakuin* (Combined Index to the Tables of Contents of Official Handbooks), Kyoto, mimeo.

Rowe, W.T., (1992), "Women and the Family in Mid-Qing Social Thought: The Case of Chen Hongmou", *Late Imperial China,* 13/2:1-41.

—. (1993), "State and Market in Mid-Qing Economic Thought: The Career of Chen Hongmou (1696-1771)", *Études chinoises,* 12/1:7-40.

—. (1994), "Education and Empire in Southwest China: Ch'en Hung-mou in Yunnan, 1733-38", in Elman - Woodside (eds.), *Education and Society in Late Imperial China, 1600-1800*: 417-57.

—. (2001), *Saving the world: Chen Hongmou and Elite Consciousness in Eighteenth-Century China*, Stanford: Stanford University Press.

Saeki, Tomi, (1975), *Fukkei zensho goi kai* (Index to the Terms in the *Fuhui quanshu*), Kyoto: Dōbōsha.

Wakeman, Jr., F. – Grant, C., (eds.), (1975), *Conflict and Control in Late Imperial China.* Berkeley: University of California Center for Chinese Studies.

Watt, J.R., (1970), "Leadership Criteria in Late Imperial China", *Ch'ing-shih wen-t'i*, 2/3:17-39.

—. (1972), *The District Magistrate in Late Imperial China.* New York: Columbia University Press.

Will, P.É., (1989), "Bureaucratie officielle et bureaucratie réelle á la fin de l'empire", *Études chinoises,* 8/1:69-142.

—. (1994), "Développement quantitatif et développement qualitatif en Chine á la fin de l'époque imperial", *Annales: Histoire, Sciences sociales,* 44/4:863-902.

Zhang, Fang, (1993), "Qingdai rexin shuili de Chen Hongmou" (Chen Hongmou, an Enthusiastic Hydraulician of the Qing Period), *Zhongguo keji shiliao,* 14/3.

CHAPTER TWELVE

WHAT STATUS FOR SERVICE TO THE LORD? THE CLERKS AT THE MINT AND GENERAL WAREHOUSE OF KANAZAWA

GUILLAUME CARRÉ

The Retainers' Matrix

The warrior regime which dominated Japan during the Edo (1600-1867) progressively engendered "bureaucratic" systems of government that were not really known under the medieval Shogunates. But the word *kanryôsei*, frequently employed to characterize forms of feudal lord control over society, is merely a translation of the expression "bureaucratic system", as it is used in sociology or in western political science. It reinforces therefore the idea of an administration run by State functionaries: the term *kanryô* has since then been used to designate functionaries in contemporary Japan (perhaps with a certain predilection for the upper ranks of the administration or central administrations in general). In the Edo period, such concepts were not used, even if related words can be found in political thought modeled on Chinese studies. The preferred term for designating individuals who constituted the cogs of administrative apparatus in early modern times was *yakunin*, the "officials", or, more exactly, "those who realize a service" under charge by seigneurial power, identified with Public Authority. Since the new disposition of authority through administration blossomed in the heart of the territories of the seigneurial principalities ruled by the great feudal lords, or daimyô (there were around 270 fiefdoms or "domains" in the 1860s), there was no essential difference between the administration of a seigneurial principality and that of the Shogunate: in practice the latter dealt particularly with the lands of the Tokugawa clan and with some exceptions did not exercise control over the governing of the principalities.

The principalities managed their own affairs in an autonomous manner, and reproduced, on a reduced scale, the same organs of government that were installed in the Shogunal capital of Edo.

Therefore, if there was a "bureaucratic system" under the Tokugawa, it never culminated in a political unification under the aegis of a single state structure, controlled from a sole center of decision making for the totality of the archipelago.[1] The building up of such administrative apparatus certainly tried to replace the forms of direct domination over populations exercised by certain feudal powers (that of vassals over villages, and also of religious institutions). But the administrative forms of the Edo were in no way an attempt to recover the centralized patterns of government based on an elite of civil and military functionaries that had more or less worked between the eighth and the eleventh centuries, when Japanese leadership had tried to imitate Chinese state and council models. The unification of the archipelago by a State administration was not achieved until 1871, with the Meiji era, and the modernization of Japan following western models.

The bureaucratic apparatus of the seigneurial principalities of the Edo period were in fact an extension of the functions of vassal band (*kashindan*), that is to say the feudal military organizations which defined the condition of warrior and assured the power of the daimyô over the warriors dependent on their authority. The historian Fukaya Katsumi (1993: 41) has pointed out that at the beginning of the Tokugawa regime, as the country accustomed itself to pacification after a long period of warfare between fighting clans, there were no real administrative organizations to direct the principality: in these pioneer times, the only tangible organ of seigneurial power, and its first concern, was still the vassal bands that retained a strong military character and the need to exploit the lands on which they were installed as forces of occupation.

---

[1] Except in certain very concrete cases, the government of the Shogunate did not nominate direct representatives under its authority in seigneurial domains, and it contented itself with sending inspectors (or their spies). The marks of allegiance of the *daimyo* houses to the Shogunate authority were not less numerous and constraining: the obligation of residence in Edo for one out of every two years, of leaving their hostages as well as submitting to the rules and edicts dictated by the Shogunate, the obligation to have its territorial rights confirmed by the Shogunate in the case of successions, etc.. The structure of the regime remains marked by its feudal origins, with an organization very different from the centralized administrative systems within their core an imperial or royal court, as in China and in Korea in the same period.

The studies on "bureaucracy" in the Tokugawa era are therefore especially interested in the origins of this warrior administration (Takagi 1990; Fujii 1999), in its development and in the recruitment of its members,[2] even to the patterns by which government was installed in rural areas (Kurushima 2002). Evidence has been presented regarding the progressive distinction of the functions of civil administration at the heart of the vassal bands, with the constitution during the seventeenth century of a hierarchy parallel to military ranks. The positions attributed to warriors in the vassal band of the Maeda clan, the powerful lords of the domain of Kaga, were thus divided between the military grades of *kumikata* and missions of an administrative nature or the personal service of the prince (*yakukata*). A similar kind of order can be found in the Shogunal vassal band itself with the military positions of *bankata*, and the civil offices (that were always assigned to warriors), also called in this case *yakukata*.

The establishment and stabilization in the way the organs of seigneurial government functioned towards the middle of the seventeenth century pointed to the need to find an effective way for a stable vassal band to function even under circumstances that might render the supreme seigneurial authority (the daimyô) unable to govern, such as death or long-term incapacity. However, these transformations in the manner of exercising power were often accompanied by a broad political reflection which rested on the heritage of Chinese thought, and particularly on the importance of neo-Confucianism that had become the dominant intellectual reference in early modern Japan. These influences helped the development of the seigneurial power, encouraging it to become more self-conscious and more careful about the effect that its actions might have on the whole of the social body, as well as more aware of its responsibilities in relation to its subjects. Having started from the primitive desire to assure the vassal band as a resource to maintain order, seigneurial powers evolved towards more ambitious conceptions of political action, for example in economic matters. During the entire Edo period, government organs became more complex and progressively extended their domains of action, all the while specializing and assigning designated personnel for specific duties. Therefore, from the end of the eighteenth century onwards "fiefdom schools" (*hankô*) multiplied. These were dedicated to the formation of the warrior personnel of these bureaucracies[3], and provided an education which completed the fundamental basics dispensed in

[2] See, for example, Isoda 2003.

[3] On this question, Dore 1965.

Samurai houses that, over several generations, had produced experts who could meet the needs of different administrative offices (Isoda 2003).

Despite a tradition of political thought, largely constrained by Chinese models, the warrior bureaucracy of the Tokugawa era never managed to set up a system for the recruitment of a civilian elite based on examinations. Conceived within the vassal bands to improve the efficiency of warrior domination, they could not subvert the principles that ordered feudal hierarchies. Consequently, birth and rank within warrior lineages remained the fundamental criteria for access to administrative office, even if rules were put in place, particularly after the eighteenth century, to attempt to favor competition between individuals. On the other hand, it would be wrong to believe that the creation of administrative positions in the Edo era had transformed all those who held the status of warriors into armies of functionaries. It is true that during the two and a half centuries of peace imposed by the hegemony of the Tokugawa, governmental and administrative posts took on more and more importance within the vassal band, and became as a result the most coveted way to accede to individual or family success. Nevertheless, recent studies such as those of Morisihita Tôru on the fiefdom of Hagi (Morishita 2011), have shown that administrative functions were filled by a very reduced number of vassals (at the most 10%, according to him), while the majority of warriors continued to fulfill, at least formally, missions of a military nature (guard duties, escorts, etc.).

This warrior bureaucracy, therefore, appears to us as outstandingly light, not only in relation to the contemporary overall situation, but also when compared to the administrative apparatus of imperial China or of premodern Korea. Even if posts were frequently doubled and exercised by a system of relays, warrior personnel assigned to an administrative task remained astonishingly weak, given the missions they were sent on or the jurisdictions they were responsible for: around 300 persons, for example, for the entirety of the two prefectures which governed the 500,000 inhabitants of the bourgeois neighborhoods of Edo.[4] In fact, even if practical measures and the increase of government rules demonstrated the will of leaders to more effectively control the society under their authority, nevertheless they did not envisage taking charge any more than necessary to assure their own interests and the general stability of the regime.

[4] Of course, the military at hand for the maintenance of order could be included in the personnel of the Prefecture, but this study only takes into account the civil administrative positions of the Prefecture.

Premodern Japan, like the France of the Ancien Régime, was in effect saturated by a daily communitarian social control organized by neighbors, or by different groups (familial, professional, etc.) into which individuals were incorporated, and warrior power did not anticipate changing this form of control, even supposing that such a challenge were to arise.

Townsmen Positions

Nonetheless, this warrior administration did not contain all the bureaucratic apparatus that existed in Tokugawa Japan. The principles of self-administration among the population, recognized by warrior power, naturally required interlocutors and the lesser relays of these, so as to be able to exercise their authority. These were also people or institutions that came from different areas or categories of the population. These individuals, placed at the head of their group, or of the occupation they represented—peasants, fishermen, artisans, merchants, and so forth—often saw their position recognized as *official* by a title (the "village officials", *mura-yakunin*, for example), but the constituencies that they represented, either geographical or corporative, could also be defined by the populations themselves. Therefore, thanks to these various gatherings of commoner officials and of associations (syndicates bringing together several villages, work-derived corporations and so on), there was a network covering society as a whole to the extent that could be qualified as "infra-bureaucratic".[5] Accordingly, seigneurial administrations could fulfill their tasks with greatly reduced effort: one single warrior intendant (*daikan*), an official charged with representing the authority of the lord or the Shogun in the countryside, could therefore be responsible for a whole district with several dozen villages, supported by only a few assistants in his office, but relying on an entire network of village chiefs (*shôya* and *nanushi*) and on general trustees (*ôjôya*), who would be responsible for several rural communities.

If we limit ourselves to the specific case of the towns, those neighborhoods inhabited by plebeians by warrior standards (commoners, *chônin*, i.e. merchants, artisans, but also day-workers, domestic servants, and people of similar low rank), were under the authority of warrior institutions,

[5] This term of "infra-bureaucratic" is adapted from the notion of "infra-judiciary", developed by Nicole Castan in his studies on Ancien Régime justice in Languedoc, and used by him to characterize the ways and means by which conflicts are mediated outside of the institutions of the Royal State.

specific administrative organs, but also of those administrative organs controlled by these groups of people themselves.

Town dwellers responsible for the affairs of their communities, therefore, did not constitute a municipal power, since their jurisdiction did not extend beyond the sections attributed to warriors or to religious buildings. It was common in "castle towns" (*jôkamachi*), the capital of fiefdoms that constituted the core of the urban network of Japan in the Edo era, for warriors and commoners to live in separate neighborhoods that were not under the same authorities.

These "offices" (as institutions *yakusho*) left for the city commoners to fill have been the subject of numerous monographic descriptions, especially from an institutional point of view,[6] but Japanese historians seem to find it difficult to integrate them into their conceptions of a "bureaucratic system". Doubtlessly, such reticence is due to the fact that the administrative mechanisms charged with overseeing lower-class neighborhoods and town-dweller activities were subordinate to the organs of warrior administration. Although they could circulate internal memoranda within their administrative networks, the city officers (*machi-yakunin*) at the head of such organizations could not issue decrees, since such proclamations were the exclusive preserve of the urban Prefects (*machi-bugyô*), vassals who represented seigneurial authority in commoners' neighborhoods. They were responsible for "policing" them in the broadest sense, that is, they did not just maintain order and control urban activities (questions of traffic, of buildings, of regulating markets, and so forth), but they were also an organ of justice. Supreme power, be it executive, legislative or judicial, was in fact always held by representatives of the warriors in Japanese towns and countryside during the Edo period.

The functions and prerogatives of these city officials were therefore strongly limited by their statutory subordination in a firmly hierarchical society based on rank. In the majority of cases, the city commoners' officials (*machiyakunin*) inherited their position (this was the case for example in Edo itself, but not in the city of Kanazawa, object of this study), and thereby apparently did not have a genuine "career" to fulfill within the administrative apparatus, and much less any examinations by which to be approved.

From this evidence, from certain Japanese historians whose concepts of bureaucracy have been strongly conditioned by the reading of Marx or Weber, these city officials appear rather as auxiliaries of the seigneurial

---

[6] Tanaka 1984; on the city commoners officers of Edo: Yoshiwara 1980.

authority, as subordinates charged with facilitating the exercise of feudal power within the cities, and it would be a mistake to include them within an administrative organization conceived of as centralized and unitary. But the bureaucratic systems always remain the emanations of the social order that has produced them. Therefore, even if such organizations were conceived during the Edo era so as to better impose the authority of seigneurial governments, they could not subvert the status assigned to men and social groups in a rank-ordered society and consequently such forms of administration concealed the significance of a social status, exterior and pre-existent to the administrative system itself, that conditioned both its formation and its function.

The City Officials of Kanazawa

We shall study here in greater detail the case of the castle town of Kanazawa, capital of the fiefdom of the Maeda. The seigneurial house of Maeda was the most important of the "exterior *daimyos*" (*tôzama daimyô*), that is to say it did not belong to the Tokugawa vassal band; although of course they still submitted to the authority of the Shoguns of Edo. The Maeda had received three provinces in fief, and the seat of their government, Kanazawa, was without doubt the fourth or fifth largest city of the country, with a population estimated at more or less 120,000 inhabitants, of which around 60,000 were plebeians.

To begin with, let us familiarize ourselves with the status of the city officials (*machiyakunin*) that we have been speaking about at such length. The word *yaku*, often translated by "service", in other words the "service of the lord" (*go-yô*), was an expression that designated a form of relationship between Public Authority (*kôgi*) that was personified by either seigneurial or Shogunal power, and those who were subject to it. A certain number of obligations had to be fulfilled in deference to this power in order that it would guarantee public order. Such obligations or "yaku", consisted in a sort of forced labor or "corvée", offered in exchange for a recognized status (*mibun*) granted by the feudal power. The service involved could be either individual or collective (applied for example to corporations or to groups with a collective social status). It was a question of an individual acquitting a personal charge for the seigneurial power, and one spoke therefore of "*yakunin*", translated in English by "officer" or "official".

The city officials of the town of Kanazawa were, like their warrior betters, also named by the representatives of the seigneurial power, naturally without being able to pretend to an equality of rank: they remained under all circumstances their subordinates, and under their command. Unlike in many other Japanese towns of the period, these posts were not hereditary, even if the most outstanding positions circulated among a limited number of great bourgeois houses of the town, a kind of "commoners aristocracy" that maintained privileged links with the warrior aristocracy. Another important fact: as in the rest of Japan, these offices were not in principle venal, and, at least officially, could not be made the object of economic transactions.

A list drawn up in 1785 gives us an over-all view of the principal tasks of the city officials of the town of Kanazawa.[7] In general terms, the situation can be considered as similar to the period we are studying here—the beginning of the eighteenth century. The list names around three hundred officials, each with their rank in a hierarchy appropriate to such an ensemble: the most important among them, some twenty in all, enjoyed having a seigneurial "right of audience", a protocol honor which essentially consisted of being able to go to the castle to present best wishes for a new year in the name of the dwellers of the town. Such a distinction, the "right of audience" was also important to the warrior condition, and thus elevated up to a certain point the status of these officials in contrast to other plebeians. But in fact, these twenty or so officials at the top of their city's hierarchy of honors were responsible, above all, for the management of the most important commoners' organs of the city: the City Hall (*machikaisho*), the central headquarters for the administration of the commercial district, and the Ginza (the mint).

If one examines the titles and responsibilities of these commoners' offices of Kanazawa (see Table 1), one quickly perceives that they can be classed in three principal categories: first and foremost, the management and administration of town dweller neighborhoods, with the Elders (*toshiyori*), who headed the City Hall, and a long list of neighborhood chiefs. Immediately after that, one finds the representatives or the parties responsible for the different guilds, merchants and artisans. And finally come the people who, to different degrees, are responsible for the handling of money and of the funds linked to warrior power, whether for providing loans (above all to vassals) under the control of the fief, or as a guarantee of quality, as in the case of the organizations we are going to study more precisely here. All these offices were coordinated by the City Hall, the

[7] "Kanazawa machikaisho shissan kiroku 1, Tenmei go kinotomi Kanazawa machiyakunin-chô", in *Ishikawa kyôdoshi gakkai kaishi*, 1970.

main liaison organ with the warrior authorities, but which, regrettably, has not yet been studied in depth.

Therefore, one can remark that the responsibilities of these city officials remained restricted to areas or domains specifically linked to their status. The fact that there were only three hundred officials for a plebeian population of around 60,000 inhabitants in Kanazawa reminds us of earlier observations about the administration having relatively few operatives. However, the functions itemized in this list do not represent more than the higher ranks of the commoners' officials, those who were fully recognized as such. But there existed other, more numerous positions at lower grades, whose incumbents assisted them in their tasks.

The Ginza and the Public Regulation of Money

Let us turn our attention more precisely to one of these offices, the Ginza. Originally this term meant a "silver guild". From the last years of the sixteenth century up to 1669, the fiefdom of the Maeda cast its own silver coinage, a task undertaken by this organization that bore the same name as the Shogunate mints at Edo or Kyoto. The Ginza, which had always at least two commoners' officials assigned to this mission, and often more, was a kind of both semi-public and semi-commercial body linked to the casting of money and always working under the control of warrior authorities. In 1669, the fiefdom of the Maeda was forced to stop producing these local coins and to adopt those of the Tokugawa. Nevertheless, the organization was maintained with two fundamental objectives. First of all and most important, since silver was weighed coin, the Ginza of Kanazawa had to value the silver that was entrusted to it as representative of the seigneurial authority, and to package it in envelopes which certified the weight and the value. Logically, and second to this, it was charged with detecting counterfeit money and discovering any envelopes with fraudulent or forged silver coins. Since the criteria for certification that the Ginza used were considered very strict, it enjoyed such a high reputation in the town that individuals or money changers, also, were encouraged to request that this body certified and packaged their own sums of silver. The Ginza carried out this service for a commission, of which a part in turn went to the seigneurial treasury. Besides the Ginza of Kanazawa, there were six other bodies of this type in other towns within the Maeda's domain, all placed under the control of the Kanazawa Ginza. In addition, it monitored similar institutions, one in each of the two linked fiefdoms of the Toyama and the Daishôji, both cadet branches of the Maeda House.

As we can see, the tasks undertaken by the Ginza were of a somewhat technical nature, and we could consider it a misuse to assimilate them into a bureaucracy, more so when the tasks involved could have been accomplished without great effort by private money changers appointed by the lord. But these tasks were essential for the administrative apparatus of the fiefdom to function well, as they permitted the physical movement of silver, and the establishment of accounting controls. The archives of the Ginza of Kanazawa[8] show that above and beyond the fundamental mission of positive and negative certification of silver money, this body was also responsible for all liaison between seigneurial authorities and the city's financial professionals, and therefore for exercising a sort of control over the corporation of the money changers. On the other hand, after the introduction of new coinage in the decades of the 1710s, we can see that it was the Ginza that informed warrior authorities of the commoners' expectations and was charged with both circulating information and with drawing up measures to ensure the proper functioning of money exchanges throughout the entire fiefdom, thereby avoiding panic in money markets, and the consequent outflow of gold coin from seigneurial territory. In sum, the Ginza had become a public organ that guaranteed the correct circulation of money and precious metal in Kanazawa and in the city of Kaga. It thus represented the public guarantee for the use of money at a local level. Even if the process which brought about that result was not managed directly by the warrior leaders, even if the pressure of circumstances and of merchants' demands (for example, for money to be recast) all played a great role in its development, it was the Ginza who took on, in the name and on behalf of the seigneurial government, tasks which had not apparently worried medieval powers to the extent of creating specific institutions.

One particular aspect of these city commoners' institutions that contrasts with warrior offices is the fact that they informed the rulers about the mood and circumstances of town society, but that they also relayed and filtered demands from below. But whatever degree of autonomy was involved in the decisions of the directors of the Ginza, the application of

---

[8] For these studies there have been two principal private archival sources used, reproductions of which are preserved in the "Center of Pre-modern Archives of the Municipal Library of Kanazawa": the Ishiguro and the Morishita collections. The figures attributed are the provisional studies used by the authors in the years 1990-2000 of the *History of Kanazawa* (*Kanazawa-shi shi*).

these was made effective only because this organ was an emanation of seigneurial power and acted in constant liaison with the warrior administration. Given that the Ginza was under the control of bureaucratic instances above it, warrior administration and the City Hall, those in charge of the former mints were obliged to refer any concerns to their superiors (City Elders, Urban Prefects, Prefects of the Court of Accounts, or more commonly, their subordinates). They produced numerous reports, kept their documentation up-to-date, constituted archives, ensured accounts were kept, and fulfilled other similar obligations. These were their principal roles, as bourgeois officials of high rank, given that the testing or weighing of coins was left to their subordinates.

At the beginning of the eighteenth century there were no more than two officials responsible for the Ginza, but as was common in all offices of the Edo period, such doubling permitted each of the two individuals entrusted to rotate their jobs every month, always consulting their partner while they were on duty. In the case of the Ginza, it was possible that one of the two officials in charge might have some other professional activity, as in the case of Fukuhisaya (Ishiguro) Shin'emon, a pharmacist who co-directed the Ginza between 1709 and 1719. One was nominated to this post because of one's personal honorability or because of one's lineage, and not because of any professional proficiency in the trade of silver-making or money making: it seems clear that no money changer ever obtained this position and such exclusion may have been quite purposeful. Whatever might have been the status of officials at the head of the Ginza, in the hierarchies of the bourgeoisie they were regarded quite highly, since the protocol put them second only to the City Elders.

We can thereby trace the direct and even cordial relations between the privileged notables put in charge of the Ginza and the three first lords of Kaga, at a time when the warrior-bureaucrat apparatus and that of the commoners neighborhoods was not yet stabilized. Because at the beginning of their rule the Maeda clan leaders still relied on people whom they could trust to govern, they maintained such personal links. But the situation changed after the second half of the seventeenth century, and from then on the lord had direct contact only with the high rank warrior officials of his vassal band. City officials such as those of the Ginza then had scant opportunity to meet their lord beyond the most formal ceremonies of the protocol.

The figure of the high ranking city official can therefore appear to us as quite different from that of the functionary. The post in itself, whatever real responsibilities it entailed, was also a mark of worthiness. Such a post was not necessarily the only, much less the principal, professional occupation of its title holder. Without doubt, such a task was attributed to individuals considered competent, and who could have shown their merit in earlier missions under the lords' orders, but the merits recognized in this way might be something other than simply the actual working competence of the administrator. It was also a matter of the social reputation of a house or lineage, of that person's credit within merchant society, of several generations of tasks of vassalage. All of these might be taken into account alongside his professional activities in relation to warrior rulers, such as being their official medicine purveyors in the case of Ishiguro-Fukuhisaya. Nevertheless, one should note, throughout the Edo period, a process of professionalization and job specialization among these city officials. There are early signs of the posts evolving in this way, from the second half of the seventeenth century onwards, in cities like Edo, where such posts were hereditary. Kanazawa was not an exception. The control exercised by certain families (the "great bourgeois houses", *iegara-chônin*) over such prestigious positions allowed them, with the backing of seigneurial power, to maintain their rank in urban society despite the continual regeneration of economic elites. Holding and accomplishing such missions of an administrative nature became the identifying mark of a house, which over several generations developed specific expertise regarding their inherited tasks.

The Organization of the Ginza and of the General Warehouse

Each head of the Ginza led a team with a varying number of members, between five and ten, depending on the employees at their disposition and the overall service needs. It was in fact these team members who had to guarantee the daily working of the mint. Such lower ranking personnel were divided into two categories: at the top were the "experts in silver" (*kanemi*) who were expected to know the different kinds of pieces in circulation, and be able to evaluate their quality as well as the authenticity of the marks of certification (seals, etc.) that such coins and packaging could bear. These were therefore specialists, men with a particular competence and who, as a result, remained for a rather long time at their posts. These were, for example, the individuals who informed their superiors, those responsible for the Ginza, about the history of the organization, the variation in its rules, the contents of its archives and so on and so forth. They supervised the work of the clerks (*tedai*) who were more specifically charged with preparing the weights and the packaging of sums of money. However, these ten or so people did not work all together at the same time: they took turns among themselves according to a system of shifts, and except in times of intense activity, only half of the personnel could be found at the Mint on the same day.

Another entity was also under the authority of Ginza directors. Other experts in silver and other clerks were assigned to the seigneurial treasury called "the General Warehouse" (*shohô o-dozô*) located inside the castle. These men, also of commoner status, carried out the same tasks as their equivalents in the Ginza, and therefore examined, weighed and packaged the silver before entrusting it to the seigneurial coffers. The general warehouse also received each month a part of the receipts of the mint.

The Ginza and the entities to which it was tied, because of their nature and mission, and the commoner status of their personnel, depended on a crisscrossing of administrative authorities: insofar as they were bourgeois and charged especially with business matters that interested merchants and financiers, the officials of the Ginza depended on the City Hall, but they also had to report directly at a higher level that was the Urban Prefecture. Nevertheless, their tasks also linked them to the Prefecture of the Court of Accounts (*sanyôba bugyô*), in charge of the finances of the fiefdom, and with other warrior offices which derived from this. This was particularly true of tasks entrusted to the experts and clerks of the seigneurial coffers. Such a multiplicity of warrior authorities, all charged with controlling the activity of the Ginza, could often lead to conflict and displays of bad temper on the part of one or other of the warrior officials who considered that the rules had not been properly obeyed or that their prerogatives had been impinged upon.

In Figure II, an organizational chart that outlines the relationship of the Ginza with the administrative organs of the Kanazawa and of the fiefdom of Kaga, we can see a peculiarity of the bureaucratic hierarchies of the Edo era: their composition appears singularly compacted, an effect of its scant personnel. This is far from today's image of a "bureaucracy", usually pictured as a vast labyrinth. The organ above the Urban Prefecture was none other than the seigneurial Council of Great Vassals, the Seniors (*karô*), the supreme instance of government in the fiefdom of Kaga. Certainly the prefects were very busy, and the heads of the Ginza frequently had to make do with subordinates when interceding with them, or rather when contacting them, with the elders of the cities acting as intermediaries. But the heads of the mint could also be addressed directly by the Seniors, that is to say, the ministers of the fiefdom.

The Clerks of the Ginza and of the General Warehouse

If the experts and clerks of the seigneurial coffers also depended on the officials of the Ginza, this was due to the rules of recruitment of these organisms. The experts in silver, as we have pointed out, remained at their jobs for a very long time, and in practice when a new head of the Ginza was named by the fief, he apparently retained, at least at first, his predecessor's team of experts and clerks, so as to assure a smooth continuity in services. Given their scant opportunity for job mobility, we have a poor understanding of what was required of candidates for the post of expert in silver, but, in compensation, the archives of the Ginza for the early eighteenth century contained numerous documents regarding candidates requesting placement as clerks of the Ginza.[9] For the most part, they are sons of commoners of the city, sometimes even sons of lesser members of vassal band. The hiring, and doubtlessly also firing, of such personnel remained at the discretion of the heads of the Ginza: documents requesting employment and the pledges assumed by their warrantors were all addressed to the heads of the mint.

Clerks seemed to change jobs frequently, since promotions were always possible, and one can assume that these opportunities made the job attractive. There was an additional opportunity to be placed at the head of one of the five or six other offices that controlled the fiefdom's money, either when the previous titular died or when he resigned from his post. The diaries of Fukuhisaya Shin'emon record many cases of this.[10] Up until 1717, such nominations were always made on the recommendation of a head of the Ginza. But the clerks could also be nominated for an appointment to the General Warehouse, always of course subject to a proposal from the head of the Ginza. However, in contrast to what happened in the employment of clerks in the Ginza, where apparently the only judges of a candidate's suitability were the heads of the Ginza, proposals for posting at the General Warehouse had to be ratified by the City Elders and by the warrior authorities (both the Urban Prefects and the Prefects of the Court of Accounts) in order to be considered valid.

[9] Ishiguro Archives, E-91, E-92, E-93, E-94, E-95, E-96, E-97, E-98

[10] The oldest examples can be retrieved in the extracts of the books of Kamiya Matabee, responsible for the Ginza in the year 1660. This document is preserved in the Morishita Archive (C-12).

Nevertheless, the choice was made by the head of the mint who, in this function, had also to answer for the conduct of his personnel, even in the General Warehouse although he did not have authority over that.

Any nomination to the General Warehouse had an impact on the status of the persons so recognized. As they handled silver from the seigneurial coffers, or could exercise their functions inside the castle itself, they were entitled to the position of "official" (*yakunin*). Doubtlessly, in the context of a society of ranks and orders in which each person's position must be made evident in the actions of their daily life, it would have been considered inconvenient and even incongruous to allow simple employees, almost servants, without any mark of social distinction, to touch the money of their lord. Even if, strictly speaking, they carried out the same tasks from a technical viewpoint, the clerks of the Ginza did not enjoy the same status as officials. Salaries were consequently higher in the General Warehouse, given that according to a rule of 1695, all the clerks of the seigneurial treasury received the same sum of 600 *monme* of silver, a level of payment that in the Ginza was reserved only for the experts.[11] This sum was furthermore paid directly by the fief, while in the case of the Ginza payment was advanced on the revenues of the institution.

It should therefore be underlined that two more or less similar tasks were treated differently. The clerks in the Ginza and those in the General Warehouse had different ranks. The statutory hierarchy of the seigneurial administration symbolically accorded a higher rank and higher recognition to those who exclusively handled the silver of the lord for the daily running of the warrior bureaucratic apparatus than to those who guaranteed, in a general fashion through their work, the proper circulation of money throughout the city and the fiefdom. The presence of clerks in the castle, but also at the heart of the financial workings of the seigneurial administration must have meant that warrior authorities underlined the great importance of service in the General Warehouse by the symbolic granting of the rank of official. The discovery of anomalies in the overall deposits at the General Warehouse therefore brought serious consequences and a full enquiry into the organs of the warrior administration. On the other hand, these anomalies would be simply treated as police matters when it was a question of money circulating between individuals in the Kanazawa or its surroundings, matters which could even be resolved by responsible authorities within the Ginza.

---

[11] Ishikawa-Ken, 1938 (reprint), Genroku 8/2/29. The *monme* is an accounting unit of silver, of 3.75 grams.

Another consequence of this distinction in status accorded to the clerks of the General Warehouse was that, apparently, they had to be owners of a house, or at the very least of land within the town on which they could build, a condition necessary in order to be fully recognized by the authorities as a rightful *chônin* (city commoner). Only property owners of real estate, a fundamental gauge of honorability, could thus accede to the rank of official. The mere fact of being, as was underlined by one of the City Elders "so little that one is a public official",[12] therefore forced the General Warehouse clerks to seek authorization from their superior authority (those responsible for the Ginza, the City Elders) to request a mortgage. Nothing would indicate to us that the clerks of the Ginza were subject to the same control, nor even that they were all property owners. It was also obligatory to provide a family genealogy, with whenever possible, a catalogue of merits accumulated by ancestors, before any nomination to the General Warehouse could happen.

In truth, it seems that certain officials of the General Warehouse also carried out another activity parallel to the handling of seigneurial money. This is at least what can be seen in a request addressed in 1712 by the Ginza head Fukuhisaya Shin'emon to the City Elders:[13] one of the clerks in the General Warehouse wanted to go to the town of Usshitsu on business as part of his trade in handicrafts for the tea industry. The situation was evidently intriguing, for the Ginza chief attracted comments from one of his superiors, an Elder. However, the Elder, while questioning the compatibility of these two occupations, especially in terms of the obligation of his service to the Ginza, finally gave him authorization to go. In practice, the treatment meted out to these lesser city officials was equivalent to that accorded to an *ashigaru* infantryman, the lowest category of the warrior condition, whose income was not based on the possession of a fief provided by their lord, but on a salary that was notoriously insufficient for living comfortably in town. Doubtless this is also the reason that, in 1716, eight clerks of the General Warehouse—that is to say all of them—jointly requested to be appointed by the lord as brokers in the rice market at the same time as they carried out their official

[12] Ishiguro Archives, E-89, "Hôei rokunen yori Shôtoku sannen made tomechô" ("Records of the Sixth Year of the Kan'ei Era to that of the Third Year of the Shôtoku Era"), Hôei 6 (1709) /5/7 (the dates are given in reference to the Japanese order: name of
the era and year, lunar month, and day).

[13] Ibid., Shôtoku 2 (1712) /2/17.

duties, a petition that was denied.[14]

As we shall now see, the importance of that mark of honor accorded to a treasury clerk should not be exaggerated. The granting of the rank of official to clerks of the General Warehouse did not have any real practical consequences for the way in which the warriors and the heads of the Ginza dealt with these lesser personnel in their perception of the social hierarchy.

Between the Store Clerk and the City Official

Despite the status distinction between the General Warehouse and the Ginza, the identity of the term of "clerk" to designate the two functions confined those so described to a low-ranking position. Strictly speaking, the term *tedai* was not specific to organizations such as the Ginza: it was a generic name for the employees of a house of commerce, the reason that we translate that term with the word "clerk". Note, however, that among merchants, there was nevertheless a distinction between employees who worked in the store and those responsible for trading, common laborers or other servants.[15] This was also the case in the Ginza, where so-called *komono*, menials, worked, about whom we know very little.

There were store clerks of every age, but most commonly they were young men who had been placed by their parents as apprentices in a commercial house. As we have seen in the case of the Ginza, the taking on of clerks frequently took this form—the placing of a son—and we can often come upon proof in the form of explicit requests by a father for his child, by an uncle in favor of his nephew, and so on. Access to a position in the Ginza seems to have been characterized by a certain analogy with the way that workers were taken on by a commercial house: the employee became a "servant", *hôkônin*, a general expression which served just as well to designate the employees of a business as it did any sort of domestic. And the first years of work in the Ginza were considered as a form of apprenticeship (*minarai*). We should add, that as far as we know, the word *tedai* should not ever be used under the system of vassal band to designate warriors who assume tasks in either the civil or the military administration, no matter the rank. In summary, the similar vocabulary used to define the employees of a public organization such as the Ginza and those of merchant houses, serves without doubt to illustrate the fact

[14] Ishiguro Archives, E-101 "Ginza obeogaki" ("Memorandum of the Ginza"), Shôtoku 5 (1715) /2/24.

[15] On those questions, see Yoshida 2002, and Nishizaka 2006.

that the mint belonged to the world of the town elite or the commoner, but that it is also an index of employment categories pointing to forms of personnel management appropriate to merchants.

After all, this situation was really quite natural: those in charge of the Ginza could themselves be active merchants, who might employ in their own business a relatively large number of clerks. One can deduce the common criteria for the Ginza employee and his equivalent in a merchant house, since it was often the case that when the need arose, the merchant clerks could be called upon to help in the packaging of coins.[16]

To sum up, the heads of the Ginza managed this entity in more or less the same way as they would handle their family business. Employees of a commercial house in effect would be subject to the patriarchal authority of their boss, an authority that depended as much on the latter's position as head of a business as his legitimacy as head of a family. On the other hand, things do not seem to be quite the same in the case of the clerks of the General Warehouse. Even though the Ginza authorities were de facto the hierarchical superiors of those who ran the Warehouse, they were not normally present in the General Warehouse, while they had to go regularly to the Ginza to ensure its proper functioning. We should remember that the General Warehouse was located inside the seigneurial castle and not in the town. It therefore remained a warrior space over which the Ginza heads could not exercise direct authority, even if, to a certain extent, they were responsible for the actions of personnel that they had recommended to work there. One can suppose, therefore, that daily control of such treasury clerks was within the domain of the prefects of the General Warehouse who were warriors. Because of the somewhat peculiar position of these clerks, there was a confusion about their status (were they clerks or officials?) which gave them an opportunity to defend themselves against the tutelage of the heads of the Ginza.

Securing their Status

In 1709, six clerks of the general Warehouse signed a collective letter to the directors of the Ginza that they submitted using as intermediaries the two experts in silver who were their intermediate superiors.[17] The document thereby implicated all the personnel of the General Warehouse. It was a request, addressed to the prefect of Kanazawa, and motivated by

[16] Ishiguro Archives, E-89, Hôei 6 (1709) /5/24.
[17] Ibid., Hôei 6 (1709) /11/18.

the recent death of one of their colleagues, a certain Tadaya Shichirôbee. Shichirôbee had succeeded his older brother, a man named Hanbee, who had worked for some twenty years as a coin packer, and as an expert in silver at the General Warehouse. When Hanbee resigned his position, his brother took it on and he, too, occupied the same post for almost twenty periods, until he died. Such remarkable stability in jobs at the General Warehouse, lasting over several decades, allows us to suppose that the clerks held onto their positions and did not quit them readily. The letter itself offers another proof, because those who signed it made themselves spokesmen for the late Shichirôbee, who on his deathbed had sworn them to request the succession in his "service" for his nephew Heiemon, the son of that Hanbee who had previously held the same post. Furthermore, Hanbee was still apparently alive at that time, although quite elderly, one might assume, perhaps over sixty. In any case, the letter stressed that the mourning he was subject to had prevented him from presenting the request himself.

Although the petition was presented in proper hierarchical fashion up to the heads of the Ginza, it was addressed to the Prefecture of the city. Therefore it was the warrior administration that the clerks were asking to appoint an individual, in this way short-circuiting the usual procedure that relied upon the recommendation of the chiefs of the mint. They, of course, could not easily accept that their subordinates had paid so little attention to their prerogative, and although they passed the letter on to the Prefecture, they carefully added a memorandum addressed to the City Elders in which they explained just how dimly they considered this initiative.

The directors of the mint were enraged. How could they accept, said Heiemon, the taking on as a clerk of the General Warehouse someone who had not yet "cut his hair at the front", in other words a child who was not yet fifteen years old? The biting remark was significant, because in the merchant houses, one could enter as an apprentice clerk at the age of twelve, before having achieved maturity. The Ginza chiefs reasoned carefully. They recapitulated all the assignments a clerk at the General Warehouse was expected to fulfill and they were careful to make the Elders, and through them the Prefects, understand that such tasks could not be accomplished by a novice, much less by a minor. In particular, they insisted that the clerks of the General Warehouse could be called to the rescue of the Ginza should the number of coins they had to deal with be excessive, and that meant that they therefore needed well-qualified personnel. They stressed that they could also be required to help other offices of the warrior administration, such as the office of "common payments" (*koharaidokoro*).

The other objection raised by the Ginza chiefs referred to the process of choosing clerks from the General Warehouse. The Ginza heads insisted that clerks were chosen among their own personnel as a reflection of their "merit", after having "worked there for a long time". In all probability, this requirement was motivated by the need for Warehouse workers to know their job inside out, so as to be able to handle seigneurial silver. In fact, as soon as there was a vacancy at the General Warehouse, custom had it that those Ginza clerks interested in the position would make a statement to that effect to their superior, and the latter would recommend a name to the competent authority.

Consequently, two different logics confronted each other in this affair: the way that the General Warehouse clerks proposed to choose their successor conformed to a certain patrimonial logic and also showed they understood the position to be a mark of honor and merit, important enough to distinguish the identity of a family. As we have already pointed out, it is easy to notice the ascendency of officials in the bourgeois households of worthies, even when the positions were theoretically due for circulation. Therefore, these great bourgeois houses tended to keep such signs of honorability within the family line, even when this meant changing posts or jumping over a generation. This was also the case at the head of the Ginza: in 1709 the two official chiefs included high-ranking bourgeois officials among their ancestors.

By asking for a nephew to succeed to the office, the clerks, who in this way evaded a direct succession, were perhaps searching for a way to keep up appearances according to the official norms of the time. But the succession between brothers, or from uncle to nephew, ultimately showed a way of keeping a post in a General Warehouse within the family. Furthermore, by addressing themselves directly to the Prefects of Kanazawa, the clerks pretended to ignore the fact that their nomination depended on the Ginza chiefs. It is quite remarkable to find that all the clerks plotted in this maneuver by co-signing the letter. This indicates a style of behavior and a *esprit de corps*, already shown by Morishita Tôru regarding lower-ranking warrior officials in the fiefdom of Hagi, where the army valets, who could be individuals of quite low extraction, got together to present their claims and resist the requirements of their superiors (Morishita 2011).

When confronted by this coalition of clerks, the Ginza chiefs quite naturally expressed a completely different attitude: in practice, they wished to promote the personnel of the General Warehouse along the same line as their own store clerks. Just as a pyramidal system of promotion by merit ruled commercial houses (Nishizaka 2006), the heads of the Ginza understood that it was their right to choose among their subordinates those who merited a move to the General Warehouse and so they made such a nomination a type of recompense for the most zealous. This should also have been the case for the nomination of one of the six other posts of expert in silver in the fief. In short, for the directors at the Ginza and at the General Warehouse, whatever might be the nature or importance of their responsibility, the clerks remained no more than employees, subject to a patriarchal authority.

Thus, in an office which fulfilled a public function one could find two different logics of nomination, two visions of "service" which clashed head-on, but neither of which truly corresponded to our conception of "bureaucracy". This kind of contradiction was, furthermore, not exclusive to commoner-run organizations. The same contradictory principles could also be seen among the Samurai, in the distribution of functions in the system of vassal band, and most especially in the warrior administration. On the one hand, there stood the birth, the rank of a house, and the inheritance of positions that permitted the formation of specialists within the same family. On the other, there was personal competence and talent that should equally be factors for promotion. Both were regulated by the different levels of authority incorporated into vassalage. This co-existence of the logic of status and of outstanding individuals could therefore generate tensions in the whole chain of office holding, but basically the progressive principle of lines of descendancy linked to administrative work relied on both principles.

Revindications and Compromise

Another affair noted in 1713 in the journals of the Ginza[18] showed that warrior authorities, as well as the leadership of the mint, were well aware of the desires of lower-ranking bourgeois officials to perpetuate their official status. Both elites were willing to accept such pretensions within measure. That year, a certain Kikuya Tôemon, having achieved the venerable age of 82, resigned from his position as neighborhood chief,[19]

---

[18] Ishiguro Archives, E-89, Shôtoku 3 (1713) /2.

[19] The chiefs of the quarters (*machi-kimoiri*) were city commoners' officials in charge of assuring the liaisons between the commoners' areas and the city authorities (the City Hall). They were responsible for one or more of the major

and asked that that post be granted to his grandson, Shichibee. It was not a matter of highly prestigious responsibility, since it affected a popular quarter of the city. The urban Prefecture and the City Hall did not accept this hereditary succession, as was to be expected. Nevertheless, the Prefect decided to place as chief of the quarter a certain Shôemon who had until then worked in the General Warehouse, while the alternative candidate, the grandson Shichibee, took the latter's place, apparently without previously going through a job in the Ginza warehouse. In this case, doubtlessly because the request came from a neighborhood chief who had submitted his petition to the City Elders, the whole business was settled between them and the Prefects, and the final decision notified afterwards to the Ginza authorities for confirmation.

On this occasion, therefore, the process of nominating someone to the General Warehouse completely escaped the hands of the Ginza and came exclusively within the decision-making chain of the town neighborhood, that is, the City Elders and the urban Prefects. The author of the Ginza journal, Fukuhisaya Shin'emon, considered that "perhaps it should have been up to him to nominate the successor" at the General Warehouse, but that since the decision had been taken by the Prefects, his colleagues and the warrior officers counseled him not to protest. Perhaps on this occasion the age of the postulant did not pose a problem (this was not made clear). But in any case, since he apparently had never before carried out this type of work, it was considered he should enter the General Warehouse as an "apprentice" (*minarai*).

When one examines the names of those who signed the 1709 petition, one sees that the Shôemon who left his place at the General Warehouse to become neighborhood chief in 1713, must have been a relation of a certain Kikuya Shôemon; it is therefore probable that he was in fact a relative of Kikuya Tôemon. This means that the game of musical chairs between the different offices and services must have tended to keep certain minor official positions within this family, with the consent of the authorities. One can see therefore that lower-ranking posts in the administration were complementary to, or even substituted for, family identities based on the inheritance of commercial or artisanal businesses by certain city dwellers of modest rank. The titular holders of posts in the General Warehouse would not have been great bourgeois, since the positions occupied in the

streets and there were differences in rank between those responsible for the central quarters, in which the richest population lived, and those of the outlying quarters, with poorer inhabitants.

offices corresponded to a given social rank. So the position of clerks, even in the General Warehouse, must have necessarily devolved onto individuals who were not socially excluded because they occupied low-ranking jobs. As we have seen, these clerks often came from bourgeois, merchants' households, money changers among others. Careers in the Ginza mint or in the General Warehouse perhaps offered a possibility of entry for the junior members of these families. Such positions seem to have been rather more accessible insofar as they did not require real specialized knowledge.

Whatever the case, and in the absence of a more pleasant prospect, being named as an official of the General Warehouse at the very least assured a stable income and the protection of a fief, a considerable advantage for those without much money and perhaps exposed to the hazards of existence. This would doubtlessly explain the fierceness with which these small townsmen would fight to obtain some way of guaranteeing their status within the administration (such as was permitted by the families of notables). That would also help solve their problem of recognition by the warrior authorities who basically saw in them folk of such low rank that they could not possibly have any genealogical reputation to preserve.

We have another example in 1717.[20] According to the Ginza archives, in that year two individuals, managing, respectively, the entities delivering monetary control of the towns of Usshitsu and Imasurugi, asked at the same time to nominate their own successors—their sons. Simultaneously, an expert in silver at the General Warehouse also demanded to be able to choose his successor. The first two considered that it should be their sons, while the expert in silver, it would seem, because as the text states "his own son was sick", wanted to cede the post to another clerk, unnamed, who was then in the service of a notable of the Kanazawa. What makes this interesting is that these requests with a similar goal both involved people holding posts at Kanazawa and in other towns of the fief who had probably all formerly been clerks at the Ginza. Even if it is unclear if the requests were made in a coordinated fashion, such a coincidence of demands suggests some method of understanding between lower-ranking officials. It proves that a consciousness of common interest and, without doubt, a certain *esprit de corps* continued to link clerks of this type, even after their promotions had dispersed them.

The request was again in this instance rejected by warrior authorities,

[20] Ishiguro Archives, E-101, Kyôhô 2/8/28/.

who on this occasion convened the Ginza authorities to tell them clearly that "town dwellers of such mediocre background are not to request their succession". Instead of such insubordination, the authorities and, one may well suspect, the bourgeois city councilors imposed a kind of "rotational system by list", a method that had already been put into effect the previous year for the designation of seigneurial intermediaries in the rice market. This system is not explained in detail. But it would seem to consist of establishing in advance an order of priority among the clerks working for the great bourgeois officials of the Kanazawa (and therefore not only the Ginza authorities but also the City Elders). Such ordering of priority was imposed upon those suitable to fill positions in the General Warehouse as they opened up, or positions at the head of one of the six money exchanges outside Kanazawa. But two of the City Elders had previously taken charge of the Ginza. It is just possible that their clerks had also been Ginza personnel who had not been able to achieve promotion in the General Warehouse or in another town during their time of service. As we have already seen, the experts in silver usually remained in place after a change of direction at the head of the Ginza, but we do not have enough information about the clerks. However, it is quite possible some of them followed their former boss at Ginza to his new appointment, for example to the City Hall.

The system that replaced people by listed turn seems to have been a compromise solution, tending to reconcile several contradictory understandings of the lower-ranking jobs. Above all, it prevented job holders becoming fossilized, carrying out functions that remained monopolized by the same families. It is interesting to note that this arrangement seems to have been set up to coincide with the nomination of new city Prefects, possibly indicating that the position of clerk always remained unsure, tentative, and subject to sudden change of opinion amongst the representatives of seigneurial power. This would not mean that the higher-ups were hostile in principle to a certain level of hereditary function within the administrative apparatus. But as the City Prefect reminded them, job inheritance was not suitable for "mediocre townsmen". Put differently, such recognition would grant them an unjustified market status, above their background, that could have encouraged them to ask for even more that went beyond their low-ranking role.

The fact was that by reserving the positions of clerk for those who had completed service with high ranking bourgeois officials, the power of the latter was undoubtedly reinforced, and the authorities apparently adhered to the principle that outstanding merit was necessary for such promotion, a requirement emphasized in 1709 by the heads of the Ginza. Nevertheless, one should not forget that in the case of the substitution of Kikuya Tôemon in that same year, even if direct heredity of office was rejected, care was taken nevertheless to reserve a place for everyone in the city organization. To sum up, the warrior administration of the City Hall thereby ensured from generation to generation a stable breeding ground of agents ready to fill positions in the lowest echelons of the hierarchies of power and the administration.

Conclusion

An evaluation of the overall situation of the clerks, the Ginza, and the General Warehouse of Kanazawa provides a reason for crosschecking the work of Japanese historians in the last few years. We have already cited the research of Morishita Tôru regarding domestic warrior service in the seigneurial town of Hagi. This work has shown how servants, assigned offices in the administration of the fief, attempted to hoard such posts and use them as a lever to transform their rank as unqualified workers into some kind of low-ranking post within the warrior apparatus, an ambition which was always thwarted by seigneurial authorities (Morishita 2011; 2007). The position of the *tedai* of Kanazawa was not exactly that of domestics or valets but had a certain indeterminate status that was designated by Japanese historiography as the "urban margins", that is to say from mendicants to small artisans and street merchants, and so on, rising up as far as day-workers. The *tedai* were thus among the social categories who were forced to find the means to assert and defend their interests in the extremely hierarchical society of the Tokugawa, a subject on which there has been much work done recently in Japan.[21] The pretensions associated with official jobs in the town, working for the seigneurial power, encouraged modest townsmen to try to create for themselves some kind of specific status as lower-ranking officials. One can see therefore the development of civil administrative organization, within the framework of the Japanese "society of orders" of the Edo, utilized by certain categories in attempting to ensure their social position, by conforming, at least apparently, to the criteria imposed from above (the status and privilege of being "officials") while in fact attempting to subvert the logic of the whole system. What best illustrated this in the

[21] On this question, see Carré 2011.

social and ideological grammar of the period was quite simply the appearance of social milieus who built up, as best they could, their career horizons and those of their kin within the frame of various offices of public seigneurial Authority.

A second point to be made is that, as in the case of Qing China (as pointed out in the work of Pierre-Etienne Will, 1989), the study of work and bureaucratic organization in Tokugawa Japan should not stop at the tasks and positions most often cited in the documentation, and that only in fact represent positions of management and direction. At all levels, administrative work involved more numerous personnel, but they were often invisible because the chores that were accomplished, however indispensable, were assigned to persons of such low rank that it was not considered necessary, nor even perhaps desirable, to include them in the nomenclatures of the bureaucracy. Such a bureaucratic hierarchy was not only a hierarchy of function, necessary even today for the better organization of an administrative mission. It also retained at that time a statutory dimension of rank or honorability.

Nevertheless, if we take into account the personnel that we have studied, we must change our understanding of bureaucratic systems and of their place in Japanese premodern society. Thus, reading the Ginza archives one can perceive that its chiefs had the capacity to bring modest townsmen into their office, and to assure them of a career, limited to be sure, but with a certain degree of job security (let us keep in mind the length of time implied by service in the General Warehouse). Such minor posts perhaps helped to reinforce the prestige of town councilors and notables among the great commoners officials and helped sustain their networks of influence even if such "big men", despite their institutional character as an élite, with the passing of several generations, were not necessarily at the head of the most flourishing commercial activities of the city.

The last point to be made is more specific. It concerns the location and formation of bourgeois administrative institutions. The day-by-day functioning of an entity such as the Kanazawa mint shows us quite clearly that it was only a piece in the overall plan of warrior government, and directly connected to the bureaucratic organization above it. It is correct to say, however, that such an institution is not only an extension of a vassal band and warrior rule. As city commoners or as an urban institution it could act sometimes as a voice for the professional business groups of the city (money changers, wholesalers). Furthermore, during long periods of tension about coinage, one can see that urban society could demonstrate certain fears on its own behalf and make certain reproaches over the Ginza activities (for example regarding the quality of weighing precision balances, and similar complaints), that could not be expressed directly to the warrior administration.

This somewhat hybrid nature, at the same time a seigneurial delegation and a city commoners' institution, stemmed partly from the status compartmentalization between warriors and townsmen which neither allowed in practice, nor permitted the very idea of, the fusion of administrative structures. Therefore, it was not possible to establish a separate status of functionary which could obviate these differences, since the framework of power was firmly established on the vassal band, a precept at the very basis of the warrior condition that accorded all rank distinction in an extremely hierarchical social setup.

Consequently, it would be a mistake to consider city commoners' offices as merely a way of transmitting seigneurial power. Far from being mere agents of execution, the chiefs of the Ginza or the Elders of the City had a real capacity to initiate and propose, encouraged by the behavior of the warrior administration itself which seemed to prefer to have the least possible contact with the internal business of those of plebian background. City commoners' offices, about whose origins we are quite ill informed, seem to have been as much secreted and fashioned by the merchant societies in Kanazawa as created by the power of Maeda. As the Japanese historian Asao Naohiro has remarked, the institutional system which governed and laid rules for urban and peasant populations was in fact fundamentally a product of their community organizations, diverted by warrior power to serve its own interests (Asao 1995: 123-174).

In fact, the very constitution of the administrative apparatus, or the extension of its missions in the case of the Ginza, appeared as a progressive elaboration under the pressure of circumstances as the best way of responding to new problems and to the expectations of urban society. The mint, without doubt originally a semi-commercial enterprise, in the second half of the seventeenth century became an official organ to certify coinage. Later, at the beginning of the eighteenth century, in a context of monetary crisis, the Ginza and the Urban Prefecture came together to regulate gold and silver markets in Kanazawa. All these evolutions appeared as a result of often improvised measures, rather than as the effect of some clear will to "rationally" organize an administration that united the warriors in charge and the city officials. The amalgamated needs of the growing complexity of seigneurial policies and the economic environment inexorably pushed the Ginza and its personnel towards an integration that was progressively higher up in a bureaucratic system piloted by warriors, a system which always affirmed its roots in society while expanding its own ambitions and objectives. But the "service of the lord" remained a notion doubly determined by conditions of origin and not by the mission accomplished.

The ambiguity about the status of the clerks of the seigneurial Treasury reflected a contradiction between the unwieldy ranks of those subject to a traditional society based on hierarchy and the birth of new categories of employees linked to an emerging administrative apparatus, in which "the service of the lord" or of the "Public Authority" were representations that began to take shape freely as distinct and different activities.

In short, when we look at the establishment and progressive development of seigneurial administrative systems in the Japan of the Edo period we should not simplify. Rather than the germination of a "rationality" struggling against obsolete forms of domination in order to finally become a modern bureaucracy, it would doubtless be wiser to consider these succeeding administrative constructions above all as temporary hook-ups which mixed the constraints of a "society of orders" with the demands of efficiency and the new ambition to achieve it on the part of those governing societies. The results did not necessarily announce the administrative forms inspired by the West that the Japanese adopted during their modernization in the Meiji era. The bureaucratic apparatus of the modern Japanese State was created at the end of the nineteenth century under the stimulus of leaders like Ôkubo Toshimichi. One of the most important statesmen in the beginning of the Meiji era, Ôkubo, took Bismarck's Germany as his practical model, so as to build an administration entirely devoted to realizing ministerial policies. But both the formation and growth of bureaucratic models during the early modern period indicate that, in any case, throughout the Edo period the definition of government increasingly took into account society as a whole. And the progressive elaboration during the seventeenth and eighteenth centuries of composite administrative structures uniting the rule of the fiefs and the institutions representing the city commoners are also a sign of an emergent consciousness: public authority could no longer fulfill the mission assigned to it without going beyond the ruling class and working through people of diverse social status.

Sources

"Kanazawa machikaisho shissan kiroku 1, Tenmei go kinotomi Kanazawa machiyakunin-chô", in *Ishikawa kyôdoshi gakkai kaishi*, 1970.

Ishiguro Archives, Kanazawa

References

Asao, N., (1995), "Sôson kara chô he" ("From the Village Commune to the Military Quarter") in *Toshi to kinsei shakai wo kangaeru* ("Reflections on Premodern Town and Society"), Tokyo: Asahi shinbunsha: 123-174.

Carré, G., (2011), "Les marges statutaires dans le Japon prémoderne: enjeux et débats", *Annales, Histoire, Sciences Sociales*, 4, "Les statuts sociaux au Japon" : 955-976.

Castan, N., (1980), *Justice et répression en Languedoc à l'époque des Lumières*, Paris: Flammarion.

Dore, R.P., (1965), *Education in Tokugawa Japan*, London: Routledge & Kegan Paul.

Fujii, J., (1999) *Edo jidai no kanryôsei* (The Bureaucratic System of the Edo Period), Tokyo: Aoki shoten.

Fukaya, K., (1993), *Taikei Nihon no rekishi 9 Shi-nô-kô-shô no yo* (The World of the Four Statutes), Tokyo: Shôgakkan.

Isoda, M., (2003), *Buke no kaikeibo* (The Account Books of a Warrior House), Tokyo: Shinsho shinchô.

Ishikawa-Ken, *Ishikawa kenshi*, vol. 3, Kanazawa, (1938) (reprint), Genroku 8/2/29.

"Kanazawa machikaisho shissan kiroku 1, Tenmei go kinotomi Kanazawa machiyakunin-chô", in *Ishikawa kyôdoshi gakkai kaishi*, (1970).

Kurushima, H., (2002), *Kinsei bakuryó no gyôsei to kumiai-mura* (The Administration of the Shogounate Territories and the Associate Villages), Tokyo: Tôkyô daigaku shuppankai.

Morishita, T., (2007), *Kinsei buke hôkônin to rôdô shakai* (The Warrior Domestic Sphere in the Premodern Period and the World of Work), Tokyo: Yamakawa shuppansha.

—. (2011), "Les guerriers et leurs domestiques dans la ville seigneuriale de Hagi", *Annales*, 4, "Les statuts sociaux au Japon" : 977-1004.

Nishizaka, Y., (2006), *Mitsui hôkônin no kenkyû* (Studies on the Employees of Mitsui), Tokyo: Tôkyô daigaku shuppankai.

Takagi, S., (1990), *Nihon kinsei kokka-shi no kenkyû* (Studies of the History of the Premodern Japanese State), Tokyo: Iwanami Shoten.

Tanaka, Y., (1984), *Jôkamachi Kanazawa* (The Seigneurial City of Kanazawa), Kôjunsha.

Will, P.É., (1989), "Bureaucratie officielle et bureaucratie réelle: sur quelques dilemmes de l'administration impériale à l'époque des Qing", *Études chinoises* 8/1: 69-142.

Yoshida, N., (2002), *Seijuku suru Edo* (Edo in Its Maturity), Tokyo: Kôdansha.

Yoshiwara, K., (1980), *Edo no machiyakunin* (The city commoners officers of Edo), Tokyo, Yoshikawa kôbunkan.

CHAPTER THIRTEEN

COMMENTS ON THE TEXTS ABOUT ASIA

JOSEP MARIA DELGADO,
JOSEP MARÍA FRADERA AND MANEL OLLÉ

The Status of the Lord's Subordinate Servants in the *Han* of the Maeda

Josep María Delgado

Guillaume Carré analyses the development of a system of bureaucratic government that was unknown in the medieval shogunate (*kanryôsei*). The administrative apparatuses that were developed in seventeenth-century Japan did not attempt to resurrect the bureaucratic forms that had functioned between the eighth and eleventh centuries. From that point on, the administrative functions were organized on the local level in the framework of the *han*; the *daimyo* governed autonomously just as the territories that belonged to the Tokugawa lineage were ruled.

The starting point of this evolution has to be defined as the day after the Battle of the Sekigahara (October 21, 1600) at a time when there were no administrative organizations other than the vassalages of military origin. Historical studies tend to focus on the genesis of the administration by the Samurai or the *yakusho* offices, ceded to the bourgeoisie. These posts had a distinctive institutional character and were subjected to the jurisdiction of the *bushi*; they had limited functions as part of a society strictly organized in estates that excluded the possibility of pursuing a career in the administration based on merit.

The definition of bureaucracy here should not be focused on nominative or career-based criteria but rather on practices in the workplace, the exercise of authority, and a certain way of viewing the social reality and its control. This bureaucracy was perfectly integrated into the social order that had produced it and was dependent on the society of estates. The object of this study is the seigneurial city of Kanazawa, capital of the *han* of the Maeda. More than half of its 120,000 inhabitants did not form part of the military estate, and were completely segregated, for while the warriors lived inside the castle's walled enclosure, the bourgeoisie resided in separate neighborhoods.

The Bourgeois Officials of Kanazawa

The representatives of the seigniorial power made the appointments to these offices that were not hereditary, unlike those in other cities, although the most important ones circulated among a limited number of the city's most important bourgeois families, linked by privileged ties to the *bushi* aristocracy. As they were not venal offices, it was impossible to incorporate them into a family's patrimony.

A register from 1785 provides an overview of the principal functions that the bourgeois bureaucrats of Kanazawa carried out at the beginning of the century: 300 offices organized in a clear hierarchy. Their elite was formed by about twenty of them, who enjoyed the right to have audiences with the lord, and this in turn enabled them to be spokesmen for the city's bourgeoisie. They therefore had a special status in relation to the rest of the commoners. These twenty offices were in charge of directing the city's most important organizations for the bourgeoisie: the town council, mint and urban prefects (the *machibugyo,* who administered the bourgeois neighborhoods).

They carried out three different kinds of functions:

- management and administration of the bourgeois neighborhoods, with the elders (*toshiyori*) as the highest authorities.
- representation of the different offices, merchants, and artisans.
- activities concerned with handling the currency and funds designated to facilitate the power of the warriors, whether they were for lending transactions (especially to vassals) or for guaranteeing their quality. All of these offices were supervised by the government of the elders coming from the town council.

In short, the powers of these bourgeoisie functionaries were limited to realms associated with their rank or considered as such, such as the handling of precious metals. We recognize that a total of 300 individuals out of a population of 60,000 commoners could appear to be very few employees, but only the highest-ranking category of bureaucrats was examined here.

The Ginza and Public Regulation of Currency

The Ginza was the mint where the Maeda clan coined its own silver money until 1669; the mint of the shogunate was also granted such a monopoly and had the same name.

In 1669, the mint stopped coining its own money in order to make way for the Tokugawa currency. From that moment on, its employees' activities were centered on acting as the inspectors of the weight of the currency and attesters of its value. At the request of the territorial authorities, the coins were weighed to determine their value and put in containers that certified their weight and value. The bureaucrats of the Ginza were also authorized to detect false or tampered-with currency, as well as fraudulent containers. These functions required certain skills, which conceded a high standing to those that exercised them; this prestige was then put to use for the benefit of the individuals that could certify and pack the sums received for verification. All of this was carried out in exchange for a commission that swelled the seigneurial treasury and served to cover the costs of operations, including the workers' salaries.

There also existed five other similar organizations in other cities of the dominion, which were subject to the Ginza of Kanazawa.

In addition to these eminently technical functions, the Ginza's employees were in charge of relations between the seigneurial authorities and the world of finance in Kanazawa. They thereby exercised functions on behalf of the authority that involved supervising the corporation of money changers and fluctuations in the relative value of the gold and silver coins, in addition to informing the authorities about the introduction of new currencies in the exchange market. In brief, they guaranteed the circulation of money in Kanazawa and Kaga. In any event, the employees' powers were neither sovereign nor statutory for they were delegated by the seigneurial authorities, who could diminish or increase them at any moment.

They were equally obligated to constantly inform their superiors who then made their decisions based on the information received about the circulation of money and the dominion's finances. These specific functions of controlling and supervising the monetary circulation did not exist during the period before the shogunate.

The number of functionaries varied from two to four. At the beginning of the eighteenth century, two from the highest-level of the hierarchy were positioned just below the council of elders. As they took turns holding the position, they could simultaneously exercise another office. Their selection was a function of the honorability of their lineage and not of the professional competences demonstrated in the workrooms of the mint. A private money changer never acceded to these positions.

Organization of the Ginza and the General Depository

We find that each person in charge led a team of ten men that completed the everyday tasks. The subordinates were divided into two categories with the first judging the authenticity of, and supervising the work of the second:

- experts in money (*kanemi*) that knew the different types of currency that circulated
- packers and weighers of the physical money.

Located inside the seigneurial castle, the General Depository was under the authority of the Ginza so the money that was deposited in the seigneurial treasury could be examined, weighed, and packed.

The Employees of the Ginza and General Depository

Let us begin by seeing who could apply to these positions. The applicants were generally the sons of the city's bourgeoisie and sometimes lower-ranking *bushi*. The possibility of professional promotion existed, for the structure also included the five inspection offices for currency in the dominion. The appointments to the Ginza were based on the recommendations of those that were in charge of the institution though in order to accede to the treasury of seigneurial castle, it was necessary to be approved by the elders and military authorities (urban and auditing prefects). The appointment to the General Depository represented a promotion in the employee's status that, in addition to providing a better income, elevated the person above those that worked for the Ginza. The proximity to the seigneurial power resulted in more recognition and had a greater symbolic value even if the two jobs were technically similar.

The functionaries of the General Depository could also engage in other professional activities; the terms of address they received were equal to that of an *ashigaru.* Social status and birth were the essential criteria in order to enter the seigneurial administration.

In any case, the employees of the Ginza and the General Depository were however subordinates. Recommended by their parents or a close relative, the employees started to work as young men, and completed their apprenticeship within the Ginza, just as store clerks did, who were designated by the term *tendai*. In fact, the men in charge of the Ginza could work at the same time as private merchants and administrators of the lord's affairs, as if it were a bourgeois trading house.

Ensuring their Status

Professor Carré analyzed the collective action of six of the General Depository's employees, who asked the prefects of Kanazawa to consider allowing one of their nephews to succeed a deceased functionary. The request was denied by their supervisors, who felt that their subordinates wanted to transgress the election process that necessarily included the authorities' own choice of nominees. In addition, the applicant was a minor. This case brought face-to-face two distinct criteria: that of the employees of the General Depository, who hoped to elect their own successor, making use of a logic that defined the post as patrimony that should remain in the same family—as experience demonstrated really happened (patrimonialization of the position). On the other hand, those that were in charge of the Ginza defended a logic of promotion by merit when it came to occupying new positions and this gave priority to the functionaries that already worked under their supervision and had demonstrated more merit and zeal. It has to be kept in mind that the employees were subjected to a patriarchal type of authority. Patrimonialization and meritocracy were the two guiding principles that progressively consolidated the public service administration in the context of the society of estates that predominated under the Tokugawa.

Vindications and Compromise

The military authorities were well aware of the subordinate bourgeoisie officials' wish to perpetuate their status and could accept it to a certain point; the occupations in the Ginza or General Depository granted the possibility of providing work for younger members of the family, a stable income, and the protection of the dominion, an aspiration that was nevertheless at odds with the limited respect the military authorities had for those of common lineage.

In 1717, two inspectors of outlying mints and an inspector of the General Depository asked to be allowed to choose their successors. The first two selected a son and the third an employee that was in the service of a dignitary. Do these examples illustrate the awareness of their common interests or an *esprit de corps*? These proposals were rejected by the warriors. The authorities opted for a meritocratic solution, even if on numerous occasions succession was accepted as an indispensable way to get candidates to compete for the lower-ranking positions, and this became the base for professionalizing generations of administrators.

Conclusions

The members of the lower strata of the bourgeoisie tried to find a way to establish themselves and defend their interests in a society of orders, creating the specific status of subordinate official, respecting the established criteria but at the same time, trying to subvert them. All of this underlines the need to pay attention to the lower levels of the seigneurial administration. In the Ginza, the high-ranking plebian functionaries had the power to introduce humbler plebeians into their trade and guarantee them a limited but very stable job; this ability obviously reinforced the prestige of these higher-ranking bourgeois positions.

We are therefore in the presence of a distinctive administrative apparatus, the extension of a mechanism based on vassalage, though it in turn interacted with the most dynamic elements of the bourgeois society such as money changers or merchants, that is, it had a character that could be described as being "hybrid". It is necessary to consider the long-term evolution of the bureaucracy by analyzing this hybrid character of its apparatuses, where some bourgeoisie classes accepted the limitations of the society of estates, as they in fact undermined them from within through their strategies of social reproduction. In any case, we should not forget that the dominion of the Maeda line is most probably the richest in Japan, and in some aspects rather atypical. As a result it would be necessary to expand this study the future so as to include other dominions of that epoch.

The Transformation of Collaboration: Knowledge and Bureaucracy in the Formation of the East India Company

Josep M. Fradera

The days in which historians divided up the East India Company's activities into two fundamental stages—a purely commercial one from its initial centuries until 1757, followed by the second one of state building in the context of the British Empire between 1757 and 1857—have now quite definitely ended. Today we tend to see both stages as a historical continuum, in which, in any case, it is necessary to go about making finer distinctions, establishing nuances, and pointing out the changes in the performance of the British company with its privileged status in relation to commerce with Asia.

Professor Kapil Raj's article very convincingly forms part of this analytical approach. The position that it defends is ultimately resolved by analyzing two vectors that intersected for more than two centuries. The first one functioned essentially by accumulation. Here, we are obviously referring to the gathering of the know-how that the Company had at its disposal in the different areas in which it operated. In order to fulfill its mission, the Company indeed required administrative information, accountants, access to credit, diplomatic, and in some cases even military, activity. It therefore needed not only to get to know and operate in the limited territory where it was initially established—the remote origins of what would subsequently become the three presidencies in Calcutta, Madras, and Bombay—but also to gather information about the subcontinent in broader terms. In short, the merchandise that the Company was interested in, as well as the political equilibria that guaranteed its presence, did not depend on the strictly local setting or, even more generally, on the regional space in which they were produced. A wider knowledge proved essential for survival and for being able to trade successfully while dealing with such different societies. How was this knowledge obtained?

In this case, the question to be considered is how the border was crossed between the British world and the world of those who were already settled there, a world made up of the Portuguese, the Armenian, and other diasporas, that is, groups that were not strictly local. The necessary information could be accessed through two channels. The first was formalized knowledge through texts or through the Company's own administrative processes and that of the British state bureaucracy. The other channel was knowledge derived from exchanges with groups of local experts. Few doubts can be raised about which of the two constituted the more substantial stock of knowledge. It was obviously the latter, at least until a very late period, when its legal formalization by *lettrés* had gained greater relevance (one of the principal concerns Warren Hastings had as director in Calcutta, starting in 1774). Previously, the relative weight of each source of information was not clearly differentiated since they derived from formal and informal contacts with the local world. Professor Raj is an eminent specialist in the history of the formation of knowledge and its transmission through strictly formal systems as well as more informal ones. In this case, both were certainly vital, although the relative proportions could change according to the places and epochs.

Before the great changes that occurred during the second half of the eighteenth century, the Company administered small territories discretely on both coasts of the subcontinent. Even in these circumstances, it never limited its activities to merely mercantile ones, that is, those commercial activities it was privileged to be exclusively authorized to perform. The establishment of the Company in Madras or Calcutta certainly required certain skills, not only those commonly attributed to merchants. In effect, even when the Company was an incipient project, its abiding presence on the coasts of the subcontinent forced its functionaries to deploy skills that are most commonly attributed to diplomats, magistrates, and on certain occasions, the military. It was essential to gain a suitable space, prevail over others, and extend the Company's activities beyond the *entrepôts* authorized by the native powers.

The Company's functionaries therefore established stable relations over a long period of time with certain social groups that were already established there. They included the *banyans* (merchants), present throughout the subcontinent, and the *karanams* (magistrates-mediators) of Madras, who were a local example of a specialization that existed in other areas, though with other particularities. The latter became absolutely indispensable collaborators for the survival and prospering of Company's representatives in an environment about which they lacked corroborated information before their establishment on site. In addition, as the Company's functionaries were very young when they reached the Indian ports and lacked any specific training, the relationship and, in a certain way, the alliance with the representatives of the local world were entirely inevitable and generally desirable for both sides. Neither group—*banyans* or *karanamas*—ever restricted itself to providing exclusively the specific knowledge it possessed. The Indian merchants generally doubled as bankers, but at the same time they provided political information about the small states or inner workings of the Mongol Empire or Marata Confederation. Local scholars or magistrates were simultaneously experts in languages, religions, and, above all, possessed a very valuable understanding of the legal framework that regulated life in the locality and/or even on a larger scale. Without such knowledge, whether it was transmitted formally or informally, involving military force or not, the expansion in the activities of the Company as we know it would have turned out to be very problematic. If it is clear that the British needed to learn and absorb a great deal from their collaborators on site, it seems reasonable to suggest that the latter in turn learned from their European associates—the skills with which those foreigners projected their priorities onto remote places and also about their systems of religious, economic, or political values. The nature of the exchange was certainly not the same. No Indian deemed the British Isles as the place through which his world could be expanded. Nonetheless, the concept of colonialism is not really applicable to the description of the initial contacts between two worlds during the first centuries of relation and exchange.

We know (retrospectively) that something very distinct would begin to take shape as a result of the particular manner in which the Company set itself up in Bengal. The liquidation of a previous British establishment in Hugli (nominally a Dutch colony) resulted in an inevitable shift in strategy thanks to the Company's artfulness: the purchase of almost one thousand hectares further south in 1698 for the foundation of Calcutta. In this space, located on the periphery of a province of the Mongol empire, the Company no longer shared its installations with the other commercial diasporas; its employees started to administer justice and a few other modest functions that had been linked until then to the local powers to which it was accountable. Then, the administrative spaces were articulated step by step, and this was indispensable for administering a locality that expanded rapidly until it became a city of a certain size. Once again the British were not the only ones administering and organizing the city, even though in the 1730s the Company had established the Mayor's Court where justice was dispensed.

In a very influential compilation, C.A. Bayly underlined this ability to export a legal system, based on the English model, as a distinctive note of the mature British dominion in the Indian enclaves. The formalization of a magistrature in Calcutta was nevertheless not limited to the British. It also little by little took charge of administering justice to the local people, notably when conflicts arose between the British and them. It required a greater knowledge of the law or even better yet, of the distinct judicial system with its very diverse linguistic bases that served very disparate groups, and that entailed appealing to interpreters and Hindu and Muslim magistrates. It was therefore not surprising that Warren Hastings' mandate was dominated by the idea of bringing the Indian world under control through knowledge and more extensive training for the British functionary, the only way to gain access (with more guarantees and depth) to that information provided by the intermediaries between both worlds.

It does not appear to be very daring to define this stage of selective collaboration by evoking the image of shared spaces; in many cases no established hierarchy defined everyday contact and the general interrelation between power and knowledge. The distant power of the British world compensated to a certain extent for the proximity of the competing indigenous powers in the second half of the eighteenth century. It was, nevertheless, the growth of the Europeans' power in India itself that gave rise to a notable change in the Company's strategies. The increase of exchanges, shortage of cash, and expansion of the British country traders' field of action accelerated the expansion of British interests in Asia, and as a result, whetted the Company's functionaries' appetites for taking over the collection of taxes in some territories. This change of strategy, which was added to previous demands concerning the administration of justice, required the formation of a more professionalized administration that was trained on site. This vocation provided the basis for Hastings' policies and their ultimate failure. The famine in Bengal, and the perception in London that the imperial state needed to establish limits that the East India Company should not transgress, led to the famous inquiry and the establishment of a sophisticated system of control based in the Parliament. In this context, the previous forms and frameworks of the collaboration between the Indians and the British would progressively be altered until they resulted in something quite distinct: the outline of a colonial hierarchy.

This greater colonial density was reinforced by the results of the Seven Years' War and its prolongation in a second phase during the Napoleonic wars. If the collection of the *diwani* or Mongol fiscality was indispensable for financing and invigorating commerce with Asia, it was even more necessary for paying for the territorial acquisitions that were intended to protect the British positions from French ambitions. In 1797-98, British isolation, the Napoleonic expedition to Egypt, and dalliance with the sultan Tipu of Mysore confirmed that the development of a fiscal-military model (that of the Wellesley brothers) was absolutely indispensable, even though its shareholders complained of its high cost. The strategy that would then be implemented would dominate the history of the Company in the subsequent decades, as well as the formalization of British domination over the entire subcontinent "from conquest to conquest" as David Washbrook summed it up. In this context altered by the war, information and knowledge both contributed to the development of a British administration that was more complex and better prepared than the previous ones had been. Only decades later in the 1830s and 1840s, when the Company was lord and master of the subcontinent, did the progressive weakening of the constant, informal connection with the collaborators from previous centuries diminish the acuity of the rich vision that the British had of the local needs and moods of very complex populations. It does not seem necessary here to mention the far-reaching consequences of this victory of "Orientalism" over participatory observation.

The Transformations of China's Bureaucratic System

Manuel Ollé

In the last centuries, some essentializing generalizations have been postulated about China, alleging that it has more civilization than history because of its cultural determinism. They represent yet another avatar of the already long-standing cliché of an atavistic China, enclosed in its walls and always the same. Rigorous historical studies, clearly explained and based on new documentation—such as those by Christian Lamouroux and Pierre-Étienne Will in this volume—serve as the best antidote to these generalizations. These studies are based on new documentation about specific features of the formation and development of the bureaucracy in two exceptional periods of the history of the Chinese empire (respectively the beginning of the Song dynasty—eleventh century—and the peak of the Qing dynasty—eighteenth century). Despite the substantial historiographical advances made over the last decades, the understanding of China has been reformulated to some extent since the eighteenth century by one sector of Sinological historiography, and even more implicitly in certain characterizations of the subject that are found in textbooks and in general syntheses and that continue to have some impact in the global university sphere. This situation dates far back, at least from when Voltaire the Sinophile affirmed that the core of the Chinese empire had survived with all its splendor for more than 4000 years without its laws, customs, language, or even the way its inhabitants dressed undergoing any noticeable change.

According to the alternative Sinophobic paradigm, the biological conception of culture that formed the foundation of Herder's works identified in China an infantile nature "full of filial submission to its despots". In his *Lessons on the Philosophy of History*, Hegel defined China's static and unhistorical essence when he considers that China is the most ancient state yet nevertheless, it lacks a past: "Empires belonging to mere space, as it were—unhistorical History;--as for example, in China, the State based on the Family relation; (…) This History, too is, for the most part, really unhistorical, for it is only the repetition of the same majestic ruin".[1] Despite his harsh criticism of Hegel's conception of history, Marx adopted his predecessor's ideas about China's stagnation. Marx defined the Asian mode of production as a cul-de-sac outside of the linear progression of the historical process (in the Marxist conception of history), that is, an area without history, in which the weight of the state in all the economic and social spheres had neutralized the "historical energy" of the oppressed. If the Chinese had any history, it would be the history of religion; once again, more civilization (Confucian) than history. Wittfogel's theories about Oriental hydraulic despotism, or Max Weber's diagnostic according to which Confucianism blocked (through the iron rule of the bureaucracy) China's economic development and the rise of capitalism in the Middle Kingdom, insist on this essentialist paradigm of China's millennial immobility. (This specious argument has been precisely employed in the past few decades in the opposite sense, notably by affirming that the disciplined, laborious subordination of the individual to the groups made up by the family and the state explains the success of the Asian Confucian and principally authoritarian… dragons and tigers).

In the specific field of study about Chinese bureaucracy that concerns us here, these essentialist and culturalist perspectives found in Weber's theories a thorough diagnostic that subsequently had great influence. The early development in China of the meritocratic system of the reproduction of power, the generalizing of the imperial exams in the eighth century, the perception that the Chinese bureaucratic system was centralized in a codified hierarchy, and the territorial impact of the imperial power throughout centuries all led Weber to believe that Chinese society was absolutely dependent on, and shaped by, an omnipresent highly-efficient

---

[1] G. W. F. Hegel, *Lecciones sobre la filosofía de la historia universal*, Madrid, Revista de Occidente, 1974, p. 238.

bureaucratic system that guaranteed the Chinese Empire's great ability to prolong its spatial and temporal continuity.

Any description of the Chinese bureaucratic system that is to some degree based on this type of Weberian approach is no longer completely defensible, to the extent that in-depth studies about different periods allow us to examine objectively the intervention of other agencies and distinct specific dynamics that occurred in the interplay of complex tensions and were not essentially different from those that existed in other empires, on the margins of this idealized schema. The landowning elite, mercantile networks, religious organizations, family loyalties, and dynamics of local or regional particularities wove and renegotiated relations with the bureaucracy and other intermediaries of the imperial power and this led to a changing reconfiguration of the shares of power, loyalty, or influence that cannot be overlooked. In this process the bureaucracy was a mechanism of coercion as well as a means of exerting influence, and of promoting and projecting sectorial or territorial interests.

Despite the mirages of the imperial system and the centennial continuity of the bureaucratic system, its reiterative reconfigurations and transformations present very noteworthy variations. Thus, for example, the dialectic between the "external court" (based on the bureaucratic system that was diffused throughout the territory) and the "internal court" (theoretically centered on service to the emperor) was not always resolved in the same manner. We can identify emperors that did not accept a merely ritual and religious role, for they even went so far as to promote from the internal court their hold over the territory, and to delegate administrative and fiscal tasks to groups such as the eunuchs, who were not initially envisioned for this kind of work. Likewise, we can see, from the fringes of the ordinary channels of exercising power, the territorial elite could take advantage of the direct influence they held in the palace by placing family members in collectives such as the eunuchs or concubines of the internal court, close to the imperial pinnacle. Finally, it is essential to take into account the network of interests and effective exercise of territorial power by members of the imperial family itself, as it had great scope and remarkable influence during certain periods. These were superimposed on the formal hierarchy of the bureaucratic system or even clashed with it.

In his article, Christian Lamouroux demonstrates how the bureaucratic system constructed during the initial period of the Northern Song dynasty (960-1127) fixed its roots in the decades of crisis and fragmentation that followed the fall of the Tang dynasty (620-907), thereby incorporating influences from Central Asian forms of organization that were brought in by the so-called "Sinized dynasties" (the Liao, Jin) from the north. It consequently refutes Chinese historiography's most cherished account that interprets the bureaucratic splendor of the Song period (described by Jacques Gernet as a "Chinese Renaissance") as the culmination and continuation of a process that started at the height of the previous great unified dynasty, the Tang, thanks to the generalization of the system of imperial exams. We thus see how the perception of a process marked by Sinocentrism remains debatable; it cannot even conceive of the reception of foreign influences, for it understands its relation with the periphery in terms of cultural paternalism, with China representing, in this schema, the center that influences and civilizes the barbarianism of foreign peoples. It understands its relation with the periphery in terms of a tributary hierarchy, when precisely during the reign of the Song inter-imperial taxation occurred the other way around, as it was China that bought peace in exchange for the silk, tea, or silver handed over to the northern kingdoms.

During the period that Christian Lamouroux studies, the idealization originating in Chinese historiography's self-perception tends to place more emphasis on the ideological factor (imperial exams, Confucianism, the unity of the empire) than on the singularity and complexity of the process. His own analysis clarifies and refutes this ideological version by the explication of a historical process that does not emerge from a preconceived plan for the deployment of a self-conscious system of bureaucracy, but rather corresponds to a complex, dynamic configuration, with turnabouts, unanticipated actors, diverse influences, and the presence of exogenous factors. In the period under examination, the process of constructing the bureaucracy presents the apparent paradox of being founded on—by virtue of the autocratic exercise of imperial power—a human and organizational base that originated in the military estate while, at the same time, the civil values that arose among the learned functionaries were spread and replicated after the establishment of the imperial exams.

The bureaucratization of a sector of the military estate contributed to the political centralization of the period. Chinese historiography reflected and partially encapsulated this process in the exemplary tale that wound up creating an adage referring to the exercise of political power: 杯酒释兵权 *beijiu shi bingquan*, meaning literally, "dissolve the military power in a glass of wine". This expression is used for what is understood to be a wise way of removing someone elegantly and discretely from power. Traditional Chinese historiography related that during the very first year of the Song dynasty, on August 20, 1061 precisely, the emperor Taizu, heeding the advice of his advisor Zhao Pu, invited the different heads of the military provinces, conspirators that could plot to overthrow him, to a banquet in the palace. In the toast, the emperor Taizu, in a subtle, diplomatic, and seductive manner, suggested to his regional commanders that it would be a good idea for them to give up their military authority, leave the court, and become bureaucrats in their prefectures, where they would be granted spacious mansions as a perk. According to traditional Chinese historiography, the emperor's power of persuasion was so strong that by the next day, almost all of the regional military commanders had already resigned from their posts, making way for reorganization and subordination to the civil power. The replacement of these old powerful commanders by young men of proven loyalty neutralized the threat and underscored that feature of the processes that was ideologically reflected in the "mirror of princes", as it was conceived of by history in imperial times: a characteristically subtle, harmonious, and intelligent exercise of power. The other factors and processes that were obviously involved in the process were left out of the tale.

Focusing on the eighteenth century, Pierre-Étienne Will starts from the apparent paradox of a bureaucratic system that, remaining numerically comparable to those of previous centuries, was nevertheless able to govern during a period marked by the rapid increase in a population that grew at a much faster rate than arable land expanded. This vibrant economic setting had to be subjected to taxation, and monitored in view of service to the imperial power, all in the context of wars of expansion in central Asia. Chinese agriculture reached its highest point of development during the eighteenth century. It managed to make the most of the land by complementing the traditional crops (millet, rice, wheat, barley) with new ones (potato, corn, sweet potato, sorghum) that allowed peasants to make good use of the winter, and of poorly irrigated lands. Some of these new crops originated in America and entered China through the Spanish colony of the Philippines. During this period, crops for industrial use (cotton, tea, sugarcane) were also developed, and the domestic raising of pork and fowl as well as fish farming also increased.

The institutional milieu played a decisive role in this development. Launched at the end of the seventeenth century, the agrarian and fiscal policy of the Qing dynasty adopted an approach that greatly favored small-scale peasantry, which then enjoyed the period characterized by the lightest tax burden in its history. This parallel growth of the population and production of food fell into a period of crisis by the mid-eighteenth century. At that moment, the amount of arable land per person clearly started to recede.

The viability of the models of ideological coercion and reformulation of the systems of mutual vigilance and collective responsibility established in families and on the local level (the *Baojia* 保甲 system), which led to social and fiscal autoregulation, has been adduced as one of the explanations elucidating the apparent paradox of an increase in population accompanied by the preservation of a stable contingent of functionaries. It has equally been argued that the ability to involve intermediary groups drawn from the networks of merchants or landowners, in order to subcontract elements that did not form part of the bureaucratic hierarchy, would enable the bureaucratic system to acquire capillarity and effective territorial scope. By itself it was incapable of reaching the base of the pyramid constituted by the territorial hierarchy. Finally, other approaches suggest that the efficiency of the bureaucratic system possibly increased during the period under consideration.

Studying in depth this last explanation centered on the initiatives aimed at increasing bureaucratic efficiency, Pierre-Étienne Will explores and analyzes different top-down initiatives directly promoted by the summit of the empire, notably by emperors such as Yongzheng (1723-1735) and Qianlong (1763-1795) that were deeply involved in duties related to governing. The commitment of the Qing emperors to political action has been interpreted in psychological or even cultural terms. The fact that the Qing royal family belonged to the Manchu ethnicity, rather than to the Han, the central ethnicity that dominated the course of Chinese history, could explain this need to gain legitimacy and win the favor of subjects who, in principle, could perceive the newcomers as members of an illegitimate foreign dynasty. Moving beyond this type of cultural explication, Pierre-Étienne Will adduces the anxious concern the good ruler would have to resolve the difficult structural tensions caused by the growth of the population and stagnation in new lands being tilled. It is possible to distinguish between two schools of thought or tendencies in the plan that underlies these governmental actions: the minimalist or conservative approach that points to *laissez-faire* and the interventionist leanings, marked by campaigns and supervised initiatives.

In his text, Pierre-Étienne Will analyzes distinct acts or dynamics from that period aimed at achieving bureaucratic efficiency. He examines the manuals for functionaries and the synchronization of the system of couriers and the communication that assured the rapid circulation of orders and information. It even allowed the emperor to supervise and direct faraway proceedings in a tangible effective manner.

Pierre-Étienne Will studies in more depth several edicts and campaigns for auditing and overseeing land taxes, as well as those geared toward generating awareness, reading, assimilation, and general mobilization through imperial orders, ordinances, and edicts directed at the functionaries. In these consciousness-raising activities, some sectors of the historiography have identified a certain "family" resemblance to the movements (*yundong* 运动) of ideological formation and dissemination that characterized the era of Mao. Although similarities can obviously be detected, there are also clear institutional, discursive, and formal differences. While the former processes were limited to certain sectors or positions on the bureaucratic ladder, the Maoist campaigns sought to indoctrinate the entire population. And while some processes simply aimed to improve the efficiency of the bureaucracy, the objective of the others was to change the mindset of the entire population, in the interest of constructing a "new man" and of transformation. So, although the rituals partially coincide, the recipients and intentions were distinct.

We see a similar case of possible historical parallelism, and an example of the total involvement of the emperor in remote affairs, at the beginning of the eighteenth century when the Manchu emperor Yongzheng insisted on personally monitoring the minor details of the inquiry to unmask a plot against the Manchus. He was equally obsessed with obtaining, at any price, the self-incrimination and written self-criticism of the scholars that headed the conspiracy against him. It allows us to see how the palace drove forward and recorded the slightest advance in the case. The emperor Yongzheng ordered the compilation of the letters exchanged with the anti-Manchu insurgent in a book entitled *Awakening from Delusion*. He then dictated that most of the Chinese population should read and study the book in fortnightly sessions. All of this sounds quite familiar to anyone versed in Maoism's methods of indoctrination and collective re-education. It could appear to be directly copied by the Maoist obsession for self-criticism, public confessions, and the pedagogical rehabilitation of public enemies who recognized their mistakes and turned themselves over to the party's infinite will. Thus, for example, the case of the last Manchu emperor, Pu Yi, working as a gardener in Peking after having been subjected to long sessions of self-incrimination and reeducation (and after having published their outcome in the book *From Emperor to Citizen*) appears to be a literal carbon copy of the case involving a conspirator who rose up against Yongzheng at the beginning of the eighteenth century: he was also magnanimously and benevolently released by the emperor, who had previously subjected him to a process of reeducation through an epistolary exchange and personal encounters.

The Sinologue Jonathan D. Spence narrates this incident in detail as a novelized account in *Treason by the Book* that represents an exemplary model of narrative historiography; it is crowned by a more than one hundred-page appendix, where the documentary sources that support its veracity are individually identified. We also find an obsession with maintaining a submissive and harmonious educated class in the service of the state prefigured in the Manchu emperors' subsequent literary inquiries. The trial of literary persecution undertaken by the emperor Yongzheng and described by Jonathan Spence can vividly remind us of the repression of Chinese intellectuals that was already, in the heroic times of Yan'an in 1942, the subject of theorization signed by Mao Zedong, intensified after the Campaign of 100 Flowers and reached its climax during the Cultural Revolution. We began by emphasizing the absence of essential characteristics or cultural atavisms. Such an assertion does not prevent us from taking into account continuities and influences between periods. We could perhaps even now endorse Mark Twain's words when he wrote that "History doesn't repeat itself, but it does rhyme."

The two articles that have been commented on here contextualize and expound, provide data, bibliographical traditions, and fundamental interpretations for a more complete understanding of the peculiarities of each specific dynamic of the Chinese bureaucratic system.

GLOSSARY OF SPANISH TERMS

Adelantamiento: military district inherited from the Middle Ages; it was delegated to the *adelantados*, whom the king appointed to govern and impart justice in the assigned jurisdiction.

Alcalde: magistrate in general: word that derives from the Arabic *alcadí*, which has designated the official in charge of administering justice at the local level since the Middle Ages; from the nineteenth century it has been used to refer to the person that heads a municipal government.

Alcalde de Hermandad: judge, usually without a formal legal education, appointed to a rural area.

Alcalde ordinario: magistrate that formed part of medieval and modern *concejos* in Spain and *cabildos* in America.

Alcalde mayor: in medieval Castile, this position was assigned to administering justice, whether the appointee had a legal education or not. He assisted the governor of a territory by completing the relevant judicial tasks. In colonial America, it became the highest municipal authority, and presided over the *cabildo*, appointing its officials and employees and exercising jurisdiction over civil and criminal cases, thus ranking higher than the *alcaldes ordinarios*.

Alcaldes de Casa y Corte: judges of the chamber of justice of the Royal Court; their jurisdiction was limited to the five leagues that surrounded the Court's seat except for cases of robbery, when it was extended to a maximum of twenty leagues.

Alcaldes de crimen or *Alcaldes de Chancillería*: professional "robed" judges, who were members of the criminal courts in the *audiencias* and chanceries. They were designated by the king, who selected them from a short list of three candidates proposed by the *Cámara de Castilla*.

Alcaldes de hijosdalgo: these professional "robed" judges, as members of the chamber for the lower nobility (*Hijosdalgo*) in the chanceries of Valladolid and Granada, were in charge of the lawsuits that involved the *hidalguía*.

Alcaldes de la Mesta y cañadas: judges whose jurisdiction included cases concerning the *Mesta*, a Castilian institution of medieval origin. This corporation for stockbreeders offered its members diverse prerogatives and privileges, such as grazing rights, access to drovers' roads and specific legal exemptions.

Alcaldes de las sacas y cosas vedadas: judges in Castile that had the power to institute legal proceedings in the case of offenses against the laws that prohibited exporting articles specified in these dispositions, which specifically referred to any form of gold, silver or other precious metals.

Alcaldías mayores: territorial jurisdiction presided over by an *alcalde mayor*, who was the king's representative entrusted with the matters of government and justice in his respective circumscription. In Spain, the *alcaldes mayors* answered to the *corregidor*, while in America, fundamentally in New Spain, their territorial jurisdiction was similar to the one that the *corregidores* possessed in the viceroyalty of Peru.

Alcaidía: the jurisdiction of an. *alcaide*

Alcaidías de Fortaleza: posts filled by men designated by the king or a lord to defend and guard a fortress. Most of these offices were sold in perpetuity throughout the sixteenth and seventeenth centuries while at the same time they acquired a merely honorific character.

Audiencia: high court of justice and organ of governance; for example, the *Audiencia* replaced the Viceroy or the General Captain in case of death or legal impediment.

Ayuntamiento/s: municipality and sometimes *cabildo*.

Asientos: contracts drawn up between the monarchy and entrepreneurs for the provision of certain goods, generally for the army and navy. The individuals that signed the contracts were known as "*asentistas*" (contractors).

Bailío: king's delegate put in charge of administering justice in the Kingdom of Aragon and Low Countries

Caciquismo: term widespread throughout Spain during the nineteenth and twentieth centuries referring to all those practices of social control used by local strongmen to dominate the political, economic, and social life of towns and to monopolize relations between their inhabitants and the State; examples include corruption, nepotism, patronage, and electoral fraud. This term derived from the word *cacique,* which Indians from the Caribbean used to designate their tribal chiefs.

Cámara de Castilla: council that formed part of Hispanic Monarchy's polisynodal system. Its function was to advise the king about appointments and administer the royal *gracias* and *mercedes*. It was linked to the Council of Castile.

Capa y espada: the "*capa y espada*" councilors were royal officials who had a military career; they were designated thus to differentiate them from the councilors that had a more formal legal education, in particular when both groups served simultaneously in the same institutions.

Capitanes proponentes: military officials or those that aspired to join the ranks that offered to muster, at their own expense, cavalry companies for King Charles III in exchange for receiving the commissions for captains and designations for lieutenants and second lieutenants. By selling these appointments, the "*capitanes proponentes*" could defray the expense that the recruitment of such companies necessarily implied.

Cartas ejecutorias: documents issued once judicial proceedings were finalized and the court had pronounced its verdict, that is, for lawsuits that were actually concluded. They ordered the resolute *execution* of the sentence and were generally issued at the request of an interested party.

Casa de Contratación: after having been founded in Seville in 1503, this institution was moved to Cadiz in May 1717. It took responsibility for everything related to navigation and commerce between Spain and America before it was dissolved in 1790.

Censo eclesiástico: pecuniary payment derived from contracts for real estate that some bishops and other ecclesiastical dignitaries annually received, although Castilian law stipulated that lower-ranking bishops could also benefit from such levies.

Cisplatina: name given to the Eastern Province of Uruguay when the Portuguese ruled the territory.

Consejeros: ministers that sat on the monarchy's different councils. They were appointed by the king, who selected them from among the candidates proposed by the *Camara de Castilla* or appointed them directly through his own decrees.

Consejo Mayor del Rey or *Consejo Real*: organ of government and justice in Castile; its members, who were sometimes clergymen, provided assistance and counsel to the king. It would progressively be subdivided into more strictly defined councils starting in the sixteenth century (*vid infra*).

Consejos: organs of government and counsel for the king dealing with the diverse matters that constituted the monarchy's political organization. It is possible to distinguish three different types of councils: the territorial ones (Council of Castile, Council of the Indies, Council of Aragon, Council of Italy, Council of Portugal, Royal Council of Navarre and Council of Flanders); those that had a defined sphere of jurisdiction throughout the monarchy and took responsibility for specific areas (Council of State, Council of War, Council of Treasury, Council of Military Orders, Council of the Inquisition and Council of the Cruzada); and the two chambers, those of Castile and of the Indies that were in turn bound to their respective councils for matters relating to *gracias* and appointments.

Corregidor: In Castile, the term was used from the fifteenth century onwards to designate the delegates named by the royal power to rule the municipalities. They were also established in America from the beginning of the Spanish Conquest, being appointed by the Crown to the *cabildos* for terms of three, four or five years after nomination by the Council of the Indies.

Corregimientos: jurisdiction of the *corregidor*.

Cortes: Spanish designation for the nineteenth-century parliamentary assemblies (starting with the *Cortes de Cadiz* from 1810 to 1814), which were supposed to revive the tradition of the assemblies of the estates representing the kingdoms of Castile, Aragón and Navarre, which had taken place during the Middle Ages. The word is used in the plural form (*Cortes*) because as a singular noun it has a completely different meaning, referring to the king's retinue in his palace.

Covachuelistas: derogatory term used in Spain during the eighteenth and nineteenth centuries to designate the office workers of the public sector; it likened the *secretarías del despacho* or ministries to small caves *(covachuelas),* gloomy places associated in the collective imagination with havens for thieves.

Chancillería: the high court of royal justice in the Castilian monarchy. In America, *chancillerías* were not established as they had been in the Peninsula (Valladolid, Granada), but the same term was used to designate the highly-placed official of the Council of the Indies (*chanciller*) who was in charge of dispatching and endorsing the privileges, "favors" (*gracias*), "gifts" (*mercedes*), and titles that the Crown granted to American subjects.

Derecho de entrada y ejercicio: gentlemen-in-waiting that really did perform the duties their office entailed; they therefore had access to the king's chambers. The inclusion of the term "*entrada y ejercicio*" made it possible to differentiate them from the gentlemen with neither the right of "*entrada*" nor of "*ejercicio*", as they only possessed honorific titles.

Diputació del general: entity that governed the Kingdom of Valencia.

Diputación provincial: the elective organ of provincial governments during the constitutional regime that was inaugurated by the Constitution of Cádiz in 1812. These representative organs had a clearly liberal tenor, as they had an elective composition in which the provincial towns were represented. Their responsibilities were expanded to include areas such as tax sharing, public education, thoroughfares, and charity. After the independence of America, provincial councils have subsisted until the present-day.

Dobla: name given to the different gold coins that circulated in the Iberian peninsula, from the Early Middle Ages to the beginning of the Modern Era.

Ducado: coin that was initially minted in gold and eventually became currency. By the end of the fifteenth century, a golden *ducado* was worth eleven silver *reales* in Spain while each *real* was equivalent to thirty-four *maravedís*.

Empleomanía (from *empleo* = employment and *mania* = mania): a pejorative term that was coined in the nineteenth century to criticize the alleged obsession with obtaining a permanent post as a civil servant in order to ensure one's livelihood.

Fiscales: ministers of the *audiencias* and chanceries that defended the public interest or that of the monarchy. In criminal suits, they acted as plaintiffs in accusing the defendants charged with having committed a crime, whether the case resulted from a denunciation or was an *ex officio* action. In civil suits, they defended the rights of the Royal Chamber in the matters that implicated the monarch's own interests.

Fuero: legal privilege or exemption, essentially understood as relating to the application of the law and administration of justice.

Gentilhombres de boca: the principal function of this office was to serve the monarch's table in the royal household. When the king ate in public, he was waited on by three gentlemen-in-waiting. There existed two categories of these *gentilhombres*: those that actually exercised the post in the palace and those that only possessed the title for honorific reasons.

Gentilhombres de cámara: position that served the king directly in his palace. Their principal responsibility was to assist the monarch when he dressed or undressed. In addition to the men that actually performed this function, there also existed merely honorific titles of "*gentilhombres de cámara*", which were granted to men that did not perform any real function in the palace.

Gobernador: a generic term used in Spanish America to refer to the supreme authority within a territory.

Grandes (*Grandes de España*): the highest rank of the Spanish nobility, constituted by all who held the title of duke, in addition to those of count or marquis that the Crown would have expressly granted to the *grandeza de España*.

Gracia Real: royal prerogative that allowed the king to grant pardons and *mercedes*. It was believed that only the monarch, by *Gracia Divina*, could make use of this power.

Hidalguía: social status that the nobility enjoyed. *Hidalgos* formed part of the lower ranks of the nobility and their position was set apart by the possession of a series of rights and privileges, which differentiated them from the commoners. Their principal privilege consisted of not being included on the register of the *pecheros*, which amounted to exemption from paying taxes.

Intendente: a post created by the Bourbonic reforms in the eighteenth century, in peninsular Spain as well as in Hispanic America. Derived from the French system, the figure of intendant had powers in fiscal, administrative, and military matters for a specific territory, an *Intendencia*.

Jefes Políticos: denomination given by the *Cortes* of Cádiz (in 1813) to the governors of the Spanish provinces; it was also used in Spanish America after independence. Although the figure's title (provincial governor, civil governor…) and respective powers were modified, its essence remained essentially unchanged throughout the nineteenth and twentieth centuries. These men were the national government's delegates in the provinces, charged with directing relations between the municipalities and central power and coordinating the services provided by the state's administration in the area, with a particular emphasis placed on controlling public order.

Jueces delegados: officials that were commissioned by the king or a competent authority to try a particular case or lawsuit; they were generally expected to hear the concerned parties and resolve the conflict within a fixed period of time.

Jueces pesquisidores: judges that were ordered by the king or highest courts to carry out a *pesquisa* (enquiry) in a small town or locality. The enquiry would be decreed because of a denunciation or formal written request reporting the occurrence of a serious dispute or crime. These judges sometimes had executive powers, that is, the authority to pronounce sentence.

Juicio de residencia: judgment that the monarchy's agents had to undergo once they had finished exercising their post; they were sometimes assessed by a specially appointed judge while in other cases they were judged by their successors in the same office.

Junta de Medios: meetings held by the king's ministers for the specific purpose of trying to look for supplementary financial resources for the monarchy. The *juntas de medios* were convoked during particularly difficult periods that were generally co-incided with the onset of costly warfare or its expansion.

Jurados: low-ranking municipal officials in charge of organizing the districts of Castilian cities.

Limpieza de sangre: requisite for gaining access to certain positions, offices or institutions in the Spain of the Ancien Régime; it notably required that neither the candidate nor his family had Jewish or Moor blood or had mixed with such groups.

Maravedíes: coins with different values that were generally used to define the amount of fines. They could be minted in gold, silver, and other less valuable metals for everyday use.

Maestres de plata: officials that were in charge of monitoring the silver and gold that arrived in the fleets originating in America as well as the unloading of the precious metals in Spain. Between 1598 and 1615 they were appointed by the *Casa de Contratación* and from 1615 onwards, by the Council of Indies. Most of these positions were granted in exchange for the payment of a set amount of money during the reign of Philip IV.

Media-annata: fee equivalent to six months' salary that all of the king's servants had to pay for any royal appointment that was not to a military position. Those that received honorific *mercedes* also had to pay half of their assessed value.

Merced: pardon that the king granted by making use of his *gracia real,* generally freeing the beneficiary from having to serve a sentence.

Mercedes: different forms of concessions (property, honors, positions, and offices) that monarchs made to their subjects or the most powerful lords to their vassals, thereby conferring the right to or possession of something previously held by the authorities. These *mercedes* were almost always granted in return for services rendered.

Mercedes de hábito: distinctive title of nobility that the king granted to a servant, conferring the honor of belonging to one of the military orders (Alcántara, Calatrava, Santiago, San Juan y Montesa).

Mercedes de pasos de oficios: favors that the king conceded to his servants, those that served him in the palace, so that the positions that they held could be passed on to members of their family. This system permitted the patrimonialization of these same offices.

Merinos: In Medieval Spain, this term was used to designate the man appointed by the king to rule and impart justice in a small town or specific locality; the area placed under his responsibility was known as a *merindad*. This position remained linked to the task of administering justice. The *merinos mayores*' judicial authority and powers were largely comparable to those attributed to the *adelantados* (*Adelantamiento, vid supra*).

Montepío: starting in the eighteenth century, this term referred to the fund that was created with the sums deducted from the salaries of a specific professional group; it was allocated to helping its members by providing them with pensions and assistance when they fell ill or grew old. Their families were likewise helped when members died as their widows and orphaned children were provided with pensions.

Oidores: judges or magistrates that "heard", judged, and sentenced lawsuits and cases in the *audiencias* and chanceries in Spain as well as in America.

Pecheros: referred to those that were required to pay *pechos* (taxes). All non-exempt individuals had to pay their *pechos* in the locality where they owned real estate, even if they did not reside in it, or where they were established as freemen (*vecino*).

Pena de doblo: clause included in contracts, generally for sales on credit, between individuals; it stipulated that if the buyer did not pay the debt within the established time frame, the arrears would be doubled.

Promotor fiscal or *procurador fiscal*: representative of the treasury or Royal Chamber in lawsuits and judicial proceedings (vid supra *fiscales*).

Propios: *bienes de propios* (literally "own property") or simply *propios*, were the goods and property rights that a municipality possessed; they were used to obtain the revenue that the local government needed to support itself.

Regalía: the king's ultimate right over a property or branch of the government.

Regidor: term used in Castile from the fourteenth century to designate the members of the municipal council that ruled a city. The term was subsequently employed in America for the members of *cabildos*.

Regidurías: positions held by *regidores*.

Repúblicos: Latinized designation, generally laudatory, used to designate the urban patriciate in the seventeenth century.

Sala de Alcaldes de Casa y Corte: court of law that constituted the fifth courtroom of the Council of Castile. Its jurisdiction encompassed up to five leagues surrounding the court's residence, except for cases of robbery, when it was extended to a maximum of twenty leagues.

Secretarías de Despacho: institutions where the *Secretarios del Despacho* carried out their duties. Their principal function consisted in "dispatching" dossiers along with the king, namely getting the monarch to resolve the cases he had to examine. At the beginning of the eighteenth century, when the system of councils was marginalized, the *Secretarías del Despacho* were divided into various branches specializing in specific departments, as their workload had significantly increased. At the same time, the *Secretario del Despacho* ended up becoming a sort of minister, as they took complete responsibility for the policy of their respective departments.

Señoríos: autonomous jurisdictional entities that were dependent on a lord.

Situado: method of financing that the Spanish Monarchy employed that involved placing a debt that had been contracted on a specific fiscal income or tax. In Spanish America, the same term was used during the colonial period to refer to the amount of money that a royal *caja* had to earmark each year to pay for the defense of a designated territory.

Superintendente: highest-ranked official after the viceroy in the *Intendencia* System.

Tercios: military units that were characteristic of the army of Spanish Habsburgs. This designation appeared for the first time around 1536. They remained the fundamental military structure until about 1702-1703 when the system of regiments replaced them. A field master led each *tercio*.

Vecino: Member of an urban corporation that had full rights and the ensuing obligations.

Visita: Inspection tour of a predetermined jurisdiction (viceroyalty, provincial government…) conducted by a functionary.